To Megan,
One of the
great welsh

Edwards

Terrell

THE WELSH LIBERALS

The History of the
Liberal and Liberal Democrat parties
in Wales

Also available from Welsh Academic Press

**SNP – The History of the Scottish National Party – 2nd Edition (Peter Lynch)
978-1-86057-057-5**

*'The definitive reference work on the nationalist strand of Scottish politics and
Scottish history'* **Scottish Affairs**

**Tommy Sheridan: From Hero to Zero A Political Biography (Gregor Gall)
978-1-86057-119-0**

'A timely and rigorous biography of Scotland's most flawed politician'
Paul Hutcheon, The Sunday Herald

**Hugh MacDiarmid: Black, Green, Red and Tartan (Bob Purdie)
978-1-86057-027-8**

*'Shows convincingly that the most substantial and enduring of MacDiarmid's
political convictions were two contradictory ideas, communism and Scottish
nationalism. On the first of these his ideas were widely different from those of
the British party and he allowed his membership of the SNP to lapse, but he
was always strongly in favour of Scottish independence.'*
Paul Henderson Scott, Scottish Review

Plaid Cymru – An Ideological Analysis (Alan Sandry) 978-1-86057-116-9

*"Valuable ... controversial ... this book deserves wider notice from those inter-
ested in political parties and ideological relations within them."*
David S. Moon, Political Studies Review

**Mebyon Kernow and Cornish Nationalism (Deacon, Cole and Tregidga)
978-1-86057-075-9**

*'... Fascinating and detailed ... in providing the first and long-awaited defini-
tive academic study of Mebyon Kernow and its position in the wider Cornish
movement, this timely book provides a valuable addition both to the growing
literature on European sub-state nationalist movements.*
Adrian Lee, Cornish Studies

For further information visit: www.welsh-academic-press.com

THE WELSH LIBERALS

The History of the
Liberal and Liberal Democrat parties
in Wales

Russell Deacon

Welsh Academic Press

Published in Wales by Welsh Academic Press, an imprint of

Ashley Drake Publishing Ltd
PO Box 733
Cardiff
CF14 7ZY

www.welsh-academic-press.com

First Impression – 2014

ISBN
978-1-86057-096-4

British Library Cataloguing-in-Publication Data.
A CIP catalogue for this book is available from the British Library.

Typeset by White Lotus Infotech Pvt. Ltd., Puducherry, India.
Printed and bound by CPI Group (UK) Ltd, Croydon, CR0 4YY

CONTENTS

This book is dedicated to Alexandra and Tracey Deacon who supported me throughout my writing journey. It is also dedicated to all of those who continued to carry the Liberal flame despite the electoral odds stacked against them. Without them there would have been no book to write.

FOREWORD

The Welsh Liberals have had a long and distinguished history, during which they have gained a Westminster presence in every part of Wales. This remains a remarkable record unmatched by any other political party. It is also remarkable that this long and rich history has never previously been recorded in a single volume as it is with this book. We therefore owe Russell Deacon a very genuine vote of appreciation.

As we chart Liberal Party history we can see it go from the strength of the 1906 landslide, when the party in Wales won nearly every Welsh parliamentary seat, to the low points in the 1960s, 1970s and 1990s when the party in Wales was, on one occasion, reduced to just one parliamentary seat.

Importantly, however, we must also remember that Wales has never been never entirely without a Liberal presence at Westminster and, as a result of the much fairer proportional system, has always been represented at the National Assembly.

In the first decade of this new century I feel we have once more witnessed a stabilisation of Welsh Liberalism, with the revival of the Liberal heartlands of Montgomeryshire, Cardiganshire and Brecon and Radnor where, whilst the seats can still be won or lost, the Liberals are seen as the main contender. This has been added to by the strong foothold established in Cardiff. The Welsh Liberal presence in the House of Lords is also currently at its strongest for many years.

At a local government level, the Party has also been re-establishing itself. This has been reflected in the large towns and cities of Wales such as Cardiff, Newport, Swansea, Wrexham and Bridgend, which have each had Liberal Democrat Leaders in recent years including our first female leader, Cheryl Green, at Bridgend Council. In a way, after the Liberals disappeared from much of local government in the post-war period, these recent local government successes, often from a minimal support base, have become even more remarkable than increases in Parliamentary strength.

When I look back at Wales' history I can now see that Welsh identity has often been intertwined with the evolution of the Welsh Liberals. In 1847, 'the Treason of the Blue Books' (Brad y Llyfrau Gleision) showed the deplorable state of education in Wales but by the century's end the Liberals had improved the Welsh school system and established the University of Wales. The Liberal record on building Welsh nationhood is also impressive but, sadly, now widely forgotten. Similarly the great Tithe Protest led by Liberals like Thomas Gee of Denbigh started the process that led eventually to the Disestablishment of the Welsh Church, something that was of vital national important then but seems somewhat distant now. At the same time David Lloyd George and Tom Ellis were amongst those regarded as giants of the political scene, with Lloyd George's fame and reputation becoming world known. Yet at his heart we must remember that he was always a Welsh Liberal.

As the twentieth century developed many of Wales' Liberal MPs such as Clement Davies, Emlyn Hooson, Megan Lloyd George, Roderic Bowen and Rhys Hopkin Morris also become well respected figures on the British political scene. In more recent times Alex Carlile, Geraint Howells, Richard Livsey and Lembit Öpik always combined strong local representation of their rural seats with a wider projection on the British political stage.

For every successful Welsh Liberal MP, however, there are many great names that did not taste electoral success, and it was Westminster's loss that other outstanding Welshmen like Dr Glyn Tegai Hughes, Martin Thomas and Alun Talfan Davies never made it to the House of Commons. Today, the Welsh Assembly has opened up the opportunity for a newer generation to gain elected office and I am also delighted to know many of the younger generation of Welsh Liberals and recognise their outstanding talent. It is clear that they have the potential to continue that great Liberal tradition of Wales that has stretched back over two centuries.

Welsh Liberal history is always evolving, and as a living party with long roots I'm certain that there will be much more to write about in the future. But for now let us just enjoy this marvellous book from Russell Deacon to remind ourselves of the long and illustrious history of The Welsh Liberals.

Lord Roger Roberts of Llandudno
October 2013

ACKNOWLEDGEMENTS

There are many, many people to thank in respect of this book and in particular I would like to thank the late Emlyn Hooson and Richard Livsey, both greatly missed, as well as Martin Thomas, Alex Carlile, Michael German and Glyn Tegai Hughes for providing me with detailed information.

Thanks must also be extended to Dr John Graham Jones and Steve Belzak for looking at the various drafts of the book and to Roger Roberts for writing the Foreword.

I'd also express my thanks to my publisher, Ashley Drake and to Charlie Harris for the proof reading.

Finally, I would also like to express my everlasting gratitude to my wife Tracey Deacon and my daughter Alex Deacon for their support during the long but enjoyable process of writing this book.

GLOSSARY OF TERMS

ALDC	–	Association of Liberal Democrat Councillors
AM	–	Assembly Member
AMS	–	Additional Member System
CLLR	–	Councillor
DSO	–	Distinguished Service Order
EEC	–	European Economic Community
LCA	–	Liberal Central Association
LPO	–	Liberal Party Organisation
LRA	–	Liberal Registration Association
MBE	–	Member of the British Empire
MEP	–	Member of the European Parliament
MP	–	Member of Parliament
NLF	–	National Liberal Federation
PPC	–	Prospective Parliamentary Candidate
PR	–	Proportional Representation
QC	–	Queen's Council
SDP	–	Social Democratic Party
STV	–	Single Transferable Vote
SWMF	–	South Wales Miners Federation
UN	–	United Nations
WLF	–	Women's Liberal Federation
WLW	–	Welsh Liberal Women's organisation
WSPU	–	Women's Social and Political Union
WUWLA	–	Welsh Union of Women's Liberal Associations

INTRODUCTION

To date there is no book that comprehensively covers the history of the Welsh Liberals, Welsh SDP and Welsh Liberal Democrats. This is the first such attempt. I began this book in order to fill in this large gap in Welsh political history. Any scholar or person interested in knowing more about the history of Liberals in Wales would have found that there was little material to satisfy their appetite. Of course, a number of histories of Plaid Cymru and the Labour Party in Wales have been written and many books exist about David Lloyd George. Some of these extensively cover Liberal politics in Wales in the late nineteenth and early twentieth century, but these are not the same as a history of the Welsh Liberals. This book is therefore far more than a revisiting of the life and loves of David Lloyd George, and though his influence over the history of the party is still important, many others have played equal or even greater parts. This book therefore covers all aspects of Welsh Liberal history. It embraces more than three centuries of the history of the Liberals in Wales. It should be noted from the outset, however, that the book only covers the history of Liberalism within the Welsh Liberal Party, Welsh Liberal Democrats and SDP. It does not cover elements of political Liberalism that may exist or may have existed in other political parties.

It has taken me around seven years to gather the information required to put together this wide ranging history of the Welsh Liberals. The book makes use of the historical records of the party found in the Welsh Political Archives at the National Library of Wales and the London School of Economics and also in many party and individual sources. It also draws on over 50 interviews with Liberals, Liberal Democrats and SDP members, who were either part of various Welsh parties or were connected with them during the period covered by this book.

The book has striven to cover all relevant periods of Welsh Liberal history. The period prior to the arrival of the Internet has had to be reconstructed painfully by putting together information from a variety of archive sources, interviews and secondary texts. Over the last decade or so, however, the historical record has been well documented in the Welsh Liberal Democrats' own records and by the media themselves. The arrival of the World Wide Web has provided historians with a wealth of detail and information concerning dates and events at the touch of a button. This has meant, therefore, that contemporary information has been relatively easy to source accurately. It has also meant that the need to interview elected Liberal Democrats and party officials has been reduced, unlike earlier periods. Many current and former Liberals were contacted during the writing of this book. Some provided valuable information, others stated they would provide information but didn't, whilst others chose not to reply at all. This history of the Welsh Liberals, therefore, goes beyond written records to encompass the oral history of those Welsh Liberals who have so far never made it into print.

Readers should also be reminded that this is a history of the lifespan of the Welsh Liberals, and that there may be periods which may appear to merit more detail.

Unfortunately, owing to the constraints of the word length of any affordable book, some details and events, which were not central to the Liberal story have had to be omitted. A further explanation for other omissions lies in the fact that most of the Welsh Liberal Party's records no longer exist. Therefore, details of its activities and events can only be put together from the scraps of information found in newspaper accounts, biographies or other records of the period. In some areas, such as those relating to the Welsh Union of Women's Liberal Associations and the various other women's groups linked to the Welsh Liberal Party, there is no written record at all. This has made coverage of Welsh Liberal women's history difficult to investigate.

Should readers find any inaccuracies in the text, I would be grateful to learn about these for future revised editions. I also apologise in advance if the reflection of the historical record inadvertently portrays any individual in what is felt to be at odds with historical records. Every effort has been made to check the accuracy of facts, people and information in this text. Ivor Thomas Rees' 2005 book, *Welsh Hustings 1885–2004* has proved to be an invaluable source in checking the accuracy of candidate data. Anybody who seriously studies Welsh political history should have this text in their collection. Please also note that in dealing with constituency names, I have tried to use the English or Welsh title of the seat referred to most commonly in the Welsh Liberal-Liberal Democrat records of that time.

Readers may note the paucity of primary written sources on some periods of the Welsh party's history. Let me reiterate that this is because many of the party's historical written records have now gone. The Welsh Liberal Party's main archives were damaged by water and mould and subsequently destroyed in the 1970s. What little remains is at National Library in Aberystwyth with some additional material being located in the London School of Economics and Bristol University archives. Local party records are also very limited. In the period after the Second World War most constituencies in Wales with previously active Liberal organisations ceased operations and their record were lost. Thus most historical material on the party can only be found in newspaper records, oral history or the biographies of Liberals with connections with Wales. This has meant that on occasions during the writing of this book there was no significant material to consult and the detail on certain periods of history was limited. In some chapters there has therefore been a concentration on key Welsh Liberal figures, on whom material can still be found. In addition, we must also be aware that the Welsh Liberal Party of the post war period was very small by both historic and modern standards. In terms of numbers, there were only around 40 or so key party activists in Wales between 1951 and 1966, and these only operated in a handful of constituencies. Across much of Wales in the interwar and post war years therefore there was no real Welsh Liberal story to tell.

1

WALES, THE LIBERAL NATION (1859–1898)

Introduction

The respected Welsh historian, K. O. Morgan, noted about Wales between 1880 and 1914 that 'Liberalism permeated Welsh life at every point during this period. Every major transformation in Welsh life owed something to it'.[1] As Morgan notes, it is quite accurate to say that Wales was once a Liberal nation, in which its representatives controlled virtually every political prize of note. These ranged from the position of the humblest town mayor to that of the Prime Minister of the British Isles. For a period of just over three decades between 1885 and 1922, Welsh Liberalism dominated political life in Wales to an extent that no political party had ever before or would ever again. Not even the 'mighty' Labour Party, which would come to lead Welsh politics from the 1920s onwards, would ever be able to boast of winning control of every county council in Wales in the same year or having an MP in every Welsh constituency who took their Party Whip. Before they achieved their dominance, however, the Liberal Party had to go through a birth process, which encompassed the turbulent struggles of nineteenth century democratic political reform in Wales. There were painful political battles to be fought which would transform the Liberal Party into the first political party both to represent not only the Welsh working and middle classes but also the aspirations of the Welsh nation. This first chapter looks at the origins and development of the Liberal Party in Wales during the reign of Queen Victoria and how it came to be part of the very lifeblood of the nation.

The Origins of the Liberal Party and its Development in Wales

Welsh politics was very different in the first half of the nineteenth century from what it is today. There were no distinctly Welsh political parties or groupings at this time. All politicians in Wales were fully integrated into the British system of government. It was only those aspects of the Welsh constituencies' geographical isolation, some cultural differences and the presence of the Welsh language that made its politicians different from those in England. Most of the politicians in Wales and the wider ruling Welsh elite saw no differences between themselves and their counterparts in

England. In addition, many were married into the English or Scottish ruling classes and also held estates and business interests across the United Kingdom. They did not see themselves as belonging distinctly to the nation called 'Wales'. The development of Liberalism in Wales was, therefore, initially inseparable from the development occurring in England. Developments there, in turn, owed much to the evolution of a loose political grouping commonly known as the Whigs.[2] The Whigs, who were always strongly supported by nonconformist Christians in Wales, began to wane in political dominance in the early nineteenth century and, as a result, a new political grouping emerged. In 1859 this new political grouping took on the name of the 'Liberal Party'.

This new Liberal Party, from which would spring the Welsh Liberals' own distinctive brand a few decades later, emerged, after a meeting of key Liberal Victorian political figures in the Willis Tea Room in London. The Liberal Party was thus constructed from a Whig/Peelite coalition which covered a wide range of opinions and views. The Peelites were followers of the former Tory Prime Minister Sir Robert Peel who had changed allegiance.[3] The Liberal Party was given life as a formal entity when on the 6th of June 1859, 274 'Liberal' MPs in the political factions headed by Viscount Palmerston, Lord John Russell and the radical, John Bright, came together as a Liberal Party.[4] They were joined by the remaining Peelites. The Liberal Party was therefore formed from a coalition of different interest groups. This meant that for the next hundred years the Liberal Party developed as a party of coalescing ideologies and regional interests, which, on numerous occasions, would unravel into internal civil war, as the different factions clashed.

Although there were no major Welsh representatives at the Willis Tea Room meeting, it was not long before politicians with quite strong Welsh connections were at the heart of the new party. The first politician with a major Welsh connection was the acknowledged father of the Liberal Party. Although both Prime Ministers Viscount Palmerston and Lord John Russell vied for the position of the first modern Liberal Prime Minister, they are today regarded by historians as 'the last of the old (Whig) regime rather than the first modern Liberal prime minister'.[5] It was Palmerston's and Russell's Chancellor, William Ewart Gladstone, who took over as Leader of the Party in 1867, who is now seen as the party's founding father. Gladstone had close links to both Wales and the developing Liberalism within Wales. In fact, Gladstone was not a Welsh MP or even Welsh, and was born just across the Welsh border in Liverpool. He was, however, connected to Wales by marriage. In 1839, he had married Catherine Glynn, whose family seat was the Hawarden Castle in Flintshire. Gladstone then took over the castle and estates himself and for the rest of his life made frequent visits there, which gave him a Welsh base and outlook on Welsh life.

The Development of Politics in Wales in the Nineteenth Century

Before looking at the development of the Liberal Party in Wales, it is worth taking a brief look at politics in the period that preceded the Party's arrival. From its Union with England, in the reign of Henry VIII, the gentry and the landowners had dominated internal politics across the Welsh nation. Each county had its own dominant land-owning family or families. Names such as the Mostyns in Flintshire or the Morgans in Monmouthshire were well known to people who lived in those counties. Unlike much of the Irish gentry, the Welsh gentry was not always an alien race of absentee landlords. They were often Welsh by birth and name. They were, however, normally English by tongue, education, religion and custom. This anglophile connection separated the ruling class across much of Wales from the non-conformist, Welsh speaking population, which still had a close association with the older language and traditions of Wales.[6]

The Welsh landed gentry was thus able to keep a firm hold on Welsh parliamentary seats for over the three centuries after union with England. This practice continued for much of the first half of the nineteenth century. Most people living in the constituencies were excluded from the voting process entirely. When an incumbent MP died or retired the seats were merely passed on from brother to brother, uncle to nephew and father to son, often without a vote being cast. Only occasionally was there even a contested election for the seat and even then the electorate often consisted of less than 200 people. In the general election of 1802, for instance, Colonel W. Keen was re-elected to Montgomeryshire with 62 votes compared to his opponent's, Sir James Cockburn, 21 votes – a grand total of 83 votes in a constituency which today has over 44,000 voters. During this period, MPs did not stand under any firm party labels and tended instead to form loose group alignments based on geographical locations. In time, however, immense political pressure from those excluded from the franchise compelled the ruling classes either to make the system more democratic or face the prospect of a revolution. The first step on the road to reforming the political system to the system that we know in Wales today occurred after the First Reform Act (1832). The Act divided Wales into 32 seats which were broken into county (rural) and borough (town) seats and from then on, in Wales and elsewhere, candidates started to be identified more clearly with either Whig (early Liberals) or Tory (Conservatives) political groupings. Old habits took some time to die, and the Whigs, until the mid-nineteenth century, were still subdivided into regional groupings, which often had no common cause.[7] In Wales these always took county allegiances rather than national Welsh ones.

The limited size of the electoral franchise and the 'corrupt practices' of the voting process which went with them meant that from 1835 to 1865, it was only the political elite that selected the Welsh MPs. As the elite tended to come from the Tories, they took the majority of seats in Wales in each election. Few constituency elections were contested. The tradition of the lack of competition for most Welsh parliamentary seats continued until the 1865 general election. In that year, only seven of Wales' 29 elected MPs fought contested elections. Where there were elections, the electoral system remained grossly distorted in favour of the limited wealthy electorate in the seat, who were mainly Tory voters. In 1852, the Tories gained 18 seats to the Whigs' 14. In the year that the Liberals became established as a political party, that of 1859, there were 15 (Whigs) Liberals returned in Wales as opposed to 14 Tories. Despite this apparent Liberal victory, their voting strength was only a fraction of what it would have been had the electoral franchise had been fully widened.

As the electoral system evolved, it began to yield political dividends for the Liberals. However, it still had massive imbalances in terms of the parity of constituency sizes. In 1865, the largest electorate in the whole of Wales was in the county of Glamorgan with some 6,759 voters, whilst the smallest was Brecon (town) with 281 voters, which was four per cent of Glamorgan's electorate, yet both returned one member to Parliament. The 1867 Second Reform Act, inspired by Liberal Prime Minister William Gladstone, did much to redress the inherent unfairness in the electoral system and led to a more equitable redistribution of seats in Wales. At the same time, all men living in urban areas were enfranchised (those renting or owning property valued over £10). In addition to these two improvements, a limited number of men in the countryside with long leases on property gained the vote. This had the effect of increasing the Welsh electorate by a massive 250 per cent.[8] It ensured that the Liberals were able to significantly increase both their vote and number of MPs. The number of voters in Merthyr Tydfil, for instance, increased from 1,387 to 14,577 and, as a result, the town was allowed an extra MP. In turn, Merthyr Tydfil elected two Liberal MPs one of whom was Henry Austin (H. A.) Bruce, who became Gladstone's Home Secretary, and later, Lord Aberdare. As the electorate in Wales widened and the franchise spread, Liberal fortunes rose and Conservative fortunes declined. The first general election after the Second Reform Act established the Liberal Party's hegemony in Wales. The 1868 election was Wales' most fiercely fought election to date. The number of uncontested seats was also greatly reduced from 1865; 23 of Wales' 32 seats were contested in contrast to a mere seven in the election of three years earlier.

The 1868 General Election Puts the Liberals Firmly in First Position

The 1868 general election saw 22 Liberal and 10 Conservatives elected. At the same time, it resulted in the political patronage and power of Conservatism in much of South, Mid and North Wales being overthrown in favour of Liberalism. The legacy of the 1868 general election, therefore, became the stuff of Liberal political folklore. This was not just because of the removal of many of the Conservative gentry as political masters but also owing to the subsequent backlash this caused. In Caernarfonshire, Camarthenshire and Cardiganshire, farmers were evicted for having voted for the Liberals instead of for their Tory landlords.

In Caernarfonshire, a Liberal defeated the son of the controversial Conservative slate magnate and sugar plantation owner, Lord Penrhyn. To avenge his son's defeat, many tenant farmers were subsequently evicted by their 'Tory' landlords for 'voting the wrong way'.[9] This action by a Tory landlord and others like him caused outrage amongst Welsh Liberals for generations, becoming part of the folklore of Liberal Wales. Donald McCormick, in his biography of Lloyd George, graphically described the practice:[10]

> The election ballots were not secret in those days and many tenants who had not voted for Tory candidates were evicted from their land and cottages. This happened at Llanystumdwy, and Lloyd George's earliest memories must have been of neighbours – often mothers in the last stages of childbirth – thrown out into the street with their few belongings and driven into the fields to find what shelter they could in some distant hayrick. Even then they might be charged as vagrants

and hounded out of the district. Other landlords were more subtle. They merely raised the rents of those who had voted Liberal and reduced those of their faithful Tory voting tenants. Liberals who owned shops were boycotted; their children were brought before the courts often on some trumped up charge of poaching.

These memories remained deeply ingrained in the Liberal consciousness even by those who had not lived through those times. Over a century later, the Welsh Liberal MP Geraint Howells (Ceredigion) still harboured the resentment of these events which had almost led to his grandmother being thrown off her farm for voting Liberal; a sentiment which inspired him to continue to embrace the Liberal cause.[11] Welsh Liberals of the nineteenth century were determined that in the future no elector should be punished for voting Liberal. In 1869, Parliament therefore set up a Commission under Lord Hartington, the former member for the Radnor District (1868–69) to examine these cases of electoral persecution.[12] Almost a hundred cases were proven in Wales, which led directly to the introduction of the Secret Ballot Act in 1872. These reforms meant that no landlord would be able to discover how his tenant had voted.

Despite evictions and other acts of intimidation, the Conservatives could do little in the long term to redress their declining fortunes. The subsequent Liberal ascendancy in Wales can be seen in Table 1.

Dominant as the Welsh Liberals became in the House of Commons, they could never hope to match the Conservatives' numbers in the House of Lords. There were far fewer Liberal peers from Wales than Conservative ones. Just like their Conservative counterparts, however, Welsh Liberal Lords and even Welsh Liberal MPs prior to 1868 still came from the gentry: 'almost to a man'.[14] Many Welsh Liberal peers were also not really 'Liberal' in politics. The peers were on the whole committed to their own families' concerns rather than party interests and were not great financial supporters of Welsh Liberals either. It would still be another few decades before there would be a significant number of Welsh Liberal peers in the Upper House. The 1868 general election changed the way that the political parties organised themselves in Wales. Prior to 1868, at general elections both Liberals and Conservatives often simply formed *ad hoc* election committees to contest proceedings but had not bothered with any such committees at local elections. Now with a wider franchise that included many more Liberal and Conservative voters, both parties set about establishing a

Table 1   The Number of MPs Elected by Party: The Liberalisation of Wales 1852–1880[13]

Year of Election	Liberal (Whig)	Conservatives
1852	12	20
1857	15	17
1859	15	17
1865	18	14
1868	22	10
1874	19	13
1880	28	4

constituency association in every Welsh parliamentary seat. Elections and politics in general would now adopt a more professional and permanent appearance.[15]

In the House of Commons, helped into power by these new Liberal Constituency Associations, a new breed of Welsh Liberal politician now came to the fore. Examples of these new MPs abounded in the 1880s. The champion of Welsh non-conformity, the Reverend Henry Richard, was elected for Merthyr Tydfil. Morgan Lloyd replaced an old Whig MP in Beaumaris. Lloyd was a barrister and a founder of Bangor Normal College and later campaigned as the Secretary for the 'Movement for a Welsh University'. When it was established he became the Honorary Secretary of the University of Wales. Following this University of Wales connection, the treasurer of the University College of Aberystwyth, the millionaire railway pioneer, coal mine and dock owner, David Davies, also replaced Sir T. D. Lloyd as the MP for Cardiganshire. In Denbighshire, the Welsh nationalist barrister George Osborne Morgan was elected. He would be instrumental in the development and chairing of the Welsh Parliamentary Party. As Judge Advocate General, Morgan would also later on become famous for being responsible for abolishing flogging in the British army. This influx of new Liberals meant that, over the coming decades, the Liberal parliamentarians in Wales would become a Parliamentary party more in tune with their supporters' interests than any political party across Wales had been before.

Early Issues of Ideology

In the last half of the nineteenth century, British Liberals were united ideologically about a number of fundamental issues. This ideological binding was given written form by Herbert Spencer among others. His classic work on Liberalism, 'Man Versus the State', written in 1880s, crystallised Liberal values. In essence, they 'represented a move for freedom from the remaining feudal and monarchical controls' which many Welsh Liberals were also seeking to break. As part of this notion Spencer and other Liberals sought to make sure that Liberalism didn't facilitate the replacement of the 'tyranny of the Kings' with a 'tyranny of Parliaments or the state'.[16] Resistance to this 'tyranny' involved the support for the 'freedom of membership of all groups, freedom of belief and speech'. This found particular popularity with the nonconformist Welsh Christians in their battles to remove themselves from the grip of both the landlords and the Church of England. This Liberalism also supported economic theories such as *laissez-faire* or free trade, endorsed by the Liberal railway barons and coal and steel exporters of Wales.[17]

Linked by these ideological issues, the Liberals in Wales began to equate Liberal ideology with the passions of civil and religious injustice that were most important to them in Wales. Chief among these was the large scale support for the issue of land reform amongst tenant farmers. This issue became part of Liberal folklore with the song 'The Land'. Sung to the tune of 'Marching Thro' Georgia', it became a battle cry for Liberals in the time before mass media and communication changed political campaigning for good. The first two verses and the chorus are the most relevant:[18]

> "Sound the call for freedom boys, and sound it far and wide,
> March along to victory for God is on our side,
> While the voice of Nature thunders o'er the
> rising tide, "God gave the land to the people!"

Chorus:
The land, the land, 'twas God who made the land,
The land, the land, the ground on which we stand,
Why should we be beggars with the ballot in our hand?
God made the land for the people.

Hark the sound is spreading from the East and from the West,
Why should we work hard and let the landlords take the best?
Make them pay their taxes on the land just like the rest,
The land was meant for the people.

Even today the song 'The Land' is still sung at gatherings of both British and Welsh Liberals either at conferences or meetings, such as those of the Lloyd George Society. 'The Land', however, was not solely a Welsh issue and united Liberals across the British Isles. In the 1868-1874 Parliament, issues that predominantly affected Wales, such as the role of the Church of England, started becoming more prominent. Around this time, the party in Wales began to establish its own sense of identity and the British Liberal Party, in 1877, was also exploring an outlet for the mass of its own members through the formation of the National Liberal Federation (NLF). The NLF was in essence a 'grass roots' organisation that was formally independent of the Liberal Parliamentary Party.[19] Wales would soon mirror this structure in the establishment of its own federations and a Welsh Parliamentary Party.

Wales and Liberalism in the Age of Empire (1880–1900)

During the Victorian era, parts of Wales developed into some of the most industrialised societies on earth. The agricultural and rural south was transformed into an industrial and over populated south. Booming industrially with the rise of coal mining and steel production, the population of South Wales exploded in size. Whilst this drew in hundreds of thousands of migrant workers, who mainly lived in abject poverty, it had the opposite effect on the wealth of the gentry who owned the Welsh coalfields. The scale and profit of the coal and steel industry transformed the gentry, who owned land in Wales, into powerful and wealthy political dynasties. The industrialisation of Welsh society and the ramifications of this, in turn, drove the middle and working classes to demand more economic and political power over their own lives. At the same time, as we noted in the song 'The Land', the feudal nature of the tenant farmers of Wales was also facing pressure for change. The Liberals were now at the heart of channelling these demands for change into the political system.

The concept of Wales as a nation was also changing. In the last half of the nineteenth century, the orthodoxy of the Conservatives and much of the Liberal Party had been that 'there was no such country as Wales'. The political and religious establishment reinforced this view.[20] The Welsh Bishop, Basil Jones, made this clear when he stated that Wales 'was but a geographical expression'.[21] This phrase could have been attributed to, however, most of those in the British establishment. In the 1870s and 1880s this view was famously encapsulated in the *Encyclopaedia Britannia* entry 'For Wales, See England'. This view was soon to change radically amongst most senior Liberal politicians, including the party's own leader.[22] In June 1887, the Liberal leader William Gladstone addressed a party rally in Swansea, declaring: 'I affirm that Welsh nationality is as great a reality as English nationality'.[23] Gladstone's own views on Wales had been altered over time as he recognised that Wales through its language, religion and culture was distinct from England. This was the first time a major political figure had recognised Wales's national distinctiveness. And Gladstone did not rest at just acknowledging Welsh distinctiveness. A year later when he spoke to the Welsh national Eisteddfod he fully endorsed the use of the Welsh language by the Church – which had been politically unthinkable only a decade earlier. The Welsh people's own aspirations and the status of the Welsh language, which most of the Welsh population spoke as a first language, became issues of political importance within a party of British government for the first time.

Just as Gladstone's views on Wales had changed, it was only a matter of time before the Houses of Parliament in Westminster accepted Wales as a nation – distinct from England. This acceptance was greatly aided by the campaigning of the nonconformist temperance of Welsh Liberal MPs. They helped bring about the first piece of modern Welsh legislation. This was the Wales Sunday Closing Act 1881, which dealt with the selling of alcohol in public houses on the Sabbath. Parliament had now officially accepted that a nation called Wales existed in its own right. After this Act was passed, separate legislation for Wales, although still rare, was accepted as being possible and sometimes necessary by all politically parties. It was not until 1967, however, that the word 'England' in an Act of Parliament was no longer deemed to automatically include Wales.

The Formation of the Welsh Liberal Federations

The first large scale 'Liberal' group in Wales was the Welsh Liberation Society which was formed in 1844. Its primary aims were the disendowing and disestablishing of the Church of England in Wales. It membership included many future Welsh Liberals and was led by men such as Thomas Gee (1815–98) and Henry Richard (1812–88). Gee, an influential Liberal North Wales newspaper owner, propagandist and nonconformist, was the editor of the Welsh language paper *Baner ac Amserau Cymru*. He pursued disestablishment directly with Gladstone placing it above even that of Home Rule.[24]

As noted earlier in this chapter, the British Liberal Party was formed in the 1859 Willis Tea Room meeting. The first tangible structural result of this meeting occurred two years later when the Liberal Registration Association (LRA) was formed. By 1877, the LRA had developed into the Liberal Central Association (LCA). The LCA helped create a modern structure necessary for the building of a party system by ensuring the establishment of constituency organisations throughout the United Kingdom.[25] This was supplemented by what was known as 'club government' – a term used to describe the formation of numerous Liberal (social) Clubs in working-class districts, which helped develop the mass of the working-class Liberal movement into a more cohesive force. There were numerous Clubs across England and Wales. They acted as the social and political heart of the mass Liberal movement in Wales, particularly in the south of Wales.

The Welsh Liberation Society ensured that the disestablishment issue remained central to Welsh politics. The Society's members were integral to Welsh Liberalism in 1868, and they also paid for five Welsh election agents for Welsh Liberal constituencies.[26] These agents directly supported those MPs and candidates who also desired disestablishment. The Welsh Liberation Society, however, began to get frustrated by the lack of progress in achieving disestablishment within a Liberal government. The pushing forward of the cause was restricted by the fact that the sole method the Welsh had of influencing the actions of MPs in parliament was by county associations addressing resolutions to the annual conference of the National Liberal Federation.[27] This proved wholly unsatisfactory as far as the Welsh Liberation Society and many Welsh Liberal nationalists were concerned. There was no time in a British annual conference of the National Liberal Federation to debate and pass enough motions concerning Wales. The constant fears of the Welsh Liberation Society and Welsh Liberal nationalists were that they would not even get the opportunity speak on the conference platform or that their important motions would be voted down by the more powerful English party. They therefore needed a more powerful voice. It was felt that only the establishment of Welsh Liberal Federations could do this. These federations, they believed, would then debate the issues more thoroughly and then give them a voice in determining the national policy agenda.

The first substantial step in establishing Welsh federations occurred in late 1886. In North Wales, the Liberal Agent for Wrexham, Mr Tilsen, put forward plans to establish a Welsh Liberal Federation for all Welsh Liberals. Neither Liberals in North or South Wales would accept such as body, however, as both feared domination by the other. Thus on the evening of 14th December 1886, at a meeting in Rhyl Skating Rink, North Wales and Mid Wales Liberals agreed to set up a Liberal Federation for North Wales.[28] Prominent North Wales Liberals also saw the Federation's establishment as a means to address their own political agenda. The prominent North Wales Liberal Thomas Gee, for instance, was able to ensure that the issues of tenant farmers rights in Wales were inserted into the new Federation's list of immediate priorities before it had even had its first official meeting.

In Mid Wales the Liberals in Montgomeryshire, under the Chairmanship of Arthur Charles (A.C.) Humphreys-Owen, a large Liberal landowner and Gladstone's personal friend and the MP, Stuart Rendel, wanted to form their own Mid Wales Federation.[29] The Northern Liberals felt this split would dilute their power, so at their first meeting, they elected Rendel as their President, Humphreys-Owen their chairman and Tilsen their Secretary. After persuading the separatist Montgomeryshire Liberals to join them in the North Wales Federation, Humphreys-Owen and Rendel soon forgot their desire for a Mid Wales Federation. The North Wales Liberal Federation, now consisted of nineteen delegates; thirteen for the North Wales Liberals Associations and three for Mid Wales. Interestingly, Liverpool also sent three delegates to the North Wales Federation as representatives of the Welsh population there. By the start of 1887, the North Wales Federation was in operation.

The Liberals in the South were not far behind those in North and Mid Wales in establishing a federation. On the 24th of January 1887, a meeting of South Wales Liberals in Cardiff responded to events in the North by setting up the South Wales Liberal Federation. Richard Hall became the new Secretary in the South and over the coming decades was to vie with Tilsen in the North for the public face of 'Welsh policy' determination. Once established, the North and South Wales Federations played an official part in the development of both British and Welsh party policy through the

NLF. Welsh policy was now given a platform to influence British Liberal policy.[30] Over time, the Northern Federation would earn the reputation of being 'the more conservative' and the Southern Federation, 'the more militant' of the two Welsh Federations.[31]

The Formation of the Welsh Parliamentary Party

The establishment of the new Federations inspired the Welsh Liberal nationalists to give Welsh Liberalism a more united structure. To this end, the Welsh National Council was created on the 7th of October 1887. It was established in order to bring both North and South Wales Liberal Federation together in a national forum. The Council consisted of the executive committees of both Welsh Federations. It was designed to bridge the gap left in policy-making between the Federations and Welsh Parliamentary Party.[32] In theory, it should have been a powerful mechanism from which to pursue a distinct Welsh Liberal policy agenda. In reality, its opinions were always of secondary importance when compared to those of the North and South Wales Liberal Federations, which it did not always reflect.

It was not just the Welsh Liberal Party's structure that was taking on a Welsh identity; this was spreading to its Parliamentary group. In 1888, Montgomeryshire MP, Stuart Rendel, became the first Chair of the newly formed 'Welsh (Liberal) Parliamentary Party' and, in essence, the unofficial leader of the Welsh party. Although Rendel was an English churchman, who had made his fortune through the Armstrong arms manufacturers, he had become a convert to Welsh issues. He was also a close confidant and supporter of Gladstone.[33] Rendel organised the Welsh Parliamentary Party into a formal structure with a chairman, two whips and a differing Welsh policy agenda to the main party.

The establishment of the Welsh Parliamentary Party did not go unnoticed in Westminster. As a result of Rendel's work, there were soon concerns in Westminster that the Welsh had organised themselves in the same way as the Irish MPs, who were demanding 'Home Rule'. English Liberals began asking the question: 'Would the Welsh soon be as militant as the Irish?' After all, Rendel himself had said in 1886 that the 'Irish question is helping Wales by helping to make a Welsh question'. There was also widespread sympathy for the Irish nationalist and religious causes within Wales. The two national groups of Irish and Welsh, however, never formally worked together and Welsh policy never became as radical as its Irish counterpart even under Rendel's stewardship. The establishment of a Welsh Parliamentary Party in itself, however, was a further acceptance that Welsh Liberalism saw itself as different from English or British Liberalism. How this was to be developed in the future was still open to conjecture. On the 28th of June 1892, Rendel in a speech to his constituency at Newtown was able to talk of the progress in developing Welsh Liberalism. He stated:

> "There is undoubtedly a Welsh Party, that Party is not made of one pattern of man, any more than it is made up of men of one height, or one age; it has diverse elements which contribute to its strength, and its unity. The creation of a Welsh Party is an accomplished fact."[34]

Rendel was right but the Welsh Party was never as united in its nationalist aims as he or other Welsh nationalist MPs would have liked. Over the coming decades, the Welsh Parliamentary Party was to influence government policy on Wales in subtle rather than radical ways. The difference between Wales and Ireland was that many (if not most) of the Welsh Liberal MPs and their general supporters, outside of the disestablishment of the church, always felt issues of Welsh nationalism to be of less importance than the wider political struggles and causes of the Welsh population. They did, however, accept that there was a distinction between them and England and, as a tangible result of this, they held the first Welsh conference in Llandrindod Wells in May 1893. It was addressed by some of those Welsh Liberal MPs who would become defined as the Welsh Liberal Radicals: David Lloyd George, D. A. Thomas, S. T. Evans and Frank Morgan. This was the first time in history that a political party had held a political conference in Wales that was separate from the aegis of English politicians.

Welsh Liberal Fortunes after the 1883–85 Reform Acts

The Liberal ambition to reform the electoral system continued apace during the 1880s. It was seen earlier how the redistribution of parliamentary seats within Wales and the increase in the franchise benefited Liberal representation in Wales. Furthermore, Gladstone, during his second ministry, laid the foundations for some important elements of electoral reform in Britain. He introduced the Corrupt Practices Act (1883) which set a limit on electioneering expenses, and the Third Reform Act (1884) which gave the vote to around 60 per cent of the adult male population. The latter increased the county vote in Wales from 74,936 in 1880 to 200,373 in 1885. There was also a fairer distribution of seats between rural and industrial areas. Wales now had 12 borough (urban) members and 22 county (rural) members due to the Redistribution Act (1885). The general election of 1885 therefore became the first general election in which the majority of the male population were allowed to vote. Now that they could vote, they voted overwhelmingly for the Liberals.

The General Election 1885	
Liberal	29
Conservative	4
Lib-Lab	1

The first modern general election, post the Third Reform Act, proved a triumph for most Liberal candidates in Wales and the 1885 general election increased the number of Welsh MPs by four more to a total of thirty-six. In the 1880 general election, the Conservatives had been reduced to just two MPs in Wales. At this election there had been a massive rise in support of the Marquis of Salisbury's Conservative Party in England but this was not mirrored in Wales. There were only a small number of Conservative gains in Wales. The Liberals lost Denbigh Boroughs, Radnor and Montgomeryshire Boroughs to the Conservatives but at the same time regained Carmarthenshire East. Although the result doubled the number for the Conservatives in Wales, their victory and the size of their majorities was marginal. Every Welsh Conservative seat had a majority of less than 600 votes and two of these had majorities of less than 100 votes (less than five per cent majorities). This was in marked contrast to Liberal seats, where the majorities for all but five of their MPs were well over ten per cent of the total vote.[35]

The 1885 election was not just significant because the Liberals asserted themselves once more as the dominant political power in Wales. It also sowed the seeds of a political party that in time would replace the Liberals themselves throughout Wales. Since 1868, the trade unions had been sponsoring candidates at general elections. These candidates were known as Liberal-Labour or Lib Labs.[36] This election saw the first of Lib Labs elected in Wales. William Abraham, a miner's agent (nick named 'Mabon'),[37] was elected in the Rhondda mining constituency. Mabon was elected with a majority of 867 votes (12.6%) over the Liberal candidate Frederick Lewis Davies. With his election there developed speculation that a parliamentary Labour party was developing, but this was still some years off and for the moment the Liberals, despite being defeated by Mabon, would welcome him to their side. Far from being a socialist radical, Mabon became a model 'Liberal' playing a key part in the development of the South Wales Liberal Federation and establishing a close personal friendship with both Gladstone and Lloyd George.[38] Mabon and the other new MPs had little time to settle into Westminster, however, as a serious separation of factions within the Liberal Party plunged Britain into another general election.

The General Election 1886

Liberal	26
Conservative	6
Liberal Unionist	1
Lib-Lab	1

The 1886 general election was to be the first in a series in which different Liberal factions fought each other for the control of various Welsh constituencies. Joseph Chamberlain, the arch nonconformist, who had a great following in Wales, had fallen out with Gladstone over Irish Home Rule. Gladstone was very much for Home Rule and Chamberlain very much against it. This caused a split within the Liberals between those who supported either side. It was one of the biggest splits in a ruling party in British history. Some 78 Liberal Unionists MPs left the party in support of Chamberlain; 191 stayed to support Gladstone. The political repercussions took decades to settle down and the immediate effect in Wales was direct electoral contests between Liberals of both camps.

There were seven contests in the 1886 general election in constituencies that were between Liberals and Liberal Unionists in Wales and a further fifteen between Liberals and Conservatives. The party, as a whole, was greatly weakened by the rift but in Wales it managed to remain largely united behind Gladstone.[39] Although Gladstone's Liberals were much reduced across the United Kingdom, this was not the case in Wales. Here the Liberals lost only a handful of seats. The Conservatives gained Haverfordwest and Pembroke Boroughs, Monmouth Boroughs and significantly, for an up-and-coming David Lloyd George, Caernarfon Boroughs. The Liberals also regained Montgomeryshire Boroughs. There was just one Liberal Unionist victory. The Liberal Sir William Cornwallis-West had joined the Liberal Unionists and was subsequently unopposed by the Conservatives and also by the Liberals in Denbighshire West. Thus Cornwallis-West took the seat because the Liberals did not stand against him. Confusingly, Sir Hussey Vivian, a Liberal Unionist also won

Swansea Boroughs unopposed but then took the Liberal Whip at Westminster and was therefore categorised as a Liberal rather than a Liberal Unionist.

In many ways Welsh Liberals were heartened by the general election of 1886. They had successfully fought off challenges in most seats from both Conservatives and Liberal Unionists. Tom Ellis and other Welsh radical Liberal nationalists saw this rejection of the Conservatives and their Liberal Unionist allies as proof of an alliance of the Celtic people of Wales, who would unite to push forward their nationalist issues such as Home Rule and disestablishment. Soon, however, Ellis and his fellow Liberal nationalists were to discover that the first battle facing them was not against the Conservatives and their allies the Liberal Unionists, but between themselves and the Liberal traditionalists in their party.[40]

The Political Demise of the Tory Landlords

The 1865 general election removed many of Tory aristocrats from their Westminster seats and now, in January 1889, another Welsh political milestone occurred at a local government level. A year before, the 1888 Local Government Act had led to the establishment of 15 newly elected county councils in Wales.[41] These councils had taken control over many local affairs that had been overseeen by unelected justices of the peace who ran the local boards. It was now time for the election of these newly established county councils. Later, Liberal folklore would have it that many rural councils had, from the outset, been run by independent members outside of formal political parties. This was certainly not the case at those councils' inception. Political party competition between Liberal and Conservative Party was so intense that only three per cent of candidates stood as Independents, as opposed to around a quarter of council candidates a century later. Local elections during the nineteenth century were almost exclusively a party political affair.

The election results indicated that across Wales the Liberals had been elected with a two-to-one majority over the Conservatives, taking control of every council except Breconshire.[42] The justices of the peace who had previously run the counties had mainly originated from the land-owning classes. This meant that the Tory landlords and their appointed justices of the peace, who had ran much of the educational and municipal systems were now driven from power throughout most of Wales by the new Liberal county councillors. These new county councillors were often tenant farmers, small-scale businessmen, and nonconformist clergy and middle class radicals. Their victory was a repeat of the expulsion of the Tories from Westminster two decades before. Whilst the Tory landlords, however, were largely removed from direct political control in 1889, the Liberal (Whig) land-owning families were able to continue to exert their control of Welsh rural constituencies until after the First World War.[43]

These new elected Welsh county councils and town councils were to become a central part of the political driving force of Welsh Liberalism across Wales from then on. Some fifteen years after these first elections, Lloyd George was able to unite the Welsh counties to fight against the hated Conservative government's 1902 Education Act. This would establish them as an important political force for Welsh policy determination and serve as the clearest example of a democratic Welsh political structure that successfully united Wales, until the arrival National Assembly for Wales over a hundred years later.

The 1890 Caernarfon Boroughs By-election and the Arrival of David Lloyd George in Westminster

The Caernarfon Boroughs by-election became one of the most significant events in Liberal history. It was not the significance of the place but of the person elected and his future role in shaping the Liberal Party that was important. It involved the election of David Lloyd George. Caernarfon Boroughs, also known as Caernarfon Districts, was one of the oldest constituencies in Wales, stretching back in time to the Welsh-English union of 1536. Since the Reform Act of 1832, the constituency had been 'middle of the road' in politics, with its most prominent characteristic being the loyalty of the constituency voters to the incumbent members.[44] Caernarfon Boroughs contained six North Wales' town boroughs: Bangor, Caernarfon, Criccieth, Conway, Pwllheli and Nevin. With their populations combined, the constituency had a population of some 30,000 people.[45]

David Lloyd George had been adopted as the candidate for the seat about fifteen months before the death occurred of the sitting Conservative MP, Edmund Swetenham. Both Lloyd George and the local Liberal Association expected another two years or so to pass before the next general election was called. The Association, nevertheless, soon came up with funds to fight the by-election. The Conservatives were also unprepared for an election and their candidate Ellis Nanney, the squire of Llanystumdwy, only stood after great pressure was put on him. Nanney was known to be a pleasant man but of nowhere near the political calibre of Lloyd George. In his election campaign, Lloyd George styled himself as 'the cottage bred man' whose time had now dawned, as opposed to that of the 'gentry whose time had now passed'.[46] Despite his considerable appeal within the constituency, combined with the added benefits of the popularity of Gladstonism Liberals and rising Welsh nationalism, Lloyd George managed a victory only by the margin of just 18 votes.

Caernarfon Boroughs By-election Result 10th April 1890

Candidate	Party	Vote	Percentage
David Lloyd George	Liberal	1963	50.2%
Hugh John Ellis Nanney	Conservative	1945	49.8%
	Majority	18	0.4%
	Turnout		89.5%

Once elected, Lloyd George would in time become one of the world's premier politicians, but he never forgot his political roots in Caernarfonshire politics. These resonated in the background throughout his Parliamentary life, which became apparent to all those who observed him at close hand. Viscount Samuel, later leader of the Liberal Party, described Lloyd George's good qualities as a leader, which he thought came directly from his formative years in Wales. Samuel wrote:

"His fixed points were those which had been set in his mind when he was a poor lad in a Welsh village – a lively sympathy for all who suffered from poverty and social injustice; and a fervent Welsh nationalism, which afterwards expanded into a championship of all small nationalities. Beyond this he was frankly an opportunist."[47]

As Lloyd George settled into life in Westminster, another general election was just over the horizon. This would once again test the extent to which the Liberals dominated politics in Wales. In the run-up to the election there had been considerable disagreement between the North and South Wales Liberal Federations over issues of policy. Whilst both agreed on the issue of disestablishment, the North wanted to see the issue of free school education to take a central role in the campaign and put it into its MPs' manifestos but those in the South demurred.

The General Election 1892

Liberal	30
Conservative	3
Lib-Lab	1

As in the 1886 the general election, the general election of 1892 saw Chamberlain's Liberal Unionists contest a number of Welsh seats in collaboration with their Conservative allies. Distinguishing between Liberals and Liberal Unionists became increasingly difficult. In some cases, such as Herbert Monger's Liberal Unionist address in Swansea Boroughs, and Morgan Lloyd's address in Anglesey, the Liberal Unionist message was almost identical to that of the Liberals.[48] The Liberal Unionists did, however, differ in their appeal to Welsh nonconformists in voting against the 'Liberal supporters of the Roman Catholic Church', as a message of support for the Protestant 'nonconformists of Ulster'. The other difference was that little attempt was made by the Liberal Unionists to appeal to the 'claims of Wales' in their addresses – so ignoring Welsh nationalism.[49] Many Liberals, in contrast, pleaded directly to the Welsh electorate to support their programme of Welsh issues, especially those concerning disestablishment, land reform, Welsh home rule, temperance reform and education.[50]

The competition in the general election consisted of ten 'Liberal versus Liberal Unionist' contests, with a further 22 Liberal versus Conservative contests to be held. There were also three Liberals who gained their seats unopposed (Carmarthen West, Caernarfonshire – Arfon, and in Glamorganshire) and one Lib Lab, William Abraham (Mabon) who gained the Rhondda unopposed. Despite the extent of the electoral competition, the 1892 general election proved to be far more rewarding for the Liberals than the 1886 election had been. Both Liberalism and *Cymru Fydd* provided wide appeal electorally. The Liberals' share of the Welsh vote subsequently rose from 54 to 65 per cent. Liberal candidates consequently benefited from this rise in their share of the vote. For the Liberal Unionists in Wales, however, it was a poorer election than before.

Amongst those benefiting from the Liberal Unionists' decline in fortune was Major Evan Rowland Jones, a 'hero' of the American civil war at Gettysburg. Jones returned to the country of his birth and regained Carmarthen Boroughs from the Liberal Unionist, Sir John Jones Jenkins. He won by some 225 votes (4.8 per cent). Similarly, a Methodist timber merchant, Herbert Roberts, defeated the Liberal Unionist, Colonel W. C. Cornwallis-West, in Denbighshire West by over 2,000 votes. Outside of Carmarthen Boroughs, however, where, for example, Sir John Jones Jenkins was to contest the seat twice more as a Liberal Unionist, the Liberal Unionist threat had all but disappeared. The election established the nature of Welsh Liberal parliamentary representation. It now consisted mainly of Welsh born, non public school educated men who were either from the legal profession or from industry/business rather than the landed gentry. They were also mainly religiously nonconformists who had become considerably more nationalist in outlook than their predecessors.[51] The Conservatives, on the other hand, were now a party of the Welsh margins, both politically and geographically where they had been restricted to three Welsh border counties (Denbighshire, Monmouthshire and Montgomeryshire).

Liberals Back in Government

When the voting finished, Gladstone's Liberals had 273 seats; their Irish nationalist allies 81. The Conservatives had 268 seats and the Liberal Unionists 47. The result meant that Liberals were once again back in power. There were great expectations from Welsh Liberals, both radical and traditional, concerning the newly elected Gladstone government. The Welsh radicals saw the first indication that their loyalty to Gladstonian Liberalism had been rewarded when the leading Welsh radical, Tom Ellis, was offered a post in the government. The *South Wales Daily News* saw the appointment as 'a compliment to Wales and the Young Wales (Cymru Fydd) contingent, a recognition of conspicuous ability and an earnest desire that Welsh affairs will now have due regard!'[52]

For his part, Tom Ellis sought to push through Welsh legislation on land and the Church. He was only partially successful, and his efforts within the government were partially thwarted by his attempts to placate the greater demands of Welsh radical nationalist MPs such as Frank Edwards, Lloyd George and Herbert Edwards. They were rebelling over the lack of a positive Welsh agenda in the Liberal government's programme.

In its three year term in office, the Gladstone government introduced some Welsh policies, specifically the setting up of the University of Wales. Whilst some Welsh Liberal radicals were heartened by this achievement and the movement towards land reform and the disestablishment of the church in Wales, others were not. It was felt that the government had sapped the unity of the Welsh Liberal nationalists and this meant a poorer deal for Wales. Amongst the leading Welsh Liberal Nationals, Tom Ellis had now become part of the Liberal ruling establishment. Lloyd George was spending as much time fighting against his party as supporting it, and Stuart Rendel was busy with trying to solve the Irish problem. The unity of opposition was fading rapidly whilst the party was in government.

In March 1894, the Earl of Rosebery took over as Prime Minister from Gladstone. Rosebery was an imperialist and one of his first acts was to state publicly that there would be no Home Rule for Ireland until the largest of the three kingdoms, England (the others being Scotland and Ireland) agreed. Welsh ambitions, by implication, would also have to wait for a nod of approval from England because it was designated as a principality rather than a kingdom. Unsurprisingly, this attitude did not go down at all well with the Liberal Welsh nationalist radicals. As time progressed, Rosebery fell out with more of his own MPs, particularly with Sir William Harcourt, who would shortly become a Welsh Liberal MP. The party became increasingly divided. Tom Ellis wrote to Sir Robert Hudson, one of the leading British Liberals that "The disease of the party is deep-seated. Time alone can eradicate it, and time will take ten good years to do the job.'[53]

Added to the problems of the divided party was the onset of an agricultural depression, which led to support from the farming community in a number of Welsh constituencies being switched in protest over Liberal agricultural policies to the Conservatives.

The Birth of the Liberal Radicals and the Failure of *Cymru Fydd*

We have already used the terms 'Liberal nationalist' and 'Liberal radical' earlier in the chapter. It is therefore worth spending a little time explaining how the two terms developed together in Wales. Up until the mid 1880s, nearly every prominent Liberal in Wales had ideologically followed the Liberal-Whig tradition on issues of governance and policy. This meant that Welsh Liberals were almost indistinguishable from their counterparts in England. Between 1886 and 1892, this relationship was reshaped as the old Welsh Whigs faded away and a generation of Liberal politicians dedicated to bringing change in Wales in a 'radical' manner emerged. These radical Welsh 'nationalist' Liberals would soon boast Tom Ellis,[54] Lloyd George,[55] (John) Herbert Lewis, Llewelyn Williams, Ellis-Griffith, William Jones and Frank Edwards among them. They demanded sweeping 'radical' changes in the lives of their constituents and an acceptance of the Welsh nation as a political reality. Both radical Welsh MPs and councillors were committed to changing Wales into a self-confident nation, which was no longer tied so directly to the 'apron strings' of the English Church, Parliament and land-owning aristocracy. They did not seek independence but sought to have Welsh issues addressed more fully.

Two of the most important of these Welsh radicals, Tom Ellis and David Lloyd George, came from neighbouring constituencies in North Wales. George Dangerfield described Lloyd George's arrival in his book, *The Strange Death of Liberal England,* as:

"When he first exploded into English politics, an angry little solicitor from an uncouth, starved district in Wales, he brought with him something alien and dangerous. He was less a Liberal than a Welshman on the loose. He wanted the poor to inherit the earth, particularly if it was the earth of the rich English landlords; and he wanted this with a sly, semi-educated passion which struck his parliamentary colleagues as being in very bad form."[56]

Lloyd George soon became as noticed at Westminster as one of the more traditional Liberal Cabinet heavyweights from Wales, such as Sir William Harcourt, Henry Richard and Stuart Rendel.[57] Tom Ellis and Lloyd George were not the only two prominent new Welsh radicals. There were a number of others worthy of some mention here.[58]

Alfred Thomas was the MP for East Glamorgan. Thomas had been a member of Cardiff Borough Council for the Roath ward in 1875 and had been the Cardiff mayor from 1881–82. In 1891 and 1892 Thomas introduced the National Institutions (Wales) Bill, which, together with proposing a Welsh Secretary in the Cabinet and a national council, would have introduced a national museum and a host of Welsh government departments. The failure of two Bills to gain

Royal Assent due to lack of Parliamentary time was seen by the Liberal radicals as an example of the need to push forward for full Home Rule.[59] Thomas had the reputation of having great practical skills, even though he was a weak orator in Parliament. He was elected as a *Cymru Fydd* treasurer, and although he failed to progress with many of his proposals, he was one of the most significant of the radical Welsh Liberal MPs in Wales in the nineteenth century.

Samuel Thomas (S. T.) Evans was elected to Mid Glamorgan in a by-election in February 1890, which had been caused by the death of former MP Christopher Talbot (The Director of the Great Western Railway who gave his name to Port Talbot). Evans was the son of a grocer who went on to become a barrister. He became one of Lloyd George's closest political allies. Evans permissive personal life, however, earned him an unsavoury reputation and the nickname of the 'merry widower'.[60] Fellow Welsh Liberals, therefore, saw him as an unhealthy influence on the early Parliamentary development of Lloyd George. Despite this disagreeable reputation, however, it did not block Evans' political advancement and he later became Attorney General in Asquith's first government.

John Herbert Lewis[61] was the first chairman of Flintshire County Council from which he went on to become the MP for Flintshire Boroughs in 1892. Lewis was born into a wealthy commercial family and enjoyed an extensive education, which he finished by studying law at Exeter College, Oxford. Lewis was also a long time confidant of Lloyd George but one whose personal life met Welsh Liberal Victorian standards of sobriety, marital faithfulness and devotion to nonconformism. He was committed to furthering the cause of Welsh nationalism; he later became Secretary of the Welsh Parliamentary Party, treasurer of the North Wales Federation and later a Junior Lord of the Treasury and Minister at the Department of Education. It was Lewis who was the key to the tangible aspects of the Liberals' Welsh nationalism stance. He achieved this by gaining funding and government support for the University of Wales, National Library and additional support for Welsh school education.

In Parliament, the new Welsh Liberal Radicals joined with the more traditional Welsh Liberals in supporting Gladstone over his support for Irish Home Rule. They did this despite Joseph Chamberlain's assertions that this loyalty to Gladstone would, in fact, cost the Welsh Liberals dearly by not having their own ambitions fulfilled. Welsh radicalism was consolidated whilst the party was in opposition to Lord Salisbury's Conservative Government from 1886 to 1892. The case for a greater measure of political control for Wales gained further support. On issues of Welsh nationhood, Welsh Liberal Radicals or even Welsh Lib-Labs became increasingly involved in pushing for a better deal for Wales at Westminster. The Welsh Liberals now had their own distinct policy on church disestablishment, education, temperance and land reform that were separate from those policies or practices that applied to England.

The issue of the Welsh language started becoming political for the first time during the Victorian period. In 1892, for instance, Lloyd George put down a motion regretting the appointment of non-Welsh speaking judges in Wales. The Lib-Lab Mabon stressed the importance of the motion during which he 'launched into an unbroken flow of Welsh'.[62] Some members on the Conservatives benches then broke into laughter. Mabon, however, continued until their laughter subsided and then informed them that they had been laughing at the Lord's Prayer. At around the same time, Mabon's efforts led to the formation of the *Society for the Utilisation of the Welsh Language* (Welsh Language Society), which later developed into *Cymdeithas yr Iaith Gymraeg*. He and other Liberals pressed for the inclusion of Welsh in the list of subjects enumerated in the Education Codes during 1887.[63] Simultaneously some other Welsh Lib-Labs urged that all mine inspectors in South Wales should be able to speak Welsh. This was one of the first instances of an attempt at positive discrimination in employment practices concerning the issue of the Welsh language, and would start a political trend that continues until this day.

Lloyd George constantly put down motions in Westminster in support of the language. Both he, Mabon and other Welsh Liberal nationalists worked together in the House of Commons to promote issues concerning Wales. Buoyed by their success in raising Welsh issues to the political forefront, the Welsh Liberal nationalists felt that it was now time for a united Welsh political movement. This was also part of Lloyd George's own personal agenda of leading a united Welsh political movement, just as Parnell was doing in Ireland. Others, however, were not so keen to see the flames of Welsh nationalism given any more fuel. However, it was not just on the Tory benches that Welsh radicalism did not meet with agreement or even sympathy. Such animosity also emanated at times from English Liberals and some older Welsh Liberal MPs. One case which heightened Liberal concern about Welsh nationalism occurred in 1892. On this occasion, Welsh Liberal radicals David Alfred (D. A.) Thomas, Lloyd George, Samuel Evans, and Wynford Phillipps, angered the senior members of their party, including Gladstone, when they obstructed the Clergy Discipline Bill of 1892. They did so by moving amendments to the bill for the promotion of Welsh national interests.[64] Although harsh words were exchanged on this occasion between senior Liberals and the Welsh rebels, 'Welsh revolts' were, on the whole, much tamer than those that occurred with Irish MPs. For 'radicals' such as Lloyd George, S. T. Evans and Tom Ellis, their personal ambitions of serving on the Liberal frontbench would always be more important than pursuing Welsh issues on the backbenches.

Cymru Fydd – Welsh Liberal Nationalism Peaks

The first concrete step in attempting to produce a united Welsh political movement came in 1886. This was in London, not in Wales. It occurred when Tom Ellis helped establish a group of Welsh Liberals in the capital whose ideals represented Welsh nationalism. Their drive for this was their connection to the history, literature, art, social values and political institutions of Wales. In time, the group became known as *Cymru Fydd* (Wales To Be). Among its central aims was the demand for disestablishment and self-government for Wales (Home Rule). *Cymru Fydd* was initially limited to the Welsh political community in London rather than to any specific parts of Wales.[65] Lloyd George was at the helm when it came to taking the concept of *Cymru Fydd* to the wider Wales far from London. His style of oratory was seen by the Liberal faithful as more passionate and arousing than the more senior Tom Ellis. In one of Lloyd George's first public meetings, he declared that 'Welsh Nationalism is not anti-Liberal. It is Liberal enthusiasm worked up to glowing red by blasts of patriotism'.[66]

It was with such passion and enthusiasm that he believed he could lead this Welsh nationalism to gain great things for Wales, including the prize of Welsh Home Rule. The wider Liberal movement was itself heartened by the changing political scene in Wales in the late Victorian era. Many of the initial aspirations of *Cymru Fydd,* for wider Welsh self government were gaining ground and had begun with the removal of the dominance of the Tory Welsh land-owning aristocracy through the increase in the Liberal Welsh parliamentary electorate and the introduction of elected county councils throughout Wales, which took over from the magistrates boards. These advances fuelled further campaigning between 1894 and 1896. *Cymru Fydd* now expanded as a movement and branches were established throughout Wales. It had a full time secretary. Beriah Gwynfe Evans, formerly secretary of the Welsh Language Society. It now contained many of the leaders of the mainly Welsh language speaking parts of Wales. This represented about half of all Welsh Liberal MPs, with Lloyd George at their head. *Cymru Fydd* now wanted to fuse with the Liberal Party in Wales to make one mass political movement for Wales.

Though *Cymru Fydd* was increasing in its momentum and Tom Ellis still seen as the premier Welsh nationalist, Ellis halted his nationalist campaigning when he became the Liberal Chief Whip. Ironically, Ellis then had to deal with his former Welsh radical colleagues such as Lloyd George, Herbert Lewis and D. A. Thomas when they failed to turn up for crucial votes.[67] It was Lloyd George, however, who eventually took Ellis's crown as the unofficial leader of the Welsh nationalists. When the Liberals fell from power in 1895, he took over the leadership of *Cymru Fydd* and toured Wales trying to make it into a genuinely mass movement for Welsh nationalism. Whilst Lloyd George's activities gained the admiration of many Welsh nationalists it also caused some resentment amongst other Welsh Liberal MPs. They felt that Lloyd George was building up *Cymru Fydd* as much to support his own ambitions as those of Welsh nationalism.[68] John Bryn Roberts the Liberal member for Caernarfonshire, Eifion, thought Lloyd George's activities threatened the unity of British Liberalism. Whilst Merthyr Tydfil's D. A. Thomas, treasurer of *Cymru Fydd*, President of the South Wales Federation and now political rival of Lloyd George, suspected his motives as merely self-serving.

Lloyd George's scheme, through *Cymru Fydd*, was to organise a highly disciplined Welsh Party that could link up with the Irish Parliamentary Party to challenge Westminster's view of Wales and to force the Liberal Party to endorse Home Rule. Lloyd George made unsuccessful overtures to this effect through the Irish Nationalist leader Charles Stewart Parnell's mistress, Kitty O'Shea. There was no real enthusiasm for Parnell amongst most Victorian nonconformist Welsh Liberal MPs who were well aware of the Irishman's adulterous liaisons. D. A. Thomas was furious because overtures had been made through 'a mistress'. The fact that Lloyd George was himself also being cited in a divorce petition, while these contacts were being made, made matters worse. When Lloyd George put his proposed plan to a small group of prominent Liberals concerning a united Welsh political party, it was treated in some quarters with outright hostility. D. A. Thomas angrily asked Lloyd George:

"Do you want to repeat Parnell's blunders by ruining everything for Wales' future? You seem to think that the Irish have everything to teach us. It would be better to learn from the lesson of where Mrs. O'Shea will lead Parnell – to Home Rule or the Divorce Court!"[69]

The Lib-Lab MP 'Mabon', whilst pro Welsh, was also anti *Cymru Fydd*. He there-fore tried to no avail to prevent Lloyd George spreading his *Cymru Fydd* message in the Rhondda Valleys.[70] This South Wales hostility to Lloyd George's *Cymru Fydd* vision was not paralleled in the North of Wales. Here *Cymru Fydd* went from strength to strength. The North Wales Liberal Federation amalgamated with *Cymru Fydd* in April 1895. This move was partially aided by Lloyd George's own standing and the background work of his close North Wales ally, Hebert Lewis.[71] On the 1st of June 1895, the North Wales Federation Executive under Thomas Gee's presi-dency formally requested that the South should now merge with it and become one Federation.[72] The cynics in the South Wales Liberal Federation, under the influence of D. A. Thomas, did not feel the same enthusiasm for union. Here it was widely felt that the English language Liberal speaking party of South Wales and their support-ers would be dominated by 'Welsh ideas' from the North led by Lloyd George. In January 1896, Lloyd George's ideas for a united political movement were debated and thoroughly rejected by the Southern Welsh Liberals. Robert Bird, a native of Bristol and co-founder and chairman of the Cardiff Liberal Association stated: 'There are from Swansea to Newport, thousands of Englishmen as true Liberals as yourselves ... who will never submit to the domination of Welsh ideas'.[73]

The anti-Welsh nationalism feeling was strongest in Newport, with the Conservative paper *The Western Mail* accurately portraying the town as a 'radical bear-pit' opposed to 'Welsh domination'.[74] D. A. Thomas and a number of other members of the South Wales Liberal Federation remained very much against Lloyd George's aspiration of union with the south. Such a reaction to a cause so close to his heart was not treated lightly by Lloyd George. He fumed with rage regarding with the reaction in the south to *Cymru Fydd*. Lloyd George asked of the Welsh nation whether it was 'prepared to be dominated by English capitalists who sought to take everything from the nation but put nothing back?' As far as the Liberals of Newport and much of South Wales were concerned, the answer was 'yes'. They rejected *Cymru Fydd*, which would turn Lloyd George against the very notion of Home Rule in Wales.[75]

The failure of *Cymru Fydd* to amalgamate with the South Wales Liberal Federation proved a fatal blow to the movement. If the North and the South could not unite, the hope for the Welsh nation of a united nationalist movement was lost. Although there were *Cymru Fydd* meetings in the South in 1897 and 1898, they no longer held the same conviction. The ideals of *Cymru Fydd* did not completely fade away with its demise but they were severely weakened. The bitterness between Lloyd George and D. A. Thomas would continue long after plans for *Cymru Fydd* had faded, although Thomas would later become a Lloyd George supporter until his death in 1918. The opportunity for the Welsh Liberals to totally dominate the nationalist agenda was also greatly diminished. Over half a century later when a variation of *Cymru Fydd* once again came forward with some force, it was not the Liberals but Plaid Cymru that lit the hearts of most nationalists in Wales, but with nowhere near the same mass appeal as *Cymru Fydd*.[76]

The Westminster By-elections of 1892–1895

Following their general election success, the Liberals performed well in the Welsh by-elections over the next three years. Between 1892 and 1895, there were four by-elections in Wales. All these elections were Liberal victories, although only one was contested. The first by-election was just six weeks after the general election. It was caused by Tom Ellis going into Gladstone's Cabinet as Lord Commissioner in the Treasury. At this time, MPs entering the Cabinet were required, by convention, to resign and stand again for their seat. Ellis was re-elected unopposed for his Meirionnydd constituency. Just under a year later, in June 1893, William Williams was also returned unopposed for Swansea Districts, as his predecessor Sir H. Hussey Vivian became Lord Swansea. In June of the same year, William Bowen Rowlands was elected unopposed in Cardigan. Rowlands had been forced to stand for re-election after being appointed as Recorder of Swansea.

The final by-election, in March 1894, in Montgomeryshire was the only contested one. Here the sitting MP Stuart Rendel was elevated to the Lords as Baron Rendel, and the Liberal barrister, (A.C.) Humphreys-Owen, narrowly defeated the Conservative Robert William Williams-Wynn by 225 votes (3.4%). Williams-Wynn's vote had been boosted by the Montgomeryshire farmers sending out a protest vote against the Liberal government for their failure to react adequately to the agricultural recession. Rendel's ennoblement also meant that a new chairman of the Welsh Parliamentary Party was required. This went to Sir George Osborne Morgan (Denbighshire East) who was widely respected as a Welsh political campaigner and politician of some stature by both Welsh and English Liberal MPs.

The National Federation Meets in Cardiff

In January 1895, the annual meeting of the Council of the National Liberal Federation was held in Wales for the first time. The Council had been meeting since 1879 but had never before met outside England. It was the main gathering of the British Liberal Party and the dynamo behind national policy-making and its chosen location was Cardiff. This caused some conflict between the Liberal controlled Cardiff Corporation and the effective 'owner' of Cardiff, the Conservative supporting Third Marquis of Bute. The Third Marquis did all he could to stop the Federation from coming to Cardiff, as he did not want his political foes so openly flaunting themselves in what he regarded as 'his own town'. He forbade the renting or provision of any buildings to the Liberals. To get around this, the Liberals erected a massive hall at Canton Market. It held over 10,000 people and for most of the time 'was packed to overflowing',[77] making it the largest ever official political event in Wales up to that date. The record of proceedings indicated that '…the attendance was of a most representative character, and the cordiality with which the Federation was received and entertained left the pleasantest recollections, and stamped the gathering as one of the most successful yet held.[78]

Much of the Council's time was taken up addressing the issue of the disestablishment of the Welsh Church and the problems the Liberal government was having with the House of Lords. It was the first time in history that a British political party had held its main political meeting in Wales and had dedicated so much time to key Welsh policy issues. The National Federation meeting made sure that few in the Liberal hierarchy were now ignorant of the fact that Welsh Liberalism and Wales, in some areas, wished to develop their own political agenda.

The General Election 1895	
Liberal	23
Conservative	8
Liberal Unionist	1
Lib Lab	1

Although the government, under the Liberal Lord Rosebery, should have fallen because of its internal splits over Home Rule for Ireland, it did not. Its fall from office came about instead due to continued minor scandals concerning army reforms. When the election came, the Conservative vote was boosted across the United Kingdom by a generally unpopular Liberal government. The Liberals lost 90 seats across Britain. In Wales they lost six seats. It was to be the Conservatives' best election victory in Wales until 1983, nearly 90 years later. The Conservatives won Swansea Town, Cardiff Boroughs, Pembroke and Haverfordwest Boroughs and Glamorgan South. The Liberal Unionist, Sir John Jones Jenkins, a popular local industrialist and owner of the Beaufort tinplate works, won his former Carmarthen Boroughs seat back.[79] In other seats, Liberal MPs just held on. There was one Liberal gain in Montgomeryshire, where the 1894 by-election winner, (A.C.) Humphreys-Owen won again, but this time by just 52 votes. His majority of just 52 votes was one of the smallest in Wales (1%). David Lloyd George's 194 (4.4%) majority ensured he was not far behind either the reduced totals of Humphreys-Owen or Jones Jenkins. D. A. Thomas and Pritchard Morgan saw their majorities in Merthyr Tydfil fall by over half and the Conservatives came within 2059 (8.1%) votes of winning a seat there.

The 1895 election was not bad news for every Liberal in Wales. Tom Ellis gained over 70 per cent of the vote in his election and a 40 per cent majority in Meirionnydd over his Conservative opponent. Nine other Liberal MPs in Wales had majorities over 20 per cent and a further four with a majority over 10 per cent. In contrast to this, no Conservative MP had a majority above 7.2 per cent in Wales.[80] Although newly re-elected Tom Ellis was one of Wales' most prominent home-grown Liberal MPs, his majority was not the largest in Wales. This belonged to a newly arrived and newly elected Welsh MP, but one who held greater seniority and prominence than Ellis. This was Sir William Harcourt who won nearly eighty per cent of the vote in Monmouthshire West and had a majority of some 57.4 per cent. Harcourt was important as a Liberal, not just because of his large majority but also because of his stature as one of the foremost Liberals and Leader of the Liberals in the House of Commons. He was the effective forerunner of the next Liberal Prime Minister, Sir Henry Campbell-Bannerman.

Parliamentary By-elections 1895–1900 and a New Welsh Party Chairman

There were just three by-elections between 1895–1900 (Denbigh East, Meirionnydd and Pembroke). The first by-election was due to the death of the Denbigh East MP and Welsh nationalist chairman of the Welsh Parliamentary Party, Sir George Osborne Morgan, in the summer of 1897. He was one of the first Liberal MPs to campaign openly on Welsh issues ranging from the appointment of Welsh-

speaking judges to nonconformist burials on Church of England land. The subsequent Denbigh East by-election resulted in the election of the Liberal barrister
Samuel Moss with a considerable majority: 2327 (29%). This was a five per cent
increase on Morgan's own 1895 election victory, but unlike his predecessor, Moss
was no Welsh nationalist and instead concentrated on building his own legal career,
eventually becoming a county court judge in 1906.

In 1897, along with a new MP for Denbigh East, the Liberal Party also required
a new chairman of the Welsh Parliamentary Party. In the ensuing contest, both
Lloyd George and Brynmor Jones (Swansea District) were nominated but both
declined to stand. Lloyd George's South Wales rival D. A. Thomas (Merthyr Tydfil)
had left the parliamentary party over a dispute about interference in South Wales
affairs and so wasn't in the running. Sir Reginald McKenna persuaded the meeting that a senior Welsh Liberal was needed for the post and therefore Pontypridd's
Welsh nationalist MP, Alfred Thomas, was elected unopposed.[81] The selection of
Thomas as Chair was seen a mixed blessing. He had, after all, tried in 1890, 1892
and 1893 to set up an elected council for Wales and to appoint a Welsh Secretary
to the Cabinet through his Welsh Institution Bills. Despite these nationalist credentials for some Liberals, however, his appointment was seen as the start of the
decline of the party in Wales. Humphreys-Owen (Montgomeryshire) noted in 1901
that 'the Welsh Party committed suicide when it put that old pantaloon Thomas into
the Chair'.[82] Other Welsh Liberals saw Lloyd George's rejection of the post as the
first indication that he did not intend to be tied solely to Welsh matters, but wanted
to apply his political talents on wider political field. In a time of increasing concern
over radical Welsh Liberal nationalism, senior Liberals, however, saw Thomas as a
'safe pair of hands' and were glad he was at the helm of the Welsh party.

The next by-election occurred in Pembroke in February 1898. The election
was caused by the appointment of the Liberal MP, William Rees Morgan Davies,
as Attorney General of the Bahamas. Sir John Wynford Phillips (the Thirteenth
Baronetcy of Picton) became the Liberal candidate. Phillips was a Pembrokeshire
land-owning barrister who had the distinction of defeating Keir Hardie when he had
previously stood in Mid Lanarkshire. He won the Pembroke seat with some ease with
a 1664 vote (19.6 %) majority over the Conservative Hugh Frederick Campbell (the
Fourth Earl Cawdor). He later became a key figure in the Liberal Party, President of
the Welsh National Liberal Council (as Viscount St Davids from 1908) and a key
ally of Lloyd George.

The third by-election of this Parliament was a consequence of a tragedy for Welsh
Liberalism and Welsh nationalism. The party had lost the Welsh nationalist MP
Sir George Osborne Morgan in 1897, but at 71 years of age his death had not been
totally unexpected. Two years later, there was an even greater loss for the Welsh
and British Liberal Party. The Liberal nationalist and Welsh Liberal supporting
newspapers' favourite Welsh radical MP, Tom Ellis, died after a long illness. Ellis's
early death, at the age of 40, was seen by many Liberals as depriving the Welsh
and the national party of a major talent. Ellis was also the only Welsh Liberal MP
able to match the growing talents and stature of David Lloyd George.[83] Although
Lloyd George and Tom Ellis had become firm friends, it was expected that at some
time these great politicians would compete together on the national stage. This contest would now never occur and Lloyd George would forever remember Ellis as a
political ally, rather than rival. The subsequent Meirionnydd by-election in May

1899 was not contested by the Conservatives or by anyone other than the Liberals. Therefore the Oxford academic, Owen Morgan Edwards, also the joint editor of the *Cymru Fydd* newspaper, became the hastily imposed candidate. He was duly elected for one year before stepping aside at the next general election to continue his academic career and later, in 1907, he would become the first Chief Inspector of Schools for Wales under the next Liberal government.

The Dominance of Liberals in Wales Prior to 1900

By the end of the nineteenth century the dominance of Liberals and Liberalism within Wales had spread to all the four geographical corners. Many of the Welsh constituencies were so strongly Liberal supporting that they were regarded as safe havens for any Liberal politician lucky enough to be elected there. Often these politicians were not challenged even at election times and kept their seats unopposed. The emergence of Welsh nationalism – the religious fever that had embraced Welsh Liberals – combined with the expansion of the electoral franchise and electoral competition, meant that the Liberals dominated Welsh politics during the late Victorian and Edwardian period to an even greater extent than the Labour Party was to do so half a century later. It is worth examining the extent to which Liberalism dominated Wales during the late Victorian and early Edwardian era. Outside of the Parliamentary dominance, Liberalism was present in:[84]

The press. Liberalism was evident in the majority of the Welsh press. Between 1856 to 1886 the number of newspapers produced in Wales increased from 18 to 83.[85] Many of these new papers were founded by Liberals themselves to become part of the Liberal political machine. The public was informed and became opinionated mainly via local, regional and national newspapers. Many prominent Liberals such as David Lloyd George, Llewelyn Williams and Tom Ellis expressed their views in the Welsh press through regular columns. Papers such as *The Rhondda Leader*, *Cardiff Times*, the *Caernarfon and Denbigh Herald* and the *South Wales Daily News* were effective supporters of the Welsh Liberals.[86] Welsh language papers were also prominent with Liberal journalists, authors and publishers such as Thomas Gee, editor of *Baner ac Amersau Cymru* taking leading roles in society.

Commerce and industry showed close affiliation with Liberals. The chambers of commerce for Swansea, Cardiff and Newport tended to reflect Liberal attitudes. Welsh industrialists such as: Christopher Talbot, D. A. Thomas and David Davies in coal, railways and ports; John Cory and Henry Radcliffe in shipping and Lord Glantawe in tinplate, supported the Liberals.

Culture – Wales experienced a period of cultural renaissance particularly in poetry and literary criticism. The Eisteddfod flourished more than ever before.[87] These were endorsed by leading Liberals from Gladstone to Tom Ellis and Lloyd George.

Local government was dominated by Liberal councillors. After the Local Government Act of 1888 opened up Welsh counties to elections, the Liberals soon dominated. The Liberals in many areas became a party of the 'little man' against the landed gentry. The January 1889 elections in Cardiganshire for instance, saw the Liberals gain a majority of 37 to 10. The 37 Liberals elected included 13 tenant farmers, 11 small businessmen and four nonconformist ministers. The rise of the so called 'little man' continued within all counties. In 1904, every county council in Wales returned a Liberal majority. The calibre of the Liberal councillors, however, often disappointed Liberal radicals such as Tom Ellis, who saw them as being consumed by 'petty detail'.[88]

In education, partly as a result of local government dominance, the Liberal dominated Central Welsh Board appointed 'Liberal' supporting inspectors, who imposed Liberal values on the new 'county schools' headmasters, teachers and pupils. The result was the production of Liberal minded pupils who pursued Liberal ideals in Wales for a further generation. Liberal politicians and supporters also helped create and build up the University of Wales and its colleges at Aberystwyth, Bangor and Cardiff.

In the late nineteenth century, and early twentieth century Liberalism in Wales ruled the political roost. If you believed in social progression, Welsh nationalism or just wanted to go with the political tide, you were a Liberal by party. In addition, it provided Wales with another defining political difference from its English neighbours where the Conservative party still tended to dominate. Wales was first and fundamentally a Liberal nation, to the exclusion of all other political creeds. To this extent, Liberalism's presence was felt everywhere.

Conclusion

In 1859, when the Liberal Party was formed, Wales was not recognised by many politicians as constituting a nation. The Tory landlords and MPs who dominated Welsh political life, although Welsh by birth, were English by nature and saw themselves as part of the English establishment. Similarly, the newly formed Liberal Party in Wales showed very little of the Welsh nationalism it would later develop. Yet during the later Victorian period, this view of Wales would change forever. Wales was evolving rapidly politically. As the various Reforms Acts modernised the Welsh constituencies and widened the franchise, the Liberal supporting electorate in Wales exercised its vote in ever increasing numbers. In the year the Liberal Party was formed, the general election removed much of the Welsh Tory squirearchy. At the same time as Wales was losing its Tory MPs, it was also losing the conservatism of the Whigs, whose removal from the Liberal Party brought about a renaissance in the politics of Welsh cultural and national identity.

Over the ensuing decades, the rise of the Liberal Party in Wales saw the start of the development of unique policy desires. Welsh nationalism flourished in the 1880s and 1890s to the extent that no one could any longer doubt that Wales was developing politically as a nation. It appealed not only on account of it opposition to the dominance of the Tory anglophile 'landlord, brewery and the bishop' but also by virtue of the Liberals' desire for Welsh people to have a greater say over running their political affairs and establishing their national institutions. The Welsh Liberal party which had, however, been internally split between support for and against *Cymru Fydd* had survived the riven with the Liberal Unionists virtually unscathed. The end of *Cymru Fydd* did, however, indicate the high water mark of Welsh Liberal nationalism but not its political peak, as the party had its 'golden age' still to come.

Notes

1. Morgan, Kenneth O. (1982) Rebirth of a Nation, Wales 1880–1980, Oxford University Press, p. 52
2. The Whigs emerged between 1679–80 as a group agitating for the exclusion of James, Duke of York, on the grounds of Catholicism. The name was thought to have come from the militant Scottish Presbyterian the 'Whiggamores'. The Whigs primarily backed the principles of the 1688 Glorious Revolution and the limitation of the role of monarchy in British politics
3. Peelites were broadly reform minded in economic, political and social issues. They therefore blended well with the Whigs who had become associated with the new industrial interests, nonconformity, and reform
4. Boothroyd, David (2001) Politico's Guide to The History of British Political Parties, Politico's Publishing, p. 158
5. Little, Tony (1998) Viscount Palmerston and Bloy, Margie (1998) Lord John Russell, in Dictionary of Liberal Biography (1998) Duncan Brack [ed] Politico's Publishing
6. Morgan, Kenneth O. (1980) Wales in British Politics 1868–1922, University of Wales Press
7. Vincent, John (1976) 2nd Edition, The Formation of the British Liberal Party 1857–1868, Harvester Wheatsheaf, p. 51
8. James, Arnold, J. and Thomas, John E. (1981) Wales at Westminster, Gomer, p. 67
9. Grigg, John (1997) Lloyd George: The Young Lloyd George, Penguin, p. 41
10. McCormick, Donald (1963) The Mask of Merlin: A Critical Study of David Lloyd George, Macdonald, pp. 34–35
11. Lord Howells to author
12. Morgan, Kenneth, O. (1980) op. cit., p. 26
13. Vincent, John (1976) op. cit., p. 52
14. Vincent, John (1976) op. cit., p. 48
15. Deacon, Russell (2010) 'Statues and newspaper wars': Cardiff town and city politics in Cardiff (1868–1908) Morgannwg: The Journal of Glamorgan History, Vol. LIII, 2010
16. Pearce, Malcolm (1992) British Political History 1867–1990, Democracy in Decline, Routledge p. 45
17. Robertson, David (1986) The Penguin Dictionary of Politics, Penguin, p. 187
18. Words by Henry George (1839–1897) who lead a movement that believed that land belonged to the community rather than any one individual
19. Rasmussen, Jorgen Scott (1965) The Liberal Party, Constable, p. 62
20. Morgan, K. O. (1960) Gladstone and Wales, Welsh History Review, Vol. 1, No. 1, p. 70
21. Morgan, K. O. (1960) op. cit., p. 70
22. Deacon, Russell (2006) Devolution in Britain today, Manchester University Press, p. 124
23. Morgan, K. O. (1960) op. cit., p. 82
24. *The Times*, Monday, Jul 14, 1890, p. 9
25. Self, Robert (2000) The Evolution of the British Party System 1885–1940, Longman, p. 32
26. Vincent, John (1976) 2nd Edition, The Formation of the British Liberal Party 1857–1868, Harvester Wheatsheaf, p. 71
27. Nelmes, Graham, V. (1979) 'Stuart Rendel and Welsh Liberal Political Organisation in the Late Nineteenth Century', Welsh History Journal, Vol. 9, No. 4 December 1979, p. 467
28. Watson, R. Spence (1906) The National Liberal Federation 1877 to 1906, T. Fisher Unwin, p. 68
29. Nelmes, Graham, V. (1979) op. cit., p. 473
30. Nelmes, Graham, V. (1979) op. cit., p. 470

31. Jones, Wyn (1986) Thomas Edward Ellis 1859–1899, University of Wales Press, p. 43
32. Nelmes, Graham, V. (1979) op. cit., p. 478
33. Morgan, Kenneth O. (1960) op. cit., p. 72
34. Rendel, Stuart (1892) The Land Question and the Farmers' a speech delivered by Rendel at Newtown, 28 June 1892
35. Cardiff Boroughs, Caernarfon Boroughs, Pembroke and Havefordwest Boroughs, Flint Boroughs and Monmouthshire
36. Boothroyd, David (2001), Politico's Guide to The History of British Political Parties, Politico's Publishing, p. 148
37. William Abraham adopted the bardic name of Gwilym Mabon in 1869. He was subsequently known by the surname of Mabon
38. In this respect Mabon addressed the Caernarfonshire voters on behalf of Lloyd George in 1890 and in 1914 appealed to the miners for their support in the war on behalf of Lloyd George – Evans, E. W. (1959) Mabon: A Study in Trade Union Leadership, University of Wales Press, p. 39
39. Little, Tony (1999) Out from under the umbrella, Journal of Liberal Democrat History, Issues 25, Winter 1999–2000, p. 13
40. Masterman, Neville (1972) The Forerunner, The Dilemmas of Tom Ellis 1859–1899, Merlin Press, p. 85
41. Although there was no provision in the Act for Parish Councils in Wales, Tom Ellis, was able to put in an amendment for their inclusion at a later date
42. Davies, John (1994) A History of Wales, Penguin, p. 457
43. The Stepneys of Llanelli and the Hughes of Tre-gib for instance controlled the Liberal Party in East Carmarthenshire until August 1912 (Morgan, Kenneth O. 1991, Wales In British Politics, 1868–1922, University of Wales Press, p. 245)
44. Between 1837 and 1945 William Buckley Hughes and David Lloyd George served 94 years between them representing the constituency
45. This made it a much smaller constituency than the Welsh average at the time, which was 45,000 people – Grigg, John (1997) op. cit., p. 81
46. Grigg, John (1997) op. cit., p. 81
47. Samuel, Viscount (1945) Memoirs, The Cresset Press, p. 88
48. Morgan, Kenneth O. (1991) Wales In British Politics, 1868–1922, University of Wales Press p. 118
49. Morgan, Kenneth O. (1991) op. cit., p. 118
50. Morgan, Kenneth O. (1991) op. cit., p. 119
51. Morgan, Kenneth O. (1991) op. cit., p. 119
52. Jones, Wyn (1986) op. cit., p. 59
53. Douglas, Roy (1971) The History of the Liberal Party 1985–1970, Sidgewick and Jackson, London, p. 18
54. Thomas Edward Ellis (1859–1899) M. P. Meirionnydd (1886–1999) Liberal Chief Whip 1894–9
55. David Lloyd George (1863–1945) President of the Board of Trade, Chancellor, Minister for Munitions, Prime Minister and Liberal Leader
56. Dangerfield, George (1935) The Strange Death of Liberal England, Serif, p. 29
57. Graham Jones, J. (1988) 'Early Campaigns to Secure a Secretary of State for Wales, 1890–1939, Transactions of the Honourable Society of Cymmrodrion, p. 154
58. Grigg, John (1997) op. cit., pp. 95–96
59. Graham Jones, J. (1990) Thomas's National Institutions (Wales) Bills of 1891–92, The Welsh History Review, Vol. 15, No. 2, p. 219
60. Grigg, John (1997) op. cit., p. 97
61. Morgan, Kenneth O. (2007) Lloyd George's Flintshire Loyalist: The Political Achievements of John Herbert Lewis, Journal of Liberal History, Vol. 57, Winter 2007–8, pp. 18–30
62. Evans, E. W. (1959) op. cit., p. 40
63. Evans, E. W. (1959) op. cit., p. 39
64. Morgan, Kenneth O. (1960) op. cit., p. 65
65. Davies, John (1994) op. cit., p. 454
66. McCormick, Donald (1963) op. cit., p. 43
67. *The Times*, Thursday, Apr 19, 1894 p. 6
68. This was first but not the last time that Lloyd George's campaigning split the Welsh party

69. McCormick, Donald (1963) op. cit., p. 46
70. Grigg, John (1997) op. cit., p. 201
71. Morgan, Kenneth O. (2007) op. cit., p. 22
72. *The Times*, Monday, Jun 03, 1895, p. 8
73. Davies, John (1994) op. cit., p. 466
74. *The Western Mail* 25/1/96, p. 4
75. Jennifer Longford to author 20/2/07, Lloyd George after this event feared that the English South would dominate the Welsh North in any parliament and became opposed to Home Rule
76. Davies, John (1994) op. cit., p. 466
77. Watson, R. Spence (1906) op. cit., p. 171
78. Watson, R. Spence (1906) op. cit., p. 171
79. Morgan, Kenneth O. (1991) op. cit., p. 159
80. The highest majority was W. H. Wyndam-Quin (Glamorgan South) with a majority of 7.8 per cent
81. *Aberdeen Weekly Journal* 15/3/1898, p. 8
82. Morgan, K. O. (1991) op. cit., p. 167
83. Grigg, John (1997) Lloyd George: The Young Lloyd George, Penguin, p. 221
84. Morgan, Kenneth O. (1982) op. cit., pp. 50–51
85. Vincent, John (1976) op. cit., p. 65
86. *The Western Mail* was the main Welsh Conservatives paper of this period funded by the Bute Estate in Cardiff
87. Parry, Cyril (1973) The New Liberalism and the Challenge of Labour: The Welsh Experience, 1885–1929, Welsh History Review, 1973, p. 289
88. Jones, Wyn (1986) Thomas Edward Ellis, 1869–1899, University of Wales Press, p. 41

2

THE LIBERAL ZENITH: THE 'GOLDEN AGE' (1899–1918)

Introduction

The chapter starts in 1899, a year in which Welsh soldiers, as part of the British Empire force, were launched into a colonial war in South Africa – the Boer War. The prosecution of this war had the effect of once more dividing the Liberal Party in both Wales and elsewhere; this time into pro- and anti-war factions. Some two decades later another conflict would similarly split the party, although this time it would be over the conduct of the First World War. Welsh Liberals played a central role in both splits and were similarly placed in both camps. In between these splits, however, was the zenith of Welsh Liberalism, the landslide general election of 1906. An election in which 33 of the 34 Welsh MPs took the Liberal Whip at Westminster. This was truly a 'Golden Age' for the Welsh Liberals. This momentous election heralded an era of Welsh political Liberal giants, leaders such as Reginald McKenna, Sir Alfred Mond, D. A. Thomas and David Lloyd George, whose names were not only familiar in Wales and Great Britain but also across the wider British Empire. They projected the presence of the Welsh Liberal nation onto the political world to an extent never seen before or since.

As the Edwardian era progressed, it seemed as if Liberalism in Wales would turn the nation into a one party state but the Liberal dream began to fade almost as soon as the Edwardian period came to an end in 1910. This second chapter seeks to explain something of the Welsh Liberals in their 'Golden Age' and also explore in some detail the start of their subsequent political decline.

The Liberals in the Edwardian Period

Although the Welsh Liberals dominated most of Wales politically, the twentieth century started poorly for them. They entered the century with much of the rebelliousness and nationalist inspiration of *Cymru Fydd* fading, with some key figures, such as Sir George Osborne Morgan and Tom Ellis, dead, and with their supporters searching for a new inspirational figure to follow. Whilst the statures of some Welsh MPs, in particular the young Lloyd George, were growing nationally, Welsh party policy was still closely associated with the issues of 'beer and Bible' (temperance and church disestablishment). Whilst these remained popular issues amongst Liberal activists, they were becoming more remote from needs of the growing labour and industrial problems that were affecting the sprawling working-class populations of industrial south and north Wales. A party that was prepared to deal with these issues was the newly founded Labour Representation Committee (soon to be the Labour Party). Founded in 1900, it was still a small-scale political grouping at the end of Victoria's reign, but it was starting to find its feet in Wales where Keir Hardie (Merthyr Tydfil) would be their first Welsh MP and party leader. Three years later, in 1903, the Labour and Liberal parties made an electoral pact, the so-called Progressive Alliance, which stopped them directly contesting seats where the other was felt to have the best chance against the Conservatives. Although this greatly increased the number of Labour MPs, unions such as the South Wales Miners' Federation, with a membership of over 100,000, still backed the Liberals. By 1909, however, their resources would be affiliated to the Labour Party. The wider trade union movement was also for a period uncertain about whether it would create its own political party or back the Liberals. Within the coming decade, this decision would be made and the result of their decision would be bad news for the Liberals.

The 1900 'Khaki' General Election

Liberal	26
Conservative	6
Lib-Lab	1
Independent Labour Party	1

On the 11th of October 1899, the Boer Republic of South Africa declared war on the British Empire. From then on, this war became unimaginatively known as 'The Boer War'. Many Welsh Liberals, especially Lloyd George, were against the war. This was because, ideologically, they believed that the British Empire should consist of many different nations that, in turn, would form a huge confederacy of nation states – each with its own rights of self determination over domestic issues. Britain therefore should not interfere with the domestic politics of the Boers. The Conservatives and Liberal Imperialists, on the other hand, believed in an Empire of close conformity with Great Britain (mainly England and Scotland) at its heart, acting as its guide and mentor to the other nations of the British Empire. These two ideological approaches clashed openly with the onset of the Boer War. A concept that involved defining the question: 'What sort of Empire should Wales be part of?'

The anti-war camp contained David Lloyd George, who was joined by other Welsh Liberals such as his close ally, Herbert Lewis (Flint Boroughs), Sir Frank Edwards (former MP for Radnor), (A.C.) Humphreys-Owen (Montgomeryshire), John Bryn Roberts (Eifion Division, Caernarfon) and the Scottish MP and future Liberal Prime Minister, Henry Campbell-Bannerman. Lloyd George toured Wales and England, attacking the policy behind the war of the Marquis of Salisbury's Tory government, rather than the conduct of the war itself. In his speeches he drew parallels between the Boer Republics and Wales. Lloyd George, who always supported the little nations in their struggle against the bigger ones, noted that the population of the Boer Republics was similar in size to Carmarthenshire. The 'British Empire against Carmarthenshire', he mused. It was 'the little nations against the mighty Empire'.[1] This was akin to his arguments on the need for Home Rule for Wales – the small Welsh nation being dominated by its big English neighbour.

The war, however, was not generally unpopular in Wales; in fact, quite the contrary. Many Welsh regiments such as the South Wales Borderers and The Welch Regiment fought in the conflict. The Welsh public in the first year of the war was mainly pro-war, caught up in the patriotism of supporting its soldiers and the jingoism of Empire. Whilst the Liberal Party was divided on the war, a general election was called to make the most of Liberal divisions and Tory unity. On the 18th of September 1900, Parliament was dissolved. The Tory government sought to make use of the popularity it had gained concerning the war – hence the term 'Khaki' election.[2] The general election campaign was led for the Conservatives by the Liberal defector, Joseph Chamberlain (Salisbury's health was deteriorating). Despite the fact that many Liberals supported the war, Chamberlain ran the campaign stating: 'A vote for the Liberals is a vote for the Boers'.[3] The tactic worked; although in the end it only enabled a short term boost for an otherwise unpopular government. It was enough for the Conservatives to return with a 134 seat majority. In Wales they were not so successful, where they actually lost two seats.

In Wales, ten candidates, including Lloyd George, had declared themselves publicly to be against the war. Despite the hostility they faced, all but John Albert Bright, who fought marginal Montgomery District of Boroughs, won their seats. Despite their determination to makes gains from the Khaki election, the Conservatives were unable to take advantage of their situation in Wales. They left the Liberals with eleven seats, unopposed, compared to just one in 1895. This gave the Liberals over a quarter of the total of Welsh seats before even one vote had been cast. For the Liberal Unionists, Sir John Jones Jenkins was the only candidate to stand in Wales. He lost his Carmarthen Boroughs seat to the Liberals' Alfred Davies. The Liberal tally of seats was now 27 out of the 34 seats.[4] Frank Edwards won back Radnor by 166 votes. The Swansea Town and Cardiff constituencies were also won from the Conservatives.

In England, the Conservatives made substantial gains but in Wales, Monmouth Boroughs was their only gain. Here the arch Conservative Imperialist Dr Rutherford Harris won the seat. He was a close friend of both Cecil Rhodes and Dr Leander Starr Jameson, the protagonists behind the Boer war.[5] The contest was damaged, however, by Harris' spectacular corruption in defeating Liberal Albert Spicer. Spicer soon petitioned to have the election result annulled and was successful, and Harris was unseated for corruption. The result did not, however, benefit Spicer. Another Conservative, Joseph Lawrence, won the seat in the May 1901 by-election, although the Conservative majority halved to just 343 (3.8%) from the general election victory just eight months earlier.

Another Period in Opposition

Between November 1885 and December 1905, the Liberals were in power for just three short years. They spent 18 years in opposition. During these 18 years their main consolation in Wales was that they had won outright victory electorally at every election. Despite this Liberal dominance, the Liberal leadership of the British party was shifting from Wales to Scotland. In 1899 the Welsh Liberal MP Sir William Harcourt, after falling out with the Liberal Imperialists led by Lord Rosebery, stepped down as Liberal leader in the Commons and his position was taken by the Scotsman,

Henry Campbell-Bannerman. After the Boer War ended in 1901, it was felt to be the right time for Campbell-Bannerman to try to bring the Liberal Party together again. Campbell-Bannerman had the ability to bind the party after its numerous splits. He was able to straddle the gap between Liberal Imperialists and the anti-war Liberals. Campbell-Bannerman led the Liberals in the last of their long periods of opposition and got them into the position of being a potential party of government once more.

The Welsh Liberal Rebellion against the Education Act 1902

The first issue to help unite the Welsh Liberals occurred shortly after the end of the Boer War. Its cause was the Conservative Party's Education Act 1902. This sought to ensure that all schools, with the exception of private schools, were funded by the local council rate. Previously, voluntary schools, mainly run by the Anglican and Catholic churches, were funded by parents and the church. The Board Schools (state run) were either secular or nonconformist and taught about two-thirds of the pupils in Wales. What the Welsh Liberals led by Lloyd George did not want was for Church of England and Catholic schools to be supported on the rates without the local councils having any influence on the running of the schools. Thus Anglicanism and Catholicism were pitted directly against Christian non-conformism over the Conservative Prime Minister Arthur Balfour's Education Act. The battle against what became know as 'the Balfour Act' had the effect of uniting the Welsh Liberals against common foes, the Conservatives and the established state church. Only the Liberal MP, William Jones (Arfon), was in favour of the Act. All other Liberal MPs were initially either indifferent or opposed to it. Despite attempts to make a compromise for Wales, the Act came into force without a compromise and therefore against widespread opposition. The county and town councils refused to implement it and the March 1904 county council elections were then fought on this issue. The Liberals were united against the Act and won massive majorities in every council in Wales (Table 1). Balfour then brought in the Education (Local Authority Default) Bill in order to force Welsh authorities to take voluntary schools on the local rate. The *Daily News* described it as the 'Coercion of Wales Bill' and it soon became known as *Y Mesur Gormes*.[6] Councils, however, continued to refuse to support Anglican or Catholic voluntary schools, especially after being encouraged to do so by Lloyd George and his fellow Welsh Liberals. Despite the intervention of the courts, the matter remained unresolved till the 1906 general election. It did, however, become one the major electoral issues of the 1900–1906 period.

Cardiff Becomes the First Welsh City

Liberalism had a strong pedigree in Cardiff. It was the largest constituency in Wales with 26,475 voters and, therefore, it also boasted the largest number of Liberal members. Constant electoral spats occurred between the Cardiff Liberal Association and the Conservatives, controlled mainly by the Fourth Marquis of Bute and his various companies. On the 28th of October 1905, Cardiff became a city much to the delight

Table 1 **Welsh County Councillors Elections –**
March 1904 [7]

Council	Liberal	Conservative
Anglesey	48	8
Brecon	39	21
Caernarfon	59	6
Cardigan	54	10
Carmarthen	60	8
Denbigh	53	11
Flint	40	16
Glamorgan	75	13
Meirionnydd	52	3
Montgomeryshire	37	19
Monmouth	50	18
Pembroke	50	14
Radnor	22	10

of both political parties. It was now the 14th biggest city in the British Empire. The move was mainly because of the Conservative government's attempts to gain some votes in the 'new city' in the forthcoming general election. The city council, far more anglicized than anywhere else in Wales, was controlled by the Conservatives – the only council in Wales under their control. They also held the Cardiff parliamentary seat. This was because in 1904 the sitting Liberal MP, Sir Edward Reed, had crossed the floor to join the Conservatives because of his support for trade tariffs. The Liberals were wholly against the introduction of trade protection. In 1905, however, he declared that he was too old and ill to carry on as MP and James Fortescue Flannery became the new Conservative candidate. The Liberals had selected Ivor Churchill Guest, a sitting Conservative MP and industrialist who had just joined the Liberal Party, over the issue of free trade (both were strongly in favour of it).[8] He crossed the floor on the issue with his cousin, Winston Churchill.

Guest's family, despite moving the Guest family seat to Dorset in the 1840s had retained strong links with Wales and with Glamorganshire[9] in particular. Despite his Welsh credentials, it was the fact that he was a former Conservative candidate that did not go down well with many of the Cardiff Liberals, the Trades Council, or even with neighbouring Welsh Liberals MPs such as D. A. Thomas.[10] Nevertheless, Guest would successfully spend the next few years integrating himself with the Cardiff Liberal establishment to obtain enough of a Liberal pedigree to win the seat.

Free Trade

It was free trade that had brought Ivor Guest to Cardiff, and it was a cause that was close to most Welsh Liberals' hearts. The issue of free trade had to do with whether or not to introduce import taxes (tariffs) on imported goods. This policy was aimed at protecting those British industries which had become vulnerable to cheaper foreign imports. Liberals, however, felt any trade tariffs against foreign goods would be reciprocated by other countries thereby damaging Welsh exports. In the

Conservative government of 1900–1905, Joseph Chamberlain and Arthur Balfour became increasingly pro trade tariffs and anti free trade. They argued that free trade was outdated and harmful to the country and that the British economy should be rebuilt behind a wall of tariffs.[11] The call for trade tariffs had virtually no support in Wales. Free trade had been one of the articles of Welsh Liberalism since Samuel Roberts of Llanbrynmair's declarations in the 1840s had achieved widespread approval with the party.[12] Most Welsh jobs were dependent directly or indirectly on the export trade. By 1905 Wales was exporting 50 million tons of coal and five million tons of steel annually and employing nearly a million workers. There was a lot to lose by ending overseas trade. The Welsh Liberal establishment was well aware of this threat to its livelihood. Liberal ship owners, mine owners and mine workers – all opposed tariffs with the full vigour of the vested interests they represented. The issue of free trade was therefore an easy cause for the Liberals to unite behind.

With so much Liberal enthusiasm in their campaigns on education and free trade, it is unsurprising that these were therefore placed at the heart of the Welsh Liberal campaign during the 1906 general election. Added to these two causes was that of the disestablishment of the church. Some Welsh Liberals were prepared to stake their political careers on these issues. Sir Alfred Thomas, Pontypridd MP and chairman of the Welsh Party, stated that he could not support any government that did not put Welsh disestablishment emphatically at the top of its policy agenda.

By-elections of 1900–1906

There were only two parliamentary by-elections during this government. Neither was won directly by the Welsh Liberals. The first election in Monmouth Boroughs, noted earlier in the chapter, was a victory for the Conservatives. The second by-election in Monmouth West was caused by the death of former House of Commons leader, Sir William Harcourt, in late 1904. Harcourt had announced his retirement in early 1904, so a new candidate, the Lib-Lab Thomas Richards, was already in place to succeed him. The fact that it was to be a Lib-Lab and not a Liberal candidate succeeding the former Liberal Commons leader was an early indication of the growing power of the Labour movement as a political entity. Thomas Richards was also treasurer of the powerful South Wales Miners' Federation. Yet the local West Monmouthshire Liberal Association wanted a Liberal candidate to stand and not a Lib-Lab. They had, in an internal ballot, voted 116 to 66 against allowing a Labour candidate in. In the event, Herbert Gladstone, the former Prime Minister's son and Liberal Chief Whip, overruled them. He desired a Labour candidate in place as part of the pact agreement between the Liberals and Lib-Labs over future power-sharing in government. This meant that although there was a Liberal nominee, J. Wormington, he was rejected for Richards. He, in turn, agreed to take the Liberal Whip, which meant that the West Monmouthshire Liberal Association, in a vote, then narrowly decided to back him. In the by-election, he was opposed by the Tariff Reform candidate, Sir John Cockburn, former Premier of South Australia (1889–91). Despite Cockburn's strong political background, Richards still had a confortable victory of some 4635 (40.8%) votes. The story of the Monmouth West by-election eventually concluded in the February 1910 general election when Richards dropped the 'Lib'(eral) part of Lib-Lab and became a fully-fledged Labour MP. Labour were then to hold this seat and its successors for the rest of the twentieth century and beyond. Monmouth West would never again be a Liberal seat. It was to be one of the first of many Liberal victims to succumb to the rise of Labour in Wales.

This period of political collaboration in both the Welsh Liberal and Labour parties' history is referred to by historians as the 'Progressive Alliance'. In this period, the two parties worked closely together at Westminster and made electoral arrangements not to contest each other at elections. Although this broke down in some constituencies, it stayed mainly intact until the end of the First World War. During this period, however, the Labour Party built and consolidated its strength in working class industrial seats across Wales that had previously been the domain of the Liberal Party.

The Formation and Development of the Welsh National Liberal Council 1895–1918

In 1895, outside of the elements of the British Liberal Party that co-ordinated Liberalism in Wales, the Liberal Party in Wales was effectively run by five bodies: The South Wales Liberal Federation; the North Wales Liberal Federation; the Welsh National Council (consisting of the executives of the two Federations); the Welsh (Liberal) Parliamentary Party and the individual Liberal Constituency Associations interrelated with the numerous Liberal Clubs. Related to these were the various Liberal Women's bodies and the League of Young Welsh Liberals. Between 1885 and 1895, Stuart Rendel MP was the glue that helped hold these varies Liberal bodies together either as President, Chair and or political heavy-weight inside them, as an executive officer or outside of them as advisor and confident.

When Rendel stood down in 1895 from his various posts, his fellow Welsh Liberals soon made attempts to re-organise the structure of the Welsh Party's various organisations into one overall body – *Cymru Fydd*. This concept failed and with it the concept of a united Liberal Welsh National Federation seemed also to have failed. A further attempt to form a Welsh National Liberal Association failed in February 1898, when it was blocked by the Cardiff Liberal Association. The Cardiff Association was far more anglophile and feared domination by the Welsh nationalist Liberals. This meant that the Welsh Liberals now had to rely on the Welsh National Council, which also later became the Welsh National Federation, and the Welsh Parliamentary Party to co-ordinate any distinct Welsh Liberal interests. Both these bodies effectively excluded any input from the wider Constituency Associations. In 1898, therefore, David Lloyd George promoted the idea of revising the Welsh National Council into an all-encompassing 'Welsh National Liberal Council'. This council would have equal representation from all Welsh constituencies. Whilst most Welsh Members supported the idea of a revised council, a number of prominent Liberal MPs, including Bryn Roberts, Sir Alfred Thomas (the new Welsh Party chairman) and Humphreys Owen, did not. They still remembered clearly the unhappy episode of *Cymru Fydd*. They sought to ensure that the new Council would not come about. Once again the Cardiff Liberal Association became the strongest opponent of the idea of promoting a Welsh National Council. Supported by the Liberal leaning publication *The South Wales Daily News,* it sought to either replace it entirely with four Welsh regional bodies or to ensure that the number of non-elected members of the executive was greater than those elected. The effect of this would be that the

Welsh National Liberal Council had 'no teeth' to control Liberalism in Wales. In the end it was agreed that each constituency could nominate one representative in 3000 electors. Even after its foundation, on this much weakened basis, Cardiff Liberals continued to try to restrict the role of the Council in determining any united Welsh Liberal policy. In 1899, they were able to get a motion passed that removed the rights of non-elective bodies such as the remainder of *Cymru Fydd* (based in London) to sit on the Council. The Council then became, in effect, a mouthpiece for the more dominant South Wales Liberal Federation and its general adoption of 'English Liberal policy' in Wales. In 1899, Lloyd George contemptuously described their sum achievement in eighteen months as being 'the appointment of a secretary.'[13] Yet the Council did not fade away as the South Wales Liberals had wished; it continued in its greatly subservient position to the Welsh federations.

For the first five years of the twentieth century, the Council continued to meet annually, but the frustration of its members only continued to grow as its own inadequacies became ever more apparent. In 1905, Lloyd George became chairman of the Council. In 1907, he dismissed the Council, as being 'little more than a committee, drawn from the locality of where ever it meets'.[14] Lloyd George moved to enhance the status of the Council and, together with the Treasurer, C. E. Breeze, and Secretary, W. H. Hughes, he sought to reconstitute it. They brought in further representation from the Women's Liberal Federation, labour, free church and temperance organisations, the Liberal organisation in England and the Welsh Party. Although Cardiff Liberals resisted the changes, they were still carried out and Viscount St Davids (formerly J. Wynford Philipps) became President of the newly constituted body in 1908. The Council now moved being from a 'mouthpiece' of British Liberal policy to much more of a Welsh electioneering organisation. In this newly defined role, one of its first moves was to organise the successful Pembrokeshire by-election victory of July 1908. Ironically, this very election had been called by the Welsh Council's President, Lord St Davids' elevation to the peerage.

Following the by-election, the Welsh National Liberal Council held its first 'Great National Convention' at the Albert Hall, Swansea on Thursday the 1st of October 1908, where it was addressed by its chairman Lloyd George. The four resolutions passed were on supporting the licensing of alcohol sales, the reversal of the Balfour Education Act, disestablishment and free trade. They were at the core of the Welsh party's principles.

The Council had now become more prominent in Welsh Liberal life than ever before. It went on to play a major role in the two general elections of 1910. From that year onwards it also had a full-time salaried secretary (W. H. Hughes) who co-ordinated activities of the party across Wales. The Council was able to get some important issues of policy accepted by the wider party across Wales. In August 1911, for instance, E. T. John (Denbigh East) and Beriah Gwynfe Evans were able to get the Council to endorse Welsh home rule.

The Council became adept at rallying the party's supporters on issues of Welsh Liberal principle. In 1911, Cyrus J. Evans took over from Hughes as secretary. Evans helped develop the Council's role as far as possible and in 1912 organised 500 meetings across Wales on issues such as Irish Home Rule, Free Trade, National Insurance and disestablishment. Evans also helped in the by-elections in East Carmarthen in August 1912 and Flint in January 1913.[15] For large rallies, the Council made arrangement for special trains and cheap fares on Great Western Railway trains.

Helped by this, the party organised the largest political demonstration ever held in Wales on disestablishment in Swansea on Whit Tuesday, the 28th of May 1912. Over ten thousand Liberal supporters attended this mass rally held by the Council.

The Welsh Council chose Cardiff as its headquarters. Its offices were at 35, Charles Street, Cardiff, which was about five minutes walk from the St Mary Street office, from which the Welsh Liberal Party would have as its headquarters some eight decades later. The Welsh Council's executive committee was re-elected every year. Despite its campaigning efforts attempts to introduce new blood into the Council, executive meetings were generally poorly attended. Lloyd George was busy as Chancellor of the Exchequer and did not attend many meetings. Others felt the Council to be of limited value outside its being an electioneering and debating forum for Welsh Liberal policy. Thus, by 1912, the list of those attending meetings showed that Lloyd George and D. A. Thomas attended just one out of six possible meetings and some other MPs, such as Sir Alfred Thomas, the former Welsh Party chairman, had never turned up at all. Only the chairman Lord St Davids, who, by then, in effect, controlled the policy outputs of the Welsh Council, had attended all of the meetings.

Initially, those on the Welsh National Liberal Council were critical of the Liberal government of 1906 for its failed Liberal pledges on disestablishment. Somewhat embarrassed by this criticism, Viscount St Davids when in government, was then tasked by Lloyd George with weeding out this dissent, which he duly did. From then on the Welsh Council became a more loyal supporter of the Liberal government's policies on many occasions, but also pursued a Welsh agenda on issues such as disestablishment and Home Rule, which the party in London had little real interest in. When the party split in 1916, the Scottish and English Liberal Federations followed Asquith, but the Welsh Council, thanks to St Davids' presence, backed Lloyd George. Asquithian Llewelyn Williams tried to change this but St David's kept him and other Asquithian supporters out of the Council.[16] When the parties came together again in 1923, the Welsh National Liberal Council changed its name to become the Welsh Liberal Federation to bring together, at the same time, the separate North and South Wales Federations under one body. David Davies MP (Montgomeryshire), its President, warned Lloyd George that, bearing in mind the past animosity between the Liberal north and south of Wales, the Welsh Federation would split in time. This duly happened with Tom Waterhouse heading the reformed North Wales Federation and the retired school teacher, Walter Jones, heading the South Wales Federation, both in turn wishing to form new 'Liberal' federations alongside their own visions of what Liberalism was.

Outside of Wales, there was also the London Welsh Liberal Association, which, for a long period, was chaired by leading London Liberal, Woodward Owen. It was open to all members in London who paid a subscription of one shilling or more a year and lasted into the 1930s. It often acted as a meeting group and planning body for many aspects of Liberalism in Wales.

Bridging the Ideology of the Two Centuries – the 'Radical Liberals'

The years 1886 to 1906 saw the Welsh Liberal MPs at their most 'radical'. The brief Gladstone-Rosebery government of 1892–95 had only dimmed the radicalism for a short while. The demands of being the party of government had little impact on many of the Welsh radicals. With the exception of Tom Ellis, the other radical Welsh Liberal MPs were also then too junior to play an active part during the short three years of Liberal government.[17] In opposition, the radicalism was therefore channelled into political writing, electoral contests and open resistance to the Conservative governments on various issues. Many of the crusades were inspired by what Welsh Liberal demonology referred to as the 'Unholy Trinity'.[18] These were the Brewers (temperance) the Bishops (disestablishment of the church) and the Squires (tenant land reform). Added to these causes was also a substantial political sympathy to events that occurred in Ireland. On many issues, such as those of Home Rule and the need for religious reform, the events occurring in Ireland were felt to parallel those occurring in Wales. This meant that Welsh Liberal nonconformists MPs, such as Tom Ellis and David Lloyd George, often united with the Irish Roman Catholic MPs in and outside Westminster because their grievances were felt to be similar in many respects.[19]

Campaigning on one issue or another was part of the *raison d'être* for Welsh Liberal radicals. To be a 'radical' meant that you were wedded to a cause or causes that would be at the very soul of your political being. As a result, the Liberals in Wales were involved in many political crusades. Some of the most prominent Welsh crusades have been mentioned in passing earlier, but it is worth pursuing them in more detail in order to determine the extent to which Welsh Liberal radicalism sought to change the political, social, economic and cultural face of Wales. These crusades concerned:

- The issue of land and tenant farmers. Through the radical Liberal MP Tom Ellis in Westminster and because of the campaigning of the Welsh Land League, there was a change in the law to support tenant farmers' rights of tenure against their 'Tory landlords' rights of eviction. Ellis introduced a Land Bill in 1892 which led to the setting up of a Welsh Land (Royal) Commission. Its findings helped deal with the numerous injustices suffered by Welsh tenant farmers. The issue of land reform would remain a key policy issue of Welsh Liberals, even when the party went into decline in the 1920s.[20]
- *Welsh nationalism.* Liberalism and Welsh Nationalism had become fused during the late nineteenth century. The Liberals were the only party with a visible Welsh identity and, therefore, provided a vehicle for its growing national consciousness.[21] Liberalism worked as a nationalist organisation through both *Cymru Fydd* and outside it. Despite never implementing the main devolutionary measure desired by the Liberal radicals, the 1906–1914 Liberal Governments facilitated the decentralisation of government to Wales with some practical measures and overall afforded much more sympathy than the Conservatives had.
- The Liberals were successful in creating a policy on abstinence from alcohol (*temperance*), which impacted on the Welsh populace. As we saw earlier in chapter 1, the introduction of the first specifically Welsh legislation, the Wales Sunday Closing Act 1881, led by Liberal MP John Roberts (Flint district), made areas in some Welsh counties 'dry' on Sundays for the next century. Lloyd George, with his temperance background, went on to help ensure the regulation of the liquor trade during the First World War to get the workers out of the pubs and into the factories. His efforts to get the munitions workers away from the pubs

became legendary and in 1915, he famously announced that 'Britain was fighting 'Germany, Austria and Drink'. The end of this 'industrial scale drunkenness' had been one of the dreams of the Welsh temperance nonconformists for generations. Lloyd George sought to bring this about, and he pleased his Free Church supporters in the process. Ever the politician, however, Lloyd George did not want to alienate working-class Liberal voters. His solution was to close the pubs on Sundays but to allow the workingmen's clubs to remain open.

• *School education.* The Balfour Education Act, as noted earlier, was a particular cause for Liberal radicalism. As we mentioned in chapter 1, university education was also important to the Liberals when they established the federated university of Wales in 1893. The background to this came fourteen years earlier when Liberal MP Hussey Vivian (Glamorgan) introduced a motion on the 1st of July 1879 to remedy the 'deficiencies of Welsh higher education'. Gladstone spoke in support of and sanctioned the appointment of a departmental committee under Lord Aberdare. In 1881, they recommended the creation of one college in the North and one in the South of Wales. Then, in 1885, Gladstone sanctioned the sum of £8,000 per annum to each of the two Welsh university colleges at Bangor and Cardiff. At around the same time as this was happening, the Liberal MP, Stuart Rendel (Montgomeryshire) was also acting as a benefactor to the University College at Aberystwyth. This is indicated today by the fact that the Chair of English and one of the Halls of Residence still bear his name. Other Welsh Liberals, such as Hebert Lewis (Flint Boroughs), also supported both secondary and University education in Wales with passion, becoming directly involved it getting various Liberal and Coalition governments to increase funding to them.[22]

• *Social reform and health issues.* David Lloyd George was one of the greatest social welfare reformers. In addition to him there were, within Wales, other MPs involved in social welfare. David Davies, the millionaire coal owner and railway magnate and the Liberal MP for Montgomeryshire, inaugurated a national campaign against tuberculosis; a disease which was killing thousands in Wales each year. He went on to launch the Welsh School of Social Services at Llandrindod Wells in 1911. In many local councils during this period, socially concerned Liberals were introducing social welfare policies. The Welfare Liberals were now displacing their Gladstonian predecessors, whose own ideas of social welfare were related to the principle of an self-reliance as the cure to social problems.

• *Establishing Welsh institutions.* Stuart Rendel MP presented Groythan, Aberystwyth as a site for the National Library of Wales. The Conservative government under Arthur Balfour later went on to establish both the National Library and the National Museum of Wales in 1905, in addition to granting Cardiff city status. These events occurred partially because of Conservative attempts to gain Liberal votes in the forthcoming elections.[23] It was, however, the Liberal government that gave these new Welsh institutions their Royal Charters in 1907.

Of all the great Welsh Liberal causes, the one that continued to be important in the hearts of Welsh radical Liberals was that of Home Rule or what was later known as devolution. This became a central theme of Welsh Liberalism across the generations and, in this respect, it unites all the chapters in this book. It started in the era of the Victorian Welsh Liberal Radicals and would outlast them by more than a century.

The Great Cause of 'Home Rule for Wales'
1886–1906

In the nineteenth century, many Welsh Liberals desired Home Rule (political devolution) and for them the day of its deliverance could not come soon enough. For the wider Westminster political world, the concept of Home Rule became associated as a potential solution to the problems in Ireland. Yet the arguments for Home Rule in Wales were felt by Welsh Liberals to be just as strong. They felt that Wales had a distinct nationality every bit as good as Ireland's and Scotland's. In fact, Welsh Liberals felt that it had a better identity in some respects. Wales had, after all, kept its own language whilst the Celtic tongues in the other two nations had all but disappeared. At the same time Welsh nationalism had no 'blood on its hands' through violent revolution, as was the case in Ireland. The Welsh Liberal Radicals, therefore, came to agree that Wales was now ready to govern many of its own affairs. They believed that the Imperial Parliament at Westminster was now too busy with the business of running the British Empire and did not have the time necessary to concentrate on the 'provincial' matters in Wales. The answer, therefore, was a Welsh Parliament which would be able to concentrate on the issues that Westminster neglected. One of the first attempts to do something concrete on Home Rule occurred in 1886 when Tom Ellis brought forward a Welsh Institutions Bill to set up a Welsh Parliament. It failed to get a second reading and so, from the outset, it looked as if progress on Home Rule would be slow. The Liberal Radicals were only too aware of the way Wales was being treated in comparison to the other Celtic nations. In 1889, Lloyd George saw the way that Wales was bring treated by his fellow Liberals, over the issue of Home Rule, as being like 'prize giving' at a country fayre, he stated

' ... Excellent little Wales' and all that. At horse shows we sometimes see a first prize of £10 given to one, £5 to another, while the third is 'Highly Commended'. That is the way that Wales is treated by the Liberal Party. Ireland deservedly gets the first prize (a series of splendid measures). Scotland take second prize. Wales, like a Welsh mountain pony, is sent away with nothing.[24]

Because of this patronising attitude, Welsh Liberals would again and again try to achieve devolution for Wales. In 1890, the National Institutions (Wales) Bill was brought forward by Alfred Thomas, the coal owner and Liberal MP for Glamorgan East.[25] The Bill was aimed at establishing a Welsh Secretary and a Welsh Office. It was seconded by Pritchard Morgan, Liberal MP for Merthyr Tydfil. The Bill was also backed by the newer Welsh Liberal MPs but did not succeed. It was reintroduced in 1891 and 1892. Although it enjoyed the support of seven Welsh Liberal MPs, including Lloyd George and Tom Ellis, other Welsh Liberal heavyweights, such as the leader of the Welsh Parliamentary Party, Stuart Rendel, opposed the measure and it failed again. They feared that a Welsh Secretary under the Tories would create a more powerful Welsh Conservative Party.[26] In 1893 Lloyd George tried to put through another Bill, which sought to establish an elected council and a Secretary of State for Wales. This Bill did not progress either. Welsh Home Rule was, however, given a substantial psychological boost when, in 1895, Rosebery himself came out in favour for Home Rule across the United Kingdom, albeit with an effective English MPs' veto in place as to whether this would occur at all. This was partly a way of solving the Irish problem but it would have also had the full endorsement of the Welsh Liberal radicals. Later in the same year, Lloyd George, assisted by Scottish Home Rulers, was able to win a House of Commons vote approving the principle of Home Rule for both nations. Both his and Herbert Lewis's (Flintshire) motion was carried by 180 votes to 170. *Cymru Fydd* also did much to ignite this passion for Home Rule. When the movement ended, however, much of the wider passion for Home Rule faded with it. Most of the Welsh Liberal middle class supporters saw no real advantage in Home Rule, arguing instead for a greater inclusion of Welsh aspirations within the existing institutions of Britain and the wider Empire. The powerful South Wales Liberal Federation, led by figures such as D. A. Thomas, had received a lukewarm response, at best, to the concept of Home Rule. A few Welsh Liberal MPs, however, continued to press for Home Rule.[27]

When the Liberals were out of power, there was little point in appealing to a Unionist Conservative government to grant a Welsh Parliament. Any further progress had to await the next Liberal government. This came in December 1905, and didn't require a General Election. The Liberals had united over the issues of free trade but the Conservatives had now become divided by the same cause. Indeed, had not Ivor Churcill Guest and his cousin Winston Churchill crossed the floor to join the Liberals over this very issue? By December 1905, Balfour felt unable to continue to hold the Conservative party together and resigned. This led to the Liberal leader Henry Campbell-Bannerman forming a minority government. Campbell-Bannerman sought to bring in as many factions within the party as possible to the Cabinet. For Wales this meant that leading Liberals – David Lloyd George and Reginald McKenna – were brought into government. Lloyd George, however, did not become Minister for Wales as some hoped he would. Instead he became chairman of the Board of Trade. He was the first native Welshman to go into the Cabinet since Cornewall Lewis fifty years earlier in 1855. Reginald McKenna (North Monmouthshire), in turn, became Financial Secretary to the Treasury. With the new Liberal minority government formed, Campbell-Bannerman decided it was time to give this new government its own mandate and called a general election for the start of the following year.

Liberal Return: In Government Again 1906–1914

The 1906 General Election

Liberal	28
Lib-Lab	4
Independent Labour Party	1
Labour	1

On the 2nd of January 1906, at the start of what was to be the Liberal Party's best ever general election result, a massive National Welsh Liberal Convention was held in Caernarfon to endorse Welsh Liberal policy. It consisted of some one thousand Welsh delegates from every Welsh Liberal constituency association. Now part of a Liberal government, Lloyd George's own opinion held greater sway than ever. What Lloyd George declared as his vision of Welsh Liberal policy became identical to that endorsed by the delegates at this mass meeting. The day after this meeting, a Welsh Campaign Committee was formed with the intention of putting this policy into practice. This was duly fed into the election addresses of many of the Welsh Liberal candidates. The actual voting process in the general election in Wales went on for just over two weeks. The first member to be returned, unopposed on the 12th of January, was Sir Brynmor Jones, for Swansea District. The last member returned was John Herbert Lewis for Flintshire on the 27th of January. In between, the party secured another 26 of the 32 remaining Welsh seats.

No other region or nation within the United Kingdom and Ireland returned a greater proportion of Liberal MPs as a percentage of the total. The two existing Lib-Labs, Mabon and Thomas Richards, were now joined by three other Lib-Labs (South and West Glamorgan, Denbigh Boroughs). In places, the contest was confusing. John Williams, the Labour candidate in the Gower constituency, defeated the Lib-Lab candidate there. Still, he described himself as a 'Lib-Lab' and continued to support the Liberals. In turn, he was backed by the Gower Liberal Association who didn't support his Lib-Lab opponent.[28] Regardless of the confusion over candidates' political labels, the tangible result was that 33 of the 34 Welsh MPs now took the Liberal whip. Only the Labour MP, Keir Hardie, (Merthyr Tydfil) failed to do so. This was also a Parliament in which those Welsh Liberal MPs who were elected were to receive great fortune. Henry Hadyn Jones (Meirionnydd), elected in 1910, noted in 1934 'that every member who was returned for a Welsh constituency at the memorable general election of 1906, would from now on be given a special bonus in the form of a peerage, a Privy Councillorship, a knighthood, a county-court judgeship, legal preferment in the way of briefs at the hands of the Treasury, or a place in the government' before the end of their career.[29]

In spite of the party's national triumph, there were some ominous signs to be seen at local levels. By the following year, in Swansea, the Liberals were in the minority on the council, in Cardiff, the Conservatives controlled the council and in Newport, the balance of power was dependent on the mayor's casting vote.[30] On many South Wales urban councils, however, the Liberals had already disappeared and been replaced by Labour, the 'Municipal Reformers' and groups of Independents. The Progressive Alliance between Labour and Liberals worked far less well in local government than it did at Westminster. Here, almost from the outset, Labour candidates had been willing to stand under a Socialist banner and take seats off the Liberals. Within a generation, the Liberal Party would disappear almost entirely from Welsh local government but, for the moment, at least, they remained Wales' supreme party in the county councils and in the Welsh parliamentary party, if not in the urban authorities.

The Liberal Government of 1906

The scale of the Liberal Welsh victory did not lead to a large Welsh Liberal agenda being implemented. Despite the strength of Welsh Liberalism, the large Liberal gains elsewhere in Britain meant that Campbell-Bannerman's government was not dependent on Welsh Liberal votes to get its policy agenda through. This, therefore, gave the Welsh Liberal radicals little leverage over the Liberal policy. Politics remained dominated by British, rather than Welsh issues. Lloyd George and Reginald McKenna kept their places in the government and were joined by a number of other Welsh MPs. Herbert Lewis (Flint) became a Junior Lord of the Treasury and later became

Financial Secretary to the Treasury. Later on there was a further Welsh contribution, with Samuel Evans becoming Solicitor General in 1908, and William Jones becoming a Junior Lord of the Treasury in 1909.[31] Some prominent Welsh Liberals, however, were left out of office and had to be given other forms of consolation. Alfred Mond, the great industrialist, failed to get a Ministerial post because, as Asquith informed him, 'The Ministerial jobs have all been promised and you are too big a man for an under-secretaryship', so he made him a Baronet, in July 1910 instead.[32]

The number of Welsh MPs serving in the government diverted prominent Welsh Liberals' attentions to the wider concerns of running Britain and the Empire rather than specific matters relating to Wales. The same enchantment with power that had diverted Tom Ellis from fulfilling the radical path in Gladstone's government was now weaving its spell on another group of Welsh Liberal MPs in Campbell-Bannerman's. Nevertheless, there were some significant measures concerning the establishment of Welsh institutions and the devolving of public administration to Wales. This would not fully satisfy the more prominent Welsh Liberals outside of government. Parliamentary Party Chair, Sir Alfred Thomas, therefore, saw that the absence of legislation dedicated to the Wales Liberal agenda made his own position 'a fraud and a failure ... the laughing stock of the Commons'.[33] Much of the criticism was, however, muted. So much so, that by 1910, Brynmor Jones (Swansea Boroughs) was aware that the previous rebellious nature of the Welsh party had gone and the party had become a 'mere appendage of the whip's office'.[34] This was not entirely true, as some of the more radical Welsh Liberal MPs, such as Llewelyn Williams (Carmarthen Boroughs) and Edward Thomas (E. T.) John (Denbigh), still helped ensure that the Parliament pursued a Welsh agenda in as many areas as practicable. One effect of this was that the Army in Wales was reorganised so that it now had its own Welsh commander. Another specifically Welsh Liberal cause was that of temperance across Wales. The Welsh Liberal policy action resulted in The Licensing Act (1908) which brought Monmouthshire into the Welsh Sunday Closing Act (1881), which was something the county had escaped until then. The removal of this anomaly had been a demand of the Welsh temperance movement for a number of years.

Most Welsh Liberal MPs were not driven in the main by issues of Welsh nationalism – whether Home Rule or the establishment of all-Wales institutions. Like their counterparts in the rest of the United Kingdom, many wanted to see widespread social and industrial reform. In this area, they were successful and made really radical progress. The Liberal government of 1906 became one of the major social reforming governments of all time. Both Campbell-Bannerman and later Asquith played their roles in determining the social and welfare policies but it was Lloyd George who was seen as the 'apostle of the New Liberalism'.[35]

In 1908, the Prime Minister, Campbell-Bannerman's health collapsed. He resigned in early April and died later in the month. Herbert Henry Asquith became his successor. Asquith had a few loyal Welsh supporters. The most prominent was the Cardiff MP and industrialist, Sir Ivor Churchill Guest. He held the celebration banquet for his new premiership at his London mansion, Wimborne House. Whilst Guest was Asquith's loyal Welsh ally, Wales' most prominent MP, David Lloyd George, had a more distant relationship with him. Despite this distance, however, Asquith recognised political talent when he saw it and moved Lloyd George from the Board of Trade to the Exchequer, as Chancellor. Asquith, himself, had been Chancellor of the

Exchequer previously and requested that he be allowed, therefore, to put the 1908 budget through the House of Commons. This he duly did by introducing old age pensions for the first time, but history, however, would remember Lloyd George as the man who introduced the old age pension rather than Asquith.

The People's Budget, 1909

Whilst Lloyd George is now seen as the grandfather of the welfare state, this book deals with the wider Welsh Liberal Party rather than the career of its most famous Liberal MP. This chapter will, therefore, just look at one of the Lloyd George's eight budgets and the one, which, perhaps, had the most effect on Wales, as it did across the rest of the British Isles. In 1909, Lloyd George was able to introduce his famous 'People's Budget'. It was so named because of its benefits to the working-class masses (the people). History was to record it as one of the most radical budgets of any British government. The central aim was to raise some £15 million in new income for both defence and old age pensions. It was the introduction of old age pensions that made it so radical. To pay for a wide scale pension system, the government needed to raise significant sums of new income. It did so by increasing income tax and death duties, as well as licensing tobacco and spirit duties. There were also new taxes on cars, petrol and land. It was the land tax which was the most contentious. This land tax was seen as a chance by Welsh Liberals to hurt the hated Tory controlled landlordism. This issue had dominated much of Welsh Liberal politics, including Lloyd George's own political agenda, over the previous decade.

The Liberals may have defeated the Welsh Tory aristocracy in the Commons but a number of Tory lords and squires still held sway across much of Wales and Britain. At Westminster they were able to block any attempt at Liberal reform through their veto in the House of Lords. To this end, the Lords rejected the budget, which then enabled Lloyd George to tackle the bastion of Tory aristocracy head on. This was in the 'Who rules commoners or gentry?' general elections of 1910. On the 21st of December, 1909, the Welsh Liberal National Council held a Great National Convention in Swansea, which included all Welsh MPs and constituency associations, with the exception of the Labour Merthyr Tydfil MP, Keir Hardie. Its purpose was to discuss both the constitutional crisis with the Lords and the general election campaign now commencing. Nearly a thousand delegates attended in order to beat the campaign drum for the forthcoming election.[36] After the Convention, between July 1909 and July 1910, the Welsh National Liberal Council ran a massive campaign in support of the 'People's Budget' and against the powers of the House of Lords. The Welsh Council:[37]

- Sent out 5,570 letters
- Created 1,694 circular letters for campaigning
- Sent 400 telegrams
- Held 45 public meetings, mainly 'People's Budget' demonstrations
- Delivered 257,000 pamphlets
- Sent three tons of posters to constituencies
- Spent £10,000 on the two 1910 general elections

Lloyd George's 'People's Budget' galvanised the Welsh Liberals as no other budget had or would again and the Welsh party as a result campaigned whole-heartedly behind him

Parliamentary By-elections 1906–1910

The Liberals maintained their political monopoly at Westminster and in the Welsh county councils but as we noted earlier they lost ground rapidly in the county boroughs and urban district councils. In the county council elections of 1907, the Liberals once again won all the counties, although this time the Conservatives increased their number of councillors, so that they now represented almost half of the Liberals' Welsh total. Between 1906 and 1910, there were six Parliamentary by-elections in Wales. They were all plain sailing for the Welsh Liberals. All but one was caused by the MPs being given jobs connected with the law, either appointments as County Court Judges (as in Caernarfonshire – Eifion, and Denbighshire East) and Recorders (as in Mid Glamorgan, Carmarthen West and Denbighshire East) or by going into the government as Solicitor General, Samuel (S. T.) Evans did in Mid Glamorgan, which legally obliged them to re-contest their own seats. Most of these by-elections were unopposed. Contests by the Labour candidates against Liberals were deliberately prevented because of the Progressive Alliance and the fact that the trade unions felt that it was better to keep 'the Liberal big guns' in their seats rather than risk a challenge by a Labour candidate letting a Tory in.[38] Thus, Evans' re-election in Mid Glamorgan was assured when the trade unions prevented Labour from contesting the seat. The Denbighshire East by-elections of August 1906 and April 1909, however, were contested. Here the Liberal candidate EG Hemmerde easily defeated the Conservative candidate in the 1906 by-election and later his Liberal Unionist opponent in the 1909 election.[39] The only other contested by-election during this period was in Pembrokeshire where John Wynford-Philipp's was elevated to the peerage as Lord St Davids.[40] In this election the Liberal candidate Walter Francis Roch defeated his Conservative opponent John Rolleston Lort-Williams by a convincing 2172 (24.8%) votes. A native of Pembrokeshire, Roch was also a barrister and one of the leading members of the Men's League for Women's Suffrage. He would hold the seat for the next decade.

The small number of by-elections wins and the county council elections in 1907, plus the distractions of now being in office did little to prepare the Welsh Liberal Party for their next great electoral hurdles: the twin general elections of 1910. The elections had been brought about, as we saw earlier, by the House of Lords' blocking of Lloyd George's budgets and by its rejection of other important Liberal legislation. This was the central issue of the early general election called by Asquith in January 1910. In this constitutional battle the Liberals, led by Asquith, asked the electorate, 'Who governs Britain – the people or the aristocracy?' Their answer was mixed.

January 1910 General Election

Liberal	27
Labour	5
Conservatives	2

For most Welsh Liberal MPs the election of January 1910 was a personal resounding success. Only one victorious MP, Sir John David Rees in Montgomery District of Boroughs, had a majority of less than 10 per cent (he had a very marginal 13 votes or 0.4%) over his Conservative opponent. Rees was a fanatical campaigner against women's suffrage, which put him at odds with the wider Liberal movement in Wales, to such an extent that he joined the Conservatives in November 1910 and did not contest the Montgomery District of Boroughs seat again. In total, some 27 Liberals were re-elected, one less than in the landslide election of 1906. It was true that two Conservative MPs were elected in Wales again but this did not cause much immediate concern for the Welsh Liberals. One Conservative had taken a Lib-Lab seat (Denbigh Boroughs) and the other defeat was in the highly marginal Radnor constituency. Even in these two seats the combined Conservative majority was just 24 votes. Thus Wales had come within a handful of votes of remaining a 'Tory free zone' once more and Liberalism appeared to remain strong there.

The January 1910 general election contest was, however, in some ways very different from the one in 1906. This time the Liberals enjoyed no unopposed seats. For the first time in 15 years every Welsh seat had been contested. The Liberals in Wales also benefited from the unevenness of the first-past-the-post electoral system. They gained 79 per cent of the Welsh seats on only just over half of the Welsh vote (51 per cent). At this election, with the exception of the defeated anti-socialist MP Allen Clement Edwards in Denbigh, who stood on the Lib-Lab ticket, the Lib-Labs had by now abandoned their Liberal connection and become fully-fledged Labour Members. This had occurred in part because the Liberal government had passed the necessary legislation to ensure that the trade unions could develop their own political party without fear of legal challenge. Relations between the two parties remained amicable but within a decade the Progressive Alliance would be fully over and the electoral gloves would come off between the two with little remembrance of the alliance they had once enjoyed. For now, however, it was only in two constituencies that the Liberals fought Labour directly. In Merthyr Tydfil, Keir Hardie won a seat for Labour; in the other Liberal versus Labour contest, in Swansea Town, Labour were not successful. Here the industrialist and prominent free trader Alfred Mond, who had recently left the Chester constituency to contest Swansea Town, beat both Labour and Conservative opponents by a conformable margin.[41]

The most ominous sign for the future of Welsh Liberalism at this election was the fact that the Labour's share of the total Welsh votes was 16 per cent despite the fact they only contested six seats compared to the Liberals contesting 30.[42] What would happen to the Liberals' working class support if or when Labour started contesting more seats?

As the Liberal-Labour partnership was fading, Welsh Liberal MPs started to show their anti-socialist credentials more fully. It was the victor of the three way challenge in Swansea Town, Alfred Mond, who would lead the anti-socialist charge. Mond was a Jewish industrialist of German origin. Despite his own religion he had an impressive knowledge of Christian theology. Mond had the necessary financial resources behind him to push the Liberal cause against often bitter personal anti-Semitic and anti-German attacks by the local media and by his political opponents.[43] Apart from Mond's election, the other significant political development was the political seat jumping of South Wales Liberal heavyweight, D. A. Thomas. He had been the MP for Merthyr Tydfil for 22 years, and had been a leading member of the Men's League for Women's Suffrage since 1907. Despite having his country estate at Llanwern just outside Newport, he played a key part in Cardiff Liberal politics and business all through his time in Merthyr Tydfil. D. A. Thomas was invited to stand by the leading Cardiff Liberal Robert Bird for the 1910 election.[44] In the selection contest he was pitted against John Cory the wealthy shipping owner and long standing Liberal city councillor, whom he subsequently beat. The incumbent Liberal MP, Sir Ivor Churchill Guest, had been elevated to the House of Lords as Lord Ashby St Ledgers on Asquith's request. This was to help strengthen the Liberal presence in the House of Lords. This gave the House of Lords a very rare father and son combination, as his father, the Liberal, first Viscount Wimborne was still alive and sitting in the Upper House. D. A. Thomas subsequently won the Cardiff Boroughs seat with a 1,555 (6.2%) majority. In his old seat of Merthyr Tydfil, Edgar R. Jones, a local Baptist and Welsh-speaking barrister became the new Liberal MP, with Keir Hardie also retaining his seat for the Labour Party in the dual seat.

Whilst in Wales, Liberal losses were limited to just one seat (Radnor), in England, there were a much larger losses of seats. The Liberals lost 125 seats overall. The Conservatives had recaptured 48 seats in the South of England alone. The Liberals now secured 275 seats against the Conservative and Unionists 273; the Irish nationalists gained 82 and Labour 40. The Conservatives, however, now had the majority of the national vote, 47 per cent compared to the Liberals 43 per cent. The Liberals could only, therefore, continue in power with the help of their Irish and Labour allies. This they now did.

In the break between the two general elections of 1910, at the age of 76, Sir Alfred Thomas announced that he would leave his Glamorgan East seat, after 25 years as MP, to become ennobled as Lord Pontypridd. He stood down, at the same time, as Chair of the Welsh Parliamentary Party. This caused an election for the post. Thomas was then replaced, at the age of 61 by the younger barrister Sir David Brynmor Jones (Swansea District). He had been nominated for the post in 1897 but had declined it in favour of Alfred Thomas. Jones himself was replaced two years later by the successful North Wales barrister Ellis Jones Ellis-Griffith (Anglesey). Ellis-Griffith had strong Liberal radical credentials and had led a revolt against the government in 1909 over its failure to agree to a Disestablishment Bill. Neither Jones nor Ellis-Griffith, despite the latter's own strong Welsh nationalist credentials, were able to use the Parliamentary Party to exert much pressure on the Liberal government at the time. Thus the Welsh Parliamentary Party remained something of a talking shop rather than a mechanism for Welsh nationalist aspirations. Around the same time that Alfred Thomas announced he would retire from the Commons, D. A. Thomas also declared he would not re-contest his newly acquired Cardiff Boroughs. He would later become Lord Rhondda and until the First World War arrived Thomas would concentrate on his considerable mining and business related interests.

The only by-election of this short Parliament was at the end of March 1910. It was caused once again by Sir Samuel T. Evans who had brought about two by-elections in the previous Parliament. This time he was appointed as President of the Probate, Divorce and Admiralty Division of the High Court, but unlike previous by-elections, Evans did not contest the election himself and left Westminster. The South Wales Liberal tin-plate manufacturer and temperance figure Frederick Williams Gibbons won the seat by 2710 votes (18%) beating Labour's Vernon Hartshorn. The Liberal Chief Whip, the Master of Elibank (Lord Murray), did not want Gibbons to contest the seat at all for fear of upsetting the Lib-Labs with whom they were in coalition but the local Liberal Association ignored his pleas. One of the founding figures of the Labour Party and, later, a prominent Labour cabinet member during the 1920s, Hartshorn had also been frustrated by failing to get the South Wales Miners' Federation (SWMF) to support him in the various election contests that he wished to fight against Liberal candidates, including this one.[45]

Despite the Liberal victory, the Lords once again refused to pass the budget. The country was only spared an immediate new election by the ill health and the subsequent death of King Edward VII in May 1910. Lloyd George held a secret conference with the Conservative Lords to try to come to some truce. This failed and the new King George V agreed to a fresh election. All of Wales was soon plunged once more into election mode. The pursuance of a Parliament Bill, which would halt the power of the Lords to stop future budgets, became the main issue in the December 1910 general election, as much in Wales as elsewhere. The fact that Welsh disestablishment was being blocked by the Lords added further fuel to Welsh Liberals demands for a Parliament Bill. The issue of the Lords sidelined other important political issues, such as the violent labour unrest at Tonypandy, which had taken place the month before, which would otherwise have been central issues for the campaign in Wales.

December 1910 General Election

Liberal	26
Labour	5
Conservatives	3

Both the Conservatives and the Liberals gained 272 seats apiece in the general election. As a result Asquith's Liberals again formed the government with Labour and Irish MPs' support. In Wales, the main difference between the December 1910 general election and the January one was that the Conservatives, as in 1906, were again unable to contest all Welsh seats. This time ten Liberal MPs were elected unopposed. This represented more than a quarter of all of the Liberals' unopposed seats in the United Kingdom. There was one Welsh Liberal gain. The Oxford educated solicitor, Sir Frank Edwards, won marginal Radnor seat off the Conservatives by just 42 votes (1%). At the same time there were also Liberal losses. The Conservative Colonel, Edward Pryce-Jones, who had lost Montgomery Boroughs in 1906, now regained it. The Conservative Lord Ninian Crichton-Stuart, third son of the Marquis of Bute, won D. A. Thomas' former seat of Cardiff Boroughs. He defeated the hastily imposed Liberal candidate Sir Clarendon Hyde by 299 votes (1.2%). In Pembroke and Haverfordwest, the brother of the former MP for Cardiff, Ivor Guest, Henry Guest, won the seat ensuring that the Guest family would represent the Liberal cause in Wales constantly between 1906 and 1918. Once again there were few direct Labour-Liberal contests. Where they occurred, as in Mid Glamorgan and East Glamorgan, the Liberal candidates easily defeated the Labour candidates set against them. In the Gower, however, despite strong support for the last minute Liberal candidate, the journalist and anti-Socialist, William Francis Phillips, Labour held the seat by 953 votes (9.6%).

Disestablishment is Back on the Agenda

Asquith introduced another Welsh Disestablishment Bill in 1909. It was, as Rosebery had predicted 14 years earlier, overthrown by the House of Lords. In 1912, it was one of only two measures, which the House of Lords applied its full power of two years' delay over; the measures had been granted to them by the 1911 Parliament Act.[46] Disestablishment was, therefore, only finally passed into law in 1914. This was mainly due to the Welsh Liberal Home Secretary, Sir Reginald McKenna's own personal drive. McKenna threatened his own resignation if the Bill was not kept in the government's programme. Even after the Bill turned into an Act, the battle was not won. Its enforcement was suspended until after the end of the First World War. It was a victory, however, on an issue that few English Liberal MPs saw any merit in and caused a great deal of resentment over the amount of time it had consumed. The Liberal grandee and convenor of the Welsh Disestablishment Conciliation Committee Chair, Sir Henry Lunn,[47] summed this up when he stated:

> 'We Liberals were using our party machinery to carry through a measure for which there was no strong demand from any but the Welsh extremists, and which was directly contrary to the feelings of that large body of voters which represents the Church of England.'[48]

Wales was eventually disestablished from the Anglican Church in 1922 during what was to be the last Liberal-led government. With an overwhelmingly non-conformist membership, very few Liberals in Wales did not support disestablishment. The days of chapel politics, however, were fading as the new religion of Socialism and the ideals of Communism with the promise of creating 'a new heaven on earth' for the working man began to take its place. Williams Jones MP (Caernarfon) predicted that the 'day that saw the passing of the Welsh Disestablishment Bill into law would also mark the end of the long regime of the Welsh party'. He was to be proved right. The party now struggled to find new causes by which to motivate a mass following. Henry Hadyn Jones, the long serving Meirionnydd MP, thought that the party should work with the farmers to end the Welsh tithe. These new causes lacked the widespread appeal of disestablishment and gained little support from the urban Liberals, weakening the party's long term appeal to its chapel-going rural supporters.[49]

The Welsh Women Liberals (1890–1945)

In her autobiography, Margaret Haig, Second Viscountess Rhondda (1883–1958) and daughter of MP D. A. Thomas looked back on her childhood as an ambitious female politician and noted:

> 'What,' as a contemporary remarked, 'is the use of college for a girl? You don't want to become Chancellor of the Exchequer! I had no word to answer her with, and I had no idea at the time why the remark irritated me so much … It never occurred to me that, or something akin to it, was exactly what, some-where deep down inside me, I did want to become.[50]

In the Victorian and Edwardian periods, women were not only excluded from elected office but were expected to either bow out of political activity entirely on marriage or, at a minimum, to endorse the political party of their husbands. Any political ambition they had was at the behest of their husbands. As a result, the political development for the female Liberals in Wales was always tied up closely with what men deemed right. In Victorian Liberal politics the main priority was to expand the franchise for men first. In this respect, the Second Reform Act of 1867, significantly increased the male electorate and also changed the way the political parties were run.[51] From then on, both general and local council elections would become more competitive and organised in a more overt political way. Politically, there was a need to campaign on an almost permanent basis and, therefore, across Wales in each constituency Liberal Associations were established, and female Liberals were active in these. The majority of local associations were also affiliated to both the Women's Liberal Federation (WLF) and the Welsh Union of Women's Liberal Associations (WUWLA) or local branches of the Liberal Social Councils, which brought both men and women together for social events. At the regional level, the South and North Wales Liberal Federations also had female sections. By the mid-1890s, the WUWLA was composed of some 57 associations and 9000 members.[52] From 1891 they held an annual conference in Wales where they pursued their own political agenda, which did not always coincide with the wider party. As well as extending the franchise to women, they were particularly keen on furthering employment rights for women. In this respect, they campaigned that no 'limitations should be placed on the hours and conditions of labour of women', that were not also imposed on men, and that female inspectors be employed to protect the welfare of women in factories and other workplaces.[53]

In 1892, Mrs. Nora Philipps, as President of the WUWLA, became the first female Liberal politician to come to public prominence. She was the first wife of the Mid-Lanarkshire (1888–92) and, later, Pembrokeshire MP (1898–1908), Sir Wynford Philipps. Nora Philipps was a founder of the Women's Institute, Pembrokeshire president of the Welsh Industry Association and Lady President of the 1913 National Eisteddfod. Although she was English by birth, she developed a great fondness for Welsh folklore and became an accomplished public speaker and gave recitals across Wales.[54] Philipps also contributed to a regular column on women's interests in the Liberal *Young Wales* magazine. She was so prominent in both Welsh and British Liberal meetings and campaigns that she would undoubtedly have been a Liberal MP in her own right if she had been given the opportunity. She was later joined in the public gaze by another prominent Liberal woman. This was Sybil Thomas, wife of the Merthyr Tydfil and, later, Cardiff MP Liberal MP and South Wales rival to David Lloyd George 'D. A.' Thomas. Sybil, a passionate Conservative before her marriage to 'D. A.' in 1882, had now become an equally strong advocate of the Liberal cause.[55] After Davies was ennobled as Viscount Rhondda in 1910, Sybil became the first Viscountess Rhondda. She became Chairwoman of the war-time government's Women's Advisory Committee and the National Savings Committee. Their only daughter Margaret also followed the family's political interest and was a keen Liberal until her marriage to her Conservative husband Humphrey Mackworth in 1908. Protocol at the time meant that she had to resign from the Liberals and support the Conservatives. She did not support the Conservative cause for long, however.

Instead, she joined the cause of female suffrage in the Women's Social and Political Union (WSPU). Membership of the WSPC prohibited membership of political parties until universal suffrage was gained for women. Margaret, therefore, threw herself into the heart of the protest movement and this included the protest marches, jumping onto the running board of Liberal Prime Minister Herbert Asquith's car in St Andrews, setting fire to pillar boxes and, as a result, serving a period in Usk Prison. Prison didn't stop Margaret's campaigning, however. Upon the death of her father in 1918, she was allowed by the King (through a Special Remainder) to become a Peeress in her own right – Baroness Rhondda of Llanwern. Margaret was now one of the few peeresses from whom the title could pass down through the female line – although in the event, she had no children and so the title ended with her.

By the time of her ennoblement, Margaret had already taken over the directorships of some 30 of her father's companies when he had joined the war-time government as food controller. She now became an even more prominent figure and role model in the advancement of women's political rights. In 1922, she led an unsuccessful campaign to allow women to sit in the House of Lords. They would not be allowed to sit there until 1958, a year after Margaret's death in 1957. In this campaign she was backed by many leading suffragettes including Millicent Garret Fawcett, the former Liberal and now Labour supporting women's rights campaigner. If the campaign for entry to the Lords had been successful, then the Second Vicountess Rhondda could have joined Viscountess St Davids, the second wife of the now ennobled, Sir Wynford Philipps, and also a peeress in her own right, as one of the two first Welsh women to sit in the House of Lords.[56] Although she was never to sit in the House of Lords, Margaret did become the first female President of the Institute of Directors in 1926 and in 1922 established and then edited the influential weekly paper *Time and Tide*.[57]

In the period before both the Viscountesses Rhondda became prominent on the British political scene in Wales, the WUWLA had expanded politically. They held weekend schools where they were addressed by MPs and other notables. There was also widespread support for women's rights throughout the wider Welsh Liberal Party, which became apparent at election times when the absence of female candidates and voters was most evident.[58] On the 18th of April 1895, for instance, a National Convention of Wales (of all Welsh Liberals) was held in Aberystwyth under the President of the North Wales Federation, Thomas Gee. It committed the Party in Wales to campaign for equal rights for women within the Liberal Federation.[59] It was not, however, able to help women get elected because women were not eligible to be elected to the Westminster Parliament until 1918.

Despite the Parliamentary bar, Welsh female Liberals still played an active part in politics. Aside from the Women's Liberal Federation, there were females serving on the committees of constituency parties. In local government, most Education Committees had female members co-opted onto them. At the same time, Liberal lady mayoresses always had a prominent role in public affairs and, in addition in the constituency, Women's Liberals groups acted as important campaigning forces. Just a few weeks after the 1904 council elections in Cardiff, for instance, Mrs. Eva McLaren, the Women's Liberal Association Chairwoman, reminded the new parliamentary candidate, Ivor Guest, that women members had played a 'vital role in canvassing and educating the ignorant voter of the correct choice, we are fighting for a Liberal majority'.[60] Guest, a former Conservative MP and cousin of Winston Churchill, outside of elections, however, had little time for supporting women in their campaign for a franchise and would prove to be a political enemy of McLaren, one of the leading Liberal campaigners for female suffrage. He went on to lead the Women's National Anti-Suffrage League as its honorary treasurer. Despite Guest's and some others' views, all candidates held separate election meetings for women Liberal members in which they were endorsed by women from the local Liberal Associations. No candidate seeking selection could avoid this. The Qualification of Women Act (1907) allowed women to be elected onto Welsh borough and county councils for the first time. Women could now stand anywhere for Welsh local government. As soon as the Act was passed, Liberals in Brecon petitioned for a well known and active Liberal, Gwenllian Morgan, to stand for election. She was duly elected, becoming the first female Welsh councillor and, in 1912, the first female Welsh Mayor of Brecon.[61] These were two notable firsts. From then on it would be slow progress for Welsh female Liberals to gain elected council office and until the 1990s they would only appear in ones or twos as councillors on most Welsh councils.

As well as those women Liberals already mentioned, the campaign for universal suffrage, which dominated female Liberal policy at the start of the twentieth century, was supported by Margaret Lloyd George, amongst others. Dame Margaret, who acted as the ever supportive wife to Lloyd George, also ran the households at both number 10 and 11 Downing Street. As well as supporting her wider political family, she also supported the Liberal cause in North Wales until her death in January 1941. On the 28th of April 1911, many of Margaret's North Wales female Welsh Liberals visited Lloyd George to press him to vote in the Second Reading of Sir G. Kemp's Bill on Women's Suffrage, which he duly committed to do.[62] The WSPU directed its members to disrupt public meetings of all Cabinet member and, therefore, there was action to be taken both against Lloyd George and the South Wales Liberal MP and Home Secretary, Reginald McKenna.[63] In 1912, for instance, suffragette disturbances directed against Lloyd George at his opening of the Llanystumdwy village institute caused the national press to focus its attention on North Wales; they also did the same when Lloyd George attended the Wrexham Eisteddfod in September 1912.[64] McKenna, as Home Secretary, was also directly involved in dealing with the hunger strikes of women suffragettes in prison, introducing his so called 'Cat and Mouse Act'. This allowed female prisoners out of prison when they were close to starvation and brought them back in again when they recovered. One of the mice let go by McKenna was Margaret Haig, the future Second Viscountess Rhondda. Imprisoned in Usk Prison for a month she went on hunger strike. Haig was released after five days but did not go back to prison because her fine was then paid.

During this period of political turmoil for women, two of Wales' most famous Liberal philanthropists, Gwendoline and Margaret Davies, followed a more sedate path. They started to develop the arts, music, education and various Liberal causes throughout Wales. The sisters' brother was the Montgomeryshire Liberal MP, David Davies. They had benefited from a multi-million pound inheritance from their grandfather, the Liberal MP railway and coal pioneer, David Davies senior. From the 1900s onwards both sisters collected mainly Impressionist paintings and made various gifts and bequests that would later form the main collection of the National Museum of Wales.[65]

On the 21st of November 1918, the Parliament (Qualification of Women) Act came into law and allowed women to sit in Parliament as elected MPs. The following year, the Sex Disqualification (Removal) Act (1919) allowed women to sit on juries and become JPs. In the coming decades, Welsh female Liberals would start to trickle into politics. Most prominent Welsh Liberal females were prevented from seeking seats in Wales by the overwhelming male dominance in the constituencies, which meant that they had to seek them elsewhere. Dr Betty Morgan, a prominent Welsh Liberal and close friend of Ramsay Muir,[66] for instance, unsuccessfully fought a seat in Sunderland in the 1929 election.[67] Winifred Coombe Tennant, the leading South Wales Liberal and art collector, fought but failed to win the Forest of Dean seat in 1922. Despite the Welsh Liberal Federation supporting votes for all women in its conference address in 1921, it did nothing practical to ensure that any woman from its own party was able to be elected in Wales.[68]

In order to challenge Wales' male-dominated political scene, the Welsh Liberal Women's organisation (WLW) continued to operate and promote the female political agenda until it was disbanded in 1988. In the post-war period, Megan Lloyd George was the President of the North Wales Liberal Women's Federation. Elsewhere the WLW continued to be supported by leading male and female Welsh Liberals. Rosa Hovey, the principal of Penrhos College for Girls in Colwyn Bay, was, for instance, the Vice President of the Northern Federation in the 1920s and 1930s.[69] She was a prominent educationalist from Denbighshire who projected a strong presence for female Welsh Liberals. Similarly, Lilian Richards from Cardiff was a prominent member on the Welsh National Liberal Council between 1923 and 1927. Many female Liberals of the time, with the decline of the Welsh Liberal Party, went into the forgotten and unrecorded past of Welsh Liberal history of which only a few fragments have survived mainly in the Political Archive section of the National Library of Wales. One other significant Welsh woman Liberal who we have not mentioned here in detail is Megan Lloyd George. Her story will be told more fully in the following chapters.

Liberal Moves towards Welsh Devolution 1906–1922

Although there was much criticism by Welsh radicals and nationalists that political and administrative devolution had been forgotten, there were, in fact, a number of more concrete measures undertaken by the Liberal governments to increase Welsh autonomy over administrative and cultural areas. In March 1906, there was a meeting of the Welsh National Liberal Council containing, amongst others, representatives from county councils, church and chapel. At this meeting, Brynmor Jones MP had a resolution passed that called for Welsh administrative devolution.[70] Its resolution stated that a Welsh National Council should be established with powers over the Board of Education in Wales, Board of Agriculture and Central Welsh Board.[71] The Council would also have had a Welsh Government Minister in charge of its relationships with Westminster. The Bill supporting this council was introduced to Westminster and passed by the House of Commons in 1906 and supported by all Welsh MPs but it was then rejected by the House of Lords. There would therefore be no Welsh National Council and the Welsh Liberals had to settle with gradual measures of devolution, which were passed down by the Liberal government. These started with 'Standing Order 86', established in 1907. This Order ensured that all Welsh MPs could, in future, have the right to scrutinise legislation

Table 2 **Political and Administrative Measures Undertaken by the Liberals and Coalition Governments, 1906–1922**

Standing Order 86	1907
National Library of Wales (Royal Charter)	1907
National Museum of Wales (Royal Charter)	1907
Welsh Department of Education	1907
Welsh National Insurance Commission	1911
Welsh Board of Health	1919
Welsh Office of the Board of Agriculture and Fisheries	1919

that was solely for Wales.[72] The measures of Welsh administrative devolution are shown in Table 2 above.

When the Irish Home Rule Bill passed through the House of Commons in 1912, Asquith indicated that Welsh Home rule would follow. The September 1913 annual general meeting of the Welsh National Liberal Council consequently resolved to press the government to act and introduce Home Rule for Wales. Sir David Brynmor Jones, the newly elected chairman of the Welsh Party, supported this. He had just replaced Sir Ellis-Griffith, who joined the government. In its November 1913 meeting in Shrewsbury, the Welsh National Liberal Council convened and appointed a sub-committee of eight to prepare a campaign for Home Rule for Wales. In 1914, once again, Jones and E. T. John joined together with Scottish Liberals and were successful in getting the Welsh Home Rule Bill brought before the House of Commons on 13th February 1914. This specified the powers and type of Parliament Wales was to have. It would have 95 elected members in charge of virtually all issues affecting Wales. The only significant powers to remain at Westminster would be customs and excise, foreign and defence policies.[73] The Bill failed to progress. The Welsh National Liberal Council then discussed the fate of the Government of Wales Bill in June and July 1914, but in the dying days of peace it failed to make any further progress. Home Rule would have to await the outcome of what would become known as 'The Great War for Civilisation'.

Liberal By-elections 1910–1914

There were four by-elections in Wales prior to the outbreak of the First World War. All were minor affairs. The first was an unopposed contest in Caernarfonshire, Arfon, in February 1911. Here the sitting MP, William Jones, was appointed as Lord Commissioner of Treasury. He, therefore, had to stand for re-election and was subsequently elected unopposed. The next by-election was contested. William Llewelyn Williams' appointment as Recorder in Swansea in January 1912 resulted in him putting himself up for re-election. In the subsequent three cornered contest, his opponents were Conservative and Independent Labour candidates. Williams had been elected unopposed in 1910; in 1912 he won the by-election with a 1,281 (19.5%) majority over the second placed Conservative candidate, Henry Bond.

The two remaining by-elections were caused by the deaths of the sitting Liberal MPs. The first concerned the death of the elderly barrister Abel Thomas, in

Carmarthenshire East in July 1912. The new Liberal candidate was Reverend Josiah Towyn Jones. He was not a popular choice within the party. Lloyd George thought he was a 'thoroughly bad candidate' and the Liberal MP for Carmarthen Boroughs, Llewelyn Williams, described him as 'full of conceit and vanity'.[74] The electorate, however, failed to see these failures and gave him a 2,728 (30.6%) majority over his Conservative and Labour opponents. The final by-election was in Flint Boroughs in January 1913. The Liberal MP John Williams Summers, who had been elected for the first time in 1910, had died. In a two horse race between local Liberal barrister Thomas Henry Parry and Conservative John Hamlet Roberts, the Liberal won, but the majority was more than halved from 1910, to 211 votes (5.2%). Despite the drop in votes in Flint Boroughs, the election meant a 100 per cent record for the Liberal Government in defending its Welsh seats up until the start of the First World War. This was a war that would unite the Conservatives and Liberals against a common foe – Germany. It was also a war, in which both Parry and Roberts would be fighting together as commissioned officers overcoming domestic political differences.

Labour Unrest

As we alluded to earlier in the chapter, in 1910 there was a series of violent mining labour disputes and riots across South Wales which resulted in the army being called in to quell the disturbances. As Liberal MPs were frequently involved in the ownership of both the coal mines and coal related businesses, such as shipping, railways and docks, many of which were the object of these disputes, a rift was appearing between these Liberals and organised union labour. The South Wales Miners' Federation and its sponsored Welsh Labour politicians were now pitted directly against the industrial South Wales Liberals. The Liberal mining establishment was extensive and consisted of many well known names, such as D. A. Thomas of Cambrian Collieries, and numerous other Liberal industrialists, such as David Davies MP (railway and collieries), Sir John Cory (ship owner and coal exporter), Henry Radcliffe (ship owner and coal exporter), W. Thomas (Maerdy Colliery owner) and W. Jenkins (Ocean Colliery owner). The labour disputes, therefore, became largely ones between Liberal industrialists and Labour supporting unionists and miners. This labour unrest, however, was not as damaging as it might have appeared. Despite the size of the mining industry, only one in five of the electorate was directly connected to the mines in South Wales and therefore the Liberal industrialists did not feel totally doomed by these labour disputes. The Liberal industrialists also felt themselves to be both enlightened and good employers who had been given a bad press by the unions. They, therefore, sought to fight back against the rising tide of Labour activism. They did this in part by re-establishing the 'Liberal Five Hundred'[75] as a mass supporters' movement in South Wales constituencies.

The intense rivalry of later decades between Liberals and Labour was not yet fully apparent across Wales. Between 1910 and 1916, because of mutually shared interests and the continuance of the Progressive Alliance, Labour MPs still propped up the Liberal administration of Asquith. Many Liberals outside the industrial south still felt politically unthreatened by the Labour Party. Liberal MPs were returned by healthy majorities and their main foe was still seen to be the Conservatives. Prior to the First

World War, the Liberal Party remained firmly in the number one slot in Welsh politics, effectively fighting off challenges from outside and sometimes from inside the party. Often it was the Labour party rather than the Liberals who were on the defensive at election time. Yet, at the same time, the signs that Liberal support in South Wales was waning were apparent for astute observers. Aside from the mining disputes that were radicalising many miners away from Liberalism, fewer and fewer people were going to chapel, the very institution that was the bedrock of Welsh Liberal support. The Christian Puritan ethic and cause of non-conformism was having less and less appeal in the South Wales coalfields.[76] The First World War would see the final demise of the Progressive Alliance, which had done much to keep Liberalism and Socialism from clashing head on. It was this Socialism that had already displaced the Welsh Liberals in local government across urban parts of Wales even before the Progressive Alliance ended. In the November 1912 council elections, Swansea town council saw its first Labour mayor, with no Liberals contesting the seats there; the same was true of many councils in the industrial south from Merthyr Tydfil to Aberavon and Neath.[77] Here few, if any, Liberal council candidates could be seen on the ballot papers. In these areas, the Liberals still held the Parliamentary seats but their presence in the council chambers was drying up or had already evaporated.

The Welsh Liberals and the Great War

Germany's invasion of Belgium in August 1914 soon turned all Welsh Liberals' attention away from domestic issues to the war they in which were soon all embroiled. The Welsh nation enthusiastically backed the war and, proportionately, would soon send more of its men to fight than any other part of the British Isles. Council elections stopped after 1915 and the general Westminster elections would not recommence until 1918. The nation focused its attention on war. After a hesitant start, Lloyd George played a key role in the government, first as Chancellor, then as Minister for Munitions and later as Secretary of State for War.

The progress of the war, however, did not go anywhere near as well as the British and French had anticipated. In 1916, after two years of mounting causalities and military stalemate, the wartime Cabinet of the Liberals became increasingly unsustainable. Military failures, such as the Dardanelles, the aftermath of the 1916 Easter rising in Dublin and the huge casualty lists from the Somme (in which Asquith's own son Raymond was killed), pushed the Cabinet further apart.[78] The government suffered continual backbench revolts from issues as diverse as McKenna's 33 per cent wartime tax on tea and the implementation of conscription. In Wales, these tensions came to the surface as various MPs fell out with Lloyd George. Llewelyn Williams, the MP for Carmarthen Boroughs, for instance, took issue with Lloyd George over conscription in 1916, and went on to become a thorn in Lloyd George's side until his own death some six years later. Similarly, David Davies (Montgomeryshire) also split with Lloyd George over his running of the war and failed to support him. Ironically, this was only after he and other Liberals had canvassed secretly to get some hundred Liberal MPs, including Welsh MPs such as Herbert Lewis, to support a Lloyd George, rather than an Asquith, Premiership.

In December 1916, the withdrawal of Conservative support from Asquith's government and its support for Lloyd George Premiership led Lloyd George to oust

Asquith from his premiership in what was called a 'palace revolution'.[79] Thanks to the previous work done by some of his fellow Welsh MPs, Lloyd George was aware of those who would support him as opposed to Asquith. Lloyd George then carried on with running the gruelling war campaign. This split had the side-effect of dividing the Liberal Party into supporters of Asquith (Asquithians) and supporters of Lloyd George (Lloyd Georgites), leaving bitterness between the two families that would last for the next half century. Although this book does not have the time to go into Lloyd George's premiership in any great detail, its sufficient to say that Lloyd George was seen by many as the man who led the British Empire to victory in the Great War. From a Welsh historical perspective, it is important to note that Lloyd George brought a number of Welshmen into the government with him as parliamentary aides, civil servants and advisors and, for the first and last time in the history of the Welsh language, Welsh was frequently used in the business of running 10 Downing Street.[80]

Asquith's departure led to the division of the Liberals across the United Kingdom between Asquithians and Lloyd Georgites Liberals. At first Asquith gave the new government his support and, therefore, the divisions within Liberalism caused by Lloyd George's ascension to the Prime Ministerial office did little to undermine the general cohesion of the Liberal Party. The divisions within the party started to widen in May 1918 after the infamous Maurice Debate in which Asquith led the 98 Liberals into the opposition lobby against Lloyd George's government.[81] These included anti-Lloyd George Welsh MPs, such as Llewelyn Williams and Reginald McKenna. This was seen as an act of open disloyalty and split the Liberal Party in two. Shortly after the Maurice Debate, the Liberals supporting Asquith who had taken part in the revolt set up their own Parliamentary organisation in Wales and the rest of Britain and were then known as 'Wee Frees'.[82] The Liberal Party split into two organisations, an official one still led by Asquith and a second one led by Lloyd George from the Treasury Offices in Downing Street. For the rest of the war the Lloyd Georgites continued to increase the size and scope of their organisation in order to match the Asquithians Liberals. The confusion in the minds of the general public (and even the Liberals themselves) over who was the real representative of 'Liberalism' was suppressed by the war-time election truce but would come into the open in the general election later that year.

Liberals Who Served in the War-Time Government

Apart from Lloyd George, there were a number of Welsh Liberal MPs or Peers who became prominent in the war-time government. Reginald McKenna was Home Secretary between 1914–15 and Chancellor between 1915–16. As mentioned earlier, McKenna fell out with Lloyd George and left the government after Asquith's departure in 1916. With one Welsh Liberal MP leaving government, another came in. This was Sir Alfred Mond (Swansea) who was rewarded for being a keen supporter of Lloyd George and a substantial contributor to party funds[83] by being made First Commissioner of Works. This was regarded as one of the most important posts outside the Cabinet.[84] A close ally of Asquith, Lord Ashby St Ledgers (formerly the Cardiff MP, Ivor Churchill Guest) was appointed Lord Lieutenant of Ireland from 1915 to 1918. He was there during the troubled 1916 Easter Rising and was involved directly in suppressing the revolt and its aftermath.

There were a host of other Welsh parliamentary appointments. David Davies served as Parliamentary Private Secretary to Lloyd George as Minister of Munitions. Herbert Lewis was Parliamentary Secretary to the Board of Education and Sir Ellis-Griffith (Anglesey) was Parliamentary Secretary at the Home Office. Lloyd George's old South Wales rival, Lord Rhondda, became Parliamentary Under Secretary for Food Control in 1917 and became known as the 'man who ended the (food) queues'. The Reverend Towyn Jones (East Carmarthenshire) became the Welsh Liberal Whip and a Junior Lord of the Treasury, in 1917, and Clement Davies (later Montgomeryshire) became an adviser in the Board of Trade about enemy activities in neutral countries. All these Welsh MPs and Lords helped ensure that Welsh Liberalism was represented at the heart of the war effort. Lloyd George's eldest daughter Olwen served in the Red Cross in France and also at times became central to the Anglo-French meetings held in Downing Street. This was because Olwen was fluent in French and German and often translated directly for her father, although in spite of her excellent knowledge of French, she sometimes struggled with the translation of phrases such as 'barbed wire entanglement'.[85]

Those Liberals Who Served in the Front Line

Some 280,000 men from Wales served in the armed forces during the war. In Wales, the most notable casualty politically was Lord Ninian Crichton Stuart, son of the Fourth Marquis of Bute, and the Conservative MP for Cardiff Boroughs. He was killed in action in 1915. Crichton Stuart was, fortunately, the only Welsh Parliamentary Member killed in action during this bloody conflict.[86] However, many prominent Welsh Liberals lost members if their families. One of Lloyd George's most prominent supporters in South Wales, Winifred Coombe Tennant, for instance, lost her son Christopher at Flanders in 1917 aged just 19. Charles Stanton, the Liberal MP for Aberdare, 1918–1922, also lost a son. Lord Rhondda ('D. A.' Thomas) and his daughter the Second Viscountess Rhondda narrowly escaped death when they were travelling on the liner *Lusitania*. The ship sank after being torpedoed off the coast of Ireland in 1915. The *South Wales Daily News* duly declared 'Great disaster at sea, 'D. A.' Saved.'[87] Thanks to his role as Food Controller, Lord Rhondda was well known. He wasn't just prominent in Wales though. When he died on the 2nd of July 1918, just a few months before the end of the war, condolences were sent from the King and statesmen from around the world, including US President Woodrow Wilson. Every newspaper in the United Kingdom carried extensive obituaries of him.[88] His political legacy would now be carried out by his equally dedicated daughter, the Second Viscountess Rhondda, until her death in 1958.

Although there were no deaths amongst their Parliamentary representation, a number of prominent Welsh Liberals served directly in the conflict. The most prominent elected Liberal MP, at the time, to serve in the conflict was David Davies (Montgomeryshire). He fought in the trenches during the war as Colonel in the South Wales Borderers and a Royal Welsh Fusiliers. David was appalled by the tragedies of the battles of the Somme, Ypres and Passchendale.[89] Henry Guest, the Pembroke and Haverfordwest Liberal MP, also served as a Colonel in France between 1914 and 1915, and Thomas Henry Parry (Flint Boroughs) served as a Lieutenant Colonel in the Royal Welsh Fusiliers in Gallipoli, Egypt and Palestine from 1914 to 1918. The most prominent future MP who was in active service was the Prime Minister's own son, Gwilym Lloyd George. He served as a Major in the Royal Artillery in France.

Although initially protected by his father from the front line, who made sure that he served as an *aide-de-camp* to a general, he served in action from 1916 to 1918. There were many other future Welsh Liberal MPs who were also in active service. These included Major Goronwy Owen, Gwilym's brother-in-law and future MP for Caernarfon (1923–45), who gained the DSO.[90] There was also Lieutenant General William (W. N.) Jones, who held Carmarthen for one year between 1928 and 1929, and Captain Richard Thomas (R. T.) Evans – who later represented Carmarthen from 1931 to 1935 who served with the South Wales Borderers. Similarly, Sir Rhys Hopkin Morris (Cardiganshire 1923–32 and Carmarthen 1945–56) served as an officer in the Royal Welch Fusiliers. He was mentioned twice in dispatches and awarded the MBE (Military Division) for an action in which he was severely wounded and carried shrapnel in his leg for the rest of his life.[91] Sir Henry Morris-Jones (Denbigh 1929–50) also gained the Military Cross for his service in the Royal Army Medical Corp. Professor William John (W. J.) Gruffydd, later MP for the University of Wales, served as a Lieutenant in the Royal Navy from 1915 to 1918. In addition, Sir Geoffrey Crawshay, a key Liberal candidate and an active supporter of the Welsh Party until the 1930s, served with the 3rd Welch Regiment at the battle of Loos, where he was severely injured.

Not only male Welsh Liberals played a key part in the war effort. Winifred Coombe Tennant served as the Deputy chairman of the Women's Agricultural Committee for Glamorgan and also as chairman of the War Pensions Commission for Neath and District.[92] The wives of other prominent Welsh Liberals were also drawn very much into the war. Unable to stand for office themselves, they used their prominence to help aid Welsh soldiers in 'flag days' and fund raising campaigns, often deputising for their husbands. On St David's Day 1918, for instance, Margaret Lloyd George in the company of other prominent Liberal women, drove around 'The City of London' in a decorated car, in order to gain money for the Welsh servicemen. Apart from Margaret, the female Welsh Liberal aristocracy boasted the names of Lady Rhondda, Lady Lloyd Mostyn, Lady Griffiths, Lady Armstrong-Jones, Lady Price and Viscountess St Davids. They set up shops and restaurants in army depots in London for the sale of souvenirs, such as metal leeks and gilt daffodils.[93]

The By-elections of the Great War

There were six by-elections during the First World War in Wales. The war-time coalition meant that the other political parties did not contest these elections, allowing instead the party who held the parliamentary seat to nominate a candidate. The first such election occurred in August 1914 and Sir David Brynmor Jones was appointed as the Recorder of Cardiff. It went by without incident and Jones was once again returned unopposed as the MP for Swansea Boroughs. The next by-election, however, also unopposed, provided the Liberal Party with a much greater headache. This was the Swansea District by-election of 1915.

Swansea District By-election 1915[94]

On the 7th of December 1914 the Swansea District Liberal MP Sir David Brynmor Jones was appointed Commissioner in Lunacy. Under the terms of the First World War 'party truce', it should have been a simple matter of appointing a new Liberal candidate, but in Swansea this process nearly tore the constituency and the wider Welsh Liberal Party apart. This was because Charles Masterman, who was already a member of the Liberal Cabinet, wanted the seat and was supported by senior Liberals in London. Masterman had lost his own seat to the Conservatives in February 1914, after having to step down and contest it again upon entering the Cabinet. He was against two local candidates: Thomas Jeremiah Williams, a barrister and the chairman of the Beaufort works in Swansea, and the son of the former Liberal MP for Swansea District from 1893 to 1895; and Dan Thomas, the private secretary of the member for Swansea Town, Sir Alfred Mond.

Most Swansea Liberal members wished to see a local man in post – whether Williams or Thomas – rather than Masterman. Williams proved to be a stronger local candidate than Thomas and the contest appeared to be between Williams and Masterman. Senior Liberals, therefore, desperate to see Masterman regain a Parliamentary seat, stepped up the pressure on Williams to step down. They failed to persuade Williams to stand down, mainly because he was aware that he enjoyed the overwhelming support of the membership of local Liberal bodies, such as Swansea Liberal Club, which backed him unanimously. He was also supported by the Welsh Liberal press. Both local candidates also enjoyed the support of the local Liberal press, with the *South Wales Daily Post* duly condemning the 'English carpet-baggers' who were 'obviously in the House of Commons to advance not the interest of the electors but their own'. Lacking local support, Masterman subsequently withdrew from the contest and from the Cabinet and Williams secured the nomination and the seat. He then served as MP for the constituency until 1918 when the seat became Swansea East, which he represented for another year before his death in 1919 at the age of 47.

The Remaining By-elections of the War Years

The next Parliamentary by-election in July 1915 saw the barrister Griffith Caradoc Rees replace, unopposed, the recently deceased William Jones in the Arfon district of Caernarfonshire. Rees was soon part of the government as Sir John Simon's (Home Secretary) Parliamentary Private Secretary. In November 1915, the Conservative James Herbert Cory (of the Cardiff Tory shipping family) was brought in to replace the recently deceased Lord Ninian Crichton Stuart. Some two weeks later, a more controversial by-election occurred. Labour pioneer Keir Hardie had died and therefore a by-election was held in Merthyr Tydfil. Hardie and the Labour Party had opposed the war, yet all of the other political parties in Wales and the majority of trade unionists in South Wales had supported it. The Labour Party put up their candidate, James Winstone, who was also President of the South Wales Miners' Federation. He was then opposed by a new political party – the pro-war National Democratic and Labour Party. This party's candidate was Charles B. Stanton, a former miners' agent. Both his sons were serving in the war. The Liberals had declared that they would not stand against a candidate who was pro-war.[95] Stanton was pro-war, and so he was backed by the Liberals, Conservatives and other pro-war groupings. This support was enough to ensure that Stanton was able to win the seat off Labour with a 4,206 vote majority.

In July 1917, the much decorated soldier and Liberal MP Major-General Sir Ivor Herbert was elevated to the Lords as Lord Treowen. This left a vacancy in his Monmouthshire South constituency. This vacancy was to be the last Welsh by-election before the end of the First World War. Unlike so many wartime by-elections, this one was not unopposed. It was, however, a contest between Liberals but not the Asquithian and the Lloyd George Liberals. Instead, it was a battle between two Welsh Liberal Thomases, both of whom believed they stood for Welsh Liberalism. Sir Abraham Garard Thomas stood as the official Liberal Party candidate and B. P. Thomas as the independent Liberal candidate. In the event, the official Liberal Sir Abraham Garard Thomas won with a massive 90.3 per cent of the votes albeit on a much reduced wartime turnout of 32.6 per cent.

The 1918 'Coupon' General Election

Within one month of the end of the First World War, Wales was plunged into a general election – its first for eight years. Despite the fact that since July 1918, a Committee under the Liberal radical, George Addison, containing among others the Welsh National Liberal Council president Viscount St Davids, had been planning the election, almost everyone, including the Welsh Liberals (mainly Lloyd Georgite – Coalition Liberals), was ill-prepared for it.[96] It was almost two whole parliamentary terms since the Liberals had last tested their full electoral strength in Wales. On the positive side, since then, with the help of the war-time coalition, they were successful in every Welsh by-election in which one of their members had stood down. In addition, they had one of their own MPs, Lloyd George, leading the country and the Empire and acting as a world statesman. On the negative side, this was no longer the unified Liberal Party of the 1906 landslide election or even the Liberal Party of the 1910 elections. They had entered those elections full of enthusiasm to beat the Conservatives and introduce their own radical programmes for government. Now many Welsh Coalition Liberals would be fighting to keep those same Conservatives in government against former (Asquithian) Liberal and Labour colleagues, who had been on the same side only two years earlier. The Liberal Party was now firmly split between the Asquithians and Lloyd Georgite Coalition Liberals (also called 'Coalies', short for Coalition Liberals).[97]

The 1918 Welsh General Election

Coalition Liberal	19
Labour	10
Conservative	4
Liberal	2
National Democratic and Labour Party	1

To coincide with the 1918 general election, there was a fundamental redistribution of parliamentary seats across Wales. This was needed because the Welsh constituencies were nowhere near equal in size in respect of their electorates. At their extreme, Cardiff Boroughs had become a constituency of some 185,000 electors, whilst Montgomery Boroughs had just 16,000 electors. As a result of this long overdue redistribution of seats, those in Glamorgan and Monmouthshire increased from 14 to 22 but those in the rest of South Wales fell from 8 to 5 and in the North they fell from 12 to 8. At the same time, with the exception of Caernarfon Boroughs (nobody dared to tinker with Lloyd George's seat), all the boroughs seats were merged with those of the surrounding rural counties. In addition to these changes, thanks to Welsh Liberals' pressure, a new seat was established for the registered graduates of the University of Wales. It was done to match those who were already represented in the university seats established in England and Scotland.[98]

The general election of 1918 became known in Wales and elsewhere as the 'Coupon election'. This was because in order to be nominated as an official Coalition candidate, people needed to receive an official letter (a coupon) to stand. Without one, they were not official candidates. Welsh Liberals critical of Lloyd George, such as Llewelyn Williams, were kept away from the coupon. Loyal Coalition support- ers, such as Pontypridd's Thomas Arthur Lewis, were rewarded with the coupon to prove their legitimacy as coalition candidates. The coupon didn't always stop Coalition Liberals and Conservatives contesting against each other. In Swansea West and Pontypridd, the Conservatives ignored the Liberal candidates' coupons and stood against them. The Conservatives also stood against some of the nine Asquithian Liberals in Wales without the coupon. Unlike in England, however, with the exception of Caernarfonshire, Asquithian Liberals did not fight in the same seats as Coalition Liberals.

Asquithian Liberals were nowhere near as popular as Coalition Liberals in either Wales or elsewhere. This meant few gains for the Asquithian Liberals. In Wales only the Asquithian Liberal shipping owner Sir William Henry Seager in Cardiff East and Henry Haydn Jones, who was returned unopposed for Meirionnydd, gained seats. Other loyal Asquithians, such as Walter Roch the Pembrokeshire MP, didn't seek re-election. In the whole of Britain the Asquithians only secured 28 seats: Herbert Asquith, himself, failed to secure one.

The Liberal MP, David Davies, refused the coupon but did not openly support Asquith. He was offered the coupon and was duly endorsed by the Coalition Liberals, but refused it. Having parted company with Lloyd George during the First World War, Davies didn't seek to reunite with him now because of the 'coupon'. He described the coupon as 'an unsolicited testimonial, I assure you I have never asked for it ... A great many people are beginning to protest against the kind of labelling which is going on at present.'[99] Instead, Davies saw himself as a semi-independent Liberal.

The election in Wales was fought over the issue of Lloyd George being 'the greatest Welshman ever' and he led the campaign here. After all the ballots were counted, some 19 Coalition Liberals had won seats in Wales.[100] They were joined in Wales by four Coalition Conservatives and one member of the National Democratic and Labour Party. Outside Wales, however, the Coalition Liberals were not in the majority. There were another 116 Coalition Liberals elected but there were also 335 Coalition Conservatives. From then on, Lloyd George and the Coalition Liberals were entirely dependent on the Conservatives' support and votes in the Commons and Lords.

The 1918 General Election and Changing Liberal World

The 1918 general election was significant for the Welsh Liberals, as it was the last time they gained the highest number of votes in Wales, of all the political parties contesting seats. Even as Lloyd George romped home in Caernarfon Boroughs, with a massive 12,898 votes (85.4%), the Labour Party was advancing into Liberal constituencies throughout South and North East Wales.[101] Some prominent Liberals of the pre-war era such as E. T. John had now joined their number and were also standing as Labour Party candidates in Wales.[102] Although for the moment many Liberal seats were still retained by the party, the Coalition Liberals majorities were kept artificially high by the absence of Conservative competition for most seats. The true size of Liberal support, therefore, remained untested. As a result, the Liberals still retained significant majorities in some Welsh industrial seats. Lewis Halsham won in Newport by 3,846 votes (15.4%) and tin-plate manufacturer Thomas Williams won Swansea East by an impressive 4,730 votes (27.2%). Even the barrister Sir Edgar Jones, was able to beat Labour in Merthyr Tydfil by 1,445 votes (5.4%).

Ominously though, where there were three party competitions, such as in the three new Cardiff constituencies, Labour was now outperforming the Liberals in both Cardiff Central and Cardiff South. Even in Cardiff East, the Liberals' strongest Cardiff seat, Labour was only a few thousand votes from taking the seat. In Swansea West, the industrialist, Sir Alfred Mond, put Labour into third place by some 3069 votes, though Labour had more than doubled its votes since it had last stood in the seat in February 1910 (from 12% to 25.6%). Mond's victory was obtained despite a vicious personal campaign against him in which his Conservative opponent David Davies fought the seat on the issue of Mond's German Jewish ancestry that made him 'unfit to stand for the British Imperial Parliament'.[103] He was also accused by Davies and the local press of being a German spy and a war profiteer but successfully sued for libel and was backed by both Lloyd George and Bonar Law in this action.[104] Whilst the Welsh Liberals and the Conservatives, who were meant to be allies in a coalition government were fighting, the Labour Party was making inroads across Wales, including Liberal North Wales where it had doubled its Welsh tally of seats from 5 to 10.[105]

University of Wales Seat Becomes a Liberal Bastion

The political scene in Wales was evolving. In the new University of Wales seat, for the first time there came the opportunity for registered graduates to vote for their own MP and also for a female candidate. The first female candidate in Wales was the Education Professor Hettie Mackenzie. She was not a Welsh Liberal but a Labour representative. Mackenzie lost to Lloyd George loyalist Herbert Lewis, the former MP, for the recently dissolved Flint Boroughs seat. Lewis, in alliance, with Lord Kenyon was responsible for reversing a defeated amendment to the Representation of the People Act which would have allowed for a University of Wales seat to be established.[106] This acted in his own interest. His support for the University of Wales, whilst he had served at both the Treasury and Education Departments was well known. This was a fact which did nothing to harm his vote and consequently secured him a 61.6 per cent majority in the actual election. Thus the Liberals won the University of Wales seat on its first election and, with the odd exception, the party would win it every other time there was an election for the next thirty years. In the future, it often proved to be a refuge for Liberal MPs in Wales, like Lewis, fleeing Parliamentary seat redistribution or electoral failure elsewhere. With the new university seat established, Wales now had 36 parliamentary seats.[107]

Conclusion

Even in 1918, the last year covered by this chapter, Welsh Liberalism was by far the most powerful political force in Wales. Although the Progressive Alliance between Liberals and Labour, which had divided the Welsh seats between both parties almost for a generation had ended, a new alliance with the Conservatives in the Coalition government seemed to be almost as rewarding. This meant that the Liberals, unlike any other party in Welsh history, politically dominated nearly all of Wales at a Parliamentary and county council level. There was not one town or village that at some time was not represented by a Liberal MP or covered by a Liberal-controlled council during this period. The party represented the worker, the industrialist, the businessman, the nationalist, the unionist, the non-conformist, the tenant farmer and even in some places the landlord. It was a broad political church and there were few prominent Welshmen of the late Victorian and Edwardian period who did not worship at its altar sometime during their career. The outlook for Welsh Liberalism was apparently good. Welsh Liberalism, on the surface, appeared to be uniquely well equipped to withstand the challenge of Labour in the years before 1914. In virtually every straight electoral contest it triumphed over the Labour Party.

The Liberal Party in Wales described in much of this chapter was still a large, democratic, populist national movement, associated with the aspirations of Welsh society and with Welsh cultural awareness at every level. It helped inspire the imaginative prose of John Edward Lloyd and Owen M. Edwards, the poetry of Gwynn Jones and the rhetoric of Lloyd George. Yet what would happen to it now? As the Great War came to a close, the Liberal Party, even in Wales, was split into factions between Lloyd George Coalition Liberals and the Asquithian Liberals. The end of 1918 saw the public support for Lloyd George outpace that of the Liberal Party itself. His own ambitions, supported by this popularity, kept the party divided, which signalled its downfall. Lloyd George's dominance of the party in Wales, however, ensured that the party on the whole remained united under his leadership. Nevertheless this was a distressing end for Welsh Liberals, who had less than a decade earlier, been so dominant.

Notes

1. Griggs, John (1997) op. cit., p. 102
2. Khaki was the colour of the British soldiers' uniforms
3. Massie, Robert K. (1991) Dreadnought, Random House, p. 212
4. This figure includes William Abraham (Lib Lab) Rhondda and Keir Hardie (ILP) Merthyr Tydfil who both took the Liberal whip
5. Both men were deeply involved in the events that led to the start of the Boer War
6. Morgan, Kenneth O. (1991) op. cit., p. 206
7. Morgan, Kenneth O. (1991) op. cit., p. 191
8. Ivor Guest was also 1st Viscount Wimborne, and grandson of the Duke of Marlborough
9. Ivor Guest's grandfather, Josiah John Guest, had been the first MP for Merthyr Tydfil (1832–52) where the family was instrumental in life of the town. The family's company was Guest, Keen and Nettlefords. They were Britain's leading steel manufacturer with works in Merthyr Tydfil, Cardiff and Newport. John Davies, Nigel Jenkins, Menna Baines and Peredur L. Lynch (2008) The Welsh Academy Encyclopaedia of Wales, University of Wales Press, p. 341

10. Deacon, Russell (2005) 'From Gladstone Primary School to Lloyd George Avenue: Cardiff Liberal Council Politics in the centenary year', speech to the Lloyd George Society, February 2005
11. Davies, A. J. (1995) We, The Nation: The Conservative Party and the Pursuit of Power, Little Brown and Company, p. 21
12. Davies, John (1994) op. cit., p. 394
13. Morgan, K. O. (1991) op. cit., p. 171
14. Morgan, K. O. (1991) op. cit.
15. Welsh Liberal National Council records, 1908, National Library of Wales
16. *The Western Mail* 27/4/33
17. Although Sir William Harcourt (Monmouthshire West) was Chancellor during this period his seat was in Derby at the time and only had a Welsh seat in 1895 after the Liberals were out of office.
18. Morgan, Kenneth (1973) Lloyd George, Family Letters 1885–1936, University of Wales Press, Oxford University Press, p. 13
19. Morgan, K. O. (1960) op. cit., p. 71
20. Packer, Ian (2001) Lloyd George, Liberalism and the Land, The Royal Historical Society, The Boydell Press
21. Parry, Cyril (1973) op. cit., p. 290
22. Morgan, Kenneth O. (2007) op. cit., p. 22 Lloyd George's Flintshire Loyalist: The Political Achievements of John Herbert Lewis, Journal of Liberal History, Vol. 57, Winter 2007–8, p. 25
23. Morgan, Kenneth O. (1981) op. cit., p. 57
24. Grigg, John (1997) op. cit., p. 55
25. Alfred Thomas got some reward for his service to Welsh Liberal nationalism when he was awarded a knighthood in 1902
26. Nelmes, Graham V. (1979) op. cit., p. 483
27. Davies, John (1993) op. cit., p. 465
28. Cleaver, David (1985) Labour and Liberals in the Gower Constituency, 1885–1910, Welsh History Review, Vol. 12, No. 3, 1985, p. 403
29. *The Western Mail*, Junior Member for Treorchy, 22/11/34
30. *The South Wales Daily* Post 11/11/1907
31. Morgan, K. O. (1991) op. cit., p. 216
32. Bolitho, Hector (1933) Alfred Mond First Lord Melchett, Martin Secker Ltd, p. 66
33. Morgan, K. O. (1991) op. cit., p. 241
34. Ibid.
35. Ibid.
36. Welsh Liberal National Council records, 1909, National Library of Wales
37. Welsh National Liberal Council, List of Speakers, 1910
38. Stead, Peter (1969) Vernon Hartshorn: Miner's Agent and Cabinet Member, in Stewert Williams' Glamorgan Historian Vol. 6, D. Brown and Sons Ltd, pp. 83–94
39. E. G. Hemmerde stood in two byelections because of the precedent of having to stand for re-election on undertaking an outside position in the judiciary. He stood down for Denbighshire East in 1910 before becoming the Liberal MP for Norfolk North West 1912–18 and then defecting to become the Labour MP for Crewe 1922–24
40. Lord St David's remained one of the main figures of the Liberal Party in Wales and nationally for the next three decades
41. In Swansea Town by over four times the Labour vote 6020 to 1451
42. Labour could not contest more seats at the time because financial support for the Labour Party was limited by the Osborne case of 1909. This had adjudicated that the trade union's political levy was unlawful. As the unions paid the bulk of money to their working class candidates and MPs (MPs were not paid a salary until 1911) Labour campaigning was therefore severely reduced
43. Bolitho, Hector (1933) op. cit.
44. Alderman and President of Cardiff Liberals 1893–1903, D. A. Thomas, Records of, National Library of Wales
45. Stead, Peter (1969) op. cit., p. 86
46. Cross, Colin (1963) The Liberals in Power, Pall Mall Press, p. 167
47. Ibid
48. Bentley, Michael (1977) op. cit., p. 199

49. Western Mail 16/11/33
50. Rhondda, Viscountess (1933) This Was My World, MacMillan, p. 92
51. Morgan, Kenneth. O (1980) *Wales In British Politics 1868–1922*, University of Wales Press, p. 57
52. Masson, Ursula (2007) 'Liberalism, gender and national memory', University of Wales Institute Cardiff, Centre for Humanities Open Seminar series, 3/5/07
53. *The Western Mail* 14th March 1895
54. *The Times*, 31st March 1915, p. 10
55. Rhondda, Viscountess (1933) op. cit., p. 142
56. Nora Phillips had died in 1915
57. Dictionary of Welsh Biography 1941–1970 (2001), The Dictionary of Welsh Biography 1941–1970, The Honourable Society of Cymmrodorion, p. 264
58. Morgan, Kenneth O. (1980) op. cit., p. 252
59. Liverpool Mercury 19th April 1895, p. 7
60. *South Wales Daily News*, 25th November 1904
61. *Brycheiniog*, Volume XII 1966/67
62. The Times, 28/4/11, p. 8
63. Rhondda, Viscountess (1933) op. cit., p. 148
64. Graham Jones, J. (2002) Lloyd George and the Suffragettes at Llanystumdwy, Journal of Liberal Democrat History, Issue 34/35 Spring/Summer 2002, pp. 3–10
65. Fairclough, Oliver (2007) 'Things of Beauty': What Two Sisters Did For Wales, National Museum Wales Books
66. Professor Ramsay Muir was a leading figure in the Liberal Summer School movement and the National Liberal Federation
67. *Daily News*, 3rd January 1930
68. Dictionary of Welsh Biography 1941–1970 (2001) op. cit., p. 23
69. *The Times*, 19/10/32, p. 16
70. Randall, P. J. (1972) Wales in the Structure of Central Government, Public Administration, Autumn 1972, Vol. 50, p. 353
71. Morgan, K. O. (1991) op. cit., p. 223
72. Deacon, Russell (2002) The Governance of Wales: The Welsh Office and the Policy Process 1964–99, Welsh Academic Press, p. 121
73. Davies, John (1993) op. cit., p. 467
74. Morgan, Kenneth O. (1973) op. cit., p. 163
75. The term 'Liberal Five Hundred' referred to five hundred regular paying Liberal members supporting campaigning in the constituency. It was seen to reflect the strength of the constituency.
76. Morgan, Kenneth O. (1973) op. cit., p. 303
77. *South Wales Daily Post* 1/11/1912
78. Brock, Michael, 'Asquith' in Dictionary of Liberal Biography (1998) Duncan Brack [ed] Politico's Publishing, p. 19
79. Brock, Micheal, (1998) op. cit., p. 19
80. Dr. Thomas Jones was one example, he became Deputy Secretary to the Cabinet in 1916. He then served all Prime Ministers from Lloyd George to Ramsay MacDonald in 1930. His daughter Eirene White was the Labour MP for East Flintshire (1950–70). She was the only Welsh female Welsh Office Minister and government minister in the twentieth century. She later on became Baroness White of Rhymney. In June 1995 she told the author of her father and Lloyd George's use of Welsh in conversation in order for it to remain secret when dealing with Michael Collins and the Irish Nationalists in the drawing up of the 1922 Treaty. Collins and his team in turn had spoken in Gaelic to avoid the British knowing what they were saying.
81. It was called the Maurice debate as it referred to allegations made by the sacked Director of Military Operations, Major-General Sir Frederick Maurice, that both Lloyd George and Bonar Law had made false statements concerning British military strength in France. Asquith demanded a Select Committee to inquire into the allegations; Bonar Law Law recommended a tribunal of two judges instead. A division was held over the issue and Asquith then led the 98 Liberal MPs into the division lobby against the government.
82. This being an analogy with a small and strict Scottish Presbyterian sect – the Wee Frees, Douglas, Roy (1971) op. cit., p. 137

83. Wilson, Trevor (1968) The Downfall of the Liberal Party 1914–1935, Collins, p. 39
84. Graham Jones, J. (1998) 'Sir Alfred Mond' in the Dictionary of Liberal Biography (1998) Duncan Brack [ed] Politico's Publishing, p. 265
85. Carey Evans, Olwen (1985) Lloyd George Was My Father, Gomer, p. 74
86. Today the statute commemorating his death lies only some fifty metres away from the statue of his political adversary, David Lloyd George, in Cathays Park, Cardiff.
87. The *South Wales Daily News*, 8/5/1915
88. D. A. Thomas's personal papers at the National Library of Wales have two large volumes of obituaries from around 100 newspapers in the United Kingdom.
89. Davies, W. R. (1995) Laying the Foundations: The Contribution of Lord Davies of Llandinam in Davies, W. R. (ed) The United Nations at Fifty: The Welsh Contribution, University of Wales Press
90. Distinguished Service Order – a military decoration for bravery
91. The Dictionary of Welsh Biography 1941–1970 (2001), The Honourable Society of Cymmrodorion, p. 190
92. *The Times*, 1/9/56 p. 11
93. Jones, Emrys (2001) The Welsh in London 1500–2000, University of Wales Press on behalf of The Honourable Society of Cymmrodorion, p. 233
94. David, E. I. (1970) Charles Masterman and the Swansea by-election 1915, Welsh History Review, Vol. 5, No. 1
95. Mor-O-Brien, Anthony (1985) The Merthyr Borough Election, November 1915, The Welsh History Review, Vol. 12, No. 4, 1985
96. Wilson, Trevor (1966) op. cit., p. 142
97. *The Observer*, 10/12/21, p. 12
98. This was part of what was called plural voting, in which graduates of universities and those with business premises, were allowed to have two or more votes at election times
99. Graham Jones, J. (2001) op. cit., p. 21
100. Sidney Robinson in Brecon and Radnor, John Hinds in Carmarthen, M. L. Vaughan Davies in Cardigan and David Davies in Montgomeryshire were all returned unopposed
101. Boothroyd, David (2001) Politico's Guide to The History of British Political Parties, Politico's Publishing, p. 151
102. E. T. John lost his Denbigh seat to the coalition Liberal Sir David S Davies by a massive 11,815 (66.6%) of the vote. He was to stand twice more for Labour in 1922 and 1924 in Brecon and Radnor but he lost there was well.
103. Bolitho, Hector (1933) op. cit., p. 211
104. Bolitho, Hector (1933) op. cit., p. 211
105. Parry, Cyril (1968) Gwynedd Politics, 1900–1920: The Rise of a Labour Party, Welsh History Review, Vol. 4, No. 2, pp. 313–328
106. Morgan, Kenneth O. (2007) op. cit., p. 27
107. Davies, John (1993) op. cit.

3

THE LEGACY SPOILT (1919–1945)

"The issue, therefore, for the electors is whether they will entrust the destinies of the country to the Liberal Party, which can show a long record of great and enduring service to the nation, and which can command today amongst its leaders a number of able and experienced men ..."

David Lloyd George – The 1929 Liberal Party General Election Manifesto

Lloyd George's persuasive words in his party's 1929 manifesto were to be rejected by the general public in the election results of that year. The general election results for the Liberals showed clearly that the Liberals were no longer in the running for power in their own right. Yet what might be thought of as Lloyd George's overconfidence was not totally unjustified, at least from a Welsh perspective. In 1914 the Liberals were by far the most powerful political party in Wales. They held 26 of the 32 Welsh parliamentary seats, they were in government and they also had a number of MPs holding powerful positions in the government. A few years later, with David Lloyd George as Prime Minister, the presence of Welsh Liberalism was felt internationally, including at the peace conference at Versailles. The Welsh party's strength was then formidable and there was little thought of any possibility of rapid electoral attrition in the near future. The Liberals, however, fell from their position of dominance in a very short period afterwards.

The ten years that followed the end of the First World War saw a transformation of politics in both Wales and the rest of the United Kingdom. From 1918 to 1924, the Labour Party changed from being the third small party of British politics to an actual party of government. It was significantly aided in part by gaining many former Liberal Party parliamentary seats. For a while the Liberal Party remained a significant force in British politics, though it was increasingly squeezed between the Labour and Conservative parties, but after the 1929 general election, it became marginalised and then split once more.[1] In Wales, Liberalism remained a strong force for much longer than it did in England. Here, it continued to outshine the Conservatives electoral record long after it had ceased doing so elsewhere. Even in Wales, however, its strength was faltering. This third chapter charts the events behind the fading Liberal fortunes across Wales and why they appeared to come about so suddenly.

The Welsh Liberals and Post War
Welsh Policy Agenda

The Lloyd George (coalition) Liberals had put out a joint general election manifesto with the Conservative Party under the leadership of Andrew Bonar Law in
the 1918 general election. It talked mainly of its success in winning the war and the
potential future of 'our Empire and the nations of which it is composed'.[2] Despite
Lloyd George's Welsh heritage and his warm words about Wales whilst he was
Prime Minister, he did not mention Welsh aspirations in the manifesto. The former
Welsh radical had the British and the international stage as his main political focus
now. Herbert Asquith replied with his own manifesto for the non-Coalition Liberals,
which consisted of just over three hundred words, and similarly made no mention of
Wales or the Welsh, although the Asquithian Welsh Liberal Federation later proposed
establishing an elected Council for Wales.[3] Most Liberals now focused on reshaping
the post-war world rather than going back to the pre-war Welsh nationalist agenda.

With the omission of Wales from both the Liberal manifestos, the question arose
about what now remained of the pre-war Welsh Liberal nationalism. The issues of
the nonconformist church had ended with the disestablishment of the Welsh church.
The post-war era with its legacy of war, growing mass unemployment and problems
with the division of Ireland gave the appearance of belonging to another age entirely.
The Montgomeryshire MP, David Davies and a few other Liberals promoted a
national conference at Llandrindod Wells, during the Whitsun of 1918, to discuss
a measure of devolution for Wales.[4] No invitation was sent to Labour 'nationalists',
so the conference was, in effect, only a Liberal Party affair. The organisers were
convinced that Wales would soon be afforded a Parliament as part of the all-round
solution to the Irish problem. Twenty-two delegates were chosen from the gathering
to attend a subsequent meeting to flesh out the details and report back to their local
authorities. In the event, only seven of the twenty-two delegates turned up at the
next meeting, which led to *The Western Mail* describing it as a 'Home Rule Fiasco'.[5]
It was not, however, the end of the move towards Home Rule and the following
year a further conference was held. The 1919 Llandrindod Wells Whitsun Home
Rule Conference was much better attended and included Liberal MPs, local government representatives and prominent academics. Unanimous support was given for
a motion calling for 'full local autonomy in Wales'. Support for a Welsh Secretary,
however, was only given a lukewarm reception. The conference had moved devolution forward but not by much.[6] It was, therefore, left to the Parliament to move the
question of Welsh devolution forward.

In the Commons, following the second Llandrindod Wells conference, the Tory
MP Major Edward Wood (Ripon) successfully put down a motion that called for an
inquiry into the question of devolution for England, Scotland and Ireland. Despite
the objections of the Welsh Liberal MPs Sir Robert Thomas (Wrexham), T. A. Lewis
(Pontypridd) and John Hugh Edwards (Neath) who asserted that the exclusion of
Wales from the motion 'implied Welsh inferiority', it was carried by 187 votes to 34.
Lloyd George's response to the issue of Home Rule was to appoint a political committee from across the British Empire, known as a Speaker's Conference, to examine the
whole question of devolution. Its report in May 1920 did little for Welsh nationalist
aspirations when it recommended a variety of options ranging from the setting up of

'regional grand councils and subordinate parliaments'. These anti-Home Rulers were able to effectively dismiss the report as inconclusive. In Wales, the growing power of Socialism focused its attention on gaining power in Westminster rather than using Home Rule to do so in Wales. No Progressive Alliance would, therefore, be forged between Labour and Liberals to unite in a campaign for a Welsh parliament.

A small group of Welsh Liberal MPs called directly on Lloyd George to create the post of Welsh Secretary but he urged them to 'go for the big thing', implying that they should pursue a Welsh Parliament rather than just a Cabinet post.[7] David Matthews' (Swansea East) attempt to present a Bill calling for a Welsh Secretary in February 1921 came to nothing without government support. Later, in 1921, Lloyd George dismissed the idea of Home Rule for Wales entirely. In September 1921, Lloyd George told at a meeting of the Welsh Parliamentary Party that devolution to Wales was too expensive an option. He stated that as 'Prime Minister of the Empire, and custodian of the National Resources'[8] he would oppose a Home Rule Bill. This about face may have been more to do with the fact did not trust the now Labour dominated south of Wales to govern the mainly Liberal north in any Welsh Parliament.[9] Whatever his reasoning, this meeting proved a huge disappoint to those MPs who remembered the Welsh radical Lloyd George of the 1890s and early 1900s and his support for Home Rule. In February 1922, Hugh Edwards' (Neath) Westminster Committee on Welsh Home Rule recommended introducing a Welsh Parliament consisting of an upper and a lower chamber with substantial law making and tax-raising power (Part of the Scotland and Wales Bill). The head of the Parliament would to be known as 'Lord President of Wales'.[10] This was followed up by a well attended conference on Welsh Home Rule in Shrewsbury on 30th March 1922. The Welsh Liberal Party was unable to agree at this meeting to endorse this Bill. The conference could not manage even to agree to support the Home Rule Bill and following on from Lloyd George's private concerns, the Northern Welsh Liberals expressed their fears that they would be dominated by the 'Bolshevism' of South Wales.[11] The rural and north Wales delegates also felt that Home Rule would mean excessive taxation. In addition, they felt that the Welsh capital should be in Caernarfon or Wrexham rather than Cardiff. This put them at odds with the South Wales Liberals. It was these same arguments that had destroyed *Cymru Fydd* a few decades earlier and kept the Welsh Liberal Party from truly uniting.

However, despite the Shrewsbury meeting and Lloyd George's rejection of Home Rule, this did not stop Sir Robert Thomas, the Liberal MP for Wrexham, from introducing, together with the Scottish Member, Murray MacDonald, the Government of Scotland and Wales Bill on the 22nd of May 1922. This Bill, like others before it, was once again a failure. The Government of Scotland and Wales Bill was 'talked out' on its First Reading at Westminster. Six months later Lloyd George was out of office and the issue of any immediate prospect of devolution vanished with him.

Home Rule for Wales aside, Lloyd George had done a few things for Wales and the promotion of Welsh Liberal interests while in power. In 1921, for instance, he refused to allow Pembroke Dock Naval Dockyard in the Liberal Pembroke seat to be closed in the 'interests of economy'.[12] This would not have the lasting legacy a Welsh Parliament would have brought but it helped the Liberals retain the seat. Therefore, it would not be Home Rule but British social reform that dominated the Liberals' policy agenda in Wales from 1918–22. A series of social measures were passed concerning education, health, housing, unemployment insurance and pensions, which took up most of Welsh MPs' time at Westminster. Despite the wide-spread endorsement for these policies by Welsh MPs, the Liberal Party was still divided between the Coalition Liberals and the Asquithians. The division almost developed into a fully-fledged civil war.

The Liberals and the Labour Party Post World War One

Despite the relatively peaceful and, at times, co-operative pre-war relationship between the Liberals and Labour in Wales, things were to change dramatically after the First World War. Labour abandoned its six decades of close cohabitation with Liberalism and pursued its own agenda.[13] Already with a substantial local government presence, the Labour Party further expanded its base in the first local government elections to be held in six years in the Welsh urban council elections in November 1919. They made 26 gains across Wales and in Llanelli, Swansea, Carmarthen and Brecon not a single Liberal candidate stood for election.[14] Lloyd George was aware of the potential that Labour would have if Liberalism failed to tackle the widespread 'social problems'. He tried to limit the appeal of the Labour Party with his various Acts on health, unemployment insurance, education, land reform, old age pensions and housing.[15] After the war, however, there was a desire for more radical change amongst returning service men and this found its way in Wales through direct support for the Labour party. Communism and Socialism, which underpinned the rise of the left, with their 'workers ownership' through nationalisation, offered an answer to the returning service men's desire for change. Labour's fortunes in the industrial areas of South and North Wales blossomed. The Labour leader Ramsay MacDonald and the Labour party now sought nothing less than the annihilation of the Liberal Party. As they moved closer to government they sought to be portrayed as a moderate party that could be trusted. Whilst they required the support of the Liberals to get into power, they did not want to return to the pre-war Progressive Alliance of Liberals and Labour. Instead, they planned to replace it wholly by the Labour party.[16]

In addition, the trade unions, such as the South Wales Miners' Federation, that had often not wanted to contest Liberals seats directly in the pre-war period in order not to undermine the Progressive Alliance against the Tories, no longer felt the need to exercise such restraint now that the Lloyd George's Liberals served with them.[17] As their own party launched from crisis to crisis, lacking its own ideological drive and linking itself with the Conservatives, many Coalition Liberals began to lose faith with their party. In turn, those Asquithian Liberals, on the more radical side, were not unsympathetic to these Socialist cries of change and declarations that the Liberals' time had passed and that they were the new radicals. A number of Welsh Liberals, including the Liberal radical nationalist MP of the pre-war years E. T. John, had already crossed the road to join the Labour. In South Wales, Sir Alfred Mond wrote to Lloyd George in 1922 that Labour was coming to regard the South Wales coalfields as 'the Eldorado of their Utopian hopes'.[18] Mond attacked both the Labour Party and Socialism at almost every opportunity. As the Liberal MPs pondered his warnings and other things about their party's future, a quarter of all the Welsh Parliamentary seats were to undergo by-elections.

Parliamentary By-elections 1918–1922

The first by-election to occur in Wales after the 1918 general election was in Swansea East in July 1919. The sitting Liberal MP Thomas Jeremiah Williams had died and the subsequent by-election was a straight fight between Coalition Liberals and the Labour Party. The Coalition Liberal David Matthews retained the seat. The Labour Party, however, had reduced the Liberal majority from 27.2 per cent to just 6.2 per cent. The next by-election did not see a Liberal candidate enter the contest at all. When Labour's Thomas Richards retired from the Ebbw Vale seat in July 1920, the Coalition Liberal Junior Whip for Llanelli, the Reverend Towyn Jones, advised the party not to contest the seat. The Liberal constituency party there had by then become defunct and there was no resistance to this stance from the wider Welsh Coalition Liberals. Labour's Evan Davies won the seat unopposed. Five months later the Liberals managed, however, to contest the Abertillery by-election. This coal mining seat had been established just two years before. William Brace had taken it for Labour unopposed in 1918. Brace had not been MP for this new seat for long when he took up the full-time position of Chief Labour Adviser to the Government Mines Department. Therefore, a by-election was necessary. This time the Coalition Liberals challenge took Labour head on. The wealthy Liberal barrister Sir George Hay Morgan was set against George Baker, a former miner and decorated Zulu war veteran. The Liberal manifesto of 'anti-Bolshevism and anti-Socialism', however, ran counter to both the sentiments of the working-class and the rallying-call of the Labour Party. Morgan consequently lost by a hefty 7,650 votes (32.8%) to Baker.

Liberal Versus Liberal 1921 Cardiganshire By-election[19]

It was not just the Labour Party that was the political foe of the Coalition Liberals. They also competed on occasions with the Asquithian Liberals who, a few years earlier, had been their loyal comrades. Administratively and politically, the Lloyd George faction dominated the co-ordinating Welsh Liberal National Council and ensured that it supported the Coalition and excluded all Opposition Liberals from the Welsh Executive Committee. As we noted earlier, Lloyd George's key ally, Lord St. Davids, presided over the Welsh Council, making it the only national Liberal council in Britain that the Asquithians had failed to take control of. However, Lloyd George did not have it all his way; his Welsh opponents led by Llewelyn Williams, Judge J. Bryn Roberts, Ellis W. Davies and Rhys Hopkins Morris established a rival body to the Welsh Liberal Council and called it the Welsh Liberal Federation.[20] This pursued its own policy agenda which was much more Welsh in nature than that of the Coalition Liberals. They campaigned, among other Welsh issues, for renegotiation of the disendowment clauses of the Welsh Church Act 1920, to give greater benefit to nonconformity, further temperance legislation and, importantly for Home Rulers, the setting up of an elected Council for Wales.[21]

Although Lloyd George Liberals were dominant in Wales after the split in 1918, battles with the Asquithians still became unavoidable. The bitterness between the Lloyd George Liberals and the Asquithians reached a peak in Wales in 1921. In

February of that year, a by-election occurred in Cardiganshire. This was to pit the Asquithians directly against the Coalition Liberals in open electoral warfare. These two were the only candidates in this election. The by-election was caused by the incumbent Liberal MP and chairman of the Welsh Parliamentary Party, Matthew Lewis Vaughan Davies, being elevated to the Lords as Lord Ystwyth. In Cardiganshire, there was considerable support for the Asquithians Liberals with the rejection of the Liberal Coalition which was being maintained with the support of their traditional political foe, the Conservative and Unionists. The Coalition Liberals were represented by Captain Ernest Evans (an Aberystwyth barrister and former private secretary to Lloyd George). The Welsh Liberal National Council supported Evans' candidature in the Cardiganshire by-election, when it met by 43 to 5 votes. A barrister, the anti-conscription and former newspaper editor, William Llewelyn Williams, was an Asquithian Liberal candidate who was duly backed by the Welsh Liberal Federation. A Liberal civil war centred on Cardiganshire was now set to occur.

The campaign was fought mainly over tariff reform ('Evans for reform' with 'Williams against') and Evans avoided engaging in more specific Welsh matters, such as temperance and nonconformism (those supported by Williams).[22] Politicians from both sides weighed in to support the candidates; Margaret Lloyd George, the Prime Minister's wife, and Lady Violet Bonan Carter, Asquith's daughter, spoke on numerous occasions in support of their respective candidates throughout the county. The by-election caused major urban-rural and religious splits within Cardiganshire, which would take a generation to die down. The Methodist and urban population tended to support Evans whilst the rural population and Congregationalists supported Llewelyn Williams. In the event, Evans beat Williams by some 3,590 votes. Evans had also picked up much of the Conservative vote as the coalition candidate, whilst Williams picked up the Labour vote. The split within the Liberal Cardiganshire divided its Liberals into two rival associations and two separate Liberal Clubs were now established in Aberystwyth. There was even a split between the local papers, with the *Cambrian News* supporting Evans and the *Welsh Gazette* supporting Williams.[23]

Cardiganshire By-election 18 February 1921

Candidate	Party	Vote	Percentage
Ernest Evans	Liberal (Coalition)	14,111	57.3
William Llewelyn Williams	Liberal (Asquithian)	9,959	42.7
	Majority	3,590	14.6
	Turnout		80.1

After the Cardiganshire by-election, the coalition government contested all the remaining by-elections in Wales up until November 1922, even though in many of the seats, the Liberal organisation had by then collapsed and the agents departed. The Liberals, therefore, continued to lose heavily to the Labour Party in seats they had until recently held. They lost by 4,741 votes (18.7%) in Caerphilly in August 1921, by 3,455 votes (15%) in Gower on the 20th of July 1922 and a week later by another 4080 (14%) votes in Pontypridd. Here the sitting MP, Thomas Arthur (T. A.) Lewis, had been forced to resign because he had been appointed a Junior Lord of the Treasury. In the subsequent by-election, the Labour campaign was based mainly on painting Lewis as something of a 'war profiteer', an accusation that appeared to stick with the electorate, despite there being little evidence to substantiate it.[24] Whilst the South Wales Liberals contemplated their losses, in respect of British politics, the most important Welsh by-election ever was just about to occur. After its conclusion, Welsh and British politics would never be quite the same again.

The 1922 Newport By-election and the End of the Liberal Governance of Wales

Lloyd George was worried that the Cardiganshire by-election would destroy the coalition. In fact, it was another Welsh by-election that ended the coalition and his reign as Prime Minister. In the summer of 1922, the former Monmouth Boroughs and latterly Newport Liberal Coalition MP, Lewis Haslam, died after an operation for gastric problems. Haslam had been born in Bolton and had kept his Lancashire roots strongly there during his 66 years of life; he remained a JP there until his death. He had previously been the MP for the Monmouth district between 1906–18.[25] Normally this would have been a straight fight between the Coalition Liberals and the Labour Party. This time, a by-election spanner was thrown into the coalition works not by an Asquithian Liberal[26] but by Reginald George (R. G.) Clarry, an 'anti Lloyd George Conservative'. Clarry stood in open breach of the electoral pact between the Conservatives and the Liberals not to stand against each others' candidates. The Coalition Liberals selected the Liberal, Lyndon (W.L.) Moore. Many prominent Liberals had been asked to stand for the seat but had declined, leaving the field open for Moore, a solicitor and local coroner. The Newport Liberal Association, despite having a Coalition Liberal MP, was against the coalition and, therefore, wished its own local candidate to promote only 'traditional Liberal values'. Moore was thought by the Newport Liberals to have the personal popularity to win the seat by bringing the severed sections of the party together in the seat (the Coalition and the Asquithians Liberals).[27] Moore, however, was not given the free reign to speak that the local Liberals had wished for and had to fight the campaign unable to criticise an increasingly unpopular coalition government. This was in contrast to his Conservative and Labour opponents who both called openly for an end to the coalition.[28]

The Coalition Conservatives and Liberal Whips tried every trick they knew to stop the vote from being split between Clarry, Moore and the Labour candidate, J. W. Bowen. It failed and the Liberals went from first to third place, with the rebel Conservative Clarry coming first. The Conservatives, out of sole electoral power since 1906, had previously believed that they could not survive outside the Coalition government. The Newport by-election allayed this major fear of the Conservative MPs. As a result, almost instantly, the Conservatives MPs withdrew their support from the Coalition and decided to seek government office alone.

Newport By-election 18 October 1922

Candidate	Party	Vote	Percentage
R. G. Clarry	Conservative	13,515	40
J. W. Bowen	Labour	11,425	33.8
W. L. Moore	Liberal (Coalition)	8,841	26.2
	Majority	2,090	6.2
	Turnout		79.2

The Newport by-election had therefore caused the downfall of Lloyd George's Coalition government and remained the only by-election in British history to remove a government. It also signalled the end of Welsh Liberals at the heart of government and spelled the end of the Welsh Liberalism as a major political power in the urban south of Wales.[29] Lyndon Moore, the failed Liberal candidate, now took solace in becoming the longstanding inter-war leader of Newport's Liberals.

The Three General Elections – Hope and Then Despair

Every year from 1922 to 1924, there was a general election in the United Kingdom. These three general elections saw the fall, the rise, and then the collapse in the number of Liberal MPs in Britain. Although Welsh Liberal fortunes changed much less than in England and Scotland, the next three general elections, nevertheless, shaped their fortunes in Wales as much as elsewhere.

The 1922 General Election

Conservative	6
Liberal National (Collies)	9
Liberal	2
Independent Labour	2
Labour	18

The 1922 general election was significant for the Welsh Liberals, as it saw the demise of the largest political party in Wales after almost half a century. Although the political map of Wales still had a considerable Liberal presence on it, the nation was becoming increasingly Labour and Conservative in orientation. As this political repositioning occurred, the Liberals still remained a much divided party. Although the feud between Asquith and Lloyd George was less rancorous than before, neither side still forgave the bitterness of the 1918–1922 parliamentary divide, and the insults that had been hurled during the Cardiganshire by-election the year before only added fuel to this dispute.[30] In Wales, as elsewhere, the Liberals were once again split between the Coalition Liberals ('Collies' or Liberal Nationals because they had supported the national coalition) and the Liberals (Asquith supporters were now labelled simple as 'Liberals'). In Wales, the Collies and the Liberals only contested four of the same seats. Although in two of these the Asquithians Liberals came close to taking the seats, in Cardiganshire they were 515 votes (2%) short of victory and in the University of Wales seat 46 votes (3.6%) short. They did not win any seats off the Collies. Partially this was because of the Collies' strength and also because of the reluctance of Lloyd George. The Collies were still against reunion with the Asquithians and, in Wales, only the senior Welsh and British Liberal, Sir Alfred Mond, argued that they should now fully separate from their 'distinguished Tory allies' and 'take a stand as Liberals desiring reunion'.[31] Whilst they remained against reunion, the Welsh Collies tactically fought the 1922 general election with one hand behind their back, unable to attack their former Conservative coalition partners to any effective degree because they had both been supporting the same policies. Labour, however, could attack both the Collies and the Conservatives with impunity and did so. Across the United Kingdom the Collies retained less than half the number of their 1918 seats[32] (62 MPs as opposed to 133 MPs). Lloyd George was left with 62 Collies supporting him, eight of whom were in Wales. The Asquithian Liberals almost equalled them with 54 seats, of which only two were in Wales (Meirionnydd and Montgomeryshire).

Although David Lloyd George was returned unopposed, and his son, Gwilym, was elected with a massive 11,866 majority (38%) in Pembroke, the Collies lost 11 of their seats in Wales. The shift in working class support from Liberals to Labour was of seismic proportions. Swansea East recorded a swing from Liberal to Labour of 14.5 per cent and Neath a massive 23.3 per cent. The Liberals lost six industrial seats to Labour (Aberavon, Aberdare,[33] Llanelli, Merthyr Tydfil, Swansea East and Neath). In one blow, the Welsh Liberals had lost almost their entire industrial support base. In North Wales, Wrexham and even Liberal Caernarfonshire and Ynys Môn were lost to Labour. The losses of the seats of Ynys Môn and Wrexham were directly connected to the same man – Sir Robert John Thomas. Wrexham had been Thomas' seat before he moved on to contest Ynys Môn in 1922. In Wrexham, Thomas had been an absentee member and had instead concentrated on his shipping and insurance business to the exclusion of party campaigning. This meant that the Wrexham Liberal Constituency Association became inactive at a time when the Labour Party was becoming extremely active in the seat. The Liberal constituency executive, in fact, met only once between December 1919 and December 1920. With Wrexham's fortunes declining, Thomas moved on to fight in Anglesey – a seat in which he could let the more active local Ynys Môn Liberal Association undertake the work, although in the event he had not been successful in such a ploy. The Wrexham Liberal Association failed to motivate itself to support Thomas' successor, Evan R. Davies. Many local Liberals there didn't support Evans because he was seen as 'Lloyd George's placeman', supporting an unpopular coalition government and also being selected over more local candidates.[34] The fact that Davies had been in Lloyd George's secretariat in Downing Street, came from his Caernarfon Boroughs constituency and was even related to Lloyd George, made many Wrexham Liberals suspicious. They were uncomfortable about having such a strong Lloyd Georgite as their candidate. Evans subsequently lost the seat to Labour by 1098 votes (3.2%). Thus, Thomas had directly participated in the loss of two Welsh Liberal seats to Labour in the same election.

The Conservatives now contested the majority of Welsh seats, dividing the vote between themselves, the two Liberal factions and Labour. It was their best Welsh election for over twenty years. The by-election winner, Reginald Clarry, who had caused the general election, also held Newport for the Conservatives. This time he only faced a Labour opponent, as the Liberals were unable to find a candidate to contest him. The Conservatives won all three seats in Cardiff, along with Barry and Llandaff, and in addition they took Monmouthshire unopposed. The Cardiff East seat saw the well respected[35] industrialist Sir William Henry Seager fail to pass on the seat to the Ocean Collieries' director, the Liberal, Sir Henry Webb. So bad was the Liberal result that Webb almost lost second place to Labour in a seat Seager had secured in 1918 with a majority of almost 2,000 votes (10.1 %).

As both Asquithians and Lloyd George Liberals licked their post-electoral wounds, it became apparent that if either was to have a future they would need to work together. This was going to be a hard process of reconciliation. In August 1922, Lloyd George still felt that the Asquithians were preoccupied by their 'vendetta' against him, which he felt was 'absorbing and poisoning their thought and energies ... like a bad tooth'.[36] The Asquithians Liberals still felt deep resentment about the events of 1916 and 1918 and desired an apology from Lloyd George for his 'betrayal' in moving the Liberal Party into coalition with their traditional Tory foe. On the 14th of March 1923, at a meeting of the Collies, Lloyd George claimed he had held the Liberal faith as strongly as any Asquithians and that the record of Coalition Liberals was as good as any Liberal Government in history'.[37] At the same time as the rhetoric was flying between the two groups, there were signs that the ice between them was starting to melt. A month earlier, on a debate on the King's Speech, H. A. L. Fisher, Lloyd George's former Minister of Education, had moved an amendment to the address on behalf of both factions of the party. In March, events in Wales were to bring the two sides even closer together. The Independent Labour MP for Ynys Môn (Anglesey) Owen Thomas died. In the subsequent by-election both groups of Liberals agreed to endorse the same candidate, Sir Robert John Thomas. Thomas, the candidate who a few months earlier had helped lose both Ynys Môn and Wrexham, now had a chance to regain one of these losses. With both Liberal factions now working together, Thomas won the seat with a massive majority of 22.8 per cent and the total Liberal tally of seats went up to 12 in Wales – a third of the total Welsh seats. In the process, Thomas beat the Liberal Welsh nationalist defector E. T. John convincingly enough to help keep Labour out of the seat again for the next three decades.

Ynys Môn By-election 7 April 1923

Candidate	Party	Vote	Percentage
Sir Robert John Thomas	Liberal	11,116	53.3
E.T. John	Labour	6,368	30.5
Richard Owen Roberts	Conservative	3,385	16.2
	Majority	4,748	22.8
	Turnout		76.4

The resounding Liberal win in Ynys Môn helped quicken the pace of Liberal reunion, which would be consolidated even further over the coming months. In May 1923 the Conservative Prime Minister Bonar Law was diagnosed with throat cancer and resigned. He was succeeded by the Leader of the House of Commons, Stanley Baldwin. On the 25th of October 1923, Stanley Baldwin suddenly decided in favour of economic protectionism as a means of aiding the fight against rising unemployment. Both the Asquithians and the Lloyd George Liberals had always been pro-free trade. Baldwin's policy, therefore, had the effect of uniting both wings of the Liberal Party under a common economic cause. On the 13th of November 1923 Asquith and Sir John Simon met the other Liberal faction represented by the two Welsh Liberal MPs, Lloyd George and Sir Alfred Mond, in order to bring the Liberals together in one party. The meeting was held in Mond's St Stephen's House office in Westminster.[38] Despite Mond's initial scepticism, the meeting was a success and both jointly declared that at the next general election that 'all candidates will be adopted and described as Liberals, and will be supported by the whole strength of the party without regard to any differences'.[39]

The results of this meeting were seen immediately. The coalition Liberal organisation in Wales and those elsewhere were disbanded and the *Lloyd George Liberal Magazine* did not appear after the November 1923 issue. The Welsh Liberal Council joined with the Welsh Liberal Federation, taking the latter's name. For the first time, the North and South Wales Federations were joined as one body. Lloyd George supplied vital funds to enable the new united party to effectively contest the majority of seats at the general election. These funds would soon be needed, as Baldwin had called another general election.

December 1923 General Election

Liberal	11
Labour	20
Conservative	4
Independent Liberal	1

The Conservative Prime Minister, Stanley Baldwin's decision to fight the December 1923 general election on the issue of protectionism provided a short term boost to Liberalism across Britain. The cause of trade tariffs brought a popular cause back into Liberal politics in Wales. It was an issue that the Liberals could use to turn on the opposition rather than divide themselves with. The strength of having a worthwhile cause to fight for brought back into the fold candidates such as David Davies who had remained politically aloof and thought of leaving politics altogether. He was now persuaded to return to fight another election.[40] As for Lloyd George, despite the hostility of a number of Welsh Asquithian Liberals and senior British Asquithian Liberals to having him return to the Liberal Party, he was still adored by rank and file members. When Parliament was dissolved for the forthcoming election on the 13th of November 1923, a joint press statement was issued by both factions, which said that the Liberals would be fighting the election as a united party. The portrait of Lloyd George, formerly consigned to the cellars of the National Liberal Club, was now reinstated to a place of honour in the smoke-room.[41]

The 1923 general election, however, was to be the last in which the Liberals came close to matching Labour in the national vote and gained enough Parliamentary seats to have a serious presence at Westminster. It was also an election in which the three main parties' share of seats came closest to their percentage share of votes. The Liberals gained 159 MPs, which was 43 seats more than the combined number that the Coalition Liberals and Liberal MPs had in the 1922 election. They were aided in part by former Conservative voters who supported free trade and were now voting Liberal. It was neither the Liberals nor the Conservatives who formed the next government. It was the Labour Party under Aberavon MP, James Ramsay MacDonald, which now formed a minority government. Welsh Labour MPs were getting their first taste of national power, although they were still dependent on Liberal MPs' support in Westminster. Labour, while using this Liberal support, only looked at it as a short term measure. Its objective was to be viewed as a moderate and sensible party of government and then take over the Liberals' support base to achieve sole power. The leading Labour member Hugh Dalton made clear his party's view on the Liberals. He bluntly stated: 'I hope we shall be able to avoid giving the Liberals either Proportional Representation of Alternative Vote this Parliament. They may not live to ask for either in the next'.[42]

Despite the 1923 general election, which saw the Welsh Liberals take some 11 of the 35 Welsh seats, the Liberals were now plainly playing second fiddle to Labour in Wales. The party's inquest of the general election came up with many factors for failure, but it failed to reveal two key things:[43]

1. That Liberalism's bid for power on traditional lines had finally failed
2. That the Labour Party had taken Liberalism's place as the alternative government to that of the Conservatives.

In Wales, things did not appear to be totally lost. The Conservatives were still a distant third electorally with just four Welsh MPs. The Liberals had also had a number of new victories in 1923. Across Wales Sir Henry Webb reversed his 1922 defeat and won Cardiff East from the Conservatives, Goronwy Owen won back Caernarfonshire off Labour, and Sir Roger Thomas held Anglesey, although this time unopposed. The Liberals, however, failed to regain any of the mining and industrial seats they had lost in 1922 and only Pontypool with a 326 vote (1.2%) majority and Wrexham with a 1881 (5.6%) majority were now Labour–Liberal marginal seats. The other lost industrial seats now had substantial Labour majorities rising up to a figure of 37 per cent in Merthyr Tydfil. Liberalism was failing to win these industrial seats due to weaknesses in party organisation, morale and a failure to effectively extend its policy beyond the chapel-politics of the pre-First World War era against a more adept Labour opponent.[44]

United but Still Divided – Rhys Hopkin Morris, the Independent Welsh Liberal Victory

Despite the Asquithians and the Lloyd Georgites coming together, not every Liberal candidate stood under the new united banner. The battle scars that had occurred just two years before were reopened in Cardiganshire. There was once again a battle between two Liberals. Llewelyn Williams had died but another Independent Liberal, Rhys Hopkin Morris, took his place. Hopkin Morris won the seat off Enrest Evans with a substantial 5078 (19.2%) of the vote. The legacy of these contests and the defeat of Lloyd George's close aid, Evans, was to divide Rhys Hopkin Morris and David Lloyd George for the rest of their political careers. The scale of Morris's victory put him in no mood to bury the hatchet. At the Welsh Liberal Party conference in Llandrindod in June 1924, Hopkin Morris asserted, 'I am not a follower of Mr David Lloyd George, and I have no intention of being one'.[45] Although he later rejoined the Liberals, Hopkin Morris always voted against accepting Lloyd George as leader when it came to a vote. Upon his death in 1956, in an ironic twist of fate, David Lloyd George's daughter Megan succeeded him, though now as a Labour MP, in his new Carmarthen seat.

Welsh Liberalism Seeking to Find a Policy Role

Even with the battle cry of 'Free Trade', there was little in the policy field to distinguish the Welsh Liberals' present policies from their pre-war appeal of 'Chapel

Politics'. In many seats, the election slogans revolved around the old Liberal motto of 'Peace, Retrenchment and Reform'.[46] The world had changed greatly since the days when this motto had widespread appeal. Revolution in Russia had overthrown the capitalist system there and brought in a 'workers' state' – an idea that appealed to many of the working class voters of South Wales. In Neath, for instance, the Liberal Thomas Elias fought the 'determination to abolish all private ownership' by appealing for 'a sane, circumspect course'.[47] These plain words failed to impress an electorate that had seen plans for 'Socialism and the Capital Levy' advocated by Labour. Elias lost to Labour by 8,202 votes (24.6%). Many Welsh Liberals nonconformists were still anti-Socialist and regarded it as atheist. This, however, did not help their electoral appeal greatly as the role of religion declined. Welsh Liberalism, therefore, remained at it strongest in the rural Welsh speaking areas of Wales where the appeal of the chapel remained strong.

The Liberal industrialist, Sir Alfred Mond, who had been at the heart of the Liberals reunification, was the central figure in its campaign against the electoral threat of Socialism. He toured the country utilising anti-Socialist campaigning tactics, which were designed partly to woo Conservative voters in these industrial seats. This campaigning, however, failed to save the anti-socialist Liberals. Despite his anti-socialist rhetoric, Mond lost his seat in Swansea to Labour by 115 votes. He wasn't the ideal Liberal constituency candidate. As well as spending much of his time outside the constituency during the campaign, his political secretary also noted that Mond was easily sidetracked by political detail, such as reviewing the latest attacks upon him in the *Morning Post*. He would become engrossed in these at campaign meetings and would often shut himself off from the Swansea West Liberal Association campaign team, which, in turn, alienated them and they came to regard him as eccentric and aloof.[48] Mond was, despite his flaws, an astute and hard working politician and was, therefore, back in Westminster within nine months. He did this by winning the Carmarthen by-election in August 1924, caused by the retirement of the sitting Liberal MP Sir Ellis Jones Ellis-Griffith. Despite Mond's rapid electoral recovery, most of Welsh Liberalism that had covered industrial Wales had collapsed in the face of the Socialist onslaught. In the south of Wales Liberal organisations had faded away to nothing. The historian C. P. Cook noted that:

"Many constituencies on the eve of the 1923 election presented a dismal sight: thus, in November 1923 the Cardiff Liberals possessed no agent, no executive and no offices within the city. At Merthyr, the Liberal organisation had collapsed; it was equally non-existent at Newport. In Abertillery neither Liberal nor Conservative had done any propaganda work in the last twelve months. Likewise, nothing had been heard of the Liberals in the Bedwellty division; although Bedwellty produced an eleventh-hour Liberal in 1923, none had appeared in the constituency since then."[49]

The *Glamorgan Free Press*, then a pro-Liberal paper, observed that 'in the market place is a scene of desolation and silence as far as the Liberal vendor is concerned.'[50] The party entered the next general election in this perilous state.

The Short Term Legacy of the 1923 Election – Starting to Redefine Liberalism

After the 1923 election was over, Asquith and Lloyd George were able to work together on a united course for the first time for seven years. In the following year, at the Welsh Liberals' June Conference in Llandudno, there was a formal coming together of both sides of the Liberal Party. In the next three general elections in Wales, the Liberals fought together. Their new challenge was to compete against the ever growing appeal of the Labour party despite the fact that the Liberals had supported them in government. As the Liberals' chances of forming a government in their own right faded, a dilemma occurred which would remain with them for rest of the century. This concerned which side the Liberals should support – the Conservatives or Labour. On the 22nd of April 1924, in a public meeting, Lloyd George summed up this problem to his Caernarfonshire constituents when he said:

> "If we dare to criticise the Labour Government then we are visited with 'pee-vish resentment'. Liberals are expected to be the 'oxen to drag Labour over the rough roads of Parliament' for two or three years, and at the end of the journey, when there is no further use of us we are to be slaughtered."[51]

Lloyd George believed that the only way to break this 'yoke of the oxen' was to get back the support of the working classes taken from them by the Labour Party.[52] In Wales the first place to start would be to retake the initiative in the industrial south and meet the Socialists head on. The task, therefore, was to come up with a popular policy on mining and power generation. Thus, over the next few years, there was a stream of policy commissions formed by Lloyd George aimed at giving his party policies that would appeal to the working classes and undermine the appeal of Socialism. In the event they would prove to be more divisive in his own party than appealing to the working class voters they had lost.

The first new policy came forward in March 1924 and was called *Coal and Power*. It rejected the Socialist polices of Syndicalism (the 'Mines for the Miners') and Nationalisation (the 'Mines for the State'). The document stated that the state should buy out the royalty owners and other landlords and then grant leases to companies or co-operatives that could prove more efficient operation of the mines. Labour's Prime Minister, Ramsay MacDonald, and Conservative leader Stanley Baldwin ignored *Coal and Power* entirely. Neither party wanting to give credence to what they both hoped was a dying party. The South Wales Miners' Federation (SWMF), which dominated much of industrial Welsh politics, also turned it down as it fought for their own policy for the nationalisation of the mines. This enraged Lloyd George, as the MacDonald government, while giving a massive loan to the newly recognised Communist Russian government, refused to buy the mineral rights to Welsh mines. On the 10th of September, in Penmaenmawr, he declared that owing to the extent of the depression in Wales in mining and elsewhere, then this Russian money should be spent at home, and to do otherwise was an 'act of criminal recklessness'.[53] His words were ignored by both the SWMF and the Labour government.

The Labour government's term in office, however, was short-lived. In July 1924, J. R. Campbell, the acting-editor of the *Communist Workers Weekly*, published an

article exhorting soldiers, sailors and airmen to refuse to fire on their fellow workers in 'war or class conflict'.[54] The Labour Attorney General, Sir Patrick Hastings,
brought a prosecution under the Mutiny Act (1795). On the second hearing, the
Campbell Case was dropped as the prosecution accepted that it was not an attempt
to seduce men in the armed forces but only to prevent them using military force to
suppress industrial disputes. Still, many prominent people in public life, including
the King, were disturbed by the prosecution being brought at all. MacDonald tried to
continue in government despite this growing concern over the Campbell case but in
September, the Liberals put down a motion which would set up a select Committee
to inquire into the circumstances of the prosecution. The Conservatives joined the
Liberals in the divisions lobby and the government was defeated by 263 votes to
198. MacDonald treated this as a vote of 'No Confidence' in his government and
tendered his resignation to the King the next morning, asking for an immediate dis-
solution. This would be the third general election in two years and the most significant for the Liberals.

The Liberal Party was poorly positioned financially to fight another election.
Most of the money for the campaign, some £60,000, came from the Lloyd George
Fund. This fund was a personal fund of Lloyd George's which had been generated
mainly from the controversial sale of honours during his premiership. Although the
exact amount of money in the fund was never known either publicly or in the Liberal
Party, it was said to be worth millions of pounds. The price of a donation from Lloyd
George's fund to the Liberal Party was that the number of candidates nationally was
to be reduced from a projected 500 to a more affordable 343. Lloyd George was not
prepared to pay for campaigning costs in what he thought were 'hopeless seats'. Many
of these hopeless seats were in South Wales where the Labour Party had built up their
political strength during the days of the Progressive Alliance. As a result of Lloyd
George's ruling, some 14 seats in Wales were now uncontested by the Liberals, as
opposed to just four in 1923. This meant that the Labour Party had a free run in a number of Welsh seats. They took seven seats in Wales unopposed, almost half of their
seats in Wales. For the Liberals, however, only Rhys Hopkin Morris in Cardiganshire
had an unopposed seat.

Despite the Liberals putting forward one of their most comprehensive manifestos
ever, including the mining proposals in *Coal and Power*, the campaign was not really
dominated by issues of unemployment or conditions in mining, housing or any specific policies related to Welsh working class concerns. Instead, the main issue was
described in the manifesto as 'The Russian Blunder'.[55] At first this 'Blunder' just
concerned the loan to Russia, but then the Campbell Case became entwined with
it. The icing on the cake of Labour's defeat was, however, the scandal associated
with the so-called 'Zinoviev Letter'. This concerned an 'alleged letter' by Zinoviev,
the Russian head of the Third Communist International, to the Central Committee
of the Communist Party of Great Britain. It set out plans to overthrow the 'ruling
classes' in the United Kingdom and thereby exposed the Soviet Union as a hostile
nation. This was the same Soviet Union that the Labour Party had recently recognised as a new nation state. The letter was widely published in the press and although
it was declared to be a fake by both the Russian *Charge d'Affaires*, Rakovsky, and
the Labour Party, the damage was done. The Liberals claimed that the Labour
Government had become nothing more than a tool of the revolutionary extremists

and was supporting Britain's enemies. In this atmosphere of plots, the country went politically to the right in what became known, after the Zinoviev letter, as the 'Red letter' general election.

October 1924 'Red Letter' General Election

Liberal	11
Labour	16
Conservative	9

The election was fought by the Liberals on supporting British Parliamentary democracy against the supposed extremism of the Labour Party – 'Constitutionalism against anti-Constitutionalism'.[56] The Liberals, however, were widely unprepared for the election so soon after the last one. On the day that Parliament was dissolved, only three seats in Wales had chosen their Liberal candidates. This caused the Welsh press to express their surprise at the lack of the Liberal preparation; the *Cambria Daily Leader,* for instance, noted that 'Liberalism in West Wales has been caught napping. The battle has come much sooner than anyone had anticipated'.[57]

What was true for West Wales was true for the rest of the nation. Publicly, even though their motion had brought down the government, the Liberals were widely seen to have been propping up an unpopular Labour government. Liberal votes in Wales dropped by 12 per cent, almost exactly the same percentage as in Britain as a whole. The 1924 'Red Letter' general election was a disaster for the Liberal Party as a whole but, in Wales, the party was still supported in the Welsh speaking nonconformist heartland. The Liberal election results in Wales, therefore, despite the large drop overall, were not unduly severe. It resulted in four Liberal losses to the Conservatives and three Liberal wins from Labour. The wins entailed the shipping magnate and anti-Lloyd George Liberal, Walter Runciman,[58] retaking Sir Alfred Mond's old seat of Swansea West by the narrow margin of 845 votes (3%). Ernest Evans came back from his defeat in Cardiganshire the year before and won the University of Wales seat off Labour with a 336 vote (18.8%) majority. In Wrexham, despite general Liberal inactivity, the Liberal Association Chair, Alderman Edward Hughes, was able to persuade the Conservatives not to contest the seat in order not to split the anti-socialist vote. This enabled the steel manager, Christmas Price Williams,[59] to win the seat off Labour by 3,863 votes (11.2%).[60] At the same time as these wins, there were a number of Liberal casualties to the Tories. The most prominent one was Gwilym Lloyd George who lost his Pembrokeshire seat by 1,530 (4.2%).

In Cardiff East, Sir Donald McLean was relegated to the third position under both the Conservatives and Labour. McLean, who had gone to Haverfordwest Grammar School, was the father of the future Soviet spy Donald Maclean, adding something of a twist to this Red Letter election. He was also a prominent anti-Lloyd Georgist and chaired the Asquithian Liberal Party from his Scottish Peebbles and Mid Lothian seat between 1918 and 1922. McLean had been an MP before and would be an MP again in North Cornwall in 1929. In Flint, Thomas Henry Parry lost his seat to the Conservatives by some 4683 votes (13.6%) after some 11 years. Parry failed to inspire party activists in this campaign, as he had in the others. He did not provide party workers with much encouragement and this affected morale and encouraged an air of apathy and arrogance.[61] The same was true in Montgomeryshire, though with a different result. Here David Davies' animosity to Lloyd George and his reluctance to adhere to the party line made him, in effect, an Independent Liberal representative, but the lack of a Conservative opponent and the strength of both the Liberal tradition and the Davies family name in the seat were more than enough to get him elected with a healthy 54.6% majority.[62] William Albert Jenkins lost the Brecon and Radnor seat to the Conservatives by 2,460 votes (7.3%).[63] It was a seat that the Conservatives hadn't contested since 1910 and one in which all three parties now contested with some vigour. The Liberal Welsh nationalist defector E. T. John, who was the Labour candidate in the seat, now took part in his final parliamentary contest and came just a few hundred votes behind Jenkins.

Unlike in Brecon and Radnor, six of the Welsh Liberal victors were helped by Conservatives not standing in their seat, including that Lloyd George's own seat. With the exception of Goronwy Owen's Caernarfonshire seat, with a small 469 (1.6%) majority, the other Liberal MPs enjoyed majorities of over 10 per cent. In the only seat in which there was a straight Conservative-Liberal contest (Denbigh), the Liberal MP, Ellis Davies, held it by a much decreased majority. The collapse of the Liberal-Conservative coalition a few years earlier had allowed the Conservative organisational strength to grow back. The Conservative candidate was the formidable Lady Annie Brodrick who was just 1,421 votes (6%) off taking the seat. The success would have made her Wales' first female MP and for the next five years she would work on winning the seat.

In Wales, the party escaped relatively unscathed, losing only one seat overall. Wales now had over a quarter of the remaining Liberal seats in Britain. Amongst the casualties elsewhere was Asquith himself. He had lost his seat once again and was never again to return to the Commons. Lloyd George now became the Leader of the Liberal Parliamentary Party, although initially this was only to be until Asquith 'returned' to the Commons. Despite the fact that they had fared much better than the rest of Britain, the 1924 general election result awakened the Welsh Liberals from their complacency. One of the reasons the Liberals had survived so well in North Wales over the last few elections compared to the South, was the fact that they had 'capitalised on the advantages they enjoyed … their roots lay deep in the cultural fabric of the region'.[64] This was to keep the party alive there for another two decades. But Liberalism even in North Wales was changing. Reflecting on the election, Ellis Davies was quoted in the *Liverpool Daily Post* on 27th March 1925 saying:

"… It is felt that Liberalism does not mean the same to the old as it does to young: that young men are not encouraged to become candidates, they believe that some of the old leaders, who have done good work in their day, are dangerously out of touch with modern political thought, and there is far too much speaking [as] if Gladstone were still alive and if nothing had changed in the last fifty years."[65]

The editorial in the *Pembrokeshire County Guardian* on the 7th of November 1924 summed up the rapid decline of the traditional dominance of the Liberal Party across Wales:[66]

It seems incredible to many that the Party of Gladstone and Campbell-Bannerman, Asquith and Lloyd George should 'fold their tents like Arabs, and silently steal away … It is not the first time that one or other of the great Parties have been submerged, but it is the first time there have been three great parties struggling for supremacy. The Liberal Party is between two fires (Labour and Conservatives) and must suffer accordingly.

Outside Wales the Liberal Party was in an angry mood concerning its losses and was looking for some internal retribution. On the 11th of November 1924 over a hundred defeated Liberal candidates from Wales, Scotland and England assembled at the National Liberal Club and demanded that the resources of the 'Lloyd George Fund' be put fully at the disposal of the party. Lloyd George held back from committing to this, stating that the money would come to the party when its organisation and candidates were fit enough to deserve it. This opened up new splits in the party. On the 2nd of December, a group of 10 Liberal MPs, including Rhys Hopkin Morris, with Walter Runciman as their chairman, declared themselves to be the 'radical Group' who would not work with Lloyd George. It was clear that as long as Lloyd George was in the party it would remain divided. Yet at the same time he remained one of their greatest assets, a political hero for both introducing pensions and winning the war and a tremendous crowd puller at election times.

'I'd sooner go to hell than Wales': Asquith's Demise and Lloyd George's Reprieve

The speech Asquith made in favour of the motion on the need for an enquiry into the Campbell case that had brought down the MacDonald government in 1924 was his last on the green benches of the House of Commons. At the age of 72, Asquith fought his fourth and last campaign in Paisley. This time, however, he lost his seat in a straight fight with Labour. His Commons career was over. Although he was offered the possibility of a safe seat in Wales, he declared to Charles Masterman, who himself had been denied a 'safe' Welsh seat a decade earlier, 'I'd sooner go to hell than Wales'.[67] For Asquith, the contemplation of coming under the direct control of Lloyd George's Liberal Wales was too much to bear. In the event, the King offered him a personal peerage and he took the title of the Earl of Oxford. For the next few years, Asquith attempted to restore a united Liberalism across the country. As part of this process, the failed Cardiff East candidate, Sir Donald Maclean was given the national job of chairing a committee to find out what had gone wrong in previous elections with the view to putting it right in the future. The committee toured the country, meeting Liberal Associations and hearing complaints and gathering suggestions. Its efforts to penetrate Wales were rebuffed by Lloyd George. Maclean was simply informed that the Welsh could sort out their own house without outside interference, thus ignoring his recent Welsh electoral experience in the process.[68]

Wales was not sorting out its own house, however, and was continuing to lack the necessary cohesion to move forward. Key figures who should have been driving the party were seeking opportunities elsewhere or wished to remain outside any Liberal Party run by Lloyd George. Lloyd George's son, the ex Pembrokeshire Liberal MP Gwilym Lloyd George, was now out of Wales, acting as the director of his father's newspaper *The Daily Chronicle*.

Moreover, three Welsh MPs still loathed and distrusted Lloyd George's stewardship of the party. These were David Davies, Rhys Hopkin Morris and Walter

Runciman. They made their feelings well known. Hopkin Morris, for instance, told his Constituency Executive in February 1927 that 'Mr Lloyd George has leased the Liberal estate for a term of years uncertain and the rent reserved was equally uncertain. The only certain thing is that he has acquired shooting rights.'[69] Hopkin Morris and his Cardiganshire Liberal Association, therefore, remained aloof from Lloyd George for the rest of his leadership. Davies did likewise and Runciman now chaired the Liberal Council, an anti-Lloyd George grouping. The remaining Welsh Liberal MPs, for the time being, retained more cordial relations with Lloyd George and continued on the whole to support him.[70]

Changing the Liberals' Policy Agenda

Between 1924 and 1929, there was once more a serious attempt to address the appeals of both Socialism and Conservatism by the Liberals in what would, half a century later, be referred to as 'The Third Way'. Lloyd George set up a number of enquiries. Using money from the Lloyd George Fund, the enquiries were as well-financed and staffed as Royal Commissions. It was noted earlier that *Coal and Power* was published before the 1924 general election and did not make much of an impact on the electoral fortunes of the Welsh party's lost mining seats. The next report, however, by the Liberal Land Committee, had much greater impact in Wales. In October, its report on agriculture, *The Land and the Nation* (known afterwards as the 'Green Book') came out and went down badly with the traditional Liberal voting farming free holders.[71]

The Green Book proposed 'cultivating tenure' in the form of quasi-nationalisation of cultivable land. It was due to be debated fully and, if accepted, endorsed in February 1926. Lloyd George was keen that these proposals be accepted and offered a contribution of £20,000 a year for three years to the Liberal Party, on the condition of a favourable decision regarding the land reports.[72] In the rural areas it was difficult to find any real support for the plans. Although the prominent Cardiganshire Liberal, Professor Levi,[73] supported the plan, there was little enthusiasm elsewhere and the policy was rejected by most Welsh rural Liberals and their Constituency Associations.[74] Sir Alfred Mond was so against the policy that he crossed the floor to join the Conservatives over the Green Book.[75] In a letter to Alderman John David, chair of the Carmarthen Liberal Association, he made it clear that he would never 'accept universal land nationalisation' as supported by Lloyd George.[76] One of the few remaining Liberal industrialists who was still a Welsh Liberal MP, David Davies of Montgomeryshire, was similarly appalled by the Green Book and the way in which the Liberal Party encouraged such plans, as was his Montgomeryshire Liberal Association. For those Liberal MPs, such as Denbigh's Ellis Davies, who supported the proposals, there were open revolts over the issue within their constituency organisation. As a result, in the Denbigh constituency, stalwart Liberals worked openly for Lady Brodrick's (the Conservative candidate) victory at the next election because of their dissatisfaction with Ellis Davies's support for the Green Book.[77] This didn't affect the result of the next election in Denbigh, as Ellis Davies didn't contest Denbigh again. In 1934 he would join the Labour Party, though he later left them to join the Liberal Nationals in 1939. By the time of the next election, however, Lady Brodrick was also too ill to contest the seat. She died shortly after the election. This ensured that these two bitter rivals would never again lock horns in a parliamentary contest.

Carmarthen By-election 1928

When Mond was elevated to the peerage in 1928 as Lord Melchett of Blandford,[78] a by-election was held in Carmarthenshire. Lord Melchett now stood on the election platforms encouraging support for the Conservatives whom he had so bitterly opposed in past elections. Despite understanding the reasons behind Mond's defection two years earlier, the Carmarthen Liberal Association resented Mond changing party and having an MP who now supported the Conservative Party, their traditional political foe. This helped spur the Carmarthen Liberals into a concerted action to return the seat to the Liberal fold.[79] Mond had gained a majority of over 9,000 at the previous election but then there had been only a Labour candidate against him; now all three parties would be fighting the seat. This was the only Welsh by-election of the 1924–1929 parliament, so it would also provide an indication of Liberal fortunes in Wales. Lloyd George nominated Captain Richard Levi Thomas (R. T.) Evans who was pro Green Book but the constituency rejected him and chose as their candidate Lieutenant General William Nathaniel Jones, who was a strong opponent of the Green Book and was, therefore, able to scrape in by a narrow majority of just 47 votes, despite Mond's support for the Conservatives and a strong Labour challenge. The defeated Conservative candidate, Sir Courtenay Cecil Mansel, was a Liberal defector like Mond. In 1926, he had been Vice-President of the Carmarthen Liberal Association and had been on their short-list of candidates to stand for the Liberals at the subsequent election. He had also previously been the Liberal MP for Penrhyn and Falmouth from 1923 to 1924. His decision to stand against his former party as a Conservative saw the Tories drop to third place behind Labour in Carmarthen.

Carmarthen By-election 28 June 1928

Candidate	Party	Vote	Percentage
William Nathaniel Jones	Liberal	10,201	35.5
Daniel Hopkin	Labour	10,154	35.4
Sir Courtenay Cecil Mansel	Conservative	8,361	29.1
	Majority	47	0.1
	Turnout		76.6

The narrow Liberal margin of victory and the rise of the Labour vote in the seat was seen at the time as indicating that West Wales could soon go the way of South Wales in replacing the Liberals with the Labour party. Therefore, the Liberals became even more anxious to find a policy that could wrestle working class support from the Labour party and restore their fortunes.

The Yellow Book – 'We Can Conquer Unemployment'

After the 'Green' and 'Brown' Books came the most famous of all of Lloyd George's Commissions reports: the 'Yellow Book', also known as *We Can Conquer Unemployment*. This advocated massive state intervention in the economy to stimulate employment. Lloyd George's Commission advisers were all Englishmen (Maynard Keynes, Walter Layton, Seebohm Rowntree and Hubert Henderson). It was radical, and gained much broader support than the Green Book had. Even Hopkin Morris in Cardiganshire who continued to reject Lloyd George's leadership and William Jones in Carmarthen, who had denounced the Green Book, now supported the Yellow Book. Liberal candidates, who were taking on the Labour strongholds, such as James Jenkins, the candidate in Merthyr Tydfil, and Dapho Llewellyn Powell in Ogmore (a Cardiff shipowner and barrister) were able to boast a new policy that would 'remedy the depression in the coalfields'.[80] The Yellow Book was also endorsed by a host of Welsh industrialists, from textiles to iron and steel, inside and outside the party. Thus, Lloyd George's 1929 general election address was able to extol the virtues for *We Can Conquer Unemployment* and become the first political party to adopt what became known as Keynesian economics.[81] These policies, however, were mainly British in their nature but there had been some Welsh planning. For example, some £42 million was planned in improvements to the London–Oxford–Aberystwyth road, which would bring employment to a number of Welsh Liberal constituencies. The Liberals then put out full page adverts in the local Welsh press such as the *Cambrian News* to highlight these job creation policies.[82]

The May 1929 (*We Can Conquer Unemployment*)
General Election

Liberal	10
Labour	25
Conservative	1

This election was to be the last to be fought under Lloyd George's leadership of the Liberal Party. Asquith's recent death had allowed Lloyd George to firmly resume the leadership, unchallenged once more. Although Lloyd George had nearly split with the party a number of times, most notably over his Green Book and over his lack of support for the government during the General Strike of 1926, he enjoyed the endorsement of the Parliamentary Liberal Party, the Liberal National Federation and the Candidates' Association as their leader. It was with their backing that he now campaigned mainly with his Yellow Book. Lloyd George threw himself wholeheartedly into the election campaign with the assured belief that he would be the next Prime Minister. He toured Britain from Newcastle to Plymouth, taking time to speak for his daughter in her Anglesey contest and his son in his attempt to retake his old Pembrokeshire seat.[83]

The 1929 election, unlike that of 1924, was not a rushed affair. This time the government was not forced into a sudden election. In reality, the Liberal Party had been placing its candidates in Welsh seats since 1927. The Liberal heavyweight and future party leader Sir Herbert Samuel, on his campaign trail in Monmouth on the 15th of April 1929, was therefore able to declare that 'there are thirty-six constituencies (in Wales) and Bedwellty is the only one where a Liberal candidate has not yet been selected'.[84]

In the event, Bedwellty, the 'one seat' with no Liberal candidate would not have one at this election. The rest of Wales did, and, despite Labour accusations of a 'Lib-Con' pact, this was not the case in Wales. The Welsh Liberals were running the most well-organised and professional election since 1910. They were also outspending their Labour rivals in Wales by an average of £813 to £452 per candidate.[85] Technology meant that sound amplifiers and loudspeakers could now make a politician audible not just to the large crowd to whom the politician was addressing directly, but to an audience fifty or sixty miles away. On the 3rd of May 1929, in South and West Wales, for instance, surrounded by 250 of Pembrokeshire's leading Liberals, David Lloyd George made a speech to a crowd of over 10,000 in Milford Haven. The speech was relayed by this new technology to large audiences in Carmarthen, Swansea, Neath and Port Talbot.[86] Despite the occassional use of new technology, however, campaigning throughout Wales for all parties in this pre-television age still relied on personal contact with voters by leaflets, newspaper advertisements, the use of large and small election rallies, numerable talks and hustings at village, town and school halls throughout each constituency.

As we noted previously, the Liberals' main message in the election was on how the Yellow Book would tackle the growing unemployment within Wales. The Lloyd George Fund gave the party sufficient campaign money. The poster and leaflet campaign took place on a massive scale. The head of the Liberal Organisation, Lieutenant-Colonel T. F. Tweed and Lloyd George had even brought in the former advertising manager of *The Times* to run the poster and advertising campaign. The Liberals remained in a very bullish mood. When endorsing Megan Lloyd George, Sir Robert Thomas, her predecessor in Anglesey, told the meeting there would be '250 Liberal MPs and the next Prime Minister would be the father of your candidate'. Lloyd George himself, in his last pre-election day speech in Caernarfon, spoke of a 'sensational revival of Liberalism'. The Liberals were caught up in their own election fever.

The Green Book and its mention of the nationalisation of farming land still proved as unpopular in traditional Liberal territory as it had been in the Carmarthen by-election. The Welsh Liberals, therefore, almost universally declared that the Green Book was only a discussion document and never party policy and they would not support it. The more popular Yellow Book and its proposed cure for unemployment, however, did not reignite Welsh Liberal electoral hopes as the party had expected. Whilst the Liberal share of the vote was a third of the Welsh total or some 442,623 votes, it was still 10 per cent less than Labour. It was, however, still 12 per cent above the Conservatives. Virtually every seat in Wales was now part of a three-way contest, which in many ways did not help either the Conservatives or the Liberals. Whilst the Conservatives lost every seat but one in Wales, the Liberals lost three seats and gained two. The three seats lost were:

- Swansea West-where Lieutenant Colonel Charles Kerr lost to Labour's Howell Samuel by a slim majority of 643 votes (2%). Kerr would later attempt to go back into Parliament via Daventry in 1929, only to be forced to stand down as candidate when the sitting MP became the Speaker. In 1932 he would become the Liberal National MP for Montrose Burghs in a by-election and was ennobled by them in 1940, as Baron Teviot of Burghclere. He was never again a member of the Liberal Party.
- Carmarthen-where the by-election winner, Lieutenant Colonel William Jones, significantly increased his share of the vote but by not enough to defeat his Labour opponent who won the seat by 653 votes (1.6%).
- Wrexham-where the Liberal Association was this time unable to prevent the Conservatives from contesting the seat which decreased Christmas Williams'

vote and chances considerably. Williams' vote fell from 55.6 to 31.5 per cent allowing Labour's Robert Williams to gain the seat with a healthy 6,587 votes (14.9%) majority.[87]

Swansea West and Carmarthen had been marginal losses but the Liberals had not anticipated any Welsh losses and were expecting to make at least three gains in Pembroke, Brecon and Radnor[88] and Flintshire.[89] There was even some talk about winning Llanelli and Pontypool, which had popular Liberal candidates – former captains, Richard Thomas (R. T.) Evans (Llanelli) and Geoffrey Crawshay (Pontypool).[90] Both candidates came nowhere near winning their respective seats as the Labour vote remained rock solid. In the event, only two of their target key seats were won; both these were taken from the Conservatives:

- Gwilym Lloyd George regained his Pembroke seat. This time he had a handsome 4815 vote (10.5%) majority. The Pembrokeshire Liberals were so delighted at him retaking the seat that his agent Mr. E. T. Thomas and other supporters attached ropes to a car and 'he was borne in triumph through the streets of Haverfordwest'.[91]
- The Caernarfon born and Aberystwyth University educated solicitor Frederick Llewellyn-Jones won the Flintshire seat from the Conservative barrister E.H.G Roberts. Llewellyn-Jones gained a 4,476 vote majority (8%).

The remaining Welsh Liberal victors, with the exception of Clement Davies (7.8%) and Goronwy Owen (9.3%), had majorities over 10 per cent. This was also the first election in which the Liberals put forward any female candidates: Miss Anne Grace Roberts in Caerphilly and a Miss Megan Lloyd George in Anglesey. Roberts had been the organiser for the Asquithian Liberals in Wales. In the election campaign, apart from touring the country and supporting other female candidates, including Miss Roberts in Caerphilly, Megan was the voice of the Liberals in the special BBC broadcasts 'By and for Women'. Only one female Liberal candidate was a victor. At the age of twenty-seven, Megan Lloyd George was elected to Anglesey by 5618 votes (21%). She became the first Welsh female MP and one of only eight Welsh women MPs to serve in the House of Commons in the whole of the twentieth century. Roberts failed to get elected to Caerphilly and two years later defected to the Labour party. In 1932, she was short-listed for the Liberal stronghold of Cardigan but failed to get selected.

David Lloyd George now became the first politician in British political history to have both a daughter and son representing constituencies in Westminster at the same time as their father.[92] Important as the election was for the Lloyd Georges, the future of Welsh and British Liberalism would not ultimately be in their hands but instead in those of another Welsh Liberal elected at this time. It was the election of a young barrister called Clement Davies in Montgomeryshire who would ultimately decide the fate of the Liberal Party. This was because he was to become the postwar Liberal leader who kept the party from disappearing entirely in the post war period, see chapter 4. This was the last parliamentary election Davies fought before he became leader in 1945. He was to have the luck of being unopposed in the following two general elections, which were then followed by the long wartime Parliament of 1935–1945, during which no general elections were held.

Another Liberal MP, who was elected in 1929 but who did not come to such prominence, was Dr Henry Morris-Jones (Denbigh). Dr Morris-Jones was a Welsh speaker and a nonconformist. In contrast to Major Alan Crosland Graham, his Conservative opponent, he was a well-known local figure.[93] What makes Morris-Jones interesting from an historical point of view is that he published a biography in 1955 entitled *Doctor in the Whip's Room*. The title alluded to his former profession and his later position as a Liberal National Whip. The biography gives us a useful insight into the life of a North Wales Liberal constituency MP during the 1930s and 1940s. Morris-Jones' seat, Denbigh, was at that stage classified as a safe Liberal seat. With this in mind, Morris-Jones described his selection in the 1929 general election:[94]

> "Opportunities of a safe seat do not come frequently; and there was a vacancy in the Denbigh Division. There was no dearth of candidates … I travelled over one of the largest constituencies in Britain … It was necessary to call on most of the men and women who were leaders of the Party in their neighbourhood to solicit their support. When I arrived at the (selection) meeting at two o'clock the room was crowded with delegates. My speech, which I had no time to prepare, could not, I surmised, have converted a single doubtful supporter. I was, however, accepted by a substantial majority. Adoption in West Denbigh then meant election."

Morris-Jones was duly elected with a 8,189 majority over Major Graham. Graham, however, had the consolation of later becoming the MP for the Wirral, just over the border in England. The 1929 general election ended with the Liberals' total of seats in the United Kingdom at 59. This was just 13 seats up on the number the Liberals held when Parliament had been dissolved. The Liberals were now also a party of the Celtic fringes with eight seats in the mainly Welsh-speaking constituencies, two in the mainly English-speaking Welsh seats, five in Cornwall and seven in the Scottish Highlands and Islands. A third of its total seats now came from the Celtic fringe. Labour had made substantial gains and was now the largest party in the House of Commons, for the first time, with 287 seats against the Conservatives 260.

The Welsh Liberals had made a net loss of one seat. In some areas of Wales, however, they were still very much the most important party, and in the whole of Wales no Liberal candidate scored less than 20 per cent of the vote. In North Wales they held every seat with the exception of Wrexham. In the rural counties of Mid and West Wales, they held every seat, with the exception of the Carmarthen and Brecon and Radnor constituencies, both of which Labour had gained with the help of the substantial mining votes in each constituency.[95] In the industrial south of Wales, however, they did not hold a single one of the 23 seats. The nearest seat that the Welsh Liberals held to the nation's future capital in Cardiff was now Cardiganshire over eighty miles away. For the first time in Welsh Liberal history, there was no longer a Welsh Liberal MP to speak for the south of Wales.

The Economic Depression and Lloyd George's Last Spell as Leader

The former Labour MP for Aberafon and now MP for Seaham, (Co. Durham), Ramsay MacDonald, once again became Prime Minister. Labour was now governing without

Liberal support. This enabled some of the new Liberal MPs to bed in as opposition members, as opposed to quasi-coalition partners of the Labour government, as had been the case in 1924. It still remained a confusing period for many in the Liberal Party, unsure of whether they were supporting Labour, the Conservatives or going their own way. This lack of direction gave some Welsh MPs a chance to spread their parliamentary wings and Megan Lloyd George seized this opportunity. As the only female Liberal MP and the party leader's daughter, she gained a high public profile through, amongst other things, regular slots on the BBC's *The Week in Parliament*. For the rest of her life Megan would remain in both public and media demand.

The Ending of Welsh Liberal Ambitions in the South of Wales

In February 1930, Ramsay Muir was appointed chairman of the British Liberal Organising Committee. He was aware that one of the reasons for Liberal inactivity was the fact that constituency parties 'mistakenly believed there was an inexhaustive fund at headquarters which in the long term sapped the vitality of associations and federations'. In Montgomeryshire, for example, there had been no contribution from central party funds since 1918. The multi-millionaire, David Davies, had bankrolled the constituency, which ensured the constituency's[96] executive had remained inactive with regard to fund-raising or attempts to increase membership. Similar stories occurred elsewhere with rich Liberal MPs being selected as candidates, mainly because they could fund the local Liberal Association. This practice would continue within the Liberal Party in Wales right up until the end of the century. The Liberal Party, if it was to expand, however, had to attract the same calibre of working-class candidate that the Labour Party had done. They would have to rely on the local Liberal Associations to raise the necessary finance. The 1929 campaign had cost the party centrally £254,000 because local parties had not been able to raise the money and there were many lost deposits. In a memo to Herbert Samuel in May 1930, Muir divided all of the non-Liberal constituencies in the UK into five categories. These ranged from an 'A' category, which was allotted to seats they were most likely to win to an 'E' category for those they could either not contest or, if they did so, then their deposits would be lost. Muir concluded that there were no more than 300 seats in the country that were worth the Liberals contesting with any possible chance of winning. What this meant was that whilst north, mid and west Wales constituencies would be contested; most of the south would not. For the next four decades, for the Liberals, the south would become a series of what would later be termed 'derelict' constituencies. Only Cardiff East and Swansea West now fell into the 'A' or 'B' camp.

In North and Mid Wales, most seats fell into the 'A' or 'B' grouping. As a result in northeast Wales, the divisional associations were spurred, on through the encouragement of party headquarters and their respective agents, to look to the future and expand their membership base. In Wrexham, activists attempted to keep Liberal spirits buoyant. The defeat at the hands of Labour in 1929 had been the source of great disappointment. Moreover, the resignation of their former MP, Christmas Williams, as their candidate in August 1930 compounded their misery. In Flintshire and Denbigh, however, members were more optimistic. The prospects for the Flintshire party appeared extremely rosy, and in September 1930, the Flintshire Liberal Association chair, Thomas Waterhouse, noted that through strict control of their finances they had managed to stay out of debt and were on a sound footing for the future.[97]

The Great Depression Arrives

Wales had been suffering an economic slump for nearly a decade before the Western World itself experienced the worst of the period known as the 'Great Depression'. This period resulted from the economic crisis that followed the 'Wall Street Crash' in the United States in 1929. During this time, the MacDonald government became increasingly helpless in the face of the rising mass unemployment. This rising tide of jobless men became symptomatic of impoverished economic life in virtually every constituency in Wales. Emigration from depressed areas was widespread and unparalleled levels of unemployment for the next decade caused the virtual break-down of community life in parts of Wales. The Liberals urged the use of Keynesian economics to deal with the problem but the Labour Chancellor Snowden rejected this notion. Unemployment continued to rise into the millions and, as a result, MacDonald in June 1930 sought to call a three party conference to tackle the dire economic situation. Baldwin, the Conservative leader, refused to attend any such meeting but Lloyd George did agreed to meet and, for around six months, Labour sat with the Liberals in discussion but with little result. In February 1931, Lloyd George rejected a personal appeal by the soon to be Labour Party Leader, George Lansbury, to the Liberals to join with the Labour Party. Lloyd George could see that the Labour government was falling apart internally and replied to Lansbury that the merging of the two parties would do nothing to help cure unemployment. The Liberal support for this was there already; the Liberals would therefore remain independent.

The majority of the Liberal Party, still mindful of the problems that had arisen from coalition government a decade before, had little desire to repeat the experience at this juncture. On the 25th of March 1931, their MPs voted 34 to 17 against going into a pact with either the Conservatives or the Labour Party. They were still uncertain about what their role should be. During these turbulent times, Lloyd George maintained an active Liberal presence in the House of Commons through support from his son and daughter and fellow Caernarfonshire MP and son-in-law, Goronwy Owen, who had been appointed Chief Whip. Yet Lloyd George's presence was not enough to keep the party together. As Labour continued to push for a pact with the Liberals or the Conservatives, a group of right-wing Liberals split from the party, determined to stop this. Sir John Simon, with former Lloyd Georgite, Leslie Hore-Belisha as his first lieutenant, left the party in June with 19 other Liberals, to, in effect, join Baldwin's Conservatives. Sir John Simon had close Welsh connections; he was the son of a nonconformist minister in Pembrokeshire.[98] He had a close relationship with Clement Davies and his legal background had brought him into contact with many Welsh barrister MPs. The former Asquithian MP for Cardiff, Ivor Churchill Guest, now Viscount Wimborne, also became the first Chair of the Liberal National Party together with a number of other Welsh Liberals.

There was little love lost between Lloyd George and Sir John Simon. They had been political adversaries since the start of the 1920s. Their enmity had stemmed from the 1919 Spen Valley by-election, in which the Coalition had put up a candidate to obstruct Simon's chances of election as an Asquithian Liberal. Later on, the Coalition had tried to smear Simon by stating that he was unpatriotic and that he had tried to mount a legal challenge to the war in 1914. Unsurprisingly, Simon became one of Lloyd George's fiercest internal critics.[99] Simon never engaged in hostile public banter with Lloyd George; on the surface, he appeared mild mannered and polite man but many of his contemporaries saw him as as insincere and overly ambitious. Despite these flaws, he was an elegant speaker and was considered 'a man of brilliance' by his supporters.[100] The group of Liberal MPs and Lords, most of whom had also fallen out with Lloyd George at some time, that came to follow Sir John Simon, became known as 'the Simonities' or 'Liberal Nationals'.[101] They were termed 'Liberal Nationals' because they supported a National Government of all parties and were particularly close to the Conservatives. The Liberal Nationals were determined to stop a Labour government that was believed to have become overbearing and anti-capitalist. This left-wing doctrine was perceived to be against the core Liberal faith of individualism. Simon asserted that 'socialism … is a poisonous doctrine because it seeks to substitute for the Gladstonian principle that money is best left to fructify in the pockets of the people, the wholly different principle that the State will manage money better than we shall'.[102] In Wales three MPs were persuaded by Simon's views enough to join him. They were Dr John Henry Morris-Jones (Denbigh), Frederick Llewellyn-Jones (Flintshire) and Clement Davies (Montgomeryshire). Within a few months their Liberal National group had established an organisation that was preparing for re-election in Wales. The tangible representation of this was a South and North Wales Liberal National Organisation.

The three North Wales Liberal MPs did not join the Liberal Nationals without consequences to themselves or their constituencies. The *Liverpool Daily Post* columnist 'Celt' speculated that many Liberal supporters in Denbigh would be dismayed with Morris-Jones' decision to leave the Liberals and join the Liberal Nationals.[103] The *Denbighshire Free Press* recorded that both the Denbigh and Ruthin Liberal Associations had also expressed their condemnation of Morris-Jones' decision. There were calls by Denbigh Liberals for the former MP, Ellis Davies, to be reinstated but his fragile health meant that he was unable to fight the seat again. The Liberals in the seat became even more dismayed when the Conservatives, their bitter opponents, gave Morris-Jones unqualified support.[104] The resentment against the Liberal Nationals was also apparent in Flintshire where the senior North Wales Liberal figurehead, Thomas Waterhouse said:

"We have too many Whigs left in the Liberal Party. We want a radical programme and to go forward with courage. The great word 'Liberal' has been prostituted by men like Sir John Simon with their 'Liberal Nationals'. The Liberal Nationals are out to destroy the Liberal Party. Their intention at the next election is secure our seats with Conservative votes. Today we are fighting from within the party to Radicalise it … we want rid of all the Liberal Nationals first, and all the Whiggish elements afterwards, and the sooner they go the better." [105]

Waterhouse was therefore unable to endorse the Flintshire MP Fred Llewellyn Jones who was now prepared to accept the implementation of trade tariffs, and to contest

Flintshire under the banner of the Liberal Nationals. Jones, during the election, justified his change of loyalty by saying, 'however much I disagree … with the Tory party … it would be infinitely better for this country to have (Lord) Beaverbrook[106] and his policies applied than to have the policies of a Socialist applied'. Waterhouse described this address as the 'best Conservative speech I have listened to in my life'.[107] The Flintshire divisional Liberal Party disbanded after this, ending active Liberalism within the county for a short period. In Montgomeryshire, the Liberal Association remained unhappy with the move over to the National Liberals and refused to affiliate with them.

The Elections and By-elections of 1929–1931

There were two Welsh by-elections during the 1929–1931 government. The first was because of the Labour MP, T. I. Mardy Jones, who stood down in Pontypridd in March 1931 because he had illegally allowed his wife to make use of his MP's pass on the railways. Ironically, Mardy Jones had taken his seat off the Liberal MP T. A. Lewis, in part by constantly referring to him as a war profiteer and thereby unfit to hold office. Now because of Mardy Jones' activities, he was also deemed to be unfit to hold office, though unlike Lewis, he would not win a parliamentary seat elsewhere. The Liberal candidate was Geoffrey Crawshay from Liberal Merthyr Tydfil supporting iron masters. He had previously performed well for the Liberals in Pontypool in 1929, where he had gained some 36 per cent of the vote. In the Pontypridd by-election of 1931, Crawshay got a quarter of the votes, well ahead of the Conservatives but still some 12,319 votes (35.7%) behind Labour's D. L. Davies. This was a drop of 12 per cent in the Liberal vote on the 1929 general election but this was to remain the best Liberal vote there for the next fifty years. On the death of Vernon Hartshorn, the other by-election occurred in Ogmore in May 1931. It was not contested by the Liberals, despite the fact that they had achieved almost 30 per cent of the vote there two years previously, a decision that serves to indicate the party's continuing decline in operations in South Wales.

In the three Welsh borough council municipal elections of November 1930, the Liberals remained the largest political party in Cardiff and second largest in Swansea, but despite this pre-eminence, they did not gain or even contest a single seat in Merthyr Tydfil where they had, in effect, been out of the running since the council was founded in 1904. Cardiff was now one of only four borough councils in the United Kingdom where the Liberals were still the largest party. In the whole of the United Kingdom, the Liberals now controlled only one borough council outright – Huddersfield. In Wales, much of the Liberal success was thanks to local co-operation with the Conservatives, which squeezed the Labour vote. Such a tactic in Cardiff, therefore, ensured that in the 1931 borough elections only one Labour councillor was elected.[108] It also needs to be noted, however, that a number of Welsh authorities candidates, who had previously stood under the Liberal banner, were now standing under a variety of titles, often in collaboration with Conservatives or Independents within some 'anti-Socialist' grouping. This means that is not possible during this period to gauge the full strength of the Liberal Party at a grassroots level by simply looking at council election results.

Another General Election Arrives – 1931

The Liberals who followed Lloyd George soldiered on at Westminster and, in July 1931, discussions with the Labour Party indicated that a coalition might be possible with Ramsay MacDonald as Prime Minister and Lloyd George as Foreign Secretary. At this critical moment in the nation's history, Lloyd George was taken seriously ill with prostate problems. Whilst Lloyd George was recovering from an operation, MacDonald now met the King and gained his authority to form a National Government to deal with the massive rise in unemployment caused by a crisis in the economy. In the new government of all parties, Sir Herbert Samuel and Lord Reading went into the Cabinet on behalf of the Lloyd George Liberals. The only Welsh Liberals to participate in this government were Gwilym Lloyd George, who was appointed parliamentary under-secretary at the Board of Trade, and Goronwy Owen who became the Liberals' Chief Whip. There was still no role for the Simonite Liberals – Welsh or otherwise in the National Government.

The single Welsh Liberal Federation which had been in operation since the Asquithians and Lloyd George Liberals had come back together was now breaking up once more. In 1931 Walter Jones from Cardiff was the chair, Lloyd George, the president. Even before his period of poor health, Lloyd George often failed to turn up at any meetings; in 1930 he did not attend the British Liberals' Barmouth Conference, which meant that Hadyn Jones was the only Welsh Liberal MP present.

Seabourne Davies, later the Liberal MP for Caernarfon Borough, Lloyd George's seat, was a radical Welsh Young Liberal at this time and was publicly very critical of Lloyd George's failure to attend the Welsh Federation's meeting or support it financially. Such inaction by Lloyd George took its toll, and on the 29th of August 1931, the Welsh National Liberal Federation's Cardiff office was closed by a decision of the Management Committee of the Federation. The Welsh party's income-raising capacity was less than £500 per year whilst expenditure amounted to over £2,500. Overall income had dropped significantly since the Liberal Party in London had stopped funding the Welsh Federation directly, when it too had run into financial difficulties. Pleas for income from within Wales to support the office had fallen on deaf ears.[109] For awhile, the Secretary, Mr. D. L. Salathiel, ran the Welsh Federation from his home in Caerphilly. Then on the 12th of September 1931, a separate federation for the north was discussed at Colwyn Bay and endorsed. It was felt to be needed because the interests of Liberalism in the North could best be served by their own organisation there. The move in the north was lead by Waterhouse and Gomer Owen of Rhyl, Chair of the North Wales Liberal Society Agents.[110] There were similar moves to restart a Federation in the south. This meant that Wales was once more split into separate North and South Wales Liberal Federations. The Welsh National Liberal Federation continued but in a much weakened form and would from then on take second place in the presence of the reinvigorated regional Welsh federations.

It was made clear to Lloyd George that this new National Government would only last as long as the sterling crisis continued. Lloyd George still saw a role for himself in the government and was determined to stand against any early Westminster elections which might change the status quo. From his sick bed he sought pledges from Samuel and Reading to this effect, but they would not give them and allowed an election to be called for the 27th of October 1931. Lloyd George felt betrayed by

Samuel and those Liberal MPs who been complicit in this decision. He said, 'You have sold every pass we held!' and informed them that he would no longer support them.[111] As a result of his decision, Gwilym and Gorowny Owen[112] left the government immediately, as did Lord Reading. The other Liberals stayed in the government, which proved not to be an unpopular move with most Welsh Liberals. Even Gwilym's Pembrokeshire Liberal Association was against his withdrawal from the Samuelite Liberals. Samuel himself asked Gwilym not to resign in haste but to sleep on the idea. In the event, Gwilym could not go against his father's wishes.[113] Samuel tried to keep Lloyd George in the Liberal camp and adapted the manifesto to please him in order that he would endorse it. The ploy did not work and his family group stayed outside the Liberal Party.

As the election date drew close, the Liberal Party split into three parts – those who followed Lloyd George, Sir John Simon or Sir Herbert Samuel. Importantly, however, the split between the Lloyd Georgeites and the Liberals was on matters of tactics rather than policy. Both were still linked firmly together on traditional Liberal principles.[114] Only some 160 candidates from all of the Liberal factions fought the 1931 general election. No faction could claim to be a party capable of government, but only a party of potential coalition.

October 1931 General Election

Labour	15
Conservative	6
Liberal National	5
Liberal	4
Independent Liberal	4
National Labour	1
Independent Labour Party	1

The election was another 'coupon election' and Samuel instructed Lieutenant-Colonel T. F. Tweed, as head of the Liberal Party Organisation, to meet with the Conservatives to ensure that neither party contested the other. Lloyd George was furious with this and forbade Tweed to take part in this. In the event, however, only 10 of the 173 Liberals who stood in 1931 had Conservative opponents.[115] Three of these ten opposed were the Lloyd Georges – David, Gwilym and Megan. Those supportive of the national government had few worries in this election. In 1931, the Denbigh Liberal National MP Morris-Jones wrote:

"My adoption by the Executive was carried by forty-six against twenty-two …
When the result became known I received a private message from the President of the local Conservative Party asking me to meet him … As I was supporting a National Government and was against Socialism, he would advise his party not to put up a candidate."[116]

Morris-Jones now gained his seat unopposed not only by the Conservatives but also by the Liberals and Labour. Clement Davies in Montgomeryshire had a similar discussion with the Conservatives in order to avoid a contest.[117] The different Liberal groups gained 72 seats in the three factions and the Conservatives 417 seats. The

Labour Party, however, was decimated, gaining just 52 seats. Although they lost seven seats in Wales, the Principality still contained a quarter of their parliamentary members. Wales had now become a refuge for the Labour Party just as it had to the Liberals a decade before. In Wales the total of all Liberal groups in all factions was 13 – for the first time in a decade this figure came close to equalling Labour's seats in Wales. These consisted of:

Liberal Nationals – There were thirty-five Simonites who won seats and joined the new MacDonald government across Britain. The five Simonites in Wales were Aled Owen ('O'.) Roberts (Wrexham), Dr (John) Henry Morris-Jones (Denbigh), Frederick Llewellyn-Jones (Flint), Lewis Jones (Swansea West) and Clement Davies (Montgomeryshire). Lewis Jones was elected for the first time. He took Swansea West off Labour with a majority of 6016 votes (17%), helped by the Conservatives' decision not to contest the seat, which gave Jones most of their vote. Lewis Jones was now, incidentally, the third MP for Swansea East who had left the Liberal Party to join another. Alfred Mond had joined the Conservatives and his Liberal predecessor Charles Kerr had become a Liberal National MP for his new Montrose Burghs seat. Like Lewis, the former teacher, Llewellyn Jones, was similarly helped by Conservative endorsement. In Wrexham, the Liberals adopted Aled Owen Roberts in June 1931 in his first foray into politics. He abandoned his commitment to free trade and a national agreement between those parties participating in the newly formed national government meant that the Conservatives did not contest the seat.[118] Despite no Conservative opposition, Roberts won a narrow victory only over Labour of 1821 votes (4.2%). Both Dr Henry Morris-Jones and Clement Davies gained their seats unopposed. After the election, during the formation of the government, Sir John Simon became Foreign Secretary. The success of his Welsh supporters in securing government positions was less evident, however. Morris-Jones became an Assistant Whip; the others took no position at all.

Liberals – There were thirty-three Samuelites elected in Britain, four of whom came from Wales. There was (R.T.) Evans (Carmarthen) who defeated both Conservative and Labour opponents to win the seats with a slender 1214 (3.2%) majority. Rhys Hopkin Morris (Cardiganshire) only had a Labour opponent and was able to defeat him handsomely by 13752 votes (52%). In Meirionnydd, the long-serving Merchant Slate proprietor, Henry Hadyn Jones, was returned against both Conservative and Labour opposition with a 1949 (8.2%) majority. Lastly, Ernest Evans (University of Wales) gained an easy victory over Plaid Cymru's Saunders Lewis with a 1315 (41.8%) majority. They joined the governing coalition with their party leader, Sir Herbert Samuel, serving as Home Secretary. In the few councils that were still overtly Liberal in Wales, it was the Samuelities who on the whole were the most prominent. In Cardiff, for instance, Sir Charles Bird (the interwar leader of Cardiff Liberalism) and other leading Cardiff Liberals, such as Alderman F. H. Turnball, C. F. Sanders and J. E. Emlyn-Jones, also supported and endorsed Sir Herbert Samuel wholeheartedly at election times.[119]

The last group in the Welsh Liberal tripartite grouping were the 'Independent Liberals' in the (family) group. They were collectively called the family group because they were technically all related. This Lloyd Georgeites group consisted of, as would be expected, of the Lloyd Georges, David (Caernafon Boroughs), Gwilym (Pembroke), and Megan (Ynys Môn). There was also Major Goronwy Owen who had married Gwilym's sister-in-law. There was one member of the group who was not related to Lloyd George - Frank Owen. Owen was a fiery 23 year old Liberal radical, and future biographer of Lloyd George,[120] who barnstormed the traditional Tory seat of Hereford for the Liberals in 1929. He had previously been Lloyd George's parliamentary researcher. Owen, however, now lost his seat to the Conservatives and was out of Parliament for good. Those Lloyd Georgeites elected now constantly followed the Samuelites closely in Parliament, being almost indistinguishable from them in the division lobbies at Westminster.[121]

The Ottawa Conference Shakes up Welsh Liberalism

The problems of the British economy were examined at the Imperial Economic Conference of the British Empire opened in Ottawa, Canada on the 21st of July 1932. The Samuelites were concerned that Prime Minister Ramsay MacDonald would use the occasion to introduce a system of Imperial (British Empire) preference in international trade. These concerns were heightened by the fact that no Samuelite or free trader was included in the British delegation. The Ottawa conference did not exactly consolidate protectionism but, at the same time, it did nothing of real value to enhance free trade. Samuelites saw this as the last straw on free trade. Samuel declared that as there was no national peril, there was no reason for the Liberals to now stay within the government. They then left it.

The ramifications of Ottawa were felt across Wales. The North Wales Liberal Federation, at the Liberal Party Assembly at Clacton in April 1932, called on the party to withdraw from the government and lay down their own policy on Ottawa, which it did a few months later.[122] Then the Wrexham MP, Aled Roberts crossed over to the Simonites in 1933, and was supported by most of the right leaning and anti-socialist local Wrexham Liberal Association under the Chair of Edward Hughes. He then reformed it into the Wrexham Liberal National Association, with a rump of Liberals refusing to join and forming their own rival radical Action Association.[123] In Flintshire, the divisional Liberal Party reformed in June 1932. They had severed their links with Liberal National Fred Llewellyn Jones, who, until the end of 1932, enjoyed only Conservative party support in the seat. In September 1932 he relinquished his ties with the National Government. This decision caused much anger in Tory ranks but indifference within Liberal ones. Like Roberts, he felt he had no choice but to cross over to a different group. He objected to the recommendations of the Ottawa conference. Despite doing this, Jones was not invited then or later back into the ranks of the Flintshire Liberals. In 1934, he told Henry Gladstone that neither he nor his family had been invited to any Liberal Party meeting or function in the seat since October 1931 when he had joined the Liberal Nationals. Gomer Owen, Secretary of the Flintshire Liberal Association, and Herbert Gladstone, now worked to unify the party. They both wanted him back in the Liberal Party as the Flint MP and put this before the Liberal Association. Consequently, the Executive Committee in November 1933 reluctantly endorsed him.[124] This political manoeuvring, however, occurred too late as, Jones, fed up with the internal squabbles of the party, had tendered his resignation as prospective Liberal candidate in February 1934. With the departure of this popular local MP the chances of keeping Flint as a Liberal seat also vanished.

The Cardiganshire By-election 1932

In the Summer of 1932, one of Lloyd George's most fierce Welsh Liberal critics, Rhys Hopkin Morris, resigned from his Cardiganshire seat to become a Metropolitan Police Magistrate. Hopkin Morris had been a Samuelite and it was the Samuelites who had now to defend their own seat. Cardiganshire Liberal Association refused to select a candidate other than a Samuelite as they did not support the coalition. Their candidate was the Welsh barrister, a Cardiganshire man from the south of the county and the son of a tenant farmer, David Owen Evans. The Conservatives demanded a free run at the seat as they were coalition partners with the Samuelties in the National government. The Cardiganshire Liberal Association dismissed this request. In turn, Evans sought to get them to stand down by pledging support for the National Government but the Conservatives, in turn, rejected this and fielded a candidate against him.

Cardiganshire By-election 22 September 1932

Candidate	Party	Vote	Percentage
David Owen Evans	Liberal	13,437	48.7
Col. E. C. L. Fitzwilliam	Conservative	8,866	32.1
Rev D. M. Jones	Labour	5,295	19.2
	Majority	4,571	16.6
	Turnout		70.4

Evans won the seat with a considerable majority for the Welsh Liberals. Despite the fact that this victory, in the heart of the Welsh nonconformist territory, should have been certain, it still came as a huge relief to the Liberal Party.[125] Then on the 28th of September, the Samuelite Ministers resigned from the government over the imposition of trade tariffs through the Ottawa agreement. They continued, however, to support the government at Westminster and did not go into opposition as Lloyd George had done. Their Simonite (Liberal National) counterparts, however, stayed in the government, signalling a permanent split between the two Liberal factions.

It may have come third in Cardiganshire but, outside this constituency, it was the Labour Party that was continuing to advance across Wales. They made big advances in the municipal elections of November 1933 and took control of Swansea outright for the first time. At the same time, the Liberals made significant losses in Swansea and elsewhere in Wales.[126] Labour was also consolidating its hold of its Westminster seats but the Liberals still had significant support in some of these seats. In the remaining by-elections of the Parliament, the Liberals gained a respectable result in Rhondda East. Here Solicitor William Thomas gained 23.6 per cent of the vote and put his party third behind the Communists. In Merthyr Tydfil, barrister and university Law lecturer John Victor Evans (J. V.) gained 28.9 percent of the vote. He came second, but this time well ahead of the Communists. Although these were by no means bad results, they were still a significant way off from winning these seats.

The Liberals Struggle on...

In North Wales, Thomas Waterhouse became chairman of the recently re-established North Wales Federation. For most of the 1930s both he and W. Rees Edmund, the South Wales Chair, were also the Welsh representatives of the Liberal National Federation. They also worked together with J. W. Jones as the chair of the much weakened Welsh Liberal National Federation. Waterhouse was a close ally of Lloyd George's and tried to get him to play a more prominent role in Wales during the 1930s. In turn, Lloyd George said of his loyal ally: 'I fear you are the only one who will put up a fight for radicalism'.[127] In 1933, Waterhouse had endeared himself to Lloyd George further by declaring that 'it was the duty of every Welsh Liberal to leave the Coalition government',[128] which was something Lloyd George strongly advocated. A year later, in February 1934, he called on Lloyd George to lead a great Liberal revival throughout the country.[129] Although Lloyd George did not take up this challenge, he did frequently attend North Wales Liberal Federation meetings, which was more than he had done for the Welsh Federation ones. For his seventieth birthday he addressed a rally of 7,000 in Caernarfon. Here he made it clear that he had no intention of resigning, even at the age of seventy and expressed his love for the people of Wales, particularly those in the North.[130] Samuel had also approached Lloyd George to lead a Liberal revival in Wales. This got widespread support in Wales amongst Liberals of all factions and there were stirrings that this might come together in one group.

In February 1933 the Liberal D. O. Evans (Cardigan) and the Liberal National Aled Roberts (Wrexham) formed the Welsh Liberal Group, which was chaired by Lloyd George. It was designed to provide a forum for all Welsh Liberal MPs. For the first meeting, 10 of the 13 Welsh Liberals of all factions attended.[131] After its initial success, however, the splits between the Liberals hardened, which ensured that the Welsh Liberal Group never developed into an effective political body for Welsh Liberalism and, in time, withered away entirely. Whilst all of this was happening the Meirionnydd Liberal MP, Henry Haydn Jones, became Chair of the Welsh Parliamentary Party. Jones was on the right of the Liberal Party and although he never became a National Liberal, he remained hostile to Labour and Socialism throughout his long political career. It was this stance and his long tenure that, in part, helped secure his knighthood in 1937.

The Last Inter-War General Election – November 1935

The November 1935 General Election Results

Labour	18
Liberal	7
Conservative	6
Liberal National	3
National Government	1
National Labour Organisation	1

In June 1935, the Conservative Stanley Baldwin took over from the ailing National Labour Ramsay MacDonald as Prime Minister. Within a few months an election was called. The Liberals had been electioneering for some time and the previous January, Lloyd George, in a much publicised speech in Bangor, had launched his 'New Deal' campaign linked to Keynesian economics. The Lloyd George Liberals were now moving back together with the Samuelites. His speech was aimed at uniting all those Liberals who opposed the National Government.[132] Despite his widespread appeal both inside and outside of the Liberals, Lloyd George was still outside the mainstream of the party. During the campaign, Neville Chamberlain described him contemptibly as 'an old friend who most of us have forgotten'.[133] He was not forgotten in much of Wales, where his comments and statements still gained widespread coverage by the Welsh press. To the Welsh public, by and large, he remained a potent political icon who drew huge crowds. In the 1935 campaign, when Lloyd George went to speak on behalf of his son Gwilym at Pembroke Dock, he was able to attract an audience of over five thousand people. Lloyd George wasn't just a political 'crowd puller', he also held the purse strings for important revenue that the party could use for fighting elections. His absence from the mainstream of the Liberal Party, however, left the wider party starved of the vital funds needed to contest more than a minority of seats. At the same time the National Government's candidates were well-financed and resourced. In this, the last peace time general election, the Liberals were able to contest just 14 of the 36 Welsh seats, which resulted in nine south Wales seats subsequently falling to Labour unopposed. After all the ballots had been counted, there were seven Liberal victors in Wales – now just one ahead of the Conservatives.

The Liberal Nationals fared comparatively well in Wales considering the fact that they had contested so few seats. All three seats contested were won by them. Clement Davies stood once again as a Liberal National but only after he had triumphed in a showdown with his Montgomeryshire constituency executive, whom had wanted him to stand as a Liberal. Davies was unopposed and therefore he knew he was an MP as soon as nominations closed. Of the two other Liberal Nationals elected, Lewis Jones in Swansea East became the last of the South Wales 'Liberal' MPs, beating Labour by some 2,081 votes (5.8%). Henry Morris-Jones in Denbigh became the third Liberal National victor with a 5,043 vote (14.5%) majority.

The Liberal Nationals were now in an electoral concordat with the Conservatives and had become indistinguishable from them electorally and ideologically.[134] This led to the increasing disillusionment of the Welsh Liberal Associations who had Liberal National MPs. In Denbigh, Morris-Jones' appointment as a National Government Whip led the Liberal branches to disassociate themselves from him, as had occurred before in Flintshire with Llewellyn-Jones. He was sent to political Coventry and, as a result, no Liberal group would entertain his presence and he was forced to attend only Conservative functions. Yet Morris-Jones always gave a plausible argument for his support of the National Government, saying that 'it was a time of economic crisis'.[135] In 1931, this had the desired effect of preventing the Liberals from putting up a candidate against him but, by 1935, this argument would no longer hold water with the local Liberal Association. He was directly challenged by a Liberal candidate. Morris-Jones' Liberal opponent was John Cledwyn Davies, the former National Liberal MP for Denbigh (1922–23) and the county's Director of Education. He was persuaded back into the political arena because of his belief that Morris-Jones was failing to represent the true Liberal cause. Davies' notion was not without a grain of truth. Although the two had been friends for over forty years, Davies branded Morris-Jones as a 'turncoat' and attacked his personal integrity.

Morris-Jones did not respond with a personal attack and was supported by Tory voters and some powerful Liberal supporters, including Lord Clwyd.[136] As a result, Morris-Jones won with a handsome 5,043 (14.5%) majority. Denbigh was only one of two seats in Britain, the other being Oldham, where the Liberals also contested the Liberal Nationals.

There was one other Liberal supporting MP elected in 1935, Ivor Grosvenor Guest, the National Government MP for Brecon and Radnor. He supported the Liberal Nationals and later would become their Chief Whip in the House of Lords. Guest was the son of Lord Wimborne, the former Cardiff Liberal MP, Sir Ivor Churchill Guest, who himself had become a National Liberal. He had been selected as the National Government candidate by the Brecon and Radnor Liberal Association in collaboration with an agreement with the seat's Conservative Association.

When the nationwide results came in, the Liberals continued in their status as a minor party, with just 21 seats gained in total. Only in Wales, which returned seven of their 21 members, were there still what could be described as concentrated Liberal strongholds. Their three seats in Scotland and 11 in England were scattered 'without rhyme or reason'.[137] Of the powerful Liberal government of 1910, Lloyd George was now the only remaining senior member who was still an MP and connected to the Liberal Party in some way. His family group took the seats of Caernarfon Boroughs (David), Pembroke (Gwilym), Anglesey (Megan) and Caernarfonshire (Goronwy Owen). They campaigned mainly on the issues of: 'unemployment to be cured by great public works, the dangers of the armaments race with Germany and support for the League of Nations'. It was, however, the Lloyd George family name, rather than their policy ideals that helped them retain their seats.[138] After the election the group came back into the party fully, and to provide evidence of this fact, David Lloyd George even chaired the first meeting of the newly elected Liberal MPs. He no longer desired the leadership role in this much-diminished political party and refused the Chairmanship of the Parliamentary Party, passing it on to Sir Archibald Sinclair, the former Chief Whip.[139]

The remaining Welsh Liberal MPs won their seats without too much difficulty. In Cardiganshire the recent by-election winner D. O. Evans was able to defeat his Labour opponent on the anti-Socialist messages of 'it is but a short step from Socialism to Communism' and 'nationalisation means dictatorship, which is the negation of Liberalism'.[140] Evans secured a majority of 5,761 votes (22.2%), despite the fact that the president of the constituency's Liberal Association complained that political interest in the seat was failing as the young people of Cardiganshire 'know more about Greta Garbo than they do about politics'. Despite this, there were enough older voters to secure the seat for the Liberals.[141] Ernest Evans won the University of Wales seat with a 22.6 per cent majority over Labour's Ithel Davies. He was the only Liberal elected in all 12 university seats in Britain. Both Liberal MPs were joined by Haydn Jones (Meirionnydd) who gained a 1,149 majority (4.8%) over Labour in a three cornered fight.

As in the rest of Britain, there were Liberal losses in Wales too. Three Liberal seats were lost in total. In Carmarthen, R. T. Evans's 1,214 vote majority was demolished by the Labour candidate, who now had a 5,235 vote majority (13.6%). The mining vote was necessary to win the seat and this had gone firmly to Labour. In Flintshire, the Liberal candidate, the Cardiff-based Liberal and former MP for North

Dorset (1922–24), John Emlyn Jones, lost the seat previously held by the ostracised Llewelyn Williams. He was a veteran politician closely aligned with Lloyd George. Emlyn Jones was also a free trader and defined his brand of politics as 'Liberalism with kick in it' but he lacked the personal appeal of Llewellyn Jones. He was also committed to hoist the free trade banner in a seat where there had been many job losses from cheap overseas competition. Flint would never be a Liberal seat again. In Wrexham, Aled O. Roberts stood as a 'real Liberal' opposed to pacts with either Labour or the Conservatives. Although the Conservatives didn't stand this time in Wrexham, Robert's stance alienated the Conservatives and the Chairman of the Wrexham Conservatives advised Conservative voters to abstain. This they did and Wrexham had its lowest turnout (75.5%) since 1918,[142] as few Conservatives either voted or backed Roberts.[143] The result was a Labour victory over Roberts by another Roberts (Richard) by 5,283 votes (12.6%). The Liberals were ousted from Wrexham for good. Although the Liberal National Association in Wrexham continued even into the 1950s under Edna Edwards, they received little support from the Liberal National Party in London and, as a result, became subordinate to the Conservatives there. Wrexham now became a safe Labour seat but the Conservatives continued to use the Conservatives and Liberal National tag on their Westminster candidates, right up until the 1960s.[144]

As the new Parliament began its term, Ernest Evans put down an amendment to the King's Speech on behalf of the Welsh Parliamentary Party. This received signatures from nearly all his colleagues, regretting that the speech had contained no reference to matters relating to Wales.[145] The amendment was heavily defeated but Evans had continued in the Welsh Liberal radical tradition of ensuring that Westminster remained fully aware that the Welsh nation still existed. Both he and other Welsh Liberal MPs of various factions would continue to pursue Welsh matters in the coming Parliament, though in a greatly diminished pool of Welsh Liberal MPs compared to the Liberal radicals' heyday of some three decaded earlier.

The Last Years of Peace

The last years of peace were divided between events concerning the oncoming war and continuing with the everyday business of politics in Wales. The North and South Wales Federations continued in weakened forms to issue policy statements and discuss general policy issues. The South Wales Federation was now without any MP. The financially weakened state of the party also led to the failure to appoint a new Welsh Liberal Party Agent after the outgoing official stepped down in 1935. There was now no one to co-ordinate Liberalism across Wales in the Welsh National Liberal Federation beyond its officers and nor would there be for another decade.

There were other important events that involved the Liberals outside the run-of-the-mill party politics in this period. The most important was the coronation of a new King, George VI, and the events which went with celebrating this. For Welsh MPs, the Coronation tour of Wales by King George VI led to Morris-Jones, Megan Lloyd George and Wrexham's Labour MP, Robert Richards, being entrusted by Liberal National leader and Home Secretary, Sir John Simon, to organise a spectacular investiture at Caernarfon castle. This they did and in July 1935 some 3,000 notables gathered in the castle to greet the new king. It was the last great civic occasion co-ordinated by leading North Wales Liberals and was deemed a glorious success by all involved.[146] A year later Megan enjoyed a 'coronation' of her own when she became President of the Women's Liberal Federation, which continued to reinforce her role as one of the most prominent female MPs of her time both in Wales and the rest of Britain.

Policy and Activities

In 1935, David Lloyd George organised a band of mainly Welsh experts whom he named the Council of Action for Peace and Reconstruction. He revived his 1929 government programme under the title *Organising Prosperity: A Scheme of National Reconstruction.* The programme was based once more on the Keynesian economics model then being used by the US President Roosevelt in his 'New Deal'.[147] Lloyd George's proposals were formally considered by the government but rejected by the Cabinet, marking the last venture through which Lloyd George sought to pursue his economic policy ideals.[148] Other Welsh Liberal MPs also continued to pursue their own policy objectives. Perhaps the most notable was the Liberal National Clement Davies who in November 1937, won second place in the ballot for Private Members Bills. Over the previous year he had been supporting the moves of the Welsh Parliamentary Party, which had been campaigning for the establishment of a Secretary of State for Wales. Davies was strongly supported in his efforts by one of the former Lloyd George group members, Goronwy Owen. He included this in his Private Members Bill. Although the issue got some Parliamentary support from the other parties, the Prime Minister, Neville Chamberlain, showed no interest in the issue and would not meet Davies to discuss the issue further. The Bill failed on the 3rd December one to of lack of Parliamentary time.[149] Once more the establishment of a Welsh Secretary would have to wait for another day.

Even before Clement Davies' Bill had been rejected, however, there had been British Liberal endorsement for further Welsh devolution. At the 1937 Buxton (British) Liberal Assembly on the 28th of May 1937, a policy motion which called for 'a reasonable system of devolution, particularly for Scotland and Wales' had been endorsed. Recognising, however, that the national entity of Wales had hitherto received inadequate recognition, the Assembly urged the immediate appointment of a Secretary of State for Wales and the creation of Welsh Departments of State, as a min-imum acknowledgement of the national status of Wales. The government, as it would later on with Davies' Bill, ignored the motion. Despite this, two years later in May 1939, at Scarborough, the Liberal Assembly reaffirmed its support for 'the demand for a Secretary of State for Wales, and emphasised the importance of such an appoint-ment with regard to the Social Services in the Principality, and for dealing with the claim made by the people of Wales that Welsh shall be of equal status with English as an official language in all Courts of Law in Wales'. On the eve of another world war, however, this further plea for Welsh devolution would soon get lost in ensuing events. Yet all was not lost and, as we shall see shortly, the Liberal policy regarding the Welsh language in the courts would soon stand a chance of becoming reality.

Clement Davies had more positive results in the area of Welsh social issues dur-ing the late 1930s. He was one of the first MPs to raise the issue of rural poverty and, in 1938, he chaired the Welsh Committee of Enquiry into tuberculosis. Entitled the 'Clement Davies Report,' it was published in 1939 and was vivid in its portrayal of the squalid and unwholesome conditions that led to tuberculosis in Wales. The report was equally scathing with regard to Welsh local authorities for their neglect in combating tuberculosis. Sweeping changes were set to occur in Wales in tackling the disease, which were halted by the outbreak of war later in the year.[150] Nevertheless, Davies' enquiry led to the more successful treatment of tuberculosis in Wales through the establishment of widespread isolation hospitals.

Welsh Liberal at the Polls

Electorally, with differing varieties of Liberalism offered, which was confusing for the Liberal Associations and also the Welsh public, it was perhaps unsurprising that there were mixed results for the Welsh Liberals in the Westminster by-elections of this Parliament. In the only two by-elections they contested, in Llanelli (1936) and Pontypridd (1938), they gained between a third and forty per cent of the vote. Yet in these two horse races with Labour, as the Tories stood aside for them, the Liberals were still running a distant second to Labour. In Brecon and Radnor, the National Government MP, Ivor Grosvenor Guest, who was, in effect, a Liberal National was now elevated to the Lords upon the death of his father, Lord Wimborne. The Brecon and Radnor Liberal Association nominated E. Davies, a Cardiff solicitor, as their candidate. The Conservatives then claimed that there had been a gentlemen's agreement that the nomination would revert to them once Guest stood down and, therefore, named their own candidate Richard Phillips, the son of the Conservative peer, Lord Milford. The issue was then referred to both parties' co-ordinating committee which tied on party lines with five votes each. The Conservatives announced Phillips as the candidate and the Liberal Nationals backed down stating that they had to place the 'interests of the National Government higher than that of the party's'.[151] The by-election was eventually won by Labour. Thus the Brecon and Radnor Liberal Nationals lost the seat to the Liberals for the next 46 years by failing to stand firm. In other by-elections of the Parliament, Liberals of either faction failed to field candidates. This further indicated the weakened status of Liberalism in Wales.

In the local government the council elections during this period, Labour was still encroaching further on Liberal territory. The 1937 elections saw Labour win over a quarter of Denbighshire's council seats pushing Liberals out of coalition control; in South Wales the Liberals' fall was such that, outside the coastal urban councils, they had been reduced to a few isolated councillors on urban and rural district councils.[152] In other areas, such as in West Wales and parts of North Wales, however, the Liberals remained strong and retained a significant number of council seats, though not always overtly representing the party. In this respect the senior Liberal figure, Thomas Waterhouse, became the Chairman of Flintshire County Council in 1938 and many of Wales' rural counties still retained a strong Liberal presence in both their membership and in the chairing of committees. Elections, however, would soon be of minor importance to the Liberals, as a year later the Welsh nation, together with the rest of the British Empire, was plunged into a new world war. This meant that the general election scheduled for 1939 or 1940, at the latest, had to be suspended and a political truce was introduced this that meant that, for the duration of the war, the main political parties would not contest each other's seats should a parliamentary seat become vacant.

The Welsh Liberals during World War Two

Just as the First World War had impacted on the Liberals' views of the world, so the Second World War would also shape these generations of Welsh Liberal politicians. Some future Welsh Liberal MPs served in the conflict. Roderic Bowen served as a captain in the Army. Emlyn Hooson served in the Fleet Air Arm and Emrys Owain Roberts served as a staff officer with the rank of Squadron Leader with the RAF. Many future Welsh Liberal candidates also served in this conflict. In various ways the Second World War would shape the future generations of Welsh Liberals, just as the First World War had shaped the previous generation into a party of peace-supporting internationalists and pro-Europeans.

Welsh Liberal Wartime Activities

All the Liberal MPs in Wales played numerous roles in the war. Some roles were controversial most were not. Lloyd George, because of his meeting with Hitler in 1936, had gained the reputation of being an appeaser. In October 1939, he called for an international conference to prevent further conflict. This did not go down well with many Liberals, especially with the Liberal Nationals. Sir Henry Morris-Jones was particularly aggrieved with what Lloyd George had requested; he declared that he 'had done a great disservice to this country. Wales should be ashamed of the words he uttered'.[153] Similarly, the ideas behind the conference were widely dismissed. Lloyd George, however, was in reality no appeaser. The following year, in May 1940, both Lloyd George and Clement Davies played an important role in the replacement of the Prime Minister, Neville Chamberlain, with Winston Churchill.[154] Lloyd George's oratory in the chamber and Davies' political skills outside it helped bring about the necessary pressure that led to Chamberlain stepping down.

Because of the wartime truce, there was little electioneering or overt political point-scoring during the war. Most political activity was limited to promoting wartime morale, raising money for wartime causes and taking part in events in the House of Commons. Party business continued as normal to a degree and, with the exception of the years 1940 and 1944, Liberal Assemblies were held annually. Many agents and organisers were away at war or involved in wartime activities and consequently, Liberal Constituency Associations did not meet as often.[155] However, from time to time, there were meetings, which would be of great significance later on. The most notable perhaps was that held by the Montgomeryshire Association on the 8th of August 1942. Under the Chairmanship of Lord Davies, it took the constituency and the Liberal National MP, Clement Davies, back into the Liberal Party through re-affiliation. With this one step, the Welsh Liberals had regained an MP and the Liberal Party as a whole had gained a future leader.

Welsh Liberal Wartime Policy

In the 1930s, the Welsh Parliamentary Party, an amalgam of all Welsh MPs, had enabled some of Wales' Liberal MPs, of both Liberal and Liberal National parties, to pursue a Welsh agenda together. In 1941, the Liberal National MP, Henry Morris-Jones, was elected as the Chair of the Welsh Parliamentary Party. One of its successes under Morris-Jones was putting through lesgislation the Welsh Courts Act 1941, which recognised Welsh as equal in status to English in the legal system in Wales. This Act helped redress anti-Welsh language legislation which dated back to the Acts of Union.[156] Morris-Jones was helped by Lord Davies to get it through the Upper House. This legislation had fulfilled a policy commitment made at the 1939 Scarborough Liberal Assembly, which had committed the Liberals to enacting a Welsh Courts Act, as part of their support for the Welsh language. Thus, the first Act, of Parliament to support the equality of the Welsh language was originated by the Welsh Liberals.

The Welsh Liberals had been successful in their legislative support for the Welsh language, but what of political devolution? The earlier campaigns to get a Welsh Secretary had come to nothing though in November 1936 the Welsh Parliamentary Party had begun a new campaign for a Welsh Secretary. Clement Davies pursued this at Westminster a year later but once again to little effect.[157] This campaign continued to be supported by the Liberals during wartime and, in 1943, Thomas Waterhouse pushed through a motion at the local authorities' conference in Shrewsbury in support of a Secretary of State for Wales.[158] But it was wartime and this campaign once again proved fruitless. There was some success, however, in 1944 when Megan Lloyd George, as Chair of the Welsh Parliamentary Party, secured a 'Welsh Day' in the House of Commons. It was far from the Welsh parliament that the Welsh Liberals longed for but, it meant that in the future, for at least one day in the year, a parliament would debate Welsh issues.

The Wartime Government

Despite the 'Party Truce', the Liberal Party Organisation constantly reminded its remaining associations in 1940 that they were to continue to be active 'otherwise it would be impossible to resurrect them after the war'.[159] As we noted earlier, however, many Liberals had now been called up or were involved in other aspects of war work. The more prominent ones had also been called upon to serve in the wartime government. In 1940, when it looked like Chamberlain would be replaced, there were rumours that the former war-time Premier Lloyd George would be brought back as the next Prime Minister. In reality, he was now thought to be too old to lead the country.[160] Instead, he was invited by Churchill to be either Food Controller or Ambassador to Washington but he declined both roles, anticipating that a greater prize would come his way.[161] There was, however, still one Lloyd George in the government. Gwilym joined the government in June 1940 as an Under Secretary at the Ministry of Food. In doing so, he became the last Welsh Liberal MP to serve in a Westminster government. He was one of only six Liberal MPs to serve in the wartime government.[162] Gwilym later became the Minister of Fuel and Power in 1942 and served in this post for the rest of the war. Lord Wimborne, another prominent former Welsh Liberal MP (former MP for Brecon and Radnor) also served as an Under Secretary at the Air Ministry under the Liberal leader, Sir Archibald Sinclair. Wimborne also became the Liberal National Chief Whip in the Lords in 1944.

Apart from Gwilym and Wimborne's participation in the government, Welsh Liberal activity was limited to constituency issues, supporting the war-time coalition and general campaigning on war issues.[163] In July 1942, Captain Ernest

Evans (University of Wales) led a parliamentary revolt against Regulation 18b (imprisonment without trial). In the House of Commons, Evans gave a speech which *The Times* described as 'moderate and forceful' and the Labour Members who followed him described as 'extremely persuasive'.[164] Although some twenty-five MPs, mainly Liberals, supported Evans, his motion was defeated by a considerable margin.[165] On another occasion, in April 1943, Megan Lloyd George, along with other notable Liberals, signed a Liberal motion calling for the 'immediate and boldest measure of rescue to help save the Jews from Nazi massacres'.[166] Clearly, this motion had no impact on Nazi Germany but it illustrated the fact that Welsh Liberals were well aware of the outward manifestation of the Holocaust, two years before it was to become fully apparent to the world these Liberal voices were clearly to be heard condemning this atrolity.

Liberal Factions in Opposition

On several occasions during the war, discussion took place between the Liberal Party and the Liberal Nationals about uniting again. The main sticking point was that the Liberals wished to remain an independent party, whereas the Liberal Nationals wished to be an anti-socialist party working directly with the Conservatives. The Liberal Nationals' days in Wales were, however, numbered. Henry Morris-Jones briefly left the Liberal Nationals between 1942 and 1943 and Clement Davies left them for good during the war. This meant that only Swansea's Sir Lewis Jones stayed with the Liberal Nationals throughout the war years. The question whether all Liberal factions would reunite both in Wales and elsewhere was resolved on the 20th of November 1944. On this date, a letter was written by Sir Archibald Sinclair, leader of the Liberals, to Ernest Brown, Leader of the Liberal Nationals. The letter made it clear that, despite both Liberal groups having close ideological similarities, they differed substantially on the extent to which they would co-operate with other political parties. This issue of whether it was to be total independence, co-operation or collaboration proved to be insurmountable and, after this date, both sides ruled out formal co-operation between Liberals and Liberal Nationals.[167] Despite having worked closely together in Wales, the Liberals and Liberal Nationals would now take different paths. In the same year they decided to part company, the Caernarfonshire Liberal MP Goronwy Owen became the last North Wales Liberal MP to receive a knighthood. Although he was then unaware of it then, Owen would also lose his seat within the year and, therefore, also be the last Liberal knight to represent a North Wales seat.

Even before the break between the Liberals and the Liberal Nationals was fully cemented, there was plenty of Welsh Liberal criticism regarding the wartime coalition government. A number of Welsh Liberals wished to be more active in holding the government to account for wartime misadventures. To this effect, in 1941, two of the Welsh Liberal MPs, Clement Davies and Megan Lloyd George, joined the Radical Action Group (formerly known as the Liberal Action Group). Professor Gruffydd, the future Liberal MP for the University of Wales, also later joined this group. Part of the group's agenda was to place the Liberals back in opposition to the government, rather than to support 'cosy all-party coalition' that then existed. This would end the Parliamentary truce on by-elections and put the party in Wales back into campaigning mode.[168] Although it only numbered five Liberal MPs in total with a few other prominent Liberal figures in its membership, it brought together a number of Welsh Liberals as a 'radical' team, who in a few years would be working together as some of the few remaining post-war Liberal MPs in Britain.

The University of Wales By-election 1943 and Other By-elections

The Liberal MP for the University of Wales seat, Ernest Evans, had been appointed as a County Court Judge in 1943. This led to a by-election in January 1943. Professor William John (W. J.) Gruffydd emerged as the Liberal candidate. He had been Professor of Celtic Studies at University College Cardiff since 1918. Although five candidates stood in the election, the real battle was between two Welsh political heavyweights – Professor Gruffydd and Saunders Lewis. Lewis was a Welsh Nationalist hero, poet, writer and ex-President of Plaid Cymru. Professor Gruffydd had also been a prominent member of Plaid Cymru since its foundation but had resigned in 1939 from the party because of its pacifist stance on the war. He was an immensely respected literary and academic figure in Wales. The by-election campaign was active and on occasions heated. Both Saunders Lewis and Professor Gruffydd produced lists of eminent and not so eminent supporters to impress the University electorate and the press. Finally, the seat was won by Professor Gruffydd for the Liberals. Alun Talfan Davies, who would later be a prominent Welsh Liberal, also stood in this election as an Independent and came third.

University of Wales By-election 25–29 January 1943

Candidate	Party	Vote	Percentage
Professor William John Gruffydd	Lib	3,098	52.3
Saunders Lewis	PC	1,330	22.5
Alun Talfan Davies	Ind	755	12.8
Evan Davies	Ind Lab	634	10.7
Neville L Evans	Ind Lab	101	1.7
	Majority	1,768	29.8
	Turnout		53.4

The Death of David Lloyd George

On the 19th of January 1943, Lloyd George reached 80 years of age. Both Houses of Parliament gave him a luncheon to celebrate this milestone.[169] Two years later Lloyd George's life was drawing to a close. Even before his death, a by-election had been called for his Caernarfon Boroughs seat. This was due to his ennoblement as Earl Lloyd George of Dwyfor and Viscount Gwynedd in early 1945. Lloyd George died a short period after his ennoblement on the 26th of March 1945, ending once and for all his dominance over Liberal and Welsh Liberal politics, which had lasted for nearly half a century. He had been an MP for fifty-five years, the same length of service as another Liberal Prime Minister, William Gladstone, under whom he started his political career. Lloyd George was buried on the banks of the river Dwyfor within sight of Snowdon and the heart of the Caernarfon Boroughs seat which he had represented. Sir Winston Churchill, his political ally for the last forty years, described him as 'the greatest Welshman which that unconquerable nation has produced since the age of the Tudors'.[170]

While still grieving, the Welsh Liberals had the problem of a by-election in the closing months of the Second World War. Lloyd George's constant supporter, Frank Owen, recounted a story:

> One day in the House of Commons, during the Government of the Snores (1931–35), Baldwin had been lounging on the Front Bench, deeply immersed in a handbook and paying no attention to the debate. A colleague edged up to him to see what he was reading. It was Dod's Parliamentary Companion, which contained a detailed record of elections. 'I think', said the Prime Minister, reflectively, 'if the Old Man (Lloyd George) goes, we [the Conservatives] should stand a very good chance of winning Caernarfon Boroughs.[171]

This did not occur at the Caernarfon Boroughs by-election in which the London University Professor of Common Law, David Seabourne Davies, was the candidate. The former Aberystwyth University student had been Chair of the Welsh Young Liberals and ironically, in view of the seat he was now contesting, he had been a frequent critic of Lloyd George. Because of the wartime electoral truce, he successfully secured more than three-quarters of the vote over his Plaid Cymru opponent, with no Conservative or Labour opponents contesting this seat.

Caernarfon Boroughs By-election 26th April 1945

Candidate	Party	Vote	Percentage
Professor David Seabourne Davies	Lib	20,754	75.2
Professor J. E. Daniel	PC	6,844	24.8
	Turnout		58.8

Within a few days of the result Hitler was dead, Parliament was dissolved a few weeks later and a general election would wipe the Caernarfon Boroughs election result off the political map, with Professor Seabourne Davies having to resume his academic career once more, this time in Liverpool University. Never again would the Welsh Liberals gain such a resounding victory in North Wales.

Conclusion

The Liberal Party had started this chapter as the dominant political force in Wales, even though it was already suffering from the ills that would cause it much stress over the rest of the century. The First World War had left the party split between the Asquithians and the Lloyd Georgites and these splits were to continue on and off until the rift between the Liberals and the Liberal Nationals resulted in the party dividing for good. The electorate was often confused about what Liberalism stood for, as were the Liberals themselves, which in turn resulted in defections, moribund constituency associations, poor morale and, frequent defeats at the ballot box. During this period most of the wealthy industrialist Welsh Liberal MPs either died, retired, went into the Lords or even joined another political party. Thus, the days when the local Liberal MP not only represented people in the constituency but also employed a good number of them had passed into history.

Whilst the Liberals were experiencing internal problems that caused divisions, and the loss of its industrial MPs, the Labour Party was becoming the dominant political force for the majority of the Welsh population. The Liberals had lost the support of the working class in the south and by the general election of 1945 all vestiges of Parliamentary Liberalism had been driven out of South Wales. In the north, the party was weakened and lost seats but still managed to hold on to some of its former support. Only in Mid Wales, with the lack of real competition from the Conservatives and Labour, did the party feel relatively secure but even here the picture was no longer what it had once been.

The majority of radical young, politically ambitious men in Wales no longer saw the Liberals as the party that would give them a route into politics in the same way as their forebears had. Labour and the Conservatives now offered more direct routes into power. Those Welsh Liberals, who wished to remain loyal to the cause, had to focus on other professions, such as the Law, Education or the Church as a means for survival rather than politics. Others were able to pursue their Liberal ideologies through non-party pressure groups such as the international movements, just as some had in the 1930s when people had pursued the League of Nations Union causes.[172] A decreasing few, however, would continue to hold the Liberal banner high in Wales and remain as MPs and become part of an ever decreasing group that would soon find itself keeping the British Liberal Party alive.

Notes

1. Dutton, David (1992) Simon: A political biography of Sir John Simon, Aurum, p. 75
2. Dale, Iain (2000) Conservative Party: General Election Manifestos, 1900–1997, Routledge, p. 21
3. Dale, Iain (2000) Liberal Party: General Election Manifestos, 1900–1997, Routledge, pp. 36–37
4. Graham Jones, J. (2001) The Peacemonger: David Davies, Journal of Liberal Democrat History, Issue 29, Winter 2000–01, p. 18
5. Davies, D. Hywel (1983) The Welsh Nationalist Party, 1925–1945: A Call To Nation Hood, University of Wales Press, p. 20
6. Davies, D. Hywel (1983), op. cit., p. 21
7. Davies, D. Hywel (1983), op. cit., p. 21
8. Madgwick, P. J., Griffiths, Non and Walker, Valerie (1973) The Politics of Rural Wales: A Case Study on Cardiganshire, Hutchinson, p. 55
9. Jennifer Longford, Lloyd George's daughter to author
10. *The Manchester Guardian*, 09/02/22, p. 10
11. *The Manchester Guardian*, 01/04/22, p. 14
12. *The Western Telegraph*, 14/11/35, p. 2
13. Morgan, K. O. (1980) Wales In British Politics 1868–1922, University of Wales Press, p. 292
14. South Wales Daily Post 3/11/19
15. Owen, Frank (1954) Tempestuous Journey: Lloyd George His Life and Times, Hutchinson, p. 677
16. Dutton, David (2008) Liberals in Schism: A History of the National Liberal Party, Tauris Academic Studies, p. 13
17. Stead, Peter (1969) Vernon Hartshorn: Miner's Agent and Cabinet Member, p. 92

18. Morgan, K. O. (1973) op. cit., p. 304
19. Some information taken from Welsh Political Archive, National Library of Wales, also from Graham Jones, J. (2002B) op. cit.
20. Douglas, Roy (1971) op. cit., p. 149
21. Graham Jones, J. (2002B) 'Every vote for Llewelyn Williams is a vote against Lloyd George' Cardiganshire, 1921, Journal of Liberal Democrat History, Issue 37, Winter 2002/03, p. 9
22. Madgwick et al. (1973) op. cit. p. 47
23. Madgwick, P. J., et al. (1973) p. 47
24. Belzak, Steve, The life of Thomas Arthur Lewis MP', Conference Paper, British Liberal Political Studies Group, Birmingham Conference, 19–21st January 2007
25. *The Manchester Guardian*, 13/9/22, p. 8
26. The Asquithian Liberals did think of putting up their own candidate but failed to do so. *The Times*, 19/9/22; p. 5
27. *Western Mail* 19/4/34
28. *The Times*, 7/10/22 p. 10
29. Wrigley, Chris (1998) op. cit., p. 227
30. Jenkins, Roy (1964) Asquith, Collins, p. 497
31. Wilson, Trevor (1968) The Downfall of the Liberal Party 1914–1935, Collins, p. 226
32. 62 MPs in 1922 as opposed to 133 MP in 1918
33. Aberdare had been held by National Democratic and Labour Party which despite its name supported the coalition and fought against Labour in 1918. It is regarded therefore by historians such as C. P. Cook as a Liberal win
34. Jones, Sian (2003)) The Political Dynamics of North East Wales with special reference to the Liberal Party 1918–1935, Ph.D, University of Bangor, p. 63
35. Jones, Arthur Herbert (1987) op. cit., His Lordship's Obedient Servant, Gomer Press
36. Bentley, Michael (1977) op. cit., p. 88
37. Owen, Frank (1954) Tempestuous Journey: Lloyd George His Life and Times, Hutchinson, p. 665
38. Bolitho, Hector (1933) Alfred Mond First Lord Melchett, Martin Secker Ltd, p. 243
39. Douglas, Roy (1970) op. cit., pp. 170–171
40. Graham Jones, J. (2001) op. cit., p. 21
41. Owen, Frank (1954) op. cit., p. 675
42. Dutton, David (2008), op. cit., p. 13
43. Owen, Frank (1954) op. cit., p. 676
44. Morgan, K. O. (1980) op. cit.
45. Graham Jones, J. (1998) 'Sir Rhys Hopkin Morris' in the Dictionary of Liberal Biography (1998) Duncan Brack [ed] Politico's Publishing, p. 270
46. Cook, C. P. (1968) 'Wales and the General Election of 1923', Welsh History Review, Vol. 4, No. 2, p. 392
47. Cook, C. P. (1968) op. cit., p. 392
48. Bolitho, Hector (1933) Alfred Mond First Lord Melchett, p. 247
49. Cook, C. P. (1968) op. cit., p. 393
50. *Glamorgan Free Press*, 14 December 1923
51. Owen, Frank (1954) op. cit., p. 678
52. Owen, Frank (1954) op. cit., p. 678
53. Jenkins, Roy (1964) op. cit., p. 503
54. Owen, Frank (1954) op. cit., p. 678
55. Dale, Iain (2000) op. cit., pp. 44–48
56. Graham Jones, J. (1982A) Wales and 'The New Liberalism', 1926–1929, National Library of Wales Journal, Vol. XXII, p. 321
57. *Cambria Daily Leader*, 10 October 1924 cited in Graham Jones, J. (1982A) op. cit.
58. Runciman had previously been MP for Oldham 1899–1900 and Dewsbury 1902–18.
59. He was called Christmas Price Williams because he was born on Christmas Day 1881
60. Dutton, David (2008) The Glyndŵr Manuscripts: Denbighshire Record Office, Ruthin, Journal of Liberal History, Issue 61, Winter 2008–9, p. 22
61. Jones, Sian (2003) p. 127
62. Jones, Sian (2003) p. 131
63. William Albert Jenkins continued his political life in Swansea where he was elected onto the Borough Council in 1927 and served as Lord Mayor there from 1947–49. He was knighted in 1938.

64. Jones, Sian (2003) p. 127
65. Cited in Jones, Sian (2003) p. 129
66. *Pembrokeshire County Guardian*, 7/11/24
67. Jenkins, Roy (1964) op. cit., p. 505
68. Wilson, Trevor (1968) op. cit., p. 318
69. Madgewick et al. (1973) op. cit., p. 51
70. Jones, Mervyn (1991) A Radical Life: The Biography of Megan Lloyd George, Hutchinson, p. 71
71. It was called the Green Book not due to the 'environmental nature of 'green' but simply due to the fact that the book had a green cover. There was also a 'Brown Book' published by the Liberal Land Committee in 1925 on urban land entitled 'Towns and the Land'
72. Douglas, Roy (1971) op. cit., p. 192
73. Professor Thomas Arthur Levi (1874–1954) was a well respected and influential professor of English Law at Aberystwyth University. He was appointed to the University of Wales as professor at the age of just 27. Levi headed the Law faculty until he retired in 1940. Despite refusing on a number of occasions to be the candidate for the Liberals in Cardiganshire Levi was a strong supporter and campaigner for Liberalism starting off and encouraging many Welsh Liberal students including the future MPs Roderic Bowen, Emrys Roberts and Emlyn Hooson. Levi was himself a fierce campaigner against capital punishment. From 1922 onwards he was Honorary Permanent Chairman of the University College of Wales Liberal Society, a body of which, sadly no record now exists.
74. Madgewick, P. J., et al. (1973) p. 49
75. Emy, H. V. (1973) Liberals Radicals and Social Politics 1892–1914, Cambridge University Press, p. 280
76. Bolitho, Hector (1933) op. cit., p. 262
77. Jones, Sain (2003) op. cit., p. 139
78. It was around this time that Mond merged his company Brunner, Mond and Co together with a number of others to form Imperial Chemical Industries (ICI). The new company manufactured 5,000 products and the assets were worth over £100 million, and in its first year it made profits of £4.5 million. Mond was from German Jewish ancestry and was a Zionist and centrally involved in developments around the establishment of Palestine
79. *The Times* 27/6/28, p. 9
80. Morgan, K. O. (1973) p. 311
81. Dales, Iain (2000) op. cit., p. 51
82. Madgwick et al. (1973) p. 50
83. Jones, Mervyn (1991) op. cit., p. 78
84. Graham Jones, J. (1982A) op. cit., p. 335
85. Graham Jones, J. (1982B) op. cit., p. 178
86. *The Pembrokeshire County and West Wales Guardian* 3/5/29, p. 4
87. Dutton, David (2008) op. cit., p. 23
88. Brecon and Radnor became one of the closest three-way marginal seats in Welsh history with each of the three parties getting a third of the vote. Labour's Peter Freeman won with 14,511 votes 187 votes ahead of W. D'Arcy Hall (Conservative) with 14,324 and the Liberal E Wynne Cemlyn Jones with 14,182 votes
89. Graham Jones, J. (1982A) op. cit., p. 338
90. Crawshay was part of the famous ironmasters family that had been the driving force behind the industrialisation of Merthyr Tydfil and much of the surrounding South Wales valleys.
91. *The Pembrokeshire County and Western Telegraph* 7/6/29, p. 3
92. *The Pembrokeshire County and West Wales Guardian* 3/5/29, p. 3
93. Jones, Sian (2003) op. cit., p. 143
94. Morris-Jones, Henry (1955) Doctor in the Whips' Room, Robert Hale Limited, pp. 80–81
95. Graham Jones, J (1982) op. cit., p. 198
96. Cited in Jones, Sian (2003) op. cit., pp. 203–4
97. Jones, Sian (2003) op. cit., p. 207
98. Hooson, Emlyn (1999) Clement Davies: An Underestimated Welshman and Politician, Journal of Liberal Democrat History, Issue 24, Autumn 1999, p. 4
99. Cott, Nick (1999) Tory cuckoos in the Liberal nest?: The case of the Liberal Nationals: a re-evaluation, Journal of Liberal History, Winter 1999/2000, p. 29
100. Dutton, David (2008) op. cit., p. 44
101. Douglas, Roy (1971) op. cit., p. 213

102. Cott, Nick (1999) op. cit., p. 28
103. *Liverpool Daily Post* 15/10/31
104. Jones, Sian (2003) op. cit., p. 218
105. Cited in Jones, Sian (2003) op. cit., p. 218
106. Lord Beaverbrook was the Conservative supporting press baron who owned the *Daily Express* newspaper group
107. Cited in Jones, Sian (2003) op. cit., p. 218
108. Cook, Chris (1975) 'Liberals, Labour and Local Elections' in Gillian Cooke and Chris Cooke, The Politics of Reappraisal, Macmillan, pp. 170–171
109. *Manchester Guardian* 12/9/31
110. *Manchester Guardian* 14/9/31
111. Owen, Frank (1954) op. cit., p. 720
112. Goronwy Owen's two month tenure as Liberal Chief Whip made him the shortest serving Liberal Whip ever
113. Douglas, Roy (1971) op. cit., p. 219
114. Douglas, Roy (1971) op. cit., p. 221
115. Jones, Mervyn (1991) op. cit., p. 91
116. Morris-Jones, Henry (1955) op. cit., p. 94
117. Wyburn-Powell, Alun (2003) Clement Davies Liberal Leader, Politico's Publishing, pp. 50–51
118. Jones, Sian (2003) op. cit., p. 226
119. The Cardiff Liberal Association had collapsed at the end of the 1920s and it was not revived again until November 1933 under the chairmanship of D. T. Salathiel the Liberal Agent for Cardiff East and Cardiff South divisions, and was later chaired by Arthur Smith. *Western Mail* 16/11/33
120. Frank Owen wrote a biography of Lloyd George entitled 'Tempestuous Journey' published in 1954 and cited in this book
121. Douglas, Roy (1970) op. cit., p. 224
122. *Manchester Guardian* 18/4/32
123. Dutton, David (2008) op. cit., p. 25
124. Jones, Sian (2003) op. cit., p. 226
125. De Groot, Gerard J. (1993) Liberal Crusader: The Life of Sir Archibald Sinclair, New York University Press, p. 100
126. Cooke, Chris (1975) op. cit., p. 184
127. Letter from Lloyd George to Thomas Waterhouse, 23/1/33, National Library of Wales Political Archive
128. The Dictionary of Welsh Biography 1941–1970 (2001), The Honourable Society of Cymmrodorion, p. 278
129. Cook, Chris (2002) op. cit., p. 121
130. *Manchester Guardian* 20/1/33, p. 2
131. Jones, Sian (2003) op. cit., p. 232
132. Cook, Chris (2002) op. cit., p. 121
133. *The Western Telegraph* 14/11/35, p. 2
134. Douglas, Roy (1971) op. cit., p. 236
135. Jones, Sian (2003) op. cit., p. 231
136. Jones, Sian (2003) op. cit., p. 238
137. Wilson, Trevor (1968) op. cit., p. 411
138. *The Western Telegraph* 21/11/35
139. Douglas, Roy (1971) op. cit., p. 237
140. Madgwick, P. J. (1973) op. cit., p. 56
141. Madgwick, P. J. (1973) op. cit., p. 57
142. 10 per cent less than in 1931
143. Dutton, David (2008) op. cit., p. 24
144. Dutton, David (2008) op. cit., p. 26
145. *Western Mail*, 27/10/35
146. Morris-Jones, Henry (1955) op. cit., p. 103
147. This meant curing the problem of mass unemployment by direct state involvement in stimulating the economy through massive public works programmes.

148. Campbell, John (1975) 'The Renewal of Liberalism: Liberalism without Liberals' in Gillian Cooke and Chris Cooke, The Politics of Reappraisal, Macmillan p. 109
149. Wyburn-Powell, Alun (2003) op. cit., p. 62
150. Roberts, David (1976) opt. cit., p. 191
151. *The Times*, 24/7/39, p. 19
152. Jones, Sian (2003) op. cit., p. 286
153. McCormick, Donald (1963) op. cit., p. 282
154. Roberts, David (1976) op. cit., p. 208
155. Wyburn-Powell, Alun (2003) op. cit., p. 125
156. Morris-Jones, Henry (1955) op. cit., p. 125
157. Roberts, David (1976) op. cit., p. 189
158. The Dictionary of Welsh Biography 1941–1970 (2001), The Honourable Society of Cymmrodorion, p. 278
159. Liberal Party Organisation Bulletin No. 6 April 1940
160. Roberts, David (1976) op. cit., p. 209
161. Jennifer Longford to author
162. Samuel, Viscount (1945) Memoirs, The Cresset Press, p. 281
163. Liberal Party Organisation Bulletins during the wartime period constantly record the frustration of Liberal Associations not being able to stand candidates in by-elections because of the party truce
164. *The Times* 17/7/42
165. Liberal Party Organisation Bulletin No. 34 August 1942
166. Liberal Party Organisation Bulletin No. 41 April 1943
167. Watkins, Alan (1966) The Liberal Dilemma, MacGibben and Kee, p. 47
168. Wyburn-Powell, Alun (2003) op. cit., p. 127
169. Liberal Party Organisation Bulletin No. 38 January 1943
170. Thorpe, Jeremy (1999) In My Own Time, Politico's Publishing, p. 58
171. Owen, Frank (1954) op. cit., p. 721
172. Morgan, K. O. (1973) op. cit., p. 310

4

THE BRUSH WITH EXTINCTION
(1945–1959)

'I must guard myself carefully against any suggestion of uttering what are called blandishments to
the nine representatives of the Liberal Party, most of whom we see in their places under the guidance so generously provided by the Principality of Wales'.

Winston Churchill, House of Commons, 7 March 1950[1]

These comments by Winston Churchill[2] provide an indication of not just the decline
of the British Liberal Party but also the staying power of Liberalism in Wales. For
much of the period covered by this chapter, the Liberal Party in Wales represented
both the survival and future hopes of the wider Liberal Party in Britain. In the past,
Wales had supplied the Liberal leadership in the form of Sir William Harcourt and
David Lloyd George; now it would do so through Clement Davies. It would also
be Wales that now supplied the bulk of the Parliamentary Liberal representation up
until the late 1950s; and it was also this nation that offered the best prospects of new
Parliamentary gains. This meant, however, that in the late 1940s and 1950s these
Welsh Liberal MPs were so closely tied up with keeping the national party alive that
Welsh Liberalism and British Liberalism became almost indistinguishable. At the
same time, in Wales, much of the old world of Welsh Liberalism was rapidly fading.
The electoral lights were going out in the Welsh Liberal heartlands after more than a
century and would never again be re-lit.

It must also be said that the Liberal Party of Wales lacked a clear electoral or
ideological strategy after 1945. For much of the time, it struggled with its own survival. Labour, and the Conservatives' increasing dominance of the political scene,
brought the remaining Welsh Liberals' divisions over aims and values evermore to
the forefront. The party continued to produce manifestos at election time and have
meetings but its very existence often depended on the strength and drive of one or
two individuals. This was to be a period of the Welsh Liberal Party's struggle for
survival and its brush with the prospect of extinction.

Welsh Liberalism Enters the 'Nuclear Age'

The wartime coalition government had not been popular amongst a number of Welsh
Liberals. They felt controlled by the government. At the Liberal Assembly 1943, former MP for North Dorset, John (J. E.) Emlyn Jones, now a member of Cardiff East

Liberal Association had put forward a motion calling for the Liberal MPs to leave the National Government after the war 'because of its strong Conservative nature'.[3] Two years later this is what the Welsh Liberal MPs did, with the exception of Gwilym Lloyd George. The Welsh Liberals now felt free of the shackles of the collective responsibility of government and able to pursue their own agenda once more.

The 1945 July general election was held just one month before the Americans dropped their atomic bombs on Hiroshima and Nagasaki. As Wales was entering the nuclear age, the Liberal dominance of North-West Wales began to crack. It had been ten years since there had been a general election in Wales. The Liberals had kept a strong hold on North-West Wales during the 1935 election, even though they had been weakened or removed from elsewhere in Wales. They had held their own in the wartime by-elections but they had not been tested against any effective opposition. During the previous decade, David Lloyd George had died and his presence, which helped hold his own family group of four Welsh Liberals together, was gone. Within the time frame of the next two general elections, the remaining members of the group, Megan, Gwilym and Sir Goronwy Owen would all be defeated at the ballot box. For a short while, however, in 1945, the Welsh Liberals could still believe that they were a serious political party, at least in Wales. The July 1945 general election saw them take a fifth of all Welsh seats.

The 1945 July General Election

Liberal	7*
Labour	25
Conservative	3
National Liberal	1

* Gwilym Lloyd George gained his Pembroke seat as a Liberal candidate but in effect became a Conservative almost straight away, serving in their shadow cabinet.

The Welsh Liberals fielded candidates for under half of the parliamentary seats in Wales during the 1945 general election (17 out of 35). At the heart of Liberal policy nationally was the concept of abolishing 'Need and Want'. This concept of 'Social Security' for people, advocated by the Liberal MP, Sir William Beveridge, in his 1942 Report on Social Insurance, was key to this policy.[4] The Liberals' national manifesto also advocated devolution for Wales in the shape of a Welsh Parliament.[5] These were two policy areas that the party thought would appeal to both the working class and nationalist population of most of Wales. But would they even be noticed in a Britain that was fast becoming a two-party contest between Labour and Conservatives? For the Liberals, with David Lloyd George dead, other Liberal leaders were now needed in Wales to encourage voters to join the Liberal cause. They were sadly not forthcoming and the election saw only Beveridge, and the former leader Viscount Samuel, tour the North Wales constituencies to try to drum up support. The remaining Liberal MPs didn't stray too far from their own constituencies for fear of being squeezed out by Labour or the Conservatives.[6]

When the results came in, it was a landslide victory for the Labour Party and a virtual annihilation of Liberalism across much of Britain. *The South Wales Echo and Evening Express* headline on 26th July 1945 read:

Socialist Landslide: Eleven Ministers Defeated – Liberal Party Debacle

A host of famous and not-so-famous Conservative and Liberal MPs lost their seats, including future Conservative Prime Minister, Harold Macmillan, and Liberals, Sir William Beveridge and Sir Archibald Sinclair, the Liberal leader. Across Britain, the Liberals were routed. For the first time at a general election, there were no Liberal MPs elected in Scotland, the Midlands or the County of London. The Liberal candidate in Cardiff Central, Peter Morgan, who was only selected only the previous month, lost his deposit.[7] All he could say to console his supporters in his losing address was: 'I thank the Cardiff Central voters who stood for the Liberal faith, Cardiff and the country at large will still need Liberalism'.[8] His fellow Liberal candidate for Cardiff East, a former Liberal MP, Emlyn-Jones also lost his deposit but was clearer about why he had done so. In his losing address he stated:

'It seems evident that the determination to evict the representatives of the coalition government found expression in the Socialist vote and the electors choose between the Tories and the Socialists, leaving the Liberals high and dry between them'.[9]

In Wales, the Liberal result was bad but not as bad as elsewhere. They secured 14.9 per cent of the Welsh vote against a UK average of 9 per cent and won seven seats. Although this represented the worst Liberal performance in Wales ever, it still meant that the Welsh party represented more than half of the UK party's total seats, which were now just 12. There were Liberal losses in Wales too. Caernarfonshire and Caernarfon Boroughs were lost. Sir Goronwy Owen lost to Labour's Goronwy Roberts by some 6,406 votes (16 %). David Seabourne Davies, who had won the Caernarfon Boroughs by-election just months before, was this time in a four party competition. The addition of both Labour and the Conservatives to the contest resulted in his vote dropping by almost half. It was Plaid Cymru's presence in the seat, however, which was felt to have deprived Seabourne Davies of ultimate victory. Although they gained only 1,560 votes, this was more than four times the eventual majority in the seat. Seabourne Davies lost the seat by 336 votes to the Conservative Lieutenant Colonel David Algernon Price-White and with it the Lloyd George Liberal heritage that belonged to it. A short while later, a young Emlyn Hooson, later Liberal MP for Montgomeryshire, was selected to contest the seat at the next general election. By the next general election, however, the Caernarfon Boroughs seat was scrapped and Hooson would fight part of its successor seat, Conwy.

The 1945 general election was not all doom and gloom for the Welsh Liberals. In Carmarthen, David Lloyd George's old political Liberal foe Rhys Hopkin Morris came back from his post as the first BBC Regional Director for Wales to win the seat from Labour. With local Liberal stalwart P. W. Trefor Thomas as his agent, Hopkin Morris won partly by the sheer force of his personality. He was helped by the fact that previous Labour member, Ronw Moelwyn Hughes, himself a former Welsh

Liberal, was not regarded as very impressive by his constituents.[10] It was one of only three Labour losses in the 1945 general election and ensured that West Wales (Pembrokeshire, Carmarthenshire and Cardiganshire) became the most notable example of concentrated Liberal presence in Britain. Hopkin Morris had a 1,279 majority (3.4 %) over Labour. He was helped by the fact that the Conservatives did not contest the seat and, therefore, it was a two horse race between the Liberals and Labour. The same was true for:

1. Roderic Bowen, newly elected in Cardigan, where he gained a 9,194 majority (27.6%). Bowen had been chosen as a late candidate when the sitting Liberal MP, David Owen Evans, had died shortly before the election. Bowen was described by the *Daily Herald* as 'a plump Welshman with a polished manner'. He had been chosen in preference to the other Liberal contenders, including Liberal grandee Sir Ifan ab Owen Edwards, Alun Talfan Davies and John Morgan Davies.[11]
2. Megan Lloyd George in Ynys Môn where she gained a 1,081 majority (4.4%)
3. Gwilym Lloyd George in Pembroke where he gained the seat with a small 168 majority (0.4%) over Labour. This now became the most marginal seat in Wales and a key Labour target for the next election. Gwilym had stood as a 'Liberal candidate supporting the National Government', which set him apart from the other Welsh Liberals who did not support the National Government.

The Labour Party had not contested two other winning Liberal seats but either the Conservatives or Plaid Cymru had. These contests were:

1. Clement Davies in Montgomeryshire, who gained a 3,123 majority (12.6%) over the Conservatives
2. Professor W. J. Gruffydd, who gained a 3,543 majority (51%) over Plaid Cymru's female candidate Dr Gwenan Jones.[12] The strength of Liberalism in the University of Wales postgraduate community and Professor Gruffydd's own personal reputation within the University ensured he had a healthy majority.[13]

Only in Meirionnydd did Emrys Roberts face a full slate of opposition candidates. Here the barrister, just demobbed from the RAF at the age of 35, successfully won the seat with a small 114 votes (0.4%) majority over Labour. His Liberal predecessor Sir Henry Haydn Jones had just stood down after holding the seat for some 35 years. Jones was on the right of the party. Roberts, however, was the son of a Caernarfon shopkeeper who had been devoted to Lloyd George. In turn, Roberts had become a 'Radical Liberal' who could, he felt, also have stood for Labour. His closeness to Labour ideals and the Lloyd George tradition made him Megan's closest Liberal soulmate in the following Parliament.[14] Roberts' narrow margin of victory meant that the 1945 general election left four of the seven Welsh Liberal MPs (both Lloyd Georges, Hopkin Morris and Emrys Roberts) with very small Parliamentary majorities.

With the exception of the Lloyd Georges and Professor Gruffydd, the four Liberal MPs elected were all barristers at law. The Welsh Liberal barrister MPs were as prominent in the Welsh party now as they had always been and would remain at its heart until the end of the century. Despite their differing professions, one factor that united all of the MPs was the fact that they were all Welsh speakers; something that was essential to keep their seats in Welsh-speaking Wales.

The Evolution of the Welsh Political Order

The Welsh electorate was becoming increasingly reluctant to vote Liberal in anywhere near the numbers needed for a Liberal revival. A 'Mass Observation Report' of June 1945 had shown that while there was general goodwill towards the Liberals in Britain, it was felt that a vote for them was a wasted vote and the main objective of the election was to defeat the Conservatives.[15] In Wales, the voters mainly saw the battle as being between the forces of socialism and conservatism. Over half of the electorate in Wales (58%) consequently voted in Labour MPs to represent 70 per cent of Welsh constituencies. They rewarded the Conservatives with just 17 per cent of the vote and 8 per cent of the seats. The results were repeated in the November council elections in which Communist council candidates were now more common than Liberal ones, with no Liberal candidates to be found at all on the majority of Welsh councils.[16] To be 'up and coming' politically in the Welsh Westminster and council politics theatre, now more than ever meant supporting Labour. Yet not every politician saw Labour as their future. The National Liberal in Denbigh, Henry Morris-Jones, whose party gained 13 seats across Britain in this election, was quite happy to collaborate with the Conservatives. As was Gwilym Lloyd George, whose move to the political right, as outlined earlier, came as a bitter blow to the Welsh Liberals.

Gwilym Lloyd George Leaves the Liberal Fold

In 1938 his father had predicted that 'Gwilym will go to the right'.[17] He had stood in July 1945 as a Liberal appealing to both Liberal and Conservative voters but had not left the wartime coalition government like his fellow Liberal and Labour MPs. His 1945 election posters had read 'Vote for Gwilym Lloyd George. Vote for Churchill'.[18] In the election Gwilym had sold himself to the electorate as 'an Independent Liberal who is answerable only to his county association'.[19] Within Pembrokeshire there had been continued concern expressed by the Liberal Association over his support for the National Government, which came into conflict with Liberal colleagues' views. However, this criticism became muted. The fact that he remained the anti-Socialist candidate best capable of defeating Labour was, as far as both the Liberals and the Conservatives in the seat were concerned, his most important asset.[20]

Gwilym continued to receive copies of the Liberal Whip until 1946 but he never again attended a Liberal parliamentary meeting.[21] He continued to use the label of 'Liberal' until his defeat in 1950, but he refused to become either Chairman of the Liberal MPs or Chairman of the Liberal National Party. In 1946, after having voted more often with the Conservatives than with the Liberals in the Commons, he had the Liberal Whip withdrawn. In his public speeches, Gwilym insisted that no major issue divided the Liberals from the Conservatives and that both parties were united in their opposition to Socialism.[22] This view was held only by his fellow National Liberals and not by Liberals MPs. The loss of the 'Lloyd George' name to the Conservatives' fold, although Gwilym's own name was now hyphenated, was a depressing sign of things to come. By the next general election, the Liberal Party of Wales would publicly declare that Gwilym was no longer a candidate that the Liberals should support.[23] Yet Gwilym continued to claim that he was a Liberal and no Liberal stood against him to disprove this. At his adoption meeting in June 1945, he stated 'I have been in the National Government for five years. I entered it without hesitation, and if I may say so my Liberalism has not been weakened one little bit since I entered'.[24]

Alderman George Howells, who was the chairman of the Pembrokeshire Liberal Association, backed him as the Liberal candidate. The Liberal activists of Pembrokeshire similarly supported Gwilym. In November 1947, the Pembrokeshire Liberal Association indicated that it would 'welcome help from any quarter in the fight for our liberties'.[25] The result was an 'official parley' with Conservatives, which was in direct opposition to the chair of the Liberal Party of Wales, J.E. Emlyn-Jones. Despite gaining the support of both the Conservatives and the Liberals, Gwilym was seen by some elements of the Welsh press as being one of the former Coalition government ministers most likely to lose his seat at the next election.[26] In February 1950, it was, therefore, the Liberal voters he once again appealed to for victory in the seat, declaring 'I have been brought up in the Liberal tradition, and I can say, without fear of contradiction, that I have never let the Liberals down'.[27] No Liberal MP, including his own sister, Megan, would have agreed with this statement. Once more he received the backing of the Pembrokeshire Liberal Association, but this time the Liberal supporters within it were no longer united in their support of Gwilym. A number had started to favour the Labour cause and the enthusiasm of the Liberals to campaign for the re-election of the now clearly Conservative Gwilym was now waning. Gwilym would shortly lose the seat, abandon Wales and head for a safer English Conservative seat in Newcastle Upon Tyne.

The Liberal Seed Box – University of Wales College, Aberystwyth

The University of Wales College, Aberystwyth, had, in part, been formed mainly as a result of Liberal paternalism. The university was in Cardiganshire, which was one of the strongest Liberal seats in Britain. Both Liberal MPs Stuart Rendal and David Davies had done much to provide the university with buildings and resources. It had also produced Liberal MPs, such as Professor David Seabourne Davies, the last Liberal MP for Caernarfon Boroughs (Lloyd George's former seat). In the 1940s, many of the professors and lecturers at Aberystwyth were known to be broadly Liberal. The legal expert Professor Llwelfryn Davies was a well-known Cardiganshire Liberal. Another prominent member of the Welsh Liberal Party there was Professor Thomas Levi, Head of the Law department and a very active campaigner. He had inspired a number of Liberals to stand successfully as candidates, including Roderic Bowen and Emrys Roberts.[28]

It was only in 1947, however, that a Liberal society was set up in the university. Emlyn Hooson, who was returning from his National Service, decided to set up a Liberal Party Society in the College. There already existed Socialist, Communist and

Welsh Nationalist Societies but until then there was no Liberal Society. Professor Levi became the honorary Life President and Professor Llwelfryn Davies its President. An undergraduate law student, Emlyn Hooson, took on the role of chair. Apart from organising speakers and discussions, the Liberal Society's greatest achievement became its production of a magazine titled *The New Radical.*

In October 1947, for the price of one shilling, the first edition of *The New Radical* was published. Emlyn Hooson was the main ideas man with Dewi C. Jones and Elwyn Thomas as the organisers. In the magazine there were messages of support from Phillip Fothergill, Chairman of the Liberal Executive and Frank Byers MP, the Liberal Chief Whip. In Welsh, there were also messages from MPs Professor Gruffydd and Emrys Roberts. The magazine tackled the issues of policy, defining Liberalism in a Welsh context and illustrating its pro-European credentials.

The enthusiasm behind *The New Radical* showed how the Liberals, who had seen little sign of resurgence, were delighted at the publication. The Aberystwyth Liberals swiftly received postal orders for 50 copies each for Alderman Sir George Hamer (Hooson's future father-in-law) in Montgomeryshire, Alderman David Tudor in Meirionnyddshire and Alderman Emyr Thomas in Caernarfonshire. Clement Davies was also soon communicating with them. *The New Radical's* appearance soon attracted the attention of other Liberals in other universities. Glyn Tegai Hughes, for instance, a leading Young Liberal, contacted Hooson from Cambridge, was keen to get involved. Over the coming half-century, the Liberals from Aberystwyth would continue to play a prominent role in the Welsh party, with many contesting and sometimes winning Parliamentary seats.

Clement Davies Becomes the Liberal Party Leader

Sir Archibald Sinclair, the leader in the House of Commons, had been marginally defeated in his Caithness and Sutherland seat. Although he was expected to return to the House soon, in a by-election, a temporary leader was needed. By far the most important of the new Welsh Liberals in the immediate post-war period was the new House of Commons Liberal leader, Clement Davies. His leadership of the Liberal Party was meant to be only temporary. Davies had returned to the Liberal fold a few years before; prior to this he had been an independent Liberal for a year and as a younger man, he had spent ten years as a National Liberal. Such a pedigree meant that he did not enjoy universal trust within the party as a whole. Before Davies' appointment, the longer serving Welsh Liberals MPs had also been closely involved in the problems of national leadership selection. The Liberal Chief Whip, Sir Percy Harris, first approached Gwilym Lloyd George. He had refused, stating that he could not afford the incidental costs that went with the office. Rhys Hopkin Morris similarly refused to allow his name to go forward as Chairman. Clement Davies was then offered the position and took it on a temporary basis.[29] Davies was chosen because he was seen as experienced in politics and a compromise candidate between the struggle for left and right within the party. He was, however, not an elected leader but given the title of Chairman of the Parliamentary Party and was meant to hold the office only for that Parliamentary session. Sinclair remained the leader of the party outside the House. With the passing of time and Sinclair's failure to be re-elected at the general election in 1950, Davies became fully accepted as the Leader of the Liberals both inside and outside Westminster but would never be elected into that post by his fellow MPs.[30]

A Party in Search of a Policy Identity

With the exception of the Liberals' united views on the need for a wider European political federation and the importance of the welfare state, there was little policy direction throughout Wales and outside it from their MPs and leaders. Commentators at the time considered the Welsh Liberals to be generally more favourable to the new Attlee government than their counterparts elsewhere. Clement Davies had generously endorsed the Labour government in his first speech as leader when he said: 'We can all rejoice at the end of the Tory regime, at the end of reaction and chaos ... we wish this government well'.[31]

The Welsh Liberals, nonetheless, did not consistently support either the government or the opposition. In December 1945, Gruffydd and Hopkin Morris failed to back the government against an opposition censure motion. The following year, when the Welsh Liberals voted against the Labour Party's Transport Bill aimed at the nationalisation of transportation, Megan Lloyd George was the sole Liberal to vote for it.[32] It was hard to pin down the ideology of the Welsh Liberals. As a result, there was some speculation over how long the party would hold together. Gwilym had, in effect, left the party in 1945, but what about Megan? The senior Welsh Labour nationalist, Huw T. Edwards, described her as 'the only ... radical left in the Liberal Party' and appealed to her to join Labour in October 1948.[33] Almost a year before, at the start of December 1947, the *Evening Standard* U.K. published a story airing a Westminster rumour that Megan would soon join Labour. Another paper shortly afterwards stated that Hopkin Morris had reached an agreement with the Conservatives. Both reports were denied, but it illustrated the extent to which it was difficult to clearly identify Welsh Liberal ideology; something that resulted in W. J. Gruffydd declaring 'I was elected to the House as a Liberal, which means, as things are at present that I can be eclectic in my politics'.[34]

The Welsh MPs did not always know which side they would support on policy issues but they did know that they supported Welsh devolution. In July 1946, the six Welsh Liberal MPs sponsored an amendment to the National Health Services Bill that would transfer to Wales the administration of its own hospitals and specialist units. This was blocked by Welsh Labour MPs.[35] Megan Lloyd George continued to support the Parliament for Wales Campaign along with Women's Rights – two Liberal policy areas that were still more radical than Labour's.[36] Megan spoke at Liberal Assemblies and further afield throughout the 1940s in support of these two causes. In 1947 and 1949, she ensured that motions supporting a Welsh Parliament were passed at Liberal Assemblies.[37] She condemned the Labour Government's setting up of a consultative Council for Wales instead of a Welsh Secretary or Welsh Parliament as 'the fobbing off the Welsh people with a scraggy bone without meat or marrow in it ... a half-hearted concession to Welsh public opinion'.[38] This was seen as the first 'firing shot' in the development of the Parliament for Wales Campaign.

Welsh devolution was a frequent conference policy item in both the Welsh and the national party. At the 1947 Bournemouth Assembly, the Solihull Liberal Division in Birmingham put forward an amendment regarding a future Welsh Parliament. It sought to remove devolved power to a future Welsh Parliament for trade, commerce and industry. It called for these to be given to a 'Welsh Office' instead. This enraged the Welsh Liberals and the Rev. J. Herbert Jones from Abergele stated the case for Wales on behalf of the Party Executive. He was backed by numerous Welsh representatives including J. Walter Jones and Emlyn Jones from Cardiff. Martin Rees, secretary of the Meirionnydd Liberals Association, wrote to the chairman of the Liberal Party in London and stated that if the motion was passed it would 'without a doubt be serious blow to Liberalism in Wales. It would gravely damage the prospects of the Liberal Party in rallying its forces in the North and South of Wales'.[39]

The strength of their argument and passion for a Welsh Parliament with full powers was so great that in the end only the mover and the seconder of the Solihull amendment voted for it.[40] Devolution, an issue on which they were always united on with varying degrees of enthusiasm, would now remain at the heart of Welsh Liberal policy.

The Liberals were aware that failure to be active on the devolution front would move more support to Plaid Cymru. J. Walter Jones of the Neath Liberal Association pointed out that in his view in 'at least five constituencies', there was a danger that the Nationalists might wreck Liberal representation in North Wales'.[41] On New Year's Eve 1949, the Liberal Party started actively supporting the Parliament for Wales Campaign.[42] From the outset, there was concern amongst the Liberals that Plaid Cymru and Labour would steal the credit for the Parliament for Wales Campaign. One member of the Meirionnydd Liberal Party wrote to Emrys Roberts: 'It will be difficult to get Meirionnydd's Liberals to wholeheartedly back the campaign, but it should be made clear that it is not the 'Blaidd's' campaign, but a Liberal one'.[43]

The policy of the wider Liberal Party continued to veer between left and right, although it was mostly felt by members and observers to be on the right. The Liberal Party had not been formed as a middle way between Conservatism and Socialism. It had been formed as an alternative to the Conservatives. Yet Socialism was now seen as fulfilling this role. Therefore, for both those inside and outside the party, Liberalism was coming to represent the middle ground between Socialism and Conservatism. In this respect it still had its own policy agenda. The Liberals remained strongly part of the Free Trade and the United Europe movement. Post-war there was still a strong desire within the party to put 'great store upon the uniqueness of the individual, upon the value of personality, upon the private conscience and the private judgement'.[44] These commitments were supported by the Welsh Liberals who made up the bulk of the Parliamentary Party. Emrys Roberts led a campaign within and outside the party to reject the continuance of conscription during peacetime. He and most of the Parliamentary Party viewed peacetime conscription as a 'violation of individual liberty'. At the 1947 Liberal Assembly, Roberts sought to prevent the wider party from endorsing the continuance of conscription. Despite an impassioned speech, the Liberal Conference overruled the views of the majority of the Liberal Parliamentary Party and endorsed conscription.[45]

The Welsh Liberal Nationals Leave the Liberal Fold Forever

In May 1947, Lord Woolton, the chairman of the Conservatives, arrived at an agreement with Lord Teviot of the Liberal Nationals. The Liberal Nationals changed their name to 'The National Liberals' in 1948.[46] This was done for two reasons. Firstly there was no longer a national government for the Liberal Nationals to be part of, so it was felt that a new name was needed. The second reason was that it was now felt safe to use the terms 'National Liberals', which had in 1931 been seen to be too close to the Lloyd George Coalition Liberals of the 1918–22 coalition government.[47] They had also used the term, 'National Liberal'. This move paved the way for the merger of the two parties. In some Welsh constituencies, such as 'Pembrokeshire, the process of merging the two parties was already occurring in practice, if not in name. Although the National Liberals did not finish as a separate political party until twenty years later, 1948 marked their effective end and with it the realisation that they would never again return to their Liberal roots. The fact that the Liberal Nationals were no longer seen by the Conservatives as equal partners hastened their demise. Mergers were forced by the Conservatives in most constituencies, often excluding entirely the local Liberal presence. This Liberal National-Conservative combination caused mass confusion over who were the 'Liberals'; was it the Welsh Liberal Party or the Liberal Nationals and Conservative candidates? In Wales, it was in only Denbigh, Pembroke, Wrexham and some constituencies in and around Swansea, however, that the National Liberal and Conservative candidates stood in the 1950 general election. In seats where Liberal National Associations were still active, they were finally assimilated by the Conservative Association in the mid 1950s.

The problem over the use of the Liberal name would remain a thorn in the Liberal Party's side for decades. Despite pleas from the Liberals to the Conservatives and a letter from Clement Davies to Churchill threatening legal action, the practice of Conservatives using the 'Liberal National' name persisted. The Conservatives and Churchill insisted that the names would not change for a number of reasons. Among the foremost of these was that there were more National Liberals in Westminster than Liberals.[48]

The Welsh Liberal Party Wobbles

In 1946, after a lapse of ten years, the post of Welsh Liberal Agent and Secretary was filled once again by a long term Liberal activist Hywel Rhys. Rhys set about trying to re-establish a number of now derelict Liberal Associations across Wales. The Chairman of the Liberal Party of Wales, Major Parry Brown, from Newport helped him in this task. Whilst attempts were being made to revitalise the Welsh party, Churchill, via Lady Rhys Williams, had asked the Liberals to form a pact with the Conservatives in September 1947. On the 27th of October 1947, the Liberals in Westminster considered and rejected it. The Welsh 'radicals', in the shape of Megan Lloyd George and Emrys Roberts who wanted the party to remain anti-Tory, rejected it out of hand. Even Clement Davies who had moved the party to the right saw little virtue in it and thus it was totally rejected.[49]

The constant pressures between left and right within the party, however, meant that in 1948 an attempt was made by some of the radical left MPs to replace Davies as leader by Megan. Davies, however, refused to resign and the other MPs did not push the issue further. As a result, however, in January of 1949, Megan was appointed Deputy Leader.[50] This was a position that had not existed in the Liberal Party since 1929. Publicly, it was stated that the appointment had been to help an overworked Davies with his heavy duties. Privately, it was seen as appeasement to Megan's supporters and a way of keeping both Megan and her supporters within the party's folds.[51] At the Liberals' London Assembly in 1950, with Megan's blessing, the Welsh party then flexed its devolutionary credentials once more. There was a joint motion proposed by Major Parry Brown and Dr L. T. M. Gray, the Chairman of Scottish Liberal Party, supporting Parliaments for both nations plus the appointment of a Secretary of State for Wales, as an interim measure. The motion was soundly endorsed. After the vote, Parry Brown declared to *The Manchester Guardian*'s reporter that it was the Liberals who were leading the calls for devolution and it was they who would call together all political and non political organisations in Wales after the general election to form a convention on Welsh devolution.[52]

Devolution would also prove to be a strategic electoral issue when the 1945 Parliament drew to an end in 1950. Clement Attlee called an election in the February of that year. To consolidate their position in North Wales, the Liberals stated that they would not oppose Labour candidates who supported the 'Parliament for Wales Campaign'. This was, however on the condition that, they would allow the Liberals a free run elsewhere.[53] The proposal was ignored, as Labour's London headquarters opposed deals and had its mind set on taking three Liberal seats (Meirionnydd, Pembroke and Ynys Môn). At the same time, both Hopkin Morris and Roderic Bowen avoided openly endorsing the campaign, which led to accusations that the Liberal Party's support for devolution was sometimes 'anaemic'.[54]

The 1950 General Election

Liberal	5
Labour	27
Conservative	3
National Liberal	1

The Liberal grandee, Lady Violet Bonham Carter, stated in 1946 that one of the main reasons for Liberal voters not supporting the party in sufficient numbers was that they did not field enough candidates to form a government. This idea was accepted by Clement Davies and there was a tremendous effort by him to increase greatly the number of Liberal candidates at the next general election.[55] This broad front strategy resulted in some 475 candidates being put up. There would be enough candidates, if all were elected, to form a government. In Wales, however, they only managed to put up 21 candidates in the 36 seats. This was just two more than in 1945.

Clement Davies led the election under the slogan 'The Liberals Can Win' and 'At last you can have a Liberal Government'.[56] In Wales, the message seemed farcical when the party had failed to field candidates in fifteen Welsh constituencies. Even the Liberal candidates' own supporters often also saw the contest as being between only Labour or Conservative candidates: as in 1945, the Liberals were seen as a relic of the past. In the 1950 campaign, the Labour Party ignored the Liberal presence entirely and insisted that the only contest was that between Labour and the Conservatives. Churchill, on the other hand, sought to both recognise and solicit Liberal votes, emphasising the Liberal values of individual liberty in the current Conservative Party.

The Welsh Liberal campaign material was distinct from that in England. As expected, it sought to be Welsh. The election leaflets often produced in constituencies made great use of the Welsh Dragon.[57] Although the Welsh Liberals now boasted the biggest names in the British party, Megan Lloyd George and Clement Davies spent much of the election ensuring that their own seats were secure rather than trying to win seats elsewhere. Despite her leanings towards Labour, Megan Lloyd George still refused to endorse Labour candidates in seats in which they were unopposed by a Liberal candidate in Wales and elsewhere.[58] Around the same time that Megan was becoming closer to Labour, her family's Liberal rival was becoming closer to the Conservatives. Violet Bonham Carter (Baroness Asquith – 'Lady Vi') was not only unopposed by the Conservatives but was also publicly endorsed in Colne Valley by Sir Winston Churchill. There was, however, no use of the so-called Huddersfield formula in Wales, whereby the Conservatives stood down in favour of the Liberals in order to let them have a clear contest with Labour. In some seats, such as in Carmarthen, the Conservatives tactically decided to step down in order to avoid splitting the anti-Labour vote, however.

When all of the general election votes were counted, it became apparent that only nine Liberals had been elected in Britain. Five of these came from Wales. The abolition of the University of Wales' seat by the Electoral Reform Act 1948 had removed Professor W. J. Gruffydd. He was unwilling to seek another seat and retired from the House of Commons, thus depriving the Welsh party of one of its greatest Welsh intellects.[59] There was another defeat; Gwilym Lloyd George (now a Liberal National and Conservative) lost his seat by just 129 votes. In Pembrokeshire, a joint Lib-Con pact had been formed for the re-election of the now National Liberal and Conservative Gwilym. The Labour Party had come to regard Pembrokeshire as one of its most likely successes in 1950 and brought the political heavyweights of Clement Attlee and Aneurin Bevan into the seat to campaign for Desmond Donnelly. He won the seat for Labour, but ironically some two decades later, was himself expelled from the Labour Party and joined the Conservatives.[60] In Pembrokeshire, however, the Liberals had now been banished forever. Although they continued to score up to 26 per cent of the vote in the Pembroke seat (in 1987), they were never again to be serious challengers there.

All sitting Welsh Liberal MPs – with the exception of Rhys Hopkin Morris (Carmarthen) – now had three-way contests, and, in the case of Meirionnydd, a four-way political competition. Yet they all survived, albeit in some of Wales' most marginal seats.[61] Despite the fact that her seat was also contested, this time by a Tory, John Owen Jones, Megan Lloyd George still appeared to enjoy considerable support and was endorsed by Anglesey's newspaper, *The Holyhead Mail*.[62] During the election campaign, she benefited from a high political profile and national media coverage in the form of a 6.15 p.m. party political broadcast on Friday, 10th February 1950. This was one of the four party political broadcasts given by the Liberals.[63] Megan ended the broadcast by stating in Welsh 'Nos da, Hunan Llywodraeth I

Gymru' which meant 'Goodnight – Self Government for Wales'. This meant little to English listeners but a lot to her Welsh speaking constituents on Anglesey (Ynys Môn).

Roderic Bowen, in his 1950 adoption meeting, appealed to the vanity of his Cardiganshire Liberal supporters. He stated, 'They' were of the highest character, and provided the majority of public leaders in Cardiganshire'.[64] To this was added his Liberal virtues of being clearly against nationalisation, which of course included the nationalisation of farming land. In a rural county such as Cardiganshire, and Clement Davies' neighbouring Montgomeryshire, this appeal to the farmers to prevent the state from taking over their farms had strong merit and voting appeal. Bowen and Davies subsequently won their seats with over half of the vote and enjoyed majorities of around 25 per cent over their opponents. These were the only two seats in the United Kingdom in which the Liberals secured an absolute majority in a three-cornered fight.[65] Emrys Roberts had one of the toughest fights in Meirionnydd where he gained just 38.8 per cent of the vote in a four-way contest that included Gwynfor Evans standing in the seat once again for Plaid Cymru. To add to his problems, his Liberal predecessor in the seat, Sir Henry Hadyn Jones, had fallen out with Roberts' left-leaning Liberal views and signed the nomination papers of his Conservative opponent, and was now openly backing him. Despite these challenges, Roberts improved on his narrow 1945 win and increased his 0.4 per cent majority to 4.2 per cent. At the same time Rhys Hopkin Morris appealed directly for the Carmarthenshire voters to compare present day Socialism with the Liberal Radicalism of the past:[66]

'Can anyone imagine the old stalwart Radicals voting for conscription in peace time? Can anyone imagine the old stalwart Radicals voting for the Supplies and Services Act of 1947 (nationalism) … Socialism is, in fact the very denial of Liberalism, which has ever stood out so boldly for liberty, freedom and fair play'.

Hopkin Morris' appeal had a mixed result. He kept the seat but saw his majority of 1279 votes over Labour slip to just 187 votes, becoming, after Pembroke, the second most marginal seat in Wales.

The Liberals contested 21 seats in Wales. Where there were gaps, there was the inevitable problem of whom Liberal supporters should vote for. Sometimes this resulted in the party making an extra effort to bring a candidate in. In Brecon and Radnor, for instance, the local party refused to put up a candidate, which meant that the then Liberal Peer but soon to be Conservative Peer, Lord Rennell, urged all Liberals here to vote Conservative. Clement Davies, who saw this embarrassing event occurring in his neighbouring constituency, helped bring in Malcolm Paton as an Independent Liberal but endorsed by the Liberal Party. Paton lost his deposit with just 3,903 votes (8.5%) but those Liberals in the seat now had someone to vote for. Elsewhere in Wales, only Glyn Tegai Hughes' narrow loss in Denbigh by 1,209 (2.7%) to the National Liberal and Conservative Emlyn (E. H.) Garner Evans[67] offered any real hope for the future. Ironically, Garner Evans had been the Liberal candidate in the seat in the previous election in Denbigh. His defection was typical of a number of new Welsh Parliamentarians' who, despite having a Liberal background, joined one of the two larger parties in order to get into Parliament.[68]

In Conwy, Emlyn Hooson had gained a quarter of the vote but was still some 6,000 votes behind the Labour victor. In Caernarfon, Liberal Party Executive member and social worker, Elwyn R. Thomas, had a similar tale to tell. Here he came second with a fifth of the vote, but languished more than ten thousand votes behind Labour's Goronwy Roberts. Nowhere else in Wales was there now any real possibility of a Liberal win. Elsewhere, it had become more of a task of keeping the Liberal deposit than winning the seat. In Wrexham, Dr Herbert Mostyn Lewis, the son of the first Liberal MP for the University of Wales and the Lloyd George loyalist Sir John Herbert Lewis, failed to gain more than 15% of the vote. Maldwyn Thomas, later to be Chairman and Chief Executive of Rank Xerox and a mainstay of the Welsh Liberal Party, stood in Aberafon. He lost his deposit by some four votes. Thomas was the first Liberal to stand in Aberafon for 20 years. The Liberals would not stand there for another 23 years. In Llanelli, Huw Thomas stood at the age of 22, making him one of the youngest candidates in the UK. He came second to Labour's James Griffiths, though was over 30,000 votes behind. The story was the same in most of South Wales. Yet Liberal strength in Wales was strong compared to that in much of the UK. They had lost just three deposits in Wales (Aberafon, Brecon and Radnor and Cardiff East), compared to 313 deposits in Scotland and England. In addition, there were only 24 seats in the United Kingdom where the Liberals had won more than a quarter of the vote and seven (30% of the total) of these were in Wales.[69] Nationally, Liberal hopes of survival, let alone recovery, still rested firmly on Wales.

The 1950 general election was for Welsh Liberalism something of a short reprieve. They still held five seats, more than the rest of the British Liberals combined. They might even gain another next time, in Denbigh, as they were just 1,209 (2.7%) behind the victor. At the same time, the Conservative vote had risen in Wales, although their tally of seats had not. Across the United Kingdom, the party had made considerable gains which meant that the Labour Party had been re-elected with a majority of just six seats. This left the Liberals, with their nine seats, in a moral quandary. Should they keep the Labour government going if its majority looked weak or should they let it fall? Once again, the Liberals were left to decide Labour's fate. Clement Davies had no desire to test the Labour government's strength and stated that the holding of another general election in the short term was 'unthinkable'. The position therefore became one of examining Labour's legislative programme on a case by case basis. At the same time, however, Megan and Emrys Roberts held private talks with Labour's Deputy Leader, Herbert Morrison, about how they could prevent the Tories from gaining power. In March, she and Emrys Roberts had abstained on the Liberal amendment to the King's Speech which would have censured Labour for rising prices. In the domestic economy the action caused consternation in Wales and the Liberal Party of Wales chair, Alderman Alfred E. Hughes, had to issue a statement on behalf of the Welsh party indicating that the party would not act against Megan and Roberts on this issue'.[70] The Liberal motion had been backed by the Conservatives and could have brought down the government, if it had been carried out. Roberts and Megan did not want to see a Conservative government in power and declared this publicly.[71] The abstention therefore helped ensure Labour's survival. This covert co-operation was kept secret from Clement Davies and Rhys Hopkin Morris who would never have sanctioned such a move.[72]

The Liberals decided to stay on the political sidelines at Westminster but to continue to oppose the Labour government as deemed necessary, even if it led to the danger of defeating them. One such occasion was when Welsh and other Liberal MPs came together to support the Conservatives over an amendment to the Iron and Steel Bill. Most Liberals were against the nationalisation of the steel industry, which was such a major employer in Wales. Although the days of Liberal representation in steel-making constituencies were gone in Wales, there was still a considerable Liberal presence and ambition to do well in the steel-making areas of North Wales. This was, therefore, an issue which could mean gaining valuable votes at election time. Roderic Bowen led the Liberal case in the House of Commons emphasising that the Liberals saw the nationalisation of steel as having 'very grave consequences upon the national economy and welfare of the country as a whole'.[73] Even Megan Lloyd George supported the Conservative amendment but only after she was persuaded to do by Davies and the former chief Liberal Whip, Frank Byers. The amendment failed but an important point had been made, the Liberals could and would support whichever party was closest to its own ideological ground and would not be tied to supporting one party, even if it meant that party's downfall.

Whilst the Liberal MPs were overtly supporting the Conservatives, in March 1950, a number of Liberal Peers (Lord Reading, Lord Rennell of Rodd, Lord Willingdon and Lord Cowdray) decided to support the Conservatives permanently by joining them in the House of Lords. They were joined by some Welsh Liberals, J. Herbert Jones a former parliamentary candidate and Vice President and Honorary Secretary of the Liberal Party of Wales also followed the peers in their flight in the November of that year.[74] Most of the Welsh Liberal hereditary peers by this period were also now supporting the Conservatives, a number coming from the National Liberals. Within the Liberal Party itself, there was an increase in pressure to join the Conservatives in an anti-socialist alliance. Clement Davies would have none of this, however, and on the 3rd May the Liberal Party Committee under Davies issued a statement which said 'The Liberal Party Committee assures Liberals in the country that it has no intention of compromising the independence of the Liberal Party.'[75] At the same time, there was also an attempt to shift the party to the left. North Wales Liberal, Ronald Waterhouse, supported Dingle Foot's motion that the Liberal Party should no longer fight with and should join forces with the Labour Party.[76] Both were political allies of Megan Lloyd George and, like her, would end up joining the Labour Party. The motion failed and Megan Lloyd George declared at the conference that there had clearly been 'a shift to the right'.[77] In her actions, she was now covertly, if not openly, supporting the Labour Party. Over the following six months she ensured that she was often absent from the House when the Labour government's decreasing majority was threatened by joint Conservative-Liberal motions. Despite Megan's efforts to keep the Labour government alive, the continued exhausting late-night sittings forced by the Conservative opposition and the internal strife within the governing Labour party weakened Clement Attlee's desire to struggle on in power. He, therefore, called an election for the 25th October 1951 in order to try and gain a higher majority.

The General Election 1951

Liberal	3
Labour	27
Conservative	5
National Liberal	1

The 1951 general election resulted in a Conservative victory with a small majority. For Welsh Liberals this meant being marginalised by the two main parties to an even greater degree. The Welsh Liberals were now well aware that they were being squeezed politically in their own heartlands. In over 95 per cent of the elections in the United Kingdom, either the Conservatives or Labour had achieved first place. Clement Davies wrote to his predecessor Sir Archibald Sinclair at the start of 1951 general election: 'I do not know whether I will be back here ... Even if I do pull it off, it will be a damned near thing ... Each of us in Wales will have a very tough fight.'[78] There was little financial support for the Liberal candidates for the 1951 general election. The Welsh Liberals centrally put what little resource they had into the seats that they thought they had the greatest chance of winning – existing seats, plus Conwy and Denbigh (although in both these seats the Liberals were now in third position). Other seats which they had held only a few years before such as Caernarfon and Flint East and West were now electorally abandoned. In the whole of Britain, the Liberals contested only 109 seats. In Wales, they contested just nine seats – their lowest ever to date. The Welsh party had decided at an emergency meeting of its MPs on 26th May in Welshpool that they would contest only those seats they had a chance of winning. This was accepted to be less than a third of Welsh seats.[79] Across the country, the Liberals voters who were denied a candidate voted in the majority for the Conservatives; in Wales, as we will see later, the party's two losses were not to the Conservatives, however, but to Labour.[80] The election issues in respect of Welsh Liberalism having its own distinctive agenda were limited mainly to a commitment for Parliament for Wales which was endorsed in the Liberals' British manifesto, entitled *The Nation's Task*.[81]

The Welsh Liberals' reluctance or inability to select candidates in the vast majority of Welsh seats was typified by what happened in the Swansea West constituency. Here the National Liberal, Sir Lewis Jones, had held the seat until 1945. The Liberal Association there had all but disappeared after the split in 1931.[82] In 1951 Lewis stated that he did not wish to stand again and could not be persuaded to do so. A joint Conservative and National Liberal committee decided by a small majority to select a Conservative with no connection to the seat, Captain Henry Britten Kerby.[83] The National Liberal members of the Swansea committee accepted this decision with some reluctance, as it went against the 'Woolton-Teviot' pact which had been made to preserve the status quo in former National Liberal constituencies. As late as the 28th of September, National Liberal members tried to get Sir Lewis to stand again. They failed and had to endorse Kerby. At the same time, the remnants of Swansea West Liberal Association had invited candidates to stand and one local business man was selected. After three days of deliberation, the candidate declared that 'this was not the time' and the Liberal Association then merely announced that it would not select a candidate after all for this election but hoped to do so next time. They sent copies of a Liberal questionnaire to the candidates and forwarded the replies to the *South Wales Evening Post,* which did not even publish them.[84] The Swansea West Liberal Association then gave no guidance about how their supporters should vote. This story of Liberals failing to stand was repeated virtually everywhere in the south of Wales. They did not wish to contest the seats even where Liberal Associations were still active.

The Welsh Liberal Radicals are Defeated

In the 1951 general election, the greatest loss to both the Welsh and British Liberal Party was that of Megan Lloyd George in Ynys Môn. A strong Conservative candidate, Meurig Roberts, combined with the changing character of the island, helped Labour's Cledwyn Hughes win by 595 votes. To help them the Conservatives produced a leaflet depicting David Lloyd George and the words of a speech he made in 1935 denouncing Socialism.[85] Although Megan condemned this leaflet, it provided the Conservatives with enough new votes, gained from the Liberals, to assist in her removal. In a general election, in which only 27 British seats changed parties, she became the most prominent political casualty of the entire general election.[86]

What now for the Liberals' most famous female MP? When pressed on her political future Lady Megan said, 'I am not of retiring age nor of a retiring disposition. I am ready for the next fight whenever it comes'.[87] The fact that she had led the Campaign for a Welsh Parliament meant that there was speculation that she might even join Plaid Cymru. Her political ambitions, however, remained more mainstream and invitations from senior Labour figures for her to join them started to flood in. Attlee sought to persuade her that the party of the 'Radical' was now Labour. Before long, she had been persuaded by Labour members that her future was with them.

Emrys Roberts, Megan's fellow Welsh radical, lost his Meirionnydd seat.[88] This was explained mainly by the fact that Plaid Cymru's failure to stand a candidate there resulted in their supporters' votes going to Labour. The result was Labour's Thomas (T. W.) Jones won the seat by some 1048 votes (4.2%). Meirionnydd had been held by the Liberals since 1868. Their defeat in Meirionnydd showed the extent to which Welsh Nationalist sentiments could now be contained within the Labour Party rather the Welsh Liberals. Jo Grimond wrote to Emrys Roberts: 'I thought that with no nationalist standing you were safe. It seems to have been a most cruel stroke that Labour should have gained the votes'.[89] One Liberal member, however, laid the blame for the defeat directly at the Liberal Party's own door. He stated:

> 'It's all very well blaming Plaid Cymru, but the truth is that we have not kept our organisation in order. We did less work than any other parties between elections and therefore a lot of the blame should be placed on the Liberals of Meirionnydd, myself included'.[90]

The downfalls of Megan and Roberts in Wales, and Edgar Granville's loss in the constituency of Eye, meant that all of the Liberal Radicals had now been defeated. The Liberal Party had lost the left of its party. Its three remaining Welsh MPs were on the right of the party. They had escaped Conservative opposition in their seats, as a result, and only fought Labour candidates. The Welsh Liberal MPs had not benefited from the so called 'Huddersfield arrangement'. Instead, the Conservative Central Office endorsed them because they were anti-Socialist and the Conservatives themselves lacked significant constituency organisations in these seats from which to manage a successful election campaign.[91] As a result, Clement Davies enjoyed a 9,491 (38.4%) majority; Roderic Bowen had a 10,257 (34.6%) majority whilst Rhys Hopkin Morris scraped in with a majority of just 467 votes (1%). The three Welsh MPs represented half of the British Parliamentary Party. There were now as many

Liberal seats in Wales as there were in Scotland and England combined. The Welsh party had become, in effect, the British Liberal Party.

Should the Liberal Party Continue?

The Liberal Party had already debated its future existence throughout much of the previous Parliament; and, inevitably the subject would soon resurface. Once the election results were known, the Liberals released a statement:

> 'We are disappointed. There is, however, evidence that a core of Liberalism will continue in this country. The party juggernauts have again defeated us. Our beachhead is not enlarged. But it remains.'[92]

On the 26th October, Winston Churchill accepted the King's invitation to form a Government. A few days later, on the 28th October 1951, Clement Davies met Winston Churchill at Chartwell. A fomer Liberal himself, Churchill was the only post-war Prime Minister who respected the Liberal Party and consequently, he offered Davies a post in the Cabinet. Davies had talks with leading Liberals, including Bowen and Hopkin Morris who were wholly against Churchill's offer. He then released a statement refusing the offer but indicating that the Liberals would support the Conservative government provided that they believed their policies to be in the national interest. With this simple statement Davies had ensured the continued existence of the Liberal Party. As well as being the most important act by any Welsh Liberal to determine the party's future, it was also perhaps the greatest act undertaken by any Liberal. Over the coming five years, the Liberal Party Council would continue to insist that the Liberals remain an independent party in coalition with no other, a position which was fully supported by the Welsh Liberals.

The Liberals' decline meant that there were constant moves by the other political parties to take advantage of the Party's weakness. In the 1950s the Caernarfonshire Liberal Association, for instance, resisted persistent Tory overtures to reach an electoral understanding. Their financial difficulties had meant that candidates could not be funded in 1950 and 1951 but this fuelled speculation there had been a pact. This notion was not popular and the Welsh language newspaper, *Y Cymro*, even suggested that the 'idea of a Welsh Liberal Conservative Party' was not only bizarre but like 'mixing milk and vinegar'.[93] The days of Liberal-Conservatives pacts, it seemed, had died with the National Liberals.

G. W. Madoc Jones, Major J. Parry Jones and a Few Die-Hards Keep the Party Going

By the mid 1950s, the Liberal Party in Wales, like the Liberal organisations elsewhere in Britain, was in a poor state. The Welsh Liberal Party Chairman, Glyn Tegai Hughes, noted the decline of the Welsh Party as evidenced by a Liberal Party of Wales AGM, held in Wrexham in the late 1950s:

It was badly attended. One instance involved Roger Roberts as the Welsh Party's press officer. He managed to drum up 11 journalists to turn up to one of our meetings. Only 14 Liberal members turned up, however and the hall was empty. I had to rush them into a neighbouring room in order to brief them and avoid them seeing the reality. The organisation was on its last legs.[94]

Apart from Glyn Tegai Hughes and Roger Roberts, the support of a few more Liberals from North and South Wales helped keep the party going. One of the best known Welsh Liberal organisers of the post war period in Wales was an agricultural machine salesman called Geraint (G. W.) Madoc Jones. He lived in Borthwen, Denbigh, where he had converted an outbuilding into an office-cum-storeroom for all things Liberal in Wales. Madoc Jones was officially the North Wales Liberal Federation's press and publicity officer and Honorary Secretary of the Liberal Party of Wales.[95] Unofficially, he was the reason why Liberalism held together in Wales during that period.[96] Madoc Jones' position in the party was such that he acted as the party's 'eyes, and ears, judge, jury and executioner, a shoulder to cry on and a referee on the party's many quarrels'.[97] Just as Thomas Waterhouse had been a rock of Welsh Liberalism two decades earlier and had won the admiration of Lloyd George, so now Madoc Jones kept the party together, winning the admiration of Clement Davies. Clement Davies informed him, 'I believe that the North Liberal Federation would die of inaction were it not for your enthusiasm, vigour and drive'.[98]

In 1954, Madoc Jones launched a series of newsletters entitled *Liberal Lighthouse*, which he described as a 'monthly message of comfort and enthusiasm for a party solely in need of both'.[99] This was the first real Welsh Liberal output since *The New Radical* had been launched by the Aberystwyth Liberal students seven years earlier. Although Madoc Jones was seen as perhaps the leading light of the post-war Welsh Liberal organisation, there were a number of other key figures. Dr Glyn Tegai Hughes held the position of Welsh Party Chairman for a number of years, as did Alun Talfan Davies and Martin Thomas. Jennie Gibbs from Maesteg, in Glamorgan, took over as the Honorary Secretary of the Liberal Party of Wales from Madoc Jones. Jennie with her husband John kept the Party alive in the South. As evidence of this, in 1962, they wrote to Glyn Tegai Hughes stating that the 'two of us worked from 10am to 11pm yesterday on South Wales Liberal Federation business and could do this every day'.[100]

In South Wales there was also another prominent Welsh Liberal, Major J. Parry Brown from Newport, who helped keep the South Wales Federation going. He was at times the Chairman and Treasurer of the Welsh Party and held various posts in the South Wales Liberal Federation. Parry Brown was also the South Wales Federation representative on the executive of the Liberal Party Organisation (LPO) in London. Although the LPO records for this period indicate that he seldom said anything in meetings beyond reporting back on the state of the party in South Wales, his presence on the executive was at least an indication that the Liberal Party in Wales had not died. Parry Brown was seen as a polite and affable man by his contemporaries. He was often quizzical and puzzled by the young 'Turks' in the party, raising his eyebrows at radical suggestions brought forward by them.[101] Parry Brown, therefore, earned a reputation of having a sobering influence on the party. His wife was also an active Liberal and Vice-President of the party. At the same time that Mrs Parry Brown was active in the party, one of the Lloyd Georges was also still prominent in the Welsh Party. This was Lady Olwen Carey-Evans, the second daughter of David Lloyd George, who was a Party President and also a Party Vice-President and remained a Liberal until her death aged 98 in 1990.

The Welsh Liberal Parliamentary Party Limps On

Whilst Clement Davies set about saving the Liberal Party and serving his constituency, the other two Welsh Liberal MPs, Rhys Hopkin Morris and Roderic Bowen, continued to develop their legal carers, which on occasions they also combined with constituency matters. Perhaps the most famous occasion was to do with the Upper Towy Valley compulsory purchase case in 1951. This was brought about in November 1949 when the Forestry Commission had compulsorily purchased 46 sheep farms (20,000 acres in all) in the Upper Towy Valley, Carmarthenshire, without consultation. The political pressure brought by both Hopkin Morris and Bowen ensured that an inquiry was held into the matter. Both MPs were also KCs (King's Counsel) and represented the Carmarthenshire farmers free of charge. The case was won, the farmers kept their land and the stature of both MPs was enhanced in the eyes of the constituency's farmers. Three years later, the longer-serving Rhys Hopkin Morris was knighted in the New Year's Honours list of 1954. He became the last Liberal MP to be knighted in Wales.

At the end of May 1954, the then chairman of the Liberal Party of Wales, Major Parry Brown, made an optimistic speech at the Silver Jubilee of Clement Davies' election in Montgomeryshire. He assured his listeners that a 'tremendous Liberal revival' was about to happen in Wales. This was being triggered by the recent re-establishment of local Liberal Associations in many parts of Wales.[102] In the event, this message proved to be wildly optimistic; Parry Brown later failed to get even his own Newport Liberal Association to contest seats at the general election. The rest of south Wales was similarly devoid of any prospective Welsh parliamentary candidates. The Welsh Liberals, therefore, remained electorally feeble and were about to become even weaker.

One of the successes of the Welsh Liberal Party in the few early 1950s was the founding of the Welsh Liberal Weekend Schools. These policy and discussion forums met twice or sometimes three times a year. They were founded by Maldwyn Thomas and his sister Mair, together with Glyn Tegai Hughes and Emlyn Hooson at Pantyfedwen, Borth. Over the coming decades they would bring some of the best known political and business people directly into the heart of Welsh Liberal policy formulation.[103]

1955 – A Black Year for the Welsh Liberals

After the 1950 general election, a number of prominent Liberals had joined the Conservative Party. This time after the 1951 general election, a number were also to join the Labour Party. On the 26th of April 1955, amongst much publicity, Megan

Lloyd George announced her conversion to the Labour Party. Megan had always insisted that she was a Radical and despite the continued presence of Radicals in the Liberal Party, she asserted that they no longer had a position in the Parliamentary Party or within Wales. She declared, 'in the changed situation of today it is only in the Labour Party that I can be true to the radical position'.[104]

In November 1952, Megan Lloyd George had refused an invitation to stand again as a Liberal candidate for Ynys Môn. Her main reason was that the Liberals were moving too far to the right.[105] She resigned as deputy leader of the party at the same time. Megan's distancing from the Liberal Party did not surprise her old enemy Lady Violet Bonham Carter. She wrote to Lord Samuel on the matter explaining that the Radicals were not to be trusted an inch. She went on to write that 'Joseph Chamberlain became the mainspring of Protection and Imperialism; Lloyd George sold the Liberal Party to the Tories in 1918. Such things are possible for so-called radicals – impossible for any Liberal – you – my father (Asquith) – Edward Grey'.

The main concern for the Liberal Party was that she would be used to undermine their own vote at the expense of Labour. The party's constituency executive received a press briefing note based on challenging the rationale of switching to a party in which 'freedom of speech was restricted'. Frank Byers gave the official Liberal response:[106]

> All Liberals will naturally be extremely sorry to hear of Lady Megan's decision. We cannot believe that she will find in the Labour Party the freedom of expression which she has always enjoyed amongst Liberals and which has enabled her in the past to render useful political and public service. We hope and trust that her association with the Labour Party will only be of a temporary nature.

At the same time as Megan was leaving the party, Clement Davies had become ill. He was unable to attend the April Assembly of the Liberal Party which was being held in Llandudno. At the age of 70, questions were being asked about how long he could continue. The Liberal supporting press, namely the *News Chronicle* and *The Guardian*, were running headlines such as 'Clement Davies: The big query' and 'New Leader for the Liberals?'.[107] The general election was announced whilst the Assembly was in session and it fell to Jo Grimond to give the rousing speech. The leadership of the Liberals would soon be passing out of Wales for good. In April 1955, Sir Winston Churchill retired from the Premiership. His successor, Sir Anthony Eden, called a general election for the following month.

The General Election 1955

Liberal	3
Labour	27
Conservative	5
National Liberal and Conservative	1

The Conservatives won the 1955 general election with a majority of 60 seats. Nationally, the Liberals only managed to put up 110 candidates, one more than in 1951. In Wales, they managed 10, the same number as in 1951. There was little interest by the other two parties about whether the Liberals could split the vote and 'let the Tories/Socialists in' this time. They had largely been forgotten. In only 15 seats in Great Britain, neither, Labour nor the Conservatives occupied the first and second positions in the poll.[108] Over half of these were in Wales.

The other parties, however, still vied for Liberal votes where it was tactical to do so. As feared, the Labour party exploited the defection of Megan Lloyd George whilst the Conservatives appealed to Liberal voters' fears of Socialism in seats which the Liberals did not contest. With such a small show of candidates, most of the Liberal campaigning discussion concerned who Liberal supporters should vote for in the absence of a Liberal candidate. Frances Stephenson, Lloyd George's second wife, stated that she would be voting Conservative, as did the Liberal Lord Moynihan. As could be expected, Megan Lloyd George and Dingle Foot[109] recommended voting Labour. Those Liberal Associations, in which there was no Liberal candidates were advised by the LPO to invite Conservative and Labour candidates to attend the local meetings and then to decide how to vote. In much of Wales, however, the Liberal Associations had by now ceased to function. At a local level, Liberal councillors in this period had also been reduced to isolated pockets of one or two on a small number of councils.[110] In a council by-election, for instance, in November 1948, on Pontypridd Urban District Council, Eddie Williams won a seat off Labour in the Trallwn ward. Williams would be the sole representative on the council until he stood down as a councillor in 1954.[111] Most Welsh councils did not even have that single Liberal representation.

For the election, Liberal policy in Wales had been determined in the Federations mainly by a series of 'panels' chaired by the senior Welsh Liberals. Madoc Jones chaired the Industry Group which included other notable Liberals, such as Sir George Hamer and Lieutenant-Colonel Stuart Waterhouse.[112] As in 1951 none of the three surviving Welsh Liberal MPs faced Conservative opposition. This meant that campaigning in these seats was directed against the Labour Party. In Cardiganshire, Bowen countered his Labour opponents' claims that he was an absentee 'playboy' by quoting glowing endorsements from the Cardiganshire branch of the National Farmers' Union.[113] In the subsequent election, although Bowen's majority was cut, he still had a secure majority of some 8,817 votes (30.4% majority) over Labour's D. Jones-Davies.

In Carmarthenshire, Sir Rhys Hopkin Morris enjoyed his largest ever majority over Labour. He was helped by the intervention of a Plaid Cymru candidate in the seat for the first time. Hopkin Morris' majority of 3,333 votes (6.5%) made Carmarthenshire a safer Liberal seat than it had been since 1924. In Montgomeryshire, Clement Davies vote fell but he still had an impressive 8,500 vote majority (36.2%) over his Labour opponent. Elsewhere in Wales, things looked less certain. Liberal solicitor Henry Evans Jones failed to regain Meirionnydd. In a four-cornered race, he just beat Gwynfor Evans into second place but was 2,682 votes (11.4%) behind Labour. In Denbigh, Glyn Tegai Hughes slipped back to 4,641 votes behind Garner Evans. In Ynys Môn, journalist and writer John Williams Hughes failed to regain the seat and put the Liberals second behind Labour's Cledwyn Hughes, who now enjoyed a 4,573 vote (15.8%) majority. In Flint West, the local Liberal Association Secretary, Gomer Owen, contested the seat at the last minute, when the local association decided not to put forward a candidate. Although Owen only gained half the vote that the party had obtained in the 1951 election, it was enough to retain his deposit and ensure that Flint West was just one of a handful of Welsh constituencies in which the Liberals would contest every post war election. In Caernarfon and Conwy, the Liberals lost their deposits; in Brecon and Radnor they were within a whisker of doing so. In the other 26 Welsh seats, there were no Liberals to be seen.

Nationally in its analysis of the general election, the Liberal Party felt that although it had not progressed from the previous general election in terms of either seats or share of the vote, there was a feeling that "the general trend downwards had been halted, that things had gone well; that there was a better chance next time".[114] The main complaint from candidates and agents, from over half of them, was that the party still 'lacked a proper organisation' across Britain.[115]

After the election in Wales, once again it was determined that the Liberals must contest more seats. The party started working together more on electoral strategies. There was then a series of by-elections in which the Liberal vote looked more promising. The nearest one to Wales was in Hereford which saw Frank Owen, a former MP for Hereford and a member of Lloyd George's independent group, get second position for the Liberals, just 2,000 votes behind the Conservatives in 1956. Although Owen lost, he was treated as something of a hero by Liberal Radical activists. As the Radicals came back into the fold after their fall-out with the party in 1954, he was adopted as the group's vice-president. With the Radicals back and the party having shed its more zealous right and left wings, it was more united than it had been for decades.

Clement Davies Steps Down

Clement Davies had suffered from a serious illness in the winter of 1954–55. His involvement in political campaigning had therefore become limited, and there was increasing pressure for him to step down. He was now 72 and his contemporaries, Attlee and Churchill, had retired in 1955 giving their places to younger men. Major General Grey, the Party Treasurer, approached Davies in July 1956 and urged him to relinquish the position of leader.[116] Davies accepted this advice but the problem was who would succeed him? Sir Rhys Hopkin Morris was now 67 and lacked any political ambition to be leader. The two English MPs, Arthur Holt and Donald Wade, owed their survival to the Conservatives and did not enjoy the substantial majorities the Welsh MPs had. This left only Roderic Bowen and Jo Grimond as possible leadership candidates. There was pressure from the Welsh Liberals for Bowen to stand for the leadership in order to counter Grimond's more left wing anti-Conservative views, but would he? On the 29th of September 1956, Davies stepped down as Liberal Leader, stating:

'It is time that the tiller was placed in the hands of a younger man, and that a new voice should be calling on the ship's company, rallying them to the great cause which we all have so much at heart. Fortunately, I can step down knowing that there is a worthy successor waiting – one who has fully earned his master's certificate.'[117]

Grimond nominated Bowen for the leadership but Bowen was aware that Grimond was the more popular and energetic character and nominated him instead.[118]

Jo Grimond was certainly more popular than Bowen; he received a standing ovation for his conference speech the day before he was to be elected as the new leader. Bowen, however, remained disappointed about not becoming leader and skipped the next Federal party Conference by going on a visit to the United States.[119] He failed to appreciate Grimond's desire for a 'realignment of the Left' any more than he wished to see the party align itself with the Conservatives.[120] This led to a mutual misunderstanding between the men and Bowen from then on took an independent line on many issues, often not relating them to the position agreed by the Parliamentary Party. He also came under much criticism by Grimond due to his infrequent appearances in the Commons. In a conversation with Violet Bonham Carter in July 1961, she noted:[121]

'He (Grimond) wrote imploring Bowen to be with him for the Berlin debate on Monday and to speak. Bowen replied that he has 'a function'. He does damn all in the House. As Jo (Grimond) says- why go into it?'

In 1956, although there were only six Liberal MPs left at Westminster they became a divided party once more, this time over the Suez crisis.[122] Sir Rhys Hopkin Morris and Roderic Bowen had been against the invasion whilst Clement Davies supported the Conservatives' line. The Labour Party was equally divided. The Liberals did, however, come together at the start of November when they issued a statement condemning the Government's action.

As the events in Egypt unfolded, the party across Wales continued to be in a weak state organisationally and electorally. From the North Wales Federation, Glyn Tegai Hughes reported the most optimistic news to the LPO executive. The position there was that there were three MPs plus PPCs (prospective parliamentary candidates) in West Flint and West Denbighshire. They were also negotiating for PPCs in Meirionnydd and Ynys Môn. Getting candidates for North Wales, however, was not always easy because of having to get 'Welsh speaking candidates for a number of the seats'.[123] In South Wales, Major J. Parry Brown, reported:

- 'Swansea has no association, Swansea West was a Liberal National seat and therefore there is no longer Liberal support there
- Aberavon, quite active, good local party but no candidate
- Cardiff, has three divisions one of which ought to be won if a candidate could be found
- Pontypridd, new Liberal Association
- Brecon and Radnor – new association formed who are anxious to find a candidate
- Newport – was functioning well but a small association'.

Summing up, he said that the situation in South Wales was 'not too good but he hoped in a year it would be better'.[124]

For the Liberal Party of Wales overall news was a little more optimistic. There had been some fiscal success; their overdraft of £1,300 had been reduced to £150. They had even managed to hold a rally in Aberystwyth in May with several hundred attending and the party's AGM in Builth Wells in September had gained around 80 delegates. As soon as the overdraft was cleared, the executive believed that they would be getting a part-time secretarial assistant to co-ordinate the sub-committees that had been drafting Welsh policy.[125] Although later on, in reality, this did not prove to be the case.

Disaster at Carmarthen – February 1957

On the 21st November 1956, Rhys Hopkin Morris attended the House of Commons for the last time. He fell ill there and returned to his London home in Sidcup where he died that night. *The Times* regarded his 'whole life as a plea for the liberty of the individual' and the Liberal historian, Roy Douglas, reflected that he was 'one of the finest and purest exponents of Liberalism' he had ever known.[126] During his time at Carmarthen, he had never got overly involved in constituency campaigns, nor had he any constituency staff or office, nor had he lived in the constituency, coming down at the weekend to stay in The Boar's Head in Carmarthen. Still, at each election he had managed, sometimes by the smallest majority, to retain his seat. His agent's daughter, Judith Trefor Lewis, summed up Sir Rhys Hopkin Morris style as an MP:[127] 'He was a wonderful speaker in both Welsh and English, in some ways he seemed a distant and patrician figure but ordinary people thought he was wonderful. Never patronising, he did not need to use notes or prepared speeches.' Sir Rhys' strong personality was enough to ensure that he had held Carmarthen for 11 years and ended with a small majority of 6.5 per cent. The Welsh Liberals would now have to do something they had not done since 1945 – both fight and win a Welsh by-election.[128]

The thorny issue of the Suez crisis would play a central role in this by-election. Sir Rhys Hopkin Morris had not voted with the Conservatives after a Labour motion had divided the Commons over an anti-Suez motion in October 1956. This was unlike Clement Davies and Roderic Bowen, who had supported the government. Later on he also put out a statement condemning the Suez invasion.[129] It was, therefore, perhaps somewhat ironic that the future key to winning Carmarthen would be by opposing Hopkin Morris's views. The Conservatives had given Sir Rhys a free run against Labour in 1955, but now with the Liberals firmly against Suez, but were threatening to cancel the agreement not to stand their own candidate. With the thin majorities of the past in this seat in mind, getting the Conservatives not to stand would prove vital for the Liberals.

On the 12th December 1956, the Carmarthen Liberal Association selected John Morgan Davies as their candidate. Morgan Davies was a man with a farming background who worked for the Fatstock Marketing Corporation. More importantly, he was a pro-Suez candidate. This was needed to appease the right-wing views of the members of both the Carmarthen Liberal and Conservative Associations. He got the support of both and consequently became the Liberal candidate, unopposed by the Conservatives.[130] The Association's choice was also dominated to a large extent by the endorsement of a Liberal matriarch, Mrs Trefor Thomas – known as the 'Queen of Carmarthen Town'. She was also one of the key members of the South Wales Federation.[131]

Davies's views could have come straight from the Conservative front bench. On the electoral stump, however, neither Jo Grimond nor any other Liberal was prepared to publicly contradict him. Grimond stated to the media that he believed Liberal

candidates could have their own views and 'it did not follow that [the position supported by the Liberals in the Commons which was anti-Suez] should be imposed
outside of the House'.[132] In reality, he bitterly resented having to endorse a Liberal
candiate who was diametrically opposed to his and the party's mainstream views.[133]

Morgan Davies was pitted directly against the former Liberal heroine, Megan Lloyd
George, in her new Labour clothes, as she had been selected to fight the seat. Some
Liberals had actually worn their coats backwards to her public meetings to signify their
disgust with this 'turncoat', though others found her immensely appealing. Carmarthen
town was 'agog at the fact that Megan would now fight for the Labour Party'.[134] During
the by-election former Liberal leader, Lord Simon, had to warn the Carmarthenshire
Liberals not to support her.[135] There were many Liberals who knew her only as a
Liberal and they were very upset by the fact that she had crossed the floor.[136] Jennie
Eirian Davies, a popular local figure, stood for Plaid Cymru. She was endorsed directly
by Gwynfor Evans, Plaid's President, who lived within the seat. All three candidates
toured throughout the whole constituency but the real contest was always between
Labour and the Liberals. Megan had perfected her public oratory skills, honed over
thirty years of Parliamentary performance, but the press, fellow Liberal activists and
eventually the voting public viewed Morgan Davies as 'a poor candidate and public
speaker'.[137] Davies was described by a Labour supporting *Tribune* reporter as having
'as much personality as a television set with a defective tube'.[138]

The Suez issue became more and more prominent and unpopular. Morgan Davies
could not disguise it. In their candidates' statements for the *Carmarthen Journal*
Megan put her views on Suez at the forefront of her campaign whereas Davies
relegated his right to the back. Megan brought the issue out at every public meeting around Carmarthenshire's villages and highlighted the contradictions between
the Liberals' public anti-Suez views and Morgan Davies' 'pro-Suez stance'. How
could a pro-Suez MP be welcome in an anti-Suez Parliamentary party? Megan
Lloyd George labelled him 'the Suez candidate'.[139] She pushed forward the point
that Morgan Davies needed 'Tory support to win'. She suggested, in effect, there
was 'collusion' between the Conservatives and the Liberals.[140] The Liberal Party
Organisation (LPO) in London sent down one of their helpers Peter Bessel (later
Liberal MP for Bodmin). He had been successful in organising Bodmin, and was
well aware of the significance of Liberalism in a seat. The Liberals in Carmarthen,
however, felt that Megan was bound to win because of who she was. There was
no great ideological tradition of supporting the Liberal cause in Carmarthen; the
tradition was one of supporting whom they saw as the best candidate for the seat.

Towards the end of the campaign, the chairman of the Carmarthen Conservative
Association appealed to the members to support the Liberals because of the two
parties' 'agreement that foreign policy should be in the hands of experienced
statesmen'. As the Conservatives were suffering a drop in support in other by-
elections due to Suez, Labour now felt confident to win. In the event, the Labour
vote rose by 2,600 on 1955 and the Liberal vote decreased by almost 4,000. Despite
the fact that the Liberals had 'worked like mad', when the result came in, many of
them were in tears because they felt they had done so badly. It was felt by many
voters, however, that having a Lloyd George win the seat was carrying on the father's
traditions and it was right that she should be there.[141] A Lloyd George was back in
Westminster representing Wales but not a Liberal Lloyd George.

The Carmarthen by-election made the Liberal Party think hard nationally. It was true that the Liberal Party needed all the MPs it could get, but Grimond's appearance of representing any opinion, if it was thought to win, did not go down at all well with the voters or with the party members. Some members left the party over such tactics. Miss Honor Balfour, a founder member of the old Radical Action movement and a member of the Liberal Executive, resigned from the party.[142] She accused Grimond and the Carmarthenshire Liberals of compromising over Suez to win Conservative votes. Many others in the Liberal Party held the same view but the loss of the seat to Megan Lloyd George gracefully saved considerable embarrassment and turmoil within the party in having a pro-Suez MP just as the rest of the party had agreed to oppose the action.[143] It also had the effect of reducing the Welsh Liberals MPs from three to two in number and removing Carmarthenshire from the Liberal camp forever.

Carmarthen By-election Result, 28th February 1957

Candidate	Party	Vote	Percentage
Megan Lloyd George	Labour	23679	47.3%
John Morgan Davies	Liberal	20610	41.2%
Jennie Eirian Davies	Plaid Cymru	5741	11.5%
	Majority	3069	6.1%
	Turnout		87.5%

In the Welsh municipal elections of that year the party won just 8 seats in Wales, one in Cardiff and seven in Wrexham.[144] The other Welsh municipal authorities were devoid of Welsh councillors. The year 1957 was not a good one for Welsh Liberals. Almost a year after Carmarthen in March 1958, in the Devon constituency of Torrington, the Liberals won their first by-election since the 1920s. Amongst the Welsh Liberals who came to support Mark Bonham Carter (grandson of Lloyd George's old foe Asquith) as candidate was Roderic Bowen.[145] Bonham Carter victory started what was felt to be the first new seat at a stirrings of a revival of the British Liberal Party. This result was also good news for Welsh Liberals but, unlike their growing Liberal presence over the border in England, its own presence was continuing to get scarcer. Only eight of Wales' 34 constituencies were still affiliated to the LPO. As well as most of South Wales, amongst those other constituencies no longer affiliated were: Ynys Môn, held by the party only eight years earlier and Carmarthen, lost just one year before.[146] Some sixty constituencies in Britain had Liberal memberships of over 500. In Wales only two – Conwy and Cardigan – had over 500 members. Of the remaining Welsh constituencies, Caernarfon and Denbigh had between 499 and 250 members but all other active Welsh constituencies had less than 250 members.[147] On the party's British executive the only Welsh Liberal presence there was Patrick Lort-Phillips, who served as one of the party's three honorary treasurers. Apart from Lort-Phillips the only Welsh Liberals to be seen outside Wales were its two MPs. Their occasional presence at the party conferences was the most notable evidence of the its continuing survival. Bowen put forward one motion on raising pensions at the September 1959 Liberal Assembly at Scarborough and that was the sole input from any of the Welsh party.[148] The shrinking presence of the Welsh party nationally was, therefore, a somewhat ominous sign just as Harold Macmillan called a general election for the 8th October 1959.

The General Election 1959 in Wales

Liberal	2
Labour	27
Conservative	6
National Liberal and Conservative	1

The Suez crisis, protests about nuclear weapons and problems in the African colonies, although prominent in Westminster and party politics, had made little impact on the British public. Instead, the voters were generally satisfied with a rise in living standards and the general expectation brought to them by Macmillan's Conservative government. Grimond spent much of the campaign in his constituency leaving the national campaign to Frank Byers (chairman of the Campaigns Committee) and Herbert Harris (the party's general director). The Liberal Party managed to double the number of seats contested to 216 compared to with 110 in 1955. In Wales the party hit an all time low of just eight seats being contested. Labour contested every seat, the Conservatives contested all seats except for Cardigan and even Plaid Cymru had managed to contest 19 seats.

Glyn Tegai Hughes and Emlyn Hooson together constructed the Liberal Party of Wales' General Election Manifesto entitled 'A New Deal for Wales'. Apart from the traditional calling for a Welsh Parliament and Secretary of State for Wales, it also called for:

1. Welsh agricultural support for co-operatives, hill farmers and small-scale farmers.
2. Large-scale support for rural unemployment; there was no mention of urban unemployment. Also widescale support for Welsh ports was indicated. Gwynedd and a portion of south west Wales should be designated as special development areas.
3. Road development for a north-south road as well as a bypass for Port Talbot and Queensferry in North Wales.
4. In the cultural areas there was a call for a third Welsh language television channel to be set up, for the Welsh National Opera to become professional and for the development of a Welsh National Theatre and greater support for the publication of Welsh language books.
5. Amongst other issues which were specifically Welsh was the support for compensation for quarry men suffering from pneumoconiosis; a Welsh Water Board to plan the development of Wales water and the establishment of Welsh language secondary and grammar schools across the nation.

With the exceptions of the issue of total independence for Wales and the call for the immediate appointment of a Welsh Secretary and the establishment of a Welsh Office, the Liberal Manifesto was as Welsh Nationalist as any produced by Plaid Cymru. Alun Talfan Davies, when looking back on this general election, in which he had fought the Carmarthen seat, was heartened by the fact that everywhere that Liberals and Plaid Cymru fought each other (seven seats), only in Ynys Môn did Plaid Cymru gain more votes than they had.[149] It was felt, therefore, that overall the Welsh Liberals had been the winners in the contest for the Welsh nationalist vote.

Grimond predicted that 18 to 20 seats would be won. The Liberals nationally failed to rise from their total of seats, losing the Torrington by-election gain but with Jeremy Thorpe gaining North Devon. In Cardiganshire Roderic Bowen's poor attendance record in both the House of Commons and the constituency had brought forward rumours that he would not stand again in 1959. Bowen dismissed the conjecture stating that it is 'all twaddle and nonsense. It's a hardy annual put up by the Labour boys when things go quiet'.[150] With the absence of a Conservative candidate, Bowen enjoyed nearly 60 per cent of the vote and a majority of 9,309 votes. The then Secretary of the South Wales Liberal Federation, J. Ellis Williams, proudly described it as 'the safest seat held by a Liberal Member (in the UK)'.[151]

In Montgomeryshire, Clement Davies' majority plummeted to just 2,794 (10.8%) after the Conservatives entered the electoral contest once more. They had not contested the seat in the previous election. Mary Garbett Edwards, Montgomeryshire's long-serving Liberal Party agent stated that 'this election was Davies hardest since 1929'.[152] The defeated Conservative candidate, Leslie Morgan, declared, 'This is now a marginal seat ... We will do it next time'.[153] At seventy-five, Davies decided it was time for a younger man to enter the fray. A few months after the election he announced his retirement, which made both the Conservative and the Labour Party think the seat was now theirs for the taking.[154]

In Ynys Môn, Liberal candidate and barrister Rhys Gerran Lloyd saw the Liberal vote fall to just 13.5%, placing him behind not only Labour and the Conservatives but also Plaid Cymru. This was the first time a Liberal had ever come below Plaid Cymru in a Parliamentary election. In Conwy and Flint West the Liberals got an even lower percentage, though mercifully they kept their deposits. Meirionnydd was still a strong possibility for the Liberals with Ben (B. G.) Jones chasing Labour's T. W. Jones, finishing just 976 votes (4.5%) behind. It was one of only five constituencies in Great Britain where the Liberals did not win but obtained more than a third of the vote. Carmarthenshire was another of these seats. Alun Talfan Davies, who had first stood as an Independent candidate in the University of Wales seat in the 1943 by-election came second, behind Megan Lloyd George. Talfan Davies was part of the talented 'Liberal new blood' who thirty years before would have come straight in as an MP. In Carmarthen, he had sought to counter Megan's appeal to both Labour and the Liberals by using the campaign slogan 'Don't betray your traditions'. Despite this, he had been in contention for a strong second position. But when the result came, the seat was still really a two horse race between Labour and the Liberals with Talfan Davies finishing 6,633 votes (13.6%) behind. Plaid Cymru lost their deposit in this seat with just 5.2% of the vote and the Conservatives weren't far off from doing the same. In Denbigh, Glyn Tegai Hughes failed to improve on second position and remained 4,625 votes behind the National Liberal and the Conservative candidate W. Geraint Morgan. Depressingly for the Liberal Party of Wales, South Wales was the only region in the entire United Kingdom where the party failed to field a single candidate. Outside the south, however, the Liberal vote in Wales, in the constituencies where they had stood, averaged 29 %. This made it the second strongest Liberal vote in Britain after the Scottish Highlands and Islands.[155] Still, at the same time, the highest fall in Liberal votes had been recorded in Welsh seats. Montgomeryshire was down 26.1%, Ynys Môn down 19.1%, Carmarthen down 15.2% and even Cardigan was down 6.2%. The outlook for the Welsh Liberals seemed one of terminal decline.

Towards the end of the decade the Welsh Liberals did, however, make one gain in Parliament, albeit in the House of Lords. On 19th October 1959, Lord Ogmore crossed the floor from the Labour Party to join the Liberals. Born in Bridgend in 1903 (hence the title of its river 'Ogmore' in his own peerage), David Rees Williams had been a Liberal in his youth. He later joined the Labour Party whilst enjoying a successful career as a solicitor in Cardiff. During the Second World War he served as a lieutenant colonel and chief legal adviser to Field Marshall Montgomery. Williams became the Labour MP for South Croydon in 1945 and when he was defeated in 1950 he went to the Lords and was briefly a Civil Aviation Minister in Clement Attlee's Labour government. He became a Liberal partly because of his disillusionment with Labour's nationalisation plans and partly because of his belief that a strong anti-Socialist alternative was needed to oppose the Conservative government of the time.[156] Lord Ogmore was soon at the heart of the Welsh and British Liberal Parties. He joined the British Liberal Executive in 1960, became the party's President between 1963 and 1964 and then served as Deputy Liberal Leader to Lord Rea in the House of Lords.[157] Lord Rea had warned him when he started by saying: 'Our present personnel is totally inexperienced … You may find a great amateurishness throughout our organisation which has such meagre funds compared with the big two parties'.[158] It did not deter Lord Ogmore who remained both a committed Welsh Liberal Nationalist and British Liberal until his death on the 20th of August 1976.

Conclusion

The Welsh Liberals began the post-war period considerably weakened but still as the dominant force of post-war Liberalism. Clement Davies led the British Liberal Party through much of this period. The seven MPs that the Welsh Liberals boasted in 1945 represented a high point that would not be repeated in Wales. Thus, in the 1940s and 50s, the Welsh party became less significant as each year passed. The Lloyd Georges drifted off one by one to join other political parties; the Welsh presence in the British party became increasingly thin and was being replaced by a Scottish and West Country Liberal presence. The party failed to regain its lost seats in Ynys Môn and Meirionnydd or to win in its constant near miss seat of Denbigh. They lost Carmarthen to the former Liberal, Megan Lloyd George. With the exception of Lord Ogmore's defection to the Liberal Party in 1959, there was little good news for the party. Other than it had managed to survive another year. This survival was itself owing to the efforts of a band of dedicated amateurs kept the Liberal name alive. It was their memory of a glorious Liberal past and their belief that a Liberal revival was just around the corner that kept both them and the party going.

In the decades that followed, this period in the Welsh Liberals' history would be almost totally forgotten. Firstly, this was a product of the absence of political victories that had occurred in England at Torrington and could be used as a rallying cry. The second reason was that its political activists had by now to a mere handful in Wales, concentrated in just a few constituencies. In the future, the party would have to start virtually from scratch in most constituencies with no members from this period to bridge this time gap between then and its historical heyday. Yet, as bad as things appeared in 1959, they would become still worse. The party had not yet reached its lowest point.

Notes

1. Cited in Alan Watkins (1966) The Liberal Dilemma, MacGibbon and Kee, p. 57
2. Winston Churchill nearly stood in Caerphilly as a Liberal candidate in 1923, he made frequent trips to Wales between 1905 and 1923 promoting the Liberal cause. Churchill archive to author.
3. J. E. Emlyn Jones now lived in Cardiff but had previously been the MP for North Dorset between 1922–24. He was also President of Cardiff and Barry Liberal Council and Pontypridd Liberal Association
4. McCallum, R. B. and Readman, Alison (1999) The British General Election of 1945, MacMillan, p. 64
5. Liberal Party Manifesto 1945
6. McCallum, R. B. and Readman, Alison (1999) op. cit., p. 223
7. A lost deposit resulted from obtaining less then 1/8 th of the total vote
8. *South Wales Echo and Evening Express*, 26th July 1945, p. 1
9. Ibid, p. 1
10. Judith Trefor Lewis to author
11. Graham Jones, J. (1999) A breach in the family, The Lloyd Georges, Journal of Liberal History, Issue 25, Winter 1999–2000, p. 333
12. Jones was a senior lecturer at Aberystwyth and the author of Welsh religious plays
13. McCallum, R. B. and Readman, Alison (1999) opt cit, p. 221
14. Roberts, David (1985) The Strange Death of Liberal Wales, in John Osmond's The National Question Again: Welsh Political Identity in the 1980s, Gomer, p. 78
15. Watkins, Alan (1966) The Liberal Dilemma, MacGibbon and Kee, p. 42
16. *South Wales Evening Post* 2/11/45
17. Sweeting, Andrew (1998) 'Gwilym Lloyd George' in the Dictionary of Liberal Biography, Politico's Publishing, p. 239
18. Western Telegraph and Cymric Times, 5th July 1945
19. Ibid, p. 7
20. Western Telegraph and Cymric Times, 28th June 1945, p. 7
21. Rasmussen, Jorgen Scott (1965) The Liberal Party, Constable, p. 11
22. Graham Jones, J. (1999) op. cit., p. 332
23. Wyburn-Powell, Alun (2003) Clement Davies Liberal Leader, Politico's Publishing, p. 178
24. *Western Telegraph and Cymric Times*, 16th June 1945, p. 2
25. *The Manchester Guardian*, 30/11/47
26. South Wales Echo and Evening Express, 27th June 1945, p. 3
27. *Western Telegraph and Cymric Times*, 23rd February 1950, p. 7
28. Lord Hooson to author
29. Ingham, Robert (1999) Leadership Contests of the Past, Journal of Liberal Democrat History, Issue 23, Summer 1999, pp. 3–4
30. Rasmussen, Jorgen Scott (1965) op. cit., p. 41
31. Roberts, David (1985) op. cit., p. 79
32. Roberts, David (1985) op. cit., p. 80
33. Graham Jones, John (1993A) 'The Liberal Party and Wales, 1945–79', The Welsh History Review, Vol. 16, No. 3 June 1993, p. 330
34. Cited in Roberts, David (1985) op. cit., p. 80
35. Health was not transferred to Welsh administration until 1968
36. Jones, Meryn (1991) op. cit., p. 207
37. The Liberal Party of Wales (1959) New Deal for Wales's, Manifesto for the General Election October 1959, p. 7
38. Graham Jones, J. (1992) The Parliament For Wales campaign 1950–1956, The Welsh History Review, Vol. 16, No. 2, p. 209
39. Edwards, Andrew (2002) Political Change in North-West Wales: 1960–1974: The Decline of the Labour Party and the Rise of Plaid Cymru, Ph.D, Bangor University, p. 83
40. *The New Radical* (1947) Vol. 1, No. 1, Aberystwyth, p. 21
41. Edwards, Andrew (2002) op. cit., p. 84

42. Y. Cymro, 6 January 1950
43. Blaidd is a play on words as it is Welsh for wolf, cited in Andrew Edwards (2002) op. cit., p. 84
44. Cruikshank, R. J. (1948) The Liberal Party, Collins, p. 10
45. Rasmussen, Jorgen Scott (1965) op. cit., p. 121
46. Watkins, Alan (1966) op. cit., p. 47
47. Duttton, David (2008) op. cit., p. 166
48. Watkins, Alan (1966) op. cit., p. 49
49. Watkins, Alan (1966) op. cit., p. 49
50. Rasmussen, Jorgen Scott (1965) op. cit., p. 43
51. Jones, Mervyn (1991) op. cit., p. 206
52. *The Manchester Guardian*, 30/01/50, p. 4
53. Edwards, Andrew (2002) op. cit., p. 84
54. Roberts, David (1985) op. cit., p. 86
55. Rasmussen, Jorgen Scott (1965) op. cit., p. 94
56. Watkins, Alan (1966) op. cit., p. 54
57. Nicholas, H. G. (1999) The British General Election of 1950, MacMillan Press, p. 237
58. Thorpe, Jeremy (1999) In My Own Time, Politico's Publishing, p. 61
59. Wyburn-Powell, Alun (2003) op. cit., p. 170
60. Jones, Beti (1999) op. cit., p. 186
61. This was the last time that John Bellis acted as Megan's agent. He had been with her for every election since 1929. A former cashier at Holyhead docks he had been personally endorsed by her father and had been a firm friend with Megan since 1929, Jones, Mervyn (1991) op. cit., p. 77
62. Jones, Mervyn (1991) op. cit., p. 210
63. Nicholas, H. G. (1999) op. cit., p. 127
64. Madgwick, P. J., Griffiths, Non and Walker, Valerie (1973) The Politics of Rural Wales: A Case Study on Cardiganshire, Hutchinson, p. 61
65. Nicholas, H. G. (1999) op. cit., p. 323
66. *Western Telegraph and Cymric Times*, 23rd February, 1950
67. E. H. Garner Evans had stood as a Liberal candidate for Denbigh in 1945 and was seen widely by Liberals there and elsewhere as being a 'turncoat'
68. Lord Hooson to author
69. Nicholas, H. G. (1999) op. cit., p. 323
70. *The Manchester Guardian*, 13/11/50, p. 5
71. Ibid.
72. Jones, Mervyn (1991) op. cit., p. 214
73. Watkins, Alan (1966) op. cit., p. 57
74. *The Manchester Guardian*, 19/11/50, p. 8
75. Watkins, Alan (1966) op. cit., p. 59
76. Son of Thomas Waterhouse the North Wales Liberal grandee, later Sir Ronald Waterhouse the High Court Judge. He was President of the Cambridge Liberals and fought Orpington for the Liberals. In 1959 Waterhouse stood for Labour in Flint West coming second to the Conservative Nigel Birch
77. Watkins, Alan (1966) op. cit., p. 59
78. Graham Jones, J. (2002C) 'Grimond's Rival: Biography of Roderic Bowen MP, Journal of Liberal Democrat History, Issue 34/35 Spring/Summer 2002, pp. 26–33
79. *The Manchester Guardian*, 27/05/51, p. 5
80. Butler, David (1952) The British Election of 1951, MacMillan, p. 242
81. Liberal Party (1951) Liberal Party General Election Manifesto, The Nation's Task
82. Dutton, David (2008) op. cit., p. 199
83. Captain Henry Britten Kerby had been a Second World War espionage operative
84. Butler, David (1952) op. cit., p. 198
85. Butler, David (1952) op. cit., p. 95
86. Butler, David (1952) op. cit., p. 237
87. Graham Jones, J. (1999) op. cit., p. 36
88. Ermys Roberts was offered a Vice Presidency of the Welsh Liberal Party in 1974 but rejected it. He entered the business world and became chief executive of Tootal Ties, upon his retirement he once again took part in Liberal politics before he died in 1990

89. Edwards, Andrew (2002) op. cit., p. 86
90. Edwards, Andrew (2002) op. cit., p. 86
91. Graham Jones, J. (2002C) op. cit., p. 28
92. Butler, David (1952) op. cit., p. 245
93. Cited in Edwards, Andrew (2002) op. cit., p. 89
94. Glyn Tegai Hughes to author
95. His wife Jean became President of the North Wales Liberal Federation (Lord Thomas to author)
96. Glyn Tegai Hughes to author
97. Edwards, Andrew (2002) op. cit., p. 86
98. Edwards, Andrew (2002) op. cit., p. 86
99. Edwards, Andrew (2002) op. cit., p. 86
100. Letter from John and Jenny Gibbs to Glyn Tegai Hughes 6/3/62
101. Glyn Tegai Hughes to author
102. Graham Jones, J. (2002C) op. cit., p. 28
103. Roddick, Winston (2003) Sir Maldwyn Thomas: A tribute by Winston Roddick, Papers from the Lloyd George Society Weekend School, Abernant Lake Hotel, Llanwrtyd Wells.
104. Watkins, Alan (1966) op. cit., p. 75
105. Graham Jones, J. (1999) op. cit., p. 36
106. The Liberal Party, Notes to Press Officers, 29/4/56
107. Rasmussen, Jorgen Scott (1965) The Liberal Party, Constable, p. 44
108. Sell, Geoffrey (1999) 'A Sad Business' The Resignation of Clement Davies, Journal of Liberal Democrat History, Issue 24, Autumn 1999, pp. 14–17
109. Dingle Foot was the brother of Michael Foot, future Labour Leader and MP for Ebbw Vale
110. Sell, Geoffrey (1999) op. cit., p. 14
111. Belzak, Steve (2008) 'Swinging in the Sixties to the Liberals: Mary Murphy and Pontypridd Urban District', Conference Paper, Political Studies Association Conference, Swansea, 2nd April 2008, p. 1
112. Son of Thomas Waterhouse, member of the Liberal Party Executive and Flintshire county councillor
113. Graham Jones, J. (2002C) op. cit., p. 29
114. Liberal Party Organisation, October, 1955 General Election report back
115. Ibid
116. Sell, Geoffrey (1999) op. cit., p. 16
117. The Guardian, 1 October 1956
118. Wyburn-Powell, Alun (2003) Clement Davies Liberal Leader, Politico's Publishing, p. 228
119. Graham Jones, J. (2002C) op. cit., p. 29
120. Liberal Democrat News, 7/9/01, Obituary, Roderic Bowen QC, Lord Emlyn Hooson, p. 8
121. Pottle, Mark [Editor] (2000): Daring to Hope: The Diaries and Letters of Violet Bonham Carter 1946–1969, Weidenfeld and Nicolson, p. 242
122. The Conservative Government under Anthony Eden had sent a British force to join with the French in the invasion of Egypt to seize the Suez canal which the Egyptians under President Nassar had nationalised. This action caused widespread condemnation both within the United Kingdom and abroad.
123. Liberal Party Organisation minutes 9/3/56
124. Liberal Party Organisation minutes 14/4/56
125. Liberal Party Organisation minutes 9/3/56
126. Douglas, Roy (1971) op. cit., p. 268
127. Judith Trefor Lewis to author
128. The Newport by-election in July 1956 and the Pontypool by-election in November 1958 were not contested by the Liberals, although the other three parties in Wales contested them all
129. Douglas, Roy (1971) op. cit., p. 268
130. Rasmussen, Jorgan Scott (1965) op. cit., p. 152
131. Lord Hooson to author
132. Rasmussen, Jorgan Scott (1965) op. cit., p. 152
133. Grimond, Jo (1979) Memoirs, Heinemann, p. 197
134. Judith Trefor Thomas to author
135. Graham Jones, J. (2002C) op. cit., p. 30
136. Judith Trefor Thomas to author

137. Lord Hooson to author
138. Cited in Jones, Mervyn (1991) op. cit., p. 285
139. Jones, Mervyn (1991) op. cit., p. 283
140. Jones, Mervyn (1991) op. cit., p. 287
141. Judith Trefor Thomas to author
142. Honor Balfour did have a history of resigning from the party. In December 1943 she resigned from the party's executive in order to fight the Darwen by-election as an Independent Liberal
143. Watkins, Alan (1966) op. cit., p. 75
144. *The Manchester Guardian*, 10/5/57, p. 4
145. Pottle, Mark [Editor] (2000) op. cit., p. 198
146. Liberal Party Organisation, Twentieth Report, Scarborough, September, 1959
147. The Liberal Challenge, 1959 details British Liberal constituency parties membership
148. Liberal Party Assembly Meeting, Scarborough, September 17th–19th, 1959, Final Agenda, Liberal Party Organisation p. 9
149. Talfun Davies, Alun (1960) Some Reflections on the Election, The Welsh Liberal Challenge, Spring 1960, No.2
150. Graham Jones, J. (2002C) op. cit., p. 29
151. Graham Jones, J. (2002C) op. cit., p. 29
152. Graham Jones, J. (1993B) 'Emlyn Hooson's Parliamentary Debut: The Montgomeryshire By-election of 1962, The Montgomeryshire Collections, p. 121
153. Ibid p. 121
154. Graham Jones, J. (1993B) op. cit., p. 121
155. Butler, David, E. and Rose, Richard (1960) The British General Election of 1959, MacMillan p. 193
156. *The Times*, 19/10/59, p. 10
157. *The Times*, Wednesday, 01/10/76, p. 14
158. Graham Jones, J. (1993A) op. cit., p. 341

5

THE FIRST TRULY WELSH
LIBERAL PARTY (1960–1974)

Introduction

The Liberal Party of Wales had now been in existence for generations, but was still, in effect, only an umbrella organisation for the North and South Wales Welsh Liberal federations. David Lloyd George's attempts to unite the party under *Cymru Fydd* over 70 years previously had failed because the rivalry and mistrust between North and South Wales had proved too great. These rivalries persisted and there were still splits between the North and the South Wales Federation over issues of policy, both British and Welsh. At the start of the 1960s, the Liberal Party in Wales was, therefore, in a subordinate position to the Federations.

The Liberal Party in Wales was now nothing but a pale shadow of its former glory of just half a century before. However, this was to be the period in which the Welsh Liberals would finally have both the courage and the self-interest to form themselves into an autonomous state party. The problems and divisions associated with the Liberal federations would finally be resolved. Those that formed this new Welsh state party had nothing less in their minds than the rebirth of Welsh Liberalism. This chapter explores the events that led to the foundation of the Welsh Liberal Party in September 1966 and maps how the fortunes of the party were determined in the light of the arrival of this new party structure and how the party was able to embark on the slow process of electoral regeneration.

The Sixties: 'A New Decade and New Tests'

In the spring of 1960, Liberal activity of any note in Wales was restricted to the constituencies of Brecon and Radnor, Cardiff North, Cardigan, Conwy, Denbigh, Meirionnydd, Monmouthshire, Montgomeryshire, Pontypridd and Wrexham. In the latter two constituencies, there had even been some recent council election victories over Labour.[1] On Pontypridd Urban District Council, W. L. Simmons won a seat on the Trallwn Ward, re-establishing the Liberal presence there after a gap of six years.[2] Important as this was for the Pontypridd Liberals, it was on a small scale for the Welsh party as a whole when compared to the pre-war era. Nevertheless, as Welsh Liberalism entered the 'swinging sixties' there was a new determination in the party that they would contest in all possible elections. In the former Liberal National seat of Swansea West, a new Liberal Association was formed in 1961 and now set out to contest the next general election.

The first selection for a Welsh Westminster seat was not Swansea West but that of the retiring Clement Davies in Montgomeryshire. For a Liberal seat such as this there was intense interest from across the party. Local speculation was initially concentrated on Mary Davies, the daughter of the late Lord Davies, and his son, Edward Davies, president of the Montgomeryshire Liberal Association. Also mentioned was Emlyn Hooson, described as 'the newest and most promising Silk on the Wales and Chester circuit'.[3] Unlike the others, Hooson was not related to any previous Liberal MPs; he came from a Liberal family in the Vale of Clwyd. His parents were great admirers of Lloyd George but he was the first Liberal politician in his family.[4] He had also married into as about as prominent a Montgomeryshire Liberal family as was possible. Hooson's wife's (Shirley) father was the leading Mid Wales Liberal figure, Sir George Frederick Hamer.[5]

In July 1960, the Montgomeryshire Liberal Association invited the local Liberal branches to nominate possible candidates. In the event, 17 national and local figures came to light, including Frank Byers, Mark Bonham-Carter, Mary Gabett Edwards, Major Peter Lewis, Lt Colonel Patrick Lort-Phillips and former Meirionnydd MP Emrys Roberts. Only four, however, received a substantial number of nominations: Emlyn Hooson (25 nominations), The Hon. Edward Davies (24), Stanley Clement Davies (14) and Dr Glyn Tegai Hughes (12). A number of the prospective candidates withdrew their names: Frank Byers and Mark Bonham-Carter pleaded attachment to their existing constituencies of Bolton East and Torrington.

Dr Glyn Tegai Hughes felt he could not compete against his friend Emlyn Hooson and, therefore, prevented his name from going forward once more.[6] The Hon. Edward Davies[7] also withdrew and the final short list put forward by the Association Council, on the 11th of March 1961, had Lt Col Patrick Lort Phillips, Stanley Clement Davies (the sitting MP's son) and Emlyn Hooson. Although not well-known in the Montgomeryshire seat, Lt Col Lort-Phillips came from a Pembrokeshire Liberal family with a strong Liberal pedigree. He had, however, a mixed relationship with the party. He had publicly resigned with some bitterness as the British Liberal Party's joint Treasurer in April 1960 after a Standing Party, excluded him after commencing operations to regulate affairs more closely.[8] For a short time, however, this was to be the Welsh Party's gain, as Lort-Phillips committed himself to the Welsh party as an agent in its revival. It was as part of this plan to help the party's revival and boost his own stature within that party that he had put his name forward for the Montgomeryshire seat. Stanley Clement Davies then withdrew on health grounds and Hooson became the favoured candidate above Lort-Phillips and was duly selected shortly afterwards. He now had much work to do, as the Conservatives and the Labour Party were both becoming increasingly active in the seat.

The Ebbw Vale By-election

Prior to the Montgomeryshire selection, Lort-Phillips had already made a name for himself as a Welsh parliamentary candidate. In October 1960, a by-election had been called upon the death of the Welsh Labour politician and political icon Aneurin Bevan. The Welsh Liberal Party had already discussed the by-election in late August when it had decided to send an agent to the constituency to assess possible options.[9]

Lort-Phillips, then the President of the South Wales' Liberal Federation, declared publicly that he would be standing for the Liberals without going through any form of adoption. Privately, he made it known to the Liberal Party of Wales, that if he was not supported by them he would stand as an Independent Liberal.[10] Apart from the manner in which Lort-Phillips had declared his candidacy, the main problem for the party in Wales was that he openly campaigned for unilateral disarmament, which was against the Liberal Party's defence policy. This meant that Grimond would not speak on his behalf during the campaign.[11] Grimond was aware of the problems caused in the Carmarthen by-election three years that had been earlier by supporting a candidate who held opposing views to the party's. He was no longer prepared to endorse these candidates at the expense of the wider party. Lort-Phillips responded angrily to this perceived snub. The following April he wrote in a letter to Grimond:

'The Party has ceased to exist as an effective political force, and its officers and Executive have become meaningless shadows. The Party is dead ... No previous Leader of the Party in all its history has ever treated, or tried to treat, the party with such contempt and indifference'.[12]

Yet this report could not have been said to relate to the Ebbw Vale Liberal Association. This had long since disappeared and the party had not fought a Parliamentary election there since 1929. It was reformed on the 10th of October 1960 in order to give some legitimacy to his candidacy. Accordingly, Lort-Phillips was adopted by the new Association on the 31st of October and he and his agent, Ieuan Lewis Edwards, formed a skeleton crew to start the campaign. Despite some severe criticism by the Party in London, Lort-Phillips enjoyed widespread support from the Liberals and the Liberal Party of Wales. They had already declared in August that if the Liberals did fight the election it should be with Lort-Phillips as the candidate.[13] Many admired him for taking on the role of Liberal candidate when no-one else had risen to the challenge. As a result, the party launched 'Operation Welsh Sunrise' in order to provide him with an effective fighting fund.[14] In the eventual election for Ebbw Vale, Lort-Phillips came third and secured some 3449 (11.5%) of the vote in a seat the Welsh Liberals had last fought over three decades before.[15] The Labour winner, Michael Foot, came from a prominent Liberal family that included former Liberal cabinet members and the former Liberal MP defector friend of Megan Lloyd George – Dingle Foot.

Ebbw Vale By-election Result 17th November 1960

Candidate	Party	Vote	Percentage
Michael Foot	Labour	20528	68.8
Sir Brandon Rhys Williams	Conservative	3799	12.7
Patrick Lort-Phillips	Liberal	3449	11.5
Emrys Roberts	Plaid Cymru	2091	7
	Majority	16729	56.1
	Turnout		76.1

This by-election result and the failure to secure the Montgomeryshire nomination was not the end for Lort-Phillips' ambitions. In September 1962, he sought the nomination of his own home constituency of Pembrokeshire. He failed to get it and Meurig Jones, a personnel manager, was selected by the Liberal Association instead. Lort-Phillips did not take this rejection well and shortly afterward resigned from the Liberal Party, declaring that in future he would be supporting the Labour Party.[16] He subsequently failed to find a suitable constituency with Labour and returned to the Liberals once again in 1972 but would no longer play a central role in the Welsh party.

Away from Westminster the 1961 local council elections saw the Welsh Liberals take a small number of seats on councils in Cardiff, Neath and Llanelli. Despite these modest gains, the wider non-elected representation of the party in Wales was now much smaller than the comparable party in England and Scotland. For the 1962 Edinburgh Liberal Assembly, only 15 of Wales' 36 constituencies were affiliated to the Liberal Association, 21 were not. Wales was entitled to send only 18 delegates to conference, the smallest by some considerable way of any region in the United Kingdom, with the exception of Northern Ireland. Scotland, in contrast, was now able to send 368 delegates, some 350 more.[17] At the elections for the officers to the British Liberal Party Organisation, there were no representatives from Wales despite the fact that Roderic Bowen and Lord Ogmore were two of only eight Parliamentarians attending the conference. The Welsh party by now had become all but invisible at a British level.

The 1962 Montgomeryshire By-election

Lort-Phillips had failed to set the Liberal world alight at Ebbw Vale, but a year and a half later on the 14th of March 1962, a by-election of massive political significance swept the country. Eric Lubbock turned a Conservative majority of 15,000 into a Liberal majority of 7,855 in Orpington. If this was repeated elsewhere in the country, the Liberals could be the next government. In virtually every by-election that followed, the Liberals gained a third of the vote or more, but, with the exception of Montgomeryshire, they did not win any of these seats. The Montgomeryshire by-election was caused by the death of Clement Davies in March 1962 at a London clinic. Lord Atkin of Aberdovey[18] said of Clement Davies, 'There was no high office in the land which was not his for the acceptance, when he was kidnapped by commerce and became one of the head directors of Unilever'.[19] He was widely seen as the man who had saved the Liberal Party not only in Wales but also in Britain from extinction. Montgomeryshire had benefited from his talent for over three decades but it was now time to choose another MP. The Liberals hoped it would be a barrister called Emlyn Hooson.

The campaigning in the by-election was fierce, bearing in mind the traditional and gentler methods of campaigning style Montgomeryshire was used to. The great days of public meetings had passed but this by-election helped revive them. Many Liberals came into the constituency and spoke for Hooson, including Roderic Bowen, Jo Grimond, Jeremy Thorpe and Eric Lubbock.[20] Lord Ogmore also made some powerful speeches on the decline of the Welsh rural communities at the hands of the 'Tory government'. This by-election also saw Plaid Cymru stand a candidate in Montgomeryshire for the first time. Their candidate was the novelist and playwright, Islwyn Ffowc Ellis, who subsequently lost his deposit.

In the campaign itself were the Conservatives who were seen as the main threat. Almost the whole Cabinet came out to support Robert H. Dawson, a local farmer. These included household names such as Henry Brook (Lord Brecon), the Welsh speaking Enoch Powell, Nigel Birch, Ian McLeod and Rab Butler. Dawson, however, did little to endear himself to the constituents. He campaigned on defence issues, stressing his belief in maintaining 'an independent nuclear deterrent' but this was of little interest to most voters in Montgomeryshire.[21] Dawson also frequently stated that 'he was not a swivel chair candidate' which no one really understood and, consequently, most voters felt somewhat confused and bemused by him and had no inclination to vote for him. Far worse, however, was the fact that he had refused to play cricket for Montgomeryshire; instead he played for the 'Gentlemen of Shropshire'. This was an unforgivable sin for Montgomeryshire voters, which he would soon discover as they voted against him.[22]

Tudor Davies, the Labour candidate, also benefited from high profile support. Labour Shadow Cabinet members George Brown, Jim Griffiths and Harold Wilson visited the seat together with about half of the Welsh Labour MPs who were buoyant in their hopes of repeating their victory at Carmarthen five years before. Davies, therefore, enjoyed the endorsement of Megan Lloyd George, who spoke for him in the constituency saying that Davies and not Hooson was the man to carry on the 'Radical tradition'. Only a decade before, Hooson had sat on the Liberal Executive with Megan Lloyd George endorsing his presence. Now she was campaigning directly against him. Things had changed enormously within Welsh Liberalism in just one decade. Davies' main campaign issues were focused on reversing the 'Beeching Axe' on Montgomeryshire's railway lines and providing greater subsidies for rural industry.

Both Dawson and Davies saved most of their ire not for each other but for Hooson and the Liberals. At times both Labour and Conservative candidates' teams also indicated that they would rather see the other side win rather than the Liberals.[23] The Conservative Central Office predicted on the eve of poll that Montgomeryshire would provide them with 'Orpington in reverse' although a poll by National Opinion Poll, taken the day before the vote, had suggested that Hooson would win by a considerable margin. He was elected with a massive majority, which sent reassuring waves around the Welsh Liberals and beyond. Hooson declared that it was 'a victory of the ordinary person over the party machine'.[24] He had also proved that the vote in Montgomeryshire was truly a Liberal vote rather than a personal vote for Clement Davies. Montgomeryshire was not Carmarthen; here the Liberal roots were deeply embedded, much to the relief of the Welsh Liberals.

Montgomeryshire By-election Result 15ᵗʰ May 1962

Candidate	Party	Vote	Percentage
Emlyn Hooson	Liberal	13181	51.3
Robert H. Dawson	Conservative	5632	21.9
Tudor Davies	Labour	5299	20.6
Islwyn Ffowc Elis	Plaid Cymru	1594	6.2
	Majority	7549	29.4
	Turnout		85.1

Once elected, Hooson addressed a crowd of 1,000 cheering supporters in Welshpool's main street. He declared that 'This constituency is the heart of Liberalism and that heart is in very fine fettle and very fine shape ... It was not I who achieved this victory. I merely carried the banner.'[25] After dealing with his supporters, Hooson rapidly got into parliamentary business. As part of a small Liberal team, he spoke on Defence, Law and Order and Home Affairs. *The Times* journalist Alun Jones was his adviser. Jones himself was later created a Labour Peer (Lord Chalfont) in 1964 and served as a Minister at the Foreign Office, before resigning from the Labour Party in the mid 1970s to sit as a cross-bencher in the Lords. There Hooson would join him once more in 1979.

The Post-war Structure of the Welsh Liberal Party

Writing about the structure of the post-war Liberal Party in 1965, Jorgen Scott Ramussen noted:

'The Welsh Liberals and, to a greater extent the Scottish Liberals maintain a modicum of separate organisation. But this is not so great as to warrant separate discussion. As regards federations, Wales has two and Scotland none'.[26]

The main purpose of these federations as far as the Liberals were concerned was to 'facilitate administrative decentralisation and to provide more immediate assistance to the constituency associations than national headquarters can achieve'.[27] The federations, therefore, saw their role as running the Liberal Party in their area and communicating this to the Liberal Party Organisation and the media. As we saw earlier, however, the contradictory directions followed by the two Welsh federations often proved to be damaging to the party rather than facilitating effective decentralised administration.

In 1960, the Liberal Party Organisation in London in its booklet 'This is Your Party' determined that each Federation should run on an income of around £1,500 a year. Both the North and the South Wales Federations ran on just over £100 per annum and even this amount came in only after much arm-twisting for contributions from their constituent Liberal Associations. Despite this lack of finance, the much better organised and supported North Wales Federation managed to maintain paid agents in the 1950s and early 1960s. In North Wales in the 1950s, these included Ieuan Edwards and Owen Roberts in Meirionnydd, Vanessa Ellicott in Denbigh and A. S. Phillips in Conwy. These were agents who survived on 'tiny salaries' but nevertheless provided a dedicated service in promoting the Liberal cause.[28] To aid them, a new chief Liberal organiser for Wales was appointed in 1962. He tried to get the party going again in the south of Wales but the cost of maintaining this organiser led the party into severe financial problems. The Welsh Constituency Liberal Associations were meant to pay a quota payment of £100 to the party's central organisation. Few, however, did so, much to Madoc Jones' disgust, who described the Welsh Associations' lack of response as 'a disgrace to us all'.[29]

In their structures, as well as in the constituencies, the federations also included regional representatives of the Women's Liberal and Young Liberal groups. In theory, the federations were meant to be well enough organised and financially sound enough to employ a full-time organiser. In practice, this was not the case. Perhaps, therefore, the most important role of the federation played was in the selection of candidates for the Westminster elections. It was the federations and not the Liberal Party Organisation that had the ultimate say on whether candidates could bear the Liberal name on their election leaflets. Each parliamentary candidate had to be referred to the federation before adoption. This was so 'that arrangements may be made with the Chief Whip's Office for the usual enquiries' or, in other words, they were vetted as to their suitability.[30] Not that the federations or even the Liberal Party Organisation could prevent a candidate from being selected if the constituency still desired it. The independence of the constituency association was held in such high esteem by their members, however, that the use of the central party veto on the candidate was deemed to be 'unthinkable'.[31] Welsh constituencies selected their own candidates with little interference from outside at election time.

As the Liberal Party in Wales prepared for the next general election, Hooson and Roderic Bowen would now have to work as the Welsh Liberal parliamentary team. As noted before, Bowen was not seen as a team player and was criticised for often failing to turn up at Westminster. Fortunately he was better at appearing on Liberal Party platforms in Wales.[32] Bowen could be an active campaigner when the occasion called for it and often spoke in support of Liberal candidates in by-elections.[33] He also spearheaded the pre-election campaign to 'Take Wales Ahead with the Liberals' which was launched on St David's Day on 1st March 1963 with Jeremy Thorpe in North Wales. In the south, Jo Grimond and Emlyn Hooson took the Liberal Campaign across the coastal towns and the city of Cardiff.

The General Election of 1964

Liberal	2
Labour	28
Conservative	6

The Conservative government, under Harold MacMillan and Sir Alec Douglas-Home, had been first creaking and then cracking politically since early 1961. A series of government scandals, sackings and resignations had helped the Liberals win the by-election Orpington in 1962; a number of other by-elections saw Labour wins. The Conservatives left the general election as late as they could but the October 1964 election still saw a tired Conservative government replaced by Harold Wilson's government, with the largest swing to Labour since 1945. Despite this swing, Labour still had only a five seat majority. The Liberals had had a good election on the whole, picking up three seats in Scotland, which was now experiencing the Liberal renaissance, often hoped for in Wales.

The Welsh party had produced a detailed manifesto entitled *Liberal Partnership for Wales*. Amongst a plethora of Welsh policy ideas, it proposed:[34]

1. a Mid-Wales Development Agency,
2. a Welsh Arts Trust to promote culture,
3. the establishment of a department of veterinary medicine at Aberystwyth,
4. the establishment of a Welsh ports' authority,

5. the keeping open of local railway lines,
6. the creating of a Welsh civil service and an elected council for Wales.

The Liberal electoral force behind campaigning for these manifesto ideas to be implemented covered just a third of the Welsh seats. Although some seats in South Wales were now contested, most were not. It was the South Wales Liberal Federation executives who themselves contested the key seats. The Chair, Denis (D. G.) Rees contested Cardiff North for the Liberals for the first time since 1950, gaining 16 per cent of the vote and coming third. The Treasurer Owen (O. G.) Williams stood as a Liberal in their first foray in Swansea West since 1929, receiving just under 10 per cent of the vote and losing his deposit.[35] In North Wales, however, matters had deteriorated since 1959. In Caernarfon and in Conwy, where the Liberals had put up a candidate since the war, there were no Liberal candidates. In the Welsh Liberal hopefuls, little had changed since 1959. Alun Talfan Davies was still stuck in Carmarthen 13 per cent behind Megan Lloyd George, although he had still managed three times the vote of the third placed candidate – Plaid Cymru's Gwynfor Evans. In Meirionnydd the new Liberal candidate, the Welsh speaking barrister Richard Jones, was snapping at Labour's heels, just 1,249 (5.7%) behind them in second place. In Denbigh another doctor, (this time a GP), Dr William Ellis Jones, had replaced Dr Glyn Tegai Hughes as the Liberal candidate. He kept the Liberals in second place to the Conservatives, on over 30 per cent of the vote, but he still trailed some 4,639 votes (10.8%) behind. The Liberal vote in these three seats appeared to have now reached a plateau but it was still the best opportunity the Welsh Liberals had to move forward.

In the two seats they still held, the Liberal vote was slipping downwards. In Montgomeryshire, Emlyn Hooson's majority was halved from the by-election result some two years earlier. As his opponents' votes rose, his own fell from 51.3 per cent to 42.3 per cent of the vote. For a Liberal seat, however, this still remained quite a healthy majority of some 15.6 per cent. In Cardigan a different picture was emerging. Labour had been increasing its efforts in Cardigan and had opened a new county headquarters in Aberystwyth. Bowen's infrequent Parliamentary presence – he spoke in just two debates during the two year Parliamentary sessions preceding the election – was a poor record which was beginning to damage him politically. He was seen as standing at the end of a long tradition of Welsh Liberal barrister MPs who regarded being an MP as an accompaniment to their legal careers. In an increasingly professional era of politics, it was increasingly difficult for Liberal MPs to get away with these 'dual careers'. To add to Bowen's problems, the Conservatives stood a candidate for the first time since 1950. Their candidate, Dr A. J. Ryder, took nearly 20 per cent of the vote. Labour's longstanding candidate D. J. Davies took 31 per cent of the vote. Bowen, on 38 per cent of the vote, had now a majority of just 2,219 (7.4%) down from one of 30 per cent in the 1959 election. Cardigan had now become, for the first time in over a century, a marginal Welsh Liberal constituency.

That May's council elections saw little real Liberal activity. The Liberals suffered heavy losses in national council elections but their limited number of Welsh councillors meant they had far fewer council seats to lose. In Wales just a handful of seats were contested. In the south, these elections were mainly restricted to councils in Cardiff, Swansea, Newport and Pontypridd. They managed to put up six candidates between them (five of whom were sitting councillors standing for re-election). Three of these councillors lost their seats to the Conservatives, two held their seats and the other candidate won his seat from an Independent.[36] There was some better news from North Wales where Howell Roberts became the first post-war Liberal Mayor on Colwyn Bay Metropolitan Borough Council. Howells was a rare example of Liberal success. He was not only the first Liberal mayor in Colwyn since the war but he was also the only Liberal on the council.[37] In a contest which involved around 500 Welsh councillors being elected throughout Wales, the Liberals, with only around a dozen candidates, clearly posed a serious electoral threat to nobody and seemed to most Welsh councillors something of a curious relic from days gone by.

The Liberal Party of Wales' Conference, held in Builth Wells on the 31st of July 1965, saw the new 'up and coming' Liberal MP Emlyn Hooson present but the old Liberal MP Roderic Bowen did not appear, which caused annoyance to many Liberals, including the retiring Chair Alun Talfan Davies.[38] Bowen was becoming ever more distant from the mainstream Liberal Party. It was something about which the new Chair of the Welsh Party Mr. E. Gwyn Jones was able to do very little.[39]

Towards the end of 1965, Elystan Morgan who had previously stood for Plaid Cymru in Meirionnydd in 1964 defected to the Labour Party. When he contested Meirionnydd, he had been widely seen by the party as taking enough votes off the Liberal candidate Richard Jones to deny him the seat. The Welsh Liberals were quick, therefore, to seize on the 'good news' of this defection and on the fact that he would not contest Meirionnydd again. There were soon articles in *Liberal News* speculating that Plaid Cymru would not now be able to field a candidate in Meirionnydd and that their votes could go to the Liberals. The euphoria carried on and in October Welsh *Liberal News* predicted 'that Plaid Cymru will urge all but six of its constituency organisations not to field candidates'.[40] In the event, Plaid Cymru contested 20 seats in Wales at the next general election, including finding a new candidate for Meirionnydd. The Liberals had vastly underestimated the strength of Plaid Cymru.

The 1966 General Election

Liberal	1
Labour	32
Conservative	3

Labour's governmental majority had been reduced to just three MPs by early 1966. Instead of calling for Liberal support, however, Prime Minister Harold Wilson called for an election to try to increase his majority on the last day of March 1966. After all the votes had been counted, Labour now had a 96 seat majority; they would not need Liberal support now.

Despite their distance from power, the Liberals' 1966 Welsh Manifesto had been extensively developed with political power in mind. It called once more for a Parliament for Wales, like that in Northern Ireland and also a Mid Wales Industrial Development Authority to revive the rural economy. For internal Welsh communication, a motorway between Shrewsbury and Aberystwyth along the west coast and between North and South Wales was called for. In education, there were calls to develop the University of Wales so it became truly national and to grant university college status to the Welsh College of Advanced Technology.[41] However, in most of

Wales the electorate was largely unable to vote for this manifesto, as the party contested just 11 of the 36 possible seats in Wales.

Across Great Britain the Liberals gained two seats overall but also lost a number, including one in Wales. Once again the Liberals achieved second place in Carmarthen (D. Hwyel Davies), Denbigh (Alun Talfan Davies) and Meirionnydd (North Wales Liberal Federation and Welsh Chair Edwyn (C. G.) Jones). But their vote either slipped or failed to nudge forward in each of these seats. Elsewhere in Wales there was little tactical rhyme or reason to which seats were contested. There was no Liberal candidate in Ynys Môn for the first time in the century and Cardiff North, which had been fought by the Liberals less than two years before, was left without a Liberal candidate. Cardiff South East had its first Liberal candidate since 1950 and Ogmore its first since 1929. However, neither Liberal candidate in these two seats managed to come higher than bottom of the poll. In Cardiff South-East, Cardiff County Council Liberal group leader, George William Parsons, lost his deposit but this was the first time a Liberal had contested this seat since the 1930s, which itself represented an important landmark. In Montgomeryshire, Emlyn Hooson's majority slipped slightly but he still had a considerable majority of 3494 votes (14%).

'Tragedy' as Cardigan is Lost for the Liberals

The 1966 election saw the loss of a Welsh seat that had been so solidly Liberal that there was no MP or Lord alive who knew Cardigan as anything but a Liberal seat. Over the previous decade it had been alleged by the Labour opposition in the seat that the incumbent MP Roderic Bowen was 'nothing but an absentee MP who concentrated on his legal career at the expense of his constituents'. In the end, Bowen lost the Cardigan seat, ironically, not because he devoted too much time to his legal career but because he decided to give it up for his Parliamentary one. This occurred when Sir Harry Hylton-Foster, the Speaker of the Commons, died suddenly on 2nd September 1965. Bowen was made aware that Harold Wilson wanted him to become the Deputy Speaker but, in the event, he only succeeded in getting the public endorsement of Emlyn Hooson and David Steel.[42] The Conservatives had refused to put forward an MP to fill this vacancy as it would increase the Labour government's majority. Having a Liberal fill this vacancy instead of a Conservative would have prevented Wilson's Parliamentary majority from falling to just one MP. In succeeding in his first step to becoming Speaker, Bowen had already taken the position of Deputy Chairman of Ways and Means, a post also held a few years before by Sir Rhys Hopkin Morris. It was a quasi-Deputy Speaker's position that in theory could lead him to the Speaker's post. This move put Bowen in a neutral non-voting position and prevented the Labour government's majority from falling to one. At the same time, however, it dashed the Liberals' hopes of holding the balance of power.

Bowen's desire for the Speaker's post and the ending of Liberal hopes of influencing the government caused a great deal of bitterness between him and his Liberal colleagues. They felt he had put personal ambition above the interests of the Liberal Party. Hooson had tried to persuade Bowen to make it clear to the Liberal MPs that he would only take the job of Speaker and not be tempted by anything like the Deputy Speakership or the Deputy Chairmanship of the Ways and Means. Bowen's response was to ask Hooson, 'What business is this of yours?'[43] Bowen wanted the Deputy Speakership as well as the Speakership. Hooson's pleading to the Liberal MPs to be more relaxed about Bowen's ambitions fell on deaf ears.[44] They would not support Bowen's ambitions.

When the general election came in Cardigan in 1966, Labour had been working hard on securing the seat. Their candidate, Elystan Morgan, was a young articulate lawyer, who, as noted earlier, had defected from Plaid Cymru only the year before. Morgan initially thought that Bowen would become the Speaker and there would be no contest in Cardigan. When this did not happen, he thrust his energies into winning the seat. He now benefited from the rising Labour vote there as well as from having an extensive family connection in the constituency, which helped gain even more votes. Morgan made much of the fact that Bowen wanted to be Speaker and had already become Deputy Chairman of Ways and Means. He alleged that Bowen was unable to represent them effectively because of his new position. Bowen himself put little effort into the campaign, content to rely on the County's Liberal traditions. The result was a Labour victory of 523 votes. Bowen left the constituency and the Liberal Party a bitter and defeated man. Although later on he held a string of high profile jobs in Wales, he made no attempt to have any contact with the Welsh Liberal Party or Cardigan ever again. When Geraint Howells won the seat back for the Liberals in 1974 he received no congratulations or any communication at all from Bowen.[45]

After the general election, the newspapers were full of stories about the Liberals' decline in the Celtic fringe as its strength increased in the urban areas of England. The defeats of Roderic Bowen and George Mackie at Caithness seemed proof of this. At the same time, Michael Winstanley had won Cheadle, a Manchester suburb, which had little record of support for Liberalism.[46] In the *Liberal News,* Roderic Bowen's loss was simply marked by his and George Mackie's photo with 'Two sad losses' written above it.[47] Such was the news of this defeat officially recorded.

It was felt amongst the Liberals that perhaps the one bright spot in the elections had been the failure of Plaid Cymru to make any significant headway. In many seats Plaid Cymru had lost its deposits and in those that it contested with a Liberal candidates present, it had gained only a fraction of the Liberal vote. Roger Roberts penned an article in *The Liberal News* to this effect in May 1966 under the heading 'Crisis for the Welsh Nationalists'. Roberts noted 'that nationalists only succeed where there are no Liberal candidates to vote for'.[48] It was concluded that if there was a Liberal candidate in the seat there would be no need to vote for Plaid Cymru. This was now the Liberal view and they continued to believe it in their Westminster electoral contests. At local council elections they seldom came into contact with Plaid Cymru, who were considered to be no real electoral threat to Liberal ambitions.

Another Welsh Political Storm Erupts in Carmarthen

On the 14th of May 1966, after a long illness, Megan Lloyd George died. For all but six of the last 80 years, there had been a Lloyd George amongst the Welsh MPs. Now this was to be no more. For the Welsh Liberals, this meant a chance to regain the seat.

In the general election of six weeks before, Pembrokeshire County Councillor, David Hywel Davies,[49] had gained almost twelve thousand votes for the Liberals. Although he was still over nine thousand votes short of winning the seat, he was considerably ahead of his Plaid Cymru and Conservative rivals.

Although the Carmarthen Liberal Association supported Davies' candidature in the by-election, the Liberal Party Organisation in London was far from convinced that Davies was the right man. In his investigative trip to the constituency in April, Edward Wheeler, the Liberal chief agent said about the election:[50]

'I believe that this will be crucial not only for Carmarthen but for the whole Liberal Party in Wales. I think we have got to run a really hard and exiting campaign … Basically, I do not think that Hywel Davies is the right man, and I emphasis the word 'right' as opposed to 'good' because I believe that he is the latter'.

Wheeler believed Davies was 'too short tempered' and said he would prefer 'a younger calmer man'. The main problem, aside from Wheeler's doubts about Davies, was that the Carmarthen Liberal Association, despite its 581 members in 10 branches, was all but dormant between elections with few campaigning and little leafleting going on. Since Hopkin Morris' victory in 1945, the local Liberals had grown a lot older with no new or younger faces coming to join them.[51] Despite these reservations, Davies, a Welsh speaking chartered accountant, was the Liberal candidate once again. It was also felt by local Liberals that unlike the 1957 by-election they had a much better public speaker, which would boost their chances. The *Western Mail* described Hywel Davies as a 'personable candidate, a fine platform performer, and an energetic worker'.[52] Wheeler's reservations were kept private and the Liberal press remained cheerful about Davies' prospects.

On the 10th of June *Liberal News* ran with an article titled 'The Challenge of Carmarthen.' It noted that, in the whole of the United Kingdom, Carmarthen was the sixteenth most winnable Liberal seat. The contest was between Labour and the Liberals, as it had always been. As for Plaid Cymru 'it seems unlikely that PC [Plaid Cymru] will bow out of the fight, in view of the steady increase in their vote to above the lost deposit line.' It was felt that they couldn't really cause any harm. After all, they had only started fighting the seat 11 years before and had never seriously threatened the Liberals or Labour. The article went on to note that 'the going will be tough but this seat can be won. What a tremendous shot in the arm it will give, not only for Emlyn Hooson's dream of doing for Wales what Jo Grimond has done for Scotland but to the morale of Liberals everywhere.'[53]

In the campaign itself, Hywel Davies was advised by Hooson not to attack Plaid Cymru's Gwynfor Evans[54] 'who had become something of a Nationalist Saint'. However, at a hustings at the Ivy Bush Hotel in Carmarthen, this is exactly what Hywel did. It went down well with a Liberal audience but not with the wider public.[55] Gwynfor Evans was an immensely popular Welsh Nationalist figurehead. On the platform he was also an effective performer and was able to combine the Labour Party supporters' alienation over the Wilson government's poor handling of the seamen's strike with the nationalist aspirations of the Welsh speaking constituency there. Gwynfor Evans stormed home in the seat and, in the process, lit a nationalist flame that in time would almost entirely extinguish Welsh Liberalisms support in Welsh-speaking Wales.

Evans was able to push himself from third position to first in the largest swing against a government in the post-war period. Plaid Cymru now had a seat in Parliament, 41 years after the party's founding, and the Welsh Nationalist star was now in the ascendancy. Politically, at Westminster, their one seat now equalled that of the Welsh Liberals. The political legacy of this election was to develop rapidly for Plaid Cymru over the next decade with a number of new Parliamentary victories in former Liberal seats. The Welsh Liberals, on the other hand, were now in a period of uncertainty once more. If they could not win in a recently held seat where could they win?

Carmarthen By-election Result 14th July 1966

Candidate	Party	Vote	Percentage
Gwynfor Evans	Plaid Cymru	16179	39.0%
Gwilym Prys Davies	Labour	13743	33.1%
David Hwyel Davies	Liberal	8650	20.8%
Simon Day	Conservative	2934	7.1%
	Majority	2436	5.9%
	Turnout		74.9%

The Liberals had now come third in Carmarthen in what in the future would be a Labour-Plaid Cymru battleground. The *Western Mail* noted: 'It was a Black Friday for the Liberals and a Golden Day for Plaid Cymru. Ten years ago, Carmarthen was recognised as one of the bastions of the famous Celtic fringe of Liberalism'.[56] This would never be the case again. The losing Liberal candidate, Hwyel Davis, saw the result as 'clearly a protest vote, going straight to a Welsh Nationalist Member'. Whereas North Wales Liberal activist and future Liberal Peer, Roger Roberts, writing in *The Liberal News* the week after election, explained the poor result by the uniqueness of Gwynfor Evans' political magic. On an optimistic note, he reassured Liberal readers that there was only one Gwynfor Evans and this result could not, therefore, be repeated elsewhere. In the same edition of *The Liberal News*, Wheeler, who had doubted Davies' calibre as a candidate, wrote that he felt that support for Plaid Cymru would fade and in time its supporters would return to Welsh Liberalism.[57] Once more the Liberals had underestimated the threat of Plaid Cymru.

The Problem with the Federations Comes to a Head

In 1964, on paper at least, the Liberal Party of Wales looked an impressive organisation. Its president was the Montgomeryshire Liberal and father-in-law of Emlyn Hooson, Sir George Hamer, its chairman was the respected future Judge, Alun Talfan

Davies, with two more powerful Liberals as its Treasurer, Major J. Parry Brown and Secretary, Madoc Jones (two of the key figures from the North and South Wales Federations). Its 14 vice-presidents were the sons and daughters of a number of former prominent Liberals, including Lady Olwen Carey Evans (daughter of David Lloyd George) and Dr Mostyn Lewis (son of Liberal MP Sir J. Herbert Lewis). Yet, on the ground, the Liberal Party of Wales had become almost totally ineffective as a body to push Welsh Liberalism forward.[58] The years between the late 1950s and the mid 1960s showed starkly that Liberal political power had all but vanished across much of Wales. Despite this decline, the remaining Liberal activists were still unable to unite to save the wider party.

There were constant attempts to divide the party still further at the start of the decade. An attempt by the Welsh League of Young Liberals at the 1960 Welsh Party AGM to split the party in Wales into three Federations – North, South and Mid – was rejected because the wider party felt it would be compelled to put both of its MPs into the Mid Wales Federation at the expense of the North Wales one.[59] Another attempt by Dr Mostyn Lewis in January 1961 to form a Welsh Borders' Federation failed. This would have been centred on Shrewsbury (including the West Midlands, North Wales and Brecon and Radnor).[60] It failed because the two Welsh Federations felt it was taking the 'cream of the Welsh constituencies from North and Mid Wales' into England and undermining the existing Welsh Federations.[61] This was also the only attempt in the party's history to bring united elements of the Welsh and English Liberal parties as one Federation. Despite jointly rejecting this proposal, the two Welsh Federations still distrusted each other, wouldn't work together and, as a result, often produced contradictory policy statements.[62]

In early 1962, the Federations were as far apart as ever. In late February, at a meeting of the South Wales Federation, with executives John and Jennie Gibbs, Ieuan Lewis Edwards, Alun Talfan Davies (Chair) and Lieutenant Colonel Dai Rees present, the future of the South Wales Federation was discussed. John and Jennie Gibbs wrote to Madoc Jones, the North Wales' Secretary and Liberal stalwart, describing the situation tersely:[63]

'Both Dai [Rees] (godfather of the Llanelly lot) and Parry Brown are keen on building up a strong South Wales Liberal Federation, both condemn "that lot" which is you up there (and you can look a bit like a clique at times even to my friendly eye), and both of them are in close and constant contact with the London HQ.'

Madoc Jones and Jennie Gibbs, however, were both in favour of a strong Liberal Party of Wales, although Madoc Jones believed any Welsh Party Office should be in the more active North rather than in the 'derelict' constituencies of the South. By March 1962, Major Parry Brown had changed his mind concerning the Liberal Party of Wales and now felt that it was 'the important thing'.[64] The newly appointed South Wales Liberal Federation Treasurer, Owain Glyn Williams, was also a 'strong pro-unity and Liberal Party of Wales man'.[65] The tide was turning in favour of the end of the federations and their eventual replacement, with a united Welsh state party, was becoming a possibility.

Mr. D. A. Thomas and the Strike.

Western Mail cartoon by J.M. Staniforth. It shows how D.A. Thomas (later Lord Rhondda) the MP for Merthyr Tydfil and also owner of the Cambrian Colliery company, was 'caught between management and workers' during one of the bitter coalfield disputes.

Liberal leader William Gladstone was the first Prime Minister to recognise Wales as a distinct nation.

The Right Honourable David Lloyd-George,
President of the Board of Trade.

Carnarvon Boroughs.

D. LLOYD-GEORGE	...	...	...	L.	3,221
R. N. NAYLOR	...	...	...	C.	1,997
Lib. Maj.	...	...	...		1,224

MR. DAVID LLOYD-GEORGE, M.P., was born in Manchester on January 17th, 1863, and is the son of the late Mr. William George, Schoolmaster. He was educated at the Llanystumdwy National School. In 1879 he was articled to the firm of the late Mr. Breese, Portmadoc, and five years later he began practising on his own account. In 1888 his name was put forward by the Pwllheli Liberals as a suitable candidate for the Carnarvon Boroughs; the following year he contested the seat and triumphed, and at the General Election, 1892, he increased his majority tenfold. Mr. Lloyd-George possesses all the elements of the true orator, and his speeches ring with Celtic fervour. His pluck and independence of judgment and action have been shown in the brave stand he made in the Committee on the Clergy Discipline Bill, in his skirmishes with the Welsh Bishops, and in his famous plan of campaign and revolt against the Education Act, 1902.

GREAT SUCCESS OF MESSRS. D. A. THOMAS AND LLOYD-GEORGE.

J.M. Staniforth cartoon from 1895 showing D.A. Thomas and David Lloyd George fighting for the disestablishment of the Anglican Church in Wales.

David Lloyd George, the Welsh Liberal who dominated British politics for over fifty years.

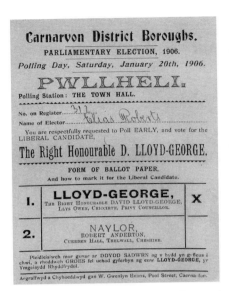

David Lloyd George's 1906 General Election leaflet. The famous 'landslide election'.

D.A. Thomas, President of the South Wales Liberal Federation and arch rival of Lloyd George.

D.A. Thomas' January 1910 General Election leaflet, when he won the Cardiff constituency, beating the Conservative Lord Ninian Edward Crichton-Stuart (The Marquis of Bute).

Reginald McKenna, Home Secretary and later Chancellor (1911-1916), the other Welsh Liberal in the Cabinet.

Photo by Alfred Freke, Queen St., Cardiff.

Rhondda.

WILLIAM ABRAHAM (unopposed).

MR. WILLIAM ABRAHAM was born in 1842, and is the son of a working miner. He was educated at the National School, Carnarvon. He married, in 1860, Sarah Williams. He has been a Miners' Agent since the year 1873. He is President of the South Wales Miners' Federation, and has been the most prominent Miners' Leader in South Wales and Monmouthshire for many years past. His popularity may be gauged by the fact that the holiday, which until recently the colliers were accustomed to take on the first Monday of each month, was known as "Mabon's Day." He has represented the Rhondda Valley District of Glamorganshire since 1885.

William Abraham (Mabon) the Lib Lab MP for the Rhondda who was a loyal Liberal-supporting MP until his retirement in 1910.

ST. GEORGE AND THE DRAGON.
(Not the Welsh one.)

'The man who won the war'. J.M. Staniforth's portrayal of Lloyd George.

'Mr Abraham did not write any address - Returned unopposed - nothing done'.

W. Evans, Mabon's election agent in the Rhondda, responding to a request for a copy of his candidate's election leaflet in 1906. Many Welsh Liberal and Lib Lab MPs were returned unopposed in this election.

Ivor Churchill Guest, MP for Cardiff 1906-10, one of three members of the Guest family to be elected as MPs in Wales and a central character in the Liberal Party.

Margaret Haig, 2nd Viscountess Rhondda, daughter of D.A. Thomas and a leading Welsh suffragette

The 1922 Newport by-election during which W.L. Moore, far right of picture, signalled the end of the Lloyd George Coalition government.

The 1922 General Election saw the defeat of Lloyd George's Liberals and their exit from the Government.

David Lloyd George, Sir Alfred Mond and Herbert Asquith in 1923.

Sir Alfred Mond (1st Baron Melchett), the long serving Welsh Liberal MP, industrialist, anti-Socialist and senior Liberal figure who fell out with Lloyd George and joined the Conservatives in 1926.

A new road linking Cardiff's City Centre to the National Assembly in the Bay was named after Lloyd George by the capital's Labour-controlled council, much to the delight of the city's Liberal Democrat councillors.

Despite never again being in government after 1922, Lloyd George left a huge imprint on Welsh politics. This statute was erected outside the National Museum of Wales in Cardiff.

In 1929, Megan Lloyd George became Wales' first female MP.

Lloyd George's land policy 'the Green Book' was widely rejected by Welsh Liberal MPs.

Megan Lloyd George's election leaflet in 1935 when she stood in Ynys Môn.

Gwilym Lloyd George, Liberal MP for Pembroke, who became a Minister in the 1939-45 wartime coalition government. He would later become a Conservative Home Secretary.

Grace Robert, aside from Megan Lloyd George, was the only inter-war female Liberal candidate in Wales when she stood for Caerphilly in 1929

Sir Henry Morris Jones, the Denbighshire Liberal MP who joined the Liberal Nationals.

Clement Davies, the post-war Leader of the Liberal Party and long-serving MP for Montgomeryshire.

Sir Rhys Hopkin Morris' 1945 election address. Hopkin Morris unexpectedly won the Carmarthen seat from Labour.

Sir Lewis Jones defeat in 1945, would spell the end of Liberal parliamentary representation in South Wales for the next 65 years.

The 1959 General Election manifesto of The Liberal Party of Wales.

The headed paper of The Liberal Party of Wales. It bears the name of party Secretary, Geraint Madoc Jones, who was instrumental in keeping the party alive in the decades that followed the Second World War.

From his election in 1962, Emlyn Hooson would be central in driving the direction of the Liberal Party in Wales for the next two decades.

Roderic Bowen's defeat in Cardigan in 1966 brought to an end over 100 years of Liberal parliamentary domination in the County.

A photograph taken at the Liberal Assembly in Eastbourne in 1970. Back-row (L to R): Lord (Geraint) Howells; unknown; Ken Rees; and Emlyn Thomas former General Secretary of the Welsh Liberal Party. Front row: Lord (Martin) Thomas; Lord Ogmore; Lord (Emlyn) Hooson; and Lord Lloyd of Cilgerran.

A 1974 election poster for David Hando, a long-serving Newport councillor, who contested the Monmouth constituency.

Alex Carlile, pictured here with David Steel in 1979, would regain Montgomeryshire at the 1983 election.

The 1974 election calling card of Norman Lewis, the Welsh Liberal Party Treasurer who fought the Caerphilly constituency.

Geraint Howells, MP for Cardigan, became the dominant figure in the Welsh Liberal Party after Emlyn Hooson's defeat in the 1979 election.

A Campaign Bulletin produced by the Welsh Liberal Party in 1982.

By the early 1990s, Liberal Democrat 'Focus' leaflets were appearing across most of the urban areas where the party was active.

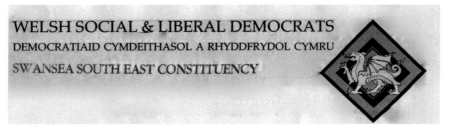

Welsh Social and Liberal Democrats headed paper from 1988, the party would soon remove the word 'Social' from its title.

John Dixon and Paddy Ashdown campaiging in the 1994 European parliamentary elections

The Welsh Liberal Democrats targeted five seats at the 1997 General Election. Disappointingly they won just two, Montgomeryshire and Brecon & Radnor.

The appeal, in 1997, to re-elect Richard Livsey in Brecon & Radnor.

Paddy Ashdown was the federal leader during the 1990s. In his book 'Beyond Westminster: Finding Hope in Britain', he wrote extensively about the Liberal tradition in Breconshire.

The Welsh Liberal Democrats frequently experienced problems getting their members to stand under the party label. Here, Councillor Bob Fox also uses the 'independent' label during the 1994 Rhondda Cynon Taff Council election.

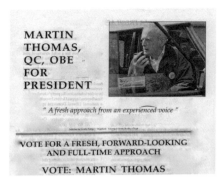

MARTIN
THOMAS,
QC, OBE
FOR
PRESIDENT

" A fresh approach from an experienced voice "

VOTE FOR A FRESH, FORWARD-LOOKING
AND FULL-TIME APPROACH

VOTE: MARTIN THOMAS

Martin Thomas' election address in the contest for President of the federal party. The election was won by Charles Kennedy.

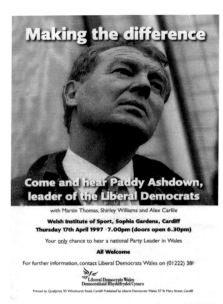

Making the difference

Come and hear Paddy Ashdown, leader of the Liberal Democrats

with Martin Thomas, Shirley Williams and Alex Carlile

Welsh Institute of Sport, Sophia Gardens, Cardiff
Thursday 17th April 1997 · 7.00pm (doors open 6.30pm)

Your only chance to hear a national Party Leader in Wales

All Welcome

For further information, contact Liberal Democrats Wales on (01222) 38

Liberal Democrats Wales
Democratiaid Rhyddfrydol Cymru

Printed by Qualiprint, 93 Whitchurch Road, Cardiff. Published by Liberal Democrats Wales, 57 St Mary Street, Cardiff

A promotional flyer for Paddy Ashdown's 1997 General Election rally in Cardiff.

A Christmas card produced by Merthyr Tydfil Liberal Democrats in 1998. By the end of the decade, the party's strength in the valleys of south Wales was growing once more.

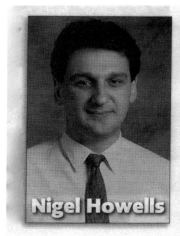

Three things to remember about Nigel Howells

- The Liberal Democrats are strong challengers to Labour in Pontypridd.
- If you want change, don't look to Labour. They've embraced the Conservative agenda. Only the Lib Dems offer a fresh, radical alternative.
- Citizens of Pontypridd know that if Labour can't do a good job in local government, they're going to find it hard to get things right at Westminster.

Liberal Democrats

Election communication
Pontypridd Constituency

Nigel Howells' election address when he stood for the Pontypridd constituency against the incumbent, Labour's Kim Howells.

The Welsh Assembly

What you need to know

Liberal Democrats Wales
Democratiaid Rhyddfrydol Cymru

Soon after the General Election of 1997, the Welsh Liberal Democrats campaigned for a 'Yes' vote in the devolution referendum held later that year.

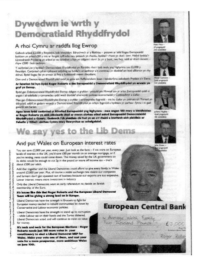

Roger Roberts, after missing out again in Conwy in 1997 and in the European elections of 1999, accepted a peerage and decided to represent the Welsh Liberal Democrats in the House of Lords.

The Liberal Democrat's 1999 Welsh Assembly election manifesto, which projected Mike German as the party's prospective Leader in Cardiff Bay.

Welsh Liberal Democrat President, Rob Humphreys, campaigning with Charles Kennedy during the 203 Welsh Assembly election.

Jon Owen Jones, the then Labour MP for Cardiff Central, with Dr Rodney Berman, the future leader of Cardiff Council, at a formal dinner. Jones would subsequently lose his seat to Jenny Willott.

The 2005 Westminster election saw a more diverse field of Liberal Democrat candidates such as Asghar Ali, the Cardiff Councillor, who stood in Caerphilly.

Lembit Öpik enjoyed a high public and media profile becoming a celebrity MP in the process

Liberal Democrat Leader, Menzies Campbell, campaigning with Jenny Randerson and Jenny Willott in Cardiff Central. Willott won the seat, becoming the first female Liberal MP in Wales since Megan Lloyd George in 1951.

The 2005 Westminster elections saw victories for Lembit Öpik (Montgomeryshire); Roger Williams (Brecon & Radnor); Jenny Willott (Cardiff Central) and Mark Williams (Ceredigion). The largest representation of Welsh Liberals in the House of Commons since 1950.

Welsh Liberals in the House of Lords in 2006. Back row (L to R): Lord (Martin) Thomas of Gresford; Lord (Alex) Carlile of Berriew; Lord (Richard) Livsey of Talgarth. Front row: Lord (Emlyn) Hooson, Baroness (Joan) Walmsley, Secretary to the Welsh Lords, Lord (Roger) Roberts of Llandudno.

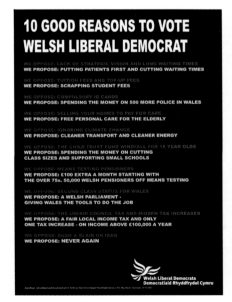

The Welsh Liberal Democrat poster for the 2005 Westminster elections.

The six Liberal Democrat Assembly Members re-elected in 2007. (Left to Right): Kirsty Williams; Peter Black; Mike German; Eleanor Burnham; Mick Bates and Jenny Randerson.

Jenny Randerson launches her bid to lead the Welsh Liberal Democrats in 2008.

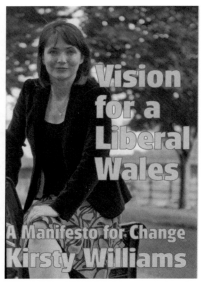

The 2008 National Assembly Liberal Democrat leadership election saw Kirsty Williams emerge victorious.

Husband and wife team, Mike and Veronica German, campaigned jointly at the National Assembly elections. Veronica would go on to replace Mike as a list AM for South Wales East when Mike was elevated to the House of Lords in 2010.

The 2010 Westminster election saw several Liberal Democrats candidates narrowly defeated such as Ed Townsend in Newport East.

The Liberal Party of Wales Finishes and the Welsh Liberal Party Arrives

The Liberal Party of Wales held a fairly well attended August conference in Builth Wells on 1st August 1965. There Hooson outlined the Welsh Radical Group's plans for revitalising the Welsh economy in their pamphlet entitled 'The Heartland'. Despite the optimistic note made in the pamphlet about the Welsh Liberals' opportunity of again becoming an alternative to Labour in Wales, the overall mood was one of desire for more radical change within the Welsh party before matters Labour could be fully challenged. The loss of Cardigan and the failure to regain Carmarthen had been bitter blows to the Welsh Liberals in that same year. Although the Party was still soldiering on, there was a general feeling that it had little breath 'left in its dying body'.[66] The North and South Wales Federations still held monthly meetings but continued to pass conflicting motions and often refused to put up candidates at council or Westminster elections. In addition, they kept their financial resources away from the Welsh party and would not disclose them. The Liberal Party of Wales was supposed to co-ordinate such resources but did not succeed in doing so now, any more than it had done when it was set up over half a century earlier. Madoc Jones stated:[67]

'Liberalism in Wales is in need of a drastic reform as to its organisation and its fighting potential as a progressive political entity. And we are all unhappy for this image of the party to continue – at peril of its total decay and final extinction.'

The federations were failing when they were needed most to revitalise the party to the growing threat of Welsh nationalism. Amongst the younger Liberals it was believed that the federations were both conservative and regressive and were stopping any prospect of a revival in Welsh Liberal fortunes.[68] Stirred by the loss of Cardigan and the slow death of the party in Wales, a group led by Emlyn Hooson MP and including senior Welsh Liberals Rhys Gerran Lloyd,[69] Councillor Lloyd Morris (Secretary of the group) and Martin Thomas came together to try to plan a more successful future. The initial objective was to bring the federations together. The idea was to separate Wales from London by having one Welsh state party, as was already the case in Scotland. The Welsh party was still financially dependent on London but there was a desire for Wales to have control over its own policy creation. Hooson's group had agreed on the vision of what the Welsh Liberals future should be. But would the wider Welsh Party?

On 11th June 1966, in a meeting in Builth Wells, the Liberal Party of Wales agreed to create a separate Liberal state party in Wales. The North Wales Federation accepted the idea first, and the South Wales Federation followed. Both Federations would be replaced by area committees under a federal Welsh state party. From now on the Welsh Liberals could, in theory, enjoy widespread autonomy from the party in London. They could now design their own constitution, create their own policies regarding a host of domestic matters, have their own administrative structure in Wales and decide how they would select candidates. These were decisions they could make independently of the party in London. This was how the federal structure of the Liberal Party was to be organised, something that was unique in British politics with its unitary political system.

The formation of the Welsh Liberal Party in 1966 was also seen in part as a way of competing head on with Plaid Cymru by stressing the Liberals' Welsh credentials more clearly. There was no resistance from London over the federal moves. The news of the arrival of the new Welsh Party was greeted with little comment by the Liberal Party in London, although Lord Byers, Eric Lubbock and Gruffydd Evans[70] of the LPO put out a joint statement 'We express no comment on the proposed changes. The model in Scotland works, we will support whatever the Welsh decide'.[71] They did, however, make it quite clear to the media that it was not a 'break-away' from the Welsh party but merely putting it on the same footing as the party in Scotland.[72]

For decades there had been a declining Welsh Liberal presence in the Liberal Party Organisation (LPO). This fact, combined with the Liberals' general enthusiasm for the devolution of political power, added to the lack of resistance to the setting up of a Welsh state party from the party in London. There was also general indifference in the LPO to the changes in Wales and a general reluctance of English Liberals to interfere in the affairs of the Welsh Liberals.

A steering committee was appointed by Emlyn Hooson to see this new party through its birth and first few months, to write a constitution and to arrange a conference. This conference was held in July 1966 and an executive was then elected. Councillor Mary Murphy[73] from Pontypridd became the first Chairman of the Welsh Party and, in doing so, became the most prominent Welsh female politician since Megan Lloyd George a decade before. Murphy was one of the party's most prominent figures in Welsh local government, close politically to the Liberal leader Jeremy Thorpe, and also chair of Pontypridd Urban District Council.[74] The Welsh Liberal Party could officially only come into existence, however, when that existence was endorsed by its members. On the 10th of September 1966, some 200 delegates attended a conference at Llanidloes, Montgomeryshire.[75] Both Murphy and Hooson spoke of the rising challenge that Liberalism and Nationalism would face in replacing Wales' current 33 Labour 'yes men' MPs. Elfyn Morris Jones, the Secretary of the new party, informed *The Times* and *The Manchester Guardian,* who both covered the event, that the result of the vote in favour of establishing the state party 'was greeted with loud applause, with delegates standing on their seats'.[76] The party's membership had thus enthusiastically backed the formation of the new state party and as evidence of this some £750 was collected during the tea break to help fund the new party.[77]

Hooson then declared to the new party that the nationalism of Plaid Cymru would, in turn, lose out to that held within Welsh Liberalism. Among its first new policies was the continued support for a Welsh Parliament, the demand for a Welsh Water Board and the rejection of the compulsory replacement of Welsh grammar schools by comprehensives. *The Manchester Guardian* saw Hooson as the man behind the rebirth of Welsh Liberalism.[78] At the end of September, *Liberal News* ran a profile on Emlyn Hooson, 'the man who led the Welsh Liberals to independence'. At the end of the piece it read: 'Montgomeryshire is the sole surviving bastion of once-Liberal Wales. Inevitably, Emlyn Hooson becomes the voice of Welsh Liberalism, and on his shoulders will fall the burden of recovery'.[79]

The coming decade would see to what extent Hooson and the newly founded Welsh Liberal Party could redress decades of Welsh Liberal decline. Hooson was determined to project the Welsh credentials of the party. At the centre of this new party's Welshness was the Government of Wales Bill (1967). On St David's Day, on the 1st of March 1967, wearing his daffodil, Hooson rose to his feet in the House of Commons and requested 'That leave be given to bring in a Bill to provide a scheme for domestic self-government of Wales.' [80]

Hooson outlined the scheme for a single chamber parliament with seventy-two elected members representing the existing Welsh constituencies. It would be a parliament similar to that then operating in Northern Ireland but in a federal United Kingdom. The Bill was naturally supported by the wider Liberal Party and Plaid Cymru's Carmarthen victor, Gwynfor Evans. The Second Reading was held on the 16th of June 1967. This time it was also supported by a Welsh Labour MP, S. O. Davies, the member for Merthyr Tydfil. The Labour government, however, refused to grant facilities for a Private Members' Bill on that day and, therefore, the Bill was killed off. Nevertheless, the Welsh Liberals had once more confirmed their commitment to devolution.

The Government of Wales Bill had been drafted by both Emlyn Hooson and the barrister Martin Thomas. Thomas had developed a promising career in the legal profession and a political one within the Young Liberals. Since the mid 1950s he had become one of the key North Wales Liberals, not only in his native Wrexham but also in the wider Welsh and British Liberal party. Thomas had stood for the Presidency in 1966, but had been beaten by George Kiloh, who had been backed by Tony Greaves, which afterwards caused a degree of friction between the two. Kiloh was part of the radical Young Liberal Group who became known as the 'Red Guards' because of their constant clashes with the leaders of party hierarchy.[81] However, Thomas would, in time, go on to play a more prominent role than that of being the President of the Young Liberal Movement and become a central figure in both the Welsh and the Federal Liberal Party.

Attempts to Revitalise the Welsh Party

The Welsh Liberal Party had been established with the idea of achieving nothing short of a full Welsh Liberal revival. With this notion in mind, Peter King chaired the Candidates' Committee and, by December 1967, was able to get some 13 candidates on two separate lists: those selected for a named constituency and those who would fight anywhere they were deployed. They could, however, fight only where there was an active Liberal Association in the constituency. Most of Wales still remained devoid of these. In its monthly meetings the Welsh Party Executive continued to examine these 'derelict' areas with the hope that some life would emerge in them, but in practice very little arose.

In South Wales, Lord Ogmore was frantically trying to make the Cardiff constituencies active. To this end, he got Ron Anderson, Chairman of the Cardiff University Liberal Students (CULS), to join with Dr Peter Bridger to reform the Liberal Association in Cardiff West. Chris Stevens, the Secretary of the CULS then agreed to send a team of students on a campaigning offensive which was launched on the 'derelict area' of Merthyr Tydfil.[82] At the same time Cardiff South East, the only active Association in Cardiff, adopted George Parsons as its parliamentary candidate, to stand against the then Labour government's Chancellor of the Exchequer, James Callaghan. The Cardiff South East Liberal Association, however, had been infiltrated by a number of right wing extremists allied to the National Front. These members also sought to form a 'City of Cardiff Liberal Party' and asked to be affiliated to the Welsh Liberal Party. This was rejected by the Welsh Liberal Party Executive in December 1967 who feared right wing infiltration. There was later an enquiry held into the Cardiff South East Liberal Association chaired by Martin Thomas. This resulted in their Parliamentary candidate George Parsons being expelled from the party in 1968 for supporting the National Front. He later became the National Front's South Wales' Area chair. Parsons later stood for them in the Cardiff South East and Penarth constituency in 1970, where he duly lost his deposit (with just 1.9% of the vote).

The Federal Party's Leadership Contest 1967

On 17th January 1967, the Federal Party's leader Jo Grimond announced that he would step down as leader. Although Grimond was credited with the revival of the party's fortunes in Scotland, the same could not be said of Wales. Under his leadership, the Welsh party had gone from three to just one MP. Grimond had, however, been as strong on supporting devolution for Wales as he had been for Scotland and had been a frequently supporter of the devolutionary cause in the Principality.[83] Since Clement Davies had stepped down as leader over a decade earlier, there had been little Welsh influence on the Federal party. Was this now the time to bring back a Welsh leader? The contest was opened and held the day after Grimond's resignation. Despite the fact that the Liberal constituencies wanted a direct voice in choosing the leader, this did not occur in 1967.[84] On this occasion the selection of the federal (British) leader was only determined by the party's MPs. Of the party's 12 MPs, Jeremy Thorpe was the most well known nationally. Whereas Grimond was related to the Asquiths, Thorpe's family was strongly connected to the Lloyd Georges, and went back five generations; Megan Lloyd George had been his godmother.[85] The Lloyd Georges, however, had, for almost a generation, aside from Olwen, not influenced Welsh Liberal politics. Consequently, Thorpe's Welsh connections were of little use to him in gaining support in Wales. This was exacerbated by the fact that Megan and Gwilym's defections to other parties had tarnished the 'Lloyd George' brand for Welsh Liberals.

Aside from Thorpe, two MPs threw their political hats into the ring: Eric Lubbock and Emlyn Hooson. Lubbock (Chief Whip), the victor of the Orpington by-election in 1962, had, however, a base in London and had never played a part in Welsh affairs. The Welsh party leader, Emlyn Hooson, tried to persuade Richard Wainwright MP (Colne Valley) to stand for the leadership but he had been a conscientious objector in World War Two and felt this would be a burden when leading the party. Failing to get Wainwright to stand, Hooson was left in a dilemma. He did not trust Thorpe to lead the party, thinking of him as a 'Jekyll and Hyde character' and, therefore, concluded that he must stand against himself.[86] Would Montgomeryshire produce another federal party leader to follow in the foot steps of Clement Davies? Emlyn Hooson had laid out his own manifesto for the leadership a year beforehand entitled 'the three conditions for Liberal growth', which, according to Hooson, were:[87]

'First, the Liberal Party must maintain absolute independence of Labour and Conservatives parties.

Secondly, we Liberals must never allow our policies and our attitudes to change in the hope of small, short term gains

Thirdly, Liberals must reaffirm strongly our beliefs that human progress comes largely through individual efforts'.

Through this brief manifesto Hooson was seen to be to the political right of the party, Thorpe and Lubbock to the left. Thorpe had the most support. When the votes were cast on the 18th of January 1967, Hooson got three votes, Eric Lubbock three and Thorpe six. Alan Watkins, a historian writing at the time, felt that many in the party saw that 'Mr Hooson is in some quarters thought to be too mild mannered, and too immersed in his legal practice, to make a wholly successful party leader'.[88] It was not, however, the party members that rejected him but his fellow MPs. Hooson would now concentrate on building both his legal and parliamentary career, whilst it would be up to Thorpe to lead the party into the next general election. Hooson's attempt at the party leadership was to be the last bid for the party's federal leadership by a Welsh Liberal MP; for the rest of the century, the British Liberal party was to be led by MPs from either the West Country or Scotland, with only the occasional Welsh federal president to show that the Welsh too were part of the wider Liberal party.

The Council Elections

Between 1962 and 1967 the future Liberal MP for Leeds West, Michael Meadowcroft, frequently toured Wales as apart of his role as the Liberal Party's Local Government Officer. Whilst in the rural mid and west, he knew that many Welsh Liberals remained under the 'Independent' councillor label. He also became aware that although there were not many Liberal councillors in Wales, they were still far from being extinct. In the south, there was a small Liberal group on Cardiff County Borough Council. They held all the seats in Plasnewydd ward and some in the Cathays ward. The group was led by a local lawyer called Ken Rees. Some two decades later these wards would be the springboard for a Liberal revival in Cardiff. There were also two Liberal Councillors on the Llanelli Municipal Borough Council, one of whom was a Sri Lankan, Bill Tilleke. In the Pontllanfraith ward of the Mynyddislwyn Urban District Council, Vernon Gapper had won a by-election in 1965 and become the only Liberal there. Across Wales there were Liberal councillors emerging in ones or twos in places such as Burry Port in the south and Wrexham in the north. Also in the north of Wales, Flintshire County Council had developed by far the largest and most well organised Liberal council group in Wales and even controlled the council for a brief period.[89]

The newly formed Welsh Liberal Party now had dreams of making Welsh councils more like Flintshire in terms of Liberal representation. Although most Welsh councils still had no Liberal candidates, one of the central figures in the party was ambitious to push the party forward on her own council. This was the Welsh Liberal Party Secretary, Mary Murphy, who put up six candidates on Pontypridd Urban District Council in the 1967 council elections. Similarly, the Monmouth Liberal Association had reformed the Pontypool-Cwmbran branch and put up five candidates.[90] Across Wales the party was able to put forward 53 candidates, a fraction of the overall seats up for election but a considerable move forward for a party that had not actively contested the majority of Welsh council seats for generations. In the event, there were nowhere near 53 victories but those few councillors that got elected were to play significant roles in the party in Wales over the coming decade. In Newport, college lecturer Hugh Clarke was re-elected to Newport Borough Council. Clarke would remain one of the pillars of the Liberal Party in Newport for the next forty years both on and off the council. Angus Donaldson was elected in Tredegar to Monmouthshire County Council. Donaldson, although on the right of the party, would be one of the key Liberals in south east Wales until the end of the 1970s, when he would leave the party to become an Independent. In North Wales, Alice Robinson, a housewife who had moved into Colwyn Bay from Lancashire, joined Howell Roberts as the second Liberal councillor on Colwyn Bay Metropolitan Borough Council. The two, however, remained the only two Liberals on the council until it was reorganised and became the Colwyn District Council in 1974.[91]

On the giant and dominant Glamorganshire County Council, the former Liberal Party of Wales Secretary, Jennie Gibbs, despite having a marked 'Home Counties' English accent[92] and already an Urban District Councillor in Maesteg, was elected onto Glamorganshire County Council. Her husband, John, was the agent. He almost won another council seat, but was finally defeated due to a large influx of postal votes for the Labour candidate.[93] In Gower, Brian Keal's victory was claimed to be that of the youngest councillor in Wales, at 27 years of age. In Pontypridd, there were three victories for the Pontypridd Liberals. They went to join Mary Murphy and Elias Evans in the councils, expanding the Liberal group. The council elections provided the Liberal group with some reward for their hard labours when Arthur Davies won in Rhydyfelin and Reg Green won in Trallwn ward. Trallwn would now remain a Liberal ward for the next forty years. Derek Lewis finished the triple victory by winning in the Town ward. Lewis, a photographer, whose shop sat next to Pontypridd's famous arched bridge, agreed a year later to stand as the Liberal candidate for Rhondda West. This, however, was subject to a local constituency association being established there.[94] It never was. Rhondda was to remain a constituency for the rest of the century, entirely devoid of its own Liberal Association. This was not the case, however, in Pontypridd. Here they now had one and they remained a little island of Welsh Liberalism in a sea of Socialist Labour for the rest of the century. In May 1968, in combination with the Independent councillors, the Liberals were almost able to gain control of Pontypridd Urban District Council. They remained just one councillor short of a majority.[95, 96]

The Liberals had had some limited success in urban councils but in rural counties, even getting a candidate to stand under the Liberal banner often proved impossible.

In the May 1969 council elections, constituency secretaries were asked by the Welsh party how many seats they would be contesting. In Anglesey, Secretary, Ellen Edwards replied that 'all elections – county and local are fought by Independents. Politics does not enter into the fight at all!'[97] Arthur Jones in Carmarthenshire informed the executive:[98]

> 'It would appear that the reaction in the past has been for the candidates of Liberal persuasion to contest the elections in the colours of an Independent candidature. It is said that the reasons behind this is, are the possibility of losing votes by introducing the party element into local administration. Whether there is any validity to this approach I would not care to say; it is true to say however that we have councillors both at local and county level who are members of the Liberal Party'.

The same reply came back from the Caernarfon, Brecon and Radnor, Montgomeryshire and Pembrokeshire Liberal Associations. East Flint, on the other hand, gave another reason for not fighting council seats. This was that it was a derelict area with no one wishing to fight, which was no better news for the party than refusing to adopt the party colours.

Welsh By-elections, Plaid Cymru and the Welsh Liberal Response

The Welsh Liberals had hoped that the foundation of their own state party in 1966 would see the start of a Liberal revival across Wales. The period between 1966 and 1970 did see a revival in Welsh politics, but it was a Welsh Nationalist one. This time, however, it was not the Liberals who were leading it but Plaid Cymru. As we saw earlier, Plaid Cymru had dashed Liberal expectations in Carmarthen and swept to victory there. Plaid's victory in Carmarthen also sent shock waves through the Labour Party. They had been defeated in a seat where they had previously had a majority of almost 10,000 votes. Less than a year after Carmarthen, on 9th March 1967, Plaid Cymru reduced Labour's 17,000 majority to just over two thousand in the Rhondda by-election. Here the Welsh Liberals could not even manage to find a candidate. Huw Thomas, the barrister and broadcaster who had stood in Llanelli in 1950, whilst still President of the Liberal Society at Cambridge, was approached but declined to stand. No one else was willing to stand either.

The Welsh Liberals tried in vain to battle against Plaid Cymru's appeal. They argued against Plaid Cymru's message of an independent Wales. On Saturday, the 25th November 1967, for instance, the Mid Wales *County Times* published a statement by the Vice-President of Plaid Cymru indicating that an independent Wales was possible because 'in terms of taxes alone, the balance of payments is very much in favour of Wales'. This assertion came from a study by Professor Nevin at Aberystwyth University. Emlyn Hooson also undertook economic research and proved the study wrong. Such studies by Liberals, however, obtained little media attention and did little to either increase Liberal support or reduce Plaid Cymru's appeal.[99]

In 1968, the staunchly anti-devolutionist Labour MP for Caerphilly, Ness Edwards, died. This time the Welsh Liberals were able to find a candidate to contest the seat – a 41 year old university economics lecturer, Peter Sadler. But their odds of victory were not good. When Sadler was out knocking on doors for the campaign with Martin Thomas, they looked down the valley to see a Plaid Cymru procession of cars going past that seemed to last for almost an hour.[100] It was a sure indication of the rising tide of Welsh nationalism. Plaid Cymru reduced Labour's 59.7% majority to 5.2%, a result that in part persuaded the Labour government to take the issue of political devolution more seriously. The Liberals were only able to muster a fraction of the supporters of Plaid Cymru and duly came at the bottom of the poll, losing their deposit.

Caerphilly By-election Result 18th July 1968

Candidate	Party	Vote	Percentage
Fred Evans	Labour	16148	45.6%
Dr Phil Williams	Plaid Cymru	14274	40.4%
Robert Williams	Conservative	3687	10.4%
Peter Sadler	Liberal	1257	3.6%
	Majority	1874	5.2%
	Turnout		75.9%

Emlyn Hooson had started the Caerphilly by-election with the rallying cry that 'it was last fought for the Liberals in 1929 and for forty years their voice has been silent … There are thousands of Liberals in Caerphilly and they must be found'.[101] The thousands of Liberals turned out to be just over one thousand. The poor Liberal showing did little to increase Liberal morale. When Roger Roberts wrote to Welsh Party Secretary, Emlyn Thomas, to express his concerns, Thomas replied:

'Caerphilly taught us a great deal and I am sure that we will profit from our short comings in the campaign. However, I would like to say this. That to me Caerphilly's result was a tremendous achievement considering that the Constituency had been in a derelict state for some forty years. Our view now, of course, is to see that those twelve hundred odd people who had the courage of their conviction to support the party are not left in a vacuum and that they be moulded into a nucleus from which ultimate success will grow'.[102]

After having stated this, the party soldiered on in Caerphilly until the next general election, in which, incidentally, it did not contest the seat again. This was left until October 1974. Attempts to join the Welsh Nationalist bandwagon and make the party more overtly Welsh, such as those of the Welsh Executive member, Ken Rees who suggested the adoption of a sticker with a Welsh Harp logo on its stating 'Get into tune with the Liberals', were rejected. The Welsh Party Executive believed ideas such as this to be too obscure yet failed to come up with any alternative to Rees' or other members' suggestions.[103] Once more it was evident that the Liberals were failing to meet the challenge set by Plaid Cymru through their own indecisiveness.

The Welsh Party Gets a General Secretary

Until June 1968, the Secretary of the Party in Wales had been Councillor Mary Murphy. She had run the Welsh Party from her home at 'Taff Villa', Berw Road, Pontypridd. At the annual Welsh party conference on 1st June 1968 at the Hotel Metropole, Llandrindod Wells, however, the party decided to appoint a permanent 'General Secretary', as well as to continue with the post of 'Secretary' of the party. The post of general secretary is now what we would refer to as a chief executive. The newly appointed Secretary was Emlyn Thomas. At that time he was Secretary to the Farmers' Union of Wales. The salary agreed was £1,800 per annum plus £600 expenses, a substantial sum of money at the time. This could be afforded because Emlyn Hooson and Rhys Gerran Lloyd had been able to obtain large contributions from about ten friends to pay for Thomas' salary for the first year.[104]

The party's headquarters then moved from Pontypridd to 17 Queen's Road, Aberystwyth, where a two-year lease was signed. Aberystwyth was the chosen location for two reasons. The first being that it was near Emlyn Thomas' home and the second being that it was in Cardigan, which was the Liberals' top target seat in Wales at the time. Within a year, there were attempts to move the headquarters to Cardiff to be nearer the 'Welsh media outlets' but most Welsh Liberal Party executives rejected this notion.[105]

From the outset Thomas' role was vague. Most Liberal executive members were uncertain about what he was actually doing, if anything. In a confidential 'Financial Report' in May 1969 it was declared that 'The Hon Secretary has no knowledge of present state of the accounts dealt with at Aberystwyth by the General Secretary, who still never consults him about any expenditure commitments made by HQ'.[106] As time moved on, it transpired that the appointment of Emlyn Thomas had proved nothing short of a disaster for the party. Some £7,000 had been spent in the Aberystwyth office between 1969 and 1970, added to which there was a trail of unpaid bills.[107] Emlyn Thomas left his post in March 1970 and went up to fight Meirionnydd for the Liberals, which in 1966 had been a Labour-Liberal marginal. At an emergency meeting of the Welsh party's executive on 25th April 1970, the executive made it clear that Thomas had not only done a poor job as General Secretary, but also that the state of the party's finances were unclear, as he had withheld the accounts from the Treasurer. The party's Treasurer, Rhys Gerran Lloyd, stated:[108]

'The cost of the Aberystwyth office was at the rate of at least £4,000 per annum. Having myself initiated the collection of the sums of money required to maintain the payment of his fees and expenses, I cannot but sympathise with many who feel that so far Welsh Liberal Party has not received the service to which it seems entitled.'

It was left to the Cardigan Liberal, Geraint Howells, to clear up much of the mess left by Thomas. He took over all the Welsh Liberal Party office papers and sorted them out, supplied the Treasurer with lists of subscribers and council members and ensured that the unpaid bills were settled. The party then resolved to put Aberystwyth behind it and move the party's offices to St Mary's Street in Cardiff from May, in time for the general election.

Troubles with Finance

Emlyn Thomas, the Welsh Party's general secretary, reported in July 1968 that in the future the Welsh party would need to raise £5,000 for the first year increasing to £10,000 for the second. This money would be used for an office and staff, of which there would be four organisers across Wales.[109] To date, in the constituencies, the system of permanent agents that existed had been both *ad hoc* and ill organised. These agents also were often temporary and their period of employment was uncertain. In 1968, Roger Taylor, the organiser for Denbigh had resigned because he believed the Executive was not democratic enough. 'It did not represent the wider Welsh Liberal Party', he declared as he left his post. In Montgomeryshire, Mrs. Wyatt Jones resigned as part-time organiser. As Montgomeryshire was one of the constituencies that frequently did not pass on its affiliation fees, the Welsh Party decided that one of their new organisers would take over this post, but that was only when Montgomeryshire's contribution was sufficient for a full-time organiser to be employed there. In Cardigan, a similar situation had occurred. The agent, Sidney Chapman, had resigned but instead of waiting for approval from the Welsh party, Cardigan constituency had appointed another agent, Ceirog Williams, themselves, partly paid for by their refusal to pay any affiliation fees or further contributions to the Welsh party. In seats where organisers were active – Brecon and Radnor (Thomas John), Carmarthen (Phyllis Bowen) and Meirionnydd (Owen Roberts) – they spent most of their time collecting the membership fees that paid their salary rather than on any issues related to campaigning to win the seat for the Liberals.[110]

In August, the Welsh executive held a special meeting in Llandrindod Wells at which the Treasurer Gerran Lloyd declared that apart from single donors, which the party had survived on so far, the only way forward was for the Welsh Liberals Associations to have 1000 members paying £3 per month (the Liberal Thousand). It was a promising idea but the party was not organised enough to see it ever come to fruition.[111] Corporate fundraising was tried; some 25 companies were approached for donations in early 1970; all declined.[112] This was tried again in 1972 when the party attempted to emulate the Conservatives by appealing to industry for funds. Once again this failed miserably. The reason, according to Lord Ogmore, was that the 'industrialists felt that the Welsh Liberal industrial policy was non-existent or non-credible', in reality, although it was more likely that they were, viewed by most industrialists as a fringe party politically in Wales with little impact on national political decision making.[113] There were few bright spots in finances. The one exception appears to be in late 1968 when Geraint Howells went on a membership recruitment drive and gained £31.8.0d from Brecon and Radnor, Cardigan and Montgomeryshire.[114] This, however, was a drop in the ocean in respect of the finances that were needed to move the party forward.

Unsurprisingly, paying for the 1970 general election proved to be something of a nightmare for the Welsh party. As a result of the losses incurred through Emlyn Thomas' negligence, the small amount available for elections was reduced by a further £1,000, which all on the Welsh Executive agreed was 'a ridiculous situation'.[115] Just a month before the general election, Gerran Lloyd reported to the annual conference that Thomas' expenditure as general secretary meant that the party was still in credit but its 'reserves have been largely used up'.[116] In 1970, in an effort to contest all 36 seats, local associations were told to raise £1,000 (another version of the 'Liberal Thousand'). Martin Thomas, the secretary of the Welsh Liberal Party, believed this scheme 'to be nonsense ...absurd, bearing in mind that many constituencies especially in South Wales could be fought for £400 given a young candidate'.[117] In short, the party was in dire straits once more. Senior figures, such as Lord Ogmore, informed the Welsh Liberal Party Executive that unless they watched their expenditure, 'they will bankrupt us all very quickly'.[118] Within the next few years, however, spending was brought under control. By late 1972, Rhys Gerran Lloyd QC, in his final statement as Treasurer was able to declare that the party was sound financially with £5,000 in cash funds and £6,000 in assets, including its Cardiff Offices'.[119]

The 1970 General Election

The preparation for the 1970 general election was once more a case of ambition being greater than reality. The Welsh party had decided in September 1968 that full-time agents should be encouraged for most constituencies but that the constituencies would have to raise the money themselves. This was far beyond their capacity. At the Welsh Liberal Council meeting on 29th September 1968, on top of the usual seats it contested in North and West Wales, it was decided to encourage candidates for Abertillery, Aberdare, Bedwellty, Gower, Merthyr Tyfil, Neath, Rhondda, Swansea and perhaps Newport. When it came to the actual general election, however, not a single one of these seats was actually contested. Attempts to recruit young Liberal members from universities to fight South Wales seats came to nothing.[120] A few months beforehand in June, Martin Thomas, now Chair of the Welsh party together with Rhys Gerran Lloyd, who was the Welsh Campaign's director, had summed up the Welsh party in a blunt and sharp way.[121] They had stated that the party could break through in Wales but that there was too much internal conflict on electoral strategy. Put simply, the party spent too much time arguing and fighting. At Barry, in March 1969, at a rally, the party declared it had 21 candidates, although in reality this was two more than it was to have at the actual general election. Despite this setback this was a marked improvement on the decade before when the party failed even to contest a quarter of the Welsh seats.

With regard to economic policy for this election, ideas were now in full flow. The Welsh party produced a wealth of plans for a Welsh Investment Bank, Welsh Industrial Bank, Land Bank, Welsh Development Agency and a Welsh Water Resources Board in January 1969.[122] Lloyd George had found out in 1929, however, that economic policies were not enough to win a general election. You also needed a strong united Liberal Party. In Wales the party's executive was weak. Its meetings were avoided by many important post holders who treated their positions as 'honorary posts'. The party had never had a proper budget or fundraising strategy. Most constituencies in Wales, even those with candidates, did not pay their affiliation fees. Fundraising was poor and there were no corporate contributions. Communication between branches and the central Welsh party were also weak. None of this helped make an effective national campaign.

To help formulate general policy for the forthcoming election, a Policy Committee was established under the Chairmanship of Mr. E. L. Morris. It concerned itself with wide-ranging areas of Welsh policy and established a number of sub-committees for issues, such as the Constitution and Wales, finance and local government. Each committee was headed by a designated expert. The ideology for the Welsh party at the time of the elections was summed up at the time by Lord Ogmore, President of the Welsh Liberal Party:[123]

'It must be realised that the Liberal Party does not form 'the middle way'. It is the only radical party. The Labour and Conservative Parties pretend to promote or attack socialism but there is no socialist society in this country to defend or attack. What there is in Britain is state capitalism on the one hand and private monopoly capitalism on the other'

The Welsh Liberal 1970 general election manifesto, 'Life to a Nation', covered a wide range of policies across Wales. Policies from creating a new polytechnic in North Wales to turning South Pembrokeshire into a 'free port' area to help promote the declining ports in that county. Gerran Lloyd was appointed officer in charge of Wales for the next general election by the federal general election organiser, Lord Byers. As well as gaining support from London, the Welsh executive decided to construct its own election leaflets based on those produced by the Scottish Liberals. They also produced their own party political broadcasts. Huw Thomas, the barrister and ITN anchorman, also a contemporary of fellow Liberals Ludovic Kennedy and Robin Day, presented the Welsh party's election broadcasts. Thomas also stood in Carmarthen, in the first election after Gwynfor Evans victory in by-election in 1966. Thomas saw a slight rise in the vote but the party was some 8,000 votes behind the Labour victor, Gwynoro Jones.

In the run up to the campaign, Jeremy Thorpe toured North Wales between the 17th and the 18th April 1970. He returned again on the 1st of June, doing a whirlwind tour of Mid and North Wales, starting at Carmarthen at 10.15 am followed by Aberystwyth, Welshpool, Barmouth and ending in a rally at Colwyn Bay at 3.30 pm. Thorpe, along with Emlyn Hooson, pushed the traditional Welsh Liberal policies of devolution, together with more support for agriculture and better communications in Wales. These initiatives were to be allied with those of the British agenda, such as creating a Human Rights Act, promoting better industrial relations in a period of mass strikes.[124]

The General Election of 1970 in Wales

Liberal	1
Labour	27
Conservative	7

Harold Wilson had called the 1970 general election with the expectation that his party would do well. The Liberals once again anticipated gains in seats. The Welsh Liberals had been set a target by the Liberal Party Organisation in London to contest all 36 Welsh seats.[125] They failed. Their 19 candidates gained some 103,747 votes (6.8%). Labour topped the Welsh poll with 781,941 votes (51.6%) and some 27 MPs, the Conservatives came second with seven MPs and 419,884 votes (27.7%) and Plaid Cymru gained 175,016 votes but no seats. Plaid had lost their one seat of Carmarthen to Labour's Gwynoro Jones by some 3,901 votes (7.9%). The Liberals won only one seat: Emlyn Hooson's in Montgomeryshire. They were only in conten-tion for one other seat, Cardigan, in which Huw Lloyd Williams, had not only failed to regain the seat, but saw Labour's majority rise to 1,263 (3.9%). Angus Donaldson came second in Ebbw Vale, but with only 14.5% of the vote, he was a massive 17,446 votes (57.9%) behind Labour's Michael Foot. In virtually every other seat that the Liberals contested, they were either a poor third or a fourth, often losing their deposit at the same time. Meanwhile, whilst Plaid Cymru had failed to gain any seats, it was a close second now in five Welsh seats, indicating that the nationalist tide was still rising, whilst the Liberal one was failing to make the grade.

The result in Meirionnydd was particularly disappointing for the Liberals. Since the seat had been lost in 1951, the party had always been in the contention for regaining it. The 1970 candidate was none other than Emlyn Thomas, the former Welsh Liberal Party general secretary, whose tenure had been nothing short of a disaster for the party. Under Thomas, the Liberal vote fell by 10 per cent and they came third. Plaid Cymru's Dafydd Elis Thomas took the number two position from which he would win the seat at the next general election. The Liberal Party was now out of the running in Meirionnydd for good. Geraint Howells had also tried for the seat but had not been selected and went instead to Brecon and Radnor, where as well as getting 18.9 per cent of the vote, he was able to restart the constituency organisation once more. Ironically for Howells and the Liberals, Thomas would return in 1979 to haunt them one more time when he contested Cardigan; this time for the Conservatives. Thomas had become the Welsh Liberals' version of the 'bad penny', always turning up when least wanted.

Dealing with Mr. Heath

Nationally, the Liberals had had a terrible general election. They had won just six seats, only half the number they had in 1966. This was their worst result since 1959 and a psychological blow for the party nationally. Despite the fact that it had been widely predicted that Labour would win the election, it was the Conservatives, under Edward Heath, who came to power with a majority of 30 seats. The Heath government, almost from the outset clashed continually with the trade unions, first as a result of the harsh monetarist policies they introduced, then because of its inadequate attempts to deal with the 1973 oil crisis, subsequent inflation and rising unemployment. Six times between July 1970 and November 1973, the government used the Emergency Powers Act (1920) to deal with dock, coal and power strikes. This was more than any government in history. Heath was also troubled with issues of foreign policy ranging from the Arab-Israeli war causing an oil crisis to the continued problems with the British colony of Rhodesia (Zimbabwe).

The Conservative were not the only party with problems. The Liberals had their problems too. They had become infiltrated by a number of Young Liberal activists whose ideology was often more closely related to Marx than Hobbes or Locke. At the Eastbourne Assembly in September 1970, they sought to hijack the party conference. Hooson publicly tried to stop 'the Young Liberal tail wagging the Liberal dog'.[126] The Young Liberals wished to take politics out of Westminster and on to the streets in community politics. An idea that appealed to many Liberals but the notion of communities 'taking and then using power'[127] smacked too much of Marxist rhetoric for some members. Hooson described them as 'anarcho-syndicalists youngsters' regarding the Liberal party as merely there for their own ideas of community politics and, therefore, alien to the practical approach to politics adopted by the Liberals since the war.[128] Nevertheless, despite Hooson's objections, an amended motion was passed at Eastbourne, which, in time, converted the Liberals to the community pavement politics they later became famous for. Some fifteen years later, this approach would also start to pay dividends for the Liberals in Wales but for now the politics remained on constituency wide basis rather than on a community nature in its approach.

At Westminster, the Welsh Liberals now concentrated their political fire on the new Conservative government. At the start of 1972, Hooson made a speech to a number of Welsh and English Liberals at Shrewsbury. He attacked the government for concentrating too much on issues in Rhodesia and South Africa and ignoring domestic issues. At the same time, he brought forward the issue of the lack of accountability in local government by Labour and Conservative councils that were failing to inform local people of what was happening.[129] The Liberal Party, in Wales, was, however, unable to provide a model of local government. The Welsh Liberals could only muster 21 candidates for the ten borough and district council elections held in 1972 – a tiny fraction of what was required to contest them all.

The Merthyr Tydfil By-election: 'Testing the Polls'

The 1970–74 Parliament was an excellent one for British Liberals in by-election terms, attracting to the party a host of prominent names.[130] The party was able to almost double its Westminster seats from six to eleven with their five by-election wins. As Britain became increasing disillusioned with the two party system of Labour and the Conservatives, crosses flowed into the Liberal or Nationalist parties' candidates' boxes at election time. In Wales there was only one by-election – in Merthyr Tydfil. Here the Liberal Party had not contested the seat since 1934. However, in this Welsh by-election, those in England, there would be no flow of disenchanted Labour voters switching to the Liberals when the other alternative to the two party system, Plaid Cymru, were also on the ballot.

Merthyr Tydfil By-election Result 13th April 1972

Candidate	Party	Vote	Percentage
Ted Rowlands	Labour	15562	48.4
Emrys Roberts	Plaid Cymru	11852	36.7
Christopher Barr	Conservative	2366	7.3
Arthur Jones	Communist	1519	5.5
Angus Donaldson	Liberal	765	2.1
	Majority	3710	11.7
	Turnout		79.5

The 1972 Merthyr by-election had been caused by the death of the Independent MP, S.O. Davies. Davies had been a maverick pro-nationalist Labour MP who, in 1970 at the age of 80, had refused to retire and stood as an Independent, and beat the official

Labour candidate by over 7,000 votes. The by-election was called at the height of industrial unrest in the South Wales' coalfields. A miners' strike had begun in January 1972. Merthyr and its hinterland were alien to the Welsh Liberals and the campaign was run on a 'shoestring budget'.[131] It came as no surprise, if a little disappointing for morale, that leading South Wales Liberal Angus Donaldson, famous for always wearing his deer stalker hat, lost his deposit and finished in a very poor fifth position. It was Plaid Cymru's Emrys Roberts and Labour's winning Ted Rowlands who bathed in the glory of the poll.[132]

Royal Commission on the Constitution (1968–1973): A Parliament for Wales?

By 1968, with the by-election results of Carmarthen, Rhondda West and Caerphilly showing a nationalist surge and the same being apparent in Scotland, Harold Wilson's Labour government announced that a Royal Commission on the Constitution would be set up to examine devolution. The Commission was initially chaired by Geoffrey Crowther, a former editor of *The Economist,* but he died. Lord Kilibrandon, a Scottish lawyer, then chaired the commission until it published its report in 1973.[133]

At the time when the commission was convening, Wales was represented in the Cabinet by a pro-devolutionist Welsh Secretary. This was Cledwyn Hughes, the Labour MP who had relieved Megan Lloyd George of her Anglesey seat in 1951. Hughes, however, had been a keen supporter of Megan when she had chaired the 'Campaign for a Welsh Parliament' movement. It was he who had proposed an elected Welsh Council to take over from the Welsh Office, but this and other pro-devolutionary initiatives were blocked by both the Labour MPs in Wales and the government in Whitehall. Hughes was replaced as Welsh Secretary at the start of the Commission by George Thomas, a Labour MP who was both fiercely anti-nationalist and anti-devolution.

The Welsh Liberals were greatly excited by the prospect of a commission looking seriously at Welsh devolution. Executive members, Judith Thomas and Winston Roddick, set up a working group to supply information to it. In the party's November 1968 meeting Lord Ogmore suggested that Dr Glyn Tegai Hughes and Ben Jones be contacted to put their names forward for the Commission.[134] In the event, neither was to serve on the Commission. Instead, it was Alun Talfan Davies the former chair of the Welsh Liberal Party and candidate for Carmarthen and Denbigh, who was selected as one of the eleven commissioners. Davies, a top barrister and later a judge, did his best to ensure that the Welsh Liberal vision of a legislative parliament emerged from the Commission.

There was much debate in both the party and Wales about what requests should go into the Commission and what should stay out. It eventually reported back in October 1973. Although the majority of Commissioners (six), including Talfan Davies, favoured legislative devolution for Wales, almost half the Commissioners and, more importantly most of the Wales Labour Party, favoured 'executive only' devolution for Wales.[135] Executive devolution was, therefore, proposed and it was this version of devolution for Wales that was to be set as the standard for the next decade.

The Party in the Early 1970s

By the end of 1971, the Liberal party was showing signs of renewed activity across much of Wales. In December, the Welsh President, Rhys Gerran Lloyd, was able to declare to the executive that 'we now have 32 constituency organisations in being, two promised with only Bewellty completely derelict ... we also have a central co-ordinating office in Cardiff from which they can get courteous and prompt replies'.[136] However, it was not all good news. In 1973, the Welsh League of Young Liberals collapsed because of inaction and apathy. This was a recurring event with the Liberals' Youth movement. They had folded in the past and would do so again. This practice occurred when most Young Liberals moved on into the main stream of the party and no new Young Liberals came in to fill the vacuum. It was, nevertheless, seen as a setback for the Welsh party, though only a short term one, because student Liberal politics was once more on the rise. The Aberystwyth University Student Liberal Society, which had closed at the end of the 1972–3 academic year, was re-established in the following year by Colin Smith.[137] He, together with some like-minded Liberal students, got it restarted between 1973 and 1974 when they began to produce a weekly duplicated sheet called "Liberals in Action", which they put under every door in the halls of residence. Along with student support for the Liberals and their constituency candidate, Geraint Howells, there was a strong link between student Liberals and a number of academic staff – particularly Richard Livsey who was at the agricultural college, Dr Merfyn Jones (a biochemist), Professor King (chemistry) and George Morrison (also member of the Welsh Liberal Party executive).[138]

International matters were always close to Liberals hearts and in 1973, many Welsh Liberals were delighted that Edward Heath was able to complete, after long drawn out negotiations, Britain's entry into the European Community. Although this was initially good for Welsh farmers and at the core of the internationalist beliefs of generations of Welsh Liberals, it did not have total support within the Welsh party. In the European Community debates, Hooson had been the sole Liberal Parliamentarian against joining the Community. He thought both agriculture and industry would take a 'hammering if we go in'.[139] In 1971, he had declared at the party's Scarborough conference that although he did not challenge the party's deep commitment to Europe, he did not share the romantic view of Europe which believed that the Common Market was the answer to all ills.'[140] Hooson's views on Europe were to put him on the right of the party during both this and the next two Parliaments and thus at odds with many other Welsh Liberals.

On domestic matters, the Welsh local government system had undergone a massive restructuring in 1973 with the old county councils, urban and rural district councils being reorganised into eight county and 37 districts. Although these authorities did not start operating until April 1974, shadow elections for them were held in May 1973. In the county elections, the Welsh Liberals were able to contest 9.8 per cent of the total seats. Labour, in contrast, contested 72.8 per cent, the Conservatives 24 per cent and Plaid Cymru 16.7 per cent. In the district elections, the Liberals fared even worse. Just 5.9 per cent of seats were contested, less than 10 per cent of Labour's 61.7 per cent. The party managed to gain just over 5 per cent of the vote in the council elections and 4.5 per cent in the districts. From this came the election of only a handful of councillors across Wales. On most counties and districts/boroughs, the Liberals gained no or, at the most, two seats. In four counties they were more successful – Gwent (3 councillors) Clwyd (4) Powys (4) and Dyfed (8). In the 37 districts only in Montgomery (3) Blaenau Gwent (3) Alyn and Deeside (4) and Taff Ely (5) were they able to display a notable presence. This was against ruling groups that could be more than 10 times their number. Only in the districts of Ceredigion (9) and Colwyn (8) were the Liberals the largest political parties.[141] The party was still a long way from power in the town and county halls across Wales.

There was one good piece of Parliamentary news for the Party in 1973. The Welsh Party's 1970 general election director, who was now President of the British Liberal Party, Rhys Gerran Lloyd, was ennobled to become Baron Lloyd of Cilgerran, named after the place of his birth. For the next two decades he would often be the Welsh Party's voice in the House of Lords and also the Liberal Whip there (1973–75). Meanwhile in the House of Commons, being in that small group that was British Liberal Parliamentary Party, meant that Hooson had to take on a number of portfolios. In November 1973, he was given the large portfolio of Agriculture, Wales and the Law by Thorpe.[142] At the time that Hooson received his new portfolios, the industrial situation in Britain became so bad, with both coal miners and power workers on strike for better pay and conditions, that a three-day working week had to be introduced, with power cuts becoming the norm. Heath found the situation of governing the country untenable and, therefore, decided to call a general election for early 1974 to determine once and for all 'who governs Britain', the government or the unions?

At the February 1974 general election, the Liberals in Wales would project their own, now very well conceived and planned, policies for Wales and beyond in the unimaginatively entitled 'This is Welsh Liberals' Policy' – a title the executive thought so good that it was kept for both 1974 general elections' manifestos. In their first 1974 manifesto, apart from the inevitable call for a Welsh parliament, the party, if elected as the government, would have established a Celtic Sea Oil levy to be paid into a development fund for Wales, if oil was discovered off Wales' coast. They also suggested a levy on Welsh water pumped to England, the setting up of a Welsh language broadcasting channel and the promotion of bilingual education across Wales. The question now was to what extent would these creative policies aid their chances of victory in Cardigan, Denbigh and their other Welsh target seats?

The General Elections of 1974

As the Welsh party went into the February 1974 elections, it was Emlyn Hooson who was the leader, with Geraint Howells as President and Chair. Councillor Gareth Morgan (Montgomeryshire) would later take over as Party Chair once Howells had been elected. The Welsh party was in high spirits for the general election. In Aberystwyth, at the town's council elections at the start of February, the Liberals had taken control of the council, winning 11 of the 12 seats they contested and taking the Labour leader's seat in the process.[143] This, in the process, convinced the Cardiganshire Liberals that they stood a good chance of retaking the seat.

Opinion Polls across the UK had put the Liberals as high as 28 per cent in the polls in the previous Parliament[144] and for over a year now they had been over 14 per cent. The Liberal Party across Britain had ready some 517 candidates, the highest number since 1906.[145] The Welsh party had managed 31 candidates, the most since 1900.[146] There was a general feeling, therefore, that the party's fortunes were on the upturn. The Liberals could genuinely put themselves forward as a prospective party of government, as an alternative to the 'failed policies of both Labour and Conservative governments'.[147] The two-party politics that was present in the UK meant that the Liberals were mainly ignored by the Conservatives or Labour parties as both turned their guns on each other, leaving the Liberals in a political 'no man's land'.[148]

The General Election of February 1974 in Wales	
Liberal	2
Labour	24
Conservative	8
Plaid Cymru	2

Despite the fact that the Welsh Liberal Party was now contesting most seats across Wales, they still focused their eyes on Cardigan and Montgomeryshire. In the Cardigan seat, the contest between Geraint Howells and Elystan Morgan (the sitting Labour MP) was intense. Judi Lewis, the future Welsh Liberal Democrat chief executive, was Howells' agent. Importantly for Howells and Lewis, Elystan Morgan had become more unpopular with the constituents, particularly with the nationalist element. They viewed him as a 'turncoat' because of his move away from Plaid Cymru in 1965. In addition, he was against the establishment of a Welsh language medium school in Aberystwyth. Howells was, therefore, able to use this to his full advantage in getting the Welsh Nationalist vote on his side. As the main nationalist contender, Howells got the Plaid Cymru supporters to back him in order to get 'Morgan out'. This pushed down Plaid Cymru candidate's Clifford Davies' vote whilst giving vital extra support to Howells'.[149]

Labour sought unsuccessfully to 'portray Howells as a bumbling peasant unfit to stand for Parliament'.[150] Things came to a head with these Labour tactics when there was an election meeting in the Great Hall of Aberystwyth University on the Sunday afternoon before the election. Howells was ill with flu and unable to attend. Winston Roddick had to stand in for him at short notice but when Morgan 'portrayed it as Howells being afraid to face him', the Liberal students became so enraged that they tried to boo him off the stage. Labour's personal slights continued to the bitter end and when the declaration was made on election night, there were attempts to drown Howells' speech out with sheep noises. Despite the bitterness of the contest, Howells managed to win the seat for the Liberals by a substantial 2,476 votes (6.9%).

In Montgomeryshire, despite the local organisation being somewhat disorganised, Emlyn Hooson's majority had almost doubled to 4,651 (16.9%) votes over the Conservatives.[151] The Liberals, after an eight-year gap now had two seats in Wales. Cardigan was their first gain since 1945. However, the Welsh newspapers on the day after the election results, did not lead with the story of a Liberal revival in mid Wales but with the nationalist surge in North Wales instead.[152] Dafydd Wigley had won Caernarfon from Labour's Goronwy Roberts who himself had taken it from the Welsh Liberals in 1945. Dafydd Elis Thomas at the same time won the Meirionnydd seat, also from Labour, who in turn had also taken it from the Welsh Liberal MP

Emrys Roberts in 1951. The Meirionnydd victory also closed the door to the Welsh Liberals on one of their most hopeful post-war target seats and relegated the Liberals' Iolo ab Eurfyl Jones to a poorly placed third position. Elsewhere in Wales, with the exception of Dr David L. Williams's good result in Denbigh where he came a strong second (30 % of the vote) to the Conservative's Geraint Morgan and Martin Thomas's 25 per cent share of the vote in Wrexham, it was a tale of lost deposits and third or fourth placed candidates. Future Montgomeryshire MP, Alex Carlile, gained third place and some 18.8 per cent of the vote in Flint East. It was Carlile's first attempt at Westminster, having originally been chair of the University's Labour Club while a student at King's College London and only moving over to become a Liberal after being inspired by a speech by Grimond.[153] Over the next decade, Carlile would become one of the most influential Welsh Liberal MPs both in Wales and at Westminster. But this was still to come.

In Between the 1974 Elections

The election result left the British Liberal Party with fourteen seats, three up on when it had embarked on the election. Although this was a great improvement on the 1970 result with some 19.3 per cent of the national vote, this was still 123 seats fewer that the party would have gained had the vote been proportional to the seats gained. The Conservatives had gained 297 seats and Labour 301 seats, the other parties, 23 seats. Still, despite the result, it was the Conservatives and not Labour who first tried to form the government. The British Liberals' leader, Jeremy Thorpe, had a series of meetings with Conservative leader Edward Heath to discuss whether he could gain Liberal support to keep his government in power. The Liberal Party agreed that the central condition for support would be the introduction of proportional representation for the Westminster elections. Although Heath was sympathetic to this notion, his party was not.[154] The wider Liberal Party, however, was not generally in favour of a pact just with the Conservatives, although many remained enamoured with the idea of a 'National Government' of all parties in which they would serve.

Heath's offer was a Royal Commission on the electoral system, a seat in the Cabinet for Thorpe and a few ministerial appointments for other Liberals. This was not good enough for the Liberals and they decided not to back Heath. At the centre of these negotiations was former Welsh party treasurer, Lord Lloyd of Cilgerran, who was now the Federal Party's President (1973–74). As time went on, Heath failed to get support from other groups including the Ulster Unionists. It became apparent that Heath would not be able to form a government. This left Harold Wilson as the only alternative Prime Minister and on the 4th of March 1974, he duly formed his a new Labour government, which immediately set about appeasing industrial unrest by going on a massive public spending spree. It was clear from the outset, however, that it would not be long before another general election would have to be called, as Harold Wilson did not enjoy a majority and could be forced into a general election at any time by a vote of no confidence. As the prospect of a new election loomed, Lord Lloyd chaired the Welsh committee to vet potential new candidates, get existing candidates reselected and encourage derelict constituencies to adopt candidates.[155] The party had money, however, only for those candidates who had severe financial hardship. The other candidates were expected to raise money for their own election expenses.

In April, Hooson warned the Welsh Liberal executive that the situation of the government was grave and that, as Labour were now avoiding controversial legislation in order to stay in power, another election was not far off. The party was now on an electoral war footing. The Welsh Liberals' Cardiff conference on 1st June presented future Welsh Liberal policy. This included the passing of a motion calling for an enquiry into the running of the Welsh National Water Development Authority. They also called for the early implementation of elected devolved Assemblies via the Single Transferable Voting system for Scotland and Wales, plus other measures on industrial democracy, Northern Ireland and reducing inflation in the economy. At the conference Dr David Williams, the PPC for Denbigh and also a Welsh Member for the General Medical Services Committee, emphasised a campaign on the NHS on issues such as:[156]

'The length of waiting lists for outpatient appointments. The inadequate pay for nurses and para-medical staff and a 10 per cent cut back on certain headings of NHS expenditure. There is also a need for non clinical care\rather than managerial proliferation.'

Newly elected Geraint Howells also continued his campaigning from the previous election, much of which revolved around his pet concern of Welsh agricultural issues. Howells knew the value of the farming vote in his rural constituency. As part of his electioneering, he held a series of Farmers' Union of Wales rallies entitled 'Save Farming Now' in September 1974. At the same time as Howells was pushing forward the cause of the farmers, Emlyn Hooson, was continuing the campaign for a Welsh parliament. He made a speech at Glantwymyn School in the Dovery Valley in late September in which he dismissed Labour's Welsh Assembly plans as no more than a 'County Council for Wales' and called for a full Welsh Parliament.[157] As the party's two MPs carried on making their campaign speeches, the country moved slowly towards another general election and Harold Wilson called the second general election for October that year (1974).

The Second 1974 General Election

The General Election of October 1974 in Wales	
Liberal	2
Labour	23
Conservative	8
Plaid Cymru	3

The October general election saw Harold Wilson win with a small majority. The Liberal Party lost two seats and gained one but none of these gains and losses were in Wales. Plaid Cymru's Gwynfor Evans regained the former Welsh Liberal seat of Carmarthen. This meant that with just two victories in Montgomeryshire and Cardigan the Liberals were now the fourth party of Welsh politics placed behind Plaid

Cymru for the first time. Despite their reduced position the Welsh Party announced after the election that they were 'pleased that they held the two seats and came third (in terms of votes won) over Plaid'. They were sorry to lose 14 deposits but 'Plaid had lost 26 and the Tories 11 in Wales'.[158] Howells had survived a fierce attempt by Elystan Morgan to regain his Cardigan seat, retaining exactly the same majority over him as before (7%). Hooson's majority had fallen slightly to 14.7 per cent. This was caused mainly by Plaid Cymru and Labour candidates' votes pushing into his share of the vote whilst the Conservative vote remained constant. The Welsh party's possible seats were beginning to look less possible. In Wrexham, Martin Thomas was now in second position (22.1%) but there was still a massive 16,366 votes (29%) gap between him and Labour's Tom Ellis. In the Denbigh seat, Dr David T. Jones, had narrowed the gap between himself and the Conservative's Geraint Morgan to some 4,551 votes (9.3%). This narrowing, however, had been down to Plaid Cymru's candidate, Ieuan Wyn Jones, taking both Conservative and Liberals votes rather than any increase in the Liberal vote. Elsewhere it was a familiar story for the Welsh Party attaining third or fourth places with little hope of winning the seats contested. One of these third places was that of the future Welsh Liberal Democrat Assembly leader, Mike German who gained a respectable although distant 17.8 per cent of the vote in Cardiff North. German, with the help of the Cardiff constituency organiser David Rees and a young accountant called Phil Davies, had campaigned using the traditional methods or doorstop canvassing and putting out the election address. The result of this traditional style of campaigning put him some 7,751 (22%) votes behind the winning Conservative MP, Ian Grist.[159] German would reflect on this greatly over the next five years.

The post election period ended with what would prove to be of immense political interest in Wales later on in the decade. The issue of Welsh language broadcasting had become more prominent. The Welsh Nationalists in Plaid Cymru and other political parties were pushing hard for a Welsh language channel. The Report of the Crawford Committee on Broadcasting Coverage recommended a fourth channel for Wales in Welsh. This had already been fully endorsed in the Welsh Liberals' 1974 general election manifestos and was, therefore, welcomed by Geraint Howells who stated that 'it means that Welsh will now have its rightful place in the broadcasting system and this will boast the morale of all who love the language.'[160]

Howells had now become the party's most effective communicator in the Welsh language and consequently drew to his side supporters who would have otherwise supported Plaid Cymru. As a result, Howells was always able to see himself as a 'Welsh nationalist and a Liberal as well' – the two to him seemed synonymous.[161] The Welsh Liberals would now want this same appeal to spread from Cardigan throughout the rest of Wales so that they could compete more directly with Plaid Cymru.

Conclusion

Ideologically, Liberalism had been swamped by Socialism in the south and north-east of Wales, but had survived quite strongly in those areas where Socialism did not ignite the feelings of the rural classes in quite the same way as it did in urban areas. By the mid 1960s, however, these same areas were more and more enchanted by the growing nationalism of Plaid Cymru and, although the Liberals had been the original Welsh Nationalists, they were unable to cope with the increasing appeal of Plaid. The internal feuding between the North and South Wales Federations that had been going on since they were formed in 1886 and 1887 ended when the new Welsh state party was formed in 1966. It was this formation in September 1966 that gave the Welsh Liberals hope for the future. This notion was tested over the next three general elections. Initially, the party struggled both financially and structurally. By the general election of October 1974, however, it was able to contest every seat in Wales for the first time since 1900.

The Welsh Liberals had started the 1960s with two MPs – in Montgomeryshire and Cardigan. They finished the October 1974 general election still holding those two seats but with two different MPs. Emlyn Hooson's victory in the 1962 Montgomeryshire by-election was the Welsh party's one shining light in that decade. Shortly afterwards, Roderic Bowen's loss of the Cardigan seat in 1966 reduced the Welsh Liberals to their lowest tally of seats ever-just one. It seemed as though Welsh Liberalism was doomed to die through a slow process of attrition. Geraint Howells' regaining of Cardigan in February 1974 was the first time the Welsh Liberals had regained a seat in Wales since 1945. It was also vital for the survival of the Welsh party and now the charismatic and popular Welsh-speaking MP in Cardigan would be important in helping the Welsh Liberals from becoming totally swept away by the rising tide of Welsh nationalism. The Welsh Liberals seemed in many ways to be turning a corner but they were restricted to their rural seats and still had some way to go before they could successfully re-enter the mainstream of Welsh politics.

Notes

1. The Welsh Liberal Challenge, No. 2 Spring 1960
2. Belzak, Steve, (2008) 'Swinging in the Sixties to the Liberals: Mary Murphy and Pontypridd Urban District', Conference Paper, Political Studies Association Conference, Swansea, 2nd April 2008, p. 2
3. Graham Jones, J. (1993B) 'Emlyn Hooson's Parliametary Debut: The Montgomeryshire By-election of 1962, The Montgomeryshire Collections, p. 122
4. Lord Hooson to author
5. Sir George Frederick Hamer was chair of a leading farming company who supplied mutton to three monarchs. Hamer also served in numerous senior positions both in the county and beyond including being mayor of Llanidloes Borough Council eleven times and Lord Lieutenant of Montgomeryshire between 1950–60, as well as many posts within the Liberal Party
6. Dr Glyn Tegai Hughes to author
7. Son of Lord Davies of Llandinam and grandson of David Davies the former Liberal MP for Montgomeryshire
8. The Times, 11/4/60, p. 6
9. The Manchester Guardian, 31/8/60, p. 1
10. Minutes of the Wrexham and East Denbighshire Constituency Association, 21/9/60
11. Rasmussen, Jorgan Scott (1965) op. cit., p. 152
12. Rasmussen, Jorgan Scott (1965) op. cit., p. 152
13. The Manchester Guardian, 31/8/60, p. 1
14. North Wales Liberal Federation Newsletter, 20/10/60
15. Michael Foot was the winner for Labour with a vote of some 20528 (68.8%) and a majority of 56.1% over the Conservatives
16. The Times, 24/9/62, p. 10
17. Progress, Liberal Party Organisation, Secretary's Bulletin for Federation and Constituencies, 1962
18. The Lord of Appeal in Ordinary

19. Hooson, Emlyn (1999) Clement Davies: An Underestimated Welshman and Politician, Journal of Liberal Democrat History, Issue 24, Autumn 1999, p. 11
20. Dr Glyn Tegai Hughes to author
21. Graham Jones, J. (1993B) op. cit., p. 125
22. Lord Hooson to author
23. Graham Jones, J. (1993B) op. cit.
24. Graham Jones, J. (1993B) op. cit., p. 129
25. *The Manchester Guardian*, 17/5/62, p. 1
26. Rasmussen, Jorgen Scott (1965) op. cit., p. 87
27. Rasmussen, Jorgen Scott (1965) op. cit., p. 87
28. Roger Roberts to author
29. Graham Jones, J. (1993A) 'The Liberal Party and Wales, 1945–79', The Welsh History Review, Vol. 16, No 3 June 1993, p. 343
30. 'Effective Organising' (1958) Liberal Publication Department, p. 61
31. Rasmussen, Jorgen Scott (1965) op. cit., p. 89
32. *Liberal Democrat News*, 7/9/01, Obituary, Roderic Bowen QC, Lord Emlyn Hooson, p. 8
33. Pottle, Mark [Editor] (2000) op. cit., p. 198
34. Liberal Partnership for Wales (1964), Liberal Party of Wales Manifesto
35. From 1931 to 1945 National Liberal and Conservatives had contested the seat but no Liberal contestant had
36. *The Liberal News*, 21/5/65 p. 2
37. Alice Robinson to author 27/4/08
38. *The Liberal News*, 30/7/65 p. 2
39. The President of the Welsh Party was the Hon Edward Davies, the son of the late Lord Davies of Llandinam and the defeated Liberal contender for the Montgomeryshire by-election three years before. From the South of Wales was Newport's Major Parry Brown as Treasurer and Councillor Lloyd Morris became the Secretary.
40. *The Liberal News*, 15/10/65 p. 7
41. The Liberal Party of Wales General Election Manifesto 1966
42. *The Independent*, 24/07/01, Roderic Bowen's Obituary, Tony Heath
43. Lord Hooson to author
44. Lord Hooson to author
45. Lord Howells to author
46. Watkins, Alan (1966) op. cit., p. 149
47. *The Liberal News*, 25/3/66 p. 8
48. *The Liberal News*, 20/5/66 p. 6
49. David Hywel Davies was also a former Chair of the Liberal Party of Wales, 1953
50. Letter to J.E.H. Roberts, Carmarthen from Edward Wheeler, Chief Agent 28/4/66
51. Judith Trefor Lewis to author
52. *The Western Mail*, 15/7/66, p. 1
53. *The Liberal News*, 10/6/66 p. 2
54. The President of Plaid Cymru and a councillor and alderman of Carmarthenshire County Council since 1949.
55. Lord Hooson to author
56. *The Western Mail*, 15/7/66, p. 1
57. *The Liberal News*, 15/7/66 p. 2
58. Liberal Partnership in Wales (1964) A Liberal Party of Wales Publication, Gee and Son Ltd, p. 1
59. The Welsh League of Young Liberals Newsletter, 31/12/60
60. Wrexham and East Denbighshire Liberal Association Minutes 17/1/61
61. Wrexham and East Denbighshire Liberal Association Minutes 22/3/61
62. Lords Hooson and Thomas, Glyn Tegai Hughes to author.
63. Letter from John and Jenny Gibbs to G. W. Madoc Jones, 25th February 1962
64. Letter from John and Jenny Gibbs to G. W. Madoc Jones, 10th March 1962
65. Letter from John and Jenny Gibbs to Glyn Tegai Hughes, 11th March 1962
66. Lords Hooson and Thomas, Glyn Tegai Hughes to author.
67. Letter from Madoc to all secretaries of constituency association' 22/5/66. Lord Hooson's papers, box 42, National Library of Wales
68. Lords Hooson and Thomas to author

69. Rhys Gerran Lloyd QC, was treasurer of the Welsh party from 1969–72. He took over from Lord Ogmore in 1972 he stepped down on health grounds. Lloyd had left the bar in 1968 to become a director of a number of companies including Target Unit Trust Wales and Aladdin Industries, Pontardawe.
70. David Thomas Gruffydd Evans (1928–92) was a former solicitor and councillor from Birkenhead who went on to become chief executive of the Liberal Party Organisation, Liberal Party President and later Lord Evans of Claughton. Despite his Welsh name Lord Evans played no direct part in the Welsh Liberal Party.
71. *The Liberal News*, 17/6/66 p. 1
72. *The Manchester Guardian*, 09/6/66, p. 4
73. Mary Murphy was originally Mary Edwards but married Thomas Murphy the Town Clerk to Pontypridd Urban District Council
74. Norman Lewis to author 12/5/07
75. *The Liberal News*, 16/9/66 p. 1, *The Times*, 12/9/66, p. 9
76. The Times, 12/9/66, p. 9
77. *The Manchester Guardian*, 12/9/66, p. 2
78. *The Manchester Guardian*, 12/9/66, p. 2
79. *The Liberal News* 30/9/66 p. 11
80. Ellis, Berresford P. (1968) Wales A Nation Again!: The Nationalist Struggle for Freedom, The Garden City Press, p. 164
81. Kiloh proved to be more blue than red and, after he beat Thomas, he served for only a year in the post and then joined the Conservatives – Lord Thomas of Gresford to author
82. Welsh Liberal Party Executive Minutes 28/10/67
83. Grimond, Jo (1979) Memoirs, Heinemann, London
84. Pottle, Mark [Editor] (2000)op. cit., p. 313
85. Thorpe, Jeremy (1999) In My Own Time, Politico's
86. Lord Hooson to author
87. *Liberal News* 21/1/66 p. 1, p. 8
88. Watkins, Alan (1966) op. cit., p. 151
89. Michael Meadowcroft to author 8/8/08
90. Welsh Liberal Party Minutes 29/4/68
91. Alice Robinson to author 27/4/08
92. Michael Meadowcroft to author 8/8/08
93. Michael Meadowcroft to author 8/8/08
94. Welsh Liberal Council Meeting minutes 3/11/68
95. Belzak, Steve, (2008) opt cit,
96. Even with the loss of borough councils in 1995 the party still retained a presence on Pontypridd Town Council.
97. Welsh Liberal Council Meeting minutes 26/3/69
98. Welsh Liberal Council Meeting minutes 26/3/69
99. Welsh Liberal Party Executive minutes 28/10/67
100. Lord Thomas to author
101. Liberal News 25/6/68
102. Letter to Roger Roberts from Emlyn Thomas 12 /9/68
103. Welsh Liberal Council Meeting minutes 3/11/68
104. Welsh Liberal Party 12/8/69
105. Welsh Liberal Party 12/8/69
106. Welsh Liberal Party 24/5/69
107. Treasurers Report May 1970 to Welsh Liberal Party annual conference
108. Emergency Welsh Liberal Party Executive Meeting 25/4/70
109. Welsh Liberal Council Meeting 27/7/68
110. Welsh Liberal Party 29/4/69
111. Welsh Liberal Party 12/8/69
112. Welsh Liberal Council Meeting 17/4/70
113. Welsh Liberal Council Meeting 19/11/72
114. Welsh Liberal Council Meeting 3/11/68
115. Welsh Liberal Council Meeting 17/4/70

116. Treasurer's Report May 1970 to Welsh Liberal Party annual conference
117. Letter from Martin Thomas to Lord Ogmore, 12/2/69
118. Letter from Lord Ogmore to Martin Thomas, 13/2/69
119. Welsh Liberal Council Meeting 19/11/72
120. Welsh Liberal Party Executive 26/1/69
121. Statement by Chair Martin Thomas to Welsh Liberal Council 28/6/68
122. Life to a nation: An economic policy for Wales, Welsh Liberal Party, January 1969
123. Statement by Chair Lord Ogmore to Welsh Liberal Council 28/9/69
124. Liverpool Daily Post, 28/5/70
125. Welsh Liberal Party Executive 22/10/69
126. *The Times*, 26/9/70; p. 13
127. *The Times*, 26/9/70; p. 13
128. *The Times*, 24/9/70; p. 11
129. Hooson speech to Shrewsbury Liberals 'What's Wrong with the Liberals?' 21/1/72
130. Cyril Smith, Rochdale, Dick Taverne, Lincoln, Clement Freud, Isle of Ely and Alan Beith, Berwick-upon-Tweed
131. Edwards, Andrew (2002) op. cit., p. 354
132. Ted Rowlands was the former MP (then called Edward Rowlands) for Cardiff North (1966–70)
133. Deacon, Russell (2006) Devolution in Britain today, 2nd Edition, Manchester University Press
134. Welsh Liberal Council Meeting 3/11/68
135. Foulkes, David, Barry Jones, J and Wilford, R.A. (1981) The Welsh Veto: The Wales Act 1978 and the Referendum, University of Wales Press, p. 25
136. Letter from President Rhys Gerran Lloyd to the Welsh Liberal Party executive 30/12/71
137. Welsh Liberal Party Executive 2/11/74
138. Colin Smith to author, 2004
139. *The Times*, 16/9/74 p. 14
140. *The Times*, 18/9/71; p. 23
141. Rallings, Colin and Thrasher, Michael (1991) Local Election in Britain: A Statistical Digest, Local Government Chronicle Elections Centre
142. *The Daily Mirror*, 22/11/73
143. *The Western Mail*, 9/2/74
144. August 1973
145. Stevenson, John (1993) Third Party Politics Since 1945: Liberals, Alliance and Liberal Democrats, Blackwell, p. 57
146. Jones, Beti (1999) op. cit., pp. 44–46
147. Steel, David (1989) op. cit., p. 77
148. Butler, David and Kavanagh, Dennis (1974A), The British General Election of February 1974, Macmillan, p. 74
149. Lord Howells to author 2003
150. Colin Smith to author 2004
151. Colin Smith to author 2004
152. *The Western Mail*, 1/3/74, p. 1, *The Daily Post*, 1/3/74, p. 1
153. Lord Carlile to author, February 2000
154. Clark, Alan (1998) p. 174
155. Welsh Liberal Party Executive 17/8/74
156. D. David L. Williams statement to all candidates on 3/6/74, Welsh Liberal Party
157. Liberal Party Press Release LPR/74/GE2/36
158. Welsh Liberal Party Bulletin on the October 1974 General Election, 14/10/74
159. Michael German to author 12/10/08
160. Geraint Howells, Liberal Party press release 21/11/74
161. Lord Howells to author 2004

6

FIGHTING ON THE MARGINS
(1975–1987)

Introduction

The Welsh Liberals had begun 1975 with two MPs. The period between the mid
1960s and 1970s, when the Welsh Liberals were on the brink of annihilation electorally seemed now to be behind them. It looked as though the party had at last halted
its decline in its traditional heartlands of Cardiganshire and Montgomeryshire. Yet
the period covered by this chapter is once again one of political turbulence, with the
party's long cherished dream of 'Home Rule for Wales' being cruelly dashed, after
which the party sank back to another electoral low point. However, a short while
afterwards, the 1980s was to provide the Welsh Liberals with a large infusion of new
blood when they were joined by the new Social Democratic Party (SDP). This new
Alliance spread across Wales to revitalise areas where the Welsh Liberals had been
in decline or absent for decades.

The Alliance would help the Welsh Liberals to reach post-war electoral heights
in terms of the popular vote and bring about the regeneration of the party's presence in both Westminster and in the council chambers across Wales. That said, the
party would still remain very much on the political margins but its presence on a
number of Welsh councils was beginning to develop beyond the one or two token
Liberal councillors of previous decades. This period would also see a spectacular
by-election win in Brecon and Radnor that would become the Welsh Liberals' only
post-war Westminster by-election gain.

The Toil Continues

Organisationally, the mid 1970s started well for the Welsh Liberals. By 9th June 1975
every constituency in Wales had a Liberal Association secretary who actually lived
in and was active in the constituency.[1] This was the first time since the mid 1960s
that the party could claim this. The level of activity in each constituency, however,
varied greatly. Most constituencies could not boast elected Liberal politicians but
there were now some areas of South Wales where the party was full of life. In Taff
Ely and Blaenau Gwent there was now a strong Liberal group on the urban district
councils. Green shoots were also springing up elsewhere. In the almost lifeless constituency of Caerphilly, a new Liberal Association started in April 1974. By May of
1975, this association had 78 members in the Caerphilly area and claimed to have
delivered over 20,000 leaflets.[2] Despite this burst of activity the whole time that the

Association was active, between 1974 and 1985, they were only actually able to gain one district councillor – in 1981. Their story of huge ambition and struggle without success was repeated across Wales as Liberal Associations in various constituencies found it almost impossible to get their candidates elected, no matter how hard they campaigned. Much of this failure was blamed on the party's low public profile. In February 1975 Welsh leader, Emlyn Hooson, sent the federal leader Jeremy Thorpe a despairing letter which stated: [3]

> "The low profile which the party has adopted since the last election is a mistake. Although there is tremendous enthusiasm among Liberals in the country, there is a general sense of the Party drifting and lacking a sense of direction ... Both Tories and Labour are going for the middle ground which is the only fruitful ground in politics for the Liberals."

Hooson and other Welsh Liberals felt that the only solution to this problem was to raise the Welsh Liberal Party's profile. Other Welsh Liberals felt that the party's problems came about not because of a low profile but because of its obsession with proportional representation (PR) in elections, at the expense of other issues. The Liberal Party had spent nearly the whole of 1975 campaigning on both devolution and what it described as 'The Great Vote Robbery' concerning the way it had lost out electorally in the 1974 general elections. Richard (Terry) Thomas, the candidate for Carmarthen also attacked the party's campaign for PR at the Welsh Council Meeting at the end of December that year. Thomas, a writer broadcaster and businessman, stated: [4]

> 'The campaign is diverting attention from the need to press forward policies on a broad social democratic front. Putting all its eggs in the basket of electoral reform far from being the salvation of the Liberal Party would be political suicide. We have to make our minds up whether we are a parliamentary party producing clear, hard hitting policies or an extra parliamentary movement chasing every good cause that comes along, such as proportional representation.'

Despite these protests, PR would be central to Liberal Party policy for the next two decades. Apart from the issue of PR, Howells continued to address specific Welsh policies, particularly what he saw as the 'crisis in Welsh farming'. On 12th March he addressed the National Liberal Club in London in terms that today would be seen as being environmentally unfriendly but then had strong support amongst his farming supporters. He made clear his belief, saying[5] '...we have enough national parks and more emphasis should be put on using all available land for agricultural production. We also need more flexible planning permission for farmers.'

Farming issues aside, Howells as one of the two Welsh Liberal MPs, was able to feed his input on many differing issues directly into Welsh policy. These ranged from rates rebates and the extension of Bronglas Hospital to the continuation of the building of the M4 motorway. It was on Westminster issues, however, that Howells was now catching the public eye. In 1975 he received considerable coverage for his denouncing the Labour government's failure to allow any Welsh Liberals to sit on the standing committee of the Welsh and Scottish Development Agencies Bill. The party, squeezed between the other three Welsh parties, now found itself out in the cold on some issues of Welsh devolution.

Howells's own political situation in Cardigan looked a bit firmer when Elystan Morgan announced he would not 'stand for Cardigan again or anywhere else'.[6] However, both the constituency chair for Labour, Deian Hopkin, and Morgan himself were confident that Labour would win the seat back. In the event they would never again be a threat to Howells. Instead it was Plaid Cymru that the Welsh Liberals feared in that seat in the 1970s. In the Welsh Executive of July 1976, the Chair, Winston Roddick, stressed that the party should pay great attention to the threat from the nationalists as 'the Plaid intended a big push here'.[7] The party was still as unsure as ever of how it could effectively deal with Plaid Cymru. Executive member, Phil Davies, stressed how much 'Plaid milked Welsh issues', such as the need to create the Welsh Development Agency (WDA). They also saw Gwynfor Evans' effective use of Parliamentary Questions (PQs) in boosting their party's Welsh profile, which both Roddick and others thought that the Welsh Liberals should try to match.[8]

Unlike Plaid Cymru, the Welsh Liberals were not developing into a mass movement. It was rather the case that they were frequently made painfully aware of how they had contracted from a mass movement over the last half century. In August 1976, the Welsh Liberal Party received a letter from Midland Bank concerning the Glyngorrwg Liberal Association, near Port Talbot. It stated that they were £24.33 in credit but the Association had been inactive since 1959. The Welsh Liberal Treasurer, Norman Lewis, noted 'The hall (a wooden shed) was demolished. The officers who signed the original mandate are now all dead … We have two similar cases in Barry and I have just come across another'.[9] The sad death of much of the post-war Welsh Liberal Party in most of South Wales was now catching up with the party. It also underlined the continued perilous state of the party's finances.

Norman Lewis, an accountant and former independent councillor from Nelson near Caerphilly, would be one of the central figures in the Welsh party in the latter part of the 1970s. It was his analysis of the Welsh party's accounts that revealed a £2,000 black hole and, as a result of this news, it was clear that the party was teetering on bankruptcy. As Plaid Cymru's fortunes rose, the Welsh Liberals were once more struggling to survive. Determined to prevent the party from disappearing altogether, Lewis now had to halt all Welsh Liberal expenditure. He also avoided an overdraft and scrapped loans which he thought would take it further into debt. The immediate side-effect of this was that the party's full-time secretary, Gwynedd Ashford, was laid off and it would be a number of years before the party's Welsh office would be staffed again.[10] In October 1976 the party decided not to take part in the centenary of the British Liberal Party (1877-1977) because it felt it simply couldn't afford to.[11] In 1976, the Wrexham Office was closed down because of the lack of funds, with Martin Thomas having to personally pay off its £200 rent arrears. Other groups and constituencies within the Welsh party were also finding times hard. The Young Liberals did not pay their affiliation fee of £8 so they too lost their voting rights and only nine constituencies in Wales paid their affiliation fee that year.[12]

In July 1976 the federal leader David Steel attended the annual dinner in Montgomeryshire and went on to a rally in Aberystwyth. It was at this time that both Howells and Hooson discussed with Steel their roles in both the national and Welsh Party. It was decided that Hooson would now concentrate on policy and Howells on reorganising the Welsh Party.[13] In the British Liberal Party's conference in March 1977, it was announced that Howells' Parliamentary role was now to be spokesman for Wales and Agriculture, Hooson would act for Defence and the Law. It was with these portfolios that they would soon enter the Lib-Lab pact.

Wales Enters Europe

Conservative Prime Minister Edward Heath had brought Great Britain and Northern Ireland into the European Economic Community in 1973. This was popular with most Liberals in Wales but it did not go far enough for one senior Welsh Liberal. Emlyn Hooson, initially sceptical about the impact of the European Common Market on agriculture, was by now in favour of even greater integration. This would be in the form of a federal Europe with cross-national issues being dealt with by a federal government. Many within Harold Wilson's Labour Party, however, did not embrace the idea of being part of the European ideal at all, let alone a federal Europe. Wilson was, therefore, forced to call a referendum on 5th May 1975 in order to both keep his party from splitting and to provide an answer to the referendum question: 'Do you think that the United Kingdom should stay in the European Community?'

Both Howells and Hooson campaigned for a Yes vote, in part because of their own convictions and in part because the farmers in their constituencies were heavily in favour of it. It was felt at the time that the Common Agricultural Policy (CAP) was providing a good deal for Welsh farmers. The Welsh result saw 64.8 per cent of the Welsh population vote yes. In Hooson's own county of Powys, the result was the highest in Wales with some 74.3 per cent voting yes. Both Howells and Hooson welcomed the result of the referendum as they felt it enhanced Wales' European connections. They called for better links with the Common Market with 'roll-on, roll off' terminal ports for Cardiff and Newport and for the Welsh Secretary to attend European Council meetings.[14] Ironically for the Welsh Liberals, from now on they would consistently remain one of the most pro-European parties in Wales but would never get an elected member of the European Parliament in which to demonstrate this enthusiasm.

Thorpe Resigns and a New Leader is Chosen

In January 1976, a sexual scandal arose which would see the resignation of the Liberals' British Leader, Jeremy Thorpe. A man called Norman Scott, who alleged he had had a homosexual affair with Thorpe in the 1960s, was taken to court for defrauding the benefit system. He then asserted in court that Thorpe had tried to have him killed the year before. Although these allegations were never proved either at Scott's trial or at Thorpe's own trial in 1979, it was enough to make him resign in May 1976. The resignation was soundly endorsed publicly by Hooson, no friend of Thorpe's, on 12th March 1976. He had already publicly called for Thorpe to stand down until he cleared his name.[15] Thorpe, however, had been popular with some Welsh members as he was seen to be a friendly figure who always mixed well with the members. Yet even his supporters, such as the Welsh Treasurer Norman

Lewis, had to concede publicly that 'he needed to step down whilst his problems were sorted out'.[16] Thorpe did this and in the subsequent leadership election, Emlyn Hooson thought about standing for the leadership once more. He stated he would publicly, in March, but did not because of the lack of party support outside Wales. This was despite a supportive campaign by Martin Thomas within the wider party and media seeking to reassure Liberals that notwithstanding Hooson's right of centre reputation, he was still a sound candidate.[17] With Hooson out of the running, at a special Welsh party meeting in Westminster on 11th May, both Welsh MPs and John Roberts, Chair of the Welsh party, declared their support for Jo Grimond to take over as a caretaker leader.[18] In the final leadership contest, however, both Hooson and Howells backed David Steel to become the leader. Steel subsequently defeated his leadership rival John Pardoe.[19]

The whole business of Thorpe's resignation was damaging to the Liberals electorally across Britain. It brought their own morale to a low ebb as their disgraced leader and later on, former leader, was dragged through the law courts. As much as the Welsh Liberals deplored the continued references to the 'Thorpe scandal' in the daily press and the impact it had on their own fortunes, there was little they could do to stop it and its political fallout.

The Welsh Liberals and the St David's Day Referendum 1979

Initially, Welsh devolution was combined with plans for that in Scotland. The Kilbrandon Commission, referred to in the previous chapter, had set out some models for devolution in 1973. The Conservative government of Edward Heath had progressed little on the proposals. Their 1974 general elections manifestos mentioned nothing of devolution outside Northern Ireland.[20] The Labour Party was, however, committed to introducing elected Assemblies for both Scotland and Wales in its manifestos. So were the Liberals and Plaid Cymru. As the Labour Party had won the October 1974 general elections by a small majority and devolution was a popular issue with the amongst the Liberal and nationalist parties at Westminster, it soon found itself in a central place on the Westminster agenda.

For the Liberals, devolution was a core policy at the heart of their desire to see the establishment of a federal Britain. Although what Labour was proposing for Scotland, and particularly Wales, was far less than what the Liberals would have introduced had they been in power, it was enough to gain the Liberals support. For the first time, both the Scottish and Welsh Liberal Parties were brought together on an issue that did not directly apply to the English party. Menzies Campbell, soon to be Chair of the Scottish Liberal Party, wrote to the Welsh Liberal Party about its co-operation in October 1975. He was replying to a letter from the Welsh Liberal Executive member, Paul Brighton, which had called for closer co-operation between both nations, saying, "I rather like your suggestion that we should be the 'Celtic Front' and not the 'Celtic Fringe'. The difference in psychology is extremely apt".[21] For the next few years the 'Celtic Front' would work together on devolution in Westminster. The Welsh party's view was as it had always been, and would remain, that there should be parity with

Scotland in devolution. This meant a Welsh Assembly elected by proportional representation with legislative powers and the introduction of unitary authorities in local government.[22] Labour offered far less than this. Their diluted version of devolution did not go down well with the Welsh Liberal Party's grass roots. It involved no PR for elections to the Assembly, no primary legislative or tax-raising powers. The more radical desires of the party's elected members and the 'conservative' nature of many Welsh Liberals supporters, who did not support devolution at all, meant that, whilst the party's MPs, Lords and senior members in Wales supported devolution, there was little enthusiasm amongst the wider Liberal voters for it.

On 30th November 1976, the House of Commons caught sight of the Scotland and Wales Bill for the first time. The proposed Welsh Assembly would take over the role and function of the Welsh Office, including its one and a half billion pound budget. It would not, however, have the legislative powers of the Scottish Assembly nor have the powers and scope that many on the Kilbrandon Commission, in 1973, had recommended. Straight away, Hooson called for a separate Bill for Wales, with the addition of proportional representation for elections.[23] He was soon proved right in doing so; within a few months the combined Scottish and Welsh Bill was collapsing because of the weight of amendments being placed on it by the Conservative and Labour rebel MPs. The Westminster Liberals had supported the Bill in its earlier readings but were now increasingly unhappy with its progress and content. With the government even failing to convince many of its own MPs of the virtues of the Bill, the Liberals themselves now also felt unable to support it. On 16th February, the Chairman of the Welsh executive, Winston Roddick, travelled up to London to try to persuade the party's 13 MPs to vote for a guillotine motion in order to try and get the Scotland and Wales Bill through in 20 days.[24] They did not take Roddick's advice, the two Welsh MPs voted with the government but the other 11 Liberals, together with 37 Labour rebels, joined the opposition and defeated the government by 29 votes. This was the most significant post-war public split between the Welsh Liberals and the rest of the party. The result would, in part, now pave the way for Hooson to lose his seat some three years later.

The Labour Government was flagging and feared the possibility of defeat at any time. To stabilise a now much weakened Labour government the Liberals entered a stabilisation pact period (the Lib-Lab pact) on the 23rd of March 1977. In part, the pact was there to ensure that any future devolution legislation would pass through the House of Commons successfully. There had already been constitutional talks between the two parties on devolution which had foreshadowed the pact. There were over a dozen meetings between the government and the Liberals to discuss the redrafting of the Scotland and Wales Bill. Only one concerned Wales. This showed the much weaker position of the Welsh Liberal Party compared to their Scottish sister party in pushing the devolution agenda and revealed the greater hostility of the Labour Party in Wales to devolution compared to that in Scotland. Geraint Howells was in charge of Welsh devolution for the party and was joined by the Scottish Liberal MP Russell Johnston (Inverness) to lead the Liberals' redrafting team for the new devolution Bills. Howells, bearing in mind the February vote, had indicated in an interview with *Barn* magazine in July 1977 that, if devolution was not forthcoming this time and lacked the support of the main Liberal Party, he would support Plaid Cymru in future.[25] Such a situation never transpired and, despite his frustrations, Howells stayed firmly in the Liberal camp.

Separate Bills for Scotland and Wales now came before Parliament. The Bills for both Scotland and Wales received their second reading on the 14th and 15th November 1977 and gained the royal assent on 31st July 1978. Throughout the whole process the government, supported by the Liberals, walked a political tight-rope. The Conservatives continually drafted motions, which undermined the role of both the Scottish Parliament and the Welsh Assembly, whilst increasing the power of Whitehall and Westminster over the devolved bodies.[26] Although the Bill gained royal assent in July 1978 the referendum was not set until 1st March 1979. This allowed the 'No' campaign to build their support both against devolution and as a means of getting the voters to punish an increasingly unpopular government. At the same time the government did not follow the example of the European Referendum in 1975 by financing two all-party organisations to campaign on each side of the argument. It was a left as a political 'free for all', with both sides having to find their own resources. The Liberals in Wales, always lacking money even for their own election campaigns, had scant resources to throw into the pot. They relied mainly on the Labour and trade union campaign for the required publicity.

Devolution was now the most important issue facing the Welsh Liberals for a generation. Winston Roddick, therefore, stood down as chair of election committee in order to concentrate on the referendum.[27] Alex Carlile, Chair of the Welsh Party (1979-83), and Howells, the party's Welsh President, both joined the cross-party 'Yes' campaign. They, together with Cecilia Barton, Phil Davies, Martin Thomas, Norman Lewis, Richard Livsey and a number of other Liberals, campaigned for a Yes Vote against what they often felt were overwhelming odds. The combined might of the various elements of the No campaign ranging from the Conservative Party, large elements of the Labour party to the Welsh county councils proved a formidable force. The Welsh Liberals, nevertheless, still toured Wales speaking on the platform with many pro-Assembly government ministers including Dr David Owen, the then Foreign Secretary.

Howells had been against a referendum when it was first put before the Welsh party in 1975, fearing it would be lost and damage the Welsh Liberal Party.[28] He would soon be proved right. As the long campaign continued, so the No campaign were able to successfully link the referendum ever more closely to a vote on not only a Welsh Assembly but whether the voters should also send a message to an unpopu-lar Labour government to call a general election. Anti devolutionist Scottish Labour MPs had introduced an amendment to the Government of Wales Act 1978, which for both Scotland and Wales, imposed a quota of 40 per cent of the Welsh electorate to vote 'Yes' for devolution to become law. In the event, unlike Scotland, there was no need for a minimum vote to be imposed on the Welsh electorate. The 'No' vote was endorsed overwhelmingly by 956,330 votes (80 per cent) to 243,048 voting yes (20 per cent). Every Welsh county voted resoundingly 'No'. The 1st March 1979 St David's Referendum was a disastrous setback for all pro-devolutionists in Wales. Norman Lewis summed up the senior party's members' reaction to the Welsh media the following day in Cathays Park:[29] 'It a sad day for Wales as we could have been a great nation projecting our voice into the Common Market. Instead we must remain silent.'[30]

Those Welsh Liberals, who had fought so hard for a yes vote, were genuinely depressed by the result. For generations they had believed that this was the system of government the Welsh people truly wanted. The rise of Welsh nationalism during the

1960s and 1970s had seemed to confirm this fact to them. Yet they had been proved wrong and it was a shock to their fundamental beliefs. In the short term it would also impact heavily on the party's electoral fortunes.

After the reflection on the referendum campaign, the Welsh Party decided that the federal referendum leaflets were seen as being shoddy and they later refused to pay for them. When the Welsh Liberal Executive met on the 3rd of March, just two days after the referendum, the general consensus was that despite the devolution failure they would remain committed to a federal Britain. They restated this fact through a press release the following day.[31] Four months later the Welsh Liberals formally withdrew from the cross-party Assembly campaign and soon would once more pursue their own vision of a federal Britain with Wales having its own Parliament. It would be almost a generation later before the Welsh Liberals would return to a cross-party Assembly campaign group.

The Lib-Lab Pact Years

In 1976, Harold Wilson handed over the reins of the Labour Party to James Callaghan, the MP for Cardiff South East. As we saw earlier, within a year the Welsh Liberals would find themselves supporting this government in the first and only post war pact with two political parties at Westminster. Before this, however, they had local elections to fight. In May 1976, the second elections to the new Welsh district and borough council were fought. The councils had now been up and running for just over two years. The Liberal Party contested 8.7 per cent of the seats, a fraction of all of the other parties in Wales. Overall the number of councillors remained virtually unchanged with a few losses and a few gains; most Welsh districts were not even contested by the party. The most significant rise in councillors occurred in Aberconwy where there were now three Liberal new councillors. One of these was one of the most prominent north Wales Liberals, the Reverend Roger Roberts. He was elected for the Llandudno East Ward. Across the rest of Wales there were still only three district councils in Wales with significant Liberal group sizes. These were Cardigan and Colwyn with six councillors each and Blaenau Gwent with five Liberal councillors.

While the 1976 district elections had been something of a mixed bag for the Welsh Liberals, the 1977 county council elections were something of a disaster. The party contested more seats in the Welsh county council elections than they had in 1973. Their vote, however, slumped further to just 3.8 per cent of the total Welsh vote. The result of the poor vote was that the Liberals then lost two councillors each in West Glamorgan, Gwent and Clwyd, and three each in Powys and Dyfed. There were now just 11 Liberal county councillors in the whole of Wales. This contrasted feebly with Labour's 181 councillors, the Conservatives' 136 and Plaid Cymru's 38.

At the Callaghan government's Autumn 1976 British Labour Party Conference, it came into the open that politically the Labour Party was now struggling to hang on to power. On top of its internal political problems, the British economy was suffering from what economists referred to as 'stagflation', in which the economy was in decline but inflation was still rising. In December 1976, the government had to borrow money from the International Monetary Fund to keep the country's economy afloat. The conditions of the loan meant that Keynesian economics had to be abandoned and a period of severe monetary restraint introduced, which impacted directly on pay rises. In a period of rising inflation this caused turmoil not only in the economy but within the Labour Party and trade union movement, as they sought to come to terms with the fact that they could no longer spend their way out of economic troubles.[32] The government's majority was also decreasing as it was defeated time after time in Westminster by-elections. The side-effect of its reduced numbers meant that they could be defeated by the opposition any time that there was a significant rebellion by any of its backbenchers. There was one spectacular defeat which concentrated the Labour government's mind on how to best survive in office. When this occurred, with the fall of the Scotland and Wales (Devolution) Bill 1977, the Labour government realised that it needed support to prevent the possibility of future defeat and an early general election. As we have previously noted, Liberals at the same time, had no desire to see the early return of a Conservative government that had now become hostile to their cherished desire for devolution. To reinforce their views, the opinion polls showed that in March 1977, the Conservatives were at 47 per cent and the Liberals were at just 13 per cent.[33] March 1977, therefore, saw the conclusion of a Lib-Lab pact, which was viewed by both parties as the best chance of preventing a Conservative government from coming in and ending devolutionary hopes altogether. Initially, Hooson and Howells were supportive of the pact. Hooson was appointed with Alan Beith and John Pardoe to serve on the Lib-Lab consultative committee: Michael Foot, Merlyn Rees and Michael Cocks were their Labour counterparts.

It was clear from the outset that the Liberals were propping up a government that was failing on many levels, from inflation and pay restraint to devolution and general industrial unrest. In his New Year message to the Welsh Liberals at the end of 1977, Hooson called for an ending of the pact and the distancing of the party from Labour.[34] His party was now languishing at just eight per cent in the polls; far from increasing support for the Liberals the pact had reduced it by a third. The Liberals, however, carried on the pact until the autumn of 1978 when they expected a general election to be called.[35] After they withdrew from the pact, the Labour government went through its aptly named 'Winter of Discontent', in which, among other problems, there were mass strikes; rubbish lay uncollected in piles on the streets and bodies went unburied because of industrial action. James Callaghan, however, held on in government until the spring of 1979 when his government was defeated in a vote of no confidence. The Liberals, however, despite their withdrawal from the pact, remained in the electorate's eyes associated with the Labour government and their electoral fortunes were therefore intertwined.

Whilst it was in operation, Hooson and Howells justified the Lib-Lab pact to themselves and fellow party members by the fact that it kept devolution alive and prevented an early Conservative victory. Hooson had always been in favour of co-operation with other parties as long as it brought some concrete results. He had stated at the federal party's September Llandudno conference in 1976, to thunderous applause, that co-operation with Labour would be worth it if it resulted in a change to the electoral system that shifted towards proportional representation (PR).[36] In the event, it did not. Both Howells and Hooson knew that the pact would be unpopular in the short term in the Liberal Party as many feared selling their principles for uncertain gains. They thought, however, that if they gained tangible results from the pact its unpopularity would end amongst Liberal voters.[37] Although they didn't achieve any form of PR, there were some small measures of success for the Welsh Liberals. The most prominent was when Howells was able to get his opposite number in the Lib-Lab pact, John Silkin – Agriculture Secretary, in April 1978, to recognise the Farmers' Union of Wales (FUW) as an official negotiating partner with the Ministry of Agriculture, Fisheries and Foods and the Welsh Office.[38] This was to be conducted on an equal basis with the National Farmers Union. It was a very popular move amongst Welsh farmers and would remain one of his proudest achievements.[39]

The opinion polls for March and April 1979 put the party on just eight per cent of the polls compared to 51 per cent for the Conservatives and 27 per cent for the Labour Party.[40] On the 28th of March the Labour government fell.[41] For the first time since 1924, a government had fallen on a vote of no confidence. The Liberals in Wales and elsewhere now entered the election very much on the defensive for having supported and kept the Labour government in power. The Conservatives entered the election buoyed by their success in the devolution referendums and with their morale rising higher and higher as each opinion poll came out.[42] Just before the election, Hooson had informed the Welsh Executive that 'Jim Callaghan's delay in calling the election may have cost us the election'.[43] As the Liberal Party went into this general election there was, therefore, a genuine feeling across the party that they were to be wiped out, not only in Wales but across the whole of the UK. The general predictions in the press were that that they would not survive as a political force at Westminster.

The General Election of 1979 in Wales

Liberal	1
Labour	22
Conservative	11
Plaid Cymru	2

The Welsh Liberal Party went into the general election under its manifesto entitled the *Liberal Programme for Wales*. Because of the massive rejection of devolution in Wales two months beforehand, for the first time since the 1880s there was no mention of 'Home Rule' or devolution for Wales in Welsh campaigning literature. Instead, the manifesto focused on plans to revive the ailing Welsh economy. The morale in the party had been greatly lowered by the failed referendum campaign and the fall-out from the Thorpe trial. It became far more difficult, than in the elections of 1974, to get candidates to stand, particularly in those areas that had been very strongly anti-devolutionist. In October 1974, the party had fought all 36 seats. On the 3rd of May 1979, they were only able to contest 28 out of 36 seats. The absent candidates were almost all in the South Wales valleys constituencies.

The Welsh Liberal Party did all it could to bring forward candidates. The Brecon Branch, for instance, did not want to fight the general election because it felt it 'did not have enough money'. In addition, some members there did not want to damage the 'Conservative chances in the seat' of winning the seat from Labour. The result of this intransigence was that a number of branch members were expelled from the party and a new branch was formed by Colonel Geoffrey Cass. They then asked

Norman Lewis to stand as their candidate.[44] Lewis, the Welsh party's Treasurer, was an accomplished local government politician who had gained some national prominence, representing the party on the Yes platform during the referendum campaign. Despite this strong profile and a well-fought campaign, he was unable to gain more than half of the vote of the previous Liberal candidate, Noel Thomas, or to unite the Liberals in Brecon to support their own candidate. A number of Brecon Liberals had still continued to withhold support for Lewis even during the campaign and, as a result, the party would be divided in Brecon and Radnor for some years to come.[45]

On top of its internal troubles, the Welsh Liberal Party now counted the costs of having being seen to support two unpopular causes; Welsh devolution and the pact supporting the Labour government. At the ballot box the tangible result of its unpopularity was represented by the loss of some 16 deposits, costing the Welsh party and candidates thousands of pounds. There were a host of soon to be familiar Liberal names that saw their party's vote drastically reduced in this election. Richard Livsey fought Pembroke where the party's vote fell by a third. The same occurred for Alex Carlile in Flint East and Michael German in Cardiff North. Bill Barrit witnessed the Liberals' vote, in the Barry seat, fall by several thousand votes, reducing their vote there from 16 to 10 per cent. Martin Thomas in Wrexham saw the Liberals slump to third position and the Conservatives become the main challengers to Labour in the seat. Geraint Howell's Cardigan vote fell by 10 per cent and the Conservatives moved into the second position. Here the Conservative challenger was Emlyn Thomas, the disgraced former General Secretary of the Welsh Liberal Party, who had come back to haunt Howells, thankfully for the last time.

Aberconwy councillor Roger Roberts slightly increased the party's vote in Conwy where he was standing for the first time. But Roberts felt that the nomination of a last minute candidate in Caernarfon (John Edwards) had been a hindrance to his campaign, as he had needed the solid support of the members in the Western area of the Conwy constituency, which had now been diverted 'fruitlessly to Caernarfon'.[46] The Conservatives in Wales gained from this election, however, with three new seats in Wales, one of which was 'Liberal' Montgomeryshire. With their 11 Welsh seats it was now possible to travel from Holyhead to Newport across Wales passing only through Conservative held seats.

Montgomeryshire is Lost

Some ninety-nine years prior to this general election, the Liberals had overturned the hegemony of the Tory Williams-Wynn family in Montgomeryshire. From 1918 the combined rural and borough seat of Montgomeryshire had been a Liberal one. Whatever fate had thrown at the Liberal Party over the last century, a candidate had always been elected there bearing the Liberal name, albeit Independent Liberal or Liberal National. The Liberals had now lost the seat. Now a Conservative, Delwyn Williams, had become a 'Tory solicitor' who had managed to unseat a 'Liberal barrister'.

This was a tremendous blow to both the Welsh party and the Montgomeryshire Liberals. After a period of self-reflection by the Liberals, it became apparent that the Montgomeryshire seat had been lost for a number of reasons. These were mainly the same reasons that had seen the Welsh Liberals obtain such a dismal share of the vote across Wales in 1979. Such was, and still is, Montgomeryshire's importance as a Liberal bastion that its loss can be considered one of the most important milestones of Welsh Liberal history. It is, therefore, worth going over in some detail how such a significant Liberal seat came to be lost. The reasons were:[47]

1. The organisation had been weak in the seat in the two 1974 elections but the Liberals were helped then by the national tide that was carrying the Liberals forward. It could not rely on this in 1979 when the opposite was the case.

2. The constituency organiser had left for another job in the autumn of 1978 and the constituency was only able to place an inexperienced "organising secretary" in place just before the election.

3. Emlyn Hooson had now been an MP for 17 years and was fighting his seventh election in the seat. He had also been the party's Welsh leader, a central figure with the national party at Westminster and a powerful voice in the St David's Day referendum campaign. All of this had left Hooson exhausted both prior to and during the election campaign and thus unable to campaign fully.

4. The Conservative candidate, Delwyn Williams was seen as something of a 'Del Boy' character by the Liberals in the seat.[48] The Liberals rather looked down on him and thought the people of Montgomeryshire would do the same. After all they had a top-class barrister against a country solicitor. Williams, however, had spent several years touring the clubs and pubs of Montgomeryshire ensuring that his profile was as well known as Hooson's.

5. The devolution referendum had taken its toll on the election result. On 1st March the Montgomeryshire boxes were strongly against the Assembly. Just a handful of Liberals had come out in support of the Yes vote in the constituency. These were mainly the then Young Welsh Liberal's leader, Colin Smith, his father, Cllr Smith, also was Mayor of Welshpool, Hooson and Cllr Hefin Bennett from Llanidloes. Despite Hooson's solid commitment over the years, the party's manifesto promises, the successive conference resolutions both Welsh and Federal, the Liberals and Liberal voters of Montgomeryshire overwhelmingly voted no. Hooson and Howell's whole-hearted support for the Assembly had brought no electoral dividend to their party. Even worse was the fact Hooson had become out of touch with the grass roots feeling in his seat, which was quite 'conservative' in nature regarding both the Assembly and other Liberal policy ideas.

6. There was a big Conservative swing in Wales in 1979. Their vote had increased by 8.3 per cent of the total vote, whilst the Liberals fell by 5.3. per cent of the total vote. Such a swing had a devastating effect on Montgomeryshire's Liberal vote.

7. The Jeremy Thorpe affair had also made campaigning difficult, as had the unpopularity of the Lib-Lab pact in which Hooson had played a central role. This aided still further to the decline in the Liberal vote. Hooson, a supporter of the pact, was constantly attacked by Williams for keeping an unpopular Labour government in power.

8. The support from the federal party was also seen to be badly timed. David Steel's only visit to Newtown, by helicopter, was early on the closing day of the campaign and seen as too late to make any impact on voters.

When the election result was declared on the Friday morning, it soon became known that Hooson had been defeated by 1,593 votes (5.4%). There was then an 'outpouring of grief'. When Hooson went off for the pre-arranged 'victory' lunch at the Royal Oak in Welshpool and did the 'victory' tour to say 'thank you', there was widespread concern in the constituency. In Llanfyllin, people lined the main street, a good many visibly saddened by what they saw as the passing of the Liberal age in the constituency. Geraint Howells was now the lone Welsh Liberal MP at Westminster. Within a few month, however, he was once more joined by Emlyn Hooson who had been ennobled as Lord Hooson. There were now once again the same two Welsh Liberal voices at Westminster, although Hooson longer enjoyed the electoral mandate of Liberal voters and was sitting in the Upper House.

The Welsh Party Licks Its Wounds

In the aftermath of the election, Mike German reported to the Welsh Liberal Executive in May that it was evident there were serious deficiencies in their local and general election campaign.[49] When the Executive met again in September they had to face a stream of criticism about the lack of support that the Welsh Liberal Party had provided the constituencies with during the election. The constituencies reported back that they had received no communication from the Welsh party during the campaign. The results had also been so poor, with numerous lost deposits, that the wisdom of trying to fight every seat in Wales was questioned once more and a widespread view was expressed that in future only the better organised seats should be fought.[50] German had come a poor third in Cardiff North. He now became convinced that the traditional style of campaigning would never allow the party to break through in Wales. He had become aware of the Liberals in the Wyre Forest District Council in England that who had used a new style of Community Campaigning based on the delivery of a regular street newspaper called 'Focus'. This had enabled them to win control of the council. In Cardiff, German went about getting the necessary financial support of members to start the regular *Focus* rounds and by the autumn of 1979 these started to be distributed in a number of the city's wards.[51]

The June 1979 European Parliament elections also provided little joy for the Welsh Liberals. The first elections for the European parliament had seen Wales divided into four constituencies; in each of which a Member of the European Parliament (MEP) was elected by the first past the post electoral system. Despite being the most pro-European of political parties in Wales, the Liberals did poorly. They gained 10.1 per cent of the vote or less in three of the four constituencies. Only one candidate, the journalist and author, Nesta Wyn Ellis, managed to get respectable 17.4 per cent of the vote in North Wales. Even this figure was only enough to gain her the fourth position behind the Conservatives, Labour and Plaid Cymru.

In November, even whilst the party discussed plans for setting up a Cardiff Liberal Club with facilities for an office in Cardiff, it found itself struggling to pay the £650 annual rent on its St Mary's Street Office in Dumfries Chambers. The Welsh party had to lay off Gwyneth Ashford, the Welsh organiser, and the office now run solely by volunteers.[52] The party was entering the 1980s at another fiscal low point.

The Welsh Party Lays Some Important Local Council Building Blocks

The Welsh party would take some time to restore its morale to campaign after 1979. The May 1981 county council election, therefore, proved difficult for the Welsh Liberals. They managed to contest just 15 per cent of all council seats and from this gained just 3.8 per cent of the total vote and 4.2 per cent of Welsh county council seats. Although this was twice the number of councillors it had elected in 1977, it was still only 24 in total for the whole of Wales. Despite this, it could now know that across Wales, with the exception of West Glamorgan, there were Liberals on every county council.

Some of these newly elected councillors would lay the foundation for future developments. Three new Liberal councillors, Walter Matthews, David Rees and Gwen Schnell were elected onto South Glamorgan County Council's Cardiff's Cathays ward. They were the first Liberal councillors in Cardiff for a decade and Walter Matthews became the group leader.[53] One of these councillors, David Rees, had already, for the previous decade, been the dynamo of building up the party in Cardiff and many other parts of Wales and he would continue in this role for the next three decades. Cathays, the city's student quarter in the centre of Cardiff, thanks to Rees and others, would remain the heart of Liberal Cardiff from now on. In Gwynedd, the North Wales Liberals had also managed to get a number of Independents to adopt the party colours, which, in part, helped them gain seven seats on the council for the first time.

A New Candidate for Montgomeryshire

As noted earlier, Hooson had gone to the Lords soon after his defeat in 1979. This meant that Montgomeryshire needed a new candidate for the next general election. Before the process was started there was a thorough constituency reorganisation in Montgomeryshire and Gareth Morgan, a Llanidloes solicitor and former Welsh Liberal Party chairman, became the constituency chairman. This reorganisation aside, many aspects of the Liberals' long-established pedigree continued to flourish in the seat, despite the fact that it was then held by the Conservatives. With Lord Davies of Llandinam (grandson of David Davies the former Liberal MP in the seat) as the constituency president, the party continued to carry on almost as before with it fundraising fetes at the big Montgomeryshire country houses of Maesmawr Hall, Milford Hall, Summerfield Park and Glansevern. But as the Liberals in the seat began to take in the loss of 1979, at these social events there was also a renewed effort to reactivate Liberal membership and to recover the seat for the party.

In the selection contest for Montgomeryshire, there was an open competition to find a candidate. Unlike 1962, there was no heir apparent in the seat, as Hooson had not been expected to lose. About six people were on the long short list and they were invited to speak at well-attended meetings all over the constituency. Martin Thomas was the early favourite because he was well known locally. Dr Jennifer Lloyd of Cardiff (who had fought Barry in 1974) was also seen as a strong contender by the Montgomeryshire Liberals. At an early meeting in Welshpool, the Liberal barrister Alex Carlile's oratory skills shone above the rest of the candidates and he became the favourite. The constituency Liberal Association executive then interviewed the six candidates and presented a short list of three to the wider constituency which consisted of Thomas, Carlile and Lloyd. There was then a well attended selection meeting at Newtown High School. The Welsh media took some interest because, unusually for Welsh politics, the contest was quite open. The selection meeting, therefore, was broadcast on the Welsh BBC and HTV news. Carlile won by a clear majority. Thomas was second and Lloyd a distant third. The result came as a bit of surprise to the Liberal establishment figures, who had favoured Thomas. Carlile and the constituency then set about retaking the seat for the Liberals. As the Liberals sought to regain Montgomeryshire, a new political party was emerging that would help transform their fortunes.

An Infusion from the Left: The Arrival and Development of the Social Democrat Party in Wales

Through most of the 1980s, the Welsh Liberal Party was steered at an executive level by three consecutive chairs: Donald Crook, then Winston Roddick (later Welsh President in 1988) and finally Councillor Cecilia Barton from Cardigan. Coming from different parts of Wales, each of the three chairs can be seen as playing a key part in ensuring that the Liberals across Wales stayed connected and united. The North Wales Liberals were particularly grateful to Crook who lived in Colwyn Bay for being their 'eyes and ears' in the Welsh party, which was often dominated by the politics of South Wales.[54] All three helped steer the party through what would be one of its most exciting periods of expansion. None of them, however, at the start of the 1980s, were aware of how the next few years would alter the nature and shape of the Welsh party forever. Some in the party, however, had already predicted the shape of things to come. In December 1975, Terry Thomas, the Welsh Liberal chair of policy, had informed the Welsh executive that the basic problem of the Liberal Party was that Liberalism did not have a clear image. He added that the:[55]

> 'Social democrats in the Labour Party were the uneasy fugitives from Liberalism, which collapsed in the 1920s and 1930s. The Liberal Party therefore lost two generations of these men and women whose only recourse was to join the Labour Party. The time is ripe for saving the next generation from the same fate and getting them back into the party.'

His words were prophetic, as from the early 1970s small groups of Labour MPs had already been meeting in order to discuss how long it would take before the Labour Party spilt into differing factions. Welsh Labour MPs Gwynoro Jones and Tom Ellis were two of these MPs, who were led by the Welshman, (and former Labour Cabinet member and then President of the European Commission) Roy Jenkins. Jones was also the Parliamentary Private Secretary to Roy Jenkins, when he was Home Secretary in 1974, before Jones lost his seat to Gwynfor Evans in the October general election. Tom Ellis was the Labour MP for Wrexham and a committed Europhile. He was a moderate who had also toyed with the idea of joining the Liberals in the late 1970s but did not change his allegiance.[56]

After losing his seat in October 1974, Jones kept in contact with Jenkins and Ellis. He was in favour of them moving to join the Liberals on the grounds that they were already an established party with sitting MPs. In 1980, Jenkins delivered the 'Dimbleby Lecture' making it clear that he was willing to make the break with Labour. Shirley Williams, David Owen (of Welsh parentage) and Bill Rodgers were also connected with this desire to split from Labour (they became 'The Gang of Four').[57]

On 26th March 1981, the Gang of Four held a press conference in the Connaught Rooms, London, in which the Social Democratic Party (SDP) was formed. Later that day Roy Jenkins and Tom Ellis MP (Wrexham) launched the party in Wales. As well as being attacked by Labour, there was also some condemnation about the lacklustre nature of the SDP and its small-scale ambitions from Liberals such as Cyril Smith MP (Rochdale).[58] To add to this impression of a slow start, it took five weeks before Tom Ellis called the first meeting of SDP members at Cardiff University. Some 150 people attended with an *ad hoc* group being formed by Cardiff solicitor Tony Jeremy. Along with Jeremy, there were a number of others who would later play prominent parts in the Liberal Democrats such as Roger Williams (later MP for Brecon and Radnor) and Frank Leavers (later candidate for the Liberals in the Vale of Glamorgan by-election, 1989). Jeremy's Steering Committee convened for the first time on the 14th May at the Wyndham Hotel in Bridgend. Jeremy was keen on providing a 'Welsh' perspective for the SDP. Leavers became the Press Officer and Co-ordinator. At its second meeting on 23rd June, Ellis became the Chair of the South Wales Steering Committee and Jeremy the Vice-Chair. They then set about creating 'Provisional Area' parties but importantly for the future, they agreed to start informal contacts with the Welsh Liberals. Although they seemed outwardly united, the SDP in Wales, as elsewhere, divided into two camps. There were the so-called 'Owenites' who supported David Owen as leader and wished to see the party remain independent from the Liberals and there were the 'Jenkinites' who supported Roy Jenkins and wanted close links with the Liberals. Most Welsh SDP members tended to be Jenkinites.[59] This meant that as Owen's star rose in the party the relationship between the Welsh and the London-based SDP deteriorated.

In July the Welsh SDP wrote to Alex Carlile, Chair of the Welsh Liberal Party, requesting a joint meeting. The meeting occurred at the Glenusk Hotel, Llandrindod Wells on 17th October. Alex Carlile and Geraint Howells represented the Liberals. Howells was now the only Liberal MP left in Wales after Hooson's defeat in 1979. This added an additional burden to his already heavy workload. Tom Ellis represented the South Wales SDP and Bert Thomas, North Wales. Other SDP representatives included Tony Jeremy, Gwynoro Jones, David Heap and Joan Colin. The signed agreement stated that:

1. All constituencies should be contested by the Alliance (shared by the two parties);
2. There should be broad parity on seat allocation in Wales and also between winnable and less winnable seats;
3. For the purposes of negotiation, Wales was to be sub-divided into: North Wales, South West and Mid Wales, South East Wales.

This was the first time that the Liberals had had to share seats with another political party since the National Liberal-Conservative coalition pact of 1922. The negotiations with the SDP had involved no real concessions by the Liberals. Howells' personal view was that the Welsh Liberal Party could not 'give them our best ten seats in Wales. 'What right have the SDP to get half of the seats when in Wales when they have just arrived on the scene?' he felt.[60] They, therefore, gave the newcomers those seats, mainly in the industrial South, that they had found difficult to contest themselves.

In November 1981, the SDP in North Wales became increasingly disgruntled with what it saw as being left out of developments by the south. This seemed to mirror the history of the two separate Liberal Federations some twenty years previously. The divides between North and South SDP were removed and one 'All-Wales Provisional Steering Committee' was formed. Gwynoro Jones became the new Welsh Chair and Frank Levers the Secretary. The new Welsh SDP Group approved of the local negotiations over the general election seat allocations with the Liberal Party. Meanwhile, the SDP in Wales was joined by both Jeffrey Thomas, MP for Abertillery, and Ednyfed Hudson-Davies, MP for Caerphilly. After their initial enthusiasm both would disappear from the Welsh political scene having made little impact on the Welsh Liberal Party. Hudson-Davies went on to contest Basingstoke for the SDP and Thomas did the same in Cardiff West in 1983 but both were unsuccessful.[61]

On 26th February 1982, the negotiating teams of both the SDP in Wales and the Welsh Liberals signed an agreement on seats at a press conference in Cardiff. Howells signed for the Liberals and Ellis for the SDP. Both the Welsh Liberals and the Welsh SDP insisted that negotiations with the Liberals should be held without interference from London.[62] Although the electoral seating arrangements seemed amicable in Wales, these arrangements of the SDP London headquarters where their background of old Labour centralism still prevailed.[63] In London, matters were far from smooth; the SDP's David Owen and Bill Rodgers were dragging their heels in and, for a time, suspended negotiations. In Wales things remained smooth. By now the two parties were referred to collectively as 'The Alliance'. The first test of the parties' new relationship would be in Swansea and Gower where local discord in the Liberal Association over having an SDP candidate imposed there, was only abated by the intervention of Andrew (Andy) Ellis, the Federal Liberal Party's Secretary, who ensured that the local Liberals co-operated with their SDP partners. This co-operation in Swansea and Gower would soon become vitally important.

Gower By-election

On 6th May 1982, Ifor Davies, the Labour MP for the Gower died. Labour had held the seat in one form or another since 1904. Davies' death caused the first Welsh by-election for a decade in Wales. Gwynoro Jones became the first parliamentary candidate for both the SDP and the Alliance in Wales. The by-election was fought in the aftermath of the Thatcher government's winning of the Falklands War, which had reversed the decline in the Conservative vote. The Alliance's polling, however, had been quite optimistic, suggesting that they would come close to Labour[64] and Jones was bullish in the press in this respect. The Alliance had made a small political gain in April 1982, when they took control of Penarth Town Council from the

Conservatives. This gave them a psychological boost for future electoral contests, including the Westminster by-elections. During the Gower by-election they campaigned right across the constituency. All of the 'Gang of Four' came to the constituency, with David Owen travelling around in the SDP's famous red Land Rover to the remoter parts.[65]

Aside from the Falklands War, the key issue of 1982 was the rising rate of unemployment. By September 1982, some 167,000 workers were unemployed in Wales.[66] The Alliance planned a massive public works programme across Wales to solve some of this unemployment. Their Labour opponents at this time, however, were becoming pre-occupied by a left wing element within their party called the 'Militant Tendency'. They had been holding training weekends in Gower and this became a central issue within their own campaign. There had been three by-elections in England prior to this one, and each had seen a rise in the Alliance vote. Gower would be no exception, with the percentage of the vote increasing by about 250 per cent from the previous Liberal vote there in 1979. Jones had come a good second in the seat and there seemed to be widespread public enthusiasm for political change in Wales that was swinging behind the SDP/Liberal Alliance.

Gower By-election Result 16th September 1982

Candidate	Party	Vote	Percentage
Gareth Wardell	Labour	17,095	43.5
Gwynoro Jones	SDP	9,875	25.1
Trefor Llewellyn	Conservative	8,690	22.1
D. Ieuan Owen	Plaid Cymru	3,431	8.7
J. Donovan	Independent	125	0.3
D. Burns	Independent	103	0.3
	Majority	7,220	18.4
	Turnout		65.4

On 10th February 1983, the Conservative MP for Cardiff North West, Michael Roberts, died. Tony Jeremy, the SDP candidate for the seat now eagerly anticipated the forthcoming by-election, as did the Alliance when Alec Jones the Labour MP for the Rhondda died on 20th March. With a general election in the offing, however, there would be no more by-elections for this parliament and no chance for the Alliance to test its strength in Wales either in these two seats or anywhere else. Jeremy's failure to contest the seat was later felt to be another missed Liberal opportunity to acquire a parliamentary seat in Wales.

The SDP Soldiers On

The SDP had spent most of 1982 consolidating its own structures and policy agenda. The party's Welsh constitution was mainly the work of Gwynoro Jones and Eric Owen from Clwyd. Graeme Holmes was the key behind much of the policy direction, whether this was at the policy seminar in the Abernant Lake Hotel in Llanwrtyd Wells in April, or at the Constitutional Conference at the Hotel Metropole, Llandrindod Wells on 26th June. The following year, policy creation would mainly be taken over by Peter Sain Ley Berry, a committed Europhile from South Wales.

Although Gwynoro Jones had not won the Gower by-election, he was soon at the top of the party in Wales. On 14th December 1982, he was elected Chair, with the lay-preacher and university lecturer Eric Owen becoming the Vice-Chair. The party then went on to hold its first conference in Wales at Llandrindod Wells on 19th March 1983. SDP leader Roy Jenkins also attended the conference. Some 175 members attended to debate the party's 60 page *Towards a Policy for Wales*. The policy document covered areas within the remit of the government's Welsh Office departments (such as agriculture, health, local government, education and transport).

As we noted earlier, the relationship between the Welsh Liberals and the SDP was extremely good in Wales. Lord Hooson's idea of a joint policy group between the Welsh Liberals and the SDP was accepted by both groups and it met for the first time on 10th April. At the same time the SDP's Welsh organiser moved into the Welsh Liberals' Cardiff St Mary's Street Office and both parties shared operations for the first time.

The May 1983 council elections were the first that the Alliance fought together. The Liberals put up 187 candidates whilst the SDP managed some 168, making a total of 355. For the first time in living memory this was more candidates than either Plaid Cymru or the Conservatives were able to field. This made the Alliance the second party of the Welsh local government at least in terms of the number of seats contested.

However, the result, when it came to winning seats, did not make the Alliance the second party of government. They were like the 'curate's egg' – 'good in parts and disappointing in others'. There was one SDP gain in Neath but the rest of the gains were for the Liberals. On Cardiff City Council there were three councillors elected, one of whom was Michael German. There were also handfuls of Liberal councillors elected on the district/borough councils of Arfon, Blaenau Gwent, Brecknock, Carmarthen, Islwyn, Llanelli, Monmouth, Montgomeryshire, Rhuddlan, Taff Ely, Ogwr, Wrexham. Only in Delyn (4) councillors Alyn and Deeside (5) Aberconwy (6) and Ceredigion (11), however, did the party have a significant number of councillors elected. Only in one district council, Colwyn, was the Alliance the largest group on the council. Even here the party did not have overall control.

The Alliance had contested 22.9 per cent of the Welsh district council seats, gained 12.9 per cent of the total vote but won just 4.2 per cent of the seats. Labour, by contrast, had contested 61.5 per cent of the seats, gained 34.8 per cent of the vote and won 41.6 per cent of the seats.[67] The same electoral imbalance that had always benefited Labour in the Westminster elections was being repeated in the council elections.

Seeking to gain some of the electoral bounce of the previous year when the Falklands War had been won, Margaret Thatcher called a general election a year earlier than she needed. The election was to take place on June 9th, 1983. Both the SDP and the Welsh Liberals produced a joint manifesto *The Priorities for Wales*. For the first time since 1974, the Liberals, with the help of their new allies, were able to contest every Parliamentary seat in Wales.

The General Election of 1983 in Wales

Liberal	2
Labour	20
Conservative	14
Plaid Cymru	1

Margaret Thatcher was proved to be right when she thought that an early general election would help her party's fortunes. The year of 1983 was the Conservatives' best election result in Wales for a century. They gained 14 seats across Wales. The Alliance gained 23.2 per cent of the Welsh vote, eight per cent less than the Conservatives. The Alliance won two seats and came second in 18 more seats in Wales. It would also be the Welsh Liberals best post-war share of the vote. For the SDP, Tom Ellis came within 1,551 votes of winning Clwyd South West from the Conservatives in a three-corned fight. The other former Welsh SDP MP, Jeffery Thomas, came a poor third in Cardiff West. Elsewhere, only in Newport East where Francis David came third with a quarter of the vote and in Cardiff North where Tony Jeremy gained 30 per cent of the vote, did the SDP have any realistic expectation of gaining the seat. For the Liberals: Roger Roberts 30.8 per cent of the vote in Conwy; this put him in strong contention for the seat. Martin Thomas gained 29.7 per cent of the vote in Wrexham but still remained some 1,800 votes behind the Conservatives who were in second place. Elsewhere, the main joy for the Liberals lay in the fact that, for the first time since the Second World War, they had not lost a single deposit.

After the general election, both the Liberals and SDP sought to get to grips with the fact that they had gained 23 per cent of the Welsh vote but gained just one seat. To summarise, these were Alex Carlile's (Montgomeryshire) and held one seat Geraint Howells' (or technically gained the newly-created seat of Ceredigion and Pembroke North seat, formerly Cardigan). Carlile's narrow victory (668 votes) was not only good for Montgomeryshire but a vital morale boost for the Welsh Liberals, who now had two Welsh MPs once more. It was also one of the Conservatives' few losses in the UK. The two seats, however, represented just five per cent of the total Welsh seats whereas in proportion to their share of the Welsh vote, the Alliance would be eligible for another eight seats. The unfairness of the Westminster 'first past the post' electoral system and its lack of proportionality in Wales was once more reinforced in the Liberals' consciousness and became fully apparent now to those in the SDP. The desire for PR was once more underlined.

After the elections, whilst Howells remained the Welsh Liberal leader and Steel the British one, the SDP had changed its national leadership with one Welshman, Roy Jenkins, being replaced by a man of Welsh parentage, Dr David Owen, the MP for Plymouth Devonport.[68] The Alliance held its election review at Llanidloes on 9th July and it was open to delegates and policy agendas from both parties. In the feedback on the general election, it was the clear that there was a wish for greater co-ordination between the parties in Wales.

The failure to gain any seat in Wales and only a handful of MPs across the UK left the SDP with severe financial problems. The SDP was now struggling to keep its Welsh organiser. Although Owen had committed himself to retaining the post, the party was desperately short of money. In September and October, the business and media man Clive Lindley contributed to resources with an effective fund-raising effort from members in Wales. He was thus able to keep both the organiser and the office open in Wales by getting them to share an office permanently with the Liberals. It was seen as something of a Welsh triumph because in the same period the SDP was forced to shut its offices in Manchester, Birmingham and Bristol.

On 12th November 1983, the Welsh Liberal Party Executive and the Welsh Council for the SDP met in joint session for the first time. They agreed the apportioning of the candidates for the June 1984 European elections. The SDP would contest the North Wales and South-East Wales seats, whilst the Welsh Liberals would contest the South Wales and Mid and West Wales seats. The two parties also moved closer together. They set up a joint office in St Mary Street, Cardiff. They also established a Joint Liaison Committee under the Chairmanship of Winston Roddick and Gwynoro Jones. It was this body that was designed to co-ordinate policy and electoral strategy for the next general election. The first fruit from this closer union was the European policy document, entitled 'Wales and Europe', produced by Tom Ellis in January 1984. In their March Conference at the Crest Hotel in Cardiff, the SDP debated 'Wales in Europe' and a host of other policies, including constitutional reform, housing and Clive Lindley's (Alliance's Defence Spokesman), motion on a nuclear weapons freeze. This was duly adopted by one hundred and eighty votes to five. This vote now put them at odds with the Welsh Liberal membership who were not in favour of unilateral disarmament.

Cynon Valley By-election

On 10th February 1984, the Labour MP for the Cynon Valley, Ioan Evans, died at the age of 56. There was then an unexpected by-election for the Alliance in Wales but they were to have almost three months to prepare, and already had a sitting candidate in place – Felix Aubel. Frank Levers became the agent and Glyn Smith ran the office there. The Labour Party took longer to select a candidate in what was regarded as one of their safest Welsh seats. Anne Clwyd, the sitting MEP for Mid and West Wales, was selected from a crowded field as their candidate. The by-election was at the height of the 1984 miners' strike. Having thought it nearly impossible that Labour would lose one of its safest seats, the Press was more interested in who would take second place. For both Plaid Cymru and the Alliance, a good second place would show that they were the alternatives to Labour in the South Wales Valleys. In the event, the Alliance's share of the vote fell slightly but the party was still a consider-able way ahead of Plaid Cymru in second place.

Cynon Valley By-election Result 3rd May 1984

Candidate	Party	Vote	Percentage
Ann Clwyd	Labour	19,389	58.8
Felix Aubel	SDP – Alliance	6,554	19.9
Clayton Jones	Plaid Cymru	3,619	11
James Arbutnot	Conservative	2,441	7.4
Mary Winter	Communist	642	1.9
Neil Recontre	Independent	215	0.6
Paul Nicholls-Jones	Independent	122	0.4
	Majority	12,835	38.9
	Turnout		65.7

The pleasure of coming second did not last long for the SDP. Although the party was far stronger in the South Wales valleys than the Liberals had been for almost half a century, from now on the story for the SDP in the South Wales Valleys was to be one of rapid decline. It did, however, engage three Welsh activists who would later play a prominent role in the party, local schoolboys Stephen Williams, Huw Price and SDP activist Mark Soady. They would soon become well-known figures within the Welsh and British party and Williams would later be elected as the Liberal Democrat MP for Bristol West in 2005. Apart from attracting these solid future Liberal Democrats, the campaign was also notable for attracting two candidates who would be in the party for now but later defect elsewhere. The SDP's Felix Aubel, a 23 year old postgraduate student, who had stood for the Cynon Valley in the previous year's general election, was reselected for the seat by the SDP. Aubel spent much of the campaign condemning the Conservative government, although his views on law and order, including his support for hanging, seemed to some local members to be less than Liberal viewpoints.[69] It was, therefore, something of shock to the SDP when Aubel defected to the Conservatives at a press conference at the Plymouth South by-election, just over a month later on 11th June. Paul Nicholls Jones, who had stood as an Independent, gaining most of his press coverage from the returning officer refusing to take his £150 deposit in coins, would later join the Liberal Democrats. In the mid 1990s, however, he would also defect to Plaid Cymru.

European and Councils Elections and the Further Coming Together of the Welsh Alliance

The Cynon Valley by-election was just over a month before the European elections of June 1984. This time the Alliance had greater expectations than in the Cynon Valley because the contests would be held in areas where the parties were much stronger. In the event, the Alliance came a dismal third in three of the four Welsh European constituencies. Only Tom Ellis in North Wales was in contention for a seat. Ellis gained some 26 per cent of the vote but was still some 12,278 votes (5.6%) behind the winning Conservative candidate Beata Brookes. Ellis' result would remain the best ever for the Alliance or their successors – the Welsh Liberal Democrats, in a European election.

The Alliance spent much of the rest of 1984 deciding on the seat allocation for any forthcoming general election. In early October, there was a considerable backlash from the SDP membership over the seat agreements. A special conference was held in Carmarthen at which the Vice-Chair, Eric Owen, resigned because he felt he could not support the agreement. An attempt was made to throw out the agreement but the mover could not find a seconder. Many members referred to the agreement as 'Gwynoro and Tom's (Ellis)' despite its having been drawn through all the SDP's democratic processes. David Owen and Shirley Williams also attended the weekend having, on occasions, 'strained' conversations with Jones over how the issue could be best resolved. The Autumn AGM of the Welsh Liberals in October viewed it as a good agreement and endorsed it by 87 votes to three. It would take a special meeting of the SDP Council for Wales in Cardiff on 3rd November before the SDP could also endorse the Welsh agreement; this time by 26 votes to none with one abstention. At the same meeting a county council official from North Wales, Ieuan Evans, became the new Vice-Chair of the SDP's Welsh Council.

The SDP continued to evolve and at the start of 1985, the SDP Council for Wales met at the Mostyn Hotel, Llandrindod Wells to consider a number of policy papers presented to it in order to establish its own Welsh credentials. In the long term, the people who presented the papers proved to be more influential than the policies themselves. These were: Peter Sain Ley Berry,[70] Russell Smart, Clive Lindley, Ieuan Evans, Simon Williams and Jacqui Gasson, all of whom were to play central roles in the development of the SDP and the Liberal Democrats in Wales over the next few years.

The Alliance was able to field some 162 candidate in 1985 compared to the 93 the Liberals had put forward in 1981. The main successes for the Alliance was the election of five county councillors onto West Glamorgan county council, nine on Dyfed and South Glamorgan, seven on Gwynedd but only one on Gwent and two apiece on Clwyd and Mid Glamorgan. The Alliance had contested 34.5 per cent of Welsh council seats, gained 12.9 per cent of the total vote and gained 7 per cent of the council seats. Despite the constant law of diminishing returns for the Liberals, this was the first time in post-war Wales when there had been Alliance councillors on every Welsh county council. In South Wales, the councillors elected would now go on to form the nucleus of the eventual Liberal Democrat council groups, which would take control of Cardiff and Swansea in 2004.

Just over a week after the council elections were announced, the SDP had a reshuffle at the top in Wales. On the Council for Wales the Reverend John Pullin was elected as Chair, Jan Dickens became Vice-Chair, Peter Sain Ley Berry – became Council Secretary and Neil Williamson remained as Treasurer. The Council also established a policy committee chaired by Gwynoro Jones, including, among others, Russell Smart[71] Marion Drake,[72] Fred Hughes and Peter Sain Ley Berry. The next day the first meeting of the Alliance Committee for Wales was held at the Commodore Hotel in Llandrindod Wells. The Liberal Winston Roddick took the role of 'executive' chair whilst Gwynoro Jones took the role of 'working' chair. The Welsh Liberals and SDP were now working effectively as a team on virtually all issues of importance. The only significant issue that divided the two was the policy over defence. As we saw earlier on nuclear disarmament, the Liberals were on the whole multilateralists whereas the SDP were unilateralist. This did not, however, cause any irreparable rift between the two. At their first joint conference, the parties had passed a joint motion on defence by 180 votes to five endorsing multilateralism, confounding critics who expected the issue to split the parties apart.[73]

Brecon and Radnor the First Welsh Liberal Gain Since 1945

On the 8th of May 1985, the Conservative MP for Brecon and Radnor, Tom Hooson, died. He had been ill for some time. Hooson was Emlyn Hooson's cousin and whilst perceived at Westminster as a bit of a loner, he was seen as a hard-working MP in the constituency. As a result, Hooson had built up an impressive majority of 8,784 votes (23.2%). In a general election this would make it a fairly safe Conservative seat. Hooson had gained almost twice the vote that Richard Livsey had for the Liberals in 1983. Brecon and Radnor, however, was now a different constituency electorally in 1985 to that it had been just two years before.

In 1982, there had been a meeting of the Boundary Commission to review the boundaries of Montgomeryshire and Brecon and Radnor. Labour had wanted the existing boundaries kept. These included the strong Labour-supporting areas of Brynmawr and Cefn Coed (Merthyr Tydfil). There were about 10,000 Labour votes there. Tom Hooson, the sitting Conservative MP argued for Brecon to go in with the Monmouth constituency, which would have created an enormous Conservative stronghold. Radnorshire would have gone to Montgomery, which could also have made Montgomery a Conservative seat. On behalf of the Welsh Liberals, Councillor Gareth Morgan and Richard Livsey both submitted evidence declaring that the current situation was untenable; there were five local authorities operating in Brecon and Radnor and the new constituency should, therefore, follow the boundaries of the existing county. This was subsequently what the Boundary Commission implemented and the result was that the political centre of gravity was moved away from the Labour urban areas to the rural ones. Little was anyone to know at the time how important this boundary change was to be in transforming the Welsh Liberal long term fortunes. The new Brecon and Radnor constituency, however, still remained one of the largest UK constituencies and had the highest rural workforce (agriculture represented some 17 per cent of the workforce, against less than three per cent for the UK population).

On 26th May, the Brecon and Radnor Liberal Association selected Richard Livsey as the Alliance candidate for the seat. Livsey, a senior lecturer at the Welsh College of Agricultural, had already been tipped off about the likelihood of a by-election by his friend Geraint Howells, who knew of Hooson's failing health. Howells had re-established the Liberal presence in the Brecon and Radnor by standing there in 1970, gaining a respectable 18.8 per cent of the vote. He was also a strong supporter of Livsey and insisted that he was the only man who could win the seat. Although Livsey had not been born in the constituency, his father had been born in Brecon where he had spent his childhood.[74] His mother had been a headmistress and a teacher in Talgarth, also part of the constituency. Thus, Livsey had strong family links with the seat. He had also built up the constituency organisation and had spent the previous two years getting to know the constituency and getting those in the constituency to be aware of him. In this by-election, one of the most senior federal Liberals, the General Secretary Andrew Ellis, became the agent, which was an added bonus.[75]

As well as getting a good candidate and an experienced agent, plus a favourable review of the boundaries that had effectively reduced the Labour vote, two other factors were to benefit Livsey and the Alliance in this by-election. First, the previous Labour candidate David Morris, who had come second in the seat in 1983, had now been elected to the European Parliament. This meant that Labour's new candidate, the academic Dr Richard Willey,[76] would not have the time to develop the constituency. In addition, Willey was closeted from the press through much of the campaign, as the Labour Party had become fearful of what it saw as a mainly Tory press twisting its views.[77] The party was still dogged by its internal struggles and the miners' strike which had only recently ended in defeat for the miners. It was also not helped by the fact that the seat did not appear in the party's 130 top target seats. The second piece of good luck was the fact that, although the Welsh Conservatives wanted the election in September or October in order to build up the chances for their candidate, Dr Chris Butler,[78] the Conservative government actually moved the writ on 10th June for the election to be held on 4th July. This totally undermined Butler, who had no direct link with the constituency and was, as a result, unable to build much of a rapport with the voters in the few weeks of his campaign there.

On 18th June, the Labour supporting *Daily Mirror* produced a poll that unsurprisingly put Labour in the first position on 39 per cent; the Conservatives in the second with 31 per cent and the Alliance in the third with 28 per cent.[79] Although all parties but Labour publicly dismissed the accuracy of the poll, it caused some nervousness in the Alliance camp. Livsey then concentrated his fire on the Conservatives who were not helped by the news that they were to cut some £175 million from child benefit and was compounded by their poor record on combating the rising unemployment. Livsey was also able to successfully draw the campaign around to the increasing unpopularity of Margaret Thatcher.[80] Towards the last two weeks of the campaign, it became apparent to campaigners and the media that the Tory vote was beginning to slump. Then on 3rd July, a MORI poll put Labour on 46 per cent, the Alliance on 28 per cent and the Conservatives on 24 per cent.[81] The contest was now seen to be squarely between the Alliance and Labour. All parties brought in virtually every political heavyweight they could muster.

The campaign was at times very dirty. All the main candidates suffered personal attacks from each other. The Conservatives labelled Livsey as 'a loser, a split choice, a ditherer, an opportunist, a political nomad and not his own man'.[82] Despite this negative campaigning, the Alliance became increasingly confident as it viewed its own canvass returns. On the very day of the election the Shuttleworth[83] figures were putting them ahead. A BBC *Newsnight* exit poll put the Alliance some one to two thousand votes ahead.[84] However, in the event, Livsey won by 559 votes, turning a strong Conservative seat into an Alliance – Labour marginal.

Brecon and Radnor By-election Result 4th July 1985

Candidate	Party	Vote	Percentage
Richard Livsey	Alliance – Liberal	13,753	35.8
Richard Willey	Labour	13,194	34.4
Chris Butler	Conservative	10,631	27.7
Janet Davies	Plaid Cymru	435	1.1
David Sutch	Loony	202	0.5
Roger Everest	Independent	154	0.4
Andre Genillard	Independent	43	0.4
	Majority	559	1.4
	Turnout		79.4

This was the first new seat to be gained by the Welsh Liberals in Wales since 1945. Brecon and Radnor had not been a Liberal seat since 1939. For much of the period between then and 1985, the Liberals had either been unable to find a candidate or had come third. For the Liberals, the Alliance and Welsh politics, the Brecon and Radnor by-election remains one of the most important in the twentieth century. Livsey became the eighteenth Liberal MP at Westminster, twenty-fifth Alliance

MP and the third Welsh Liberal MP, making this the highest total of Welsh Liberal MPs since 1956.

The Liberal Weekend School Becomes the Lloyd George Society

In August 1985, in the spirit of co-operation and equality that had pervaded both the SDP and the Liberals, it was decided to transform the Liberal Weekend School into an occasion that would more broadly reflect both parties. It was replaced by 'The Lloyd George Society'. The society was named after the most prominent Welsh Liberal of all time and was felt to be more widely accepted as a named group to bring the SDP and the Liberals together. The Society's founders, however, still had strong Liberal roots. Its main founder was the former Welsh Liberal Chair, Winston Roddick, who wanted the society to be a much more open forum than the Summer School had been. Roger Pincham (Chairman and founder of the Gladstone Club) became the President. Lord Hooson, Tom Ellis, Judi Lewis, Sir Maldwyn Thomas, Peter Sain ley Berry and Martin Thomas were strongly involved. The Society also had the endorsement of Lloyd George's surviving daughters, Lady Olwen and Jennifer Longford.[85]

On 19th October 1985, the Lloyd George Society was launched in Criccieth. A ceremony to mark the occasion was held by Lloyd George's graveyard in Llanystumdwy. Gwynoro Jones recounted:[86]

'Without doubt the most moving experience in politics I have ever encountered. A peaceful, tranquil afternoon at the graveside of an international statesman … I'll never forget lady Olwen's answer to a question from a Reporter as to what advice would her father have given to the two Davids' – she said he would probably would have told them "just to get on with it".'

The Lloyd George Society was held in the same place as the Summer Schools had been, the Abernant Lakeside Hotel in Llanwrtyd Wells. The first Lloyd George Society lecture, given by Roy Jenkins at the Alliance Conference on the 16th of November 1985, attracted 150 people. Although that would mark a peak attendance for the Society, its weekends would always be well attended from then on. The SDP activist Peter Sain ley Berry was the first organiser of the weekends, though in 1991, the former Liberal parliamentary candidate Bill Barritt became the Chair and was the inspiration, together with Roger Pincham, for most of the Society's weekends, from then on.[87] Over the coming years, the Society would attract as speakers some of the most prominent people from both the Liberal and SDP as well as those in the public world. Speakers included: General Sir Anthony Farrar-Hockley (1991); Will Hutton (1993) and Lord Kenneth Morgan (2003 and 2007). Widely supported by people from England as well as Wales, the Lloyd George Society became the longest running and most successful open weekend school connected with the Liberal Party in its post-war history and outlasting the federal party's Liberal Weekend Schools, which ceased in the mid 1990s.

The Alliance Gets Stronger

On the weekend of November 16th and 17th 1985, the SDP and the Welsh Liberals held their first joint conference. As well as some interesting debates on youth, defence and the Welsh economy, the conference was important for the passing of a vote on a Welsh Parliament. Some 139 delegates voted for a Welsh Parliament and 55 against. Welsh devolution was officially back on the Welsh Liberal policy agenda after a gap of six years. In the February of the following year Gwyn Griffiths, the Welsh Liberal Chair, and Ieuan Evans, the SDP Vice-Chair, started to examine the policy papers of the two parties in order to prepare for the next Welsh Alliance general election manifesto.

The Brecon and Radnor by-election had been a tremendous success for cementing the partnership of the Alliance in Wales, bringing both parties closely together. Almost straight away Livsey was attacking the Conservatives over the declining fortunes of Welsh farming. In February 1986, at Westminster, Livsey slammed their record on farming in an Opposition day in the Commons. 'I have been in the industry 30 years and have never seen such a time when the industry shows such a lack of confidence' he said.[88] As well as highlighting the plight of Welsh farmers, it also angered the Welsh Conservatives who now became determined to take the Brecon and Radnor seat back.

In Welsh council by-elections at the start of 1986, the Alliance was on something of a roll. It was getting 35.2 per cent of the council by-election vote, beating Labour on 28.6 per cent, Plaid on 16.2 and the Conservatives on just 2.8 per cent.[89] Both parties felt, in the glow of electoral success, that they were working well together. Howells, however, the Welsh Liberal Party leader, did not like Owen, feeling he had too much influence over Steel.[90] Yet this view was not shared at the UK level. Nevertheless, in the Easter of 1986, at the Welsh Alliance Conference in Aberystwyth, he called for a merger of the two parties:[91]

'I should like to send this message to our excellent and inspiring leaders, David Steel and David Owen. It is what ever they decide on the other side of Offa's Dyke, we here, the radicals in Wales, are in such complete harmony that we feel ready to give serious consideration to a formal merger.'

Most, but not all, in the SDP membership felt the same way about merger. They were, however, well aware that David Owen did not favour a merger. Despite this opposition, the first step towards a full merger in Wales came straight after the Easter conference when Gwynoro Jones and Winston Roddick became Joint Chairmen of the Alliance Committee for Wales.

Over the course of the next year, Margaret Thatcher's Conservative government, having survived the problems brought on by the Westland crisis[92] and the US air force raid on Libya, were enjoying the poll ratings brought about by a strong economic boom. Living standards were rising, unemployment was falling and so was inflation. At the same time, the Labour Party was still going through internal struggles under its new leader Neil Kinnock and grappling with its own policy agenda. The Alliance too had its own problems; the leadership of the two Davids, David

Steel and David Owen, was increasingly subject to criticism and comical parody. In addition, the Conservatives were able to exploit the policy differences between the two parties which they strove to keep hidden. The Conservatives had, however, done their homework on these divisions and exposed them to the public gaze. The Alliance had been leading Labour in the opinion polls in the two months coming up to the general election by one or two points, making them the main challenger to the Conservatives.[93] They had done well in Wales in the May council elections. A number of Welsh authorities now had significant Alliance groups: Aberconwy (11 councillors); Cardiff (11) Ceredigion (14), Colwyn (15), Delyn (7), Glyndwr (4) and Swansea (5). In Colwyn and Cardiff the groups were now powerful enough to ensure that they shared control of the council. The Cardiff arrangement occurred after Michael German was able to persuade the Conservatives that there was no point in the council continuing on an issue by issue basis. Labour then also joined the power-sharing agreement and, for the next four years, the Cardiff Liberals and Michael German got their first taste of power in the capital in living memory. The experience would prove invaluable a decade later when German went into another coalition government arrangement, this time at the Welsh Assembly.[94]

In these Welsh council elections, it was clear that the Liberals were winning seats mainly at the Conservatives' expense, by taking much of the anti-Tory vote from Labour. It was this fact that was one of the deciding factors in Margaret Thatcher calling the general election for the 11th June, in order to take full advantage of the split in the anti-government vote.

The 1987 federal election team saw the Welsh MPs portfolio as: Livsey to cover the countryside portfolio, Howells 'Wales' and Carlile Legal Affairs.[95] The MPs, despite their federal election portfolios, did most of their campaigning in Wales and not elsewhere in the UK. It was they who were therefore at the forefront of projecting the Welsh Alliance's manifesto entitled *Wales, The Way Forward: The Time Has Come*. This had been endorsed at both parties' spring conferences. As in 1983, the SDP and the Welsh Liberal Party were, between them, able to contest every constituency in Wales.

The General Election of 1987 in Wales

Liberal	3
Labour	24
Conservative	8
Plaid Cymru	3

The 11th June 1987 general election victory for Margaret Thatcher was the first time that a party, under the same leader, had won three consecutive general election victories. The Conservatives gained 376 seats in the UK, but only eight in Wales. They had, however, a majority of 102 seats across the UK. The Alliance gained just 23 seats across the UK, despite getting 7.3 million votes. The Alliance did not lose any deposits in Wales and, in fact, only one was lost in the whole of the UK. Their strong vote share, plus the fact that the threshold for deposits had been dropped from 12.5 to 5 per cent of the vote, helped in achieving this feat. Once again the electoral system had worked in favour of the Labour Party. With a similar share of the vote to the Alliance, Labour gained 229 seats, including 24 in Wales, four of which were taken from the Conservatives.

In Wales, the Alliance managed to hold all three of their seats. In Cardigan and Pembroke North, Howells had seen his vote dip by 6 per cent, whilst his main Conservative rival O. J. Williams' vote also fell. However, that of his Labour and Plaid Cymru opponents rose. Howells, nevertheless enjoyed a comfortable 12 per cent majority. In Montgomeryshire Carlile had increased his majority from 2.3 per cent to 8.1 per cent. Richard Livsey's majority, however, had fallen to just 56 votes above his Conservative rival Jonathan Evans. This made Brecon and Radnor one of the most marginal seats in Great Britain.[96] Elsewhere in Wales, the Alliance came third in virtually every seat. There were a few very well placed thirds, Tony Jeremy in Cardiff North was just 112 votes behind Labour on 26.5 per cent of the vote, Clive Lindley also had 24 per cent in Monmouthshire and Patrick Jones gained an impressive 26.1 per cent of the vote in Pembrokeshire. Nevertheless, they suffered the psychological weakness of being third and, therefore, not being seen as the main challenger by voters. In only two seats did the Alliance come second. In Torfaen, Graham Blackburn gained 9,027 votes but was still some 17,550 behind the winner Paul Murphy. In Conwy, however, Roger Roberts was now a serious challenger to the sitting Conservative MP, Sir Wyn Roberts. Conwy then became one of the federal party's main target seats for the next fifteen years. The Alliance campaign that had achieved these results was run in Wales mainly through Andrew Ellis, who was also the last General Secretary of the Liberal Party and the first Chief Executive of the Liberal Democrats. Ellis was a renowned pioneer of Liberal *Focus* campaigning techniques, which later would be developed to good effect across Wales.[97]

Writing in the *Liberal News* that October, Welsh Liberal Executive Member, Robin Guest, noted that the 1987 election could be compared closely with that of October 1974. There had been a slight increase in the Alliance vote across all counties with the exception of Powys (which contained Brecon and Radnor) which had risen by 12.8 per cent. There were only two realistic target seats for the Alliance in Wales. These were Conwy, where the Liberal Roger Roberts had come second, and Cardiff Central where another Liberal, Michael German, had come third. The SDP side of the Alliance had not fared as well as the Liberals across Wales.[98] There were no Welsh seats in which they were realistic challengers.

Important seeds were also now being sown for the Welsh Liberals' long term future. A few months after the election, on the 12th of October 1987, Mark Williams, future MP for Ceredigion, took office as organiser for Ceredigion and North Pembroke Liberals which he combined with a post as part-time research assistant to the Liberal Welsh peers. Just over a decade later Williams would be able to use some of the knowledge he gained in this post to project his own parliamentary career in the same seat.

Within 48 hours of the election results being known, the entire Alliance leadership with the exception of David Owen, had called for the merger of the SDP and Liberal Parties. In August, a ballot of the SDP membership voted by 57.4 per cent in favour of merger. Those in favour of joining the two parties had now won the day and David Owen soon resigned as SDP leader and would continue with his own faction of the (Owenite) SDP.[99] Some SDP members in Wales joined him, including Tony Jeremy and Marion Drake. The vast majority, however, did not. For those outside the Owenite SDP, the rest of the year would now be spent going through the preliminaries for full merger.

Conclusion

Many of the politicians, who would go on to take leading roles in the Welsh Liberal Democrats towards the end of the century, were now cutting their political teeth for the first time during the late 1970s and early 1980s. The Welsh Liberals had started 1975 with two MPs and the growing optimism that there might well be a Welsh Assembly by the end of the decade. Such a development would further boost their electoral fortunes. In the event, the Lib-Lab pact and the failure of the St David's Day referendum saw the Liberals' devolution dreams shattered and also resulted in a massive decline in Liberal support in Wales. With the loss of the Liberals' bastion, Montgomeryshire, the party was reduced to just one parliamentary seat – that of Cardigan. The 1980s, however, were much kinder to the Welsh Liberals; Montgomeryshire was soon regained and the prospect of more wins to come returned to the Welsh party. The arrival of the SDP also brought a much needed boost to both Liberal and Welsh politics in the form of the SDP-Liberal Alliance. It had the effect of revitalising the Welsh Liberal Party. So often resigned to being the fourth party of Welsh politics, it now found itself in the situation of being seen as the main challenger to Labour in Welsh election polls. In the reality of the Welsh ballot boxes, however, the Alliance remained stuck on three MPs, a fraction of the Labour total. No SDP candidate, unlike those in England or Scotland, ever won a parliamentary seat in Wales. The Alliance also failed to gain a cherished European Parliamentary seat, despite its strong showing in 1984. There were some electoral successes, however. The rising number of Alliance councillors on Welsh councils was giving some Liberals their first taste of political power. In the future it would become unthinkable not to contest a Westminster seat at by-elections or general elections.

The Alliance's presence infused much needed new blood and the self-belief of victory into the Welsh Liberal Party's psyche. This belief in the possibility of victory was vital in the Brecon and Radnor by-election win. This victory would become part of Liberal folk lore, as it represented a tremendous psychological boost for the Alliance across the whole UK. It was, in addition, the only Liberal gain in a Parliamentary by-election in Wales since 1945. The party now had three MPs. This was their highest number of Welsh parliamentary seats for a generation. The Liberal Party in Wales seemed indeed to have turned a corner in its electoral fortunes, but could it last?

Notes

1. Welsh Liberal Party Constituency Secretaries list 9/6/75
2. Summer 1975 – Caerphilly Liberal Association News
3. Memo to Jeremy Thorpe from Emlyn Hooson for discussion at the Parliamentary Meeting of 19/2/75
4. Welsh Liberal Party Executive Meeting Llaninloes, Minutes, 20/12/75
5. Geraint Howells address to the National Liberal Club on 'The crisis in farming' 12/3/75
6. *The Western Mail* 27/6/75
7. Welsh Liberal Party Executive Minutes – 17th July 1976
8. Welsh Liberal Party Executive Minutes – 17th July 1976
9. Midland Bank Ltd to Welsh Liberal Party, 6th August 1976
10. Norman Lewis to author 12/5/07
11. Welsh Liberal Party Executive Minutes – 23/10/76
12. Welsh Liberal Party Executive Meeting Minutes 27/3/76 – Llaninloes
13. Welsh Liberal Party Executive Meeting Minutes 17/7/76

14. Welsh Liberal Democrats' Press Notice 6/6/75 – Post EEC Referendum Welcomed
15. *The Times*, 13/3/76, p. 2
16. Norman Lewis statement to BBC Wales supplied to author 12/5/07
17. *The Times*, 29/5/76, p. 15
18. *The Times*, 12/5/76, p. 1
19. Steel (1989), p. 113
20. 'Britain will win with Labour', Labour Party General Election Manifesto October 1974
21. Letter from Menzies Campbell to Mr. P. Brighton, Holywell, Clwyd, 3/10/75
22. Welsh Liberal Party Executive Meeting Minutes 20/12/75
23. *The Times*, 30/11/76, p. 2
24. *The Times*, 16/277, p. 1
25. *The Times*, 29/7/77, p. 2
26. Deacon, Russell (2006) Devolution in Britain today, Manchester University Press, p. 80
27. Welsh Liberal Party Executive Meeting Minutes 6/1/79
28. Welsh Liberal Party Executive Meeting Minutes 20/12/75
29. Lewis has ended up as the party's media spokesman by default, as his business was based in Cardiff (British Gas) he was always available to give interviews
30. Norman Lewis to author
31. Welsh Liberal Party Executive Meeting Minutes 3/3/79
32. Jones, Tudor (1996) Remaking the Labour Party: From Gaitskell to Blair, Routledge
33. Butler and Butler (2000) op. cit., p. 275
34. *The Times*, 31/12/77, p. 2
35. Steel, David (1989) op. cit., p. 149
36. *The Times*, 16/9/76, p. 1
37. Roberts, David (1985) op. cit., p. 94
38. The Farmers Union of Wales (FUW), formed in 1955 due to Welsh farmers dissatisfaction with the National Farmers Union (NFU)
39. Lord Howells to author, 2004
40. Butler and Butler (2000) op. cit., p. 274
41. Steel, David (1989) op. cit., p. 150
42. Cook, Chris (2002) op. cit., p. 165
43. Welsh Liberal Party Executive Meeting Minutes 20/4/79
44. Welsh Liberal Party Executive Minutes 2/9/78 Secretary Graham Blackburn reported that on 1st September, the Brecon and Radnor Liberal Association had voted by 19 to 16 votes not to contest the election, the 16 had then formed the Brecon and Radnor election committee and decided to have Norman Lewis as their candidate. The central funds were frozen but the branches as Crickhowell and Presteigne would supply funds to the new group. The Brecon and Radnor Liberal Association then had its affiliation revoked and the Brecon and Radnor election committee was granted affiliation. Lewis was accepted as the legitimate candidate for the new constituency association
45. Norman Lewis to author 12/5/07
46. Welsh Liberal Party Executive Meeting Minutes 20/5/79
47. The points come from Ian Smith to author, 2004
48. 'Del Boy' was the fictional TV character in the BBC TV series 'Only Fools and Horses'. He was a smooth talking black marketeer
49. Welsh Liberal Party Executive Meeting Minutes 20/5/79
50. Welsh Liberal Party Executive Meeting Minutes 8/9/79
51. Michael German to author 12/10/08
52. Welsh Liberal Party Executive Meeting Minutes 3/11/79
53. *Liberal News* 20/4/82
54. Alice Robinson to author 27/4/08
55. Welsh Liberal Party Executive Meeting Llaninloes, Minutes, 20/12/75
56. Ellis, Tom (2006) A Case of Welsh Political Midwifery: Tom Ellis on the Origins of the Liberal Democrats, Planet, Issues 178, p. 69
57. Much of the historical material concerning the history of the SDP in Wales within this chapter has been sourced from Gwynoro Jones (1987), *The History of the SDP in Wales*, self published booklet.
58. *The Times*, Thursday, Mar 26, 1981, p. 2
59. Peter Sain Ley Berry

60. S4C 20/6/05 – Geraint Howells – Documentary on
61. Jeffery Thomas rejoined the Labour Party in 1988. He died the following year
62. Ellis, Tom (2006) op. cit., p. 71
63. Ellis, Tom (2006) op. cit., p. 72
64. *The Times*, 16/8/82, p. 3
65. Peter Sain Le Berry to author, February 2007
66. *The Times*, 1/9/82, p. 2
67. Rallings, Colin and Thrasher, Michael (1991) Local Election in Britain: A Statistical Digest, Local Government Chronicle Elections Centre
68. Both of David Owen's parents were Welsh born
69. Huw Price to author, February 2007
70. Peter Sain Le Berry was a civil servant in Wales whose unsual family name originated from the Basque country
71. Russell Smart was then a lecturer in economic at the Polytechnic of Wales, he had stood for the SDP/Alliance in Bridgend in 1983 and would do so again in 1987
72. Marion Drake left the SDP and joined Labour. She later became a prominent Labour councillor in Cardiff
73. Ellis, Tom (2006) op. cit., p. 73
74. Lord Carlile to author, February 2007
75. Andrew Ellis was the Secretary General of the Liberal Party and would become the Chief Executive of the merged party in 1988
76. Son of the former Labour Minister Fred Willey
77. *The Times*, 21/6/85, p. 2, Peter Mandelson's involvement, in this, his first campaign, may also have something to do with the attempts at press control which was to become so familiar a decade later with New Labour
78. Dr Chris Butler was then a special advisor to Welsh Secretary Nicholas Edwards, he would later become the MP for Warrington South, 1987–92
79. *The Times*, 18/6/85, p. 2
80. *The Times*, 20/6/85, p. 2
81. *The Times*, 4/7/85, p. 1
82. Liberal News, 12/7/85, pp. 6–7
83. Shuttleworth's was the name given to the carbonated sheets used for 'knocking up' supporters on election day
84. *The Times*, 5/785, p. 1
85. Jennifer Longford's position as the daughter of Lloyd George is disputed. Longford herself believes it to be true whilst the Lloyd George family and others believe that she was probably the daughter of Colonel T. F. Tweed
86. Jones, Gwynoro (1987), p. 7.
87. William (Bill) Barritt was a chartered accountant in the Vale of Glamorgan. He had stood as the Liberal candidate in Barry in the 1979 general election
88. *Liberal News* 21/2/86
89. *Liberal News* 7/3/86, p. 8
90. S4C 20/6/05 – Geraint Howells – Documentary on
91. Liberal News Easter 1996
92. Where Michael Heseltine resigned over the ownership of Westland helicopters passing to an American company which had been supported by Margaret Thatcher
93. Butler and Butler (2000) op. cit., p. 276
94. Michael German to author 12/10/08
95. Welsh Liberal Party Campaign Bulletin No. 17 Feb 1987
96. Richard Livsey's agent for the 1987 and 1992 general elections was Celia Thomas. She was a founding member of the Winchester Liberal Party in the 1960s, and was an election agent there in October 1974 but had a connection to Wales through among other things the Lloyd George Society. From 1977 to 2005 she was also head of the Liberal, then Liberal Democrat Whips' Office in the House of Lords. Thomas was ennobled Baroness Thomas of Winchester in 2006
97. Michael German to author 12/10/08
98. *Liberal News* 30/10/87, p. 4
99. Russell, Andrew and Fieldhouse, Edward (2005) Neither left nor right? The Liberal Democrats and the Electorate, Manchester University Press

7

'HANGING ON AND FINDING
A ROLE' (1987–1998)

Introduction

The Welsh Liberals entered the post-1987 general election period in a mood of uncertainty with regard to the merger of both sides of the Alliance. This uncertainty was at times almost as great as what they had suffered during the various splits of the 1930s. The Liberal – SDP Alliance was no more and the Welsh Liberal Party was now seeking to formally merge with the SDP in Wales. After the relative stability of the Alliance era, the Welsh Liberals were now entering into the period that would provide them with a roller coaster ride of emotions. At times, when its electoral fortunes plummeted, the new party would be racked with utter despair yet the period would end with it preparing to gain the most Welsh Liberals to be elected for over half a century. This was also the period in which a number of the party's key politicos came to realise that while they may never be elected to a Welsh Westminster seat, there was a good possibility of gaining electoral office in any new Welsh Assembly. This, of course, still depended on whether the Welsh people chose to vote for such a body should there be the devolution referendum. To achieve this goal it would be necessary to first professionalise the Welsh party to an unprecedented degree. Before all this could occur, however, the party would have to respond to a series of electoral challenges that at times would again threaten to wipe it entirely off the Welsh electoral map.

The SDP and the Welsh Liberals Merge

The year 1988 saw the merger between the Liberals and the SDP proceed at a rapid pace. On 23rd January, in the federal Liberal Party's Conference in Blackpool, the delegates overwhelmingly accepted the merger with the SDP. Just over a week later, the Council for Social Democracy similarly endorsed the merger by an overwhelming margin. The vote then went to a national ballot of both parties' members and was supported by around seven to one for the Liberals and two to one for the SDP members.[1] Not all Welsh SDP members were positive about the merger. SDP leader David Owen was not happy with the merger and in Wales, Bobbie Feeley and Philip Robinson, stated at the Wales SDP councils' executive meeting on 6th February 1988, that they would be resigning from the Executive and staying with the continuing SDP.[2] Other prominent members of the SDP, such as Peter Sain Ley Berry, Russell Smart, Roger Williams and Eve Warlow, however, stated that they would move into the proposed new party. On the very same day as this Welsh SDP executive meeting was taking place, the Welsh Liberal Party held a special conference on merger in Llandrindod Wells. There the representatives voted by 199 to four in favour of the merger. A few days later, on 8th February, they were buoyed by the news, that Haydn Mansel Thomas had won a seat from the Labour Party. He had done so by a majority of more than two to one in the Margam Ward of Port Talbot District Council. This was an area that had not enjoyed Liberal success since the 1920s. It seemed to be a positive omen for the new party. With this little piece of good news behind them, the stage for formal Welsh merger was now set. In England the process of merger did not run as smoothly as in Wales but despite this on 3rd March 1988 a new combined party was launched in Cardiff – 'the Welsh Social and Liberal Democratic Party'. Few from either party liked the new name, considering it 'far too long' and subject to ridicule by their opponents who referred to them as the 'Salads' – as an acronym of Social and Liberal Democrats.[3]

On 12th March, the final SDP council meeting ever was held in Wales. After this meeting at the Crest Hotel in Cardiff, the official launch of the Welsh Social Liberal Democrat Party occurred. It was attended by the Liberal leader David Steel and the three Welsh Liberal MPs. This launch conference also decided on the new executive of the party, although for this event only 80 representatives were in attendance. This was less than half the number that had attended the merger meeting in Llandrindod Wells just a month before.

The SDP, despite their initial surge in strength in Wales, had enjoyed little electoral success beyond those few seats they had gained in Wales in the council chambers. The Liberals, with three Welsh MPs and a number of Welsh Lords, now enjoyed much greater political strength and, therefore, a greater power base in the new party. Although both sides had always got on well, it was true that the Liberal politicians outnumbered the SDP to a significant degree and, therefore, it was the Liberals who took the majority of seats on the new combined executive. There were then allegations by disgruntled SDP members of a pre-determined whipped vote by the Welsh Liberals. Despite there being no real substance to this allegation it was, nevertheless, the Welsh Liberals who picked up the major posts. Brecon and Radnor Liberal, David McBride, became the Secretary of the Party and Cardiff City Councillor, Jenny Randerson, became the new party's Chair. In doing so she had defeated former Alliance Committee Chair, Gwynoro Jones. An embittered Jones then declared: 'We were trying to create a position of influence. But because of the mechanisms of the old Liberals, we have ended up with a raw recruit'.[4] It was, therefore, the Welsh Liberals who would dominate the new party. To reinforce this fact, the longstanding Liberal Richard Livsey became the new Welsh parliamentary leader of the new party. Disgruntled former SDP members aside, the new Welsh leadership had been selected quickly and relatively painlessly; now, however, the question which still had to be answered, was who would be the new party's federal leader?.

The 1988 Federal Leadership Election

The first election to the federal leadership posts in the newly merged party was that of the mainly honorary post of Federal president. It showed that outside Wales there was far greater potential for the former SDP members in the first federal presidential elections to the new party. Ian Wrigglesworth, a former senior figure in the SDP, beat both Des Wilson and the Welsh contender Gwynoro Jones for the post. Jones political ambitions had now been dashed not only at a Welsh level but also at a federal one. He took himself out of Wales fully and sought, unsuccessfully, to become the elected member for the former Liberal border seat of Hereford, at the next general election.

There was one other interesting Welsh issue aside from the presidential one. In both 1992 and 1994, Martin Thomas stood for the federal party's presidency. He was a long way from winning; the 1992 result was won by Charles Kennedy and the 1994 contest by Robert Maclennan. Although the Liberals had had Welsh presidents before, Thomas had set a precedent for the new Welsh Liberal Democrat politicians to seek the federal presidential office in the future.

In March 1988, Federal Leader David Steel made it clear that he did not want to continue as the leader of the new party. The SDP's leader, David Owen, had left the new party to continue with an rump of hardcore SDP activists. The remaining SDP members' new leader, Bob Maclennan, did not wish to become the leader of the newly merged party. This election would also be the first time a major British political party used an all party membership election to vote in a leader. Although there would be no Welsh candidate in the leadership election, there would certainly be plenty of Welsh involvement in the election campaign. There were two candidates who came forward for the election: Paddy Ashdown, who was seen as a radical freethinking politician with 'boundless indefatigable energy',[5] and Alan Beith 'a quiet Methodist lay preacher who embodied traditional Liberal values and beliefs'. Despite representing Berwick-upon-Tweed, an English – Scottish border constituency and not being Welsh, Beith was a Welsh speaker, which ensured he had sufficient Welsh credentials to add to his support in Wales.[6]

It was perhaps unsurprising that Alan Beith's traditional 'Liberal background' and ability to speak Welsh appealed to the Welsh Liberals more than Ashdown's more modern background. Geraint Howells chaired Beith's campaign, which included support from Alex Carlile and the Rev Roger Roberts. Gwyn Griffiths, Chairman of the Welsh Liberal Party, also threw in his support. Ashdown lacked major Welsh support and the only major Welsh politicians to back him was the then Leader of the Welsh Liberal and Social Democrats, Richard Livsey. Before the campaign proper started, Alex Carlile released a list entitled 'Fifteen reasons why Ashdown was not fit to be elected'. Beith eventually condemned the letter, after intervention from David Steel and some other senior party figures, but Carlile was quietly pleased about the publicity it had provided his candidate. It was too late, however, to stop the sour note introduced into the election.[7]

After a course of numerous hustings a clear message emerged. Beith represented the traditional Liberal soul of the party whereas Ashdown represented the future fusion of Liberal at Social Democratic parties. These two aspects became apparent to party members. Which direction would the new party take? On 28th July 1988, it was announced that Ashdown had won 71.9 per cent of the votes cast, Beith the remaining 28.1 per cent on a turnout of 57,674 votes. Ashdown was duly elected and soon had his work cut out for him both in Wales and the wider UK.

After the upheaval of the merger, the new party's morale was somewhat fragile. Whilst the party was facing an uncertain future under a new leadership, the Labour Party was re-emerging from its internal splits under its new Welsh leader Neil

Kinnock, which increased Labour's appeal in Wales. The Conservatives too, with eight MPs in Wales and the Cabinet heavyweight Peter Walker as Welsh Secretary, were still feeling very confident. The nationalists, Plaid Cymru, had gained Ynys Môn in the 1987 general election and their three MPs now equalled those of the Welsh Social and Liberal Democrats. In the council chambers they were also gaining new seats, so they too felt a spirit of optimism. With the other Welsh political parties displaying a sense of renewed optimism, the Welsh Social and Liberal Democrats felt fortunate that there were only a few council elections in 1988 in Wales to test this new shaky party. In the May 1988 council elections the party retained its 15 seats in Colwyn Borough Council. In both Newport and Port Talbot, the party lost a councillor apiece. Newport only had one Liberal councillor, David Poor, and he had stood down, leaving the council with no Liberal presence. In retrospect, the poor showing in these two councils was to prove an ominous sign for the year ahead.

1989: The Year the Welsh Social and Liberal Democratic Party Nearly Sank without Trace

The British opinion polls showed that the Social and Liberal Democratic Party was in fairly robust shape at the start of 1989 with some 16.7 per cent in the polls. For the next four months the polls would put the party in the UK at around 17 per cent of the vote. Yet in Wales, it became evident that the party was only able to gain a fraction of this vote in actual elections. On 13th December 1988 the MP for Pontypridd, Brynmor John, had died. Pontypridd had always traditionally been one of the strongest areas for the Liberals in the South Wales Valleys. Yet the local Liberals did not want to get involved with the campaign. The Liberal councillors there felt that local voters wouldn't understand who the 'Social and Liberal Democrats' were and that they should, therefore, continue to put themselves down on the ballot paper as the 'Liberals'. This was unacceptable to the Welsh party and, therefore, the campaign was supported and run by former SDP members from the Vale of Glamorgan, Rhondda and Pontypridd instead. No local Liberal wanted to stand and, therefore, former North Wales SDP MP, Tom Ellis, was selected. The local campaign team then became enthused when the Federal Chief Executive, Andy Ellis, came down and promised federal resources for the campaign. As the campaign continued, however, it became clear that it was Plaid Cymru candidate, Syd Morgan, and not the Social and Liberal Democrat's candidate who was gaining local support. Federal resources were having little impact.

On the day of the election, 23rd February, it was the Labour Party's Dr Kim Howells who romped home with 53.4 per cent of the vote. Plaid Cymru took over a quarter of the vote (25.3%) to come second, with the Tory Nigel Evans[8] on 13.5 per cent of the vote, trailing in third. All the other four candidates lost their deposits. These included Ellis who managed just 3.9 per cent of the vote. He was almost beaten by his former SDP colleague Terry Thomas who gained 3.1 per cent of the vote. The Welsh Social and Liberal Democratic Party morale now reached a low point because of the huge drop in their vote in a seat that had previously always given them a healthy result. In the general election just a year and a half before, Peter Sain Ley Berry had gained 18.9 per cent of the vote on behalf of the Alliance. In the space of 18 months that vote had almost entirely evaporated.

On the day that the Pontypridd by-election was fought, the Conservative MP for the Vale of Glamorgan, Sir Raymond Gower, was out campaigning for his party in Pontypridd when he collapsed and died. This caused another by-election on 4th May. The Welsh party, still licking its wounds from Pontypridd, did not want to fight this by-election, particularly if the remaining rump of the SDP did likewise. Sain Ley Berry helped persuade the party to contest the election with the former senior Welsh SDP figure, Frank Leavers as their candidate. From the outset, the election was a two-horse race between Labour's John Smith and the Conservatives' Rod Richards. The Welsh Social and Liberal Democrats ran the slogans 'Vote for Frank Leavers, the man at the centre' and 'The Tories are going to lose the Vale by-election but who will win? Labour or Leavers?' Their message persuaded few voters to their side and Labour's John Smith won the seat with a healthy 12.5 per cent majority.

Although Leavers lost his deposit, importantly for the party in a crowded election of 11 candidates he came third on 4.2 per cent of the vote and also beat his SDP rival, Neath councillor, Keith Davies, who gained (2.3 %). In a twist of fate, Davies returned to contest the Vale of Glamorgan in the 1992 general election, this, time for the Liberal Democrats, where he gained a more respectable 9.2 per cent of the vote.

While the by-election in the Vale offered some glimmer of hope for the Welsh party, the county council elections on the same day did not. In every county council in Wales the number of Welsh Liberal and Social Democrats councillors fell to less than four councillors per county council. In the case of Gwent their struggle ended altogether. In the European elections five weeks later, the party's fortunes fell even further when they gained just 3.2 per cent of the Welsh vote. This was even below the poor outcomes in either the Pontypridd or Vale of Glamorgan by-elections. They came fifth in each of Wales' four European constituencies, lost their deposit in each and gained only around a quarter of the vote that the Greens were able to accrue in Wales. This was the worst all-Wales' result in the Liberal party's history. It caused widespread arguments and introspection in the party in Wales, and elsewhere, that focused on why the party was doing so badly with no real solution in sight. By October, the party was down to 8.3 per cent in the UK opinion polls – its lowest level for a decade. It would be March 1991 before the party was able to recover to its position of support to over 17 per cent and thus return to where it was in 1987.[9]

Despite its low morale, the party continued with its regular business. The 1988 AGM was held between the 9th and 11th of November at the Castle Hotel, Brecon. With Gwyn Griffiths in the chair, the conference had some hard decisions to make. The party's membership records were in a mess and, in an attempt to sort them out, they were transferred from the Aberystwyth Liberal constituency office to Cardiff. Staffing the party's office and the membership administration was proving to be a financial problem and, within a short period, membership would be transferred to the Federal party in Cowley Street, London, for good. The party was also finding itself in one of its regular periods of financial hardship. It couldn't afford to keep the office at 91, St Mary Street in Cardiff going as an operational unit. It, therefore, had to move to cheaper premises just down the road in 95, St Mary Street on the third

floor, above a bookmaker. The 1988 AGM also saw a number of the seasoned executive members use the opportunity to step down to allow an intake of new blood into
the executive. These included Celia Barton, Gwynoro Jones, Frank Leavers, David
McBride and Martin Thomas. Cardiff councillor Michael German now became a
more central figure in the Welsh party. A former music teacher, and for a time deputy
leader of Cardiff City Council, he was now juggling his day job of European Officer
for the Welsh Joint Education Committee (WJEC) with his part-time party activities.
German headed the Welsh party's policy committee and was also their representative on the federal policy committee, which began to give him greater prominence in
the wider federal party.[10] The post also gave him membership of the Campaigns and
Communications committee, which he would also chair for the next decade. German
was now one of the central figures in the Welsh party.

Towards the end of the year, one of the Welsh party's most prominent Liberals
died. Lady Olwen Carey-Evans, the last surviving child of David Lloyd George and
his first wife Margaret, died at the age of 98. She had remained a loyal Liberal and
an active campaigner to the end of her life and was President of the Caernarfon
Liberals and Vice-President of the Welsh Social and Liberal Democratic Party at
the time of her death. Olwen had been awarded a DBE in 1969 for her services to
Wales and lived in her house, called Eisteddfa, overlooking Pentrefelin, the nearest
village to Criccieth, her parents' resting place. When the 'grand dame' of Eisteddfa
called in the local post office to collect her pension she would always say 'Thank
You, Father', in recognition of her father David Lloyd George's introduction of the
old age pension in 1909.[11] Her death was the end of an era; after well over a century
there would be no member of the Lloyd George family in the Welsh party. Bearing
in mind the amount of differing names the Liberals underwent during David Lloyd
George's period in the party, it was somewhat suitable that the passing of the Lloyd
Georges into history would see the 'Welsh Social and Liberal Democratic Party'
change its name once more.

The Party Shortens Its Name

The terrible by-election results in Wales in 1988 and elsewhere in the UK caused
members to look once again at the party's overly long name to see whether reducing its length would improve the party's prospects. Various options arose, including
removing the name Liberal altogether. The Welsh leader, Howells, however, insisted
that the new party be called 'Liberal Democrats' and not 'Social Democrats'. He
used his position as Welsh Liberal Party leader to effect this move federally.[12] At
the same time Carlile, Howells and Livsey declared that from then on they would be
known as the 'Liberal Democrats' and in Wales as the 'Welsh Liberal Democrats'.
They held a press conference in the House of Commons to announce their adopted
name which was duly reported in the Welsh press the next day.[13] The matter of the
name change, therefore, seemed to be settled in Wales, but it took a ballot of all
members in the UK in October 1989, before it was fully agreed to shorten the party's
name officially to '(Welsh) Liberal Democrats.[14]'

The Lead Up Starts to the Next Great Electoral Challenge

The May 1990 Welsh council elections were limited to those four councils that held their elections by thirds. In Colwyn Borough Council, the Liberal Democrats lost one councillor but, with 14 councillors remaining, they still retained control of the council in a Liberal Democrat-Independent run coalition. In Newport, as in the days of the South Wales Liberal Federation, the Liberal Democrats there had decided to bide their time and failed to contest any seats. In Port Talbot, the party remained stuck on one seat and in Rhondda, it failed to move its total of no councillors. Bearing in mind the troubles of the 1989 elections in Wales and the party's low position in the opinion polls, it was a blessing for them that the elections had been limited to these four councils and that their losses were not greater.

In November 1990, Prime Minister Margaret Thatcher was toppled from power, in part because of the actions of two Welshmen; Sir Anthony Meyer, the Clwyd North-West MP, who acted as a 'stalking horse' in order to flush out Swansea Welshman, Michael Heseltine. He then stood against her in the Conservative Party leadership contest. In the event, it was John Major (and not Heseltine) who won the contest and became Prime Minister. For the Welsh Liberal Democrats, however, it was another Roberts whose time was now passing into history and was, therefore, on the minds of the old Liberals. On the 29th October 1990, Emrys Roberts, the former MP for Meirionnydd, died. Roberts, one of the celebrated Welsh Liberal barrister MPs, had held many senior posts in Welsh society since losing his seat. These included Chair of the Development Board for Mid Wales and membership in the Court of the University of Wales. Roberts had left the party after his defeat in 1951 but rejoined in the 1980s and had returned to campaigning for the Liberals once more. He was the last of the North Wales Liberal MPs to pass on, ending a link to the glory days of North Wales as a Liberal bastion.

At the start of the New Year, on 14th January 1991, the Labour MP for Neath, Donald Colman also died. Labour's candidate for the forthcoming by-election was Peter Hain. He had been the high profile leader of the Young Liberals between 1971 and 1973. Although Hain left the Liberals and joined the Labour Party in 1977, he was still regarded by many Welsh Liberals as an 'opportunist traitor'.[15] This added a particular edge to the campaign, reminiscent in some minds of Megan Lloyd George's standing in the Carmarthen by-election three decades before. Hain won the by-election with a substantial 28.4 per cent majority over Plaid Cymru. The Welsh Liberal Democrats had chosen David Lloyd to stand against him. Lloyd, a barrister, had been a Liberal in Pembrokeshire since 1974 and a councillor on Dyfed County Council between 1981 and 1986. His strong Liberal pedigree, however, did not project him into Westminster but he was able to save his party's deposit with 5.8 per cent of the vote, despite it being split by the presence of a SDP candidate. Importantly for the Welsh party, this was the first time they had managed to save their own deposit in a Welsh Parliamentary by-election since the merger and the last time the SDP would field a candidate in a Welsh parliamentary election.

The May Welsh district, borough and city council election results of that year provided little improvement on the Welsh Liberal Democrats' political status. They still held around six per cent of Welsh council seats, putting them at the bottom of the Welsh councillors' league table, although Plaid Cymru with seven per cent and the Conservatives' nine per cent of Welsh councillors were only just above them. Far above all three of them were Labour with 46 per cent of Welsh councillors whilst the Independents with a further 32 per cent were second. These two giants showed just how far the Liberal Democrats were behind the leaders in the field.[16] There was now some positive news for the party. In Monmouth Borough Council, the Liberal Democrats gained two seats, which put them on the council for the first time since 1983. In Torfaen Borough Council two more seats were gained, making a group of three councillors, which represented the first political opposition group to Labour on the council since it had been formed in 1974. Wrexham Maelor council also saw three gains which increased the Liberal Democrat group there to six seats. This made them the largest opposition group on the Labour run council and provided the nucleus, in the form of councillors Alun Jenkins and Aled Roberts, who would go on to run the council some 15 years later. There was also some bad news; on Delyn Borough Council four of the seven council seats were lost. Alyn and Deeside, Colwyn and Glyndwr councils lost two councillors each. In Ceredigion District Council, the loss of five councillors reduced the Liberal Democrat councillors to nine, its smallest number since the 'dark days' of the Lib-Lab pact over a decade before. The fact that this also occurred in Geraint Howells' Ceredigion and the Pembroke North constituency seat sent an ominous sign of declining Liberal fortunes there to anyone who cared to notice.

For the moment, the Liberal Democrats refocused their attention away from their poor local council result and moved it towards the forthcoming Monmouth by-election. This had been called following the death of the sitting Conservative MP, Sir John Stradling Thomas. As an MP with such a low profile at Westminster, he had become known as 'The Silent Knight'.[17] Would this previous low profile benefit the Welsh Liberals? They were unsure of how they would do.

'Brown Owl' Is Chosen to Fight Monmouth

The Welsh Liberal Democrats chose their Housing Spokesman, Frances David, as their candidate. A Skenfrith school teacher, she was later dubbed 'Brown Owl' by the press.[18] She had a firm knowledge of Monmouthshire and had been active in the party since the days of the SDP. David had been one of the four SDP members to negotiate the merger in Wales and in 1983 had come a good third (25.6%) in Newport East under their banner. In a campaign in which both the Conservative Roger Evans and the Labour candidate Huw Edwards were closely minded by their respective parties, David acted as a refreshing change for voters and the media. She was the candidate with the best local credentials and the Liberals tried to exploit that as her defining feature during the campaign. At press conferences and rallies her name was always prefixed with the title 'our local candidate'. The campaign was mainly run with federal party help but the Welsh party was also actively involved in it. Geraint Howells' secretary and future chief executive of the Welsh party, Judi Lewis, acted as David's daily adviser.

Right into the last week, the Liberals' campaign remained something of an unknown quantity. Paddy Ashdown continually stated that Monmouth was natural Liberal territory and did not differ substantially from Liberal Democrat held Brecon and Radnor to the north. Livsey agreed and the Liberal Democrats were also able to acquire a leaked memo from the Labour agent, Anita Smith, stating that they 'should not underestimate the Liberal challenge'.[19] Neighbouring constituency MP, Richard Livsey, was the main Welsh MP in the campaign. He used his own tactics of winning in Brecon and Radnor to good effect by ensuring that Frances visited as many of Monmouth's tiny villages as possible in order to boost her profile. This and her own persuasive personality helped ensure that the Liberal Democrat vote was not squeezed between the two other parties as expected and she consequently gained a good third place position, with almost a quarter of the vote.

Monmouth By-election Result 16th May 1991

Candidate	Party	Vote	Percentage
Huw Edwards	Labour	17,733	39.3
Roger Evans	Conservatives	15,327	34
Frances David	Welsh Liberal Democrats	11,164	24.8
David Sutch	Looney	314	0.7
Melvin Witherden	Green/PC	277	0.6
Peter Carpenter	Independent	164	0.4
Lindi St Clair	Independent	121	0.3
	Majority	2,405	5.6
	Turnout		75.8

The Monmouth result had been the most successful by-election for the Welsh Liberal Democrats since the Brecon and Radnor battle some six years earlier. Although the whole campaign was managed by the federal party in Cowley Street, for Welsh Liberals the result reflected well on the fortunes of party in Wales, as it moved towards the next general election. In addition, Plaid Cymru had got a dismal vote, which also boded well for Welsh Liberal Democrat aspirations to regain its position as the third party of Welsh politics.

Welsh Local Government Gets Another Shake-up

The month following the Welsh council elections, John Major's Welsh Secretary, David Hunt, announced that the existing two-tier system of Welsh local government (counties and districts) would be scrapped. A system of unitary authorities would replace them. As the Liberal Democrats had very little presence on most Welsh authorities at this time, the move to 22 unitary authorities made little difference to their electoral position and generated little interest inside the party outside of those authorities, where they already had substantial council groups. There was no consultation on the process and the main issue as far as the Welsh Liberal Democrats were concerned, was the proposed structure for urban authorities in Cardiff, Swansea and North East Wales and the fate of the district councils within Powys (Brecknock, Radnor and Montgomeryshire). The party was not unhappy with the plans for unitary authorities in its council strongholds of Cardiff, Ceredigion, Conwy, Swansea or

Wrexham but it was unhappy for those in the district councils in Powys. These would be scrapped and replaced by just one unitary authority – 'Powys'. One simple Act of Parliament was required to end the centuries long existence of these historic counties, which were represented by the party's two MPs. The Welsh Liberal Democrats were wholly opposed to these plans. At the Local Government of Wales Bill's Committee stage, Alex Carlile led the resistance to the plans to scrap the three district councils in Powys. Carlile was initially successful in getting the decision reversed, much to Hunt's successor, John Redwood's annoyance. Although he was able to overturn Carlile's amendment once more on the floor of the House of Commons, the Liberal Democrats had inflicted an embarrassing, albeit temporary, reversal for the Conservatives' plans.

Powys was now to be the new county council rather than the three historic counties so dear to Welsh Liberals' hearts. The elections to both Powys and all the other unitary these councils would be at least a year away, but those related to Westminster could be at any time. Whilst talk of council change was occurring, it was also apparent that John Major, in the fourth year of the Parliament, would have to call a general election within the year and the party, therefore, began preparing for this. As part of this process, all the Welsh MPs stepped up their campaigning. Howells took a delegation of Welsh farmers to Brussels to lobby the Agriculture Commissioner on Welsh issues in early 1992. Livsey and Carlile also projected their own constituency issues in Westminster and beyond.

John Major, despite his by-election losses, had given a considerable psychological boost to the Conservative party's fortunes since coming into power in 1990. For the Conservative MPs and the party's supporters a 'change appeared to be as good as a rest'. Although the party was neck and neck with Labour in the opinion polls, Major was confident that his 'down to earth soap box campaigning' would prove a triumph over the glitz and razzmatazz of the Labour campaign. In Wales, he had his eye on retaking the by-elections losses for the previous decade: Brecon and Radnor, Monmouth and the Vale of Glamorgan. The election he called for 9th April would prove whether he was up to the task as both leader and future prime minister.

Michael German steered the election campaign from the party's Cardiff office. Lacking any significant support for the federal party or Welsh resources, German did his best to try to match the campaigning efforts of the other political parties in Wales. When it came to election policy, the 1992 manifesto was drawn up by Martin Thomas and it proposed both the Senedd (Welsh Parliament) and the setting up of 24 unitary authorities. This was partly in response to the Conservative proposals, and he also proposed a Welsh Environmental Protection Agency as the most 'Welsh' part of the policy agenda. The remainder of Welsh Liberal Democrat policy was heavily linked to the wider federal party manifesto.

The General Election of 1992 in Wales

Liberal Democrat	1
Labour	27
Conservative	6
Plaid Cymru	4

The early hours of the morning of 10th April seemed to start well for the Welsh Liberal Democrats. As some of the South Wales counts were beginning to be announced, the news came in that the Liberal Democrats had gained Cheltenham, just 25 miles over the Welsh border. Expectations rose that it might be a promising night for the party in Wales as well. As the results came in, it soon became apparent that with the exception of Conwy, where Roger Roberts had made the seat a two way marginal with the Conservatives, it had been a dreadful night of losses or poorly placed third places for the Welsh party. The following week's *Liberal Democrat News* provided a short summary of the dreadful night in Wales:

'The Welsh party had the most depressing night, losing Geraint Howells in Ceredigion and Pembroke North to Plaid Cymru and Brecon and Radnor to the Tories by just 130 votes. The strong Labour Vote let the Tories in there. Conwy saw the majority sliced down to 995 votes. Cardiff Central slipped back, with Labour gaining the seat and benefiting from being seen as the main challengers.'[20]

In other Welsh seats the party either came third or fourth. In Monmouth, which had so inspired the Welsh party in the previous year's by-election, their same candidate Frances David's vote collapsed to a poor third, on just over 10 per cent of the vote. Without federal party support the seat returned to the Conservative-Labour marginal of previous elections.[21] The local party's base here had diminished rapidly and it would be another decade until it would start coming back to life again. In only one Welsh seat outside the target list did the party gain a second place. In Merthyr Tydfil and Rhymney they were able to gain the second position, all but some 26,713 votes behind the winning Labour candidate, Ted Rowlands. In part, this was because of the fact that the Liberal Democrats' candidate also had the surname Rowland (Robyn).[22] This initial swing to the Welsh Liberal Democrats was put down by Labour to short-sighted voters misreading the names but in the following elections, sometimes with the help of the long serving agent David Williams, the party would continue to take the number two slot, proving Labour's explanation to be ill-founded.

Ceredigion is Lost Once More

In Ceredigion and Pembroke North, Geraint Howells' vote fell from 36.6 per cent to 25.1 per cent of the vote. At the same time, Plaid Cymru's vote rose from 16.2 per cent of the vote to 31.3 per cent. Howells himself put the loss down to the fact that his campaign team was weak and that his key supporters from 1974, who had got him in then, were either dead or too old to campaign. His current campaign team was more confident of victory than Howells. He stated, 'I knew that in my heart this wasn't going to be the case'.[23] Howells was right. Importantly for the Welsh Liberal Democrats, one of his Campaign Team was Howells' then constituency assistant, Mark Williams. Learning from the lessons of this defeat, Williams would be back in eight years to try to regain the seat once more for the Liberal Democrats, with himself as candidate.

Plaid Cymru's winner in Howells' seat was Cynog Dafis, who stood as a joint Plaid Cymru-Green Party candidate. The previous year, a constituency poll had indicated that such an alliance was likely to win the seat. The Green element on the ticket appealed to those born outside Wales who now lived in the constituency and were not prepared to vote Plaid Cymru.[24] The 1989 European elections in Wales and elsewhere had already shown that a sizable proportion of the Welsh population was willing to vote Green. When this was combined with Plaid Cymru's vote it was enough to topple Howells. The Liberal Democrats had always been unsuccessful in combating the encroachment of Plaid Cymru; with few exceptions Plaid always gained at the Liberal Democrats' expense.[25] For the Welsh party the loss of Ceredigion and Pembroke North had one unexpected benefit. Howells' Westminster Secretary Judi Lewis became the new Welsh party manager. Over the next five years, Lewis was the sole permanent representative in Wales and it was she who effectively kept the party together in the eyes of the media and the party's own membership on a day to day basis.

Brecon and Radnor is Lost Too

In 1992 Richard Livsey's overall vote increased by 1,338 votes from 1987. But as voter turnout increased and, more importantly, his Conservative opponent, Jonathan Evans' vote also increased even more than Livsey's, he lost the seat. Evans' vote had increased by 1,524 votes, which was enough to give him a majority of 130 votes. Livsey had not been helped by a sudden national surge to the Conservatives and by the failure to effectively squeeze the Labour vote, which under their candidate Chris Mann had remained stubbornly at 26.3 per cent. One of the central issues that affected Livsey in 1992 was hunting. Livsey was, in fact, a paid up member of the British Field Sports Society and certainly not anti-hunting. During the 1987–1992 Parliament there had, however, been a debate on a private member's bill on hunting in the House of Commons, which Livsey had not attended because of constituency business. The pro-Conservative hunting lobby portrayed his absence as lacking loyalty to the cause of hunting.[26] The Conservative vote was therefore helped by what Livsey believed to be a 'whispering campaign against him' in the seat in order to sway votes to them.[27] In a marginal constituency like Brecon and Radnor, these were enough lost votes to lose the seat and to turn a Liberal Democrat majority of 56 to a deficit of 130 votes.

Another Low Point

The Welsh party's morale was once again almost broken. Two out of its three seats had been lost; its worst defeat since 1951. The internal party's gloom seemed to be matched by a more general gloom across Wales, concerning the prospect of five years of Conservative rule. Towards the end of April, Hwyel John Evans from Ammanford wrote a letter to *Liberal Democrat News* which stated: 'I am a demoralised Liberal Democrat Member. Can anyone give me a good reason to renew my membership in the New Year? We lost six excellent MPs to defeat, two in Wales.'[28] There seemed to be little comfort for Evans or the wider Welsh Liberal Democrats, save the fact that they had not been totally annihilated. They were now once again back as the fourth party in Wales,with just one MP, Alex Carlile.

In Ashdown's portfolio reshuffle in December, Carlile was given the Employment spokesman position as well as that of the Welsh portfolio.[29] While Carlile concentrated on his new role, the party in Wales begin to lick its wounds. As part of this healing process, the defeated Howells was keen that the Liberal Democrats regain Ceredigion and Pembroke North at the first opportunity. His own poor health prevented his return as the candidate and a short while after the election he was ennobled to become Lord Geraint of Ponterwyd. In October an advert was placed for an organiser for Ceredigion[30] and a selection contest was held for the seat. Two candidates put their names forward: Dai Davies, a local accountant who was also on the district council and Jeff Clarke, a Cardiff-born barrister. Davies who had a strong local support base in the constituency won the contest and was selected.[31] With Richard Livsey set to stand again in Brecon and Radnor once more, and Roger Roberts committed again to Conwy, the party had made an early start on getting its key candidates in place before the next general election, which in the event would be in five years' time.

The Carlile Years

As we have just noted, just as in 1966 and 1979 the Welsh party was now left with one sole representative at Westminster. Not only did Carlile have to represent the party at Westminster and undertake a ceaseless tour of the Welsh constituencies, he also had to undertake virtually all Welsh media appearances.[32] There were a few others, however, apart from Carlile in the Welsh Party who were developing the party's organisational abilities. Alongside Judi Lewis, Jenny Randerson and Michael German, there were a number of prominent party volunteers. As in previous decades, the Welsh party continued to carry on because of its band of dedicated amateurs. Pauline Badger worked tirelessly as the party's Secretary and Chair of the Finance Committee between 1992 and 1994, but because of ill health had to step down, and the following year tragically died. Brian Lopez, the party's Treasurer, was also forced to step down because of illness and was replaced by the young 'Liberal Turk', Nigel Howells. Howells was a charted accountant from Pembrokeshire, who would later become a central figure in the Cardiff Liberal Democrats. A number of other Liberal Democrats also became prominent in the party during this period Kate Lloyd and Jon Burree helped the party as its Secretary.[33] Jon's brother, Nick, was the Chair of the Policy Committee from 1995 to 1998, in its build-up to the Welsh Assembly elections.[34] Both Burree brothers were fiercely loyal to the party and would be recognisable figures to many in the party, as they sat in innumerable party executive meetings and in the audience at many Welsh party conferences over the coming decades. Another member, Ruth Parry, a Welsh speaking television presenter and producer, took charge of the party's televisual output and monitoring. It was Parry who professionalised and even made possible the party's Welsh Party Political Broadcasts during this period.

Another key figure during this period was Chris Davies. He was a financer from Swansea who also professionalised the Welsh party conferences and made them significant sources of fund-raising for campaigning purposes. Davies was also a close friend of Simon Hughes, the Liberal Democrat MP for Bermondsey.[35] Hughes was Davies' best man at his wedding and Davies in turn acted as his Welsh campaign manager, when Hughes stood for both the federal leadership and presidency. Because of his Welsh background and the poor state of the party in Wales during this period, Hughes also acted as Deputy Leader of the Welsh party and was frequently to be seen at Welsh party events in the 1990s.

Davies' efforts aside, the Welsh Liberal Democrats generally remained no better at fund-raising than the Welsh Liberals or the SDP had been before them. Apart from the money the party made at conferences, its sole national fund-raising relied on the gallant efforts of a Brecon and Radnor member called Megan Rosenberg. It was she who held the raffles, sponsored balloon events, the 100 Club, sponsored knits and other forms of small scale fund-raising for which she often received very little thanks but, nevertheless, persevered.

A member of the Welsh executive, Peter Black, the leader of the Liberal Democrat group on Swansea City Council (1984–99) and civil servant at the Land Registry, became the Welsh Chair from 1994 to 1996. He became an efficient, active member of the executive in this period. It was Black, for instance, who together with other key members of the party, restyled the Welsh party's name in the 1995 Conwy Spring Conference as 'Liberal Democrats Wales'. The idea was that the party would re-define itself as being a 'Welsh' party within the federal party as opposed to appearing to be separate from it. It was thought that by putting 'Wales' at the end of the name it would be made clearer that the party in Wales was its own master, rather than just consisting of Welsh members of a party based in London. The re-definition had occurred mainly because of the fact that the party was struggling to work out how it could communicate its appeal against the threat from Plaid Cymru who had taken Ceredigion and Pembroke North from them a few years before. The strategy, however, had a limited effect partly because of the fact that there was no simple noun to call the members of the newly branded party. Whereas before they had been Welsh Liberal Democrats, now they were 'Members of Liberal Democrats Wales'. This caused problems in external communications with both the media and internal party communication and, in time, would lead to a reversion back to the previous title of 'Welsh Liberal Democrats'. As part of this process of change the Welsh party had also adopted the federal party's preamble to the constitution regarding its own Welsh constitution. This stated that:

'The Liberal Democrats exist to build and safeguard a fair, free and open society, in which we seek to balance the fundamental values of liberty, equality and community and in which no-one shall be enslaved by poverty, ignorance or conformity.'[36]

In the future, all 'Welsh Liberal Democrats' members would have this message displayed bilingually on their membership cards.

The 1995 Islwyn By-election

In early 1995, the Conservative Prime Minister John Major appointed his old Labour rival, Neil Kinnock, as a European Commissioner. The party in Wales had known for some time this would be the case, and had even selected a candidate and launched their Islwyn by-election campaign in September, at the 1994 Liberal Democrat Autumn Federal party conference.[37] The by-election held on the 16th of February went rather well for the Liberal Democrats. They came third with 10.6 per cent of the vote. This was just a few hundred votes behind Plaid Cymru who came second. Importantly, the Conservatives lost their deposit indicating their increasing electoral decline across Wales. The Liberal Democrats had almost now doubled their result here from the 1992 general election and, in the process, gained around 70 new members to the party overall and were quite pleased by the result.[38]

The building of the constituency organisation in Islwyn was guided by Cardiff councillor David Rees, who was also the party's Welsh membership officer. He was helped by a number of Scottish Liberal Democrats who had come down for the campaign. Over the next few years, Rees would extensively travel throughout Wales recruiting party members who would go on to become county councillors or key constituency activists. Despite Rees' and other's efforts in the seat, Labour's candidate, Don Touhig unsurprisingly won in this Labour stronghold, with a massive 56.5 per cent majority.

Islwyn By-election Result 16th February 1995

Candidate	Party	Vote	Percentage
Don Touhig	Labour	16,030	69.2
Jocelyn Davies	Plaid Cymru	2,933	12.7
John Bushell	Liberal Democrats Wales	2,338	10.6
Robert Buckland	Conservative	913	3.9
Others	Others	842	3.6
	Majority	13,097	56.5
	Turnout		45.1

The good result aside, the Islwyn by-election in time became more relevant to the party because of some of the central characters that took part in it. Aside from Rees, the soundest, as far as the party was concerned, was the agent for the campaign, Mel Ab Owain. He was the party's Key Seats Officer, who had been appointed the year before. Ab Owain had been the agent in Conwy in 1992, an election which had seen the Welsh party's only real move forward. Over the coming decade, Ab Owain would be at the heart of the party's gaining or regaining of seats from Brecon and Radnor to winning Hereford. The three other key Liberal Democrat people in this campaign would have differing futures outside the party. These were:

1. The candidate, John Bushell, a professional musician from Swansea who would go on to join the Conservative party two years later, and later head the 'Swansea Says No' group in the 1997 devolution referendum and then become an Agent for the Referendum Party in 1999.

2. Kevin Etheridge, a longstanding popular local campaigner who had stood numerous times for the Liberals as a local government candidate, became engaged fully in the Islwyn campaign. He was later elected to Caerphilly County Borough Council in 1999 but would, in time, leave the party and stand against it in Islwyn in the 2007 Welsh Assembly elections as an Independent. Here he came a strong second, achieving a better result than any Liberal candidate had managed in the seat since the 1920s.

3. Ken Jones, who was one of the most bizarre individuals ever to come into the Welsh party. Jones was a convicted conman with a strong Canadian accent. Despite having a somewhat 'nerdish' appearance, Jones was an excellent media operator who impressed many in the party who saw his skills in action on Islwyn. This included Alex Carlile. Soon afterwards, Jones was arrested as he had returned to his old habits. He was convicted, subsequently imprisoned and would not be seen by the Welsh party again. A potential disaster avoided.

The 1995 Welsh Unitary Authority Elections

The party's Campaign and Communications Committee, chaired by Michael German, had now become committed to the community style of politics that had become dominant across the English Liberal Democrats. This involved building up the party's representation through community politics at ward level, supported by case work, campaigns and the *Focus* newsletters. This method of politics developed first in Wales in Cardiff and Swansea and then spread across the South and North Wales constituencies. It came straight from the Association of Liberal Democrat Councillors (ALDC) training manuals. Its impact on rural Welsh Liberal Democrats, however, remained patchy. Those who followed the ALDC model closely enough were also rewarded with grants (referred to as G8 money). Jenny Randerson was the Welsh representative on this body, and the Welsh party received some £6,000 from the ALDC for the 1995 elections to further encourage their adoption of the community campaigning techniques.[39] For council candidates who were used to dipping into their own pockets for campaign funds, there was now an added incentive to follow the ALDC route. The ALDC did not just offer the Welsh council candidates funding, it also helped write its unitary authority manifesto in conjunction with the Welsh policy committee under the chairmanship of Gwyn Griffiths. To observers of the development of the Welsh party, this showed the clear dependence that the Welsh party still had on the mainly English-based party institutions for support and expertise.

At the Rhayader conference in November 1994, Carlile had set his party the task of contesting every Welsh council seat in the forthcoming May shadow Welsh unitary authority elections. In the event, they put forward 369 councillors; they won 86 seats on the new authorities, which was a notional gain of seven seats. The elections were a near landslide for the Labour Party, which swept the board across most of Wales and ended up controlling the majority of Welsh authorities. For the Liberal Democrats, the best result was in the merged councils of Aberconwy/Colwyn (which would become Conwy County Council), where both councils had previously had a strong Liberal Democrat presence. On the new council they held 18 councillors but were now playing second fiddle to a victorious Labour on 19 seats. Previously the

Liberal Democrats had been the largest party when the councillors of both authorities had been combined. In Powys, they gained nine councillors and had small groups of three to five councillors on most authorities spread across Wales.

In the new council of Rhondda Cynon Taff, which encompassed the old Liberal stronghold of Pontypridd, the Liberals lost all representation for the first time in over a century. Steve Belzak, a well known town councillor, remained the sole elected Liberal representative in a council of some 239,000 people. In Cardiff and Swansea, the Liberal Democrat representation remained nominally unchanged, with the central councillors such as Peter Black, Chris Holley and Jenny Randerson managing to transfer from old city and county council to new unitary authorities. The collapse in the Conservative vote, and the wipe-out of their councillors across Wales meant that in Cardiff and Swansea, the Liberal Democrats (in Swansea with the Independents) now became the main opposition. This was a psychological boost which would help the party take control in both cities in future.

The 1995 party's spring conference in Conwy was seen as something of a real success for the party. In their key marginal hopeful of Conwy, they made a well publicised pilgrimage to Lloyd George's grave and there they were able to launch their local government campaign for the unitary authority elections on live television. At the same time a 24 year old Liberal activist, Kirsty Williams rose to prominence as she revitalised the Liberal Democrats' Wales Youth and Students and thus projected herself to the forefront of the party. Williams had managed to build up a data base of members and put out regular mailings. She organised the Youth and Students inaugural AGM, but more importantly for her, had impressed many members with both her personal drive and her oratory skills.[40]

Carlile Steps Down and Öpik Arrives

In 1996, because of family pressures brought on by the illness of his daughter, Alex Carlile decided to step down as an MP. He first met with his agent, Brian Jones, then with constituency executive committee and later with Paddy Ashdown to inform him of the news. Carlile then used the services of Guto Harri, the BBC Wales correspondent, by asking him for advice about how to step down and by breaking the news by giving him an exclusive story. The stage was set for a new Liberal Democrat candidate to be selected for Montgomeryshire.

The selection contest for Montgomeryshire was always going to be fierce. The constituency, despite the hiccup of 1979–83, was one of the few in the party which still had a long tradition of voting Liberal. In a crowded field, the candidate that shone above the others was Lembit Öpik. Öpik, a member of the federal executive, had become known within the party as something of a 'membership drive guru'. He was famed for recruiting new members anywhere he went, from passengers on train journeys to hotel receptionists. Öpik, then in his early thirties, was already a seasoned politico. He had been a former President of the Bristol University Students' Union and a contemporary of the Welsh party's campaign expert, John Dixon. Öpik then went to Newcastle on Tyne where he established himself as both a city councillor and a prominent member of the Northern Region of the Liberal Democrat party. His sole appearance, prior to the campaign in Wales, however, had been on membership drives in the south. Yet his oratory skills, general personable manner and recognised campaigning skills impressed the constituency membership. He won the selection, with the popular local candidate Mick Bates, a farmer and branch chair of the National Farmers' Union, coming second.

The Lead up to the End of the 18 Years of Tory Rule

The period leading up to the 1997 general election was dominated nationally by a period of good fortune. From May 1993, there was a succession of four Liberal Democrats victories over the Conservatives in by-elections in England, starting with Newbury and ending with Littleborough and Saddleworth in July 1995. Then at the end of December 1995, Emma Nicholson, the Conservative vice-chairman (Devon West and Torridge) defected to the Liberal Democrats. This did much to lift the party's pre-general election morale, especially when Nicholson followed her defection with a visit to the Welsh party's Swansea Spring Conference in 1996. This attendance added some gusto to the Welsh party's pre-general election momentum. The party, therefore, both in Wales and nationally, felt increasingly confident in the period approaching the end of Conservative rule that they would do much better than they had done 1992.

At the Welsh Office, the tenure of the right-wing Conservative Welsh Secretary, John Redwood, had gone down particularly badly in Wales. His general patronising manner and lack of understanding of Welsh history, its nationalist elements and culture – in particular his inept miming of the Welsh national anthem at the 1995 Welsh Conservative Party conference – helped seal his fate and mar the fortunes of the Conservative party in Wales for the forthcoming elections.

Labour and the Conservatives became involved in a series of intractable battles over devolution under Redwood's successor, William Hague. Devolution now became the central policy theme of the period leading up to the next general election. The methods of dealing with Wales at Westminster were increasingly perceived by the opposition as both tokenistic and irrelevant in a modern era. Between December 1995 and December 1996 the Welsh Grand Committee, therefore, failed to meet because Labour and the Conservatives were not able to agree on an agenda. Since 1993 it had been meeting in Wales, sometimes in Cardiff's City Hall, which many then saw as the future home of the Welsh Assembly. Carlile boycotted the meeting declaring it a 'toothless talking shop'.[41] There was another reason Carlile failed to attend the 'Welsh Grand'. Before and since Carlile had announced his resignation from the Montgomeryshire seat, in July 1996, he had been in the process of rebuilding his legal career. The more he could stay away from the details of Welsh politics, the better it was for his legal career. Although this didn't help the Welsh party, it forced them to fill in the gaps with their own people, such as Richard Livsey, Lembit Öpik and Michael German, giving them and the media a glimpse of the faces of these key Welsh Liberal Democrat politicians.

What the Welsh Liberal Democrats always found most problematic was winning seats in the Westminster elections. With Carlile absent, the party was aware that the next election would 'make or break'[42] them. They needed to regain their two lost seats (Ceredigion[43] and Brecon and Radnor), re-establish themselves in Cardiff Central as the firm challenger and also win Conwy if they were to reassert themselves in Welsh politics. The Welsh executive had asked Michael German to coordinate the forthcoming general election in Wales for the party. German then worked with the federal general election committee headed by Lord Holme. German was also now the Welsh party's elected representative on the Federal Executive, with Roger Roberts serving as Federal Vice-President. The Welsh party geared up for the general election from mid 1996 onwards. In the October of that year, for the first time, candidates were given proper media training, run by party professionals such as Ruth Parry and John Dixon, with the help of some outside experts. The relatively new process of telephone canvassing of prospective voters, which would later become an essential campaigning tool in the next decade, was also put on the constituency training agenda as a new technique to be mastered.[44]

The party was, for once, well prepared for any forthcoming general election. As evidence of this preparedness the party had held a large candidates' meeting at the Royal Show Ground in Builth Wells on 25th January 1997 with some 32 of its candidates attending. Apart from a disagreement concerning what should be in the centralised leaflets, the day was most notable for how many constituencies already had candidates in place; around 36 of the 40 Welsh seats.[45] At the same time, the party had now professionalised itself on a number of fronts. Policy under Nick Buree's stewardship had been defined more clearly and written by a wider group than had been the case for many years. Their policy agenda over the previous three years had been made public at regular periods in the form of specific policy booklets. All of the areas to be covered by any new Welsh Assembly had specific Welsh elements of policy addressing such issues it. The Welsh Policy Committee had then, in consultation with the Federal party, produced its own version of the federal policy document entilted: *'Make the difference'*. Its own initiatives, such as creating a new Welsh Language Act, a Welsh Academy of Sporting Excellence and combining the Welsh Office departments of Health and Social Services, were added to its existing policies in respect of the proposed Welsh Senedd.[46]

At the 1997 general election, in contrast to the small campaign team in 1992, there was now a host of people connected to the running of the campaign. Judi Lewis ran overall party functions. Michael German headed the campaign; Nigel Howells monitored the finance; Ruth Parry the media; Kirsty Williams dealt with candidate training; and Mark Soady managed the visiting federal party 'celebrities', such as Shirley Williams and Roy Jenkins. In addition, they were joined by an experienced national campaigner, Stephen Dering, who was well-known in the federal party for his campaigning expertise. Peter Black and Chris Davies from Swansea also helped organise the campaign, but one of the most important members of the campaign team for the election was John Dixon. Dixon, a graphic artist, was behind the core constituency leaflets, posters and target seat literature. The party during this period had become totally reliant on Dixon to get its message across in a modernised format and consequently, for the next few elections, it was nearly always Dixon, who would be the designer behind the Welsh party's distinctive electoral printed communications.

At the 1996 October Autumn Conference, the party had set its objectives for the 1997 general election. These were to:[47]

1. Hold Montgomeryshire – with the new candidate, Lembit Öpik
2. Win the target seats (Brecon and Radnor, Ceredigion, Conwy and Cardiff Central)
3. Increase their share of the Welsh vote

4. Fight an integrated campaign
5. Increase party membership
6. Develop activists' skills
7. Develop new winnable seats
8. Use it a stepping stone to the Welsh Assembly elections

As part of the strategy of retaking the 'lost seats' the party was able to undertake a constituency wide opinion poll of Brecon and Radnor. This told the party two vital things. First, in a straight fight in the seat between all the candidates, the Labour party would win, but if the electors believed that it was a two horse race between the Liberal Democrats and the Conservatives, then the Liberal Democrats would win the seat. The party's message now became 'Labour cannot win here but the Tories can'. The message on every leaflet proclaimed that 'only Richard Livsey could defeat the Tories'. The second thing that the poll told the party was that the three core messages of education, crime and health crime were just as important in Brecon and Radnor as elsewhere. The issues of agriculture and devolution, important to many activitists in the party, were right at the bottom of voters' priorities and, therefore, the party had to alter its message accordingly.[48] Having a prestigious election team also helped Livsey. The well-respected Powys county councillor, James Gibson Watt, became his election agent, aided by Key Seats Officer, Mel Ab Owen and other experienced campaigners, such as Megan Rosenberg, Jonathan Morgan and Diana Leboff. They were joined by Liberal Democrats coming from neighbouring seats to help ensure the whole constituency was fully covered.

The party geared up for its final pre-election preparation at its Spring Welsh conference, on the St David's Day weekend of 1997 in Conwy. It was here that Roger Roberts was preparing to take the seat off the Conservatives, with the incumbent Sir Wyn Roberts stepping down from his long tenure in the seat (1970–1997). The weekend after the Welsh party conference finished, there was also another chance for the party to get its candidates to prepare for the election at the party's Federal Spring conference to be held in Cardiff that year. The main disappointment for the Welsh candidates was Lord Holmes' decision to miss the election pre-briefing session with them in order to catch an earlier train back to London. The candidates were then left, much to their annoyance about perceived federal party indifference, with Geraint Howells and Michael German ready to act as substitutes.

Devolution Starts to Become a Reality

Devolution policy in Wales had been determined since the late 1960s mainly by Martin Thomas. He had been assisted from time to time by various party members and MPs. In the mid 1990s these included Gwyn Williams, a well respected Denbighshire county councillor, and Dr Russell Deacon, a university lecturer.[49] It was Deacon who revised the party's Welsh Parliament proposals. *A Senedd for Wales: Beyond a Talking Shop*;[50] the policy document advocated a tax-raising and law-making Parliament (Senedd) of around 100 members. It also introduced the concept of a quasi-bicameral Welsh parliament through the introduction of a 'Local Government Senate', which would represent Welsh local government and have the power to 'refer back' to those Parliament policies it wished to see dropped or amended. It would have its own role and functions embedded in law which could only be removed by a 75 per cent majority of the Parliamentary members or through a national referendum.[51] The Press' launch of *A Senedd for Wales* in May 2006 was the best attended policy launch the party had held that year with both television and the paper press in attendance.[52] Still, even as the party was making concrete its own plans for devolution, it was apparent that it would soon be following the devolution plans of another party – those of the Labour Party. Carlile and Livsey had written to the Labour Party requesting that they take part in a constitutional convention similar to that which had occurred in Scotland but they rejected it out of hand.[53] The Labour Party had been in the process of revising its own devolution proposals for the previous five years. It was a totally in-house affair and all external parties were excluded from their consultation process. In the event, the party produced a marginally better version of their 1979 executive version of the Welsh Assembly.

The more reactionary ('Old') Labour party members were initially able to exclude any element of proportional representation (PR) in elections. This would have meant that few Liberal Democrats would have had the incentive to endorse this old style Assembly, as only between three and five constituencies were realistically winnable. Behind the scenes, however, Shadow Welsh Secretary Ron Davies, wary of the need for the Welsh Liberal Democrats' support, assured Carlile that there would be PR in any Welsh Assembly election. Davies, however, was not always in charge or even aware of his own party's policy direction. On 26th June 1996, Davies, in a BBC Wales debate on devolution, replied to an audience question on whether the Welsh Assembly needed a referendum. He stated that he did not believe it was necessary, as any election result which brought the Labour Party to power would be a suitable endorsement of the Assembly. The following day he announced that there 'would indeed be a referendum' after all. Tony Blair had decided that a referendum would be needed in order to 'entrench' any devolution from future Conservative attempts to remove it as being 'not wanted' by the populace in both Wales and Scotland. Davies was therefore told to reverse his and the party's position and dutifully abided by this instruction. Although this reverse in the policy on referenda caused considerable anger in Scotland, it caused only mild surprise for the pro-devolution camp in Wales, which was more sceptical about the idea of devolution ever becoming a reality under Blair. It meant that the Labour Party, with many of its own members being anti-devolutionist, needed to create a 'rainbow coalition' to support the Yes vote in the referendum campaign. This came about in a two part process. First, at a federal level. In the summer of 1996 Tony Blair and Paddy Ashdown asked Robert Maclennan and Robin Cook to explore the possibility of co-operation between the two parties in relation to constitutional reform. They formed a joint committee, which on the Labour side had Ron Davies representing Wales, but there was nobody on the Liberal Democrat side to do likewise. Carlile was not asked to join the Commission[54] and although Martin Thomas, the party's Welsh devolution expert of the previous few decades, had been ennobled as Lord Thomas of Gresford, that year, he also did not serve on the Commission. The Federal leadership, unlike in the 1970s, had decided not to include the Welsh directly in the British devolution discussions.

The Commission consisted of Scottish and English Liberal Democrats. Although Carlile had some discussions with Ron Davies on the Welsh input, the Commission concentrated mainly on Scottish devolution. The results, when published on 5th March 1997, were officially known as 'The Joint Consultative Committee' on Constitutional Reform but became better known as the 'Cook-Maclennan' pact. It committed the Welsh party to supporting Labour's plans for devolution if it were to win the next general election. At the same time in Wales both Ron Davies and Alex Carlile signed a joint declaration committing both parties to campaign for a Yes vote in any referendum and, importantly, getting the devolution process reviewed, if it proved to be non-proportional in its distribution of seats.

At the Conwy conference, referred to earlier, some 20 constituency representatives spoke against any 'pacts' with Labour, with only Carlile advocating a pro-pact position. The internal grumbling continued and when the Carlile-Davies letter became public the following Thursday, the animus against the agreement became more intense. This was particularly true of those that were serving on the policy committee. Teacher and former London SDP activist, Elwyn Jones, now in Swansea, Cardiff councillor Jackie Gasson, Dai Davies (the PPC for Ceredigion) and even the author of the party's own devolution policy, Dr Russell Deacon, spoke out against the pact. On Friday, some of those against the referendum pact started going 'on the record' with the media and the ensuing publicity threatened to overshadow the party's Federal Spring Conference to be held in Cardiff that weekend. On Saturday morning, Ashdown and Carlile called in Davies, Deacon, Gasson and Jones in order to placate their anger and stop the issue from overshadowing the conference. They were able to do so by making it clear that the agreement was post and not pre-election, and therefore, the party's own policy for a Senedd elected by STV still stood. The antagonists were appeased and with calm restored, behind the scenes the party started to prepare not only for the forthcoming general election but also for the possibility of a devolution referendum. In January, Carlile appointed Deacon to the embryonic 'Yes for Wales' campaign group being set up by former Liberals' Leighton Andrews[55] and Mari James. Initially, at these meetings Deacon acted only as an observer but later, together with Michael German, they would both become fully engaged in the 'Yes' campaign.

Old Tories Depart and New Labour Arrive

The 1997 general election started in a unique way for the Welsh Liberal Democrats. The party had never contested a general election in its entire history in which it did not have an incumbent MP seeking re-election. Yet, with Carlile stepping down, this was just about to happen. The Welsh media subsequently re-categorised Montgomeryshire as a marginal seat and spent part of the campaign period speculating on whether the Liberal Democrats would be removed from Wales altogether. The Conservative Welsh Office Minister for Cardiff North, Gwilym Jones, also made much of the fact that he expected the Liberal Democrats to be driven out of Wales in this general election.[56] This point gained widespread media coverage as part of the general cut and thrust of the forthcoming election campaign.

In this period, when the Welsh media was more substantial and therefore paid greater attention to the elections, the Welsh Liberal Democrats generally had a high profile and effective election campaign. Ashdown addressed a mass rally at

Sofia Gardens, where he was joined by Baroness Shirley Williams (the ex Labour/ SDP MP) and TV film personality Barry Norman who compèred the rally. Ashdown was then able to make visits to all the Welsh target seats and the party combined his media presence with their own daily press briefings, which at 8.00 am were the earliest of all the Welsh political parties. It was at these St Mary Street meetings that journalists were also treated to a daily cooked breakfast by two Newport party stalwarts, Doreen Harris and Megan Rees.[57] As ever with its media coverage, the party was looking at new angles to get ahead in the news. The most effective media stunt during the campaign was the 'Plaidway Man' event. This involved Nigel Howells dressing up a highwayman and going to be photographed at the Severn Bridge with a Plaid Cymru rosette on, in order to act as a 'highwayman' taking the extra taxes it was claimed Plaid Cymru would need in order to have an independent Wales. The stunt was a huge hit with the media and generated the party's most effective overall media coverage. Much of the media work for this campaign had been co-ordinated by a Monmouthshire Liberal Democrat called Chris Lines. Lines' ability to often work into the small hours shaping the party's message for the next day and still produce quality material, did not go unnoticed by those at the higher levels of the party.[58]

The General Election of 1997 in Wales

Liberal Democrat	2
Labour	34
Conservative	0
Plaid Cymru	4

The 1997 general election became a famous Labour landslide victory. In Wales nearly all Conservative losses resulted in Labour victories, as they enjoyed their best results there for over a generation. For the Welsh Liberals, the first piece of good news came around three in the morning when the party retained Montgomeryshire by an impressive 6,303 majority (19.8%), which propelled Lembit Öpik into Westminster. The Conwy result that came in around the same time saw Roger Roberts fail to improve on his 1992 second position, as he was leapfrogged by Labour's Betty Williams, who won the seat by some 1,596 votes (3.8%). Labour's national appeal and the inability of the Welsh Liberal Democrats to be seen as the main challenger to the Conservatives had thwarted the party's efforts in this seat. In addition, Roberts had been damaged by the actions of Richard Bradley, a local Liberal Democrat, who had stood in the seat as an 'Alternative Liberal Democrat'. Although Bradley only gained 250 votes and was duly expelled from the Welsh party, his actions upset the Roberts' campaign and acted as an unnecessary distraction in trying to win the seat from the Conservatives. In Ceredigion, Dai Davies' candidature in a poorly fought campaign resulted in the party's vote slumping to just 16.5 per cent behind both Plaid Cymru and Labour for the first time in its history. This was 10 per cent down on the 1992 party vote and now over 10,000 votes behind Plaid Cymru. At the time, it looked as if Ceredigion, just as with other former Liberal seats in Welsh speaking Wales, had become irredeemably lost and the party privately now wrote off their chances of regaining the seat.[59]

In Cardiff Central, Jenny Randerson had secured the second position with a quarter of the vote but was still some 7,923 (18.8%) behind Labour's John Owen

Jones. The last result to come in for Wales was the most interesting one for the Welsh Liberal Democrats. When the final result was read out in Brecon Town Hall it showed that Richard Livsey had regained Brecon and Radnor with a new majority of 5,097 votes (11.9%) over the defeated Welsh Office Minister, Jonathan Evans. Brecon and Radnor was no longer a Liberal Democrat marginal, Livsey was back at Westminster, back on the Welsh Affairs Select Committee and back as the Leader of the Welsh party. This final Welsh result also heralded a 'Tory free Wales' era for the first time since the 'Liberal Landslide' in 1906.

Apart from those constituencies mentioned, the Liberal Democrat vote tended to put the party out of contention in every other seat languishing between 14 and five per cent of the vote. Despite the generally low vote share, there was miraculously only one deposit lost; this was in Ynys Môn. Here the Liberal Democrats were now just a mere shadow of their presence there half a century before. Only in Swansea West was the third place to be relevant in the future. There the former Swansea City Councillor John Newbury, was able to increase the party's vote to 14.5 per cent in a seat that within the next decade would become one of the party's Welsh 'hopefuls'.

The 1997 election was also notable for being the 'first blooding' for a number of party members who were to reach prominence within the party in the next decade. Kirsty Williams, with Peter Black as her agent, fought a bitter contest in Ogmore against Old Labour stalwart Sir Ray Powell. Mark Williams also came a distant third in Monmouth, as did Rodney Berman in Rhondda and Eleanor Burnham in Alyn and Deeside.

Just after the election was over, the party manager Judi Lewis announced her resignation. There was now a keen desire amongst the senior figures within the party to bring in a professional public relations figure to head the party. To help them, they were able to get a substantial donation in order to facilitate this desire and, therefore, they appointed Chris Lines in early 1998. Lines was a former public relations manager and, importantly, had been a Liberal since his student days at Swansea University in the early 1980s. He was also acknowledged as a superb strategist and, as already noted, had proved his worth in the 1997 general election campaign. A new party administrator, Helen Northmore-Thomas, was also appointed shortly afterwards and it was she who would run the day to day operational side of things in the party's new office in Cardiff Bay.

The party's St Mary Street office had been falling into disrepair for some time; a leaky roof and difficulty in accessing the building meant that a change of location was sorely needed. The party took a gamble on the future location of the Assembly and moved its office down into Bay View House on Bute Street, about five minutes walk from what would be the new Assembly building. The gamble paid off and despite the fact that the party forgot to note that the building had no central heating, it proved to be a sound choice when the Assembly arrived. The Liberal Democrats became the only political party to have their headquarters in Cardiff Bay.

The Road to the Welsh Assembly

Much of the political and media debate in Wales, coming up to the general election, had been about the Welsh Assembly. It was of particular interest for the large number of frustrated Welsh Liberal Democrat politicians, who had come to realise that whilst there was virtually no chance of them winning a Westminster seat there was now every possibility that they could get elected to the Welsh Assembly either at the constituency level or through the additional members list system (the PR element of the elections). It was with this in mind that many now put themselves wholeheartedly into the campaign for a 'Yes' vote.

The 'Yes' Campaign's victory was predicated on a positive momentum for a 'Yes' vote being built up across Wales. with various groups and towns/cities/counties forming their own 'Yes' Groups and feeding into the national campaign. In virtually all these groups a Welsh Liberal Democrat presence could be found. In Swansea it was Peter Black and the future Welsh party President, Rob Humphreys.[60] In Cardiff, it was Jenny Randerson, in Pontypridd Mike Powell, and in Merthyr Tydfil Steve Belzak. In North Wales it was Roger Roberts, Eleanor Burnham and Christine Humphreys. Apart from the Liberal Democrats MPs the central figure in Mid and West Wales was Mel ap Owen, the full-time Key Seats Officer for the party who now took on the role of trying to get the Yes camp organised there. Livsey and German became the media faces of the Welsh Liberal Democrats during the 'Yes' Campaign. Alex Carlile (now the Welsh party's president) together with Lord Geraint and Thomas also played active parts in the campaign. German worked closely with the Labour Party's 'Yes Man' – Andrew Davies, as the Welsh party's central figure in the organisational campaigning behind the scenes.[61] The campaign began in earnest as soon as the 1st May general election was over. Over the coming few months, virtually every county, city and town had produced its own 'Yes' Campaign. In many instances, despite the fact that the Labour Party refused to officially endorse the 'Yes' Campaign, these were still truly cross party groupings. For politicians that had seen each other only as political foes these gave most Liberal Democrats their first taste of successfully working with Labour politicians. Within three years many of these politicians from both parties would be working together again in the Welsh Assembly in a Labour and Welsh Liberal Democrat coalition government.

Despite the fact that Labour and the Liberal Democrats had signed up to a cooperative pact to support the 'Yes' vote, in some instances relations between the parties remained distant. In Merthyr Tydfil, for instance, the Labour Party refused to do any campaigning so the campaign was run solely by a handful of local Liberal Democrats. Labour's refusal to officially join the national 'Yes' Campaign also meant that whilst all of the senior Welsh Liberal Democrats took part in the Yes Campaign group they also ran a parallel 'Welsh Liberal Democrats Say Yes' campaign with specific leaflets designed by John Dixon. These were circulated throughout the Liberal Democrat seats of Powys and in the key target seats of the Welsh party (Cardiff Central, Ceredigion and Conwy). In contrast to 1979 there was a general consensus across the vast majority of the Welsh political classes that devolution was a cause worth supporting. The main political antagonists of the last referendum, the Welsh Conservatives had been utterly defeated electorally in Wales and now consisted of a small rump of just three per cent of Welsh councillors. They had no well-known lead figure or Welsh MP to support the 'No' camp as in 1979. There were still many working for the No campaign and they were often vocal but nowhere near as effective as they had been in 1979. The only real hiccup in the campaign for the 'Yes' Campaign, therefore, was at the start of September when campaigning was suspended for a week because of the death of the Princess of Wales.

The massive majority for the 'Yes' vote in Scotland on 11th September greatly helped the Welsh cause, but nevertheless, the voting on 18th September resulted in a very close result. The Liberal Democrat influence on the 'Yes' vote was hard to gauge. In those seats, such as Powys and Cardiff, in which they were strongest, the electorate voted 'No'. Yet the Welsh Liberal Democrats here argued that the size of the 'No' vote in these council areas would have been far higher without their support for a 'Yes' vote.

On the night of 18th September and early morning of the 19th, of the referendum results were collated and read out in the Royal College of Music and Drama in Cardiff. As the night went on, the number of council areas voting 'No' appeared to indicate that the referendum result would be lost, although, in the event, the eventual majority was some 6,721 votes or just 0.6 per cent. Nevertheless, it was a victory, all but a very narrow one. In the early hours of the morning of 19th September, it was Richard Livsey who joined Ron Davies and Plaid Cymru's leader, Dafydd Wigley on the stage at the Royal College to take the public bow for the success of the 'Yes' vote. To add some more excitement to the evening, as Livsey left the count, he was mobbed by jubilant teenagers giving him the appearance of an aging rock star meeting jubilant fans. For some pro-devolutionary Welsh Liberals, the 19th of September would remain their greatest personal triumph.[62]

Choosing Who Will Serve in the Welsh Assembly

Having helped win the referendum, the Welsh party now had to thrash out how it was going to select candidates for a Welsh election in which, for the first time, it expected to win substantial seats across Wales. Apart from the Welsh MPs and Lords, virtually every other Welsh Liberal Democrat, with a political ambition, saw the opportunity to be elected to the Welsh Assembly. The party held a special conference at Builth Wells to validate its rules for the forthcoming elections. Attempts to provide a gender balance across all of the Welsh seats were defeated. The proposed system would have divided up seats on their likeliness of being winnable and into male and female ranking.

The proposed system was supported by both future Assembly Members, (AMs) Kirsty Williams and Jenny Randerson, even though it would have meant that neither would have been able to stand for seats they were eventually to win, as these, according the proposed formula, had been allocated to male members.[63] With the gender balance option ruled out and the contest opened to all, the main factor that candidates now had to consider was how to maximise their votes in the selection contest. In this respect, the dates by which constituency and regional members would no longer be able to vote for them, if they had not joined or renewed their membership, became all important. For the constituencies, this date was 30th March and for the regional list selection it was 31st July 1998. Aware of these cut-off points the candidates then went about the process of getting friends, family and supporters signed up for the forthcoming elections, aided by the transferring of membership across some seats, depending on where a candidate had set his ambitions.[64] The well scrutinised approval process for these candidates was conducted by Barry Long and Caroline Evans, with Long, a Montgomeryshire Liberal, becoming the acknowledged expert of the party's

Welsh selection procedures, which, as the years progressed, would become ever more rigorous.

Almost immediately after the selection, rules were approved and selection contests began for the 40 Welsh constituencies. The key seats selected quickly. In Montgomeryshire the runner-up to Öpik in the 1996 Westminster selection, Mick Bates was selected. Bates, a former science teacher and environmentalist, was now prominent in the National Farmers' Union (NFU) and well known in the farming circles of Powys. In Brecon and Radnor, after an intensive selection contest, Kirsty Williams was selected. In Conwy, former Colywn Borough Councillor and teacher, Christine Humphreys was selected. Finally, in Cardiff Central, the Cardiff Council's opposition leader and Westminster candidate, Jenny Randerson, was selected. With the only realistically winnable constituencies filled, the remaining hopeful Liberal Democrats' candidates then turned their eyes to gaining the first position on the regional list. Ian Barton acted in the role of National Returning Officer. A former Lampeter university lecturer, *Mastermind* runner up and 'Brain of Britain' winner, Barton was well respected in his role of overall returning officer for Wales and was able to keep candidates' frustrations under control in these often fractious selection contests.

For Michael German, the party's Head of Campaigns and a central figure in the Devolution Referendum Campaign, finding a seat to contest was something of a problem. His former constituency base of Cardiff Central now had a sitting candidate, Jenny Randerson, whom he felt unable to challenge. Fortunately for German, the South Wales East constituency had no real political heavyweight in it. The most prominent Liberal Democrats there, Alistair Cameron, a former leader of Cheltenham Borough Council and Veronica Watkins, a school teacher, were both well known activists in Newport, but not so well known by party members across the wider constituency. Chris Lines, the party's chief executive, was well known in Monmouthshire and across the wider region but forbidden by the selection rules, as a party official, from standing on the list. This left the way open for German to stand for the South Wales East list, as he was known across all constituencies. In the eventual contest, German came top of the poll, with Watkins second and Cameron third. In South Wales West, Peter Black came top of the poll,[65] with Rob Humphreys coming second. In South Wales Central, Jenny Randerson came top with Gianni Orsi, a well known Pontypridd businessman and former Mid Glamorgan councillor, coming second. Mid and West Wales did things a bit differently. There the party had insisted that the constituency candidates in the 'winnable seats' did not also stand for the list. Thus Williams and Bates remained off the list, which was topped by Brecon and Radnor farmer, and prominent local Liberal Democrat Roger Williams. In North Wales, Christine Humphreys headed the list, followed by college lecturer Eleanor Burnham (importantly for the party both were Welsh-speaking, as no other candidates in winnable positions were). Phill Lloyd, the Welsh party's Chairman, took the number three slot. With the exception of Roger Williams, all list candidates also stood for constituencies. In the constituencies, the party's future leader Michael German chose to stand in Caerphilly. This was initially because it was held by the Welsh Labour leader and Welsh Secretary Ron Davies. This was felt to give him a higher media profile. In the event, Davies resigned after his 'moment of madness on Clapham Common', reducing the media focus on the seat.

Whilst the party was preparing for the Assembly elections, two Commissions were held by the Welsh Office to prepare the ground for the arrival of the Welsh

Assembly. Each had Liberal Democrats on them. The National Assembly Advisory Group (NAAG) had Kirsty Williams as the Welsh representative. She had been selected by both Livsey and Ron Davies (Welsh Secretary) to stand as the Liberal Democrat member. NAAG, which toured Wales sounding out views on how the Assembly should operate. This proved to be a good training ground for Williams in her future Assembly and later party leadership role. The Commission on Standing Orders was selected by a more open competition of applicants and Peter Price, a former Conservative MEP and defector to the party, served on this body set up to draw up the Standing Orders for the future Assembly.

At Westminster, both Livsey and Öpik sought fruitlessly to amend the Government of Wales Bill to make the Assembly more like a Parliament with primary legislative powers. They failed to get a single amendment passed, including an attempt to move the Assembly away from the proposed Committee system to a Cabinet system. This amendment was rejected by the Labour government and then, three weeks later their own amendment was introduced and passed by them. This post referendum New Labour government, with no need for Liberal Democrats' support, was not in the mood for concessions, even if these would eventually suit its own purposes. The Government of Wales Act 1998 was, therefore, entirely a Labour creation.

Welsh Leadership Election

Before the party could swing into full election mode, it needed to have a leader for the Welsh Assembly elections. Two candidates threw their hats into the ring. These were the campaigns and election guru Michael (Mike) German and from North Wales the candidate for Conwy, teacher and former Colwyn Borough councillor, Christine Humphreys. Humphreys stood only after she had been persuaded to stand by Chris Lines. He had told her that they 'all knew that Mike would be leader but that they also needed to have a leadership contest because the publicity would be good for the party'.[66] As Mike was a South Wales male and non Welsh speaking, it was felt by the party that he needed to be opposed by a 'reverse mirror image' candidate – a female from North Wales and a Welsh speaker. This would show the wider world the breadth of the Welsh party. Humphreys therefore fitted the bill as required.

The campaign was somewhat strange in that there were no constituency hustings and the candidates were prevented from actively campaigning. They were restricted to just one leaflet to members and a Welsh hustings at Builth Wells. This was because the party did not want to appear to be divided in the period running up to an election, which was something that benefited German's higher profile within the party. When the result was declared on the 30th November 1998, Michael German was declared the winner over Christine Humphreys by 1,037 votes to 883, on a 40 per cent turnout. Humphreys was amazed about how close she had come to winning, bearing in mind the lack of campaigning. The *Western Mail* commented that 'as the contest developed it became clear that Ms Humphreys was succeeding in winning the votes of women, Welsh speakers and of the large proportion of the members who live outside the industrial south'. How they were aware of this fact is unclear, but, regardless of this assertion, German was now firmly in place as the prospective Leader of the Assembly Group. However, somewhat confusingly, he was not leader of the Welsh party, as a whole, as overall Westminster leadership remained under Richard Livsey. As German won his election, the leadership contests for both the Labour and Conservative parties in Wales were splitting rather than uniting their parties, which further boosted the Welsh party's pre-election morale.[67]

As the party was pre-occupied with the Welsh Assembly elections, an important by-election occurred in Bridgend. On 12th March 1998, a computer software expert Cheryl Green was elected for the Bryntirion, Laleston and Merthyr Mawr ward of Bridgend County Borough Council. Green was the first Welsh Liberal Democrat to serve on the new unitary authority. The council was dominated by the Labour Party which held nearly 90 per cent of all council seats. Here Green would now devote her time to what looked like the impossible task of overturning the Labour hegemony in Bridgend. Over the next five years, Green would advance the Liberal Democrat cause in Bridgend, as never before.

Conclusion

The period between 1987 and 1998 had seen the Welsh Liberal Democrats evolve from two separate parties – the SDP and Welsh Liberals. There had been periods during that time when it looked like the new party was heading for electoral obscurity. This was in 1992 when it lost two of its three MPs. Yet it managed to survive and recover some of this lost ground. By the end of 1998, they had two MPs once more, with the prospect of a considerable number of Assembly Members to swell their ranks.

It was not only the number of potential Welsh legislative members that could be elected that was evolving in the late 1990s. The very nature of its politicians was also altering. Traditionally, Welsh Liberal politicians had come from four walks of life: the Law, the Church, the landowning gentry and from the business classes. The landowning Welsh Liberal aristocracy diminished across most of Wales as a political force by the late 1930s.[68] The last senior businessman Liberal parliamentarian, Clement Davies (former director of Unilever), died in 1962; the last barrister MP, Alex Carlile, stood down in 1997 and the last prominent churchman, who had been likely to become a Welsh Liberal Democrat MP, Roger Roberts, had decided to stand down from further Westminster elections in 1997. The current and future Welsh Liberal Democrat politicians now came mainly from teaching, the public sector, business and farming,[69] no longer from the law, the Church or captains of industry. The impact this change had on the party was that it made it more closely linked to the council and community politics style of Liberalism occurring across England, than the reliance on the personal constituency vote of days gone by. Although this factor still remained important in Mid Wales, it was less important in the urban seats. There had also been something of a power shift in the party. Its key figures now, for the first time, were looking inward to possible power in a Welsh government in Cardiff, rather than outwards to the opposition politics of Westminster. The next decade would soon provide the party with some defining tests as to whether it was really ever going to be a party of government or always one of opposition.

Notes

1. Douglas, Roy (2005) Liberals: The History of the Liberal and Liberal Democrat Parties, Hambleton and London, p. 297
2. SDP Council for Wales Minutes 6/2/88
3. Gwyn Griffiths to author

4. Betts, Clive (1993) The Political Conundrum, Gomer, p. 25
5. Smith, Harriet (1999) The 1988 Leadership Campaign, Journal of Liberal Democrat History, Issue 24, Autumn 1999, pp. 18–22
6. Smith, Harriet (1999) op. cit., p. 20
7. Smith, Harriet (1999) op. cit., p. 19
8. Nigel Evans was later MP for the Ribble Valley from 1992 and became Shadow Spokesman on Wales and Scotland from 1997–2003
9. Butler and Butler (2000) Twentieth Century British Political Facts 1900–2000, Macmillan, p. 320
10. Welsh Liberal and Social Democrats, Annual General Report, 9th–11th November 1989
11. Hague, Ffion (2008) The Pain and Privilege: The Women in Lloyd George's Life, Harper Collins, p. 547
12. S4C 20/6/05 – Geraint Howells – Documentary on
13. Lord Livsey to author 12/6/07
14. Douglas, Roy (2005) op. cit., p. 298
15. Various Liberal interview sources to author
16. Deacon, Russell (1997) The Winners and Losers in Wales's First Unitary Authority Elections, in Contemporary Wales: An Annual Review of Economic and Social Research, Volume 9, University of Wales Press, p. 101
17. Various Liberal interview sources to author
18. Openshaw, Graeme (1991) High Noon or Much Do About Nothing: The significance (or otherwise) of parliamentary by-elections: Monmouth a Case Study, unpublished thesis p. 7
19. Openshaw, Graeme (1991) op. cit., p. 22
20. Liberal Democrat News 17/4/92
21. Frances David to author 28/4/07
22. Rowland was a South Glamorgan councillor who would go onto fight Cardiff North less successfully in 1997 ending third
23. Lord Geraint of Ponterwyd to author 18/2/03
24. Dafis, Cynog (2005) Plaid Cymru and The Greens: Flash In The Pan Or A Lesson For The Future? The Welsh Political Archive Annual Lecture, National Library of Wales, 2
25. There was very little cross-fertilisation between Liberals and Plaid Cymru with a few notable exceptions Councillors Dr Margaret Evans in Carmarthen and John Lopac in the Cynon Valley were two popular Plaid Cymru councillors who came across to the Liberal Democrats in the 1990s but both died prematurely, before managing to build up the Liberal Democrat votes in their own constituencies
26. Lord Livsey to author 12/6/07
27. Lord Carlile to author 20/5/07
28. Liberal Democrat News 24/4/92
29. Liberal Democrat News 11/12/92
30. Liberal Democrat News 23/10/92
31. Clarke went onto unsuccessfully fight Preseli for the party in 1997 general, as well as Alyn and Deeside in the 1999 Assembly elections before defecting to the Conservatives in 2005
32. Lord Carlile to author 20/5/07
33. Kate Lloyd was awarded an MBE for her services to the Welsh Liberal Party in 1995
34. Nick was Head of History and Politics, at St Michael's School, Llanelli. A private school from which had come his star Liberal Democrat pupil Kirsty Williams, six years before
35. Simon Hughes had moved to Cowbridge in South Glamorgan when he was eight and had been educated at Christ College, Brecon.
36. Preamble to the Liberal Democrats Constitution
37. Welsh Liberal Democrats, AGM Conference Agenda, 14 October 1995, Liberal Democrats Wales, p. 13
38. Caerphilly Liberal Democrat membership records, 1995
39. Welsh Liberal Democrats, (1995) op. cit., p. 6
40. One old Liberal from Brecon and Radnor, Councillor Phil Hobhouse, declared after her 1995 Conwy conference speech, that she displayed a 'touch of Lloyd George's eloquence'. Someone whom he had heard speak many times before in the 1930s – Author's Diary, March 1995
41. The Western Mail, 2/2/95, p. 7
42. Welsh Liberal Democrats (1995) op. cit., p. 7
43. Ceredigion and Pembroke North boundary was changed and was consequently renamed Ceredigion for the 1997 general election

44. Liberal Democrats Wales (1996B) Autumn Conference Report, 12/10/06
45. Author's diary notes 25/1/97
46. 'Make the difference': The Liberal Democrat Manifesto for Wales 1997 (1997) Liberal Democrats Wales
47. Author's diary notes 12/10/96
48. Author's diary notes 14/11/96
49. Also the author of this book
50. The word 'Senedd' being the Welsh word for 'Parliament', the reference to 'Beyond a Talking Shop' referring to the Wales Labour Party's own Executive Assembly without tax raising or law making powers
51. Liberal Democrats Wales (1996A) *A Senedd for Wales: Beyond a Talking Shop: The Liberal Democrats Programme for Devolution for Wales*
52. Judi Lewis to author 22/7/04
53. Lord Carlile to author 20/5/07, Lord Livsey to author 12/6/07
54. Lord Carlile to author 20/5/07
55. Having failed to get elected as a Liberal Democrat Leighton Andrews went on to join the Labour Party and become their Assembly Member for the Rhondda in 2003
56. It was in fact Jones who would lose his seat at the forthcoming general election
57. Megan Rees came from a longstanding Liberal Newport family and her father had been a prominent supporter of Lloyd George in South Wales. Doreen Harris also an active Newport Liberal had been a successful business woman and during the Second World War a well known BBC Radio Cook
58. Author's Diary Notes 1997, the author attended the various general election campaign meetings
59. Liberal Democrats interview sources to author
60. Rob Humphreys, was at this time a lecturer at Swansea university in adult education and was a leading light in the Swansea Says Yes campaign group and didn't actually join the Liberal Democrats until November 1997. Within a short time he was approved as an Assembly and Parliamentary candidate and then joined the party's Elections 99 Committee
61. Andrew Davies was elected as a Labour AM in 1999 and went onto serve with Michael German in the Welsh coalition government between 2000–2003
62. Lord Livsey to author 12/6/07
63. Rules for the selection of candidates for the Welsh Senedd, Welsh Liberal Democrats, 28/2/98
64. Author's diary notes and personal records as a returning officer for the Welsh party during this period
65. Peter Black was one of the most senior and experienced Liberal Democrats in the party. From the 1980 onwards he had served in various posts including: Chair of both the Welsh party and its Finance Committee, a member of the ALDC standing committee, the Federal Party's Policy Committee and its Finance and Administration Committee. Since 1984 he had been the Liberal Democrat leader on Swansea City Council and at the time of selection held the spokesperson post for the Welsh party on local government and housing
66. Christine Humphreys to author 20/4/08
67. *The Western Mail*, 30/11/98, p. 1
68. Some of the Liberal landowning families continue in a limited capacity as local councillors in Powys and Ceredigion even today, although they no longer have any impact on Welsh national politics
69. Former occupations of Welsh Liberal Democrat Assembly and Westminster representatives

8

'FROM BACK ROW TO FRONT ROW 1999–2011'

Introduction

It had been the Welsh Liberals' dream since the 1920s that they would experience a massive revival. After some eight decades of misfortune, therefore, few who had been with the party over its later period expected that the day would soon come when members of their party held substantial political power. This is what occurred but not so much through the massive revival of the Liberal fortunes they had so desired, but with more of an incremental rise in fortunes. Thus, the end of the twentieth century and the start of the new millennium would see something of the long awaited political reversal of fortune for the party. Along with the triumphs, there would also still be the inevitable near misses, failures and lost opportunities that had become synonymous with much of Welsh Liberal history.

The last decade in this book proves to be the most exciting for the Welsh Liberal Democrats for over half a century. It would turn out to be a period when the party saw a significant rise in both the number of MPs it had in Wales, its active Lords at Westminster and six new Welsh Assembly members. At the same time, there was a more substantial leap forward in local government representation, which meant that some of the largest metropolitan authorities in Wales were now headed by the Liberal Democrat council leaders, albeit in coalition arrangements. The party was also to experience its first taste the of post-war government in Wales, with Welsh Assembly Cabinet posts including that of Deputy First Minister. This decade of change was to end with one of the biggest changes of all – the party electing its first female leader. This final chapter, therefore, takes the party's history up to the period just after the 2011 Welsh Assembly election with its new leader Kirsty Williams. Kirsty's period in office became one of both consolidation and marginal decline at both Westminster and the Welsh Assembly. It was also the time of Westminster coalition government; in which the Welsh party did not take any ministerial office, but did suffer the pain caused by the unpopularity of the coalition amongst its own supporters in Wales.

The Welsh Assembly Election of 1999 – the Year Proportional Representation Came to Wales

With proportional representation now on the agenda for the Welsh Assembly, the Welsh party felt it had the opportunity to make significant political progress. With this in mind, the Swansea Liberal Democrat and experienced campaigner, Chris Davies, became the Campaign Director of the *Campaign 99 Team*. Davies and Mike German, then launched a series of high profile publicity events. In part, this involved German sweeping across Wales, to various locations, in speed boats or various other methods of rapid transport. It generated visible media images, but this style of campaigning was later felt to be slightly 'over the top', and in future campaigns, the electoral strategy took on a more traditional style of community politics, which based its activities on local campaigning. Just before campaigning started in earnest, a new and central member of the Liberal Democrats Assembly team arrived from London in March 1999. This new figure was Michael Hines, who came down from Paddy Ashdown's private office in Westminster to help German with tactical advice and image presentation prior to the elections. Hines was a workaholic, a young up-and-coming politico who added a great deal of Westminster professionalism to the Welsh campaign. Over the next few years, Hines would often be at the core of defining the Liberals' media and public images in Wales, as well as being one of the deal-makers behind the scenes.

The party now had a detailed manifesto for the governance of Wales. In his last year as Chair of Policy, Nick Buree worked on overhauling the whole policy process. In 1998 he was succeeded by Dr Gareth Jones, a well respected academic and Powys county councillor, who was also closely linked to the Welsh think-tank, the Institute of Welsh Affairs. Under Jones' direction, the Policy Committee became almost fully professionalised. Livsey, German and Kirsty Williams became regular attendees.[1] Previously, senior members had stayed clear of the Policy Committee. With little prospect of any real power it was felt to be 'a waste of time'. Now anything was possible and, with this in mind, David Laws,[2] the Federal party's policy director, and Livsey's own Westminster researcher, Nicola Davies[3], worked directly with the Welsh party over professionalising policy. They produced a document called *Towards a Citizens' Wales*, which represented the Welsh party's most extensive and detailed policy programme ever undertaken. This ended up as their Assembly election manifesto *Guaranteed Delivery*. As opposed to previous decades, the manifesto was no longer shaped by just one or two people. It was shaped by many within the party, most notably Peter Black, Nick Burree, Jean Davies and Kirsty Williams. After their input, the manifesto was further refined by numerous presentations made to the party by pressure groups, Welsh charitable and civic bodies. This gave the document a detailed and well-researched substance and body, rather than the political wish lists of earlier manifestos. As events turned out, this would prove to be the Welsh Liberal Democrats' most important post-war manifesto, so it was just as well that so much time and effort had been spent over it.

The Welsh Assembly Election Results 1999

	Constituency	List
Liberal Democrat	3	3
Labour	27	1
Conservative	1	8
Plaid Cymru	9	8

In the 1999 Welsh Assembly elections, the Welsh Liberal Democrats had talked publicly about gaining 10 seats out of 60; privately they believed they would get eight; they ended up with six. They were confident of a good result because they had always believed that they would be 'everyone's second preference'.[4] This belief meant that they thought that Labour voters would vote for the Labour Party in the constituency and that they would then realise that as Labour would not gain a list seat under AMS, they would then vote for the Liberal Democrats as their second preference. However, they were proved wrong and their campaign failed to secure a significant percentage of the second preference vote. In fact, they had one per cent less of the AMS (Additional Member System) list vote, 12.5 per cent, than the constituency FPTP (first past the post) vote on 13.5%. This came as something of a culture shock to a party that had always believed that, once a proportional system came along, they would secure a much greater share of votes and seats. Nationally, therefore, the result was seen as a campaign failure, especially in the light of Plaid Cymru's spectacular gains.[5] It did, however, get some of the party's key campaigners elected. Mike German was elected on to the South Wales East list, Peter Black on to the South Wales West list. Jenny Randerson was able to win Cardiff Central with a 3,168 vote majority. This was the first 'Liberal' in a Welsh urban constituency since 1945 and in the Welsh capital since 1923. This was an event that went unnoticed in the media because of Plaid Cymru's more wide scale victories on the night. Kirsty Williams was able to win Brecon and Radnorshire with a massive 5,852 majority and Mick Bates did likewise in Montgomeryshire with an equally large majority of 5,504 votes. In North Wales, Christine Humphreys had seen the Liberal Democrat vote in Conwy collapse to just 16 per cent, fourth position, as the seat became a Plaid Cymru-Labour marginal. Humphreys was, however, able to gain a position in the Welsh Assembly because of her position as top of the North Wales' list. Elsewhere in Wales it was once again a case of poorly placed third or fourth positions, which was most notable in Ceredigion where Dorian Evans gained fourth place with the Liberal Democrats worst ever vote of just 11.2 per cent. This was less than a quarter of the winning Plaid Cymru candidate, Elin Jones' vote.

With just 10 per cent of the total Welsh seats, the Welsh Assembly elections of 1999 clearly did not result in the Welsh Liberal Democrats forming the government in their own right. The electorate did not, in fact, give a majority to any one party, although the election was generally acknowledged as being Plaid Cymru's night and certainly not Labour's. The Assembly was one of no overall control: 28 Labour Assembly Members (AMs), 17 Plaid Cymru AMs, nine Conservative AMs and six Welsh Liberal Democrat AMs. Labour was three AMs short of a majority. To the astute observer of British politics, it would have seemed obvious that, when the Welsh Assembly election results were announced, and no one political party had an overall majority, a coalition would be the inevitable result. This was what had happened in the Scottish Parliament, in most local councils and also at Westminster in the past. When either the Liberals or Labour were the largest party nationally, one party always sought the other out as its first coalition partner of choice. This had been the case since the general election of February 1910 when Asquith's Liberals were supported by George Barnes/Ramsay Macdonald's Labour Party. It was expected to be the case once again in 1999 by both Tony Blair and Paddy Ashdown. Ashdown wrote in his diary on 10th May 1999 about his discussions with Tony Blair concerning the situation in Wales:

'Look, I don't understand why this isn't happening in Wales. We have a real opportunity to put together a stable coalition government with you in Wales ... Given the fact that there are no problems of a tuition-fees nature in Wales, I just don't understand why this isn't happening. It appears that Alun Michael doesn't want a coalition. He thinks he has a deal with Plaid Cymru. But Plaid will lead him straight into a trap. They will support him now as First Minister and then dump him later when it suits them. And the result will be that the whole thing will collapse in a year or so's time ... '

Blair looked a bit flustered and admitted that he couldn't understand it either. He would have a word with Alun Michael later ... later I heard from Jonathan Powell that Alun Michael had been contacted by Blair and had agreed to see Mike German (Welsh Liberal Democrat Assembly leader) in the morning to talk about the coalition, but, in Powell's words, 'He wants to play it long. Not the same timescale as Scotland'.[6]

In reality, Labour in Wales did not want a coalition; even though it did not have the majority of Assembly seats, the concept of a coalition government was quite alien to its nature. As proof of this Labour's First Secretary at the Assembly, Alun Michael, had already chosen his Labour Assembly Cabinet, and despite Ashdown's anger over what he saw as Blair's squandering of the chance to 'play out the project on another stage',[7] the Welsh Assembly Executive did not contain any Liberal Democrats. There would be no coalition for the time being. Carlile then had a long meeting with the First Secretary in a restaurant in London to sort out details about as possible coalition. These, however, proved unacceptable to German. Thus, for the time being, the Welsh Liberal Democrats were able to settle into office without the rigours of ministerial office and government responsibility. Their new office would be run by Chris Lines who limited his role as chief executive of the Welsh party to one day a week. Michael Hines stayed on in Wales to act as German's personal and professional media adviser. To help on the policy side, Dr Russell Deacon (the author) was brought in on secondment from the University of Wales Institute, Cardiff and Dr Rodney Berman joined the office from the University of Wales College of Medicine. The Welsh Liberal Democrats were now prepared to go into action in Wales' first legislature.

Other Elections

The 1999 Welsh council elections, held on the same day as the Assembly elections, saw the Liberal Democrats break through politically in some areas of Wales. In the Welsh capital, Cardiff, they doubled their tally of seats from 9 to 18, and secured their position as the main opposition to Labour on the authority. Swansea and Bridgend councils also saw a similar breakthrough with Welsh Liberal Democrats leading the opposition in both authorities (Peter Black leading in Swansea and Cheryl Green in Bridgend). Importantly, in Cardiff, a number of the prominent Welsh Liberal Democrat Cardiff 'Young Turks', who had been campaigning without tangible result for the previous decade, gained office for the first time. Key among these was Nigel Howells, former Welsh party treasurer, John Dixon, the Welsh campaign designer, and Dr Rodney Berman, the party's local government strategist and now Assembly policy officer. All these took up seats on Cardiff City and County Council. Rodney Berman became the Cardiff Liberal Democrat group's leader a year later, taking over from Bill Kelloway. On Conwy County Borough Council, the party lost two seats but still won 15, which was enough to ensure that the council was now run as a Labour-Liberal coalition, with the party taking six of the ten committee chairs.

After the May 1999 council elections were announced it was apparent that the party was a more serious force in local government than it had been since the 1920s. As well as in Bridgend, Cardiff and Swansea councils, it was also the main political opposition in Blaenau Gwent, Powys and Wrexham as well as jointly running the council in Ceredigion and Conwy. It even won three seats in Caerphilly (its first ever), and was able to form its own group there for the first time. In Pontypridd, there were two gains, which saw Liberal Democrats back on the council after a gap of four years.[8] After years of stagnation, these council elections saw the Liberal Democrats progress forward on a sound footing across most of Wales.

The Europhiles Fail to Shine – Welsh European Parliamentary Election

Just a month after the Welsh Assembly and Welsh council elections, those for the European Parliament were held. These elections were held on a different electoral system to the regional one that had existed previously. This time there was an all-Wales list in which five MEP places were up for grabs. The Liberal Democrats had always been the most pro-European of the mainstream British parties. In Wales, therefore, with this pro-European stance and with the possibility that they may gain a seat on this new more proportional list system, there was considerable enthusiasm to be put on party's list. Ten candidates threw their hats into the electoral ring. When the STV ballot was held one candidate gained over 50 per cent of the first preferences on the ballot.[9] This was Roger Roberts. Roberts was such a well known personality within the Welsh party that he was easily able to top the selection list for the party. After having failed to gain Conwy for the fourth time, Roberts had decided that he would have one last go at elected office and this time it would be in Europe. Although Roberts' colleagues tried to persuade him to go for the Welsh Assembly elections, he had his heart set on Europe. The former Conservative MEP, Peter Price,[10] was selected as a distant second place, with Alistair Cameron in third, Juliana Hughes[11] in fourth and John Dixon as the final name on the list.

Roberts led the campaign on the prospect of Wales benefiting from joining the Euro. His main leaflet consisted of a cheque to each family in Wales for the supposed £2,000 they'd be 'better off' if the country joined the Euro.[12] As part of this campaign Roberts went on a tour of a '1,000 Welsh villages' and aimed to visit as many as he could. This was the same tactic the party had used in the 1985 Brecon and Radnor by-election and the 1991 Monmouth by-election to much good effect. Initially Roberts received a lot of party support, as his pro-Europe message was tagged on to its council and Welsh Assembly election leaflets. After the 6th of May elections, having gained elected office themselves, most of the party's activists had lost interest in the European elections. The new Assembly Members and councillors now concentrated on their new posts and Roberts found himself campaigning with little support, sometimes even failing to get the full support of all his fellow list members. The election on 10th June was a damp squib for both Roberts and the Welsh Liberal Democrats. The eventual Liberal Democrat vote of just 8.2 per cent was about a third or less than that of the other three Welsh parties'. In no constituency in Wales, some of which it had carried with substantial majorities at the Assembly elections just a month before, did the party gain a majority of the votes. Roberts' last chance at elected office had failed and with it the party's enthusiasm and expectation that it could win a European Parliamentary seat in Wales in the foreseeable future.

Ashdown hands Over the Reins of Power

On 20th January 1999, Paddy Ashdown announced he would resign as leader once a successor had been chosen. The actual election contest for his successor was held after that May's elections, but as soon as it was known that he was stepping down, potential candidates started pre-election manoeuvres. There were five eventual candidates in the contest, none elected directly from Wales and only three who gathered any support in Wales. Simon Hughes generated the most support; with his Welsh connections, he gathered support from most Welsh party notables including Lord Howells, Chris Davies, Peter Black, Roger Roberts and Mark Soady. Charles Kennedy enjoyed the support of Öpik and Livsey. Finally, Jackie Ballard, the West country MP, had the support of a limited number of Welsh party councillors and activists. Ballard, the most anti-Labour of the candidates, attracted the support of some of those Valley councillors for whom Labour was always seen as the principal opposition. The leadership hustings in Cardiff University were chaired by Mike German who had remained neutral during the campaign. They were somewhat lengthy proceedings, as each of the five candidates had to be given the time to both make their own speeches, and answer questions posed by the audience. When the results came in on 9th August, it was Kennedy who topped the polls, with Hughes being a more distant second. Ashdown had been a popular figure in the Welsh party, often holding meetings across Wales with party members to discuss issues. Kennedy would remain a more distant figure far removed from his previous persona as the congenial 'chat show Charlie'. Hughes, on the other hand, would continue to attend Welsh party conferences and be a frequent figure at their gatherings, making him a well known and well liked figure.

As part of Ashdown's resignation honours on 25th June, Alex Carlile was ennobled as Lord Carlile of Berriew. Berriew was the village in which Carlile's Montgomeryshire home was situated. Carlile had initially been reluctant to become a peer, wishing to set his sights instead on becoming a high court judge. After two very successful years at the bar he had begun to miss politics, however, and when Ashdown offered him the chance of a peerage, which may well have been his last opportunity, he willingly agreed. The other advantage for Carlile in this offer was that he wasn't ennobled as a working peer. He, therefore, had only to attend the House of Lords when the debates were relevant to him, which enabled him to continue his legal profession.[13] This lack of party constraint also enabled Tony Blair to appoint him as the Independent Reviewer of the Terrorism Act in September 2001. This was the highest profile British post for a Welsh Liberal since the 1960s. The other significant point of Carlile's ennoblement worth noting was that the Welsh party now had four active peers, which underlined evidence of both its success in the upper house and its continued weakness in the lower one.

Whilst Carlile had gone to the Lords, his successor Lembit Öpik was seeking a deal over the tricky issue, for rural Liberal Democrat MPs, of fox hunting. The party was overwhelmingly against it. Hunting, however, was an issue that had been felt to be key to Richard Livsey's downfall in the general election of 1992, so it was clearly an extremely important issue for the two Powys MPs. Öpik, therefore, became a founder member of the Middle Way Group on hunting that proposed a statutory authority to draw up guidelines.[14] The group eventually floundered, but it enabled both Öpik and Livsey to continue to gain the support of much of the rural vote in their respective seats, by being seen as figures of compromise and at the same time not against the mainstream opinion of the Welsh party.

The Road to Forming a Lab-Lib Coalition

For reasons of geography and population, the Welsh political world is much smaller than that of England. Most people, however, have no idea how small the Welsh political world can be on occasions. This is an important point to bear in mind when it comes to understanding Welsh elections. Prior to the Assembly elections, as we saw in earlier chapters, both Michael German and Jenny Randerson were both linked closely to the Cardiff Central constituency. Both had gained their political experience in that constituency on Cardiff City Council. They had both been group leaders and both had worked closely with future Labour Assembly Cabinet Members whilst at the council. These Labour figures were Rhodri Morgan, Alun Michael and Sue Essex. German, Randerson and Peter Black had worked during the Yes for Wales Campaign with Labour's Andrew Davies (the Assembly's Business Manager). Thus, the senior Liberal Democrat members had extensive experience with working not only with Labour, but also with the very individuals who were now sitting in the Welsh Assembly Cabinet. This closeness of former working relations was not true of Plaid Cymru or the Conservatives' Assembly Members to anywhere near the extent that it was true of the Liberal Democrat and Labour Members. Both the Powys Liberal Democrat Assembly Members, Kirsty Williams and Mick Bates had played a more limited role in the 'Yes for Wales' campaign and, therefore, had little real interaction with the senior Labour figures before they joined the Assembly. The remaining Assembly Member, Christine Humphreys, had been active in the Yes for Wales Campaign but this had been in North Wales where none of the senior Labour Assembly members came from.

After a short while, the Welsh Liberal Democrats settled down in the Assembly and began to assert themselves in the Welsh party, pushing its power centre away from its Mid Wales Liberal parliamentary dominance of the last half a century to other parts of Wales. This power shift did not occur without some resistance from the mid Wales MPs and communications between the Assembly members and their party's Welsh MPs and Lords were, for a while, quite strained with neither side consulting the other about what its plans or strategies were.[15] Whilst these internal squabbles occurred, upon the horizon arose the increasingly important issue of 'Objective 1', which would come to dominate Welsh politics.

The Background to 'Objective 1'

Although 'Objective 1' may sound like the title of a science fiction film, it, in fact, refers to a stream of European Union (EU) funding that seeks to increase the growth and prosperity of economies that are currently lagging behind the European Average in terms of GDP. In 1999, the West Wales and the Valleys region qualified for Objective 1 as its GDP was less that 75% of the EU average. Some £1.2 billion was made available to be drawn from EU structural funds and around a further £860 million needed to be brought down from British public finances in order to secure this funding. This public money is known as matched funding and it was concerning the issue of matched funding that the Objective 1 debate in the National Assembly ensued.[16]

The Welsh Liberal Democrats set out the mechanisms for going into coalition at their party's Autumn AGM in 1998 in Builth Wells.[17] The mechanism was then referred to after that as the "Builth Motion". This required any possible future co-operation with other parties to be recognised as a formal partnership or coalition. Peter Black, wary of coalitions, tabled an amendment at the conference which was duly passed, it included the requirement that any coalition deal would also need to be subject to a special conference of the Welsh Party for formal approval. The Welsh party leadership was considering a coalition with Labour long before the Objective 1 debate began to rage. Prior to the Assembly elections, there had been two meetings between Labour Leader Alun Michael and Michael German to, discuss 'what if' scenarios. A Labour majority was assumed at this point, but in the event of either 'no overall control' or a hung Assembly, Michael had declared that he would bring everyone on board equally.

After the Assembly election, Michael was keen to secure Welsh Liberal Democrat support in the event of a vote of no confidence in him. He did not, however, wish to concede to a formal coalition, without any real influence for the Liberal Democrats over the Assembly government, so there was little enthusiasm for a coalition on these grounds. Michael himself was now seen as the major obstacle to the formation of a Lib-Lab coalition and to the future of the Assembly itself, by not only Liberal Democrats, but also many Labour Assembly Members. Early in the life of the Assembly, a vote of no confidence was passed on his Agriculture Secretary, Christine Gwyther. Michael failed to remove her from office. He was now seen to be authoritarian and unyielding by the Liberal Democrats, which became a further reason for them to feel they could not work with him.

The First By-election of the New Millennium Brings Liberal Hope

A few days into the new millennium, Cynog Dafis, the Plaid Cymru MP for Ceredigion and regional list AM, announced that he was resigning his Westminster seat to concentrate on his work in the National Assembly. There were three Plaid Cymru AMs who were also MPs, but Dafis was the only one who was determined not to carry on the dual role. Plaid Cymru selected Simon Thomas, a former political officer who had worked with the Plaid Cymru-Liberal Democrat-Conservative rainbow coalition on Taff Ely Borough Council to replace Dafis at Westminster.

The main political campaign issue was Objective 1. It had become the key Welsh political issue of the Assembly's first year. It was also an issue that so exercised the *Wales on Sunday* newspaper that they put up their own candidate, Martin Shipton.[18] Since Howells' defeat in 1992, Bob Griffin and Dorian Evans had begun to modernise the party and politicise it in Ceredigion. The Liberal Democrat council members, for instance, still did not meet as a political group prior to this modernisation. Then in 1999, Aberystwyth University lecturer Michael Woods and Geraint Howell's former assistant, Mark Williams, began to further build up the seat. It was Williams who was selected as the by-election candidate. He was well known by the Liberals in Ceredigion. He also had the personal endorsement of Geraint Howells and was now proving himself to be an effective constituency organiser, to rebuild the party's chances in the seat.

Ceredigion By-election Result 3rd February 2000

Candidate	Party	Vote	Percentage
Simon Thomas	Plaid Cymru	10,716	42.75
Mark Williams	Liberal Democrat Wales	5,768	23.01
Paul Davies	Welsh Conservative Party	4,138	16.51
Maria Battle	Labour Party	3,612	14.41
John Bufton	UK Independence Party	487	1.94
John Davies	Green	289	1.15
Martin Shipton	Wales On Sunday		
	Match Funding Now	55	0.22
	Majority	4,948	19.74
	Turnout		45.69

In the by-election, Mel ab Owen was appointed as the election agent, and together with the support of the federal party, was able to revitalise the constituency party's prospects in the seat. The by-election turned around the situation in the seat for the Liberal Democrats. All the resources of the federal party, including an army of volunteers, were put into seat for the first time. In addition, the Welsh party was now able to send in its own paid Assembly Members and their support staff, which together with the usual volunteers, boosted the party's profile across what, until Plaid Cymru's victory in 1992, had been a natural Liberal seat. As the campaign progressed, a stream of Liberal Democrat MPs, including Charles Kennedy and Paddy Ashdown, visited the seat, further promoting Williams. At the same time, Michael German and the other Assembly AMs spent weekends working in the seat.

The by-election meant that Ceredigion had its first modern Liberal Democrat election campaign. The party used the electoral tactics of the Association of Liberal Democrat Councillors (ALDC). This involved multiple freepost leaflets, its electoral software system called EARS, telephone and doorstep canvassing, plus a target letter to farmers and rural dwellers.[19] Williams' result was able to put the party back into the important second position, above Labour and at the same time boost the party's share of the vote by around nine per cent. Although Plaid Cymru still had a substantial majority in the seat, the Ceredigion Liberal Democrats had been revitalised. The party now felt that if the resources were there, then they could win the seat.[20]

Four months after the by-election, on 16th June, Mark Williams retired as the president of the constituency and was then re-elected as candidate for Ceredigion. Both Williams and the constituency party now had their hearts set fully on regaining the seat and started working on this straight away. Williams wasn't the only candidate who was strongly focused on winning a Westminster seat for the party. At the start of the new millennium, Jenny Willott was selected for Cardiff Central, – a seat that had been one of the Welsh party's target seats for almost two decades. Willott defeated councillors Rodney Berman and John Dixon for the nomination.[21] She was the daughter of Welsh Liberal Democrat activist Alison Willott and chief executive of the Welsh Development Agency, Brian Willott. Now aged 25, Willott had graduated from the London School of Economics after working for Oxfam in India. For the previous two and half years, she had worked for Lembit Öpik in Westminster. Importantly for Willott, she already had a track record in politics in which she achieved electoral office as a councillor in Merton, a London Borough Council. From now on both Willott and Williams would be working in parallel in their attempts to get to Westminster at the next general election.

The Welsh Liberal Democrat Approach to the Objective 1 Debate

Despite its prominence during the Assembly elections of 1999, Objective 1 was not high on the Welsh Liberal Democrats' list of priorities. Their manifesto, *Guaranteed Delivery*, made only three references to Objective 1 funding. In the Assembly, German, turned the Objective 1 debate into a moral issue by stipulating that existing Welsh budgetary provision "belonged to Wales" and should not be used to finance match-funding. The Welsh Liberal Democrats, like the other opposition parties, were not prepared to accept Alun Michael's assertion that they could trust the Chancellor to deliver the extra funding required in the Comprehensive Spending Review in the Summer of 2000. Thus, when an opportunity came for a vote of no confidence in Alun Michael, the party joined the other opposition parties. Michael was able to resign shortly before the vote was carried out against him and, therefore, avoiding having to do so afterwards. Prior to this event, he had already lost the confidence of his own AMs, who declined to re-nominate him if he resigned. This meant that his old political rival, Rhodri Morgan, now became the new First Secretary (soon to be renamed First Minister) and the coalition arrangements were back on. The Welsh Assembly Business Manager and Swansea West AM, Andrew Davies, had already privately met Michael German in a public house in Brecon on behalf of the majority of Labour AMs to seek an assurance from him that the Liberal Democrats would not back Alun Michael in a coalition arrangement. This apparent disloyalty occurred because of their desire to have Rhodri Morgan, who they believed was the rightful winner of their party's leadership election, and Tony Blair backed Alun Michael. They saw this as an opportunity to redress that grievance. The Davies-German meeting, however, ensured that the Welsh Liberal Democrats would no longer back Michael whatever he was to offer.[22]

With the removal of Michael secured, the Welsh Liberal Democrat leadership expected things to move along more quickly. They had internal party discussions about what they should do if the coalition was back on. They had also met with Liberal Democrat representatives, David Laws from the Federal Party's Westminster policy unit and Dr Richard Grayson (Federal Policy Director), who had helped to draw up the negotiating document used in the coalition discussions at the Scottish Parliament. An initial negotiating document was drafted accordingly for use in the event of coalition talks. In the event, Morgan did not initially want to 'play ball' and the coalition talks were 'put on ice' following his decision to carry on alone in a minority government.

Having initially rejected Morgan as a Welsh Labour Party leader, Tony Blair was now keen to see Morgan remain in power. The half a billion pounds, needed for Objective 1 in order to stabilise his government, arrived in order to consolidate the coalition. The Welsh Liberal Democrats had felt they achieved their first victory. They then joined the Labour Party in secret talks and shortly afterwards produced a draft partnership agreement. It was not until a week before the announcement of the Partnership Agreement that German and Morgan sat in the same room to thrash out the finer points of the deal. The whole process had been so secretive that the two parties could have walked away at any stage without recriminations. The Welsh Liberal Democrats had been advised not only to put in their manifesto commitments into the negotiations with Labour, but also to put in an expendable wish list as part of the negotiations. By comparing the Welsh Liberal Democrat Assembly manifesto with the Partnership agreement, it is easy to see why the special conference endorsed the coalition deal. So much of the manifesto had been incorporated that it was, arguably, a Welsh Liberal Democrat programme of government for the next three years rather than a Labour one.

When the coalition government was formed, it was not a simple matter for the Welsh Liberal Democrats; their constitution dictated that such a coalition had to be endorsed by the conference representatives of the Welsh party. Initially, there was great anger amongst Welsh Liberal Democrat delegates about sharing power with a party that on a local government level across much of Wales was political enemy number one. Some party members suspected that their leader Assembly Mike German was perhaps more interested in his own personal ambitions rather than the wider interests of the Welsh party. Whilst most AMs (Assembly Members), Welsh Lords and Parliamentary leader Lembit Öpik MP were for the pact, some were still against it. The Welsh Liberal Democrat AM and former Assembly group leadership contender Christine Humphreys was initially opposed to a coalition, as was Richard Livsey and the future MP for Brecon and Radnor, Roger Williams. To combat this hostility and in order to get the membership behind the pact, German toured Wales, selling the idea to members before a special conference was held on 14th October 2000. He was able to emphasize that the Liberal Democrats had got such a good deal in the coalition arrangements in getting some 114 of their policies implemented,[23] that when the conference day arrived, members felt unable to resist the coalition.

Initially, many of the delegates who had come to the special conference at Builth Wells were there to denounce the pact. As the facts fully emerged concerning the extent of Labour's concessions to the Liberal Democrats, they changed their minds and spoke for the coalition on the platform. This became such a frequent occurrence that the Chair, Lord Carlile, declared that 'the AA have announced that the road from Builth Wells to Damascus is now closed because it has so many Welsh

Liberals Democrats being converted on it'.[24] They had indeed been converted. The party generally felt it was on to a very good deal and, therefore, readily endorsed the coalition. However, it was notable that some of the older West Wales representatives, notably Juliana Hughes (Carmarthenshire) and Eric Griffiths (Ceredigion), strongly opposed the coalition at the conference. But generally the party felt it had got a good deal and later on, as evidence of the extent of good deal, just before the First Minister's second Annual Report in October 2002, Mike German, much to Labour's annoyance, was able to claim that six of the eight leading achievements of the Assembly Government that year had come directly from the Liberal Democrat manifesto.[25]

The By-election in Swansea East

On 18th July 2001, the Labour Assembly member for Swansea East, Val Feld, died. The only Assembly by-election for the 1999–2003 Assembly was, therefore, called for 27th September. This was the first Assembly election in which the Welsh party was able to put its own professional support behind it. Mark Soady, the then Chair of the Welsh party's Campaigns and Elections Committee, became the agent. Chris Lines acted as Campaigns manager.[26] The biggest campaign issue locally was the Crymlyn Burrows Incinerator that was being built at the time. This provoked a lot of disquiet in the St Thomas area of Swansea East and, consequently, a lot of public meetings.[27] Labour's Val Lloyd won with 58.13 per cent of the vote, with Plaid Cymru second on 19.15 per cent. The Liberal Democrat candidate was Rob Speht, who, in the event, gained just over one and a half thousand votes.

Swansea East Result 27th September 2001

Candidate	Party	Vote	Percentage
Val Lloyd	Labour	7,484	58.1
Dr John Ball	Plaid Cymru	2,465	19.2
Rob Speht	Liberal Democrat	1,592	12.4
Gerald Rowbottom	Conservative	675	5.2
Others		659	5.1
	Majority	5,019	38.9
	Turnout		22.6

Speht had been the general election candidate in the seat and, consequently, was reselected in the constituency hustings held to select the by-election candidate. Swansea East was a constituency the party hoped to do well in. The campaign, however, received little media attention in Wales or elsewhere, which was reflected in the low turnout. This was less than one-in-four of the Swansea East voters, the lowest ever for a Welsh parliamentary by-election. What little media coverage there was specifically for the Welsh party concerned questions over identity and how it was distinct from that of the federal party.[28] The issue of a federal and state party structure within the Liberal Democrats was not one that the Welsh media, let alone the wider UK media, was ever able to grasp, and this by-election soon faded into history.

Potential New Welsh Blood Arrives at Westminster

In March 2000, Richard Livsey announced he would step down at the next general election. Livsey was aware that he would be coming close to his seventies if he stood again and felt it right to step down almost 70 then. This was both because he didn't want to be seen as an old man clinging to power and also because he feared the inevitable resurgence of the Conservatives in the seat. He felt it was time for a younger candidate.[29] The electoral contest and hustings were both a lengthy and hard fought campaign. The three main contenders for the seat were Rob Humphreys, later the Welsh party president, Alison Willott, a well known member of the Welsh and Federal Parties' Executive, and Roger Williams. Williams, a science graduate from Selwyn College, Cambridge, had been a member of the Labour Party until he became a key figure in the Welsh SDP in 1981. Later on, he was a councillor on Powys County Council, Chair of the Brecon Beacons National Park and a livestock farmer. Williams was well known within the constituency but not much outside it. His presence in the constituency over the previous decade, plus his own dedication to campaigning, helped ensure that he was able to win the nomination. Once selected, both Livsey and Williams sought to achieve the difficult task of passing on the seat from one to the other, which the Welsh Liberals had done successfully only twice since 1945 in Wales.

The Election in Which Wales Stood Still

Whilst the Welsh party was settling into being part of the Assembly government, there was the little matter of a Westminster general election to fight. Tony Blair had called the election a year early, in part to capitalise on his own party's popularity, which was still riding high in the polls. At the same time, the Conservative party was still disorganised, low in the polls and recovering from its devastating loss of 1997. The 2001 election would see the least number of seats change hands in Wales since the two elections of 1974. Only Ynys Môn, won by Labour, and Carmarthen East and Dinefwr, taken by Plaid Cymru off Labour, changed hands. This left the electoral balance the same in Wales as it had been in 1997. It also left the Conservatives without any Welsh MPs for another parliament.

For this general election, the Welsh party had changed its name back to 'Welsh Liberal Democrats', (the name by which it was commonly known) from the 'Liberal Democrats Wales'. The latter name, as had been expected, had made no difference to their electoral fortunes and had failed to bring in nationalist voters. When it came to issues of policy, *Freedom for Wales in Liberal World*, the Welsh party's general election manifesto, was a Welsh replica of the federal manifesto with a page or two of Welsh additions, such as greater powers for the Assembly and a bank holiday on St David's Day. As in 1997, policies were now fully costed to avoid the previous accusations levelled against the Liberals of putting together manifestos made of unsustainable uncosted wish lists.

The General Election of 2001 in Wales

Liberal Democrat	2
Labour	34
Conservative	0
Plaid Cymru	4

Electorally, the Welsh party's two key seats in Powys had been affected greatly by foot and mouth disease, which had broken out across Wales and England in the early part of the year. The problem across the UK was so acute that the general election itself was set back from April to May because of the concerns of its impact. In Wales, 78 of the 188 confirmed cases occurred in Powys. This resulted in the slaughter of some 15,000 livestock.[30] In Powys and along the rest of the Welsh borders huge funeral pyres of cows blackened the skies for weeks. The dairy farming community was hit at an unprecedented rate. In the south-west of England foot and mouth disease was felt to have had a damaging effect on the Liberal Democrat vote. Yet this did not occur in Montgomeryshire; despite a 10 per cent drop in turnout, Öpik was able to see his overall vote rise to 49.4 per cent of the vote (up 3.5 per cent). Öpik was becoming increasingly well known not just in his constituency but, for after dinner speeches and media appearances, across the party as a whole. At the time many of the Welsh members were bemused by and for a time relished the publicity their new MP was generating. Soon, however, Öpik's ability to attract publicity would no longer be welcomed but at these elections it was still well received by the party across Wales.

In Brecon and Radnor, where Roger Williams was hoping to take over from Richard Livsey, the result was a close-run thing. Here the Conservative, Felix Aubel,[31] came within 751 votes of taking the seat. Williams was faced by a number of factors that were not in his favour, the foremost being both his presence as the 'new boy' in the seat and the strong campaigning by the Labour candidate Huw Irranca-Davies, which held up the Labour vote that Williams needed to squeeze for himself. The narrowness of Williams' win was almost exactly mirrored by the narrowness of Jenny Willott's defeat in Cardiff Central. Here Willott had been able to reduce a Labour majority of 7,923 to just 659. Thus, for a while on the election night, it was uncertain whether Lembit Öpik would be the leader of the three Welsh MPs in Westminster or its sole representative in Wales.

In Ceredigion, Mark Williams had been able to consolidate his good showing in the 2000 by-election with a solid second position. He was still some five thousand votes off winning the seat but, importantly for him and the Welsh party, he was now seen as the main challenger to Plaid Cymru's Simon Thomas in the seat. In Conwy, Roger Roberts' replacement, Vicky MacDonald, came a distant third, with the Conservatives now being the main challenge to Labour in the seat. With Roberts' departure, the Liberal Democrat hope of winning this constantly marginal seat also disappeared. In Islwyn, Kevin Etheridge came second but was still some 15,309 votes off winning the seat. Etheridge found he was unable to build a Liberal Democrat constituency organisation to support his attempts at the seat and, consequently, gain the financial backing he required from the Welsh party to campaign for the seat seriously. Within a year Etheridge had left the party but did not join another and remained a popular county councillor in the constituency. There was, therefore, little real joy for the Welsh party in the 2001 elections. The Conservatives were placed in second position to Labour in virtually every Labour held seat. Politics seemed to have returned to the two-party contest of old. The federal party had won 52 seats, yet only two of these were in Wales. Statistically, on 13.8 per cent of the Welsh vote, it was proportionally short of five MPs. At Westminster, it represented only four per cent of the federal party's Westminster MPs and therefore asserted little influence over the party federally.

The Ogmore By-election 2002

Within less than a year of the general election, there would be the only Welsh parliamentary by-election of the Parliament. Sir Ray Powell, the veteran Labour MP for Ogmore, died suddenly at the age of 73. Sir Ray had been a traditional Labour stalwart and anti-devolutionist, with his daughter, Janice Gregory, also being the Assembly Member for Ogmore. In a former mining constituency, the key issue became the speed with which compensation claims were being paid to former miners who suffered from ill health. Thus the Liberal Democrats, with no significant presence in any former mining constituencies, were ill equipped to campaign. The by-election was called for on St Valentine's day 2002 and Veronica Watkins was chosen as the Welsh Liberal Democrat, candidate. At the time, Watkins was a researcher for Kirsty Williams, with most of her prior political activity occurring in Newport and the surrounding South Wales valleys constituencies. In a low key campaign held during the cold dark months of winter, Watkins came a distant third, with 8.8 per cent of the vote but, importantly, she saved her deposit. Huw Irranca-Davies, the Labour candidate who had worked so hard in Brecon and Radnorshire the previous year, won the seat with some 52 per cent of the vote. Plaid Cymru's veteran campaigner Bleddyn Hancock made the main advance of the night to come second, with 20 per cent of the vote. Hancock was a long established campaigner for miners' compensation, which helped boost his vote well above Plaid Cymru's normal vote share in this seat.

The Welsh Party Seeks to Turn the Assembly into a Proper Parliament

For over a century many Welsh Liberals had campaigned for a Welsh parliament. The current Assembly was without tax-raising or primary law-making powers, which left it far behind the devolution that had been granted to both Scotland and Northern Ireland. Thus, the Assembly was only seen as a 'halfway house' between the Welsh Office and a Welsh Parliament. The party was always keen to establish a Welsh parliament and the next great opportunity for them to gain a Parliament came with the appointment of the Richard Commission in July 2002. The Commission came as part of the deal that ensured Labour-Liberal Democrat coalition government could take place in October 2000. Within the partnership document *Putting Wales First: A Partnership for the People of Wales* came the commitment to:

'Establish an independent Commission into the arrangements of the National Assembly in order to ensure that it is able to operate in the best interests of the people of Wales. This review should investigate *inter alia* the extension of proportionality in the composition of the Assembly, and of the relevant competencies devolved.'[32]

It was one of three major Commissions set up by the Labour-Liberal Democrat coalition government to enable areas of policy conflict between the two parties to be resolved. The first was the Rees Commission, which examined the issue of student finance; the second was the Sunderland Commission,[33] which examined the issue of Welsh local government reform, whilst the Richard Commission became the third and final Commission of the coalition government.

For the Chair of this important Commission, the coalition government was able to secure the services of Lord Richard of Ammanford. Lord Richard was one of the most distinguished Welsh politicians who was still active. He was a former MP, EEC Commissioner, Leader of the House of Lords and former UK Ambassador to the UN. It was also felt that his weight within the Labour Party would help bring enough *gravitas* to persuade everyone that this was a major commission. The other nine Commission Members were made up of five independent members and four political party nominees – all of considerable stature. The Liberal Democrat representative was the former Conservative MEP, Peter Price, who had been an active Welsh Liberal Democrat for much of the previous decade. The only major flaw with the Commission, as far as the Welsh party was concerned, was that it would not report back until after the next Assembly elections.[34] The Commission's terms of references were twofold. They had to consider:[35]

1. the sufficiency of the Assembly's current powers,
2. the adequacy of the Assembly's electoral arrangements.

When the Commission reported back in April 2004, it recommended that by the year 2011 or sooner if possible, the Assembly should:

1. Have its delegated powers enhanced,
2. Be given primary law making powers,
3. Have its membership increased from 60 to 80 and all members should be elected by STV,
4. Be reconstituted with a separate legislature and executive.

Reviewing Proportional Systems and Proportionality

As we noted earlier, on 7th March 1997, Alex Carlile had published a letter which he had signed with Ron Davies committing the Welsh Liberal Democrats to campaign for a 'Yes' vote in any referendum on a Welsh Assembly.[36] A sub-clause in the letter committed the Labour Party to reviewing the electoral system, if it proved to be non-proportional. The system of FPTP-AMS was proportional for some parties and not for others. For instance, Plaid Cymru and the Conservatives gained almost exactly the same proportion of seats as the percentage of their total votes. For the Welsh Liberal Democrats and the Labour Party the system was less proportional. Labour was significantly over represented by the new electoral system, whereas the Welsh Liberal Democrats were under represented. In the Assembly election of 2003, the Liberal Democrats were due one more seat and in 2007 they were due two more seats to make them truly proportional, in respect of the share of seats to votes. The Labour Party in contrast always gained a larger percentage of seats than their share of the vote.

When the Richard Commission finished its report and recommended an 80 member Assembly, elected by STV, it was seen as a blessing for the Welsh Liberal Democrats. These recommendations represented the full attainment of the party's devolution policy, although without visible credit going to the party.[37] In fact, the recommendations were so close to the Welsh Liberal Democrats' own policy for the establishment of a Welsh Parliament, that they didn't even need to consult their membership on the need for its endorsement of its outcomes.[38] There was one major problem with the Richard Commission's recommendations as the Welsh Liberal Democrats discovered. They had reported back 11 months after the Welsh Liberal Democrats had left the coalition government. As we will see shortly, the post-May 2003 Assembly elections had seen Labour elected with exactly half of the seats in the Welsh Assembly. As the other political parties did not form a coalition government between them, it left Labour in charge of the Assembly government. The Welsh Liberal Democrats had now lost any influence over the government of Wales. The Wales Labour Party, which is traditionally of a 'conservative' nature in respect to devolution, now rejected Richard's recommendation of primary law-making powers and an STV system by 'two to one' in their internal consultation exercise.[39] This was then endorsed by the Welsh Labour Party's special conference on 12th September 2004. *Better Governance for Wales*,[40] the Welsh Labour policy document produced in 2004 in response to Richard's, made it clear there would be no primary law-making powers for the Assembly in the foreseeable future. In both Assembly elections, Labour had only gained one AMS seat in 1999, and none in 2003. Importantly for the Welsh Liberal Democrats, not only would there not now be an STV electoral system but the AMS system was going to be amended to prevent candidates from standing on both the constituency and the list. The question arose, where there was a possibility of winning a seat, would they put their 'best' candidates in the constituency or on the list? The incumbent list Assembly Members (Black, Burnham and German) had now to decide whether they should go for a constituency or a list seat.

After the Welsh Labour Party had effectively ruled out the Richard Commission's recommendations, Mike German became instrumental in setting up a cross party and non-party pressure group called *Cymru Yfory* or *Tomorrow's Wales*, chaired by the Archbishop of Wales.[41] *Tomorrow's Wales* was theoretically there to promote the implementation of the Richard Commission. At the time the group, however, had little impact on persuading Labour to implement Richard's recommendation and couldn't even agree to support all the recommendations itself.[42] The group, in the end, simply limped on unnoticed by most political commentators and the Assembly government during this period.

The failure of *Tomorrow's Wales* to get Labour to back the STV recommendation ensured that the Welsh party would have to continue with its more recent tactics of electoral targeting. There had been the targeting of Westminster seats since the mid 1990s. This had not been used to the same extent in the Assembly elections in 1999 or 2003, as the party believed it could acquire the other political parties' supporters' second election preferences. Therefore, a broad-brush campaigning approach was adhered to here.

The Coalition Government's Success and Failure

Out of direct power for six decades, the Liberals had made virtually no impact on government policy in Wales until they were part of the coalition government. Getting their 1999 Assembly manifesto implemented virtually in full, therefore, was the Welsh Liberal Democrats' greatest post-war policy triumph and only substantial political legacy. The establishment of the Rees Commission and the ability, consequently, to reduce top-up fees for Welsh students was one its proudest electoral boasts. There were, however, two substantial policy failures for the Welsh Liberal Democrats – the Richard Commission's recommendations, as we have just noted, and the failure to implement the Sunderland Commission's recommendations of STV for Welsh local government elections.

Perhaps the biggest internal disappointment, however, during the Welsh Lib-Lab coalition of 2000–2003 concerned the personal problems suffered by the party's leader Michael German. In January 2001 the European anti-fraud organization started investigating the European Unit of the Welsh Joint Education Committee (WJEC) over financial problems. Mike German had been the head of the unit for most of the 1990s. The WJEC was run and operated by the Welsh local authorities, the majority of which were Labour-controlled and bitterly opposed to the Lib-Lab coalition. The Labour Party membership had not been consulted over the coalition and most saw this as a case of the 'Liberal tail wagging the Labour dog'. Whether or not the WJEC was politically motivated in its investigations on German or not, by May 2001 they called in the police to examine Michael German's claims for expenses whilst he had worked there. The police investigation eventually found 'insufficient evidence to proceed further' in a prosecution. The time taken in reaching this decision, however, was enough to take German out of the Cabinet between July 2001 and June 2002. During this period nearly all Liberal Democrats had closed ranks around German, failing to criticize him publicly or to ask him to step down, with one notable exception. This was Alex Carlile, who believed that as German had been responsible for the funding, he should have stepped down as leader until his name was cleared.[43] This would sour relations between the two politicians from then on.

Unlike the Westminster elections, the date of the Welsh Assembly elections was known four years in advance. The problem for the Welsh party was that they did not know whether they would be punished or rewarded for being in coalition with the Labour Party. In the run up to the war in Iraq, however, the election, to a major degree, was overshadowed by international rather than domestic issues.

The 2003 Welsh Assembly Elections

	Constituency	List
Liberal Democrat	3	3
Labour	30	0
Conservative	1	10
Plaid Cymru	5	7
Forward Wales	1	0

The 2003 Assembly election sought to target the Labour voters' second preference votes. It did so by seeking to exploit the Labour voters' fear of a Conservative 'list win'. This was despite the fact that in much of Labour-held Wales, the Conservatives had not been a serious political threat for several decades. To create the image of a Conservative bogeyman, however, to this end, the second regional electoral postal leaflet featured a huge picture of Iain Duncan Smith (Conservative leader)and on it, it read:[44] '83,953[45] Labour Voters elected this man's party in 1999 … Don't let it happen again – Vote Welsh Liberal Democrat with your second vote to beat the Conservatives'.

In the event, electorally the Welsh public thought even less of Mike German as a party leader than they did of Iain Duncan Smith.[46] This may have been one reason for Labour voters not to have paid heed to the Welsh Liberal Democrats' advice and supported them on the list vote. The message did, however, upset the Conservatives and some of the leading Welsh Liberal Democrats also saw it as a negative message. There was a fall-out between the Welsh leaders over the issue. Assembly leader Michael German believed it the right thing to do; Welsh Liberal Democrat President Rob Humphreys and Welsh Leader, Lembit Öpik disagreed with the negative campaigning.[47] In the post election discussion, it was felt that this type of personal campaigning should not be repeated, as it was unproductive.

The problems of both Assembly elections failing to gain a substantial number of Assembly Members led to a revision of electoral strategy. The same six Assembly Members who had entered these elections were re-elected once more. There would be no new faces in the Welsh Liberal Democrat Assembly team at this election. Apart from Ceredigion, where John Davies gained second place with 28 per cent of the vote, and in Swansea West where Peter Black did the same with 24.3 per cent of the vote, the Welsh party gained no second positions that would challenge the incumbent. Again it was third and fourth positions and a lost deposit in the Rhondda.[48] It was clear now that the future would rely on targeted campaigning in all types of elections. Although some still felt that they should neglect the second preference issue entirely, because Plaid Cymru and Labour voters may 'peel off',[49] most now believed in only targeting wherever possible. In some county councils such as Swansea, Cardiff and Bridgend, they had already been targeting the council wards they hoped to gain in the Assembly elections. The strategy had involved the targeting of prospective wards by what were termed (by the Chief Executive, Chris Lines) 'the Generation X teams' (the up and coming next generation of council seats).[50] Within a year, this was to provide the Welsh Liberal Democrats with their best ever council election results.

The 2004 Welsh Council Elections Bring 'Real Power' to the Grassroots

Local government in Wales had become an area of political targeting prior to 2004. In part this was spurred on by the grants awarded to campaigning councillors by the ALDC. However, they would only award grants for campaigning, if there was clear evidence that particular wards were being targeted. In Cardiff, the Liberal Democrats, for instance, were running their *Target 38* Campaign, which aimed to secure exactly half of the city council seats, which would give the party an overall majority. Across Wales, this target was as much for the council elections of 2008 as 2004. It was, therefore, thought by most campaigners that 2004 would be the election to position the party in a position to take power in 2008. They were wrong; the Welsh Liberal Democrats gained 37 councillors in Wales taking their total up to 148. Plaid Cymru lost 14 per cent of its council seats (28) and Labour lost 12 per cent of its seats (64). The final tally of councillors for Labour (478) and Plaid Cymru (172) still placed them both ahead of the Welsh Liberal Democrats. The Conservatives despite 39 gains remained the fourth party in Wales in terms of council numbers with 109 councillors.

When all the results were in, the size of the Welsh Liberal Democrats' influence on local government was not clearly visible. It was clear that the Liberal Democrats had done well in Cardiff with 18 gains, they were second only to Newcastle (in England) in terms of their success within the Federal Party. They made significant gains elsewhere in Wales, yet they did not control any of the new councils outright. Eight Welsh authorities were left with no one party in overall control. It was the negotiations concerning who would lead these councils which were to make the difference to the party. Within two weeks, three of these 'no overall control' councils would be led by Welsh Liberal Democrats in coalition arrangements with Conservatives, Plaid Cymru and Independents (Bridgend – Cheryl Green, Cardiff – Dr Rodney Berman and Swansea – Chris Holley). On a number of other councils (Ceredigion, Conwy, Powys), they also held Cabinet seats in non-Liberal Democrat-led coalitions. Just a year later they also took control of Wrexham (Aled Roberts being the leader). As the initial scale of success became apparent, it was evident that:

1. Targeting had been effective in making significant gains. Their total Welsh vote only increased by 0.4 per cent from 1999 from 13.4 to 13.8. Yet the number of councillors increased by over 40 per cent.[51] The council results had dictated the party's Westminster targeting for the next general, and Assembly election (Bridgend, Cardiff Central, Cardiff South and Penarth, Ceredigion, Delyn, Newport East and Wrexham now all became Welsh Liberal Democrat target seats).[52]
2. The number of Liberal Democrat-led coalition councils now made them, behind Labour, the second political party in Wales, with Cardiff being the first ever capital city to be led by a Welsh Liberal Democrat administration.
3. The Welsh Liberal Democrats had been able to make rapid pacts with Independents, Plaid Cymru and Conservatives which put them in the leadership positions. They had either refused power-sharing with Labour councillors (in Swansea) or not sought it at all (Bridgend, Cardiff and Wrexham).
4. The party now had significant representation on the Welsh Local Government Association (WLGA).[53] They held 10 of the 69 places and three of the 22 portfolios of the group. Welsh Liberal Democrats had never held more than a few positions before.[54]

However, there was not success everywhere for the Liberal Democrats. On Conwy County Borough Council, the party, with some 15 councillors, had been in coalition with Labour and had three Cabinet seats. The Liberal Democrats lost 11 councillors there because of a general collapse in their vote and the retirement of some prominent councillors with no replacement candidates.[55] Therefore, Conwy, once the most prominent and successful Welsh Liberal Democrat council, faded from the party's political map. Overall, the expansion of the Welsh Liberal Democrats' local government base brought new people into the development of the party. Its council leaders became as important and often more prominent than its AMs, MPs and Lords. The wielding of day to day political power for the party, after the loss of power in the Welsh Assembly, was now at the local level.

At the tail-end of the Welsh council elections were the European elections. The number of MEPs in Wales had been reduced from five to four. The Welsh Executive had decided that there was no chance of winning a seat and that it would not fund any campaign. The lead candidate, David Williams, a translator of Welsh descent who now lived in Germany, was, however, convinced he could win. Williams ended up borrowing money from the Welsh party to pay for an all-Wales leaflet. Although the Liberal Democrat vote improved to 10.5 per cent of the vote up over two points on the last election, he was nowhere near winning a seat. Williams having to bear this loss for no tangible gain, therefore, left Welsh Liberal Democrat politics in some acrimony. His number two on the list, Alison Goldworthy, still a Politics undergraduate student at Bath University, however, would become a central figure in Cardiff politics over the next few years.

One Welsh Lord Passes On; and Another Arrives

On 18th April 2004, Geraint Howells died after a long period of increasingly poor health. Howells had been a very popular figure in both the Welsh party and his own constituency for almost half a century. He had represented the strong Welsh-speaking Liberal link in the party which stretched back to the time of David Lloyd George. Some two months after Howells' death, the Welsh party gained a new Lord. On 30th June 2004, Roger Roberts, who had been a long-time friend of Howells and at the forefront of Welsh and federal party politics for over half a century, was ennobled as Lord Roberts of Llandudno. Roberts had been near the top of the federal party's own potential peers list since February 2000 and had seen numerous members ennobled before him. It became an increasing frustration for both him and his supporters that he had not been ennobled. Once in the Lords, however, he soon made his presence felt, as he became an Opposition Spokesman on Welsh Affairs and filled some of the vacuum left by Howells, by providing a strong Welsh language Liberal in the upper house.

The Welsh General Election Break-through 2005

The party's Chief Executive who had seen them develop in both government opposition in the Welsh Assembly, Chris Lines, left office on 1st January 2005 to become Head of Communications of the National Public Health Service in Wales. He was a difficult person to replace; nevertheless, on 2nd January, Stephen Smith, the Welsh

Party's Head of Research at the National Assembly, took over as the new Chief Executive.[56] Around the same time, Ian Walton, who had been active within the administrative and campaign side of the party both at federal level and with the sister Alliance Party in Northern Ireland,[57] became the party manager. Together with Jon Aylwin, who had developed into an experienced and well respected campaign officer, they now set about preparing the party for the forthcoming general election.

The Welsh party held its pre-general election conference in Cardiff just a few months before the May 5th of 2005 general election. There the party's newly appointed President, Simon Hughes, challenged the Welsh party to gain the majority of Welsh seats by 2020. Few who cheered him at the conference would believe that the next general election would prove to be the best for the Welsh party for over half a century. The party's manifesto as usual had borrowed heavily from the federal one, even taking the same name, 'The Real Alternative'.[58] Under the policy officer, Dewi Knight, however, the plethora of newly developed Welsh policies were costed and integrated into the federal policies into a document that clearly projected the aspirations of the Welsh party at Westminster. All the main Liberal Democrat hopefuls had their picture and policy statements displayed prominently throughout the manifesto. It looked like a polished document but it was still open to question whether it would persuade the Welsh voters to back them?

The General Election of 2005 in Wales

Liberal Democrat	4
Labour	30
Conservative	3
Plaid Cymru	3

In February 2003, federal leader, Charles Kennedy, was one of the speakers in a rally in London of over a million anti-Iraq war protesters. In March, the party's Welsh MPs joined those from the rest of the UK at Westminster supporting an amendment which declared that the case for war was 'not yet proven'.[59] Öpik and others spoke publicly about the need to avoid war. In this way, the party had clearly set itself in the anti-war camp. Yet when the war broke out, it adopted a position of supporting the troops in combat. It was evident that war and the general disillusionment with the New Labour project were also leading to growing dissatisfaction with New Labour in Wales. This was what the party in Wales was hoping to benefit from. The Labour vote dropped by six per cent of the overall vote and Welsh Liberal Democrat vote rose by five per cent. It gave the party its best share of the Welsh vote since 1983.

In Brecon and Radnorshire, the 2005 general election was different from that of 2001. The Conservative candidate who had come so close to winning in 2001, a former SDP defector, Felix Aubel, because of pressures of work, was unable to contest the seat again. The Conservatives then struggled to get a new candidate. Huw Irranca-Davies, who had kept the vote up for Labour in the constituency in 2001, was now fighting Ogmore as the incumbent MP. Roger Williams, at the same time, had been able to tour the constituency in order to increase his personal vote. The combination of these factors enabled Williams to gain a majority of 3,905 votes (10.2%) and remove the constituency from its marginal status. In Montgomeryshire, Öpik was able to bring his own vote up to some 51.2 per cent of the total, giving him a comfortable 7,173 (23.8%) majority.

In Cardiff Central, the party was also able to storm home electorally. Willott's early reselection for the seat, then Randerson's winning the seat at the Assembly again in 2003, and the dominance of the Liberal Democrats in the constituency's council seats, plus Jon Aylwin's electoral skills – all helped to ensure victory. At the same time, those seats with a university student populations saw large rises in the party's vote. Those with a Muslim population saw even higher votes swing towards the Liberal Democrats.[60] In Cardiff Central, a number of prominent Muslims had both joined and become active in the party. One of the most prominent was Asghar Ali, a councillor in Grangetown who stood for Caerphilly in this general election. The student, Muslim and loyal council vote, combined with the constant work of the 'two Jennies" (Randerson and Willott),[61] ensured that the party gained the seat with a substantial 5,593 (15.5%) majority. In fact, the party's campaign team, under Jon Aylwin's direction, had become so confident of winning the vote that in the last few weeks of campaigning they had switched a lot of their own effort over to helping Mark Williams win in Ceredigion.

The Liberal Democrat win in Ceredigion was the surprise result of the night for the Welsh party. It was generally expected that Williams would gain a strong second place in order to be the challenger for the 2009–10 general election. In the event, the decline in the Plaid Cymru constituency organisation, combined with the rise of his own support in the seat, added to the benefit of the student vote in the seat, particularly in Aberystwyth. His support from Welsh members outside the seat enabled him to sneak into the victory position by some 219 votes (0.6%). Williams had been aided by the public feud between Plaid Cymru's incumbent MP, Simon Thomas, and Labour's candidate, Alun Davies, a former Plaid Cymru executive member and, later, a Labour Assembly Member. Their public feuding during the campaign was also able to make Williams look by far the most reasonable candidate.

The election was over a year after Howells' death and many old Liberals present that night deeply regretted the fact that he hadn't lived to see it. Williams' victory meant that the Welsh party now had four MPs, its highest since 1951, which meant it now had a parliamentary group worthy of the name for the first time in half a century. But, in contrast to 1951, the Welsh party no longer represented half of the federal party but only just seven per cent of it, which was an indication that the party's fortunes had changed both in Wales and England.

Elsewhere in Wales, it was a story of mainly second and third places. These results were now more encouraging than at any time since 1983. There were some good thirds: Paul Warren came third in Bridgend with 21 per cent of the vote; John Dixon in Cardiff North had 18.7 per cent of the vote; Gavin Cox 20.3 per cent in Cardiff South and Penarth, Gareth Roberts 20 per cent in his father's old seat of Conwy and Paul Brighton[62] gained 17.4 per cent in Alyn and Deeside. There were also some good seconds: Ed Townsend with 23.7 per cent in Newport East; Mike Powell with 19.5 per cent in Pontypridd; Rob Speht with 20.1 per cent in Swansea East and Tom Rippeth in Wrexham with 23.6 per cent. Only Rene Kinzett in Swansea West, with 28.9 per cent of the vote, however, was a clear potential challenger to the incumbent Labour MP. The party also lost only one deposit in Blaenau Gwent, where a split in the Labour party had produced two rival camps that squeezed all the other parties' votes.

Campbell Replaces Kennedy

Around the time of Christmas 2005, Charles Kennedy's leadership ran into insurmountable problems. His alcoholism, which had been well known within the inner party for a number of years, finally lost him the patience of the majority of his MPs. On 7th January he resigned. Lembit Öpik had been fanatically loyal to Kennedy until he resigned, defending him publicly at every opportunity. The other Welsh MPs and Assembly members stayed on the sidelines. The federal party now went through a period of inward soul-searching and a process of seeking new candidates. Three of the main Welsh Liberals supported Menzies (Ming) Campbell, Lord Carlile, Jenny Willott and Kirsty Williams. Mark Oaten was backed by Lembit Öpik. He became his campaign manager but failed to secure any other support from Wales or elsewhere and Oaten stood down on 19th January as a leadership contender. As if this lack of support for Öpik and Oaten's campaign was not embarrassing enough, on 21st January, in the light of the fact that the *News of the World* was going to publish a story the following day about Oaten's affair with a male prostitute, he stood down as the party's home affairs spokesman. Öpik now stood on the sidelines and refused to endorse any of the other candidates. Simon Hughes, a favourite of the Welsh party members, was also damaged politically by issues concerning his homosexuality. In an interview with *The Independent* on 16th January, Hughes stated clearly to the question, 'Are you gay?', 'No!'.[63] He continued to deny being 'gay' in subsequent interviews but the newspapers had started to unearth information to the contrary and on 26th January, he was forced to publicly admit that he had had homosexual affairs. This issue had the affect of damaging significantly his chances in the leadership election.

The final candidate to join the leadership race, and the least well known in Wales, was the former MEP and now MP for Eastleigh, Chris Huhne. He was also backed by three MPs named Williams, and all with Welsh connections; Roger (Brecon and Radnor), Mark (Ceredigion) and Stephen (Bristol West). The latter, only two decades previously, had been a schoolboy activist with the SDP in the Cynon Valley. Baroness Walmsley[64] also backed Huhne but there was no further backing from Welsh Assembly Members or Lords for him. At the only Welsh leadership hustings, chaired by Rob Humphreys, at Cardiff University, it was generally felt that Huhne gave the most polished performance. German and a number of the other senior Welsh members were ambivalent about should become leader. There were no strong feelings in respect of any of the candidates. In the event, it was Campbell who won the contest with little outward enthusiasm from most Welsh members. He would for many remain a distant figure only appearing fleetingly at the Welsh party's spring conferences or supporting candidates at general election time.

Problems with Öpik: Gaining a Column but Losing a Presidency

Lembit Öpik had become something of a flamboyant figure not only in Welsh politics but on the national political and media stage as well. An accomplished public and after-dinner speaker, he had become well known within the party. Öpik was also able to work effectively with the media, having his own theatrical agent to coordinate his appearances. Thus, across much of the decade, he appeared on numerous political and entertainment programmes ranging from *Have I Got News For You* to *Who Wants to be a Millionaire*? These performances began to cause some resentment by some prominent members within the party, who were concerned about him deflecting interest from the party to his own personal publicity and partly uneasy about the amount of tabloid coverage he was beginning to generate. He was already well known for the publicity he gathered concerning his predictions of an asteroid striking the earth. Now his over enthusiastic support for Kennedy and then his disastrous support for Oaten began to cast him as a political eccentric in the public eye.

In May 2004, Öpik announced his engagement to the Welsh TV weather presenter, Siân Lloyd. For the next two years, the couple toured the show business circuit together, featuring in numerous newspapers, TV programmes and magazines as well as inside the cover of the *Hello!* magazine. No Welsh politician, let alone a Liberal one, had ever enjoyed such widespread national publicity since Neil Kinnock's period as Labour leader. Most of the coverage was positive, if somewhat and embarrassingly over-romanticised. The proposed marriage to Lloyd did not occur and the couple separated. In December 2006, Lloyd sold her story concerning their split and the fact that Öpik was in a relationship with Gabriela Irimia to the newspapers. Gabriela was a twenty-four-year-old Romanian pop singer, one in a pop group duet of identical twins known as 'The Cheeky Girls'. The story became a tabloid sensation and, for the next few months, both the federal party and the Welsh party were overwhelmed with media attention concerning Öpik, which, in turn, swamped much of the publicity they were trying to gain themselves in other areas. Öpik's life would continue to be in and out of the tabloid columns and, in 2008, he even started writing a tabloid column himself, in the downmarket *Sunday Sport*.

Even before the story of Öpik and the 'Cheeky Girl' had broken at the Welsh Party's 2006 Autumn October conference in Aberystwyth, there had been an unsuccessful attempt to remove Öpik as leader, as both Peter Black and Elinor Burnham separately had tried to gather enough signatures to force a leadership contest. They failed to start a contest against Öpik but they and others now looked on his activities with increasing despair, wondering how they could halt what they saw as his adverse publicity. They were unable to do so. The publicity died down eventually but those at the heart of the party would constantly fear that some new spark or revelation would start the publicity fires roaring again and they would be unable quench them.[65] As long as Öpik remained in the media spotlight, these stories would continue to surface and frequently embarrass or irritate the wider Welsh and federal party.

Öpik's ambition had been to become the federal party president. This he had failed to do in September 2004 when he was defeated by Simon Hughes who gained

71 per cent of the vote to Öpik's 29 per cent. At the time, supporters of Öpik put this down to the fact that Hughes was a well-known and well-liked public figure in the party and that Öpik was still building his support base. Thus, when the next federal elections occurred four years later, Öpik was committed to win. He spent four years touring the UK, building up his support base and speaking at numerous constituency dinners and events. Öpik also stood down from his federal posts in order to concentrate on the election.

The Federal Presidency election of November 2008 saw a three-way contest between Baroness Scott of Needham Market, Lembit Öpik and a political novice Chandila Fernando. Whilst Öpik had by far the biggest national profile, he failed to gain the support of the majority of MPs, Lords, activists and councillors. Even within the Welsh party, many of the Welsh councillors and their leaders, Assembly Members (Black and Williams) and Lords Roberts, Thomas and Baroness Walmsley backed Scott. Although Öpik got the backing of Mick Bates and Jenny Randerson and his three fellow Welsh MPs, this could not compensate for the fact that he was unable to gain the support of many of the elected Welsh Liberal Democrats of whom he had until recently been the leader. When the votes were counted, Ros Scott had gained 20,736 votes (72%) compared to Lembit Öpik's 6,247 (22%) votes and Chandila Fernando's 1,799 votes (6%). Öpik had, to all appearances, now gained a media career but lost his opportunity to lead his party.

The Party Continues to Develop its Policy

Following the 2003 Welsh Assembly elections, the party continued to be tied into the federal party, much more so than its Scottish counterpart. For federal policy issues, because of the fact the Federal Policy Committee made policy for England as well as Britain as a whole, Wales still needed to be represented in this. After 2001, Roger Williams represented the MPs, Jenny Randerson, the AMs and the former MEP Peter Price, the elected Welsh members. As part of the policy creation process, they had been involved in the Federal Policy Review set up by Charles Kennedy entitled *'Meeting the Challenge (2005)'*. But what exactly was the Welsh Liberal ideology that could feed into this 'Challenge'?

During a period of reflection, the party had gathered all of the respective party members together in mid-Wales in April 2004 in a 'What do we stand for?' day. Although the meeting failed to come up with any definitive answers, referred to as 'the golden bullets', it started a process of self-reflection which would continue for the rest of the decade. The reflection, however, never fully succeeded in identifying a central ideology that could differentiate the party from its opponents in Wales.

New federal money meant that the Welsh party was able to have a full-time policy officer based in Wales. Policy creation in Wales overall was now directed by Dr Michael Woods, an academic from Aberytwyth University who had also been the agent for Ceredigion. As opposed to previous decades, policy creation was now a serious business and attendance, particularly by senior elected Welsh Liberal Democrats, was frequent.[66] This helped the party to professionally develop its policy and, at the 2005 Autumn Llandrindod Wells conference, they consulted the wider membership on key issues. These entailed: continuing education; schools; rural communities; housing and health. At the following year's Wrexham Spring conference, the conditions set were for the basis of any Assembly coalition. These were the introduction of STV for local government and provision for local income tax to replace the council tax.

This Autumn conference in most people's mind was prominent not for the main issues of policy, but for two other reasons. Firstly, heavy snowfall on the Sunday meant that most delegates left and struggled to find their way home, leaving the conference floor all but deserted. The second reason was that the party had been split over a motion requesting the ending of compulsory worship in schools. The party was split broadly between its youngest student members and the older elected members, MPs, AMs and Lords. The debate was one of the most heated the party had had since merger. It was the vote, however, which caused controversy. There were four separate votes held but on each vote those against the motion were able to get more supporters into the hall, until the motion was decisively rejected. The party learnt from this manipulation of the vote and amended its Standing Orders to ensure that, in future, the doors would remain closed when a vote was called.[67]

The Party Comes to Grips with Opposition in the Assembly[68]

For the first year after the Welsh Assembly elections, the Welsh party had to get used to opposition. It also had to be wary of condemning Labour party policies that it had helped initiate when it was in coalition. With Labour AM Peter Law's expulsion from the Labour party, following his candidature against the Labour candidate in Blaenau Gwent, the electoral arithmetic in the Assembly changed from 30:30 to 29:31. Labour were once again in a minority government. From the 2005 general election onwards, the opposition parties and Peter Law forced the Welsh Assembly government to make changes on a series of its policies starting with rail infrastructure and school repairs. The 2005 draft budget was rejected in plenary, and from then onwards, the Assembly government was forced to negotiate with the opposition over its budgetary plans.

The first major government defeat occurred on 24th May 2005 when the Assembly members voted by 30 to 29 in favour of a Welsh Conservative motion not to introduce top-up fees for students in Wales. The vote came just two days before the publication of a second Rees Commission report outlining future student funding options, which recommended top-up fees for Welsh students. The defeat meant a major rethink of the Labour administration's higher education funding policy. Even more importantly, it meant that the Welsh Assembly government could be defeated whenever the opposition could unite on a common purpose. In future, Labour Assembly government defeats often appeared to be as much about embarrassing the Welsh Assembly government, as they were about issues of principle thus:

- On the 11th of October 2005, a successful Plaid Cymru motion ordered Labour to postpone the merger of the Welsh Language Board with the Assembly Government. Some eight months later the Labour administration abandoned plans to abolish the Welsh Language Board until after the Welsh general election in May 2007.

- On the 1st of February 2006, the Welsh Assembly Government was defeated in a vote over plans to change how Arts bodies in Wales were funded.
- On the 20th of June 2006, in an opposition vote on an inquiry into the funding of the Welsh Ambulance service, the Welsh Assembly Health Minister, Dr Gibbons, who had led the debate against the motion pressed the wrong button and voted for the change, and the former Health Minister Jane Hutt failed to show up. Labour lost the vote by 28 to 26 in favour of an inquiry.

The Welsh Liberal Democrats were also now able to exert behind the scenes pressure on the Welsh Labour Executive. Negotiations between the Executive and Opposition over issues ranging from the budget to simple matters of policy review now occurred. An era of 'pork barrel politics' had arrived in Wales with parties or even individual AMs able to get their own interests rewarded in order to enable the Welsh Executive to stay in power.[69]

It was not just their fellow Opposition members that the Liberal Democrats in the Assembly were speaking to on better terms than ever before. It was also their own Westminster MPs. After the 2005 general election, the Welsh Assembly Members and MPs, whose relations had at times been frosty, started to flourish. They now made sure that they knew who was responsible for specific policy issues to make sure that they would no longer contradict or replicate each other on matters of policy. MPs and AMs now met two to three times a year on 'away days', with some of the six Welsh Lords also attending. As proof of this new found partnership co-operation, over the new Government of Wales Bill (in partial response to the Richard Commission), both the Assembly and Westminster members were effective in pushing forward the party's own federal agenda with both sides putting through the same amendments. In the end, however, the only real Westminster influence the party had on the Bill was in the Lords where the stalemate over the electoral system was finally broken by the Labour government conceding on one clause. This concerned amending the D'Hondt formula for setting up committees in the Assembly, which would have meant the Liberal Democrats would have been denied a presence at all but the largest committees. The amendment now meant that the Liberal Democrats would get at least one place on all committees, provided they were able to keep their existing six Assembly seats.

The Blaenau Gwent By-elections

On the 25th of April 2006, the independent MP and AM for Blaenau Gwent, Peter Law, died from cancer. Law had left the Labour Party in protest at its policy of all-women candidates' shortlists at the 2005 general election and had managed to overturn Labour's 19,000 majority. Within a short while, his wife had decided to stand for the Assembly seat, and his former agent, Dai Davies, stood for the Westminster seat. The by-election date was set for the 29th of June and the object for the Welsh party was to maximize the vote in those council seats it already held and in those it hoped to win in the 2008 council elections.

The party's two candidates were a local councillor, Stephen Bard, who had fought the seat at the last general election. Bard stood for the Westminster seat. Amy Kitcher, who worked for Mike German, stood for the Assembly seat. Bard finished a very distant third on 7.5 per cent and Kitcher with 5.4 per cent in fourth place. Both, however, had managed to save their deposits, which the Conservatives were unable to do in both elections, and Plaid Cymru was unable to do in the Westminster election. Still, it was the Conservatives who were to bring surprise news to the Welsh Liberal Democrats and the wider political world. On 19th June, the Welsh party's runner up in the Swansea West constituency in the previous year's general election defected to the Conservatives. Rene Kinzett defected in full view of the press with Conservative Party chairman Francis Maude MP and senior members of the Welsh Conservative Party present in Abertillery, as they campaigned in the Blaenau Gwent by-elections. Until his defection to the Conservatives, Kinzett had been on the party's approved list for the South Wales West region Assembly election. He was the highest profile Welsh Liberal Democrat to defect to the Conservatives since, Emlyn Thomas, the former General Secretary of the Welsh Liberal Party had done so the early 1970s. At the time of Kinzett's defection, there was intense speculation that many others would soon follow but, in the event, none did. A year later, long-serving Carmarthenshire Liberal, Juliana Hughes, defected to the Conservatives, but she was just one defection rather than the many that had been predicted.

The Welsh General Elections 2007

With the forthcoming introduction of the Welsh Assembly's new law-making powers and other changes occurring, the Assembly had the appearance of being a more powerful legislative body. To reflect these changes the Welsh Assembly election became known as the 'Welsh General Election'. After the 2004 and 2005 election successes, the party was more confident of the future. It was looking forward to using the new primary law-making powers of the Welsh Assembly. Policy, at all its conferences since its Wrexham conference of March 2006, had been determined with the new primary law-making powers in mind.[70] The manifesto was shaped by the policy committee under Michael Woods, Assembly Members, (specifically Mike German) and its policy officer Dewi Knight who collectively helped to professionalise the document.[71] Entitled: *A Fair, Green Future* it had to compete with the other parties in Wales in what became something of a 'Dutch auction' of manifesto promises including gifts such as free lap tops for school children and even providing four-year-olds with their own toothbrushes. The Welsh party, however, avoided what it saw as the gimmickry of these 'give-aways' and concentrated instead on what it saw as a large number of tangible and aspirational policy objectives. The party aimed to gain at least eight seats in 2007.[72] Their campaign slogan was 'Trust in Wales', but the question many candidates were asking was could 'Wales trust in them'? In addition to their existing list and constituency seats, they anticipated gains in Ceredigion and Swansea. On top of the constituency gains, the party hoped to gain more regional list seats including an additional seat for the Assembly leader Michael German's wife, Veronica Watkins, in his own list constituency, South Wales East.

Welsh Liberal Democrat electoral strategy moved away from the tactic of 'give us your second vote' to 'give us both of your votes', combined with targeting of council wards.[73] The optimism concerning PR and the party benefiting from the second vote of Labour supporters had now vanished after the bitter disappointment of the 1999 and 2003 elections. The Welsh Liberal Democrats had also never benefited much from the protest votes often enjoyed by their English counterpart. The electoral strategy was now on a local level, so campaigning issues also revolved more around issues in constituencies or even individual council wards. It was now a case of saving the local hospital or post office rather than focusing on national or international issues, such as Labour's record on the Iraq war.[74]

The Welsh party had never been so prepared for an election or so well financed as it was for the 2007 Welsh general election.[75] Mike German had managed to secure £100,000 from the Joseph Rowntree Reform Trust for the campaign. Money was no longer the same problem it had been in previous elections. In addition, the party's internal organisation was now more professional in Wales than it had been at any time since the 1900s.

The 2007 Welsh General Elections

	Constituency	List
Liberal Democrat	3	3
Labour	24	2
Conservative	5	7
Plaid Cymru	7	8
Peoples Voice	1	0

However, considering all of the preparation and effort, the Welsh Liberal Democrats had a depressing third Welsh Assembly election result. The same six members who were elected in 2003 were returned once more. It was good news in that the party had suffered no losses, but bad in that there was no new blood into the Assembly group. The party felt a pervasive sense of failure draw across it. The 3rd May elections initially raised the heart beat of Welsh Liberal Democrats. Throughout the election night, rumours spread across Wales of the party winning new seats – Newport East (Ed Townsend),[76] Ceredigion (John Davies), Swansea West (Peter May) and even Pontypridd (Mike Powell)[77] where the party had just two councillors. For the list members, Black and German, the advance in the Swansea West and Newport East vote, for a time, threatened to deprive them both of their own list seats and challenged their own choice to stand on the list, rather than in a constituency. Yet as the night drew on, it became apparent that projected constituency gains were in fact all going to be good second, rather than first places. In the other constituencies across Wales, it was mainly the usual story of poorly positioned third or fourth placed candidates. In Islwyn,[78] Llanelli[79] and Ynys Môn it was also a case of lost deposits. Hope for the party to advance then shifted to the list seats, some of which were not to be counted until all the results had come in on the Friday morning. It was thought that the proportional top-up list would provide the party with one or two extra seats. In South Wales East, Veronica Watkins failed to join her husband Mike German by some 2,000 votes. Before the last constituency result was declared in South Wales Central, the party was '98.5 per cent confident' that John Dixon would be their first Welsh Liberal Democrat list member there.[80] The strong Conservative showing, however, in the Vale of Glamorgan, where they almost won the seat was transferred to their list vote. Dixon lost out by 836 votes. The nightmare had come true for the Welsh Liberal Democrats. They had remained static on six seats once again.

The Luck Goes to Welsh Labour

The Welsh general election, as in that British general election of 2001, showed remarkably little change. Labour had avoided meltdown, mainly by the luck of being on the winning side of some new marginal constituencies. Five Labour seats now had majorities of less than 1,000 votes. By gaining two lists seats in Mid and West Wales to compensate for their three lost constituencies there, they were only three seats worse off than when the Assembly had dissolved earlier that month. They had gone down from 29 to 26 seats. Labour even made one constituency gain in North Wales. Here it gained Wrexham from the independent and former Labour MP and AM, John Marek. Wrexham was also a Liberal Democrat hopeful. Bruce Roberts got 16.7 per cent there, but this put him in the fourth position, behind Labour, Marek and the Conservatives. Distressingly for the Welsh party, this was the best result for them in North Wales, where on the list result, Elinor Burnham with just 7.4 per cent of the vote, narrowly escaped being beaten by the far right British National Party, which had gained 5.08 per cent.

Randerson, in Cardiff Central and Williams, in Brecon and Radnor, had retained their seats with over half of the vote. In Montgomeryshire, Mick Bates still looked secure on his 39 per cent of the vote but his percentage of the vote had dropped by nearly 10 per cent since 1999, making the seat a two-way contest with the Conservatives. To add insult to injury, in Montgomeryshire, Bates's Conservative opponent and nearest rival on 30 per cent of the vote, Dan Mumford, had previously been Alex Carlile's researcher and Chair of the Montgomeryshire Liberal Democrats. In Islwyn, another former Liberal was also doing well. Kevin Etheridge who had left the party in 2003 and now stood as an Independent and gained 28.2 per cent of the vote and had become the main challenger to Labour in a seat in which the Liberal Democrats lost their deposit.

Plaid Cymru had a good night, vote-wise and seat-wise, coming second overall with its number of elected AMs, winning seven constituencies and eight lists seats (three more than in 2003). They beat off the Welsh Liberal Democrat challenge in Ceredigion. For the Welsh Liberal Democrats, this meant that, despite John Davies' tremendous efforts, Plaid still retained a substantial majority of 3,955 votes (13.1%). This result only added still further to the party's general post election gloom.

The Welsh Party Splits Over Whether It Wants Power

As soon as the poor election results were known, Peter Black called upon German to step down and for the party to have a leadership election. There was, however, little wider appetite for a leadership election. Instead, attention was focused on what the party might do in any coalition arrangement. German had talks with all the other party leaders to see what was possible. On 17th May 2007, in Llandrindod Wells, the Assembly Group met together with the National Executive Committee (NEC). The Assembly Group voted by four-two[81] to end discussions with Labour and go into formal negotiations with Plaid Cymru and the Conservatives. The wider NEC then endorsed this decision, although the Welsh Leader Lembit Öpik did not attend because of his television appearance on *Have I Got News for You,* which caused a lot of frustration amongst his colleagues. There was no appetite to go back into a coalition with Labour as most members felt that Labour's quick rejection of the Richard Commission, and its wider failure to consult or compromise in the previous Assembly, had made it impossible to work with them again. There was also a widespread feeling amongst the party's key activists in councils that it was in Labour seats that the next gains would be made. The party, therefore, it was felt, should not prop them up in the Assembly and once more be accused by Plaid Cymru and the Conservatives as being 'Labour's little helpers'.

The following week, the AMs, MPs and NEC met once again in Llandrindod Wells on 23rd May. This time, it looked at the policy document for the combined 'Rainbow Alliance' (Conservatives, Welsh Liberal Democrats and Plaid Cymru): *The All-Wales Accord.* In the meeting, half of the NEC believed that the Accord was too weak to form the basis of an agreement. The NEC voted on it and subsequently tied nine votes to nine votes. There was nothing under the party's Standing Orders to state would happen if the NEC tied. The process was therefore suspended. An exhausted Mike German informed the press that the party 'would return to constructive opposition'.[82] At the same time, he organized a press conference for the next day to announce he was to step down as leader as soon as possible. The next morning, however, 20 conference representatives spoke to Stephen Smith (the Welsh party's Chief Executive) and Ian Walton (Welsh party's administrator) and requested that the Special Conference be set for that weekend; it had been called off the night before, but was reconvened and the potential for a deal was back on. German then cancelled his resignation press conference.

Welsh Liberal Democrats' conference committee chair, Elgan Morgan, issued a statement on Thursday afternoon: "Under the party's rules, it is now up to conference committee to arrange such a conference".[83] This it rapidly did and on Saturday, 26th May, in the Metropole Hotel in Llandrindod Wells; in the glare of the BBC and ITV television cameras, the party held a special conference. Every MP, AM, council leader and Welsh Lord, with the exception of Lord Hooson was present. Rob Humphreys successfully steered the debate. Over three hours, 54 speakers debated whether or not to approve of the policy document that had been negotiated with Plaid Cymru and the Conservatives. For every speaker in favour, there was a speaker against. The party was not split on its normal urban-rural basis but right across the board. Only the four council leaders were unanimous in their support for the deal. Three of the four MPs were against the deal whilst only Öpik was for. Two of the Welsh AMs, Black and Williams, were against the deal. As for the Welsh Lords, the former Welsh party leaders Livsey and Carlile were also against. The debate was generally good natured, although Livsey was booed for some of his anti-coalition remarks and Öpik was slow handclapped for talking for too long after his allocated two-minute slot.

When the votes were cast, 125 conference representatives supported the deal, with 77 against. As far as the Liberal Democrats were concerned the deal was back on the agenda. This hiccup, however, was enough to ensure that there would be no future rainbow coalition. Within weeks Plaid Cymru had struck a separate deal with the Labour Party and it was this Red-Green Alliance that would dominate the Assembly politics for the next four years. The Welsh Liberals Democrats seemed destined to remain in opposition for another term. The eventual result, on the one hand, pleased those at local government level who had dreaded the prospect of another Lab-Lib coalition prior to the 2008 council elections. It also pleased those constituency members in Mid Wales who were equally fearful of a coalition with Plaid and the Conservatives damaging their electoral chances in any forthcoming general election. It did not, however, please the party's Assembly leader, Mike German, who didn't relish another four years in Assembly opposition and the ending of perhaps his last chance to be in government.

At the Westminster level in July 2007 Lembit Öpik received a promotion and became Shadow Secretary of State for Business, Enterprise and Regulatory Reform in Ming Campbell's federal shadow cabinet. This was particularly gratifying for him, having survived the publicity turmoil concerning his personal life that had broken at the start of the year. Roger Williams now became the new Shadow Secretary of State for Wales, with Lord (Martin) Thomas as Shadow Attorney General of the Welsh Liberal Democrats. The Welsh Liberal Democrats now had their strongest presence in the federal party's shadow cabinet for over a decade, although they still held none of the more prominent positions in Cabinet, such as those of Shadow Chancellor or Home Secretary that those in the Welsh party had held a century ago.

At the party's 2007 Autumn Conference, Öpik announced he was going to step down as Welsh party leader and concentrate on his federal presidency leadership bid. At the same time, Mike German, amongst much internal and external leadership speculation about his future, announced that he too would step down but in the Autumn of 2008, as the Assembly leader. In that year's Welsh party leadership election, German was nominated unopposed as the Welsh leader and was duly made leader without a vote being cast. The other members of the Assembly group, who had been quietly and sometimes openly critical of German's leadership, had decided to wait another year until German stepped down before throwing their own hats into the leadership ring. The Welsh Liberal Democrats were now united under one leader across all levels of elected representation for the first time in their history. The leadership also had passed from Westminster to Cardiff Bay, signalling that the Welsh state party's power base had finally fully arrived in the Welsh capital. The party had survived the possibility of a damaging split after its poor Assembly results, but with both Öpik and German signalling their plans to step down from the central control of the Welsh party, its future remained as uncertain as ever. At the same time Rob Humphreys also stood down as the party's president and was replaced in an election by Christine Humphreys (no relation), the former AM for North Wales, who was now making a return to active politics.

The 20th of December 2007 saw the party gain a new chief executive, Joanne Foster. Stephen Smith had left earlier in the year and the party had since then been run on a caretaker basis by Mark Soady. The 27 year old Foster became both the youngest and the first female chief executive of any state Liberal Democrat party. She had extensive previous experience in the party, working first as a case worker for Peter Black, then as a researcher for Michael German and finally as the lead

Welsh Liberal Democrat negotiator with the Labour Party in the aftermath of the 2007 Welsh general election. Foster was the third chief executive that the party had had that decade. In previous decades, the party's lack of resources had meant that chief executive or general secretaries came and went with the variable finances of the party. The fact that the Welsh party had now managed over a decade to orchestrate such an orderly succession of chief executives showed how much its finances and professionalism had improved.

A New Federal Leader from Campbell to Clegg

Before the Welsh party was to get its own new leader, the news broke that the federal leadership was also going to change. On Monday, 15th October 2007, to the shock of many of his colleagues, the federal leader Sir Menzies (Ming) Campbell resigned. The party had continued to remain low in the opinion polls and the media continually raised his age and health as twin concerns during his leadership. Despite the fact that Campbell was only 66 and was in good health, he continually had to defend himself as being young enough to continue his role in the post. Campbell had never been close to the Welsh party and some members of the party, notably Peter Black, had already called on him to resign and allow somebody else to come in and restore the party's fortunes. Despite this, however, there had been no attempts to remove him from inside the party, as there had been with Charles Kennedy.

There were only two MPs who entered the leadership contest. Neither was from Wales nor did they have any tangible Welsh connections. For the first time since 1988, both challengers were from English constituencies. Chris Huhne represented Eastleigh and Nick Clegg, Sheffield Hallam. Both had been elected in 2005, were former MEPs and journalists and Huhne had already been in one leadership contest in 2006, in which he had come second to Sir Menzies Campbell. Both, since 2006, had been undertaking their fair share of Welsh constituency dinners and fund raisers. This meant that they were well known by many in the Welsh party. For the first time in a federal leadership contest, Michael German declared himself for one of the contestants, Nick Clegg. Most of the other elected Welsh members also endorsed one of the two candidates, the majority were for Clegg. Mick Bates, Eleanor Burnham and Roger Williams were the few exceptions to this and backed Huhne. Öpik, with his previous misfortunes in backing candidates, and with his eye on the forthcoming federal presidency elections, didn't endorse either of the candidates. The main Welsh hustings were held in the Marriott Hotel in Cardiff and were attended by around 500 Welsh and English members from South and West Wales and the Bristol area. Chaired once more by the party's outgoing President Rob Humphreys, it was a lively affair lasting some two hours.

On 18th December, Clegg won narrowly by 20,988 votes to the 20,477 votes cast for Huhne. Over the next year Clegg would put Roger Williams, Öpik and Willott in prominent positions in his Shadow Cabinet. Clegg was 40 when he was elected as leader, making him the youngest leader of the Liberal Party in its history. A year later the Welsh party would also make history with a new and even younger leader.

The Party Shifts Its Political Power to the Council Chambers

In the Autumn of 2007 there had been considerable speculation about a snap general election called by the new Labour Prime Minister, Gordon Brown. The Welsh party hastily imposed candidates across Wales. In the event, however, Labour took a dip in the opinion polls and the election was postponed. The Welsh Assembly had had their own election the year before, and now thoughts moved towards the council chambers in Wales. In the May elections, for the first time since the 1920s, the Welsh Liberal Democrats would be defending their leadership of four major authorities (Bridgend, Cardiff, Swansea and Wrexham). With the party now firmly out of power in the Welsh Assembly, the emphasis for the implementation of its own policies was now transferred on to the Welsh council elections.

After the elections on 1st May, only a handful of authorities had one political party in charge; none of these would be solely Liberal Democrat controlled. There were now only four out of 22 councils controlled by just one political party; before the elections there had been eleven. This lack of one party control represented a new departure for Welsh politics. Never before, had so many Welsh local authorities been labelled by the title of 'no overall control'.

For the Welsh Liberal Democrats, these were the best council elections for some ninety years. There were now Liberal Democrats councillors on 20 of the 22 councils (only Caerphilly and the Vale of Glamorgan stood out against the trend). There were, importantly, Liberal Democrat groups of four or more councillors on 14 of these 22 authorities. In North Wales, the party made slight gains or losses of one or two seats per authority. In Wrexham, where they had led the authority before the elections, they lost two seats but were comforted by Labour losing nine seats, making them the largest political party on the authority, with Aled Roberts once more leading the authority. Amongst the biggest surprises of the night was the party gaining six seats in Merthyr Tydfil, a place they hadn't held a council seat since 1900. For more than a century, this had been a local government black hole for the party.

In Powys, some 32 of the council's 73 single member wards saw councillors return unopposed. The Welsh Liberal Democrats represented five of this number, the Conservatives, one. The rest were Independents who, as before, controlled the county council. In what was their Welsh Parliamentary stronghold, the party remained stuck on 15 seats, with some gains and some unfortunate losses. The county's group leader and Liberal stalwart, James Gibson-Watt, lost his Hay-on-Wye seat to the Conservatives. Gibson-Watt had been the backbone of Welsh Liberal and then Liberal Democrat politics for almost three decades in Brecon and Radnor. His loss, together with that of another senior group member, David Peter, removed the heart of the county's political group.[84] At the same time the Conservatives, without a seat in the county prior to these elections, gained nine seats. Six of these were in Lembit Öpik's Montgomeryshire seat, signalling potential problems for him. Ceredigion saw the party gain one seat to sit on ten. Importantly for the party and its incumbent MP, Mark Williams, was the fact that Plaid Cymru failed in its ambitions to gain control of the county (it gained three seats to sit on 19, needing three more to gain outright control). In addition, William's Plaid Cymru opponent at the next general election, Penri James, was beaten by the Liberal Democrat and well known Europhile, Paul Hinge, which boosted the party's morale locally. Importantly for the party in both Ceredigion and a number other authorities in Welsh speaking Wales, the party was also now getting Liberal Welsh speakers elected. They were able to project the party's message effectively through the medium of Welsh, an ability the party had frequently lacked over the last few decades. In Ynys Môn, Aled Morris Jones became the Chair of the council and in Ceredigion, Mark Cole helped re-establish the party's Welsh language credentials there later, as Mayor of Cardigan.

In the large urban authorities, where the Liberal Democrats led the councils before the elections, there were mixed results. In Cardiff the party, on 35 seats, remained three short of an overall majority in an election which saw the Labour party almost reduced to the fourth party – in a council which they had controlled with a large majority until 2004. This put the council once again under a Liberal Democrat led coalition headed by Rodney Berman. In Swansea there were three Liberal Democrat gains, which put them on 23 seats, but at the same time there were only two Labour losses (making them the largest party with 30 seats). This meant that, once more, there would be a Liberal Democrat-led coalition with Chris Holley as leader. The party also advanced in Newport, where it won nine seats and took joint control of the council with the Conservatives, with Ed Townsend becoming the Deputy Leader. In Bridgend, Labour gained five seats. Two of these losses were Liberal Democrats, which then put Labour on 27 seats and back in charge of the council. This removed Cheryl Green as the party's only female council leader.

These council elections had been important for the party for two reasons. First, they had shown that they could retain control, albeit in coalition in Wales' three main cities Cardiff-Newport-Swansea, plus the urban area county of Wrexham in North Wales. The second reason was that the party had continued to move forward incrementally and, in the process, gain a presence in nearly every Welsh local authority. After the stagnation of the 2007 Welsh Assembly elections, this provided the Welsh party leader Michael German now with a fine local government legacy to pass on to his successor, when he eventually stood down at the start of December 2008.

The Welsh Leadership Election 2008

The end of 2007 had seen the Welsh party with a female chief executive, Joanne Foster, and a female president, Christine Humphreys. It was now time to have a female party leader.[85] The contest would be between Kirsty Williams and Jenny Randerson. This was the first time in both the Welsh and federal parties' history that an all female contest had occurred. For Wales, it would also be the first election contest that would lead to the appointment of a woman as leader for any of main Welsh political parties. A decade before, when Christine Humphreys and Michael German had fought for the Welsh Assembly group's leadership, the party had not wanted to have a long and drawn out election contest, fearing it would damage its forthcoming Assembly election contests. With no general elections on the horizon this would not be the case.

Both Williams and Randerson had been opposed to each other in the previous year's debate on whether the party should join a rainbow coalition with the Conservatives and Plaid Cymru; Williams had been against and Randerson, for.

Still, in the event, this would receive little mention in the campaign. In the second week of September 2008, Kirsty Williams announced publicly her intention to contest the Welsh Party's leadership. Over the next six weeks Williams gathered an ever larger number of supporters, which included the Welsh Lords, Carlile, Livsey and Roberts, the MPs, Mark and Roger Williams, and the Assembly Members Mick Bates and Peter Black. Williams was also able to gain the support of the Swansea council leader Chris Holley and Newport deputy leader Townsend. Randerson, on the other hand, waited until Michael German had officially resigned as party leader on 3rd November at the Welsh Liberal Democrats' Autumn conference in Clydach. It was only after that that Jenny Randerson launched her own leadership campaign. Randerson was able to gain the backing of the MPs Jenny Willott and Lembit Öpik, plus the former federal party President Simon Hughes. She was also backed by the Assembly Member, Eleanor Burnham, and the council leaders, Aled Roberts in Wrexham and Rodney Berman in Cardiff. Michael German supported neither candidate, although his wife Veronica endorsed Kirsty Williams, for whom she had previously been a researcher and remained a close friend.

The only notes of real hostility that occurred during the campaign concerned the age of respective candidates. Randerson supporters noted that Kirsty, at 37, lacked the experience of their candidate. After all, Randerson had not only her council and Assembly experience but also the government experience of serving as acting Deputy First Minister. Conversely, Williams' supporters, aware of the recent election in the USA, detected a public preference for a younger political leader. There the younger Barack Obama, 47 years old, had recently beaten the much older 72 year old John McCain. Williams styled herself with '…the vision to succeed – A leader of the 21st century'[86] on her leaflets, whilst Randerson also portrayed herself with '…the vision to lead … the experience to deliver'[87] and also the 'candidate for change'.

Hustings for both candidates were held across various places in Wales and members were bombarded with leaflets and phone calls by supporters of either camp. In the event, it was Williams who won the battle to become the new leader of the Welsh Liberal Democrats. She won by 910 votes to 612, on the 8th December. In the process, Williams became the first woman ever to lead a major party in Wales and a Liberal Democrat state party. As Williams set about writing a new chapter in Welsh Liberal Democrat history, the period covered by this book has come to a close. The outcome of Williams' period as party leader will now have to await the record of the future.

Kirsty Takes the Helm

Due to the number of Williamses, not only in the Welsh Liberal Democrats but also throughout Welsh politics, Kirsty Williams was soon commonly known by her first name, rather than the surname traditional to politicians. Kirsty's period in office was soon to see changes in the party, not least at the Welsh Assembly. Although it wasn't predicted at the start of Kirsty's period in office, her time would see an almost total change in the Welsh Liberal Democrat Assembly group. Over the next three years, only Peter Black would remain to support her from the group of six AMs that had surrounded her in the previous decade.

How did Kirsty Change the Leadership?

Kirsty set about reshaping the party as a prelude to commencing that ever cherished dream of a Welsh Liberal revival. A substantial electoral shift was needed in order to advance from their relatively small political base in Wales. As had been apparent during the leadership election campaign, she and her supporters believed, in part, that this revival could be brought about by her relative youth and vigour compared to that of the older generation that led Wales' other political parties. This would also be supported by her acknowledged political oratory skills. It would now therefore a case of letting the voting public become fully aware of who she was and what she had to offer. Then the party believed that the voters would start voting from them *en masse*.

On the 18th April 2009, Kirsty gave her first leadership speech to the Welsh party conference at the Angel Hotel in Cardiff. By way of an introduction to her address, the party's delegates were shown a three minute musical slideshow of pictures of Kirsty in campaigning action and with her family. This type of leadership promotion was a marked contrast to German's own leadership style, which had avoided the 'leadership cult' element. The concept of establishing Kirsty as a political product was common practice with the federal leadership but new to Welsh party politics, with the exception of Öpik's self-promotion in his spell as leader. The more overt leadership promotion may also be explained by the differing electoral background of the two AMs. German represented the regional list spread across 8 constituencies, in which AMs normally maintained a low individual constituency profile. Kirsty, on the other hand, represented a constituency seat in which the personal vote was essential for the Liberal Democrats to win it. The same projection of personality was therefore now projected to the wider party and media. Those running the party now believed that, if it worked for Kirsty in Brecon and Radnor, then the same tactics could also be applied to the rest of Wales.

Despite projecting herself within the party in her conference speech, she also told the membership that it was 'time to move away from spin and sleaze in politics'. This attack was aimed at both the Labour Westminster government and Labour-Plaid Assembly government and proved popular with her conference audience. The banking crisis of the previous autumn had left the country with a massive budget deficit, which would have to be tackled in order to avoid economic bankruptcy. Even during the UK's boom times, however, the Labour and Plaid Cymru record on the Welsh economy had been poor. Wales had now become one of the poorest regions not only in the UK but also in Western Europe. This economic record would also now be one of Kirsty's central plans of attack on Labour.

Pledging to reverse the decline in the Welsh economy was a broad policy aim which would take some years to fulfil, should the party once again hold office. There was one pledge, however, that was both short-term and popular with Liberal Democrat supporters, particularly with students. Kirsty pledged to scrap tuition fees for Welsh students.[88] At the coming elections the Welsh electorate would record their own verdict on the Labour governments at Westminster and Cardiff, but they would also do the same on Kirsty's and her fellow AMs and MPs pledge to scrap tuition fees. It was this small populist pledge that would soon drive the party's electoral fortunes.

European Elections 2009

At the same Welsh Liberal Democrat Spring conference that Kirsty had pledged to scrap tuition fees for Welsh students, the federal leader Nick Clegg declared that he was "determined" to push Labour into third place at the European elections in June.[89] The Welsh Liberal Democrats, just like Liberal Democrats across the rest of the UK, were committed Europeanists. This meant that in their hearts they were committed to winning in the European elections, but their previous track verdict of failure meant that there was little expectation of a win within the party.

The selection for the candidates for the June 2009 European elections did not occur until May/June 2008. This late selection was much to the annoyance of those going through the selection process, who felt that this was far too late to develop a strong campaigning platform across the whole of Wales.[90]

There were four candidates for the European elections: Alun Butt Philip,[91] Kevin O'Connor, Nick Tregonning and Jackie Radford. When the STV count for a position on the party list took place in early July 2008, Butt Philip received 40 per cent of the first preferences, and together with O'Connor, went through into the run off for top of the list. In this second count, Butt Philip was elected and duly selected as the party's lead candidate for the European elections.

The Welsh party was keen to use the European election, in part, as a preparation for the forthcoming Westminster and Welsh Assembly elections. This meant that the party organisation in Cardiff was very supportive from July 2008 onwards. The Welsh AMs, MPs and peers engaged actively in the campaign. In addition, there was support from a number of the party's federal heavyweights. There was one visit by federal leader Nick Clegg to Newport East, three visits by shadow chancellor Vince Cable (Newport, Swansea and mid-Wales) and one by Shadow Home Secretary, Chris Huhne to Swansea West. There was also a visit by Paddy Ashdown to Newport East and it was to him that the responsibility for the financial appeal to the Welsh party's membership for donations to the European elections also fell.

Despite Ashdown's financial appeal there was, however, as always a lack of funding for the campaign. At the federal level UK level, the party's campaigns department refused to give Wales any special help, as it lacked the necessary track record of success in this area. Any funding they did provide was reserved for the Westminster target seats in Wales. This meant that Butt Philip had to raise a lot of the election funding himself. The Welsh Liberal Democrats put aside £10,000 of their own budget for the Euro-elections; Butt Philip in turn spent £15,000 of his own money and raised a further £8,000. He was also able to find one or two wealthy Welsh donors and also persuaded former Welsh leader Lord Carlile and Welsh party chair John Last to help gain further funding. The bulk of the spending, however, came from the Federal Campaigns' department budget for key Welsh parliamentary seats and from the constituencies themselves. The result of all of this fund raising was that the party spent some £82, 533 on the campaign.[92]

The federal strategy of concentrating on the ten or so most winnable Welsh constituencies was also endorsed by the Welsh party organization. This strategy was not, however, fully communicated to the constituencies who were still expecting a centrally organised free post election leaflet. They did not become fully aware of that that they would have had to fund their own leaflets until late January 2009. This left

Butt Philip in the position of having to get the additionally funding to put the leaflets out in these seats. In the end some 32 out of 40 constituencies put out electoral addresses. Although this was better than the fifteen or so seats that had put out leaflets it 2004 it was still not a full Welsh coverage.

At the start of May, with a strong candidate in Butt Philip, a significant degree of funding, the decline of the Labour vote, and a committed campaign team, the candidates and some within the party were hopeful that they could now wrest a Euro-seat for Wales, for the first time. Then, in that same week, *The Daily Telegraph* starting publishing details of MPs' claims for expenses. Although the most outrageous and fraudulent expenses claims were all from Conservative and Labour MPs or peers, the Liberal Democrats were also hit by the voter backlash and the transfer of voter support to the smaller parties. Therefore it was the UKIP candidate, John Bufton, whose party had spent less than half of the Liberal Democrats Welsh on the campaign who gained a European seat from Labour in Wales.[93] When the results were fully out on the 8th June, it was clear that Butt Philip had come fifth in Wales, with just 0.2 per cent of the vote more than in 2004 and some 14,000 votes behind the fourth placed UKIP.[94] The anti-European party, UKIP, had defeated the pro-European party, the Liberal Democrats.

In the post campaign review undertaken by Alun Butt Philip, the Welsh party's chief executive Jo Foster and campaign manager Jon Aylwin, some key factors for the failure became apparent. These were that that their campaign had been weakened by the very late selection of the party list and by the lack of a campaigning base in most Welsh constituencies outside of the target seats. There was also feedback from the federal party, whose campaigns department had informed the Federal Executive in July 2009 of their 'regret' regarding their failure to appreciate how good the prospects had been in Wales and therefore there had been a miscalculation in not targeting the whole of Wales.[95] The disappointment about not winning a European seat once more was felt throughout the Welsh party to be something of a further setback.

The Lead up to the 2010 General Election

To summarise, Kirsty had failed in her first major objective of winning a European Parliamentary seat. In the period that followed the party's electoral record did not improve. They failed to win any new council seats or even retain those where their members had stood down. Both she and the Welsh party were now looking for the general election to bring a change to the party's fortunes in Wales. The period prior to the election had been dominated in part by the huge boost in the opinion polls that the federal leader – Nick Clegg – appeared to be giving the party. Clegg's strong performance in the national televised leadership contests boosted the Liberal Democrats' showing in the polls considerably. On the 18th April 2010, *The Daily Telegraph* published a poll showing that the party was on top of the poll with 33 per cent and they were predicting the Liberal Democrats would win 134 seats across the UK.[96]

It was Kirsty who led the campaign in Wales with the occasional supportive visits by Clegg. Roger Williams, the Welsh Westminster leader played a much more subdued role leaving the centre stage to Kirsty.[97] The Welsh party's manifesto – *Manifesto of Fairness for Wales* – was closely linked with that of the federal party's.

As its name suggests, it emphasised the key aims of fairness in taxes, the economy, fairness in cleaning up politics and giving a fair chance to children. The most Welsh aspect was the commitment to give an extra £125 million green economy stimulus package to 'boost the Welsh economy'.[98]

The General Election 2010

The general election was most notable in Wales for depressing the Labour vote to its lowest share since 1918 and in a period of new leadership. It saw an overall swing to the Welsh Liberal Democrats of 1.7 per cent (20.1% of the Welsh vote) and it meant that there were no lost deposits. For the party, it was their best share of the vote in Wales since 1983.[99] It was the Conservatives, however, who made the gains in Wales, winning five seats, four from Labour and one from the Liberal Democrats. For the Welsh Liberal Democrats the message was mixed across Wales, with some seats experiencing slight falls for the party, such as Bill Brereton in Delyn with a 2.4 per cent drop, and Rob Speht who was second in Swansea East, experiencing a 1.8 per cent fall in his vote. Elsewhere, there were significant rises in the party vote such as Kay David in Caerphilly (4.5%) and Martin Blakebrough in Monmouthshire (6.6%) experiencing significant swings towards their party. Disappointingly for the party it also meant no new seats in Wales and one significant loss – that of Montgomeryshire.

The General Election of 2010 in Wales

Labour	26
Conservative	8
Liberal Democrat	3
Plaid Cymru	3

In Ceredigion, Mark Williams was defending a slender majority of just 219 votes. Williams, however, had chosen not to make a national figure of himself within the party and instead concentrated almost solely on building up his profile in the constituency. For his main opponents, Plaid Cymru, this was one of their key target seats. Their candidate Penri James was ineffective in seeking to restore his party to the seat and saw Williams's majority grow to 8,324 on a 13.5 per cent swing. Williams took half of the total vote. This was the best result for a Liberal in this seat since 1959.

In Brecon and Radnorshire, despite there being a strong Conservative opponent, Suzy Davies, Roger Williams was able to make a small 1.3 per cent rise in his vote and also saw a 0.3 per cent swing to him from the Conservatives. Roger now enjoyed a substantial 3,749 votes (9.6%) majority over the Conservatives, making this the first time in two consecutive Westminster elections that the party had enjoyed such a substantial majority in the seat.

In Cardiff Central, Jenny Willott saw a significant 8.4 per cent fall in her vote. This was caused in part by a surge of support (12.3% rise) in the Conservative candidate Karen Robson's vote and, perhaps more ominously for the future, a 1.4 per cent swing from the Liberal Democrats to Labour's candidate Jenny Rathbone. There was also a strong belief, in the seat by the Welsh Liberal Democrats, that Rathbone had been chosen in part to capitalize on the fact that her name was so similar to that of the well-known AM Jenny Randerson. Despite these reversals, Willott still enjoyed a substantial 4,576 votes (12.7%) majority in the seat, making it the second safest Welsh Liberal Democrat seat.

The Liberal Democrats Come Close but Not Close Enough

In a number of seats, the Welsh party had a series of electoral swings that did not quite reach the winning post. The foremost of these were:

- Swansea West, where Peter May saw his vote rise by 4.3 per cent but failed by 504 votes (1.4%) to take the seat off Labour. The Liberal Democrat defector Rene Kinzett now standing for the Conservatives also saw his party's vote rise by 4.8 per cent, which may well have damaged May's chances of gaining the seat.
- Newport East, where despite a 8.5 per cent swing towards him Ed Townsend failed to take the seat off Labour's Jessica Morden by 1,650 votes. In the process, depriving the party of its first parliamentary win in Newport since 1918.
- In the South Wales valleys the party was achieving some of its best results since the 1920s. Mike Powell in Pontypridd received an 11.2 per cent swing but still ended up 2,785 votes behind Labour's Owen Smith.
- In Merthyr Tydfil, a seat where the party had come second on a number of occasions but normally with less than 15 per cent of the vote, Amy Kitcher recorded a 17 per cent swing to finish 4.056 votes behind Labour's Dai Havard, on 31 per cent of the vote.
- In North Wales, Wrexham, where Tom Rippeth had come second in 2005, was seen as the party's main chance of a win. It was there that the party concentrated its North Wales' resources. In the event, however, despite a 9.2 per cent drop in the Labour vote there was only a 2.2 per cent rise in the Liberal Democrat vote. Although Rippeth was still second, he remained 3,658 votes (11.1%) behind Labour and now only marginally ahead of the Conservatives who had seen their vote rise by 5.4 per cent.

After May 2010, the party was now in contention for more seats in Wales than it had been since the 1980s but it was still, as it had been in the past, the party of missed opportunities and well-placed runner up positions.

Öpik Loses Montgomeryshire

In Montgomeryshire, Lembit Öpik, saw a 13.2 per cent swing away from his party to the Conservatives. It was by far the largest swing against the Liberal Democrats in Wales. His vote share of 50.3 per cent fell to 37.8 per cent, at the same time as his Conservative opponent Glyn Davies's rose to 41.3 per cent from 27.5 per cent in 2005. This now gave Davies a majority of 1,184 (3.5%) over Öpik. Davies had stood for the seat previously and had been the Regional Assembly member for Mid Wales, establishing his office in the constituency. Since losing his list seat in 2007, he had concentrated his efforts on the parliamentary seat and building up his own reputation of a solid constituency member. Thus his style was seen as a marked contrast to celebrity form of politics, which was often seen as being symbolic of Öpik's own style.

Far from appearing to be bitter or angry, Öpik was gracious in his defeat but was clearly surprised by it. Speaking to BBC Wales shortly after his defeat, he said:[100]

> "I leave this job with a faith – a very strong spiritual faith which I have developed quite recently and thanks to many people in the constituency – but also a faith in people and human nature, and finally a faith in the liberalism which got me into politics in the first place, which I have sought to represent as best I can in this constituency and which continues unabated as the strong, deep liberal strain which characterises Montgomeryshire. Perhaps it was my brand of politics which people weren't too keen on. Perhaps it was a big surge to the Conservatives."

The following night Öpik made a 'painful' appearance on *Have I Got News for You* in which he was plainly still in shock from his defeat the previous day.[101] Öpik would leave Welsh politics forthwith and not be seen again at Welsh party functions. His politics and show business career would now be centred on London or on various reality shows.

Apart from losing a parliamentary seat, that had historically been the safest Liberal seat in the UK, the Welsh party was also losing its longest serving and most high profile and experienced MP. Öpik was someone who may have been able to play a more central role in the events that were just about to occur in the post election period. For a number of senior members in the party, however, Öpik's loss was also greeted by a feeling of relief that the party would in future be able to project its own image more strongly than the lifestyle of just one of its politicians.

The Party Goes into Coalition Again

Post election, leading Welsh Liberal Democrats aired their views on why the party had not made the breakthrough that their share of the votes indicated it should have. Alex Carlile advocated a full review of party policies to see why they had failed to gain sufficient votes at the end of the election. Whilst Peter Black decried the over-confidence that had gripped the party with 'Cleggmania', which had made them believe they could win so many seats. This had, in turn, taken their eyes off targeting the most winnable seats.[102] While the party was still licking its political wounds, however, the overall UK election indicated that no one political party in the UK could form a government in its own right. For the next week, there were heated and often frantic discussions between the federal party leadership and Conservative and Labour parties. In the end, it was the federal party's decision to join in a coalition with the Conservative party. Unlike previous coalitions, however, there would be no Welsh Liberal Democrat representation at the senior level. This was to be purely a Scottish and English Liberal Democrat run coalition. Although those in the Welsh Liberal Democrats did not oppose the coalition, they remained very much on the side lines. Soon, however, these new developments would start to impact on all of their fortunes, whether they were minsters in the new government or not.

Tuition Fees – Resignation

As we have already noted, the Welsh Liberal Democrats played no real central role in the coalition government. Jenny Willott, however, became the parliamentary private secretary to Liberal Democrat Energy Secretary, Chris Huhne, in the Westminster government. Although it is not a paid ministerial post, a parliamentary private secretary is regarded as the first step on the ministerial ladder and therefore an important one for any aspiring politician. Willott was therefore the only Welsh Liberal Democrat with any position in the new coalition government but this was not to last for long.

During the general election campaign, Willott along with most other Liberal Democrat candidates in Wales and England signed public pledges against tuition fees for university education. Once in government, however, the Liberal Democrats, as part of the new coalition abandoned this pledge and instead set forward plans to allow universities in England to charge up to £9,000 per year for students. The U-turn marked a dramatic reversal in fortunes for the party in the UK, as the electorate decided to punish the party for what was seen as a 'betrayal' of one of their key electoral promises. Although higher education, including student fees had been devolved to the Welsh Assembly and was no longer the responsibility of Westminster, the Welsh electorate did not distinguish between education policy in England and Wales.

Willott represented Cardiff Central, a seat where the student vote had been vital in winning in 2005 and 2010. Her fellow Welsh MPs Mark and Roger Williams remained politically committed to vote against student fees. At the same time her constituency party, and Nigel Howells, who was standing for the Assembly seat also stood resolute against fees. During the period leading up to the Westminster vote on tuition fees, Willott avoided all public speculation on the issue. On the night of the vote, 9th December 2010, Willott, feeling the overwhelming pressure of holding a student constituency, resigned, and two Welsh MPs voted with her against student tuition fees. Willott was one of three ministerial aides to resign that night, but the coalition government won the vote by just 21 votes.[103] This was the first post war resignation of a Welsh Liberal Democrat in a ministerial post, albeit the most junior one. While it removed Willott from the government, the symbolism of resignation had no immediate impact on improving the Welsh party's flagging electoral fortunes.

Michael German Becomes a Lord

Shortly after the general election the Welsh party gained a new member of the House of Lords. Michael German knew some time before it was actually announced on 28th May 2010 that he was to be ennobled. He had had to wait however until the general election was over and the new government was ready to declare the new set of peers. The result was that on the 30th June, Lord German left the Assembly and finally arrived at Westminster.[104] This was some 27 years after he had fought the Cardiff Central seat, coming third but paving the way for Jenny Randerson to win the seat in 1999. German's new role saw him take himself out of the mainstream of Welsh politics and into the UK wide role of the coalition government and, in particular, the area of 'Work and Pensions'.

It was Mike German's wife Veronica (nee Watkins) who took his place as the regional Assembly Member. Veronica had been active in Welsh and UK Liberal Democrat politics for the previous two decades, as we noted earlier in the chapter. Recently, she had been the organiser for the Newport East seat in the general election and the constituency manager for Mike while he was an AM. Veronica was also a long time supporter of Kirsty Williams, who was soon to hear some sad news concerning her own political mentor Lord Livsey.

The Death of Richard Livsey

Whilst the party's newest Welsh peer Lord German was finding his feet in the Upper Chamber, one of its most well respected peers, Lord Livsey, died suddenly. On 15 September, aged 75, the victor of the 1985 Brecon and Radnor by-election passed on. Livsey had not only been the Brecon and Radnorshire MP, but he had also been the very backbone of the Welsh party for much of its recent history.

Hundreds of family, politicians and friends from all political parties gathered for Livsey's funeral at St Gwendoline's church, Talgarth on 26 September 2010. There it was apparent that he had gained wide respect across Wales and Westminster in his life in politics. It was also evident that his political colleagues, and the wider Welsh Liberal Democrat party, were in shock at his sudden death. Until recently he had appeared to be in robust health, preparing himself for the forthcoming federal conference and also gearing up for the ongoing referendum on primary powers for the Welsh Assembly. His sudden death was therefore wholly unexpected.

When Livsey had been selected as the candidate for the Brecon and Radnor seat, he spent much of his time successfully dealing with the splits in the local party. He had kept the Brecon and Radnor Liberal Democrats focused and united from that time onwards. He had successfully helped get Kirsty Williams elected in 1999 and then handed over the seat to Roger Williams in 2001. As the various obituaries pointed out, although some in and outside the Welsh party regarded him as a weak political speaker, there were very few who did not like him personally or admire him as a political operator. As the BBC Wales political affairs correspondence, Vaughan Roderick noted:[105]

> His great achievement was to make us think of Powys as being the Liberal heartland, because it wasn't before Richard Livsey. Montgomeryshire was, Brecon and Radnorshire wasn't.

The fact that he had been able to transform Brecon and Radnorshire as the third strongest post war Liberal constituency from one in which the Liberal party had been almost moribund there for the decades prior to his arrival, illustrated once more how the party's fortunes could be shaped by one person.

How had Livsey Remained Such a Dominant Figure in Liberal Politics?

From 1985 until his death in 2010, Richard Livsey had been a central figure in the Welsh party and also in the wider Liberal Democrats in Westminster. His 21 years in Westminster politics make him one of the most successful post-war Welsh Liberals. His continued success came about due to three main reasons:

The right man for the right seat. Richard Livsey with his Liberal pedigree, proven commitment to Welsh devolution and Welsh causes, background in farming and family connections to the seat appealed greatly to the constituency's electorate. With his wife Rene, the two soon appeared to the wider world and, more importantly, to the constituency voters as if they had been living in the constituency all of their lives. It was also his knowledge of and compassion for agriculture, just like that of his political mentor Geraint Howells, that made him prominent in national politics.

Fortunate timing of the 1985 by-election and the previous boundary changes. The constituency boundary changes that occurred prior to 1985 had removed many of the Labour support voting areas. This made the seat more marginal politically. The electorate that remained now rejected the traditional choices of Conservative and Labour in the seat and instead choose an alternative candidate from the Liberal-SDP Alliance – Livsey. Once he had established himself there and portrayed himself and the party as winners, he established a tradition of the Liberal Democrats being one of the main contenders for the seat.

A MP who became known to all. To maintain, what was for three elections a highly marginal seat, Livsey had to ensure that he was well known and respected. In a constituency that was the largest in England and Wales, he would spend his time going from one end to the other ensuring that he not only dealt with all constituency case work but also attended as many social and festive occasions, campaign groups meetings, public tasks and even funerals as possible. It was through this tireless amount of public engagements that he was able to gain the substantial personal vote that ensured, in 1997, that he was able to finally end the marginal status of the seat. Livsey also engaged fully in the public life of the constituency. He was a Trustee of the Campaign for the Protection of Rural Wales, Vice President of the Hay Literature Festival, Chairman of the Brecon Jazz Festival and a member of Talgarth Male Choir, to name just a few of the bodies he supported.

Only three and a half months before Richard Livsey's death, the mid Wales Liberal Democrat bastions of Brecon and Radnor, Ceredigion and Montgomeryshire had looked as strong as ever. Now with Öpik's departure in Montgomeryshire and Richard Livsey's death in Brecon and Radnorshire, the mid Wales Liberal dominance seemed to be weakening.

Bates Declares his Retirement and Montgomeryshire Selects a New Assembly Candidate

On the 18 February 2010, the Montgomeryshire Liberal Democrats selected Wyn Williams as their candidate for the next Assembly election. Williams was a local businessman and farmer who was standing for the first time for the party. His main opponent, as ever, in the seat would be the Conservatives. In 2008, they had won nine county council seats in the constituency, as opposed to the Liberal Democrats' two. Liberal Democrat strategy had often been to build a strong council base and then advance forwards to win the parliamentary seat. Now this was being done by the

Conservatives in Montgomeryshire. As the Conservatives were growing stronger in the seat the Liberal Democrats, it appeared, were growing weaker.

Mick Bates' Fall from Grace

At the start of June 2009 Mick Bates announced publicly that he would not be standing again for the Montgomeryshire seat but would be retiring from politics. This was the reason that Wyn Williams had been selected as the new candidate for the following February. Events would soon, however, mean that Bates would be leaving the Liberal Democrats far sooner than he or the party had imagined.

On the evening of 20 January 2010, Cardiff paramedics were called to assist Bates when he fell down some stairs and was knocked unconscious, suffering head injuries, at Charleston's Steakhouse in the city centre. In the series of events that followed Bates became violent and assaulted the paramedics.[106] It would be almost a year before the full trial came about and a verdict was given. During that time Bates operated outside of the Welsh Liberal Democrat group, as Montgomeryshire's first independent Assembly member. Mike German had to take over his front bench responsibilities from the start of February.[107]

Bates told the court he had no recollection of the alleged incident and brought forward expert witnesses to verify this claim. Despite this evidence, he was still found guilty of three common assault charges and three public order offences. Although the judge took into account Bates' previous good character when sentencing him, the magnitude of the crime was enough to ensure a hefty fine.[108] District Judge Bodfan Jenkins fined him £4,250, ordered him to pay £600 compensation, £625 costs and a victim surcharge - making a total £5,490.

This affair had already proved damaging to Bates personally, ending in disgrace the career record which until then had been that of a good constituency Assembly Member. It had impacted on Öpik's re-election and had, as yet, done untold damage to the party's image in Montgomeryshire. Kirsty Williams reacted to the news swiftly by declaring that despite his successful constituency activities and party record:[109]

> "The Welsh Liberal Democrats are clear that this conviction for a public order offence is incompatible with the high standards we expect of our elected representatives. Proceedings have begun to terminate his membership of the party."

Bates, however, resigned his membership before the party had even begun to start these proceedings. In the process, he became the first post-war Welsh Liberal legislative member to lose the party's membership whilst still in office. Montgomeryshire had now lost both of its elected Liberal Democrat members in less than a year.

The Selection of the Assembly List Members

Two of the existing regional list members, Peter Black and Veronica German, were reselected for their respective lists without any difficulty. Both had become well known and popular with local party members and did not face any serious challenge. In South Wales Central, the process went smoothly. John Dixon, the seasoned campaigner and Cardiff council cabinet member took the top slot with Eluned Parrott taking the number two position. Parrott had been the party's candidate in that year's general election in the Vale of Glamorgan, enjoying a two per cent rise in the party's vote there.

On the October 25, 2010, the Mid and West Wales region selected their regional list candidates. It is a region that contains the key Liberal Democrat seats of Brecon and Radnor, Ceredigion and Montgomeryshire. As a result, it had always been the region least likely to return a list member. With the Liberal Democrats already sinking substantially in the polls from that May's election, however, there was speculation that it could be different at the elections occurring in seven months time for the Welsh Assembly. Top of the list was Powys county councillor William Powell, the Liberal Democrat Powys councillor for Talgarth since 2004. Powell had stood for the Pro European Conservatives in the 1999 European elections. Shortly after that, as the Conservatives drove out many of their own pro-Europeans, Powell, like a number of others, went over to the Liberal Democrats. In 2007, he had also topped the Welsh party's list, but the electoral mathematics resulting from their success in Montgomeryshire and Brecon and Radnor, meant Powell stood no chance of winning. Since then he had become one of the Welsh party's committed Liberal Democrat campaigners with a track record of supporting winning parliamentary candidates. The same could also be said of the second on the list, Councillor Mark Cole, the Mayor of Cardigan that year and also one of the youngest councillors in Wales. Cole came from the renowned Aberystwyth University Liberal stable that had produced so many of the party's activists over the last century.[110]

It was the North Wales regional list selection, however, that produced the greatest surprise. Here the Wrexham councillor leader, Aled Roberts, defeated the incumbent AM, Eleanor Burnham. In a region where only one Liberal Democrat was likely to be elected, this result was the first post war selection defeat of a sitting Liberal member by the constituency membership. Roberts was a former solicitor from the village of Rhosllanerchrugog, who also came from the Aberystwyth University Liberal stable.[111] Roberts was the council leader in Wrexham and also one of North Wales' most prominent Liberal. Burnham had originally been selected as the number two on the North Wales list for the first Assembly elections. Now three elections later, she was back in that same position.

Randerson Becomes the First Welsh Liberal Democrat Peeress

In November 2010, it was announced that Jenny Randerson would be following her former Assembly colleague Michael German into the House of Lords. Both had unsuccessfully fought Cardiff Central for the House of Commons seat, but despite this setback, both would now be in Westminster, albeit it in the House of Lords. Randerson was the first female Welsh Liberal parliamentarian ever to sit in the House of Lords. Those Welsh Liberal peeresses, who had gone before her, had died before women were allowed to enter the House of Lords.[112]

Randerson's arrival in the Lords strengthened the Welsh team there after the recent death of Lord Livsey. At the same time, however, it removed another senior Welsh Liberal Democrat from Welsh politics at a time when it became apparent that such figures may be more needed than ever.

The Welsh Liberal Democrats
and the Assembly Powers Referendum

For well over a century, the Welsh Liberals had sought to have a law-making parliament established in Wales. The Welsh Assembly Government set up a commission under Sir Emyr Jones Parry (All-Wales Convention) in 2007 to oversee the practicalities of the electoral referendum. The Welsh party's nominee was the former Welsh party president, Rob Humphreys. There was another Liberal Democrat on the commission as well. Nicholas Bennett, a former party vice president, was also nominated as a public appointment for his roles as chief executive of Community Housing Cymru and his service as a member of the Welsh Language Board. Even without these two Liberal Democrats, there was already cross-party support for the Liberal Democrats' notion of now having a full law making parliament for Wales, albeit without the criminal law making powers still desired by the party. On the All-Wales Commission, all of the other political parties were now in favour of primary law-making powers for the Welsh Assembly. It was no surprise therefore when the All-Wales Convention reported back in November 2009 to state that the Assembly in Wales should be given full law-making powers in its devolved areas through a referendum.[113]

Tired of the lengthy and ineffective existing primary law-making powers, which meant protracted procedures within the Westminster Parliament, there was no longer any real desire to keep the Assembly as an executive body within any of Wales' main political parties. Therefore, for the first time, the Liberal Democrats joined not only the Labour Party and Plaid Cymru in supporting primary law making powers for the Welsh Assembly, but also with the Conservatives. In the subsequent 'Yes for Wales' referendum campaign, led by Labour's Leighton Andrews (a defector from the Liberal Democrats), Rob Humphreys was the Welsh party's central representative on the steering group, with Jo Foster the party's chief executive being the other representative.

As in the 1997 referendum, the Welsh party concentrated on bringing out the 'Yes' vote in its areas of strength. These were mainly the target constituency seats for the forthcoming Welsh Assembly election. The Labour Party was also using the referendum, in part, as an exercise in marshaling their activists for the forthcoming Assembly campaign. Humphreys, and the Welsh party, had to try and stop the 'Yes' campaign also using the unpopularity of the coalition government's cuts as a campaigning tool. They prevented both Clegg and Cameron's portraits being used on leaflets as 'bogey men' for the 'Yes' supporters.[114] Although some of this anti coalition message did get into the campaigning, on the whole, the campaign remained harmonious between the Welsh Liberal Democrats and the other parties. When the final result came in on 4th March, it was a resounding victory for the Welsh Liberals' long cherished aims of establishing a Welsh law-making parliament. On a voter turnout of 35.4 per cent, some 63.5 per cent of voters had voted Yes. Only 36.5 per cent had voted No. Devolution had evolved once more and now seemed to be fully accepted by the majority of the Welsh population. The Welsh Liberals' Spring conference was held on the same day as the referendum result was announced. So the party's activists who had taken part in this successful referendum campaign could bask temporarily in the glow of this significant success.

The Alternative Vote (AV) Referendum
and the Party

Unlike the Assembly's primary powers referendum there was little overt activity or even that much enthusiasm for the Yes campaign in the Alternative Vote referendum on 5 May, within the Welsh party. While it was true the party's Lords, namely German and Roberts, were keen advocates of the AV, across the rest of the party there was widespread indifference. This was perhaps due to the fact that the AV referendum clashed with the date of the Welsh Assembly elections and the additional factor of the Welsh party having already been through the primary powers referendum of the Welsh Assembly two months before. In some places in Wales the party put out pro AV literature either with its own Assembly election literature or separately. Many of the Assembly candidates had also publicly backed the Welsh Electoral Reform Society's campaign and posed for the appropriate photo calls at the party's spring Cardiff conference in this respect. The campaign played second fiddle however to the forthcoming Welsh Assembly elections.

When the results came out they revealed that every county in Wales had overwhelming rejected AV. This news appeared to be of little concern to a Welsh Liberal Democrat party that felt itself to be struggling for its very survival in the Welsh Assembly elections. Thus the AV referendum, unlike the referendum in March soon became forgotten as the party sought to cope with the consequences of the Welsh Assembly election results.

Welsh General Election 2011

In the Welsh party's leadership election of December 2008 Randerson had pledged to double the number of the party's AMs at this Assembly election.[115] Luckily for Kirsty, she had made no such pledge and as the opinion polls put the party in Wales constantly on between seven and nine per cent of the vote, this appeared to be wise political foresight.

The cross party consensus that had kept the interparty political campaigning during the Assembly powers referendum did not last more than a few hours after the results were declared. At the party's Cardiff conference, the same day as the result, in the Angel Hotel in Cardiff, a Welsh TUC anti-coalition cuts rally had attracted some 1,500 supporters and blocked the road. There was heavy security and a strong police presence at the conference, not only because of the protesters, but also because the party for the first time since the 1940s was host to its own Westminster Cabinet

Ministers in the form of the Deputy Prime Minister, Nick Clegg and the Business Secretary, Vince Cable. Despite the public unpopularity of the two figures, they were both received warmly by the Welsh Liberal Democrat audience. In fact, so cordial was the conference and such little disagreement was apparent on the conference platform, there were some complaints in a fringe meeting by party members that the party needed to avoid the impression of being so 'stage-managed'.[116]

Clegg had declared that Kirsty and the party in Wales was 'attempting to start a new age in Welsh politics'. In part, by 'doing it their own way'.[117] The party then displayed a list of the hopeful seats they hoped to both hold and gain, building on the large rise in their vote from the previous year's general election. These were:

Brecon and Radnor
Ceredigion
Cardiff Central
Merthyr Tydfil
Montgomeryshire
Newport East
Pontypridd
Swansea West

In addition, they planned to keep at least one member for the regional list seats for North Wales, South Wales West and South Wales East. If all of these seats were gained, the Welsh Liberal Democrats would have 11 seats in the Welsh Assembly, one less than Randerson's planned doubling of the seats from 2008.

The signs did not look as promising for the Welsh Liberal Democrats as they had the year before. When voters were asked, after the 2010 general election, how they would vote in the next Assembly elections, the predicted Liberal Democrat vote in Wales fell from 20.1 per cent to 15.7 per cent.[118] The party was therefore well aware, that as had occurred at every Assembly election, they would lose at least a quarter of their general election vote. In addition, as always with the Welsh Assembly elections, the problem of a weak Welsh media and the dominance of the Westminster political scene affected the party's fortunes in Wales. Whereas in 2010 the party in Wales had ridden high in the polls, riding on the back of Nick Clegg's popularity, now the opposite was true. As Clegg's popularity plummeted, so did that of the Liberal Democrats. As previously noted, the Welsh opinion polls showed the party in Wales on between 7 and 9 per cent of the vote.[119] Less than half of what they gained in 2010. This led to concern within the Welsh party that they could be reduced to less than three Assembly members, the minimum needed to be recognised as a group within the Welsh Assembly.

Kirsty launched the party's manifesto in Aberaeron on the 13 April 2011, focusing media attention on Ceredigion rather than Cardiff. This was an attempt to boost the party's prospects in the Ceredigion seat. A similar tactic had been used by the party in the 1970s and 1990s, when it had been trying to regain the seat there. Now it was being used to try and gain the Assembly seat from Plaid Cymru. In the launch, Kirsty set out pledges on reducing wasteful expenditure in the Welsh NHS, creating a fund to train unemployed people and decreasing the education spending gap between England and Wales. The Labour–Plaid Cymru Welsh Assembly government, in turn, were attacked for their failure on the Welsh economy and their ignoring 'Welsh issues'.[120] The Welsh media, however, discovered a number of spelling mistakes in the English and Welsh versions of the manifesto, including incorrect spellings of the Welsh words for 'Environment', 'Sports' and 'Politics'.[121] This undermined or perhaps highlighted the party's message about literacy levels in Wales at its own expense.

Welsh General Election 2011

	Constituency	List
Labour	28	2
Conservative	6	8
Liberal Democrat	1	4
Plaid Cymru	5	6

The party also lacked the fiscal resources it had enjoyed at the 2007 Assembly elections. As they were now seen as a party of government rather than opposition, due to the coalition with the Conservatives at Westminster, they were denied the substantial funding that had previously been made available to them in Wales by the Rowntree Foundation. What limited funding they did have, was now was used to support the campaign in Mid Wales (Brecon and Radnor, Ceredigion and Montgomeryshire) and Cardiff Central. Elsewhere the party had to rely on its own resources, which meant that a number of Welsh constituencies, where the Welsh party's fortunes were normally low, in any case did not even receive constituency leaflets.

The Election Night

The fact that three ballots had to be sorted out on election night meant that most of the counts were considerably slowed down (AV, constituency and list ballots). North Wales didn't even start counting ballots until the Friday morning. Just as they started counting a clearer picture was emerging across Wales of what had happened to the rest of the party. It was one of greatly reduced fortunes. In seats where the party had been a strong second place the year before, such as in Wrexham, Newport East and Swansea West, the same candidates plummeted into poorly placed third positions behind both Labour and the Conservatives. The party lost 17 deposits, its highest number since 1979. Its vote in some constituencies such as Blaenau Gwent was as low as around one vote in every sixty counted. At times during the election night, the Liberal Democrats in Wales feared almost total meltdown. They needed at least three assembly members in order to remain as a party group in the Welsh Assembly. That was therefore their bottom line.

It was only in Brecon and Radnor, where Kirsty won with a comfortable majority of 2,757 votes (9.73%) that the party retained a secure result and won a constituency. The hopeful wins of Ceredigion and Montgomeryshire, into which the party had poured its scant resources, saw no breakthroughs. In Ceredigion, Liz Evans achieved a swing of 3.51 per cent from Plaid Cymru, but still remained 1,777 (6.11%) behind them in second place. In Montgomeryshire, Wyn Williams saw a 9.50 per cent swing to the Conservatives', Russell George, giving them a 2,324 (10.13%) majority. This was now the second time that the seat had been lost to the Conservatives.

In Cardiff Central, until now, a strong Liberal Democrat seat, Nigel Howells lost by just 38 votes (0.16%) There was a massive 14.74 per cent swing from the Liberal Democrats to Labour. Jenny Rathbone had now reversed Jenny Randerson's victory of some 12 years previous. In a seat, which had a large student population, there seemed to be a large scale vote to punish the Liberal Democrats for their part in the endorsement of student fee increases.

Yet, despite the constituency losses, the Liberal Democrats were able to keep five of their previous total of six seats. In South Wales West, Peter Black managed to hang on by 54 votes, in Mid Wales, the strong Liberal Democrat showing in their three target seats helped William Powell win a list seat there. In North Wales, Aled Roberts, a former solicitor, restored the Welsh Liberal – legal professional link after a gap of 14 years by winning a seat on the list. In South Wales Central, although Nigel Howells had lost the Cardiff Central seat, his close friend and council colleague John Dixon, became the new Liberal Democrat list member. Only in South Wales East, did Veronica German fail to win by just 127 votes, out of the 181,000 votes cast in the region. German's defeat, after less than year in office, left South East Wales as the only region in Wales without an elected Liberal Democrat Assembly member.

Across the rest of the UK, on the same day, the Liberal Democrats suffered heavy council losses. In Scotland, the party was almost wiped out at the Scottish Parliamentary elections. Wales seemed to have been spared this wholesale slaughter. It seemed as though a mixture of targeted campaigning and the list system had come to the rescue of the party. Peter Black called it 'the great escape' and put the survival of the party partly down to the fact that Plaid Cymru's vote had also fallen by 3.7 per cent, less than the Liberal Democrats 4.2 per cent fall, but, nevertheless, enough to help the Liberal Democrats secure their list seats.[122] Whatever the reasons, the Welsh party was for once fairly happy with its final result being a loss of just one seat.

The Welsh Liberal Democrats Relief did not Last Long

The five newly elected Liberal Democrats got only as far as the first vote to elect the new presiding officer, when things began to go seriously wrong. John Dixon and Aled Roberts had to step down as soon as it emerged they were members of organisations that the National Assembly Disqualification Order (2011) did not allow them to be part of. John Dixon was a member of The Care Council for Wales and Aled Roberts was a member of the Valuation Tribunal for Wales. The membership exclusion was there to prevent members of certain organisations having any conflict of interest in the Welsh Assembly. Initially, the pair and the party expected them to be readmitted to the Assembly following a vote to override the exclusions of the Act. The party put forward a motion to this end, but it soon became evident that the opposition would not support such a motion. The party and the individuals then had to wait a series of police and Assembly inquiries as to whether the two members actions had been deliberate attempts to mislead or had been due to ignorance of the law.[123]

After almost two months of deliberation, the Assembly members accepted Aled Roberts' explanation that he had read the Welsh version of the Electoral Commissions web site in which 'The Valuation Tribunal for Wales' was not included. John Dixon's explanation that 'The Care Council for Wales' had already removed him from their board before he took office, was not accepted. Dixon was removed as an Assembly Member and the number two on the list, Eluned Parrott, a community engagement manager for Cardiff University was elected in his place. Parrott had now beaten both of the Cardiff main runners and in the process helped reverse some of the gender imbalance of the new Welsh Liberal Democrat Assembly group, which had been 80 per cent male.

The whole episode, as well as being distressing for the individuals, had made the party seem amateurish in its approach to elections. Especially, when it emerged that a number of other candidates, who could have been elected, including Wyn Williams in Montgomeryshire were also members of ineligible bodies. It also showed the partisan nature of Welsh Assembly politics at its worst, with opposition Assembly members preferring short term political point scoring to allowing effective politicians in to scrutinise the new legislative process. Although Lord Carlile pointed out the Dixon's exclusion could have been legally challenged, the party had neither the finances or desire to do so.[124] The whole saga had left it exhausted.

Conclusion

The period covered by this chapter was generally good for the Welsh Liberal Democrats, after decades in which the party was on the verge of almost total annihilation. At Westminster, they now had parliamentary groups in the Lords and Commons that were larger than at any period since the start of the 1950s. Their MPs and Lords were becoming more prominent nationally, although with Lembit Öpik's personal life, the focus of much media attention, this prominence was not always related to the activities of the party or welcomed by the more senior party members. The Welsh Liberal Democrats had believed that their breakthrough to power would come through proportional representation. To a limited extent this occurred, and thus helped them become Labour's coalition partner in the Welsh Assembly between 2000 and 2003. The party was, however, unable to build on this. This was, nevertheless, their first taste of national power since 1945.

The failure of the Welsh Labour government to pursue the Richard Commission's recommendations, particularly with regard to the enlargement of the number of Assembly Members, was both a significant setback and disappointment for the ambitions of the Welsh party. After going into opposition in 2003, the party began to plan a significant increase in its Assembly Members at the 2007 Welsh general election as a way to position itself as a significant party in any coalition arrangements. Yet the 2007 elections did not produce more AMs. The party subsequently went into a period of self-reflection and loss of confidence, which was instrumental in its failure to become part of the next coalition government. The Welsh Liberal Democrats' failure to progress, on either the Richard Commission's electoral recommendations or in the Assembly elections, resulted in it pursuing new arenas of political power more thoroughly. In turn, German and Öpik stood down as party leaders. Under the two Williamses, Kirsty in Wales and Roger at Westminster, the party entered a period of decline once more. Although it was true that the share of the vote increased in 2010, their number of seats decreased. The party lost Lembit Öpik, who now set his sights on a political and show-business career in London, rather than Wales. No Welsh Liberal Democrat played a central role in this coalition government, unlike previous periods of the Welsh party's history.

After the council elections in 2004 and then 2008, both Welsh politics and the Welsh Liberal Democrats entered a new and unfamiliar era. In a number of metropolitan areas, the party's grassroots had won enough council seats to ensure that they could lead coalition arrangements to control the authorities. These included the nation's capital, Cardiff. The period after 2004, therefore, saw the Welsh Liberal Democrats either leading or part of the leading administration of Wales' three metropolitan cities: Cardiff, Newport and Swansea. With their failure to become part of the post May 2003, 2007 or 2011 Assembly governments, real power shifted within the party, from the Welsh Assembly to the Welsh councils. It was a political force now in its own right, with the power to help improve the daily lives of people that most Liberals of the post-war era could only dream of. Still, despite this Liberal dominance in metropolitan areas, the party across parts of Wales still remained very much either limited to a few councillors or was non-existent. At the same time, the leadership of the Welsh party had transferred once more back to rural mid Wales (Brecon and Radnorshire) with Kirsty Williams from the urban South East of Wales under Michael German in 2008. This was a place where the leadership of the Welsh party had been since the 1940s. Thus, while the party seemed to be going forward with a new young female leader, the power base was also shifting back to the post-war norm. A politician who had never been a member of the pre-merger Welsh Liberal Party or SDP, Kirsty Williams now represented the next generation of Welsh Liberal Democrats in charge of the party's fortunes. Even with this change to a new younger generation of politicians, it was still quite apparent that the party still had a long way to go before it could match the electoral achievements of the Liberal Party of its forebears a century before. It was still the smallest of the four main political parties in Wales and in many areas of Wales seen almost as an electoral irrelevance. It was, however, still there in Wales as a political fighting force, despite all that the opposition parties had done to dislodge them.

Notes

1. Liberal Democrats Wales (1999) Annual Report 1999, p. 9
2. David Laws would become the Liberal Democrat MP for Yeovil in 2004
3. Nicola Davies went onto fight and narrowly lose to Labour in the July 2004 Birmingham Hodge Hill by-election
4. Michael German to author 14/4/04
5. Thomas, Alys (2001) The Liberal Democrats: Losing To Win?, Contemporary Wales, Vol. 14, University of Wales Press, pp. 113–126
6. Ashdown, Paddy (2002) The Ashdown Diaries, Vol. Two 1997–1999, Allen Lane, The Penguin Press, pp. 452–453
7. 'The Project' refers to the agreement between Labour and the Liberal Democrats in 1997 entitled Partnership For Britain's Future. It led to a Joint Cabinet Committee between both parties in the early years of Tony Blair's first New Labour government
8. Pontypridd's two gains were Mike Powell (Trallwn) and Steve Belzak (Cilfyndd). There were a few near misses for long serving local Liberal Democrats including Alan Southgate, who would eventually get elected to the town council as the councillor for Treforest

9. Liberal Democrats' lists for Europe chosen candidates 1998, Liberal Democrats web site
10. Peter Price had also tried for the London regional list but had only managed sixth place out of ten there
11. Juliana Hughes, a Welsh speaker and former teacher and broadcaster, joined the party in 1982 stood for the party continually at elections from contesting the Mid-Wales European elections in 1984 to being the second list candidate on the Mid and West Wales Assembly list in 2007. She chaired the Carmarthen Liberal Association and served on many of the party's internal committees
12. Welsh Liberal Democrats (1999) Election Communication, Welsh European Parliamentary Elections
13. Lord Carlile to author 20/5/07
14. Liberal Democrat News 13/8/99
15. Liberal Democrat interview sources to author
16. Welsh European Funding Office (2001) Objective 1 Guide 2001: The essential guide to the Objective 1 Programme, Western Mail and Echo, Cardiff
17. Liberal Democrats Wales (1998) Conference Agenda, Builth Wells
18. Although in the event Martin Shipton failed to take part in any of the campaign and remained only a paper presence on the ballot paper
19. *Liberal Democrat News* 18/2/00
20. Michael Woods to author 13/6/03
21. *Liberal Democrat News* 28/1/00
22. Michael German to author 12/10/08
23. *South Wales Argus*, 6/10/00, p. 7 stated 100, Michael German to the author 11/8/04, stated that this eventually worked out at 114
24. Lord Carlile of Berriew, Welsh Liberal Democrat Special Conference on the Coalition arrangements in the National Assembly for Wales, 14th October 2000
25. Thomas, A (2003) 'Liberal Democrats', Chapter 12 in John Osmond and J.Barry Jones Ed (2003) Birth of Welsh Democracy: The First Term of the National Assembly for Wales, Institute for Welsh Affairs and Welsh Governance Centre, p. 187
26. Welsh Liberal Democrats (2001B) Annual Report 2001, p. 5
27. Rob Speht to author 7/6/07
28. BBC News 26/9/01
29. Lord Livsey to author 12/6/07
30. Russell, Andrew and Fieldhouse, Edward (2005) op. cit., p. 227
31. Felix Aubel, a church minister, had previously stood for the SDP in the Cynon Valley but defected to the Conservatives a month after the election.
32. Welsh Assembly Government (2000) *Putting* Wales First: A Partnership for the People of Wales, Cardiff
33. The Sunderland Commission reported back in 2003 and recommended STV for Welsh council elections. Something that would have benefited the Welsh Liberal Democrats electorally. The report was quietly dropped after Labour became the sole party of government at the Welsh Assembly, post May 2003
34. Michael German to author 7/4/04
35. Richard Commission, (2004) Report of the Commission on the Powers and Electoral Arrangements of the National Assembly for Wales, p. 265
36. Carlile, Alex MP, Ron Davies MP (1997) Joint declaration on a Yes Vote, 7/3/97
37. Peter Price to author 17/8/04
38. Michael German to author 15/8/04. The only real areas of omission felt by the Welsh party concerned was that it did not go far enough on tax raising powers and did not give the Assembly the ability to borrow money
39. *The Western Mail*, 4/8/04
40. Wales Labour Party (2004):Better Governance for Wales
41. Department for Humanities, Education and Social Sciences
42. It stopped lobbying for the introduction of STV in order to gain a consensus for primary law making power
43. Lord Carlile to author 20/5/07
44. Welsh Liberal Democrats (2003b), second postal list leaflet
45. This figure represented the number of Labour list voters in 1999 in each region.
46. A poll undertaken by Richard Wyn Jones and Roger Scully (2004) in *must plaid lose?* Agenda, summer 2004, Institute of Welsh Affairs, p. 62 gave Iain Duncan Smith a rating of 4.35 as a party leader by the Welsh public with Mike German bottom at 3.5. Although this may also be because German was the least well known of the Welsh party leaders and people felt unable to rate him. Charles Kennedy's rating, who was more prominent publicly, was 4.74

47. German, Humphreys and Öpik to author
48. Rob Roffe in Caerphilly also came perilously close to losing his deposit, which he saved by just three votes
49. Rob Humphreys to author 21/9/04
50. Rob Humphreys to author 21/9/04
51. Electoral Commission (2004) Local elections in Wales 2004: The official report on the local elections 10 June 2004, The Electoral Commission, Cardiff, p. 122
52. Michael German to author 7/4/04
53. The WLGA is the Welsh councils representative body in negotiations with the Welsh Assembly over issues related to local government
54. Deacon, Russell (1998) 'The Hidden Federal Party: The Policy Process of the Welsh Liberal Democrats', Regional Studies, Vol. 32, No. 5, 1998
55. Brian Cossey to author 28/4/08
56. Smith had also been Sheffield City Council Liberal Democrats Researcher/Support Officer (1999–2003) and Cambridgeshire Liberal Democrats County Organiser (1997–99)
57. Ian Walton to author 14/8/07
58. The name referring to fact that it saw itself to be the true alternative to a Labour government, rather than the Conservatives whose ideological 'clothes' were seen as being stolen by New Labour
59. Douglas, Roy (2005) op. cit.
60. Curtice, John (2005) Disappointment or Bridgehead? The Liberal Democrats in the 2005 election, Journal of Liberal History, Issue 48, Autumn 2005
61. One of the strongest supporters of Jenny Willott was her own mother Alison, who'd been a central figure in both the Welsh and Federal party over the previous decade.
62. Paul Brighton had first stood West Flint in February 1974, Alex Carlile had stood in East Flint and between them they had coined the campaign slogan of the 'Carlile to Brighton line'
63. *The Independent* 16/1/05
64. Joan Walmsley later married Martin (Lord) Thomas which made her a 'Welsh peer' by marriage
65. Welsh Liberal Democrat interview sources to author
66. Welsh Liberal Democrat conference reports 2004–2007
67. Ian Walton to author 25/5/07
68. Deacon, Russell (2007) The Welsh Liberal Democrats: From government to opposition and then back again? The Political Quarterly, Volume 78, Issue 1, 2007 pp: 156–164
69. Stephen Smith, Welsh Liberal Democrat Chief Executive to author, August 2006
70. Welsh Liberal Democrat Policy Officer – Dewi Smith to author, September 2006
71. Stephen Smith, Welsh Liberal Democrat Chief Executive to author, August 2006
72. Welsh Liberal Democrat interview sources to author
73. Michael German to author, September 2006
74. Michael German to author, September 2006
75. With the Welsh Assembly gaining new Parliamentary powers the elections to it were now officially referred to as the Welsh general election
76. Ed Townsend, a Newport County Councillor had a journalism and public relations background at senior levels including for BT, the Welsh Liberal Democrats and Cardiff Marketing
77. Mike Powell, a plumber by trade had been a Rhondda Cynon Taff councillor since 1999 and had undertaken a number of roles in the Welsh party previously.
78. Mark Maguire, the Welsh Liberal Democrat candidate, had been the former Labour Mayor of Blackwood and had defected to the party around a year before. Maguire the sole Welsh Liberal Democrat at the count subsequently resigned from the party.
79. The candidate Jeremy Townsend was the son the Councillor Ed Townsend, who was now the main challenger to Labour in Newport East
80. Stephen Smith, Welsh Liberal Democrat Chief Executive to author, May 2007
81. The two were Peter Black and Kirsty Williams
82. BBC News 23/5/07
83. BBC Wales News 24/5/07
84. William Powell a leading member of the European Movement in Wales and a former Conservative now became one of the central campaigners in Brecon and Radnor on Powys County Council
85. The sole male left at the most senior level was Professor John Last, who Chaired the Welsh Party's National Executive. Last, from St Asaph was a former Conservative activist whose considerable skills as a both a fund raiser and an organiser were credited with revitalising the party in North Wales

86. Williams, Kirsty (2008) 'Kirsty Williams the vision to succeed' election leaflet
87. Randerson, Jenny (2008) 'The vision to lead', election leaflet
88. Welsh Liberal Democrats, 21/4/09 Press Release: 'Kirsty Pulls no Punches, Wowing Conference in Debut Speech as Welsh Liberal Democrat Leader'
89. BBC Wales web site news, 17/4/09 'Lib Dems targeting second place'
90. Alun Butt Philip to author, July 2011
91. Alun Butt Philip was a Reader of European Politics at Bath University. This academic knowledge gave him an extensive knowledge of the EU and of the structural funds so important to Wales. He had been a party member since 1957 and although he had not been active in grassroots campaigning in Wales prior to 2006 he was well known by many of those within the Welsh party. Roger Roberts and Richard Livsey (both long standing friends) and Alison Goldsworthy (a former student of his at Bath) had encouraged him to stand in Wales. This wasn't his first election attempt. Butt Philip had stood in successive parliamentary elections for Wells from 1974-1987, and fought the first European election in 1979 in the Somerset constituency. He was also on the list for South-West England when there was the first PR European elections in 1999.
92. Electoral Commission (2010) Expenditure returns for the 2009 European Elections for Wales
93. Electoral Commission (2010) Expenditure returns for the 2009 European Elections for Wales
94. BBC Wales, European Election Results, 8/6/09
95. Alun Butt Philip to author, July 2011
96. *The Daily Telegraph* 18/4/10 'General Election 2010: Lib Dems take lead in new poll', page 1
97. Scully, Roger and Wyn Jones, Richard (2010) 'What happened in the 2010 election?' Wales Governance Centre, Cardiff University and Institute of Welsh Politics, Aberystwyth University, Briefing, 26 May 2010
98. Welsh Liberal Democrats (2010) Manifesto of Fairness for Wales
99. Bradbury, Jonathan (2010) 'Wales and the 2010 General Election', Parliamentary Affairs, Vol. 63 No. 4, Oxford University Press, p. 729
100. BBC News web site, 7/5/10 'Liberal Democrat Lembit Öpik loses Montgomeryshire'
101. BBC News web site, 8/5/10 – 'Have I got news for... former MP Lembit Öpik'
102. Bradbury, Jonathan (2010) op. cit., p. 737
103. BBC Wales web site news, 9/12/10 – Jenny Willott resigns aide post over tuition fees vote
104. BBC Wales web site news, 5/11/10 – 'Ex Gwent AM becomes Lord' South Wales Argus, 30/6/10
105. BBC Wales web site news, 17/9/10 – 'Liberal Democrat peer Richard Livsey dies, aged 75'
106. BBC Wales web site news, 5/11/10 – 'AM Mick Bates "has no memory" of incidents'
107. Grayling-Institute of Welsh Affairs (2010) Assembly Bwletin Cynciilad, Issue 22, February 2010, p. 1
108. North Wales Pioneer, 10/12/10
109. North Wales Pioneer, 10/12/10
110. See previous chapters for details of those from Aberystwyth University, the later list also included Caroline Pidgeon the leader of the Liberal Democrats in the Greater London Authority
111. Welsh Liberal Democrats, 25/10/10 'Strong team selected for North Wales list for 2011 Assembly election.'
112. Women could enter the House of Lords as a life peer after the Peerage Act 1958 and as a hereditary peer after the Peerage Act 1963
113. BBC Wales News web site, 18/11/09 'More powers for Wales'
114. Rob Humphreys to author, 17/7/11
115. BBC Wales News web site, 8/12/08 'Challenges ahead for new leader'
116. Grayling-Institute of Welsh Affairs (2011) Assembly Bwletin Cynciilad, Issue 30, March 2011, p. 3
117. Grayling-Institute of Welsh Affairs (2011) Assembly Bwletin Cynciilad, Issue 30, March 2011, p. 3
118. Bradbury, Jonathan (2010) op. cit., p. 732
119. BBC and ITV/YouGov polls March – April 2011
120. Grayling-Institute of Welsh Affairs (2011) Assembly Bwletin Cynciilad, Issue 30, March 2011, p. 2
121. BBC Wales web site news, 13/4/11 'Welsh Lib Dems sorry for manifesto errors'
122. Black, Peter (2011) "Coalition Positives' Liberator, Issue 346, June 2011, pp. 8–9
123. BBC Wales web site news, 23/6/11, Lib Dem AMs told no action after police investigation
124. BBC Wales web site news, 10/7/11, Lord Carlile says Lib Dems should have fought for AM

EPILOGUE

After reading this book, you may wish to ponder the notion as to whether anything still links the party's beginnings, in Wales, to that of the modern day Welsh Liberal Democrats. It is evident that the party, like Wales itself, has undergone a turbulent and troubled evolution since 1859. The Welsh Liberal Party, at its beginning, was a mass movement, encompassing all classes of Welsh life, but its elected representatives on the whole came from the upper-middle class. They were wealthy, often financially independent individuals, mainly from the professions of law, religion or business connected with the railways, manufacturing, steel, mining and shipping. The Welsh Liberal MPs were also often men, who controlled and ran not only their own affairs, but, at times, the British government and Empire. At a British level over the years, Welsh Liberal MPs held most key positions in the Cabinet and the Liberal Party, including that of its leader. They also, in part, represented the rising of the modern wave of Welsh nationalism. Few of these characteristics could be said to be present in the modern Welsh Liberal Democrats.

The Welsh Liberal barrister MP remained the most constant factor of the party for well over a century. Even this, however, had now passed into history. It took some time to do so. As the party went through its series of splits from 1916 onwards, it would be another 81 years before the last barrister MP, Alex Carlile, stood down and ended the elected link which had been almost always constant throughout the party's history in the House of Commons. During this period every Welsh constituency, at some time or another, gradually became inactive in respect of Liberal activity and thereby severed its direct links with its Liberal past. When the Liberal Democrats re-established the party in these constituencies, sometimes over half a century after the last Liberal Association had been active there, they were reborn as totally new Liberal Associations.

That said, the link between the past and the present has not been completely broken. There is still a shadow of the old Welsh Liberal Party present in the House of Lords. Lords and barristers Thomas, Carlile, and the late Hooson and the Reverend Roberts would not have been out of place in the Liberal Party of Gladstone or Lloyd George. The elected Liberal Democrats in the Commons and the Welsh Assembly, however, now come from different backgrounds to the Liberals of the Victorian and Edwardian periods. They come from the public services, multinationals or agriculture, which was not the case a century ago. There is also now a much greater role for the 'semi-professional party person', who builds their way up through the party with years of dedicated work and then goes on to progress onto elected office, an option that was rarely possible in the male-dominated times of Gladstone, Asquith or Lloyd George.

The professional party administration in Wales today, however, is as experienced as it was in its golden age a century ago, albeit with fewer elected parliamentarians and without the trappings of governmental office at ministerial level. Whereas the party in Wales has now had experience of government in the Welsh Assembly between 2000 and 2003, it has not had so at Westminster for over sixty years. In addition, its Welsh MPs no longer hold the prime positions in the party they once did, nor does Wales represent the bedrock of Liberalism it once did. To be a Welsh Liberal Democrat AM or MP is, therefore, with rare exceptions, to be somebody who dedicates their career to being in opposition to government rather than serving in it. The party is also one in which women play a far greater role than when the party started or indeed over much of its history. By December of 2008, women held the roles of chief executive, party leader and party president in the Welsh Liberal Democrats. At its beginning and through much of its history, women were relegated to supporting roles in the party with men taking the lead. This has now substantially changed.

As has been apparent through the progression of the book, electorally, the modern-day Welsh Liberal Democrats are in a stronger position than they have been for more than half a century. They have adopted the electoral practices and campaign methods of their counterparts in England, particularly with regard to the community politics associated with the English urban Liberals. This has mean that at a local government level there has been considerable success. In some cities, such as Cardiff and Swansea, therefore, they are even stronger than they were a century ago. On the whole, however, they represent today less than 15 per cent of the size the Liberal Party was in Wales a century ago. The ending of the two party system in Wales (i.e. Liberals versus Conservatives), combined with troubles the party suffered, which are detailed throughout this book, have much diminished their electoral appeal and opportunities. In most of Wales today, they, therefore, remain the third, fourth or even fifth party in electoral contests. If the Welsh Liberal Democrats enter government at all, it is as the junior coalition partner. In the days of William Gladstone and Sir William Harcourt this would have been unthinkable; Liberal strength was unassailable in Wales, as was the party's widespread commitment to some Welsh nationalist aspirations. Whilst the modern-day Welsh Liberal Democrats remain a party deeply committed to political devolution, they have lost most of the support of the Welsh-speaking nationalists to other parties. The Welsh Liberal nationalist bastions in West and North Wales fell one by one, first to the Labour Party and then to Plaid Cymru. It is Plaid Cymru that has, therefore, taken over the popular support for Welsh nationalism in these areas, and in the process, it has almost totally removed these constituencies' support for Liberalism. Only in Ceredigion has the Welsh Liberal tradition managed to survive against the Welsh nationalist onslaught. This has been one of the most significant changes to occur in the party of today and that of a century ago.

One of the central themes of both Welsh and British Liberal history has been how the party faired when being in coalition. At a local government and Welsh Assembly level it seems it make very little difference to the party's electoral fortunes. Coalitions at the Westminster level, however, have always weakened the party in Wales, sometimes considerably. The various coalitions that the Welsh Liberals had with the Conservatives between 1916 and 1945 saw the Liberal vote collapse and the party marginalised to rural Wales. The Lib-Lab pact of the late 1970s similarly saw the party decimated across Wales. The most recent coalition with the Conservatives at Westminster has also seen the party lose much of its Welsh support at elections. From each coalition it has taken around a decade or more for the party to rebuild its strength and this may well be the case after the 2015 Westminster elections.

The Liberal political ideology across the centuries, however, still links the two strands of history together. Whereas some aspects of Gladstonian Liberalism in Wales, namely the temperance and disestablishment of the church movement, have faded into history, others such as those listed below have not:

- The central theme of a commitment to the individual and the construction of a society in which individuals can satisfy their interests or achieve fulfilment
- The toleration of the belief and cultures of others provided that they do not threaten the continuance of Liberal democracy
- The progressive incorporation of all social classes within the political community
- The commitment to free trade and no trade barriers, which is explicitly addressed today in the party's commitment to the European ideal and internationalism
- Redistribution of the burden of taxation away from the lower classes in order to stimulate economic consumption
- The commitment to efficient administration, to minimise the cost of government and promote personal responsibility
- The support for devolution of political power in Wales and the establishment of a Welsh parliament

It is, therefore, this link to their ideological past, rather than direct historical links within most Welsh constituencies, which unites Welsh Liberalism across the centuries. The party today is neither fully socialist, nationalist nor capitalist but instead seeks to combine elements from all three and combine them with its own version of Liberalism. This is how the party shaped itself a century ago and continues to do so today.

BIBLIOGRAPHY

ASHDOWN, PADDY (2002)
The Ashdown Diaries, Vol. Two 1997–1999, Allen Lane, The Penguin Press, pp. 452–453

BELZAK, STEVE (2007)
'The life of Thomas Arthur Lewis MP', Conference Paper, British Liberal Political Studies Group, Birmingham Conference, 19–21st January 2007.

BELZAK, STEVE (2008)
'Swinging in the Sixties to the Liberals: Mary Murphy and Pontypridd Urban District', Conference Paper, Political Studies Association Conference, Swansea, 2nd April 2008.

BENTLEY, MICHAEL (1977)
The Liberal Mind, Cambridge University Press

BETTS, CLIVE (1993)
The Political Conundrum, Gomer

BLACK, PETER (2011)
'Coalition Positives' Liberator, Issue 346, June 2011, pp. 8–9

BOLITHO, HECTOR (1933)
Alfred Mond, First Lord Melchett, Martin Secker Ltd

BOOTHROYD, DAVID (2001)
Politico's Guide to The History of British Political Parties, Politico's Publishing

BRACK, DUNCAN [ED] (1998)
Dictionary of Liberal Biography, Politico's Publishing

BRADBURY, JONATHAN (2010)
'Wales and the 2010 General Election', Parliamentary Affairs, Vol. 63 No. 4, Oxford University Press, p. 729

BUTLER, DAVID (1952)
The British Election of 1951, MacMillan,

BUTLER, DAVID (1956)
The British Election of 1955, MacMillan,

BUTLER, DAVID (1989)
British General Elections since 1945, Basil Blackwell

BUTLER, DAVID. E AND ROSE, RICHARD (1960)
The British General Election of 1959, MacMillan

BUTLER, DAVID AND KAVANAGH, DENNIS (1974A)
The British General Election of February 1974, Macmillan

BUTLER, DAVID AND BUTLER, GARETH (2000)
Twentieth- Century British Political Facts 1900–2000, Macmillan

CAMPBELL, JOHN (1975)
'The Renewal of Liberalism: Liberalism without Liberals' in Gillian Cooke and
    Chris Cooke, The Politics of Reappraisal, Macmillan

CAREY EVANS, OLWEN (1985)
Lloyd George Was My Father, as told to Mary Garner, Gomer

CARLILE, ALEX (1997)
Carlile, Alex MP, Ron Davies MP *joint declaration on a Yes Vote*, 7/3/97

CLARKE, ALAN (1998)
The Tories: Conservatives and the Nation State 1922–1997, Weidenfeld and
    Nicholson

CLEAVER, DAVID (1985)
Labour and Liberals in the Gower Constituency, 1885–1910, Welsh History Review,
    Vol. 12, No. 3, 1985, pp. 388–410

COOK, C. P. (1968)
'Wales and the General Election of 1923', Welsh History Review, Vol. 4, No 2,
    pp. 387–394

COOK, CHRIS (1975)
'Liberals, Labour and Local Elections' in Gillian Cooke and Chris Cooke, The
    Politics of Reappraisal, Macmillan, pp. 170–171

COOK, CHRIS (2002)
A Short History of the Liberal Party, 1900–2001, Palgrave

COTT, NICK (1999)
'Tory cuckoos in the Liberal nest?: The case of the Liberal Nationals: a re-evaluation',
    Journal of Liberal Democrat History, Issue 25, Winter 1999/2000 pp. 24–30

CREWE, IVOR and KING, ANTHONY (1995)
SDP: The Birth, Life and Death of the Social Democratic Party, Oxford University
    Press

CROSS, COLIN (1963)
The Liberals in Power, Pall Mall Press

CRUIKSHANK, R. J. (1948)
The Liberal Party, Collins

CURTICE, JOHN (2001)
The 2001 election: Implications for the Liberal Democrats, Journal of Liberal
    Democrat History, Issue 32, Autumn 2001, pp. 3–5

CURTICE, JOHN (2005)
Disappointment or Bridgehead? The Liberal Democrats in the 2005 election, Journal of Liberal History, Issue 48, Autumn 2005

DAVIS, CYNOG (2005)
Plaid Cymru and The Greens: Flash In The Pan Or A Lesson For The Future? The Welsh Political Archive Annual Lecture, National Library of Wales,

DALE, IAIN (2000)
Liberal Party General Election Manifestos, 1900–1997, Routledge

DALE, IAN (2000)
Conservative Party: General Election Manifestos, 1900–1997, Routledge

DANGERFIELD, GEORGE (1935)
The Strange Death of Liberal England, Serif

DAVID, E. I (1970)
Charles Masterman and the Swansea by-election 1915, Welsh History Review, Vol. 5, No. 1, pp. 31–44

DAVIES, JOHN (1994)
A History of Wales, Penguin

JOHN DAVIES, NIGEL JENKINS, MENNA BAINES and PEREDUR L. LYNCH (2008)
The Welsh Academy Encloyopeadia of Wales, University of Wales Press, p. 341

DAVIES, D. HYWEL (1983)
The Welsh Nationalist Party, 1925–1945: A Call To Nationhood, University of Wales Press

DAVIES, W. R. (1995)
Laying the Foundations: The Contribution of Lord Davies of Llandinam in Davies, W. R. (ed) The United Nations at Fifty: The Welsh Contribution, University of Wales Press

DAVIES, A. J. (1995)
We, The Nation: The Conservative Party and the Pursuit of Power, Little Brown and Company

DEACON, RUSSELL (1997)
The Winners and Losers in Wales's First Unitary Authority Elections, in Contemporary Wales: An Annual Review of Economic and Social Research, Volume 9, University of Wales Press

DEACON, RUSSELL (1998)
'The Hidden Federal Party: The Policy Process of the Welsh Liberal Democrats', Regional Studies, Vol. 32, No. 5, 1998

DEACON, RUSSELL (2002)
The Governance of Wales: The Welsh Office and the Policy Process 1964–99, Welsh Academic Press

DEACON, RUSSELL (2005)
'From Gladstone Primary School to Lloyd George Avenue: Cardiff Liberal Council
    Politics in the centenary year', speech to the Lloyd George Society, February
    2005

DEACON, RUSSELL (2006)
Devolution in Britain today, 2nd Edition, Manchester University Press

DEACON, RUSSELL (2007)
The Welsh Liberal Democrats: From government to opposition and then back again?,
    The Political Quarterly, Volume 78, Issue 1, 2007 pp. 156–164

DEACON, RUSSELL (2010)
'Statues and newspaper wars': Cardiff town and city politics in Cardiff (1868–1908)
    Morgannwg: The Journal of Glamorgan History, Vol. LIII 2010

DE GROOT, GERARD J. (1993)
Liberal Crusader: The Life of Sir Archibald Sinclair, New York University Press

DICTIONARY OF WELSH BIOGRAPHY 1941–1970 (2001)
The Dictionary of Welsh Biography 1941–1970, The Honourable Society of
    Cymmrodorion,

DOD'S (1950)
Dod's Parliamentary Companion, 1950, Business Dictionaries Ltd

DUTTON, DAVID (1992)
Simon: A political biography of Sir John Simon, Aurum

DUTTON, DAVID (2008)
Liberals in Schism: A History of the National Liberal Party, Tauris Academic Studies

DUTTON, DAVID (2008)
The Glyndr Manuscripts: Denbighshire Record Office, Ruthin, Journal of Liberal
    History, Issue 61, Winter 2008–9

DOUGLAS, ROY (1971)
The History of the Liberal Party 1985–1970, Sidgewick and Jackson, London

DOUGLAS, ROY (2005)
Liberals: The History of the Liberal and Liberal Democrat Parties, Hambleton and
    London

DOYLE, BARRY (1998)
Reginald McKenna , in The Dictionary of Liberal Biography edited by Duncan
    Brack et al. Politico's Publishing, pp. 237–239

ELECTORAL COMMISSION (2003)
The National Assembly for Wales Elections 2003: The Official Report and Results,
    The Electoral Commission, Cardiff

ELECTORAL COMMISSION (2004)
Local elections in Wales 2004: The Official Report on the Local Elections 10 June
    2004, The Electoral Commission, Cardiff

ELECTORAL COMMISSION (2010)
Expenditure returns for the 2009 European Elections for Wales

ELLIS, BERRESFORD P (1968)
Wales A Nation Again!: The Nationalist Struggle for Freedom, The Garden City Press

ELLIS, TOM (2006)
A Case of Welsh Political Midwifery: Tom Ellis on the Origins of the Liberal Democrats, Planet, Issues 178, pp. 67–72

EMY, H. V. (1973)
Liberals Radicals and Social Politics 1892–1914, Cambridge University Press

EVANS, E. W. (1959)
Mabon: A Study in Trade Union Leadership, University of Wales Press

FAIRCLOUGH, OLIVER (2007)
'Things of Beauty': What Two Sisters Did For Wales, National Museum Wales Books

FORMAN, F. N. (2002)
Constitutional Change in the United Kingdom, Routledge

FOX, KENNETH O. (1964)
Labour and Merthyr's Khaki Election of 1900, Welsh History Review, Vol. 2, No. 1, pp. 351–366

FOULKES, DAVID, BARRY JONES, J. WILFORD, R. A. (1981)
The Welsh Veto: The Wales Act 1978 and the Referendum, University of Wales Press

GAFFNEY, ANGELA (1998)
Aftermath: Remembering the Great War in Wales, University of Wales Press

GRAHAM JONES, J. (1982A)
Wales and 'The new Liberalism', 1926–1929, National Library of Wales Journal, Vol. XXII, pp. 321–346

GRAHAM JONES (1982B)
Wales the New Socialism, 1926–1929, Welsh History Review, Vol. 11, No. 2, December 1982, pp. 173–199

GRAHAM JONES, J. (1987)
'E.T. John and Welsh Home Rule, 1910–14', Welsh History Journal, Vol. 13, No. 4, December 1987, pp. 453–467

GRAHAM JONES, J. (1988)
'Early Campaigns to Secure a Secretary of State for Wales, 1890–1939, Transactions of the Honourable Society of Cymmrodrion

GRAHAM JONES, J. (1990)
Alfred Thomas's National Institutions (Wales) Bills of 1891–92, The Welsh History Review, Vol. 15, No. 2, pp. 218–239

GRAHAM JONES, J. (1992)
'The Parliament For Wales Campaign 1950–1956', The Welsh History Review, Vol. 16, No. 2, pp. 207–246

GRAHAM JONES, J. (1993A)
'The Liberal Party and Wales, 1945–79', The Welsh History Review, Vol. 16, No. 3, June 1993

GRAHAM JONES, J. (1993B)
'Emlyn Hooson's Parliametary Debut: The Montgomeryshire By-election of 1962, The Montgomeryshire Collections

GRAHAM JONES, J. (1998)
Megan Lloyd George in the Dictionary of Liberal Biography, Politico's Publishing

GRAHAM JONES, J. (1999)
'A breach in the family, The Lloyd Georges', Journal of Liberal History, Issue 25, Winter 1999–2000, pp. 34–39

GRAHAM JONES, J. (2000)
Liberal Party Archives at the National Library of Wales, Journal of Liberal Democrat History, Issue 26, Spring 2000, pp. 26–28

GRAHAM JONES, J. (2001)
The Peacemonger: David Davies, Journal of Liberal Democrat History, Issue 29, Winter 2000–01, pp.16–23

GRAHAM JONES, J. (2002A)
Lloyd George and the Suffragettes at Llanystumdwy, Journal of Liberal Democrat History, Issue 34/35 Spring/Summer 2002, pp. 3–10

GRAHAM JONES, J. (2002B)
'Every vote for Llewelyn Williams is a vote against Lloyd George' Cardiganshire, 1921, Journal of Liberal Democrat History, Issue 37, Winter 2002/03, pp. 3–9

GRAHAM JONES, J. (2002C)
'Grimond's Rival: Biography of Roderic Bowen MP, Journal of Liberal Democrat History, Issue 34/35l, Spring/Summer 2002, pp. 26–33

GRAYLING-INSTITUTE OF WELSH AFFAIRS (2010, 2011)
Assembly Bwletin Cynciilad, various issues, see chapters for details

GRIMOND, JO (1979)
Memoirs, Heinemann

GRIGG, JOHN (1991)
Lloyd George: From Peace to War 1912–1916, Penguin

GRIGG, JOHN (1997)
Lloyd George: The Young Lloyd George, Penguin

HAGUE, FFION (2008)
The Pain and Privilege: The Women in Lloyd George's Life, Harper Collins

HOOSON, EMLYN (1999)
Clement Davies: An Underestimated Welshman and Politician, Journal of Liberal
    Democrat History, Issue 24, Autumn 1999, pp. 3–13

JAMES, MARI AND LINDLEY, PETER (1983)
The Parliamentary Passage of the Wales Act 1978, in Foulkes, David, Barry Jones,
    J. and Wilford, R. A. (ed) The Welsh Veto: The Wales Act 1978 and the
    Referendum, University of Wales Press

JAMES, ARNOLD, J. AND THOMAS, JOHN E. (1981)
Wales at Westminster, Gomer

JENKINS, ALUN R. (1967)
'Article: Is the Liberal Party in Wales Dead Yet?' W.Y.L.O News: Bulletin of the
    Welsh Young Liberal Organisation, No. 1, Sept. 1967

JENKINS, ROY (1964)
Asquith, Collins

JENKINS, ROY (1995)
Gladstone, Papermac

JENKINS, ROY (1998)
The Chancellors, Macmillan

JONES, ARTHUR HERBERT (1987)
His Lordship's Obedient Servant, Gomer Press

JONES, BETI (1999)
Welsh Elections, 1885–1997, Yr Lolfa

JONES, EMRYS (2001)
The Welsh in London 1500–2000, University of Wales Press on behalf of The
    Honourable Society of Cymmrodorion

JONES, GWYNORO (1987)
The History of the SDP in Wales, self published booklet

JONES, MERVYN (1991)
A Radical Life: The Biography of Megan Lloyd George, Hutchinson

JONES, TUDOR (1996)
Remaking the Labour Party: From Gaitskell to Blair, Routledge

JONES, WYN (1986)
Thomas Edward Ellis 1859–1899, University of Wales Press

LEWIS, RICHARD (2000)
'Political Culture and Ideology 1900–1918' in Duncan Tanner, Chris Williams and
    Deian Hopkin's Labour Party in Wales 1900–2000, University of Wales Press

LORT-PHILLIPS (1961)
The Future of Wales, Carmarthen

LIBERAL DEMOCRATS WALES (1996A)
A Senedd for Wales: Beyond a Talking Shop: The Liberal Democrats Programme for
    Devolution for Wales

LIBERAL DEMOCRATS WALES (1996B)
Autumn Conference Report, 12/10/06

LIBERAL DEMOCRATS WALES (1997)
'Make the difference': The Liberal Democrat Manifesto for Wales 1997

LIBERAL DEMOCRATS WALES (1998)
Conference Agenda, Builth Wells.

LIBERAL DEMOCRATS WALES (1999A)
Annual Report 1999

LIBERAL DEMOCRATS WALES (1999B)
Guaranteed Delivery: National Assembly Manifesto

THE LIBERAL PARTY (1945)
General Election Manifesto

THE LIBERAL PARTY (1951)
Liberal Party General Election Manifesto 1951, The Nation's Task

THE LIBERAL PARTY (1966)
General Election Manifesto: For all the people: the Liberal plan of 1966

THE LIBERAL PARTY (1970)
General Election Manifesto: What a life! Show 'em you care!

THE LIBERAL PARTY (1974A)
General Election Manifesto February 1974: Change the face of Britain – Take power –
    Vote Liberal

THE LIBERAL PARTY (1974B)
General Election Manifesto October 1974: Why Britain needs Liberal Government

THE LIBERAL PARTY (1979)
General Election Manifesto: The real fight is for Britain

THE LIBERAL PARTY OF WALES (1957)
A Rational Policy for the Development of Water Resources in Wales, Aberystwyth

THE LIBERAL PARTY OF WALES (1959)
New Deal for Wales Manifesto for the General Election, October 1959

LITTLE, TONY (1999)
'Out from under the umbrella', Journal of Liberal Democrat History, Issues 25,
    Winter 1999–2000, pp. 5–14

HOOSON, LORD (1994)
Rebirth of Death? Liberalism in Wales in the Second Half of the Twentieth Century,
    The Welsh Political Archive Lecture 1993, National Library of Wales 1994

INGHAM, ROBERT (1999)
Leadership Contests of the Past, Journal of Liberal Democrat History, Issue 23,
    Summer 1999, pp. 3–4

MADGWICK, P. J., GRIFFITHS, NON AND WALKER, VALERIE (1973)
The Politics of Rural Wales: A Case Study on Cardiganshire, Hutchinson

MAY, EDDIE (2000)
'The Mosiac of Labour Politics, 1900–1918' in Duncan Tanner, Chris Williams and
    Deian Hopkin's Labour Party in Wales 1900–2000, University of Wales Press

MASSIE, ROBERT, K. (1991)
Dreadnought, Random House

MASSON, DEIDRE (2007)
'Liberalism, gender and national memory', University of Wales Institute Cardiff,
    Centre for Humanities Open Seminar series, 3/5/07

MASTERMAN, NEVILLE (1972)
The Forerunner, The Dilemmas of Tom Ellis 1859–1899, Merlin Press

MCALLISTER, LAURA (2001)
Plaid Cymru: The Emergence of a Political Party, Seren

MCCALLUM, R. B. AND READMAN, ALISON (1999)
The British General Election of 1945, MacMillan

MCCORMICK, DONALD (1963)
The Mask of Merlin: A Critical Study of David Lloyd George, Macdonald

MOR-O-BRIEN, ANTHONY (1985)
The Merthyr Borough Election, November 1915, The Welsh History Review, Vol. 12,
    No. 4, December 1985

MORGAN, KENNETH, O. (1960)
'Gladstone and Wales', Welsh History Review, Vol. 1, No. 1, p. 65

MORGAN, KENNETH, O. (1971)
The Age of Lloyd George: The Liberal Party and British Politics, 1890–1929, George
    Allen and Unwin Ltd

MORGAN, KENNETH, O. (1973)
The New Liberalism and the Challenge of Labour: The Welsh Experience, 1885–1929,
    Welsh History Review, Vol. 12, No .1

MORGAN, KENNETH, O. (1973)
Lloyd George, Family Letters 1885–1936, University of Wales Press, Oxford
    University Press

MORGAN, KENNETH, O. (1980)
Wales In British Politics 1868–1922, University of Wales Press

MORGAN, KENNETH, O. (1982)
Rebirth of a Nation, Wales 1880–1980, Oxford University Press

MORGAN, KENNETH, O. (1991)
Wales In British Politics, 1868–1922, University of Wales Press

MORGAN, KENNETH, O. (2007)
Lloyd George's Flintshire Loyalist: The Political Achievements of John Herbert
    Lewis, Jounral of Liberal History, Vol. 57, Winter 2007–8, pp. 18–30

MORRIS JONES, HENRY (1955)
Doctor in the Whips' Room, Robert Hale Limited

NELMES, GRAHAM, V. (1979)
'Stuart Rendel and Welsh Liberal Political Organisation in the Late Nineteenth
    Century', Welsh History Journal, Vol. 9, No. 4 December 1979, pp. 468–485

THE NEW RADICAL (1947)
Vol. 1, No. 1, Aberystwyth

NICHOLAS, H. G. (1999)
The British General Election of 1950, MacMillan Press

OSMOND, JOHN (1995)
Welsh European, Seren

OWEN, FRANK (1954)
Tempestuous Journey: Lloyd George His Life and Times, Hutchinson

PARRY, CYRIL (1968)
Gwynedd Politics, 1900–1920: The Rise of a Labour Party, Welsh History Review,
    Vol. 4, No. 2 pp. 313–328

PARRY, CYRIL (1973)
The New Liberalism and the Challenge of Labour: The Welsh Experience, 1885–1929,
    Welsh History Review, 1973, pp. 288–328

PACKER, IAN (2001)
Lloyd George, Liberalism and the Land, The Royal Historical Society, The Boydell
    Press

PEARCE, MALCOLM (1992)
British Political History 1867–1990, Democracy in Decline, Routledge

POTTLE, MARK [EDITOR] (2000)
Daring to Hope: The Diaries and Letters of Violet Bonham Carter 1946–1969,
    Weidenfeld and Nicolson,

RANDALL, P. J. (1972)
'Wales in the Structure of Central Government, Public Administration, Autumn
    1972, Vol. 50

RANDERSON, JENNY (2008)
'The vision to lead', election leaflet

RASMUSSEN, JORGEN SCOTT (1965)
The Liberal Party, Constable

REES, IVOR THOMAS (2005)
Welsh Hustings 1885–2004, Dinefwr Publishers

RHONDDA, VISCOUNTESS (1933)
This Was My World, MacMillan

RICHARD COMMISSION (2004)
Report of the Commission on the Powers and Electoral Arrangements of the National
    Assembly for Wales, Richard Commission

ROBERTSON, DAVID (1986)
The Penguin Dictionary of Politics, Penguin

ROBERTS, DAVID (1976)
'Clement Davies and the Fall of Neville Chamberlain', 1939–40, Welsh History
    Review, Vol. 8, No. 2, December 1976, pp. 188–217

ROBERTS, DAVID (1985)
'The Strange Death of Liberal Wales' in John Osmonds (ed) The National Question
    Again, Gomer pp. 75–98

RODDICK, WINSTON (2003)
'Sir Maldwyn Thomas: A tribute by Winston Roddick', Papers from the Lloyd George
    Society Weekend School, Abernant Lake Hotel, Llanwrtyd Wells pp. 1–4

RODGERS, BILL (2000)
Fourth Among Equals, Politico's Publishing

RUSSELL, ANDREW AND FIELDHOUSE, EDWARDS (2005)
Neither left nor right? The Liberal Democrats and the electorate, Manchester University
    Press

SAMUEL, VISCOUNT (1945)
Memoirs, The Cresset Press

THE SDP/LIBERAL ALLIANCE (1983)
General Election Manifesto: Working together for Britain

THE SDP/LIBERAL ALLIANCE (1987)
General Election Manifesto: Britain united: the time has come

SELF, ROBERT (2000)
The Evolution of the British Party System 1885–1940, Longman

SELL, GEOFFREY (1999)
'A Sad Business' The Resignation of Clement Davies, Journal of Liberal Democrat
    History, Issue 24, Autumn 1999, pp. 14–17

STEAD, PETER (1969)
Vernon Hartshorn: Miner's Agent and Cabinet Member, in Stewert Williams'
    Glamorgan Historian Vol. 6, D. Brown and Sons Ltd, pp. 83–94

STEVENSON, JOHN (1993)
Third Party Politics Since 1945: Liberals, Alliance and Liberal Democrats, Blackwell

SWEETING, ANDREW (1998)
'Gwilym Lloyd George' in the Dictionary of Liberal Biography (1998) Duncan
    Brack [ed] Politico's Publishing, pp. 229–230

THOMAS, ALYS (2001)
The Liberal Democrats: Losing To Win? , Contemporary Wales, Vol. 14, University of Wales Press

THOMAS, ALYS (2003)
'Liberal Democrats', Chapter 12 in John Osmond and J.Barry Jones Ed (2003) Birth of Welsh Democracy: The First Term of the National Assembly for Wales, Institute for Welsh Affairs and Welsh Governance Centre

THOMAS, W. JENKYN (1895)
'An Independent Welsh National Party', Young Wales, pp. 57–9

THORPE, JEREMY (1999)
In My Own Time, Politico's Publishing

VINCENT, JOHN (1976)
2nd Edition, The Formation of the British Liberal Party 1857–1868, Harvester Wheatsheaf

WALES LABOUR PARTY (2004)
Better Governance for Wales

WATKINS, ALAN (1966)
The Liberal Dilemma, MacGibben and Key

WATSON, R. SPENCE (1906)
The National Liberal Federation 1877 to 1906, T. Fisher Unwin

WEIGALL, DAVID AND MURPHY, MICHAEL (1986)
Modern History (1815 to present day), Charles Letts & Co Ltd

WELSH ASSEMBLY GOVERNMENT (2000)
Putting Wales First: A Partnership for the People of Wales, Cardiff

WELSH EUROPEAN FUNDING OFFICE (2001)
Objective 1 Guide 2001: The essential guide to the Objective 1 Programme, Western Mail and Echo, Cardiff.

WELSH LIBERAL PARTY MINUTES AND CORRESPONDANCE (Various years, see relevant chapters)
Welsh Political Archives, National Library of Wales

WELSH LIBERAL DEMOCRATS (2001A)
Freedom for Wales in Liberal World: The Welsh Liberal Democrats for the General Election

WELSH LIBERAL DEMOCRATS (2001B)
Annual Report 2001

WELSH LIBERAL DEMOCRATS (2003A)
Memorandum from the Welsh Liberal Democrats, Moving to a durable constitutional settlement: Evidence for Change, proposals for a solution, Cardiff

WELSH LIBERAL DEMOCRATS (2003B)
Second postal list leaflet, South Wales Central

WELSH LIBERAL DEMOCRATS (2004)
Gender Balance in the Party: A call to debate and action by the National Executive, Cardiff

WELSH LIBERAL DEMOCRATS (2010)
Manifesto of Fairness for Wales

WILLIAMS, KIRSTY (2008)
'Kirsty Williams the vision to succeed' election leaflet.

WILSON, JOHN (1973)
CB A life of Sir Henry Campbell-Bannerman, Constable

WILSON, TREVOR (1968)
The Downfall of the Liberal Party 1914–1935, Collins

WYNBURN-POWELL, ALUN (2003)
Clement Davies Liberal Leader, Politico's Publishing

DOCTORAL THESES

Edwards, Andrew (2002) Political Change in North-West Wales: 1960–1974: The Decline of the Labour Party and the Rise of Plaid Cymru, Ph.D, Bangor University

Openshaw, Graeme (1991) High Noon or Much Do About Nothing: The significance (or otherwise) of parliamentary by-elections: Monmouth a Case Study, Undergraduate thesis, university not specified

Jones, Sian (2003) The Political Dynamics of North East Wales with special reference to the Liberal Party 1918–1935, Ph.D, University of Bangor

INTERVIEWS
Over 50 interviews have been undertaken for this book with politicians and party officials connected with the Welsh Liberals, SDP and Welsh Liberal Democrats. Their details are contained in the endnotes of each respective chapter. Where possible the interview material provided by them has also been verified by orther sources to ensure its accuracy.

INDEX